Nepal

Hugh Finlay
Richard Everist
Tony Wheeler

D1445680

LONELY PLANET PUBLICATIONS
Melbourne • Oakland • London • Paris

NEPAL

THE HIMALAYA
Trek through some of the most spectacular scenery in the world

THE KARNALI
Nepal's largest river, which flows through pretty canyons and jungle scenery

ANNAPURNA CONSERVATION RESERVE
Diverse mountain cultures

ROYAL BARDIA NATIONAL PARK
Stunning untouched wilderness

THE TERAI
Varied ethnic groups of the Gangetic plain – good humoured and friendly

LUMBINI
The peaceful birthplace of the Buddha

Lake Rakastal
Lake Manasarowar

CHINA
TIBET

UTTAR PRADESH
INDIA

Burang

Saipal (7050m)

Humla

GREAT HIMALAYA RANGE

Zhongba

Pithoragarh

Kali

Seti

Khaptad NP

Karnali River

Mugu

Rara NP

Karnali

Kanjiroba (6883m)

Shey-Phoksundo NP

Mustang

Dandeldhura

Jogbura

Jumla

Dillikot

Gandaki

Muktinath

Mahendranagar

Royal Sukla Phanta Wildlife Reserve

Bilauri

Dhangadhi

THE TERAI

Karnali River

Bheri River

Jomsom

Dhaulagiri (8167m)

Manang

Annapurna (8090m)

Puranpur

Chisopani

Surkhet

Dhorpatan Hunting Reserve

Dhorpatan

Tatopani

Ghorapani

Chisopani

Royal Bardia NP

Sallyan

Liban

Beni

Baglung

Kusma

Ghorapani

Kali

Seti

Pokhara

Mahendra

Kohalpur

Tulsipur

THE TERAI

Lakhimpur

Nepalganj

Highway

Lamahl

Tansen

Nanpara

Bahraich

Taulihawa

Bhairawa

Butwal

INDIA
UTTAR PRADESH

Sitapur

Lumbini

Sunauli
Nautanwa

Hardoi

Balrampur

Bayaha

LUCKNOW

Faizabad

Gorakhpur

Ghaghara

KANPUR

Rae Bareli

Sultanpur

Azamgarh

Ganges

Fatehpur

Jaunpur

ELEVATION

6000 m
4000 m
2000 m
1000 m
500 m
0

0   50   100 km

POKHARA
Peaceful lakeside life surrounded
by the majestic Himalaya

KATHMANDU
Ancient temples & fresh faces

CHINA
TIBET

Shigatse

Lhatse

Sakya

Tingri

**SAGARMATHA
NATIONAL PARK**
Sherpa culture; plus gorges,
valleys, lakes...and Mt Everest!

Saga

Manaslu
(8162m)

Ganesh Himal
(7406m)

Langtang
Lirung
(7246m)

Langtang

Cho Oyu
(8153m)

Qomolangma,
Sagarmatha or
Mt Everest (8848m)

Gauri
Shankar
(7146m)

Makalu
(8475m)

Dhunche

Langtang
NP

Kanchenjunga
(8598m)

Dumre

Gorkha

Trisuli

Kodari

Sagarmatha
NP

Namche
Bazaar

Lukli

Mugling

Naubise

Barabise

Charikot

Jiri

Phaphlu

Patan

KATHMANDU

Bhaktapur

Dolalghat

GREAT

HIMALAYA RANGE

Narayanghat

Daman

Royal Chitwan
NP

Hetauda

Tumlingtar

Taplejung

SIKKIM

Amlekhganj

Lamidanda

Hile

Dhankuta

Darjeeling

THE TERAI

Birganj

Lalbiti

Chatara

Ilam

Raxaul

Dhran
Bazaar

Kakarbhitta

Bettiah

Bairagnia

Jaleshwar

Janakpur

Highway

Itahari

Bhadrapur

Motihari

Sitamarhi

Rajbiraj

Birpur

Biratnagar

Islampur

**ROYAL CHITWAN
NATIONAL PARK**
Elephant safaris & tiger encounters

Jogbani

Forbesganj

Muzaffarpur

Darbhanga

Araria

Kishanganj

BHAKTAPUR
Beautiful Golden Gate &
Peacock Windows

SAPT KOSI FLOOD PLAINS
Thatched villages, rice paddies
& water lillies

Saharsa

INDIA

Chapra

PATNA

Arrah

BIHAR

Purnia

Atihar

WEST
BENGAL

Marsyangdi

Buri Gandaki

Trisuli

Bhote Kosi

Sun

Kosi

Dudh

Arun

Tamur

Kosi

Sapt

Mahendra

Nepal
4th edition – September 1999
First published – October 1990

Published by
Lonely Planet Publications Pty Ltd A.C.N. 005 607 983
192 Burwood Rd, Hawthorn, Victoria 3122, Australia

Lonely Planet Offices
Australia PO Box 617, Hawthorn, Victoria 3122
USA 150 Linden St, Oakland, CA 94607
UK 10a Spring Place, London NW5 3BH
France 1 rue du Dahomey, 75011 Paris

Photographs
All of the images in this guide are available for licensing from
Lonely Planet Images.
email: lpi@lonelyplanet.com.au

Front Cover Photograph
Bisket Jatra (New Year) celebrations in Bhaktapur – hauling Bhairab's
chariot through the streets requires a massive effort. (Richard I'Anson)

ISBN 0 86442 704 2

text & maps © Lonely Planet 1999
photos © photographers as indicated 1999

Printed by The Bookmaker International Ltd
Printed in China

Contents – Text

AROUND THE KATHMANDU VALLEY   218

POKHARA   265

THE TERAI 292

Contents – Maps

MAPS

The Authors

Hugh Finlay

After deciding there must be more to life than a career in civil engineering, Hugh took off around Australia in the mid-1970s, working at everything from spray painting to diamond prospecting, before hitting the overland trail. He joined Lonely Planet in 1985 and has written *Jordan & Syria*, co-authored *Morocco, Algeria & Tunisia* and *Kenya*, was the coordinating author of the 9th edition of *Australia*, and has contributed to several other LP guides including *Africa* and *India*. Hugh's most recent project has been updating the *Nepal* guide. When not travelling, Hugh lives in central Victoria, Australia.

Richard Everist

Richard grew up in Geelong, Australia, has travelled a bit and had a wide variety of jobs. He worked full time in Lonely Planet's Melbourne office before jumping the fence to become a freelance writer. In late 1994 he was lured back into the home paddock to be Publishing General Manager. He has co-written LP's *Nepal, South Africa* and *Britain* guides, updated *Papua New Guinea*, and contributed to the shoestring guides for *West Asia*, *Africa*, *Western Europe* and *Mediterranean Europe*.

Tony Wheeler

Tony Wheeler was born in England, but grew up in Pakistan, the Bahamas and the USA. He returned to England to do a degree in engineering at Warwick University, worked as an automotive design engineer, returned to London Business School to complete an MBA, then set out on an Asian overland trip with his wife, Maureen. That trip led to Tony and Maureen founding Lonely Planet Publications in Australia in 1973, and they've been travelling, writing and publishing guidebooks ever since.

FROM HUGH

As always, I am hugely grateful for the tremendous support and assistance I received from many people during the course of my research trip.

Stan Armington, of Malla Treks, helped greatly with major and minor detail – and accompanied me on a wild goose chase (unsuccessful as it turned out) to find the start of the new highway to the Terai. Badri Adhikari, of Lucky Traveller Service, once again went out of his way to help organising a trip to the Terai. Our very capable driver on that trip, Mandeep Shrestha, proved beyond doubt that the Toyota Corolla really can be an off-road vehicle. I am also hugely indebted to Basanta Bajracharya and the rest of the staff at the Utse Hotel who allowed me many liberties with monopolising their telephone lines during a difficult time.

Thanks also to Dave Allardice (Ultimate Descents) for updating the Rafting & Kayaking chapter, and to Peter Stewart (Himalayan Mountain Bikes) for his work on the Mountain Biking chapter. James Giambrone (Indigo Gallery) gave me some excellent tips on trips around the Kathmandu Valley.

Many others also helped in their own way, and to them many thanks. In particular: Chris Beall, Bharat Basnet & Prakash Moktan (Explore Nepal), Dr Buddha Basnyat (Nepal International Clinic), Nirmal Chabba (Fulbari Dusit Thani Hotel), Sonam Gurung (Dawn till Dusk), Tony Jones & Niraj Shrestha (Himalayan Encounters), Dinesh Joshi, Martin Kromer, Tejendra Shrestha, Kishore Pandey, Carolyn Syangbo (Mountain Travel) and Kishore Thapa (Kathmandu Urban Development Project).

This Book

The first five editions of this book were the work of Nepali writer Prakash A Raj. In 1989 Tony Wheeler and Richard Everist completely rewrote the book to bring it into line with other LP guidebooks. In 1992 Richard Everist researched the 2nd edition.

Hugh Finlay researched the 3rd edition in 1996 and returned in 1999 to research this edition. The Geography, Flora & Fauna and Ecology sections were written by Lewis Underwood. The Mountain Biking chapter was originally written by John Prosser and was updated for this edition by Peter Stewart. David Allardice, operations manager for Ultimate Descents and co-author of *White Water Nepal*, who originally wrote the Rafting & Kayaking chapter for the 2nd edition, updated the chapter for this edition, with the able assistance of Ravi Fry, also of Ultimate Descents.

From the Publisher

This 4th edition of Nepal was produced in Lonely Planet's Melbourne office. Lindsay Brown was the coordinating editor before handing over to Thalia Kalkipsakis who then took it through production. Mapping was coordinated by Paul Piaia with assistance from Sarah Sloane and Leanne Peake. Paul also laid the book out and designed the colour sections. Simon Bracken designed the cover and illustrations were drawn by Michael Weldon and Simon Borg. Quentin Frayne edited the language chapter. Prof T. C. Majapuria coordinated the artwork for the gods aside.

Many thanks to Stan Armington, who helped tirelessly with the gods section, as well as Sharan Kaur, Lindsay Brown (after his escape!) and Adriana Mammarella for their invaluable advice and support.

Foreword

ABOUT LONELY PLANET GUIDEBOOKS

The story begins with a classic travel adventure: Tony and Maureen Wheeler's 1972 journey across Europe and Asia to Australia. Useful information about the overland trail did not exist at that time, so Tony and Maureen published the first Lonely Planet guidebook to meet a growing need.

From a kitchen table, then from a tiny office in Melbourne (Australia), Lonely Planet has become the largest independent travel publisher in the world, an international company with offices in Melbourne, Oakland (USA), London (UK) and Paris (France).

Today Lonely Planet guidebooks cover the globe. There is an ever-growing list of books and there's information in a variety of forms and media. Some things haven't changed. The main aim is still to help make it possible for adventurous travellers to get out there – to explore and better understand the world.

At Lonely Planet we believe travellers can make a positive contribution to the countries they visit – if they respect their host communities and spend their money wisely. Since 1986 a percentage of the income from each book has been donated to aid projects and human rights campaigns.

Updates Lonely Planet thoroughly updates each guidebook as often as possible. This usually means there are around two years between editions, although for more unusual or more stable destinations the gap can be longer. Check the imprint page (following the colour map at the beginning of the book) for publication dates.

Between editions up-to-date information is available in two free newsletters – the paper *Planet Talk* and email *Comet* (to subscribe, contact any Lonely Planet office) – and on our Web site at www.lonelyplanet.com. The *Upgrades* section of the Web site covers a number of important and volatile destinations and is regularly updated by Lonely Planet authors. *Scoop* covers news and current affairs relevant to travellers. And, lastly, the *Thorn Tree* bulletin board and *Postcards* section of the site carry unverified, but fascinating, reports from travellers.

Correspondence The process of creating new editions begins with the letters, postcards and emails received from travellers. This correspondence often includes suggestions, criticisms and comments about the current editions. Interesting excerpts are immediately passed on via newsletters and the Web site, and everything goes to our authors to be verified when they're researching on the road. We're keen to get more feedback from organisations or individuals who represent communities visited by travellers.

Lonely Planet gathers information for everyone who's curious about the planet – and especially for those who explore it first-hand. Through guidebooks, phrasebooks, activity guides, maps, literature, newsletters, image library, TV series and Web site we act as an information exchange for a worldwide community of travellers.

Research Authors aim to gather sufficient practical information to enable travellers to make informed choices and to make the mechanics of a journey run smoothly. They also research historical and cultural background to help enrich the travel experience and allow travellers to understand and respond appropriately to cultural and environmental issues.

Authors don't stay in every hotel because that would mean spending a couple of months in each medium-sized city and, no, they don't eat at every restaurant because that would mean stretching belts beyond capacity. They do visit hotels and restaurants to check standards and prices, but feedback based on readers' direct experiences can be very helpful.

Many of our authors work undercover, others aren't so secretive. None of them accept freebies in exchange for positive write-ups. And none of our guidebooks contain any advertising.

Production Authors submit their raw manuscripts and maps to offices in Australia, USA, UK or France. Editors and cartographers – all experienced travellers themselves – then begin the process of assembling the pieces. When the book finally hits the shops, some things are already out of date, we start getting feedback from readers and the process begins again ...

WARNING & REQUEST

Things change – prices go up, schedules change, good places go bad and bad places go bankrupt – nothing stays the same. So, if you find things better or worse, recently opened or long since closed, please tell us and help make the next edition even more accurate and useful. We genuinely value all the feedback we receive. Julie Young coordinates a well travelled team that reads and acknowledges every letter, postcard and email and ensures that every morsel of information finds its way to the appropriate authors, editors and cartographers for verification.

Everyone who writes to us will find their name in the next edition of the appropriate guidebook. They will also receive the latest issue of *Planet Talk*, our quarterly printed newsletter, or *Comet*, our monthly email newsletter. Subscriptions to both newsletters are free. The very best contributions will be rewarded with a free guidebook.

Excerpts from your correspondence may appear in new editions of Lonely Planet guidebooks, the Lonely Planet Web site, *Planet Talk* or *Comet*, so please let us know if you *don't* want your letter published or your name acknowledged.

Send all correspondence to the Lonely Planet office closest to you:

Australia: PO Box 617, Hawthorn, Victoria 3122
USA: 150 Linden St, Oakland, CA 94607
UK: 10A Spring Place, London NW5 3BH
France: 1 rue du Dahomey, 75011 Paris

Or email us at: talk2us@lonelyplanet.com.au

For news, views and updates see our Web site: www.lonelyplanet.com

HOW TO USE A LONELY PLANET GUIDEBOOK

The best way to use a Lonely Planet guidebook is any way you choose. At Lonely Planet we believe the most memorable travel experiences are often those that are unexpected, and the finest discoveries are those you make yourself. Guidebooks are not intended to be used as if they provide a detailed set of infallible instructions!

Contents All Lonely Planet guidebooks follow roughly the same format. The Facts about the Destination chapters or sections give background information ranging from history to weather. Facts for the Visitor gives practical information on issues like visas and health. Getting There & Away gives a brief starting point for researching travel to and from the destination. Getting Around gives an overview of the transport options when you arrive.

The peculiar demands of each destination determine how subsequent chapters are broken up, but some things remain constant. We always start with background, then proceed to sights, places to stay, places to eat, entertainment, getting there and away, and getting around information – in that order.

Heading Hierarchy Lonely Planet headings are used in a strict hierarchical structure that can be visualised as a set of Russian dolls. Each heading (and its following text) is encompassed by any preceding heading that is higher on the hierarchical ladder.

Entry Points We do not assume guidebooks will be read from beginning to end, but that people will dip into them. The traditional entry points are the list of contents and the index. In addition, however, some books have a complete list of maps and an index map illustrating map coverage.

There may also be a colour map that shows highlights. These highlights are dealt with in greater detail in the Facts for the Visitor chapter, along with planning questions and suggested itineraries. Each chapter covering a geographical region usually begins with a locator map and another list of highlights. Once you find something of interest in a list of highlights, turn to the index.

Maps Maps play a crucial role in Lonely Planet guidebooks and include a huge amount of information. A legend is printed on the back page. We seek to have complete consistency between maps and text, and to have every important place in the text captured on a map. Map key numbers usually start in the top left corner.

Although inclusion in a guidebook usually implies a recommendation we cannot list every good place. Exclusion does not necessarily imply criticism. In fact there are a number of reasons why we might exclude a place – sometimes it is simply inappropriate to encourage an influx of travellers.

Introduction

Draped along the greatest heights of the Himalaya, the kingdom of Nepal is a land of eternal fascination, a place where one visit is rarely enough. It's a land of ancient history, colourful cultures and people, superb scenery and some of the best walking on earth.

Nepal's history is closely related to its geographical location, separating the fertile plains of India from the desert-like plateau of Tibet. Its position between India and China meant the country was able at times to play the role of intermediary – a canny trader between two great powers – while at other times it faced the threat of invasion. Internally, its history was just as dynamic, with city-states in the hills vying with each other for power until one powerful king,

Prithvi Narayan Shah, overran them all. That history is very visible today with the three great towns of the Kathmandu Valley – Kathmandu, Patan and Bhaktapur – still bearing witness to their days as fiercely competitive medieval mini-kingdoms. Indeed, in Nepal it's often possible to suspend belief and mentally roll the clock right back to the medieval era.

Behind the time-worn temples and palaces of the Kathmandu Valley, above and beyond the hills that ring the valley, another 'kingdom' rises skyward. The 'abode of snows', which is what *Himalaya* means in Sanskrit, is a natural 'kingdom' and a magnet to mountaineers from all over the world. Fortunately you don't have to be a Sherpa and your surname doesn't have to be Messner or Hillary in order for you to get in among these great mountains. With a dash of enterprise and a modicum of fitness most travellers can walk the trails that lead into the roadless heights of the Himalaya. One trek is rarely enough, and many visitors soon find themselves planning to return.

Fascinating old towns, magnificent temples and great walking are not all Nepal has to offer. Many visitors come to Nepal expecting to find these things but also discover how outstandingly friendly the Nepalis are.

Nor is trekking the only activity which draws visitors – Nepal also has some superb white-water rafting opportunities, mountain biking is becoming more and more popular, and down in the jungle lowland in the south of the country, safaris on elephant-back into the Royal Chitwan National Park are another not-to-be-missed part of the Nepal experience.

Warning about Figures, Dates & Names

There doesn't seem to be any 100% correct reference for anything in Nepal. As an example we've seen half a dozen different figures for the number of square kilometres that Nepal occupies. And we lost track of how many times sources A, B and C said Temple 1 is to the right, Temple 2 is to the left while sources X, Y and Z said the opposite. It's open to contention which of the three Taleju temples in Patan's Durbar Square is which. When temples were built is also a matter of speculation: some sources will give a date of construction for a certain temple, and on the same page give the period of reign for the king who built it and yet the two will not agree.

Many temples in Nepal have alternative names. For example, the Vishnu Temple in Patan's Durbar Square is referred to as the Jagannarayan or Charnarayan Temple; the great Shiva Temple in Kathmandu's Durbar Square is sometimes called the Maju Deval, at other times simply the Shiva Temple. Where possible, alternative names that are commonly used have been given.

Mandir simply means 'temple' and generally we have used the English word except in cases where mandir is always used, as with the Krishna Mandir in Patan.

Further confusion can be caused by different systems of transliteration from Sanskrit – the letter 'h' appears in some systems, but doesn't appear in others, so you may see Manjushri and Manjusri, Machhendranath and Machendranath. The letters 'b' and 'v' are also used interchangeably in different systems – Shiva's fearsome manifestation can be Bhairab or Bhairav, Vishnu is often written as Bishnu and the Nepali word for the Tibetan thunderbolt symbol can be a *bajra* or a *vajra*.

Some confusion is also caused by different places having the same name; so for example, in the Annapurna region there are two villages called Phedi.

Finally, texts differ in their use of the words Nepali and Nepalese. In this book we have used Nepali both for the language and for everything else relating to the country and its people.

Facts about Nepal

HISTORY

In many ways – historically, culturally and linguistically – Nepal has been the meeting point between the Mongoloid peoples of Asia (Tibeto-Burmese languages) and the Caucasoid peoples of the Indian plains (Indo-European languages). In earlier times, Nepal was able to exploit its position as an intermediary in the trade between India and China. Today, the country continues to take advantage of its strategic position between these two uneasy giants.

Over the centuries, the boundaries of Nepal have extended to include huge tracts of neighbouring India, or contracted to little more than the Kathmandu Valley and a handful of surrounding city-states.

Legends recount that the Kathmandu Valley was once a great lake and that Manjushri broached the valley wall with a magical sword, draining the water and creating the Kathmandu Valley we know. Or perhaps it wasn't Manjushri; he was, after all, a Buddhist from China. Hindus claim it was Krishna who performed the mighty deed, hurling a thunderbolt to create the Chobar Gorge. Choose whichever legend you prefer, but scientists agree that the valley was submerged at one time and the rivers of the valley do indeed flow southward through the narrow Chobar Gorge.

The Kiratis

Recorded history begins with the Kiratis, Mongoloid people who arrived in Nepal from the east around the 7th or 8th century BCE (before the common era). Although they are the first known rulers of the Kathmandu Valley, and Yalambar (the first of their kings) is mentioned in the Hindu epic the *Mahabharata*, little more is known about them.

It was during the Kirati period that Buddhism first arrived in the country; indeed it is claimed that during the reign of the seventh of the 28 Kirati kings, Buddha, together with his disciple Ananda, visited the valley and stayed for a time in Patan.

Other accounts of the Kirati period include a 4th century BCE description of their sheep breeding and agricultural activities. Around the 2nd century BCE the great Buddhist Indian emperor, Ashoka, visited Nepal and erected a pillar at the Buddha's birthplace at Lumbini, south of Pokhara near the present-day Indian border. Ashoka also visited the Kathmandu Valley and evidence of four stupas he erected around Patan can still be clearly seen. Ashoka may have also enlarged the stupas at Bodhnath and Swayambhunath. His daughter Charumati was said to have founded Chabahil, a village on the road between Kathmandu and Bodhnath, which has now been swallowed up by the capital. There is a stupa, which is a smaller version of Bodhnath, and a monastery here that are claimed to date back to her time in Nepal.

Kirati domination ended around 300 CE (common era) but the Rai and Limbu people of eastern Nepal are said to be modern descendants.

The Licchavis

Buddhism faded and Hinduism reasserted itself with the Licchavis, Indo-Aryan people who invaded from northern India about 300 CE and overthrew the last Kirati king. They brought with them the caste divisions which continue in Nepal to this day but also ushered in a golden age of Nepali art and architecture.

Manadeva I established the Licchavis' political and military might; a valley inscription dated to 476 CE tells of his prowess and can be seen at the beautiful Changu Narayan Temple in the eastern part of the Kathmandu Valley. His successor, Manadeva II, left numerous stone inscriptions around his kingdom, most of them commenting on what a wonderful mother he had and how he wouldn't have got anywhere without her!

The Thakuris

Amsuvarman, the first Thakuri king, came to power in 602 CE, succeeding his Licchavi father-in-law. Amsuvarman consolidated his power with strategic family connections to the north and south. His daughter Bhrikuti married a Tibetan prince and collected the Buddha's begging bowl in her wedding dowry. She was said to be a reincarnation of Tibetan Buddhism's Green Tara, seen on many *thangkas* (Tibetan paintings on cotton). Meanwhile in Nepal, Amsuvarman constructed a marvellous seven storey palace at Deopatan near Pashupatinath and contemporary accounts speak with wonder of his luxurious life.

Amsuvarman's was the first of three Thakuri dynasties and although the centuries that followed were a time of invasion and turmoil, the Kathmandu Valley's strategic location ensured the kingdom's survival and growth. It is believed that the city of Kantipur, today's Kathmandu, was founded around the 10th century by Gunakamadeva. His Kasthamandap (House of Wood) gave the city its name and can be seen in Kathmandu's Durbar Square.

The Golden Age of the Mallas

In 1200, so another legend goes, King Arideva was wrestling when news came of the birth of his son. He instantly awarded his son the title *malla* or 'wrestler' and thus founded the illustrious Malla dynasty. This golden age saw great wealth flow to the valley and the kingdom's architects constructed many of the wonderful buildings in Nepal today, but the early Malla years actually saw a series of terrible disasters. A huge earthquake shook the valley and killed thousands, an invasion from the north-west followed and the town of Patan was destroyed in 1311.

The Hindu Mallas were followers of Shiva but were considered to be incarnations of the god Vishnu, and their tolerance of Buddhism allowed the Himalayan Tantric form of the religion to continue to flourish. An aristocracy grew up under the Malla rulers and the Hindu caste rules were strengthened and became more rigid. Hari Singh, who arrived in the valley sometime between 1325 and 1330, was one of the best-known early Malla rulers and through him Taleju Bhawani became the royal goddess of Nepal. Hari Singh's southern Indian followers may have been the Newars whose name the people of the Kathmandu Valley take to this day.

During this period Nepal began to divide into numerous, frequently feuding city-states. The hill country became more densely settled as agricultural techniques improved, but a Muslim invasion from Bengal swept through the valley leaving in its wake damaged Hindu and Buddhist shrines. The wave of Muslim destruction soon passed Nepal, but in India the damage was more widespread and many Hindus were driven from the plains, establishing more small Rajput principalities in the hills and mountains of Nepal. The country we know today was divided at that time into 46 separate small states. These kingdoms minted their own coins and maintained standing armies.

In the Kathmandu Valley the three greatest towns which remain to this day – Kathmandu, Patan and Bhaktapur – were independent kingdoms with powerful kings who encouraged the construction of many temples and the creation of many enduring works of art. Each city centred around the king's palace, with the nobility and high castes concentrated close to the centre. High walls were built to fend off the city's neighbours.

In 1372, however, Jayasthiti Malla founded the third Malla dynasty and took first Patan and, 10 years later, Bhaktapur, to unify the whole valley. In the 15th century, Malla art and culture reached their peak and during the reign of Yaksha Malla (1428-82) the kingdom extended south to the Ganges River, north to the edge of Tibet, west to the Kali Gandaki River and east to Sikkim. With his death, however, the kingdom again split into small warring states and another two centuries of conflict were to follow. Trade was booming, agriculture continued to improve and the valley towns enjoyed an orgy of temple and palace construction, but the constant squabbling of the Malla kingdoms opened the door to a new dynasty.

The Shah Dynasty Unifies Nepal

From the tiny kingdom of Gorkha, halfway between Kathmandu and Pokhara, the Shah kings gradually strengthened and extended their power while dreaming of conquering the rich Kathmandu Valley. In 1768 Prithvi Narayan Shah, ninth of the Shah kings, conquered the valley and moved his capital to Kathmandu. The Shah dynasty, which continues to this day, was established.

From this new base the kingdom's power continued to expand until a clash with the Chinese in Tibet led to an ignominious defeat. The Nepalis had first fought the Chinese in 1790, but by 1792 the Chinese army had struck back and in the ensuing treaty the Nepalis had to stop their attacks on Tibet and pay tribute to the Chinese emperor in Beijing; the payments continued until 1912.

British power on the subcontinent was growing at this time and a British envoy arrived in Kathmandu in 1792, too late to aid the Nepalis against the Chinese invasion. Despite treaties with the British the expanding Nepali boundaries, stretching all the way from Kashmir to Sikkim by the early 19th century, were bound to cause problems with the Raj, and disputes over the Terai (the lowlands that are south of the Himalayan foothills) led to war with the British.

In 1810 Nepal was approximately twice its current size but the 1816 Sugauli Treaty with the British ended its growth. Britain took Sikkim and most of the Terai, and Nepal's present-day eastern and western borders were established. Some of the land was restored to Nepal in 1858 as a reward for Nepali support for the British during the Indian Mutiny (or Indian Uprising or War of Independence as it is referred to in modern India).

The Sugauli treaty opened the door for Indian business influence in Nepal and when, a century later, new direct trade routes were established between India and Tibet, the Nepalis also began to lose their influence as an intermediary in trade between the two countries. A British resident was sent to Kathmandu to keep an eye on things. The Nepalis, less than entranced with the British, allotted him a piece of land which they considered to be disease-prone and a haven for evil spirits, but the British stiff upper lip prevailed. In fact the defeat had so rankled with the Nepalis that they shut off all foreign contact and from 1816 right through to 1951 the country's borders were firmly closed to outsiders. The British residents in Kathmandu were the only westerners to set eyes on Nepal for over 100 years.

Many Nepali eyes were, however, viewing the outside world. The British were so impressed by the fighting qualities of the Nepalis that they brought mercenaries, known as 'Gurkhas', into the British army. Gurkha mercenaries have fought in the British army ever since, even spreading fear among the Argentinians during the Falklands War in 1982. Gurkha earnings are an important element of Nepal's income today and although the importance of Gurkha troops to Britain is diminishing, various other nations are only too happy to pay for their soldiering abilities. The Sultan of Brunei, for example, has a contingent of Gurkha troops.

The Ranas

Although the Shah dynasty continued in power a curious palace revolt occurred in 1846 when Jung Bahadur Rana engineered the Kot Massacre.

Jung Bahadur was an ambitious and ruthless young Chhetri noble from western Nepal. Taking advantage of the complex, often bloody, power struggles within the ruling family, he developed his own power base. On 15 September 1846, he initiated a decisive coup. His soldiers massacred several hundred of the most important men in the kingdom – noblemen, soldiers and courtiers – while they were assembled in the Kot courtyard adjoining Kathmandu's Durbar Square. Jung Bahadur took the title of prime minister and changed his family name to the more prestigious Rana. Later, he extended his title to maharaja and then made the title hereditary. The Ranas became a second 'royal family' within the kingdom and held the real power, keeping the Shah kings as pampered figureheads.

For over a century, the hereditary family of Rana prime ministers held power and although development in Nepal stagnated, the country did manage to preserve its independence during the period when European colonial powers were snatching up virtually every country unable to defend itself. Nepal was never ruled by a colonial power, but it was almost completely isolated from the outside world right through the Rana period. Only on rare occasions were visitors allowed into Nepal and even then they were only allowed to visit a very limited part of the country.

Jung Bahadur Rana travelled to Europe in 1850 and brought back a taste for neoclassical architecture (examples of it can be seen in Kathmandu today). To the Ranas' credit, *suttee* (the Hindu practice of casting widows on their husband's funeral pyre) was abolished, forced labour was ended and a school and a college were established in Kathmandu. While the Ranas and their relations lived luxurious lives in huge Kathmandu palaces the peasants in the hills were locked in a medieval existence.

Elsewhere in the region dramatic changes were taking place. After WWII India gained its independence and a revolution took place in China. Tibetan refugees fled into Nepal when the new People's Republic of China annexed Tibet, and Nepal became a buffer zone between the two Asian giants. The turmoil naturally spread over Nepal's closed borders and while one Rana made moves towards liberalising the country's moribund political system another attempted to move towards stronger central control. Under the charismatic BP Koirala the Nepali Congress party, supported by the ruling Indian Congress party, was established by many Nepalis and even by some Rana family members.

At the same time King Tribhuvan, forgotten in his palace, was being primed to overthrow the Ranas.

The Shah's Restoration

In late 1950 the king escaped from his palace to the Indian Embassy and from there to India. Meanwhile BP Koirala's forces managed to take most of the Terai from the Ranas and established a provisional government which ruled from the border town of Birganj. Nepal was in turmoil, but there was no clear victor. Finally, India exerted its influence and negotiated a solution. King Tribhuvan returned to Nepal in 1951 and set up a new government comprised of Ranas and commoners from BP Koirala's Nepali Congress.

Although Nepal gradually reopened its long-closed doors and established relations with many other nations, dreams of a new democratic system were not permanently realised. King Tribhuvan died in 1955 and was followed by his son Mahendra. A new constitution provided for a parliamentary system of government and in 1959 Nepal held its first general election. The Nepali Congress won a clear victory, somewhat to the king's surprise, and BP Koirala became the new prime minister. In late 1960, however, the king decided the government wasn't working to his taste and had the cabinet arrested. Political parties were banned and the king swapped his ceremonial role for real control.

In 1962 King Mahendra decided that a partyless, indirect *panchayat* system of government was more appropriate to Nepal. Local panchayats (councils) chose representatives to district panchayats which in turn were represented in the National Panchayat. The real power, however, remained with the king. He retained executive power, directly chose 16 members of the 35 member National Panchayat, and appointed the prime minister and his cabinet. Political parties continued to be banned.

In 1972 Mahendra died and was followed by his son Birendra, who had been educated at Eton and Harvard. Birendra's view that Nepal now had the correct political system was not supported by everybody, however. Popular discontent with slow development, corrupt officials and rising costs simmered in the 1970s. Finally, in 1979 the smouldering anger exploded into violent riots in Kathmandu, and King Birendra announced that a referendum would be held to choose between the panchayat system and one that would permit political parties to operate.

BP Koirala, who had been in jail or in self-imposed exile since 1960, was allowed to campaign but the 1980 referendum result was 55% to 45% in favour of the panchayat system.

Nevertheless, the king had already declared that whichever way the vote went, the people would elect the country's legislature on a five year term and it, in turn, would elect the prime minister. The king, however, would continue to directly appoint 20% of the legislature, and all candidates would have to be members of one of six government-approved organisations and stand under their own name, not as a representative of any party. The first elections under this system were held in 1981.

On the surface, the panchayat system, which allowed a secret vote and universal suffrage, did not appear to be dictatorial: the constitution theoretically guaranteed freedom of speech and peaceful assembly, as well as the right to form unions and associations (so long as they were not motivated by party politics).

The reality was somewhat different. Nepal's military/police apparatus was one of the least publicly accountable in the world and there was strict censorship. Mass arrests, torture and beatings of suspected activists are well documented, and the leaders of the main opposition, the Nepali Congress, spent the years between 1960 and 1990 in and out of prison. (BP Koirala died in 1983.)

Until early 1990, the king wielded considerable power. It is difficult to know quite how much – the inner workings of the palace and the king's relationships with members of the cabinet were not made public – but the constitution guaranteed his supremacy and the National Panchayat basically acted as a rubber stamp.

The aristocracy, in general, managed to retain its influence and wealth (the king and his brothers are all married to Ranas) and the panchayat system did not seem to cramp its style. Firm figures are impossible to find, but it is generally accepted that a huge portion of foreign aid (perhaps up to 50%) was routinely creamed off into royal and ministerial accounts.

People Power

In 1989 the opposition parties formed a coalition to fight for a multi-party democracy with the king as constitutional head; the upsurge of protest was called the Jana Andolan or People's Movement. Popular support was motivated in part by economic problems caused by an Indian government blockade, and by widespread discontent with blatant corruption.

In February 1990 the government responded to nonviolent protest meetings with bullets, tear gas, thousands of arrests and torture. However, after several months of intermittent rioting, curfews, a successful strike, and pressure from various foreign aid donors, the government was forced to back down. The people's victory did not come cheaply. Estimates of the number who died reach to more than 300.

On 9 April the king announced on national radio that he was lifting the ban on political parties and on 16 April he asked the opposition to lead an interim government. He also announced his readiness to accept a role as a constitutional monarch.

Democracy

In May 1991, 20 parties contested a general election for a 205 seat parliament. The Nepali Congress and a communist party were the two major players. The Nepali Congress won power with 37.75% of the vote, which secured it 110 seats. The Communist Party of Nepal-Unified Marxist-Leninist (CPN-UML) won 27.98% of the vote, giving it 69 seats. The next largest party, the United People's Front, received only 4.83% of the vote.

In the years immediately following the 1991 election, the political atmosphere in the country was uneasy. For those on the right of the political spectrum, the king's popularity never waned. Many ordinary people, however, had unrealistically high expectations and they were unsettled by political infighting and hurt by price rises. Economic pressures were intense and in April 1992 a general strike degenerated into street violence between protesters and police, and resulted in a number of deaths.

In late 1994 the Nepali Congress government called a mid-term election. The outcome failed to give any party a clear mandate, and in the end the communist CPN-UML won out, in a coalition with the third major party, the RPP (Rastriya Prajatantra Party, the old panchayats), and with the support of the Nepali Congress. It's one of the very few times in the world that a communist government has come to power by popular vote.

The CPN-UML party presented itself as the champion of the downtrodden masses, but it's hard to see how a communist party could justify its participation in a multi-party democratic system with a constitutional monarch and supporting a free-market economy. Nevertheless, the party was well organised and began consolidating support at the grass-roots level.

Political stability remained elusive, infighting and factionalism was rife, and within nine months the Congress had withdrawn its support for the CPN, fearing the communists were becoming too well entrenched. A new Congress government was formed, with the support of the opportunistic RPP.

The main feature of Nepali democracy in the late 1990s was its changeability: coalitions (often seemingly idealistically contradictory) were formed and broken with alarming frequency, opportunism and corruption were rife, and governments came and went with startling regularity (four times in 1998 alone). In December 1998 the government, a coalition between the Nepali Congress and the Nepal Communist Party-Marxist & Leninist (NCP-ML), fell apart and was forced to resign. The prime minister, GP Koirala, of the Nepali Congress Party, immediately cobbled together a new coalition between the Nepali Congress, the Nepal Communist Party-United Marxist & Leninist (NCP-UML) and the pro-India Nepal Sadbhavana (Goodwill) Party. After the elections of May 1999 the Nepali Congress successfully formed a clear majority, with the UML in opposition, and renewed enthusiasm for a workable democratic system.

On the positive side, democracy has brought a renewed sense of national pride and optimism to many, especially the educated middle classes, although there is widely held cynicism that politicians are corrupt and simply there to line their own pockets at every opportunity. Many people now hanker after the panchayat days when, despite oppression and corruption, things at least got done.

Establishing a workable democratic system at a national level, where one has never existed before, is an enormously difficult task. One of the biggest problems lies in the attitude of many of the politicians. Having spent so many years in the political wilderness during the panchayat days, when they finally get a taste of power their first concern has been their own financial security and political survival. The interests of the country and the people seem to come a distant second.

As long as political immaturity exists, it seems unlikely that one party will gain clear majority support. There is no doubt that there exists within the nation's political parties a will to change, but as long as those in power are in such a position of insecurity, little real change is likely. In Nepal this is further complicated by a fragile economy, extreme poverty, illiteracy, and an ethnically and religiously fragmented population that is continuing to grow at a high rate.

GEOGRAPHY

In two of the three dimensions, length and breadth, Nepal is just another small country. In the third, height, it's number one in the world. Nepal stretches from north-west to south-east about 800km and varies in width from around 90km to 230km. This gives it a total area of just 147,181 sq km according to the official figures.

Within that small area, however, is the greatest range of altitude to be seen on this earth – starting with the Terai, only 100m or so above sea level, and finishing at the top of Mt Everest (8848m), the highest point on earth.

Often a visitor's overriding goal is to see the mountains, especially Everest and Annapurna. However, to exclude the people, flowers, birds and wildlife from the experience is to miss the essence of the country.

Physiographic Regions

Nepal consists of several physiographic regions, or natural zones: the plains in the south, four mountain ranges, and the valleys lying between them. The lowlands with their fertile soils, and the southern slopes of the mountains with sunny exposures, allow for cultivation and are the main inhabited regions.

The Terai & the Bhabar Seen from the air, the Gangetic plain is a flat monotonous expanse that comes to a sudden halt as it turns into mountainous relief. The last of this landscape, about 100m above sea level, encroaches up to 40km into Nepal and is known as the Terai (sometimes written Tarai). This region is a montage of paddy fields, interspersed with oases of mango groves, bamboo stands and villages beneath scattered palms.

There is an intermediate strip between the Terai and the first range of foothills, referred to as the Bhabar, which is stony with shallow soils. Due to the porosity of the soil it is virtually useless for agriculture.

Chure Hills The Chure Hills, known as the Siwalik Hills in India, are the first of the four mountain ranges and run the length of the country. They have an average height of 900m, but are as high as 1350m in places. This range separates the Terai from the Inner Terai and harbours the fossilised remains of many mammals no longer typical of Eurasia. Evidence of a large mountain ape *(Gigantopithecus)* roaming the region up to half a million years ago has fuelled

PHYSIOGRAPHIC REGIONS

CHINA

TIBET

0   75   150 km

PAHAR

MAHABHARAT

TERAI

CHURE

RANGE

• Jumla

Karnali

TRANS-HIMALAYA

Kali Gandaki

HIMALAYA

• Pokhara

Narayani

✛ KATHMANDU

PAHAR

Arun

TERAI

CHURE

MAHABHARAT

TERAI

RANGE

Sun Kosi

Inner Valleys

Inner Terai

INDIA

hope for the existence of the legendary yeti. Like the Bhabar, the region's immature soils are unsuitable for agriculture and therefore large tracts of undisturbed tropical forest remain.

Inner Terai (Duns) Between the Chures and the next range of foothills are longitudinal basins about 150m above sea level, formed by east-west flowing rivers and called the Inner Terai. Before the introduction of DDT in the 1950s, the Terai was inhabited only by the Tharus, who demonstrated a partial resistance to malaria. Otherwise, cultivation was undertaken by people who worked low-lying fields during daylight and returned to homes above 1200m before sundown. The Rana prime ministers (1846 to 1951) deliberately preserved portions of the tropical jungles to use the malarial zone as a safeguard against possible invasion from the south by the British.

After the eradication of malaria, a large resettlement by hill people looking for fertile land occurred. Over a period of less than a decade, more than 50% of the natural forest was cleared to make way for cultivated land. The establishment of Royal Chitwan National Park in 1973 helped abate this trend and preserved prime habitat for indigenous wildlife, such as the royal Bengal tiger and the one-horned rhinoceros.

Mahabharat Range Still northwards, the next range of foothills, often referred to as the Middle Hills, is the Mahabharat Range. These vary between 1500m and 2700m, and though quite steep, are characterised by water-retentive soils allowing for cultivation and extensive terracing. On the lower slopes, remnants of subtropical forests can be found, whereas on the upper reaches, above cultivation, temperate elements begin. These mountains are severed by three major river systems: the Karnali, the Narayani and the Sapt Kosi.

Pahar Zone Between the Mahabharat Range and the Himalaya lies a broad belt referred to as the midlands, or Pahar zone.

This includes fertile valleys (previously large lakes) such as Kathmandu, Banepa and Pokhara. This area, which has been inhabited for centuries, supports nearly half of Nepal's population. As a result, the central and eastern parts of this zone have been extensively cultivated. Ranging mostly between 1000m and 2000m, subtropical and lower temperate forests are found here, but have been disrupted by fuel and fodder gathering.

The Pokhara area is unique, not only because of its magnificent setting at the foot of the Annapurna massif, but also because there is no formidable barrier directly to the south to obstruct the spring and monsoon rain clouds. Consequently, it is subjected to abnormally high rainfall, which limits cultivation to under 2000m. Red laterite soils are typical of such areas, where most minerals except for iron and aluminium oxide are leached out of the soil.

Conversely, the Humla-Jumla area in the west is protected to the south by ranges over 4000m in height that prevent much of the monsoon moisture from reaching this region. As a result wide, uneroded valleys, snowless peaks and drier vegetation are found here.

The Himalaya About a third of the total length of the great Himalaya is contained within Nepal's borders, including 10 of the world's 14 peaks that exceed 8000m in height. These mountains are terraced and cultivated up to about 2700m, or to the level of cloud and mist that precludes growing crops. As a result, the high temperate forest above this to the tree line is fairly well preserved.

Inner Valleys The inner valleys are those cradled within the Himalayan ranges. These broad glacier-worn valleys, which are found in the Everest, Langtang and upper Kali Gandaki areas, are not affected by the strong winds that desiccate the valley floors. The partial rain screen of these high valleys creates still different ecologies.

Trans-Himalaya North of the Himalaya is the high desert region, similar to the Tibetan plateau. This area encompasses the arid valleys of Mustang, Manang and Dolpo, as well as the Tibetan marginals (the fourth range of mountains which sweeps from central to north-western Nepal, averaging below 6000m in height). The trans-Himalaya is in the rain-shadow area and receives significantly less precipitation than the southern slopes. Uneroded crags, spires and formations like crumbling fortresses are typical of this stark landscape.

GEOLOGY

Imagine the space Nepal occupies as an open expanse of water, once part of the Mediterranean Sea, and the Tibetan plateau, or 'roof of the world', as a beachfront property. This was the prehistoric setting until about 60 million years ago, prior to the Indo-Australian plate's collision with the Eurasian continent. As the former was pushed under Eurasia, the earth's crust buckled and folded and mountain building began. See the Continental Plates illustration later in this chapter for a pictorial explanation of the plates' movement.

The upheaval of mountains caused the temporary obstruction of rivers that once flowed unimpeded from Eurasia to the sea. However, on the southern slopes of the young mountains, new rivers formed as trapped, moist winds off the tropical sea rose and precipitated. As the mountains continued to rise and the gradient became steeper, these rivers cut deeper and deeper into the terrain.

The continual crunching of the two plates, augmented by phases of crustal uplifting, created yet new mountain ranges and once again the rivers' courses were interrupted. If the forces of erosion eventually prevailed, long east-west valleys were formed. If not, lakes resulted.

The colossal outcome was the formation of four major mountain systems running north-west by south-east, incised by the north-south gorges of not only new rivers, but also the original ones whose watersheds in Tibet are older than the mountains themselves. In conjunction with the innumerable

rogue ridges that jut out from the main ranges, the terrain can be likened to a complex maze of ceilingless rooms.

The mountain building process continues today, not only displacing material laterally, but also sending the ranges even higher and resulting in natural erosion, landslides, silt-laden rivers, rock faults and also the ever possible earthquakes.

CLIMATE

Nepal has a typical monsoonal, two season year. There's the dry season from October to May and there's the wet season (the monsoon) from June to September.

In summer (May and the early part of June, before the monsoon, are the hottest), Kathmandu can get very hot with temperatures

CONTINENTAL PLATES

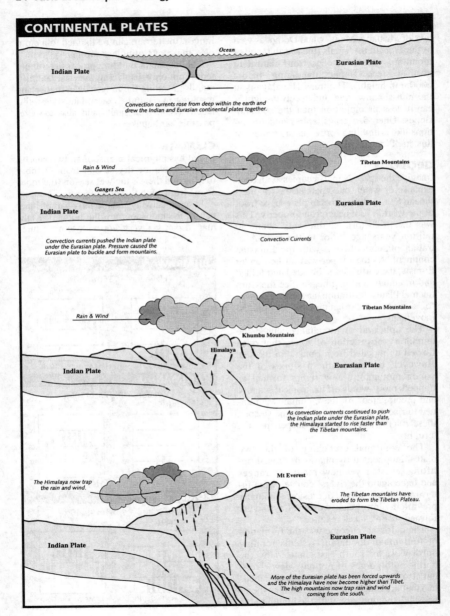

Ocean

Indian Plate

Eurasian Plate

Convection currents rose from deep within the earth and drew the Indian and Eurasian continental plates together.

Rain & Wind

Tibetan Mountains

Ganges Sea

Indian Plate

Eurasian Plate

Convection currents pushed the Indian plate under the Eurasian plate. Pressure caused the Eurasian plate to buckle and form mountains.

Convection Currents

Rain & Wind

Tibetan Mountains

Khumbu Mountains

Himalaya

Indian Plate

Eurasian Plate

As convection currents continued to push the Indian plate under the Eurasian plate, the Himalaya started to rise faster than the Tibetan mountains.

The Himalaya now trap the rain and wind.

Mt Everest

The Tibetan mountains have eroded to form the Tibetan Plateau.

Indian Plate

Eurasian Plate

More of the Eurasian plate has been forced upwards and the Himalaya have now become higher than Tibet. The high mountains now trap rain and wind coming from the south.

often above 30°C. Even in the winter the bright sunny days often reach 20°C although with nightfall the mercury may plummet to near freezing. It never snows in the Kathmandu Valley and higher up the coldest weather is also the driest weather, so snow is unusual. Due to its lower altitude Pokhara is warmer and more pleasant than Kathmandu in the winter, but hotter when the temperature builds up and wetter during the monsoon.

Surprisingly Kathmandu is farther south than New Delhi, and is on about the same latitude as Cairo, Miami and Taipei. Nepal is about 1500km closer to the equator than the Alps in Europe so the snow line is much higher.

See under Fauna in the Causes of Species Diversity boxed text later in this chapter for more details about Nepal's monsoonal climate. Also, When to Go under Planning in the Facts for the Visitor chapter has information about the importance of climatic factors in planning a visit to Nepal.

ECOLOGY & ENVIRONMENT

Much of the land between the Himalaya and the Terai has been vigorously modified by human activities and represents the lifeblood of Nepal. This land has been worked and sculpted over the centuries to provide space for crops, animals and houses. Because of this, forests lying within the inhabited zone, especially on the southern slopes, have been lopped, cut and cleared.

Farming Practices

Plant Use The Terai is widely considered the rice bowl of Nepal, though rice is usually grown up to 2000m, or higher in western parts of the county. It is usually planted before the advent of the monsoon, transplanted soon after and harvested in the autumn. The rich vibrant greens during the monsoon contrast with the subtle, diffused tones as it ripens.

If possible, wheat is planted in the cleared rice fields and harvested in spring. Fields of yellow-flowering mustard are planted for making cooking oil. Corn is also planted in

spring, especially on the hillsides, while millet is grown above the rice zone. Barley is sowed in the higher altitudes, as well as buckwheat with its pink and white flower cluster. The Sherpas grow potatoes up to 4000m, and have been doing so since the crop was introduced, probably from Darjeeling in the middle of the 19th century. Besides providing an important food staple, the prosperity attained from trading potatoes allowed Sherpas to begin building their *gompas* (monasteries) and for their culture to flourish.

In among the crops, various other food crops are grown on the berms dividing the plots, including soya beans, lentils, sesame and chilli peppers. The bright red and yellow plants with clustered seed heads seen amid the shades of green are amaranths, once an important food and medicinal grain for the Aztecs and Incas.

To keep animals out of crops, Nepalis use assorted spiny or unpalatable exotics as natural barriers. Besides prickly pear cactus and agave, there are several euphorbias used, such as the red-flowering crown of thorns, spurge and physic nut.

There are numerous trees planted around villages and fields, all for some kind of purpose, whether for shade, fruit, fodder or medicine. Bananas, mangoes, papaya, citrus fruits, peaches and apples have all brought new income to the remote hill areas.

Fodder such as rice stalks and corn sheaves is often dried and stored in trees, while seed corn is stored under the eaves of houses. A variety of fig trees provide shade for pilgrims and travellers. The magnificent mushrooming canopies of banyan and pipal trees are unmistakable, usually found together atop a stone dais designed for accommodating porters' loads. The banyan has hanging aerial roots and leathery elliptical leaves, while the pipal has a heart-shaped leaf with a long spur. The Buddha is believed to have attained enlightenment under a pipal tree, and Hindus revere the banyan as an embodiment of Lakshmi, the goddess of wealth; and the pipal is seen as an embodiment of Narayan (Vishnu).

Bamboo grows under a variety of conditions and is found throughout Nepal. Giant bamboo is common in the tropics and dwarf bamboo in the temperate regions. This grass species is used for basketry, and for building where forests are depleted, particularly in the east. The Rais work bamboo into everything from water vessels to entire houses.

Another common feature in villages are kitchen gardens comprised of greens, beans, turnips, radishes, pumpkins, cucumbers, taro and squash. Bauhinia, with its distinctive camel-hoof leaves and orchid-like flowers, is grown near houses, the former for fodder and the latter cooked or pickled. In the west, tobacco is a commonly seen plot in villages, as are fields of cannabis,

grown for hemp. In addition, stinging nettles are picked with thongs, rendered harmless by boiling and eaten as greens.

Eupatorium is a red-stemmed daisy with heart-shaped leaves called *ban mara* (death of forest) by the Nepalis. A native of Latin America introduced into the Himalaya during the 19th century, it invades subtropical and temperate zones, and is widespread. Covering deforested hillsides, it is unpalatable, even for sheep and goats, and is a prime indicator of environmental degradation.

Animal Husbandry Bovines play an important role in rural and urban Nepal. Cows are sacred and are not slaughtered, nor used as beasts of burden – they bear calves, and

KEEP Nepal Green

Ecotourism, low-impact trekking, adventure travel and cultural tours are the tourist buzzwords of this generation. Unfortunately, their meaning has been quickly debased. Package tourists consider any exposure to nature to be adventurous, and independent travellers think that because they are living on a shoestring budget they are ecologically and culturally sound.

The ugly side effects of tourism in Nepal have been widely publicised, but little has been said about what can be done to address the problems. The solution is not to cancel your visit – Nepal's fragile economy needs every dollar it can get – but it is important to be well informed, and to act accordingly. Responsible tourism doesn't take a great deal of effort, but the payoffs are enormous.

Tens of thousands of trekkers visit the Nepal Himalaya each year, so the potential for damage is enormous. In 1996, for example, a total of 88,945 trekking permits were issued by the Department of Tourism.

The average trekker consumes as much fuel wood in a day as an entire Nepali household uses in a week, but for around US$2 to US$3 a day camping trekkers and support staff (including porters) can eat food cooked on kerosene stoves. In many places trekkers are required to carry in kerosene and wood fires are prohibited.

Independent trekkers can stay in lodges that use kerosene or fuel-efficient stoves, only take hot showers when the water is heated with solar energy, hydroelectricity or back-burner stoves, and choose their meal times to coincide with other trekkers to minimise the amount of cooking time.

An estimated 50,000kg of garbage is left behind in the mountains by camping trekkers, but just eight cents a day per person covers the cost of having the rubbish carried out of the hills.

Independent trekkers should support lodges and trekking agencies that practise an environmentally sound approach, creating a financial incentive for others to adopt similar methods. They should also carry out nonbiodegradable rubbish, especially plastics and batteries.

On the cultural side, dressing in a way that is consistent with the Nepali norm will not only provide milk and multipurpose dung. In the Kathmandu Valley, the cows wandering and sleeping in the streets have been let loose by pious Hindus. Because the bull is Shiva's steed, and Pashupatinath is a major Shaivite temple, bulls are also considered holy and generally are not used to pull ploughs in the valley. The beasts of burden on the lowlands are usually castrated bulls, or oxen.

Water buffaloes belong to a different genus, but are still lumped with the bovines. These animals lose their body hair as they mature and must wallow to dissipate heat, and for sun protection. The males are used as beasts of burden and are butchered. The females produce a creamy milk, which is also converted into yoghurt. These animals tend to be skittish, a trait probably inherited from their wild ancestors, and those at the Koshi Tappu Wildlife Reserve in the eastern Terai are considered aggressive and dangerous.

Long-haired yaks, no longer found in the wilds of Nepal, are also very temperamental and are mostly used for stud service. What are generally seen are hybrids, which have confusing names. First of all, the female yak is called a *nak*. The nak or yak can be crossbred with cattle, which produces a more docile creature suitable for carrying loads. Locally, the male is called a *dzopkyo* or *zopkiok* and the female a *dzum* or *zhum*. The dzum lactates well and produces a better quality milk than the nak. The second generation of these hybrids is sterile.

KEEP Nepal Green

ease the communication gap, but also help regain respect for women, now sadly eroded by the number of female tourists who sport skimpy and skin-tight clothes.

If you want to find out more, or just want to talk to someone about where and how to trek, visit the Kathmandu Environmental Education Project (KEEP). KEEP operates a Travellers' Information Centre in Kathmandu. Located in Thamel, the Information Centre is open from 10 am to 5 pm daily except Saturday and Nepali public holidays.

Visitors can get information on how to minimise their negative impact and maximise their positive impact. Displays and hand-outs illustrate practical do's and don'ts, and there are also professional Nepali staff and western volunteers to deal with specific questions. During trekking seasons a slide show on conservation practices and a talk on prevention of acute mountain sickness is given every afternoon.

Green-Keeper's coffee shop sells freshly brewed cappuccinos, home-made cakes and cookies, KEEP T-shirts, biodegradable soaps, sun screen, lip balm, and other items useful for ecologically sound trekking. Guidebooks, periodicals and maps are available in the library. A journal records trekkers' comments on treks, and an outside notice board carries notices from people selling gear, looking for trekking partners, looking for friends ...

Although KEEP information is particularly useful for individual trekkers, it is also helpful for group trekkers, mountaineers and city sightseers – everyone is welcome. Eventually, KEEP hopes to become a clearing house for information on the environment and conservation for the entire Himalaya region.

Visitor contributions are much appreciated. An annual fee of US$20 for individuals, US$50 for businesses/institutions, US$160 for life, and US$200 to US$500 for 'Friends of Keep' entitles members to the biannual newsletter and a KEEP T-shirt. KEEP has nonprofit, charitable status.

For more information, contact KEEP (☎ 259275, email tour@keep.wlink.com.np), PO Box 9178, Thamel, Kathmandu.

In the Kali Gandaki and on the southern approaches to the Everest region, donkeys and mules are being used as pack animals. These beasts are often adorned with headgear of dyed plumes and mirrors, and collars of bells. Also, in autumn, during the prime festival season, herds of goats and sheep are driven down from Tibet to be sold for ritual slaughter and the subsequent feasts.

Conservation
As long as the Nepalis marry early, feel uncertain about infant survival, and desire sons to look after them in their old age and to perform funeral rites, the population of Nepal will continue to burgeon. With population demands, the forests will continue to be depleted, erosion caused by humans will compound that which is natural, water supplies will dry up and floods will inundate the lowlands.

The visitor should not, however, adopt the role of the vociferous critic. Nepal is making positive changes, but traditional societies require long lead times for change. There are various alternative energy schemes underway, probably the most successful being the hydroelectric project of Solu and the unit above Namche Bazaar. The Annapurna Conservation Area Project (ACAP) is also an innovative approach, not only incorporating other alternative energy developments, forest conservation and environmental education, but also being an effective strategy for getting the Nepali people directly involved in determining their own destiny.

Conservation is typically a concept of affluent countries with land and resources to spare, a luxury unknown in the Third World. With dwindling space and forests, it is difficult for a farmer to grasp why land should be set aside for tigers and rhinos, especially when they ravage crops, take domestic animals and generally make a hard life even harder.

Visitors should ensure that they minimise their impact on the environment. Trekking groups or individuals staying in lodges should insist that kerosene, as opposed to

firewood, is used for cooking meals and heating water. One should also minimise the use of nonbiodegradable products (especially plastic and batteries) as there are no facilities for their disposal. One potential nightmare is the trend to sell water in plastic bottles, which are expensive and completely unnecessary if you carry your own water bottle and iodine.

See the Trekking chapter for more information on minimising your impact on the environment.

FLORA & FAUNA
See Natural History under the Books section in the Facts for the Visitor chapter for a list of supplementary reading on flora, fauna and national parks.

Flora
There are 6500 known species of trees, shrubs and wild flowers in Nepal. In the temperate areas the flowers emerge as winter recedes and the rivers swell with snow melt, while in the subtropics, the bloom is triggered by warmer temperatures and spring showers. Americans and Europeans will recognise many of the species in the temperate areas, and residents of South-East Asia will recognise many of the subtropical species.

The height of floral glory can be witnessed in March and April when rhododendrons burst into colour. The huge magnolias of the east with their showy white flowers borne on bare branches are also spectacular, as are the orchids (there are over 300 species in Nepal). Not far behind is the blossoming of a variety of shrubs, while on the ground, blue irises and lavender primulas appear.

Unless you can identify wild flowers by their leaves or dried seed capsules, it is necessary to visit the temperate and alpine areas during the monsoon season. In order to do this, you must be prepared to sacrifice comfort and views. However, this is the time to see the true colours of the Himalaya. The southern slopes and the inner valleys are particularly lush at this time. Mints, scrophs, buttercups, cinquefoils, polygonums and composites abound in these areas, while in the alpine areas, dwarf rhododendrons, junipers, ephedras, cotoneasters, saxifrages and primulas paint over the harsh landscape.

Western Nepal, particularly the Dolpo area, is reminiscent of Kashmir in its rich variety of flora. Being in the rain-shadow area, monsoon conditions are more amenable for visitors – the region is dry and free of leeches. In order to witness the full regalia, the time to visit is July and August. From Jumla east one may recognise ground orchids, edelweiss, corydalis, campanulas, anemones, forget-me-nots, impatiens and roses. Higher up in the alpine areas, larkspurs, geraniums, poppies, sedums and saxifrages proliferate.

In the trans-Himalaya, common vegetation is primarily from the legume family, such as the spiny caragana and astragalus, as well as lonicera from the honeysuckle family.

In the post-monsoon season, when most people choose to visit, the flowers of summer are all but gone, save for some straggler blooms and those not palatable to grazing animals. However, in the subtropical and lower temperate areas, some wild flowers which have survived environmental degradation include pink luculia, mauve osbeckia and yellow St John's wort. Flowering cherry trees also add colour to the autumn village scenes as do, in the temperate areas, blue gentians. Otherwise, one can enjoy the autumn yellows of withering maples and ginger, and the reds of barberry shrubs. When the dark temperate forests are back lit, the moss appears luminescent, and the epiphytic ferns and orchids shine like tiny paper lanterns.

In the Kathmandu Valley, Australians will find familiar silky oak with its spring golden inflorescence, and bottlebrush and eucalyptus. Though fast-growing timber species in their native country, in the valley these trees are planted as ornamentals along with cherry, poplar and jacaranda. The latter, with its lavender blossoms, is from South America, as are bougainvillea and the giant poinsettias. Historically, the Nepalis have been avid gardeners of such exotics as hibiscus, camellia, cosmos, salvia and marigold.

Fauna

Birds More than 800 species are known in Nepal, more birds than in Canada and the USA combined, or nearly 10% of the world's species! Resident bird numbers are augmented by migratory species, as well as winter and summer visitors.

Eight species of stork have been identified along the water courses of the Terai. Similar in appearance are the cranes, but not as well represented, save for the demoiselle cranes that fly down the Kali Gandaki and Dudh Kosi for the winter, before returning in spring to their Tibetan nesting grounds. Herons and egrets are quite common in the tropics and subtropics, and distinguished in flight by their curved-neck posture, as opposed to the outstretched necks of storks and cranes.

Most of the waterfowl are migratory. Many can be seen at the Kosi Barrage in the eastern Terai and in the Chitwan and Bardia areas. The bar-headed goose has been observed flying at altitudes near 8000m.

Raptors or birds of prey are found in all sizes in the Himalaya, and are especially prevalent with the onset of winter. One of the first raptors to leave is the small Eurasian kestrel that must flap its wings at regular intervals, or rapidly when hovering, as compared to the Himalayan griffon, a heavy bird that must wait for thermal updraughts to allow its soaring, gliding flight. The griffon, as well as the lammergeyer, with a wingspan of nearly 3m, are carrion eaters, though often mistaken for eagles. There are, however, true eagles present, including the resident golden eagle common in the Khumbu, as well as other species that are known to migrate in large numbers in the Kali Gandaki region. Many medium-sized raptors have highly variable plumages and are difficult to identify in the sky.

There are six species of pheasant in Nepal, including the national bird, the impeyan pheasant, the male of which has a plumage of iridescent colours. These birds are known as downhill fliers, as they do not fly, per se, and must walk uphill! When flushed they will cant and swerve downhill to evade enemies such as the golden eagle. The cheer and koklas pheasants are only found west of the Kali Gandaki, while the kalij pheasant is common throughout Nepal, but with different colour phases.

Nepal hosts 17 species of cuckoo which are characterised by their distinctive calls. Arriving in March, they herald the coming of spring. The Indian cuckoo is recognised by its *'kaphal pakyo'* call, which is Nepali for announcing that the fruit of the box myrtle is ripe. The common hawk cuckoo has a repetitious call that sounds like 'brain fever', which rises in a crescendo – aptly described by British sahibs as they lay sweating with malarial fevers. Most cuckoos are social parasites, meaning they lay their eggs in the nests of other species.

Vegetation Zones

In western Nepal, forests usually extend to higher elevations than elsewhere in the country due to drier conditions. Above the temperate cultivation zone and below the tree line, the forests are less disrupted, although they do come under pressure from summer herders and wood gatherers.

Tropical Zone (up to 300m)
Sal *(Shorea robusta)*, a broad-leafed, semideciduous hardwood, dominates here. The leaves are used for 'disposable' plates, and the wood is used for construction. It varies little from east to west and is a fire-climax species.

There is also a deciduous moist forest in this zone, of acacia and rosewood, as well as open areas of tall elephant grass. The grass areas are burned off in winter, which helps preserve them – otherwise they would be succeeded by a moist forest. These two habitats are known as 'seral' communities, because if they are left undisturbed, they would both be replaced by the sal climax forest.

The red silk cotton tree *(Bombax malarbaricum)* with its thorny trunks when young, and smooth-buttressed trunk bases when older, has leafless limbs that burst into bright red flowers in early spring. It is also a part of the moist forest. The cotton or 'kapok' from these trees is used for stuffing cushions and mattresses.

These forest types are typical of the Chure and Inner Terai, though sal and silky cotton are also found in the subtropical zone.

Subtropical Zone (1000m to 2000m)
The dominant species east of the Kali Gandaki are the true chestnuts and a member of the tea family, schima. The spiky flower clusters of the chestnuts appear in the fall, while the fragrant white flowers of the schima bloom in late spring. Due to the popularity of chestnut wood as a source of fuel, it is often depleted.

In the west, the chir pine is found on all aspects. The species has long needles in bundles of three and is also found in the east, but confined to drier southern slopes.

Lower Temperate Zone (1700m to 2700m)
Evergreen oaks are indigenous to this zone. In the east, the oaks of the wet forests are festooned with moss and epiphytes and have dense understoreys. In the west, another oak preferring dry conditions is present, as well as on the sunny slopes of the east.

One of the most colourful, varied and vocal families is the timalids, or babblers and laughing thrushes, common from the tropical Terai to the upper temperate forest. They are from 8cm to 33cm in size and live in both terrestrial and arboreal habitats. They are found individually or in large, foraging parties, and can often be identified by their raucous calls. The black-capped sibia with its constant prattle and ringing song is an integral part of the wet temperate forests. The spiny babbler is Nepal's only endemic species.

There are three pairs of species among the crow family; their appearance and behaviour are virtually identical, but each species occupies a different altitudinal range. The red-billed blue magpies are residents of the

Vegetation Zones

A common wet forest that occurs mostly on north and west faces in western Nepal is comprised of horse chestnut, maple and walnut. Alder and birch are prevalent along water courses.

Homogeneous blue-pine forests occur extensively in the west, mostly on south faces, and range to the tree line. This species is hardy and fire resistant, thriving well in habitats modified by humans. It is also found throughout the east, but to a lesser extent. The blue pine is distinguished from the only other pine in Nepal, the chir pine, by its shorter needles in bundles of five, and long, pendulous cones. Both species are used for carpentry and roofing, while the resin is converted to turpentine.

Upper Temperate Zone (2400m to 4000m)
Another evergreen oak that is widespread throughout the dry forests of the west exhibits two types of leaves, the young ones spiny, while the older ones have leaf margins. In the east, this species is confined to southern slopes, but is heavily cut for fodder and fuel.

The spectacular wet rhododendron forests are interspersed with hemlock and fir. *Rhododendron arboreum*, the national flower, reaches heights of 18m and ranges in colour from red to white. There are over 30 species of rhododendron in Nepal, but these are found more extensively in the east than the west. Unfortunately, this tree is felled for fuel or turned into charcoal.

There is also a high conifer forest where blue pine is again found, occurring in the west with fir and spruce, both of which also form pure stands. In the east, firs, hemlocks and yews associate with blue pine. Firewood and roofing shingles are the common usages for these species. A mixed broad-leafed forest of maple and laurel is also typical of this zone.

Subalpine Zone (3000m to 4000m)
Silver fir mixed with oak and birch extend to the tree line in the west. East of the Kali Gandaki, only birch is found to the tree line, though under wetter conditions, dwarf bamboo and shrub rhododendron replace it. In dry areas, juniper species occur to the tree line.

Alpine Zone (4000m to snow line)
In this realm above the tree line, vegetation must cope with extremes in ground temperatures, and moisture gradients that range from nothing in winter to profuse in summer. Only the most tenacious of wild flowers thrive here, generally by being hirsute or having thick underground stems (rhizomes). A successful example is stellara, common above 5500m. In the trans-Himalaya, the vegetation is restricted to the arid-adapted species of the Tibetan plateau.

subtropical zone, while the yellow-billed species are found in the temperates. The Indian tree pie prefers the tropics while the Himalayan species lives in the subtropics and temperates. Above the tree line, two species of chough, congregating in large flocks in winter, are prevalent. Though they often overlap in range, the yellow-billed chough is found higher and is known to enter mountaineers' tents high on Everest. Another of the crow family, also bold and conspicuous in the trans-Himalayan region, is the large raven.

Besides such families as kingfishers, bee-eaters, drongos, minivets, parakeets and sunbirds, there are a host of other passerines, or perching birds, present throughout Nepal. These include 30 species of flycatchers and nearly 60 species of thrushes and warblers. Many smaller species congregate in heterogeneous flocks, not only for feeding purposes, but for protection.

In the Kathmandu Valley, sparrows and pigeons demonstrate adaptability to urban centres by their sheer numbers. Dark kites, hawk-like birds with forked tails, are common over the city. At sunset, loose groups of crows, mynas, egrets and kites fly to their respective roosts. After dark, the noisy ruckus of the spotted owlets substitutes for the cacophony of car horns. The robin dayal, with its cocked tail, is the common songster of early mornings. Pulchowki, Nagarjun and Shivapuri are excellent areas for finding birds of subtropical and temperate habitats.

In the Pokhara region, the Indian roller is conspicuous when it takes flight and flashes the iridescent turquoise on its wings. Otherwise, while perched, it appears as a plain brown bird. Local superstition has it that if

Causes of Species Diversity

Not only does Nepal's phenomenal topography range from near sea level to 8848m, but it is contained within a country approximately the size of the US state of Iowa, or that of England and Wales together. The distance between the tropical lowlands and the realm under ice and snow is, in some places, less than 100km apart. In most parts of the world these zones are separated by thousands of kilometres! In how many places in the world can one see myna birds chattering on banana fronds at 2700m before a snowy mountain backdrop seemingly close enough to reach out and touch?

Geographical Location
The 28° latitude line runs just north of Mt Everest, as well as through Morocco and central Florida. This southerly latitude is the reason the permanent snow line is above 5000m. Nepal straddles two of the world's zoo-geographical zones: the Holarctic to the north and the Oriental to the south. This means that one finds life forms from Europe and northern Asia, typical in the Holarctic and species of India and tropical South-East Asia, in the Oriental.

Climate
Nepal is subject to a monsoon-type climate where wet summers and dry winters are characteristic. Without this weather pattern, the country would be a desert with much less extensive speciation.

Every summer between June and July, the sun moves northwards and heats up the mountains, creating a massive convection cell. The subsequent rising air produces a vacuum that draws the moisture-laden air off the Bay of Bengal. This air runs into the Himalayan barriers, cools as it rises and condenses in the form of rain. Thus begins the monsoon season, three to someone about to embark on a journey sees a roller going their way it is a good omen. If they see a crow, however, it is a bad omen and the trip is aborted. Many trips must be destined for delay thanks to the presence of the common crow!

Mammals As one might expect, due to habitat degeneration from both natural and human causes, opportunities for seeing wildlife are usually restricted to national parks, reserves and western Nepal, where the population is sparse. Wildlife numbers have also been thinned due to poaching for pelts or other animal parts that are considered to be delicacies or medicinally valuable. Animals are also hunted because of the damage they inflict on crops and domestic animals.

At the top of the food chain is the royal Bengal tiger, the most magnificent cat, which is solitary and territorial. Males have territorial ranges that encompass those of two or three females and may span as much as 100 sq km. Royal Chitwan National Park of the Inner Terai and Royal Bardia National Park in the western Terai protect sufficient habitat to sustain viable breeding populations.

The spotted leopard is an avid tree climber and in general more elusive than the tiger. Like tigers, these nocturnal creatures have been known to prefer human flesh when they have grown old or been maimed. Humans are not only easy prey, but once the taste is acquired, human-flesh eaters lose interest in their natural prey. Local people have likened them to evil spirits because their success at evading hunters suggests they can read minds.

The snow leopard is often protected from hunters, not only by national parks, but also

Causes of Species Diversity

four months of high humidity, overcast skies and gentle rain. Deluges that occur during this time are due to tropical storms or squalls in the Indian Ocean.

The eastern Himalaya receives the brunt of the monsoon which loses its impetus as it moves west along the mountains. Consequently there is a distinct moisture gradient from east to west. Biogeographically, there are life forms east of the Kali Gandaki Valley associated with wet forests (typically more prolific in species diversity), while west of this line are dissimilar ones preferring drier habitats.

In winter, western Nepal experiences a reverse monsoon caused by a shift in the jet stream. This phenomenon, which drags weather patterns from the west off the Arabian Sea, brings moisture to the region in the form of snow and is essential for agriculture. The oscillation of the jet stream lasts between November and March and is not only responsible for Everest's snow plume and black appearance, but also renders mountaineering difficult.

Altitude & Aspect

Altitude and aspect (the direction that a slope faces) play equal roles in determining climate and vegetation. Temperature decreases with elevation, which affects flora as well as fauna. Conversely, rainfall increases with altitude, up to about 2700m. At this level, the clouds have spent their moisture and form a ceiling. This not only establishes the limit for crops, but affects natural vegetation distribution as well.

Aspect, or exposure, is also important in terms of moisture content, fire resistance and defining the height of the tree line. South and east-facing slopes receive more sun and therefore are drier. The shadier northern and western faces are more moist, less prone to fire and thus richer in species.

by inhabiting inhospitable domains above the tree line and sensitive border regions. Its territory depends upon the ranges of ungulate (hoofed) herds, its prey species. Packs of wolves compete directly and when territories overlap, the solitary snow leopard will be displaced.

The one-horned rhinoceros is the largest of three Asian species and is a distinct genus from the two-horned African rhinos. It has poor eyesight and though weighing up to two tonnes, is amazingly quick. Anyone who encounters a mother with its calf is likely to witness a charge, which is disconcertingly swift, even if you are on an elephant. The rhino is a denizen of the grasslands of the Inner Terai, specifically the Chitwan Valley, although it has also been reintroduced to Royal Bardia National Park.

The Indian elephant, like the one-horned rhino, is different to its African relative, belonging to a separate genus. The only wild elephants known to exist in Nepal are in the western part of the Terai and Chure Hills, though individuals often range across the border from India. Elephants are known to maintain matriarchal societies, and females up to 60 years of age bear calves. Though able to reach 80 years of age, elephants' life

spans are determined by dentition. Molars are replaced as they wear down, but only up to six times. When the final set is worn, the animal dies of starvation.

Periodically, male and occasionally female elephants, enter a 'musth' condition that makes them excitable and highly aggressive. While in this agitated state they have been known to trample villages. When a herd goes on the rampage, outsiders or non-Hindus are often summoned, as the elephant is considered a holy animal because of the much-loved Ganesh, the elephant-headed god of the Hindu pantheon.

There are several species of deer, but most are confined to the lowlands. The spotted deer is probably the most beautiful, while the sambar is the largest. The muntjac, or barking deer, which usually makes its presence known by its sharp, one note alarm call, is found up to 2400m, while the unusual musk deer, which has antelope-like features and is only 50cm high at the shoulder, ranges even higher.

There are two primates: the rhesus macaque and the common langur. The rhesus are earth-coloured with short tails and travel on the ground in large, structured troops, unafraid of humans. The langur are arboreal, with black faces, grey fur, long limbs and tails. Because of Hanuman, the monkey god in the Hindu epic the *Ramayana*, both species are considered holy and are well protected. The rhesus ranges from the Terai up to 2400m, while the langur goes up to 3600m.

In the Kathmandu Valley, rhesus macaques at the Swayambhunath and Pashupatinath temples take advantage of their holy status and relieve worshippers of their picnic lunches and consecrated food.

Two even-toed ungulate mammals are found in the alpine regions. They are the Himalayan tahr, a near-true goat, and the blue sheep, which is genetically stranded somewhere between the goat and sheep. The male tahr pose majestically in their flowing manes on the grassy slopes of inner valleys, while the blue sheep turn a bluish-grey in winter and are found in the trans-Himalayan region.

Snow leopards are solitary animals and live above the snow line.

The Himalayan black bear is omnivorous and a bane to corn crops in the temperate forests. Though it rarely attacks humans, its poor eyesight may lead it to interpret a standing person as making a threatening gesture and to attack. If so, the best defence is not to run, but to lie face down on the ground – particularly effective when one is wearing a backpack. Nepal's bears are known to roam in winter instead of hibernating.

There are some prominent canines, though behaviourally they are fairly shy. The jackal, with its eerie howling that sets village dogs barking at night, ranges from the Terai to alpine regions. It is both a hunter and scavenger, and will take chickens and raid crops.

The pika, or mouse-hare, is the common guinea pig-like mammal of the inner valleys, often seen scurrying nervously between rocks. The marmot is of western Nepal is a large rodent; it commonly dwells in the trans-Himalaya. The marmot is also found in Sikkim and Bhutan, but not eastern Nepal – such gaps in speciation are not uncommon across the Himalaya.

Noisy colonies of flying foxes or fruit bats have chosen the trees near the old Royal Palace in Kathmandu and the chir pines at the entrance to Bhaktapur as their haunts. They are known to fly great distances at night to raid orchards, before returning at dawn. They have adequate eyesight for their feeding habits and do not require the sonar system of insectivorous bats.

Pulchowki, Nagarjun and Shivapuri are good areas for possible sightings of small mammals.

Reptiles There are two indigenous species of crocodile: the gharial and marsh mugger. The gharial inhabits rivers and is a prehistoric-looking fish-eating creature with bulging eyes and a long, narrow snout. The marsh mugger prefers stagnant water and is omnivorous, feeding on anything within reach. Due to the value of its hide and eggs, the gharial was hunted to the brink of extinction, but has increased in numbers since the establishment of a hatchery and rearing centre in Chitwan. Both crocodiles inhabit the Terai.

Though venomous snakes such as cobras, vipers and kraits are present, the chance of encountering one is small, not only because of their usual evasive tactics, but also because they are indiscriminately slaughtered. The majority of species are found in the Terai, though the mountain pit viper is known higher up, along with a few other nonvenomous species.

NATIONAL PARKS & CONSERVATION AREAS

Nepal has eight national parks and four wildlife reserves that protect every significant ecological system in the country – from the tropical plains of the Terai and the fertile midland valleys, to the highest mountains in the world.

Around 16,650 sq km are protected, or 11.3% of the country's area, and you can add another 2600 sq km if you include the Annapurna Conservation Area. Considering the strength of the demand for land, there has been a particularly impressive commitment to conservation.

Travellers are almost certain to visit a protected area – the Sagarmatha National Park includes Mt Everest; the Annapurna Conservation Area includes many of the most popular treks around the Annapurna Himal; and Royal Chitwan National Park is famous for its elephant-back safaris in search of royal Bengal tigers and one-horned rhinoceroses.

All visitors are charged Rs 1000 to enter a park or reserve, and this includes the Annapurna Conservation Area. There is no fee for using a camera or video camera within the parks. The Department of National Parks & Wildlife Conservation (☎ 220912) can be contacted through PO Box 860, Babar Mahal, Kathmandu.

The problems that Nepal has faced in setting aside areas for conservation are more acute than those faced in most industrially developed countries, but the Nepalis are responding by developing new management concepts – it is not possible or desirable to set aside areas of land that are totally untouched by humans.

Firstly, very little of Nepal can be accurately described as wilderness. Most of the country is, in some way, used by humans. Virtually every possible square metre of arable land is used for farming; the remaining forests are utilised for firewood and hunting; the high country is used for hunting and grazing; and the whole country is crisscrossed with trade routes. The only exceptions are several royal hunting reserves, some of the Terai (large parts of which were virtually untouched until the 1950s) and mountain peaks at high altitude.

Secondly, developing national parks and conservation areas by following the western model would have meant totally blocking local people's access to a resource that might literally mean the difference between life and death. In most cases, therefore, the Nepalis have attempted to marry the competing interests between conservation (and tourist attractions?) on the one hand and farming (and food?) on the other.

For instance, the Sagarmatha National Park is the traditional home to several thousand Sherpas whose ancestors settled the area 500 years ago. Banishing them from their homeland would have been unthinkable, so the park management has been responsible for encouraging sustainable economic development, as well as controlling the impact of a growing number of tourists. In another example, although thousands of recent settlers were actually moved outside the park's boundary when it was declared, Royal Chitwan National Park is still used by them as an important source for thatching grass, which is harvested every year.

Despite these essential compromises, there have been some notable successes. The magnificent royal Bengal tiger has been saved in Chitwan and there have been impressive achievements in the Sagarmatha National Park and the Annapurna Conservation Area near Pokhara – in forestry, agriculture, health and education, as well as in protecting the most spectacular scenery in the world. See those sections later.

NATIONAL PARKS & CONSERVATION AREAS

CHINA

TIBET

Shey Phoksundo NP

Rara NP

Khaptad NP

Kanjiroba

Jumla

Mahendranagar

Dhorpatan Hunting Reserve

Annapurna Conservation Area

Royal Sukla Phanta WR

Royal Bardia NP

Dhaulagiri

Pokhara

Langtang NP

Sagarmatha NP

Mt Everest

Nepalganj

KATHMANDU

Bhairawa

Royal Chitwan NP

Parsa WR

Makalu-Barun NP & Conservation Area

Birganj

Janakpur

Koshi Tappu WR

Biratnagar

INDIA

0   75   150 km

National Park (NP)

Wildlife Reserve (WR)

Conservation Area

Hunting Reserve

Koshi Tappu Wildlife Reserve

The Koshi Tappu Wildlife Reserve is a small (175 sq km) reserve that lies on the beautiful flood plain of the Sapt Kosi in eastern Nepal. It runs north from the massive Kosi Barrage and the Indian border.

The reserve is often flooded during the monsoon, although mostly to shallow depths only. It is, nonetheless, home to the last surviving group of wild buffalo and several species of deer. The vegetation is mainly grassland with some mixed riverine forest. A total of 280 different species of birds – including many migratory birds – have been recorded. Local villagers harvest grasses for thatching, and also fish and collect edible fruits and ferns.

The Mahendra Hwy skirts the reserve, and the only formal accommodation option is one top-end tented camp. See the Terai chapter for more details.

Sagarmatha National Park

North-east of Kathmandu and alongside the Tibetan border, the Sagarmatha National Park covers 1148 sq km, all above 3000m in altitude. Mt Everest (Sagarmatha in Nepalis) is the main attraction, but there are a number of other well-known peaks, including Lhotse and Ama Dablam. The mountains are broken by deep gorges, glacial valleys and lakes.

Tree species include pine, fir, juniper and birch, and numerous species of rhododendron. Among the animals, there are musk deer, Himalayan tahr, black bears, wolves and fascinating birdlife. Most famous would be the beautiful impeyan pheasant, Nepal's national bird, but there are choughs, snow pigeons and Himalayan griffons, among 130 bird species.

Over 3500 Sherpas use the park for cropping and grazing (their villages are not included in the park proper) and their unique culture provides yet another reason to visit. There are several important monasteries. For detailed information on this park try to find a copy of *Mt Everest National Park: Sagarmatha, Mother of the Universe* by Margaret Jefferies, an excellent book that gives fascinating background information, and has some magnificent photos.

This is one of the most popular trekking regions in the country, but it's only accessible by foot, with the nearest airstrip at Lukla and the roadhead at Jiri. Many trekkers visit, lured by the highest and most spectacular mountain scenery in the world and by Sherpa culture. See the Trekking chapter for information on trekking.

Makalu-Barun National Park & Conservation Area

The Makalu-Barun National Park & Conservation Area, just to the east of Mt Everest, was proclaimed in November 1992. It covers 2330 sq km. Its boundaries are marked by the Arun River to the east and the Sagarmatha National Park to the north-west. Its northern boundary is the 35,000 sq km Qomolangma (Mt Everest) Nature Preserve in Tibet. Together these three parks protect a vast area around the Everest massif.

The park includes Makalu, at 8463m the fifth highest mountain in the world, and each year a small number of trekkers walk in to the base camp. Elevations range from 435m on the Arun River to the 8000m summits of the himal (a *himal* is a range or massif with permanent snow). Nearly all ecological zones, from subtropical forest to the alpine snows of the Himalaya, are found in the area. In the valleys you can find some of the last remaining tracts of pristine mountain landscapes in Nepal. The area is rich in plant and animal diversity.

The wilderness area has the status of a national park, but the surrounding regions, which are home to more than 32,000 people, are being managed according to the model pioneered by the Annapurna Conservation Area Project. The majority of people are Rai, followed by Sherpa and Tibetan-speaking groups.

There is an airstrip at Tumlingtar about 10km south of Khandbari.

Royal Chitwan National Park

South-west of Kathmandu, near the Indian border on the tropical Terai, Royal Chitwan

National Park and the contiguous Parsa Wildlife Reserve cover just over 1431 sq km. The park includes a section of the Chure Hills and the Rapti, Narayani and Reu valleys.

Sal forest covers 70% of the park, with the remainder consisting of grasslands and riverine forests. This is home to the only significant number of one-horned rhinoceroses surviving in Nepal, and to other endangered species like the royal Bengal tiger, Gangetic dolphin and gharial crocodile. Altogether, there are over 43 species of large mammals and over 450 species of birds. There are no human communities living in the park, but the surrounding countryside is intensively cultivated.

For detailed information on this park, try to find a copy of *Royal Chitwan National Park: Wildlife Heritage of Nepal* by Hemanta R Mishra and Margaret Jefferies; some of the photos are magnificent.

The park is easily accessible by road, and accommodation ranges from five star and expensive, to zero star and cheap. Many people visit for two or three days (especially if they are going to or from India) to take advantage of elephant safaris through the forest. See the Terai chapter for more details.

Annapurna Conservation Area

North of Pokhara and extending to the Tibetan border, the Annapurna Conservation Area covers 2600 sq km. It includes the Annapurna peaks, the famous Annapurna Sanctuary and a significant section of the Kali Gandaki Valley.

The conservation area is run by the Annapurna Conservation Area Project, or ACAP, a nongovernmental, nonprofit organisation which is funded by various trusts. ACAP's primary objectives are to improve local standards of living, to protect the environment and to develop more sensitive forms of tourism.

This is the most popular trekking region in Nepal, especially for individual trekkers, and this influx of visitors has added to the pre-existing problems in the mountains. The trekkers' demands for heating and hot water have led to increased deforestation,

there are litter and sanitation problems, and wildlife has been driven away from many parts.

In response, ACAP has started work on a number of projects, such as forestry nurseries, introducing wood-saving technologies (eg efficient stoves), banning fires altogether in certain areas, and building rubbish tips and latrines. Many problems still remain, and it is vital that trekkers cooperate with these and other initiatives. If you would like more information on ACAP activities, contact the King Mahendra Trust for Nature Conservation (☎ 526571, fax 526570), PO Box 3712, Babar Mahal, Kathmandu.

The treks around the Annapurna Himal are undoubtedly some of the best in the world – not only for the grandeur of the mountains, but for the variety of fascinating cultures that you can visit (Bhotiya, Tibetan, Tamang, Magar, Gurung, Thakali and others). The area is easily accessible from Pokhara and there is an airstrip at Jomsom. See the Trekking chapter for more information.

Langtang National Park

This is the nearest national park to Kathmandu, extending from 32km north of Kathmandu to the Tibetan border, and covering 1710 sq km. The park encloses the catchments for two major rivers – the Trisuli and the Sun Kosi – and several 7000m mountains.

The complex topography and geology of the area together with the varied climatic patterns means there is a wide variety of vegetation types and animals. There are small areas of subtropical forest below 1000m, then temperate oak and pine forests, subalpine juniper, larch and birch, and finally alpine scrub, rocks and snow. The fauna includes lesser or red pandas, muntjac, musk deer, black bear, monkeys and ghoral and serows (so-called goat-antelopes).

About 45 villages lie within the park boundaries (although they do not come under park jurisdiction). In total, around 18,000 people depend on the park's resources, mainly for wood and pasture land.

There are several ethnic groups, but the majority are Tamangs (settlers from Tibet and followers of the pre-Buddhist Bön religion).

There are a number of popular treks in the park, ranging in length and difficulty. There is road access to Dhunche (near the park headquarters) from Kathmandu, or you can walk in from Sundarijal, Panchkhal, or from Chatara or Tatopani on the Kodari road. See the Trekking chapter for more details.

Dhorpatan Hunting Reserve
The Dhorpatan Hunting Reserve lies in the Dhaulagiri Himal in western Nepal. It is characterised by a dry climate in the north and well developed mixed hardwood forests at lower elevations.

The 1325 sq km reserve is one of the prime habitats for the blue sheep, a highly prized trophy animal. Other 'game' animals include gboral, serow, Himalayan tahr, black bear, deer, pheasants and partridges.

The only access, unless you have a helicopter, is by foot from Jelbang.

Shey Phoksundo National Park
The Shey Phoksundo National Park is the largest park in Nepal at 3555 sq km. It encompasses the Kanjiroba Himal in western Nepal and runs north to the Tibetan border.

The park stretches across all possible vegetation zones – from the luxuriant forests of the lower Himalaya to the near desert of the Tibetan plateau. Typical animals include the Tibetan hare, Himalayan weasel and the beautiful snow leopard. Lake Phoksundo and the Shey Monastery are the two main attractions in the park, but the entire region has been little touched by the modern era.

Very few people visit this region, partly because access has, in the past, been officially restricted and entails a dangerous 14 day trek from Pokhara. Permits can be arranged through trekking companies. See *Trekking in Hidden Land of Dolpa-Tarap & Shey Poksumdo* by Paolo Gondini (available at Tiwari's Pilgrims Book House, Kathmandu) for more detailed information. According to information from the depart-ment, it takes two days to walk to the entrance gate at Sumduwa from Dunai, the district headquarters for Dolpo.

Rara National Park
In little-visited western Nepal, the 106 sq km Rara National Park was established to preserve the catchment and surrounds of the beautiful Rara Lake – a clear high-altitude lake ringed with pine, spruce and juniper forests and snow-capped peaks. The lake is the largest in Nepal (10.8 sq km) and is an important water bird habitat.

The only way to get to Rara Lake is a strenuous three day trek from the airstrip at Jumla, or a 10-day trek from the roadhead at Surkhet. Trekking in this area is much more difficult than in east or central Nepal: some areas are still closed and there are frequent food shortages. See Lonely Planet's *Trekking in the Nepal Himalaya* by Stan Armington for more details.

Royal Bardia National Park
In the western Terai, bordering the Geruwa (a branch of the Karnali River), this 968 sq km reserve is reminiscent in many ways of Royal Chitwan National Park. The relative difficulty of access, however, means it is much less popular. But there is a higher likelihood of seeing a royal Bengal tiger.

The reserve is bordered to the north by the Chure Hills, but is predominantly flat and dominated by sal forests and grasslands. Apart from tigers there is a small herd of introduced rhinoceroses, blue bull, a variety of deer and a few wild elephants. If you're lucky you might also see Gangetic dolphin in the river.

The park is 2½ hours by road from Nepalganj and there is accommodation available, ranging from budget to top of the range. See the Terai chapter for more details.

Khaptad National Park
Another rarely visited park, Khaptad covers 225 sq km in far western Nepal. Lying at around 3000m it is largely a rolling plateau with grasslands, and oak and coniferous forests.

Royal Sukla Phanta Wildlife Reserve

This 305 sq km reserve lies in the far southwestern corner of Nepal on the Indian border. It covers a riverine flood plain, dominated by sal forest, but like both Chitwan and Bardia national parks, there are also grasslands which make it ideal for wildlife observation.

Sukla Phanta is one of the last strongholds for the endangered swamp deer (now thought to number about 2000 here), but there are also around 30 tigers and an estimated 45 wild elephants, as well as leopards and a variety of birdlife.

Access to the park is by road from Mahendranagar and it is possible to stay in a tented camp. See the Terai chapter for more details.

GOVERNMENT & POLITICS

In April 1990, the Jana Andolan, or People's Movement, forced King Birendra to abandon the panchayat system that had been established by his father and under which the king enjoyed virtually sole power. (See the History section earlier in this chapter for more information.)

A new constitution was adopted in November 1990. Basically it provided for a constitutional monarchy, universal adult franchise and a multi-party parliamentary system. Members of the 205 seat House of Representatives (Pratinidhi Sabha) are elected every five years according to the first-past-the-post system.

In the May 1991 elections, the Nepali Congress won 110 seats, giving it a simple majority, and formed the government with GP Koirala as prime minister. Mid-term elections in 1994 were inconclusive, and a coalition government was formed. Over the following years Nepal saw no less than six feeble coalitions and seemingly endless political instability. After the May 1999 elections, stability again seems achievable – the Nepali Congress won a majority, with Krishna Bhattarai as prime minister.

Members of the 60 seat National Assembly (Rastriya Sabha) have a six year tenure; a third retire every two years. Thirty-five members are elected by proportional repre-

NEPAL ADMINISTRATIVE DIVISIONS

1 Mahakali	8 Lumbini
2 Seti	9 Bagmati
3 Karnali	10 Narayani
4 Bheri	11 Janakpur
5 Rapti	12 Sagarmatha
6 Dhaulagiri	13 Kosi
7 Gandaki	14 Mechi

CHINA
TIBET
Mahendranagar
Pokhara
Nepalganj
KATHMANDU
Bhairawa
Birganj
Janakpur
Biratnagar
INDIA
0   75   150 km

Maoists' 'People's War'

Any casual reader of the *Kathmandu Post* can't help but notice the daily references to 'Maoists rebels' and deaths associated with them. Since February 1996 the fiercely anti-monarchial Nepal Communist Party-Maoist (NCP-M) have been waging an insurgency against the constitutional monarchial democratic system. In the three years following the beginning of the insurgency, more than 600 people were killed.

Anti-government and anti-establishment rhetoric is predictably strong: the political parties participating in the 1999 elections were referred to in Maoist propaganda as 'reactionaries' and 'stooges of imperialists and hegemonists'. Although lying low, the Maoists boycotted the elections claiming they did not believe the elections would bring stability to Nepal.

The Maoists' influence is strongest largely in the north-western and western parts of Nepal, although they do plan to spread their activities to other parts of the country. It is hard to gauge what level of support they command, as they aim for grass-roots support.

Although they receive wide media coverage, the activities of the Maoists are not aimed at foreigners and so pose no threat to visitors to Nepal.

sentation, 15 members are elected by local government representatives and 10 members are nominated by the king.

ECONOMY

Judged by western standards, Nepal is one of the poorest countries in the world with an estimated annual Gross Domestic Product (GDP) of only US$210 per person in 1997. To a certain extent, this suggests an overly bleak picture because more than 90% of the population is basically, and will almost certainly remain, subsistence farmers operating outside the cash economy.

Agriculture

Agriculture accounts for 41% of GDP. At present, most farmers succeed in meeting their basic needs and producing a small surplus for cash sales. Indeed, aid workers have been known to bemoan the fact that they can't convince peasant farmers to work harder and produce additional cash crops.

The problem is that the rewards are not believed to be worth the effort. After all, if a family has food, a house, and perhaps access to a TV and bicycle, what more could they want – or realistically aspire to?

In the late 1970s Nepal actually exported large quantities of rice. The development of

the Terai opened up new land, temporarily relieving some of the population pressure in the hills, and the so-called green revolution (utilising improved seeds, artificial fertilisers and pesticides) led to increased productivity. The population, however, has again begun to grow more rapidly than production and Nepal has to import rice to meet its needs. It is already a net importer of food, and food imports had risen rapidly to $120 million in 1997.

The average size of land-holdings has continued to drop; it now stands at around half a hectare in the hills and a little over 1.5 hectares in the Terai. In a good year, half a hectare in the hills around Kathmandu might produce around 1000kg of rice and 500kg of mixed vegetables, but if the farmer does not own the land up to 50% of this production will go to the owner as rent. Although there are theoretical limits on the amount of land an individual may own, tenant farmers are still common and many are in debt to moneylenders.

Where possible, crops are supplemented with livestock (especially in the mountain areas), but the animals are often of poor quality, partly because there is a serious shortage of fodder, especially in winter. One of the important uses for Nepal's remaining forests is as a source for animal fodder; unfortunately this can also lead to unsustainable damage. See the earlier Ecology section for more information on plant use and animal husbandry in Nepal.

Manufacturing & Services

Obviously, for many people there's not much food to spare, especially if the rains fail. Although outright starvation is rare, undernourishment is very common, particularly in the undeveloped west of the country. A growing number of people are forced to seek seasonal work, or rely on money that is repatriated by other family members, to supplement what they can produce from their land.

Unfortunately, Nepal's embryonic manufacturing industries (mainly on the Terai) and service sector are unable to meet the demand for work, so there is significant underemployment. Manufacturing and industry now account for around 30% of GDP, up from around 20% just a decade ago.

Perhaps the most extraordinary success story of the last few decades, however, has been that of Tibetan carpets. Although weaving is an indigenous craft, in 1960 the Nepal International Tibetan Refugee Relief Committee, with the particular support of the Swiss government, began encouraging Tibetan refugees in Jawlakhel, Patan, to make and sell carpets. Today, Nepal exports more than 244,000 sq metres of rugs (down from a peak of over 300,000 sq metres in the early 1990s), valued at around US$125 million. This industry earns around 25% of the country's foreign exchange from exports, and employs around 250,000 workers.

The carpet industry has declined somewhat over the recent years, largely due to negative publicity about exploitative work practices (namely child labour) and the use of carcinogenic dyes. While both of these practices are supposedly illegal, they still continue.

For many people, however, the only accessible source of income is the tourist trade – either as a market for handicrafts and other small-scale businesses (lodges, shops, travel agencies etc) or as an employee (hotel staff, porters etc). Others work as day labourers for wealthy farmers, or try to pick up menial work in Kathmandu.

Foreign Exchange & Trade

Tourism accounts for 16% of foreign-exchange earnings, although there is some controversy over how much of this leaks out of the country again in paying for the goods and services that westerners require. Remittances, primarily from Gurkha soldiers in the Indian, British and Sultan of Brunei's armies, account for another 7.6%.

Some cynics claim that the two mainstays of the Nepali economy are really smuggling and foreign aid – there are no official figures for the smuggling, but foreign aid accounts for 23% of hard currency receipts! Almost 30% of the government's revenue comes from foreign aid and borrowing.

The country has always been an intermediary between India and China. More recently, it has become a transit point for goods from Japan, Singapore and Hong Kong. Additionally, it is claimed that many goods travel in a circuit from India to Nepal and back to India.

Nepal's trade is dominated by India and many activities within the country are Indian-owned or controlled. In the 1997-98 financial year Nepal had a trade deficit with India that amounted to over Rs 20,000 million.

Development

It is hard to be optimistic when looking at the prospects for Nepal, despite the ingenuity and decency of the Nepali people. The growing population threatens to overwhelm the developments that have already taken place, and future developments will always be hampered by the impossible terrain.

Whether the country can continue to carry the population it already has – given that soils and forests are already being exploited at unsustainable levels – might even be questioned. For a very large number of peasant families, existence appears set to become increasingly perilous. This is likely to lead to increased migration to the Kathmandu Valley (where resources are already strained), to the Terai and to India.

In Kathmandu, the gulf between rich and poor is extreme. The aristocracy wields considerable power and influence and many of its members lead lives that are extraordinarily pampered and unrealistic. These feudal survivors have been joined by a new business elite, whose strikingly ugly houses now dot the outskirts of Kathmandu. Corruption is endemic at every level of government.

The challenges facing Nepal are clearly immense. A large proportion of the population (42%) lives in poverty and nearly 75% is illiterate. Health services, especially outside the Kathmandu Valley, are limited – the ratio of doctors to people was one to 15,000 in 1991, and there were only 4700 hospital beds. The average life expectancy is 57 years.

Since most people are dependent on agriculture, this is the most important area for development. Much can be done to increase and sustain productivity, but here as elsewhere, the topography means there is an amazing diversity of problems, not least of which is reaching the isolated valleys and ridges where so many of the people live.

On the positive side, education is spreading into distant valleys, and trekkers are likely to come across thriving primary schools in the most remote areas. Also highly visible are the improvements in Nepal's communications network. The telephone system links all major towns, and roads continue to extend farther and farther into distant parts of the country. Often, however, new roads bring undesirable social changes (thanks to an influx of outsiders and trade goods, and the facilitation of migration to the cities) and some question whether the huge sums of money involved in road construction and maintenance might not be better allocated to expanding and improving the existing network of walking tracks and bridges.

Nepal's physical resources are extremely limited. There are few accessible minerals, and there is little unexploited arable land. There are, however, great hydroelectric power resources, although the market for them is likely to be found in India, and the capital and ecological costs involved in construction are huge. Perhaps one of the most optimistic trade delegations in recent times was one from Bangladesh that suggested a number of ways trade could be expanded between the two countries. Among other things, they were interested in importing Nepali boulders!

Foreign Aid

Foreign aid sounds as if it should be a wonderful industry – on the surface, totally nonpolluting and ecologically sound. Nepal has lots of it and the end result is highly questionable. If you're interested in the impact of foreign aid on a country like Nepal the magazine *Himal* regularly has articles which will provide food for thought. Two other books, ostensibly accounts of travels in Nepal, will also prove enlightening.

Peter Somerville-Large's *To the Navel of the World* (1987) contrasts the successful, heavily touristed and heavily aided Solu Khumbu region of the Sherpas in eastern Nepal with the neglected regions of the far north-west. While critics debate the damage caused by tourism it seems hardly likely that the people living in the areas where trekkers are plentiful and aid projects abound would willingly switch to the areas of Nepal which are still 'off limits'.

Charlie Pye-Smith's *Travels in Nepal* (1988) was essentially a trek from one aid project to another and what he saw was not always a pretty sight. Too often the projects were pointless, imposed without consulting the people they were aimed at, or without adequately understanding the local physical and cultural environment. Often the only people who benefited were the foreign companies who supplied the equipment and expertise and the affluent Nepalis who skimmed off a profit as the project passed by them.

Pye-Smith contends that most aid donors look for big projects (they like to have something visible to show off) and that government officials like the big ones too (there's more likely to be something in it for them). The projects that actually work, however, are much closer to ground level. He describes disastrous Japanese irrigation projects, ill-planned Austrian hydroelectric power projects and well meaning but inept US ecological projects, but also tells of a British agricultural project near Dhankuta in the east which really seemed to work and an Australian forestry project which operated on a shoestring and seemed to work much better because of that.

He concludes, however, by questioning the whole basis of foreign aid in Nepal. Along the way he turns up many interesting thoughts. Hydroelectric power, for example, is touted as an enormous energy saver but its main use is for electric lighting. Lighting with hydroelectric power-generated electricity is much cheaper than with kerosene and a great deal of expensive kerosene can be saved. But Pye-Smith argues that with cheap lighting people stay up later and when they stay up they burn firewood. The end result of providing hydroelectric power can actually be an increase in the consumption of scarce timber!

One aid project disaster he observed was a tree-planting exercise where the trees were not only badly planted but also planted in an area where the first monsoon deluge washed them away. This totally wasted plantation was fenced in by cutting down healthy trees! Even the whole horror story of Himalayan deforestation is brought into question. 'The only number which has any scientific validity at all in the Himalaya is sixty-seven', he writes. This is the factor by which estimates of per capita firewood consumption vary.

POPULATION
Nepal's population currently stands at around 22.6 million (1997 estimate). The population growth rate is a high 2.7%. The largest city is Kathmandu, the capital, with more than 235,000 people, although the population of the Kathmandu Valley is around 700,000.

In the mountains the rate of increase is lower than in the Terai, but this is because many people are migrating in search of land and work. Despite (or because of) extremely high rates of infant mortality and the life expectancy of only 57 years, the overall annual rate of population increase is high, putting enormous pressures on Nepal's fragile ecology.

PEOPLE
Like the geography, the population of Nepal is extremely diverse and highly complex. Simplistically, Nepal is the meeting point for the Indo-Aryan people of India with the Tibeto-Burmese of the Himalaya, but this gives little hint of the dynamic ethnic mosaic that has developed and continues to change to this day.

In a south-north direction, as you move from the plains to the mountains, the ethnic map can be roughly divided into layers: the Terai, the midlands or Pahar zone, and the Himalaya. Each zone is dominated by characteristic ethnic groups whose agriculture and lifestyles are adapted to suit the physical constraints of their environment. (See earlier in this chapter under Geography for more detail about the physiographic features of each area.) These zones can be further subdivided from east to west, with different groups in the east, central and western regions of each zone.

Himalayan Zone
In the Himalayan zone, the people are Mongoloids of Tibetan descent. They are known in Nepali as Bhotiya or Bhote, terms that are now often considered derogatory because the Shah and Rana regimes categorised Bhotiya as untouchables who could legally be enslaved.

Most Bhotiya identify with a particular region, and attach the suffix *pa* (people) to the name. These include the Sherpa, of the Everest region, the Manangpa of the Manang region north of the Annapurna Himal, and the Lopa, of the Mustang region. This group also includes Thakalis, the well known innkeepers from the Thak Khola (Kali Gandaki) on the Jomsom Trek, and Tamangs, around the Kathmandu Valley and the Langtang region.

With a few exceptions in the far west, all these people are Buddhist and have a similar culture to Tibetans.

Midlands Zone

In the east of the midlands zone, one finds the Kirati (also known as Kiranti) people, who are divided into the Rai and Limbu groups. These groups are also Mongoloid peoples who speak Tibeto-Burmese languages. Their religion is shamanistic – neither Buddhist nor Hindu, however Hinduism is becoming increasingly influential. They entered Nepal from the north and east and founded a kingdom in the Kathmandu Valley around the 7th century BCE that continued for 1000 years. Independent Kirati kingdoms survived in the east until the end of the 18th century.

In the central midlands zone around the Kathmandu Valley live the Newars. Some believe the Newars are Kirati, others believe they are survivors from a still older group. They have absorbed successive waves of immigrants and created a religious environment that is in many ways a synthesis of Hinduism and Buddhism.

In the central midlands around the Kali Gandaki, the two main groups are the Magar and Gurung. Both groups are Mongoloid and speak Tibeto-Burmese languages, which indicates they came from Tibet, although no-one knows when. The Gurungs tend to occupy middle elevations to the southern flanks of the Annapurna massif, while the Magars tend to occupy the lower elevations.

The Gurung's shamanistic religion is under pressure from Hinduism in the south and Buddhism in the north. The Magars have long been Hindu, and have developed close ties with the Indo-Aryan Khas, farther to the west. In many cases they have taken the high-status Chhetri (Kshatriya) caste. Until the 18th century, Magar kingdoms dominated the region. The most famous was Palpa, with its capital at Tansen, which fought alongside Gorkha at the beginning of Prithvi Narayan Shah's expansionist wars. (See the History section.)

In the western midlands, the situation becomes confusing, partly because there are few written historical records and ethnicity becomes confused with caste. The area is dominated by Khas, an Indo-Aryan people whose language has evolved into present

Two-Legged Transport

Most ethnic groups are increasingly influenced by Indian and western fashions, so it is difficult to pick someone's ethnicity by their clothing. The method someone uses to carry a load, however, often provides an interesting clue. Mountain people carry goods in woven baskets (*doko*) on their backs, but suspended from a jute headband (*namlo*) worn around the top of the head.

The people from the valleys of the Middle Hills, especially the Newars, often carry loads slung on bamboo poles balanced across their shoulders. People of the plains, more particularly women, balance goods on their heads. And western travellers carry possessions in bags suspended from their shoulders!

People of Nepal

Zone	Western	Central	Eastern
Himalaya	Khas Bhotiya	Bhotiya	Bhotiya
Midlands	Khas	Magar Gurung Newar	Rai Limbu
Terai	Tharu Abadhi	Tharu Danuwar Bhojpuri	Danuwar Mithila

day Nepali. The numbers of Khas have been continually supplemented by the arrival of Parbatiyas (Hindus of varying caste and ethnicity) from the Indian plains. In the 12th century the Khas, who controlled a large empire, were joined by Bahun (Brahmin) and Chhetri refugees from the Muslim invasion of India. Although the Khas were technically low caste, many were given the high Chhetri caste by the Bahun, and the children of Bahun men and Khas women were also made Chhetris.

The unusual fluidity of caste allowed ambitious families to adopt higher castes – the most powerful Chhetris from among the Khas and Magar became Thakuris. The Khas empire fragmented into many small kingdoms ruled by powerful families who further embellished their pedigrees by claiming royal antecedents in India. After Prithvi Narayan Shah's triumph, many Bahuns and Chhetris were rewarded with grants of land in central and eastern Nepal, and since then they have spread throughout the country. In the west, however, they are numerically dominant.

Terai Zone

Until the eradication of malaria in the 1950s the only people to live in the valleys of the Inner Terai, and along much of the length of the Terai proper, were Tharus and a few small, associated groups. Most Tharus, though not all, have a Mongoloid appear-

ance. There is considerable speculation, but no hard facts, about where they originated. Their religion is animist, with increasingly important Hindu overtones.

Along the Terai proper, a number of numerically significant groups straddle the border between India and Nepal. In the eastern Terai, Mithila people dominate; in the central Terai, Bhojpuri-speaking people dominate, and in the western Terai, Abadhi-speaking people are significant. All these are essentially cultures of the Gangetic plain, and Hindu caste structure is strictly upheld. In various parts, notably around Nepalganj and Lumbini, there are also large numbers of Muslims.

Since the Terai has been opened for development, it has also been settled by large numbers of people from the midlands – every group is represented.

Ethnic & Caste Groups

Thakalis Originating along the Kali Gandaki Valley in central Nepal, the Thakalis are a Tibeto-Burmese people who have become the entrepreneurs of Nepal. They honed these skills from the days when they played an important part in the salt trade between the subcontinent and Tibet but now they are found in many areas of modern commercial life. Originally Buddhist, many pragmatic Thakalis have now adopted Hinduism.

Most Thakalis are small farmers, but travellers will regularly meet them in their adopted roles as hoteliers. Many small hotels in Nepal are run by Thakalis; the Pokhara to Jomsom trek along the Kali Gandaki Valley is the best 'village inn' trek in Nepal, because of the numerous Thakali lodges along this route through their homeland. The actual number of Thakalis is very small.

Tamangs Tamangs are the largest Tibeto-Burmese ethnic group in Nepal, but unlike many smaller groups, little is known of their history. Tamangs are now sedentary farmers and labourers. Their appearance, language and Buddhist beliefs all bear testimony to their origins. Indeed, many of the 'Tibetan' souvenirs for sale in Kathmandu are actually made by Tamangs.

Around half the Himalayan zone of Nepal is inhabited by Tamangs, and it is likely they have been there longer than any other group. Tamangs dominate the high hills surrounding the Kathmandu Valley and the central Himalayan zone, especially in the Langtang region. Unlike the Newars, their homesteads are often solitary. Houses may be constructed out of brick or stone, but they are often modest in size with a porch and courtyard, a mud finish and a thatched roof.

Many Tamangs have been influenced in their dress by both western and Newari styles. Traditionally, women wear a colourful wraparound skirt, a blouse, jacket and

A Tamang woman.
Ta-mi means 'horse people' – some say that the Tamang ancestors were horse traders.

scarf. On important occasions they wear chunky gold or brass ear and nose rings set with semiprecious stones. Men wear loincloths or the traditional Newari pants, short-sleeved jackets and topis. Both men and women wear several metres of cloth wrapped around the waist.

Their religion is closely associated with Tibetan Buddhism (see the Religion section later in this chapter). Some Tamangs follow Bön, the pre-Buddhist religion of Tibet. In Tamang areas you are certain to come across *chörtens* (Tibetan Buddhist stupas with a square base and topped with a dome), and *mani* walls. Manis are prayer stones engraved with mantras.

Tamangs are one of the largest groups in Nepal, but they have been seriously exploited, especially since the unification of Nepal under the Shahs. In the 19th century their legally defined status was the lowest of any hill people, and much of their land was distributed to Bahuns and Chhetris.

Tamangs were relegated to bonded labour, and were dependent on menial work, particularly as porters. They were prevented from joining the government or the military (unlike many other hill groups), and they remain, in general, extremely poor, and continue to work as *thela gada* (cart pushers), rickshaw pullers, auto-rickshaw drivers and porters. They produce more than 90% of the thangka paintings sold in Kathmandu, and 70% of Tibetan carpets. Many Tamang women have been forced into prostitution, both in Nepal and India.

Tibetans Mongoloid people from Tibet have settled in Nepal for thousands of years, but the most recent arrivals have been refugees. In 1950 the communist People's Republic of China overpowered the Tibetan army. For the next eight years the Chinese made a heavy-handed attempt to bring the Tibetans into the communist fold, including the imposition of inappropriate agricultural policies that led to mass famine. In March 1959 a Tibetan uprising was brutally crushed, and the Dalai Lama, Tibet's spiritual and political leader, fled to India.

Thousands of Tibetans followed him across the Himalaya.

There are currently around 120,000 Tibetans in exile, and about 12,000 of them are in Nepal, mostly in Kathmandu and Pokhara. Although their numbers are only small, they have a high profile, partly because of the important role they play in tourism. Many hotels and restaurants in Kathmandu are owned or operated by Tibetans. They have also been responsible for the extraordinary success story of the Tibetan carpet industry, which has grown in over 30 years from nothing to being the largest single employer in the country. (See the Economy section earlier in this chapter.)

Tibetans are devout Buddhists and their arrival in the valley has rejuvenated a number of important religious sites, most notably the stupas at Swayambhunath and Bodhnath. A number of large new monasteries have been established.

Rai & Limbu These two large groups are known as Kirati people, the descendants of the Kiratis who formed the first recorded kingdom in the Kathmandu Valley. They now inhabit the eastern midlands, and many have migrated to the eastern Terai. Large numbers find employment with Gurkha regiments.

They are Tibeto-Burmese people, but their traditional religion is distinct from either Buddhism or Hinduism, although Hinduism is exerting a growing influence. The traditional religion is entirely oral and is based on the periodic appeasement of ancestor divinities and nature spirits; there are priests, elders and shamans. Rais and Limbus both bury their dead. The Limbus use a common burial site and erect a whitewashed rectangular grave marker with three tiers for a female, four for men.

The Rais and Limbus cultivate wet and dry fields, and slash-and-burn shifting agriculture is still important in places. In the hills, most villages are scattered and the houses are small, one storey edifices built of stone. Along the Arun River and in the Terai, the houses are often timber and bamboo, built on high wooden piles. In the Terai,

these houses can be large, and are often surrounded by a veranda.

Sherpas Living high in the mountains of eastern and central Nepal, in particular in the Solu Khumbu region at the foot of Mt Everest, the Sherpas are probably the best known Nepali ethnic group. Originally from Tibet, they settled in the area about 500 years ago, and were probably nomadic herders until the introduction of the potato in the middle of the 19th century. The relative increase in wealth that this new crop created allowed them to settle in permanent villages and to create a number of monasteries known as *gompas*.

The Sherpas are Buddhists, and this century their name has become synonymous with mountaineering and trekking. Not all sherpas – the small 's' word describes a trek guide or mountaineer – are Sherpas but many of them are and they've won worldwide fame for their skill, hardiness and loyalty.

A Sherpani.
Sherpas are famous world-wide for their roles in trekking expeditions.

THE GODS OF NEPAL

There are so many gods and related auspicious beings in Nepal – being able to identify some of them makes understanding and enjoying Nepali culture much easier. The definitions that follow include the most interesting and most frequently encountered 'big names' plus associated consorts, vehicles (see end of this section) and religious terminology.

Incarnations, Manifestations & Aspects

There's a subtle difference between these three possibilities. Vishnu has incarnations, 10 of them in all. They include Narsingha the man-lion, Krishna the cowherd and Buddha the teacher. Shiva, on the other hand, may be the god of 1000 names but these are manifestations – what he shows himself as – not incarnations. When you start to look at the Buddhist 'gods' their various appearances are aspects rather than incarnations or manifestations.

Brahma Brahma, despite his supreme position, appears much less often than Shiva or Vishnu. Like those gods he has four arms but Brahma also has four heads, to represent his all-seeing presence. The four *Vedas* are supposed to have emanated from his mouths.

Saraswati The goddess of learning and consort of Brahma. She rides upon a white swan and holds the stringed musical instrument known as a *veena*.

Brahma

Saraswati

Shiva Shiva is probably the most important god in Nepal – as creator and destroyer – so it's important to keep on his good side! Shiva is often represented by the phallic lingam, symbolic of his creative role. His vehicle is the bull Nandi and you'll often see this figure outside Shiva temples; there's a huge Nandi guarding the entrance to Pashupatinath. The symbol most often seen in Shiva's hand is the trident or trisul. Sadhus, the wandering pilgrims who are often followers of Shiva, frequently carry a trident.

Shiva is also known as Nataraja, the cosmic dancer whose dance shook the cosmos and created the world. Shiva's home is Mt Kailash in the Himalaya, but across the border in Tibet, and he's also supposed to be keen on smoking hashish. He takes various forms including peaceful Pashupati and destructive Bhairab.

Pashupati In the Kathmandu Valley Shiva is most popularly worshipped as Pashupati, the lord of the beasts. As the keeper of all living things Pashupati is Shiva in a good mood and the temple of Pashupati-nath is the most important Hindu Temple in the country.

Shiva

Bhairab In Nepal Shiva appears as Bhairab when he is in his fearful or 'terrific' form. Bhairab can appear in 64 different ways but none of them is pretty. Typically he has multiple arms, each clutching a weapon, he dances on a body and wears a headdress of skulls. More skulls dangle from his belt, and his staring eyes and bared fangs complete the picture. Bhairab is usually black, carries a cup made from a human skull and is attended by a dog. The gruesome figure of Bhairab near the Hanuman Dhoka palace entrance in Kathmandu is a good example of this fearsome god at his worst.

Bhairab

Tara Another deity who appears in both the Hindu and Buddhist pantheons are the Tara goddesses. There are actually 108 different Taras, but the best known are Green Tara and White Tara. They are sometimes believed to be the two wives of King Songtsen Gampo who was the first royal patron of Buddhism in Tibet. The Taras are two of the female consorts to the Dhyani Buddhas. (See the Dhyani Buddhas boxed text in the Around the Kathmandu Valley chapter for details of the Dhyani Buddhas and their shaktis.)

Shakti While Shakti the goddess is Shiva's consort, *shakti* is the creative/reproductive energy of the gods which often manifests in their consorts. A Hindu god's consort is also known as his shakti, as she is far more than just a companion. A shakti often symbolises certain parts of a god's personality, so while Shiva is the god of both creation and destruction it is often his shakti Parvati, manifesting as **Kali** or **Durga**, who handles the destructive business and demands the blood sacrifices; these are usually made not to the male but to the female and must be of male animals. She is also the energetic and dominant partner in their sexual relationship, and shakti has come to mean any goddess in her energetic and dynamic mode.

The Kathmandu Valley has numerous shrines and temples dedicated to the great goddesses including four shrines dedicated to the Joginis, the mystical goddesses who are the female counterpart to the Bhairabs. These shrines are found near Sankhu at the eastern end of the valley, at Guhyeshwari near Pashupatinath, at Pharping and at Vijeshwari. Another group of four temples are known as *varahis* and are dedicated to shaktis as she-boars. Other shrines to goddesses are dedicated to the Ashta Matrikas, mother goddesses.

Kali

Durga

Parvati Shiva's shakti is Parvati the beautiful and she is the dynamic element in their relationship. Just as Shiva is also known as Mahadev, the Great God, so she is Mahadevi, the Great Goddess. Just as Shiva is often symbolised by the phallic lingam so his shakti's symbol is the *yoni*, representing the female sex organ. Their relationship is a sexual one and it is often Parvati who is the energetic and dominant partner.

Shiva's shakti has as many forms as the Great God himself. She may be peaceful Parvati but she may also be fearsome Kali, the black goddess, or Durga, the terrible. In these terrific forms she holds a variety of weapons in her hands, struggles with demons and rides a lion. As **Kali**, the fiercest of the gods and goddesses, she demands sacrifices and wears a garland of skulls. The festival of Dasain, celebrated in her honour, is characterised by the sacrifice of animals.

Machhendranath Machhendranath is a strictly Nepali Hindu god who has power over the rains and the monsoon and is regarded as protector of the Kathmandu Valley. It's typical of the intermingling of Hindu and Buddhist beliefs in Nepal that, in the Kathmandu Valley at least, Machhendranath has come to be thought of as an incarnation of Avalokiteshvara, the Bodhisattva of our era. In actual fact the connection from Avalokiteshvara to Machhendranath is not quite so direct. Purely Buddhist Avalokiteshvara is linked with Shiva through Lokeshvara, the lord of the world. Machhendranath is then a manifestation of Lokeshvara.

There are two forms of Machhendranath based on colour and features: Seto or White Machhendranath of Kathmandu and Rato or Red Machhendranath of Patan. Some scholars say that they are the same god but for others they are different.

Parvati

Seto Machhendranath

Ganesh With his elephant head Ganesh is probably the most easily recognised of the gods and also the most popular. Ganesh is the god of prosperity and wisdom and there are many Ganesh shrines and temples in Nepal. Ganesh's parents are Shiva and Parvati and he obtained his elephant head due to his father's notorious temper. Coming back from a long trip, Shiva discovered Parvati in bed with a young man. Not pausing to think that their son might have grown up a little during his absence, Shiva lopped his head off! He was then forced by Parvati to bring his son back to life but could only do so by giving him the head of the first living thing he saw – which happened to be an elephant.

Shiva and Parvati's other son is Kumar, the god of war. He is also known as Kartikkaya.

Hanuman Hanuman is the monkey god, the important character from the *Ramayana* who came to the aid of Rama and helped to defeat the evil Rawana and release Sita from his grasp. Hanuman's trustworthy and alert nature is commemorated by the many statues of Hanuman seen guarding palace entrances. The best known in Nepal is the image of Hanuman which stands beside the old Royal Palace entrance in Kathmandu, and indeed gives the old palace its name of Hanuman Dhoka.

Ganesh   Hanuman

Vishnu Vishnu is the preserver, although in Nepal, where he often appears as Narayan, he also plays a role in the original creation of the universe. Narayan is the reclining Vishnu, sleeping on the cosmic ocean, and from his navel appears Brahma, who creates the universe.

Vishnu has four arms and can often be identified by the symbols he holds – the conch shell or *sankha*, the disc-like weapon known as a *chakra*, the stick-like weapon known as a *gada* and a lotus flower or *padma*. Vishnu's vehicle is the faithful man-bird Garuda and a winged Garuda will often be seen kneeling reverently in front of a Vishnu temple – Garuda has an intense hatred of snakes and is often seen destroying them. Vishnu's shakti is Lakshmi, the goddess of wealth and prosperity.

Vishnu has 10 incarnations starting with Matsya, the fish. Then he appeared as Kurma, the tortoise on which the universe is built. Number three was his boar incarnation as Varaha, who destroyed a demon who would have drowned the world. Vishnu was again in a demon-destroying mood in incarnation four as Narsingha (or Narsimha), half man and half lion. (See the Narsingha boxed text in the Around the Kathmandu Valley chapter for the legend behind this appearance). Narsingha statues often show a man with a lion's head and four arms holding the traditional Vishnu symbols. On the man-lion's lap will be the demon which Narsingha is about to disembowel.

Still facing difficulties from demons, Vishnu's next incarnation was Vamana, the dwarf who reclaimed the world from the demon-king Bali. The dwarf politely asked the demon for a patch of ground upon which to meditate, saying that the patch need only be big enough that he, the dwarf, could walk across it in three paces. The demon agreed, only to see the dwarf swell into a giant who strode across the universe in three gigantic steps.

Vishnu

Vishnu as the 'long strider' is often seen with his left leg raised, just about to take a mighty step.

In his sixth incarnation Vishnu appeared as Parasurama, a warlike Brahman who proceeded to put the warrior caste Chhetris in their place. The noble Rajputs of India's state of Rajasthan claim they are descended from the survivors of this clash with a god.

Incarnation seven was as Rama, the hero of the *Ramayana* who, with help from Hanuman the monkey god, rescued his beautiful wife Sita from the clutches of Rawana, evil king of Lanka. See the Janakpur section in the Terai chapter for more information on the *Ramayana*. Sita is believed to have been born in Janakpur, and this is also where she and Rama married.

Incarnation eight was the gentle and much-loved **Krishna**, the fun-loving cowherd, who dallied with the *gopis* or milkmaids, danced, played his flute and still managed to remain devoted to his wife Radha. The Bhakti cult follow this passionate and happy incarnation.

For number nine Vishnu appeared as the teacher, the Buddha. Of course the Buddhists don't accept that Buddha was just an incarnation of some other religion's god but perhaps it was just a ploy to bring Hindu converts back into the fold. Incarnation 10? Well we

Krishna

haven't seen that one yet but it will be as Kalki the destroyer, when Vishnu wields the sword which will destroy the world at the end of the Kaliyuga, the age which we are currently in.

Vehicles Each of the gods is associated with a particular animal which can either be an attendant or a vehicle on which the god may ride. These creatures are a clue to identifying a god. Vishnu's vehicle, for example, is the man-bird **Garuda** and the winged kneeling figure of Garuda in front of a temple usually indicates that it is a Vishnu temple. Similarly elephant-headed Ganesh's creature is the rat or shrew and a statue of a rat will indicate that you are in a Ganesh shrine.

Other vehicles include an elephant, which is the vehicle of Indra, the king of the Vedic gods. Agni, the Vedic god of fire, has a chariot drawn by parrots while Vasudhara, the wife of Jambhala the god of wealth, has a chariot drawn by a pig! Yama the god of death is accompanied by a crow. Ganesh's brother Kartikkaya, the god of war, has a cock. Brahma's consort Saraswati has a swan.

Nagas The *nagas* are the eight snake deities and their king is Anantnag. Snakes make many appearances in Hindu and Buddhist mythology in Nepal. Vishnu images usually have a snake somewhere in the picture and the sleeping Vishnu reclines upon a bed made from the coils of a snake. Vishnu's consort, Lakshmi, often carries a snake, but Garuda, Vishnu's man-bird attendant, has a passionate hatred of snakes and often kills them. Snakes are thought to have power over water so this means they're important for ensuring a good monsoon. They also appear guarding doorways to prevent evil entering, but if you get bitten by one you can turn to Janguli, the goddess who cures snake bites. Amoghasiddhi, the Dhyani Buddha of the north, sits under a canopy of seven hooded snakes and Vishnu's snake bed also has seven heads which form a canopy for him.

Garuda

Nagas

The Sanskrit in the picture of the nagas translates as:
Phrase 1: Aagastya, Pulastya, Bhaismyan, Sumanta, Jaiminei are five rishis who can guard you from lightning.

Phrase 2: These rishis are very powerful and those who keep this script at their door would be guarded from lightning and fire.

Phrase 3: Those who keep this script and worship the nine nagas Ananta nag, Basuki nag, Shesh nag, Padmanabh nag, Kambal nag, Sheshpal nag, Ghritrastra nag, Tachheik nag and Kaliya nag every morning and evening, they shall be guarded from being poisoned and shall always prosper.

Newars The Newars of the Kathmandu Valley, who make up around 6% of the total population, are a good example of the result of this Himalayan melting pot. They number about 600,000 and speak Newari, a language distinct from Tibetan, Nepali or Hindi, and they follow a version of Hinduism with many Buddhist overtones. See the Kathmandu, Patan & Bhaktapur chapter for more details.

Gurungs The Gurungs tend to live in higher country and generally farther to the east than the Magars (see later), but otherwise are similar to them in many respects. Their homeland is the central midlands, ranging from Gorkha and Baglung to quite high on the southern slopes of the Annapurnas. They are a Tibeto-Burmese people with a unique shamanistic religion that is gradually giving way to Hinduism and Buddhism.

They are farmers, raising rice, wheat, maize and millet. Sheep husbandry is also important, with village families contributing a handful of sheep to a larger village flock. During the summer months they move their sheep to higher pastures, then with the end of the monsoon they bring them down to the villages. Like the Magars, the Gurungs often work as Gurkha soldiers.

Magars A numerically large group (around 8% of the total population), the Magars are a Tibeto-Burmese people who are found in many parts of the midlands zone of western and central Nepal. Until the 18th century they had their own kingdoms, but they also had close contact with the Hindu Indo-Aryans in the west. This led to a gradual increase in Hindu influence and cultural assimilation. Nowadays in terms of religion, farming practices, housing and dress, they are hard to distinguish from Chhetris.

The Magars are farmers, and renowned soldiers; they fought with Prithvi Narayan Shah, and their kingdom of Palpa (based at Tansen) was one of the last to be incorporated into the new unified Nepal. Their martial qualities have been recognised by the British and Indian armies, since Magars are the single largest group in the Gurkha regiments. Gurkha earnings play an enormously

NEPAL'S MAJOR ETHNIC GROUPS

CHINA

TIBET

0   75   150 km

KATHMANDU

1 Bhojpuri
2 Bhotiya
3 Bahun;
  Chhetri; etc
4 Gurung
5 Magar
6 Maithali
7 Newar
8 Rai-Limbu
9 Rajbansi
10 Sherpu
11 Tamang
12 Tharu

INDIA

important role, both in improving living standards in the villages, and in the Nepali economy as a whole.

The Magars generally live in two storey rectangular or square thatched houses washed in red clay. Historically, these houses were often round or oval in shape. The Magars also include Thakalis (see earlier in this section).

Bahuns & Chhetris In Hindu theory there is no relationship between caste and ethnicity, so Bahuns and Chhetris are simply the two highest castes (respectively the Brahmin priests and Kshatriya warriors). In Nepal, however, most are from the Khas kingdoms that flourished in western Nepal for at least a millennia before the unification of Nepal. Today they account for around 30% of the total population.

The Khas are Indo-Aryans who migrated to Nepal over the centuries; in the Middle Ages their numbers, and their consciousness of caste, were supplemented by refugees from the Muslim invasions of India. The progeny of Bahun men and hill women were considered Chhetri, and a number of high-status families from other hill groups have also adopted Chhetri status, so some do have Mongoloid tribal ancestry.

Bahuns and Chhetris played an important role in the court and armies of Prithvi Narayan Shah, and after unification they were rewarded with lands throughout the country. The Khas' language, Khas Kura, became the national language of Nepal, and the position of Bahuns and Chhetris at the top of the heap was religiously, culturally and legally enforced. Ever since, they have dominated the processes of government in Kathmandu.

Outside of the valley, the majority of Bahuns and Chhetris, however, are simple peasant farmers, indistinguishable in most respects from their neighbours. Sometimes their wealth is reflected by relatively large houses (compared to those of neighbouring tribal groups). Most of these people live in two storey stone or mud-brick thatched houses that are washed with lime or red ochre. Many had roles as tax collectors under the Shah and Rana regimes, and to

this day many are moneylenders with a great deal of power.

All Bahuns and Chhetris are Hindu, but the Bahuns tend to be more caste-conscious and orthodox than other Nepali Hindus and this sometimes creates difficulties in their relationship with 'untouchable' westerners. Many are vegetarians and do not drink alcohol; marriages are arranged within the caste.

There is no particular cultural dress by which they can be recognised but men in both castes wear a sacred thread – the *janai* (see Janai Purnima under Public Holidays & Special Events in the Facts for the Visitor chapter).

Tharus Tharus are one of the largest ethnic groups in Nepal. The original inhabitants of the Terai, they are now often heavily exploited by newly arrived hill people, or *zamindars* (landowning moneylenders). Many have been forced by debt into a form of bonded labour (the *kamaiya* system) little different to slavery. They are generally Mongoloid in appearance, and have an animist religion that is increasingly influenced by Hinduism. See the Terai chapter for more information.

EDUCATION

While education is gradually spreading to the small villages, it has been a slow process, especially in the mountains. At 75%, the illiteracy rate in the country is uncomfortably high.

In recent years the education system has been thrown open to private enterprise. This has led to a dramatic increase in the number of schools – seemingly every town you pass through has a high number of 'English Medium Boarding Schools'. On the surface this is a good thing, but unfortunately the reality is somewhat less encouraging. With profit being the bottom line of any business, it seems many of these schools are business ventures first and foremost; the education side of things comes a poor second. Parents have to pay anything from Rs 90 to Rs 150 a month for their children to attend such schools.

It is a sad fact that the standard of education offered by the free government schools is also lacking.

ARTS

The whole Kathmandu Valley is really one enormous art gallery and museum, and the arts and architecture in Nepal are inextricably intermingled. The finest woodcarving and the best sculpture are often part of a building – a temple is simply not a temple with- out its finely carved roof struts. The crafts also reflect the uniquely Nepali melting pot where religious art has Tantric Hindu and Buddhist overtones and the dividing line between one religion and another is hard to discern.

Lydia Aran's *The Art of Nepal* is a handy and interesting introduction to Nepali art and its religious background. There are detailed descriptions of the many Hindu, Buddhist and Hindu-Buddhist deities and their associated religious terminology. This book is particularly interesting because it concentrates on the art still in Nepal, as opposed to objects in overseas museums and private collections.

Architecture & Sculpture

The earliest architecture in the valley has faded with history. The four Ashoka stupas of Patan are simply grassy mounds today and the great stupas of Swayambhunath and Bodhnath have undoubtedly changed many times over the centuries. Nevertheless these simple hemispherical Buddhist structures are essentially unchanged from their earliest appearance – they're simply a solid mound rising from the ground and topped with a spire. You can find similar Buddhist stupas in Sri Lanka, Myanmar (Burma) and Thailand.

The Licchavi period from the 4th to 9th centuries CE was a golden age for Nepal and while the temples may have disappeared the superb stone sculptures can still be found. Many temples around the valley have beautiful pieces of Licchavi craftwork in their courtyards, the temple of Changu Narayan at the eastern end of the valley is a particularly good example. The great reclining Vishnu image at Budhanilkantha is another wonderful example of Licchavi stonework. The Licchavis undoubtedly worked in wood as well but no wooden buildings or carvings survive from that era.

It was in the Malla period that Nepali artistry with wood really came into its own. The earliest woodcarving in the valley dates from the 12th and 13th centuries and includes the roof struts of the great Basantapur Tower in the old Royal Palace in Kathmandu's Durbar Square, and the Kasthamandap building, also in the square. The Uku Bahal in Patan also dates from this period but you have to go out of the valley to Panauti, near Banepa, to find one of the oldest and finest survivors in the shape of the Indreshwar Mahadev Temple.

The artistic skills of the Newar people of the valley flourished under the Mallas and not only woodcarving but metalwork, terracotta, brickwork, stone sculptures and other crafts all enjoyed a long golden age. The finest metalwork includes the images of the two Tara goddesses at Swayambhunath and the river goddesses Ganga and Jamuna, standing guard in the palace of Patan.

The popularity of the multi-roofed Nepali pagoda design in China and eastern Asia is credited to the architect Arniko, who with 24 assistants visited Tibet in the late 13th century and later also worked for the Ming emperor. The road to the Tibetan border is named the Arniko Hwy in his honour. The contact with Tibet also began to make its way back to Nepal and vivid Tibetan colours and fantastic Tibetan creatures also started to appear in Nepali art and architecture.

The last centuries of the Malla period saw temple after temple rise over the Kathmandu Valley skyline. The squabbling city-states of Kathmandu, Patan and Bhaktapur vied with each other to raise yet more glorious temples and palaces. Much of the construction was still in the traditional multi-roofed Nepali pagoda style but there was also a great deal of Indian influence, such as the stone Krishna Mandir of Patan's Durbar Square or the spires of the Mahabouddha Temple in Patan and the two temples at the top of the stairway to Swayambhunath.

With the invasion of the valley by King Prithvi Narayan Shah from Gorkha, the great age of Nepali architecture came to a dramatic end. The great woodcarved temples and palaces you marvel at in the valley today mainly date from that brilliant period prior to 1767. Although the skills used to build them have lain dormant in the centuries since then, there is no doubt that these skills are still alive and well. When the Hanuman Dhoka palace in Kathmandu and the Tachupal Tole buildings in Bhaktapur

Temple Architecture

Newar Pagoda Temples

The distinctive Newar pagoda temples are a major feature of the Kathmandu Valley skyline. While strictly speaking they are neither wholly Newari nor pagodas, the term has been widely adopted to describe the temples of the Kathmandu Valley.

The temples are generally square in design, and may be either Hindu or Buddhist (or both in the case of mother-goddesses). On rare occasions temples are rectangular or octagonal, but this depends on the god being worshipped – Krishna, for example, can occupy octagonal temples, whereas Ganesh, Shiva and Vishnu can only inhabit square temples.

The major feature of the temples is the tiered roof, which may vary from one to five tiers, with two or three being the most common. In the valley there are two temples with four roofs and another two with five (Kumbeshwar at Patan and Nyatapola at Bhaktapur). The sloping roofs are usually covered with distinctive baked clay tiles (jhingati), although richer temples will often have one roof of gilded copper. The pinnacle (gajur) of the temple is usually bell-shaped and made of baked clay or gilded copper.

The temples are usually built on a stepped plinth, which may be as high or even higher than the temple itself. In some cases the number of steps on the plinth corresponds with the number of roofs on the temple.

The temple building itself has just a small sanctum (garbha-griha – 'womb room') housing the deity. Worship is practised individually, with the devotee standing outside the door to make their supplications. The only people permitted to actually enter the sanctum are the temple priests (pujari).

Perhaps the most interesting feature of the temples is the detailed decoration which is only evident when close

Nyatapola is a fine example of traditional architecture, so well constructed that it has survived numerous earthquakes.

were restored in the 1970s the work was performed by purely traditional means and with craftwork every bit as good as in the past. More recently the Chyasilin Mandapa in Bhaktapur, completely destroyed in the great earthquake of 1934, was totally re-built in 1989-90, again using traditional skills.

Painting

Nepal has a long history of painting and some high-quality traditional work is still

---

Temple Architecture

up. Under each roof there are often brass or metal decorations, such as rows of small bells or embossed metal banners *(kinkinimala)*. The metal streamer which often hangs from above the uppermost roof to below the level of the lowest roof (such as on the Golden Temple in Patan) is called a *pataka*. Its function is to give the deity a means of descending to earth.

The other major decorative element are the wooden struts which support the roofs. The intricate carvings are usually of deities associated with the temple deity or the deity's vehicle *(vahana)*. Occasionally the designs are merely floral, and there are a number of temples where the carvings depict explicit sexual acts, often involving animals. One theory is that these have been put on temples to deter the goddess of lightning, who is a virgin.

Stupas

The Buddhist stupas of the Kathmandu Valley – particularly the stupas of Swayambhunath and Bodhnath – are among the most impressive and most visited monuments in Nepal.

The earliest stupas in India were merely domed burial mounds, but they have evolved over the centuries to become complex structures which represent the Buddha and Buddhist philosophy.

The lowest level of the stupa is the plinth, which may be simply a square platform, but may also be terraced, as at Bodhnath. On top of the plinth is the hemispherical dome *(kumbha*, meaning 'pot'), and this is usually white-washed each year.

Atop the dome is a spire which always consists of a number of elements. Immediately on top of the dome is a square base *(harmika)*, and on each face is usually painted a pair of eyes, which most people believe represent the all-seeing nature of the Buddha.

Topping the harmika is a tapering section of 13 stages, which are said to represent the 13 stages of perfection. At the very peak is a gilt parasol, which symbolises royalty.

Shikhara Temples

The second most common form of temple are the *shikhara* temples, which have a heavy Indian influence. The temples are so named because their tapering tower resembles a mountain peak (shikhara in Sanskrit). Although the shikhara style developed in India in the 6th century, they first appeared in Nepal in the late Licchavi period (9th century).

The main feature is the tapering, pyramidal tower, which is often surrounded by four similar but smaller towers, and these may be on porches over the shrine's entrances. The tower is usually built on a square stepped plinth. A good example in the valley of a shikhara temple is the Shiva Temple in Bhaktapur's Durbar Square.

Occasionally the shikhara temple follows the same basic design but is much more elaborate, with porches and small turrets seemingly all over the place. The Krishna Mandir and octagonal Krishna Temple, both in Patan's Durbar Square, are excellent examples.

being done today. The earliest Newari paintings were illuminated manuscripts dating from the 11th century and these were followed by miniature paintings influenced by the miniature styles of northern India, and then by scrolls and murals. By this time the Tibetan influence was starting to make itself felt on Newari painting, although from the 14th to 16th centuries the Newars also had a great influence on Tibetan art.

Today some of the best examples of old Newari painting are hung in temples where they are rarely seen, but the art gallery in Bhaktapur has a fine collection and is an excellent introduction to the development of art in Nepal. Newari artists have their own special caste of Chitrakar. For more information on painting in Nepal today see Thangkas in the Shopping section in the Facts for the Visitor chapter.

Music & Dance

Despite the pervasiveness of western music, Nepali music hangs constantly in the air, whether it is the plaintive notes of a flute or the gentle twang of the four stringed *saringhi*. Although the *gaines*, traditional professional musicians, are a dying breed they can still be heard. The folk music of rural Nepal still has a strong following and the gaines are often as much storytellers as musicians.

The *damais* are modern professional musicians, all drawn from the tailor caste, who form the backbone of wedding bands. This music can definitely be hard on western ears, falling uncomfortably close to the painful standards of Indian video-bus music. The blaring wail of long Tibetan horns at Buddhist religious sites probably also qualifies for the unlistenable category.

Dance also has a long and strong history in Nepal both in cheerfully performed folk dances and in the more formal classical dances. The Newars of the Kathmandu Valley are the chief exponents of classical dancing, but there are also masked dances with a Tantric background, and the colourful masked dances of Bhaktapur which are performed during the Indra Jatra festival each year.

Some of the more important traditional dances include: Bajrayogini, based on Tantric Buddhism; Bhairavkali, a classical dance of Shiva and Kali; Bhojpuri, a popular dance from the Terai; Jhagad, from the eastern Terai; Lakhe, a mask dance of the Newars; and Sangini, which is a prayer dance from the women of the Bahun-Chhetri.

Literature

Nepal does not have a long literary tradition; it dates back only to the 19th century to the works of Bhanubhakta Acharya (1814-1868). Bhanubhakta was the first person to really break away from the strong influence of Indian literature and compose truly Nepali verse. He is most famous for his rendering of the Ramayana, into Nepali. This was far more than just a straightforward translation; it was instead a 'Nepali-ised' version of the Hindu epic.

Further development of Nepali literature was hindered by the fact that until the 20th century very little written Nepali was published. The Rana regime sought to promote Nepali literature early in the 20th century with the establishment of the Gorkha Language Publication Committee in 1913. This body basically had a monopoly over Nepali publishing and due to its heavy censorship role came to be regarded with suspicion by writers and poets, who chose to have their work published in India. Indeed, a number of Nepali periodicals appeared in India for this very reason.

It was only in the 1930s that Nepal's first literary journal, *Sharada* appeared. It was published monthly right up until 1963 and gave many aspiring writers the chance to have their work published.

Important writers and poets include Lekhnath Paudyal, Balkrishna Sama, Lakshmiprasad Devkota, Daulat Bikram Bishtha and Guruprasad Mainali.

SOCIETY & CONDUCT

Nepal has always been a dividing line between civilisations and cultures, and a crossroads for the flow of commerce and culture. Here the plains of the subcontinent climb up to the high plateau of Tibet, the languages and people of India give way to those of China, and the Hindu religion blends into Buddhism. Nepal, the land at the margin, is often a complex blend of the two influences and this variation is further complicated by the diversity of ethnic groups within the country.

Cultural Considerations

The challenge for you as a visitor to Nepal is to respect the rights and beliefs of the local people, and to minimise your impact – culturally and environmentally. Remember Nepal is not an adventure park or museum established for your convenience, but home to a vital, changing culture. Life for many is extremely hard, but despite the scarcity of material possessions, there are many qualities that shame the so-called 'developed' world.

Your very presence in Nepal will have an effect – an increasing number of people say a negative one. In a totally different culture it is also inevitable that the visitor will make some gaffe at some point. Most Nepalis make allowances, but they do appreciate it when a genuine effort is made to observe local customs. Following is a miscellaneous collection of simple suggestions that will help avoid offence.

Dress Dress appropriately – shorts or revealing clothes are never suitable for women. Shorts are acceptable for men only when trekking; going without a shirt anywhere is not. Nudity is not acceptable anywhere.

Behaviour Public displays of affection are frowned upon. Nepali men often walk around hand in hand, but this does not have the same implications as it does in San Francisco!

Raising your voice or shouting shows extreme bad manners and will not solve your problem, whatever it might be. Always try to remain cool, calm and collected.

Bodily contact is rarely made, even for shaking hands, although among Nepali men with frequent western connections it is becoming more accepted. Never touch any-

thing or point at anything with your feet, the 'lowest' part of the body. In contrast the head is spiritually the 'highest' part of the body, so don't pat children on the head.

Don't inquire about a person's caste.

The Nepalis do not like to give negative answers or no answer at all: if you are given a wrong direction or told a place is much nearer than it turns out to be, it may be through fear of disappointing you!

Don't encourage begging children. If you want to help there are lots of excellent aid organisations which will make good use of your contribution and local schools will be only too happy with a gift of ballpoint pens. See the 'Begging' boxed text in this chapter for more information.

Visiting a Temple Always walk clockwise around Buddhist stupas, chörtens or mani walls. Always remove your shoes before entering a Buddhist or Hindu temple or sanctuary. You may also have to remove any items made from leather, such as belts and bags. Many Hindu temples do not permit westerners to enter.

It's the custom to give a white scarf or *khata* to a Buddhist abbot when you are introduced. The honorific title *Rimpoche* (which means 'precious one') is usually bestowed on abbots. The scarves can easily be found in Tibetan shops.

Visiting a Nepali Home Fire is sacred so do not throw rubbish into it. This particularly applies to a kitchen fire in a Nepali home and theoretically should apply to a camping site fire when trekking as well. In practice, burning the garbage before leaving camp is accepted, but it's probably best to wait until just before leaving camp before doing it, certainly not before cooking. In a Nepali home the kitchen is off limits to strangers.

Avoid 'polluting' food by inadvertently touching it or bringing it into contact with a used plate or utensil. Using your own fork or spoon to serve out more food will do this. Putting your used plate on a buffet table risks making the food still on the table *jutho* or polluted. Notice how Nepalis drink from a cup or water vessel without letting it touch their lips.

Always remove your shoes before entering a Nepali home.

Eating & Drinking Customs There are a number of 'rules' and customs relating to eating and drinking in Nepal and a number of ways in which you can make life much easier for yourself. For a start the Nepali eating schedule is quite different from that in the west. The morning usually begins with little more than a cup of tea. Not until late morning is the main meal taken. In areas where western visitors are not often seen and even more rarely catered for, finding food will be much simpler if you go along with this schedule.

You can also save yourself a lot of time and frustration if you pay attention to what you order as well as when you order it. In small local restaurants the cooking equipment and facilities are often very primitive.

Places with some experience of catering to western tastes will often offer amazingly varied menus, but just because they offer 20 different dishes doesn't mean they can fix two of them at the same time. If you and your five friends turn up at some small and remote cafe and order six different dishes you can expect to be waiting for dinner when breakfast time rolls around next day.

Begging

Begging of various kinds is relatively common in Nepal, partly because both Hinduism and Buddhism encourage the giving of alms. This presents many visitors with a heart-rending moral dilemma. Should you give? Sometimes, especially if you've just spent Rs 500 (around US$10) on drinks, it seems grotesque to ignore someone who is genuinely in need. It is often worth checking to see how the local Nepalis react; if they give, it's a reasonably safe assumption that the beneficiary is genuine.

Around the main religious shrines, especially Pashupatinath, there are long lines of beggars. Pilgrims customarily give a coin to everyone in the line (there are special moneychangers nearby who will change notes for small-denomination coins). This is a culturally sanctioned and traditional form, but most westerners find it difficult to deal with, and are not really expected to give. Sadhus are another special case, and are usually completely dependent on alms. There are plenty of con men among their ranks, but equally, plenty of genuine holy men.

The main tourist centres, especially Thamel and Durbar Marg, have also attracted numbers of beggars. Here, westerners are expected to give, although whether they should is another matter.

Thamel attracts many of Kathmandu's estimated 1000 street kids. Giving to them, however, is, at best, a double-edged sword. Firstly, the lure of easy money actually attracts kids onto the streets in the first place, and then gives them a powerful incentive to remain. Secondly, it's a dog-eat-dog world, children who are seen receiving money may well be beaten up and have it stolen.

Also highly visible are women, usually clutching one or two children. Rumours suggest that these women are often part of organised begging rings, and that the money they receive is passed on to a Fagan figure. By giving to them, you are encouraging a further influx of people into Kathmandu where very few facilities exist for them. In this case, your money could be profitably used by a number of craft shops that specialise in marketing handicrafts produced by low-income women. These are nonprofit development organisations, so the money actually goes to the craftspeople in the form of fair wages (as opposed to charity), and also in training, product development, and rehabilitation programs.

In that situation it makes a lot of sense to order the same dish six times! Not only will you save time, but you will also save cooking fuel, which is often firewood.

If you eat dal bhat, most local restaurants and roadside stalls will be able to find a spoon (with a dubious past) if you insist, but the custom is to eat with your right hand. The number one eating rule in Nepal, as in much of Asia, is always use your right hand. The left hand, used for washing yourself after defecating, is never used to eat food and certainly should not be used to pass food (or anything at all) to someone else.

Caste rules also play a part in Nepali eating habits. A high-caste Brahmin simply cannot eat food prepared by a lower caste individual, which effectively bans practising Brahmins from restaurants since they cannot know what is going on behind the kitchen door. And of course some foods are strictly taboo in Nepal. High-caste Hindus and all Brahmins are, ostensibly at least, vegetarian, but carnivore or not, beef is strictly banned from the menu since the cow is a holy animal.

If you are invited to a meal at a Nepali home you may find the women of the household remain totally in the background and do not eat with the men or with guests. As in India, even at quite westernised homes, socialising goes on before the meal

Begging

One of the best of these organisations is Mahaguthi (☎ 521493), PO Box 396, Kathmandu, which was established with the help of Oxfam. It has three shops and sells a wide range of crafts produced by thousands of people. Among other things it runs a program to rehabilitate destitute women and children.

Dhankuta Sisters is an outlet for women from the eastern hills, and Dhukuti also works with low-income women. Mahaguthi and Dhukuti have shops on the way to Patan, in Kopundol, just beyond the bridge over the Bagmati River, and Dhukuti has another outlet at Lakeside in Pokhara.

In Patan, near the well-known Kumbeshwar Temple, the Kumbeshwar Technical School (☎ 522271), PO Box 2181, Kathmandu, was established to help provide the untouchable community of Patan with skills. They now produce excellent carpets, jumpers and woodwork. See the Kathmandu and Patan Shopping sections for more information.

Although the blind and lepers are probably genuinely dependent on begging for their survival, long-term solutions are offered by See Nepal (☎ 475927), PO Box 501, Kathmandu; and the Leprosy Hospital (☎ 290545), PO Box 151, Anandban, Kathmandu.

See Nepal is an innovative and effective program well known to most Australians because of the involvement of the late Professor Fred Hollows. Many forms of blindness are dealt with in rural clinics; often, relatively simple treatments and surgical techniques can restore people's sight. See Nepal has opened a factory in Nepal which manufactures the plastic lenses used in cataract operations. Excess production will be exported to India and China and any profits will be ploughed back into the program, hopefully making it self-sustaining. In the meantime, See Nepal can do with donations.

In the countryside, visitors will quickly be discovered by small children who chant a mantra that sounds something like: 'bonbonpenonerupeeee?'. Someone, somewhere started giving children sweets (bonbons), pens and money, and it sometimes seems that every child in Nepal now tries their luck. Do not encourage this behaviour. Most Nepalis find it offensive and demeaning (as do most visitors), and it encourages a whole range of unhealthy attitudes.

rather than afterwards. As the last mouthful is consumed the guests head out the door – nobody hangs around for conversation over the coffee!

Photography

Do not intrude with a camera, unless it is clearly OK with the people you are photographing. Ask before entering a temple compound whether it is permissible to enter and take photographs. Do not exchange addresses or offer copies of photos unless you definitely intend to follow it up later. See also the photography section in the Facts for the Visitor chapter.

RELIGION

In Nepal, Hinduism and Buddhism are mingled into a complex blend which is often impossible to separate. The Buddha was actually born in Nepal but the Buddhist religion first arrived in the country around 250 BCE, introduced, so it is said, by the great Indian Buddhist emperor Ashoka himself. Later, Buddhism gave way to Hinduism but from around the 8th century CE the Tantric form of Buddhism practised in Tibet also began to make its way across the Himalaya into Nepal. Today Buddhism is mainly practised by the people of the high Himalaya, such as the Sherpas and Tamangs, and by the Tibetan refugees who have settled in Nepal.

Officially Nepal is a Hindu country but in practice the religion is a strange blend of Hindu and Buddhist beliefs with a pantheon of Tantric deities tagged onto the list of Hindu gods or, in many cases, inextricably blended with them. Thus Avalokiteshvara, the prime Bodhisattva of this Buddhist era, becomes Lokeshvara, a manifestation of the Hindu god Shiva, and then appears as Machhendranath, one of the most popular gods of the Kathmandu Valley. Is he Hindu or Buddhist? Nobody can tell. Hindu temples have been marked differently on maps, but these are obviously only a guide.

Although the vast majority of the population is Hindu (86.5%) or Buddhist (7.8%) there are also small groups of Muslims (3.5%) and Christians (0.2%).

Hinduism

India, Bali, Mauritius and possibly Fiji are the only places apart from Nepal where Hindus predominate, but it is the largest religion in Asia in terms of the number of adherents. Hinduism is one of the oldest extant religions with firm roots extending back to beyond 1000 BCE.

The Indus Valley civilisation developed a religion which shows a close relationship to Hinduism in many ways. Later, it further developed on the subcontinent through the combined religious practices of the Dravidians and the Aryan invaders who arrived in northern India around 1500 BCE. Around 1000 BCE, the Vedic scriptures were introduced and gave the first loose framework to the religion.

Hinduism today has a number of holy books, the most important being the four *Vedas*, or 'Divine Knowledge', which are the foundation of Hindu philosophy. The *Upanishads* are contained within the *Vedas* and delve into the metaphysical nature of the universe and soul. The *Mahabharata* is an epic poem describing in over 220,000 lines the battles between the Kauravas and Pandavas. It contains the story of Rama, and it is probable that the most famous Hindu epic, the *Ramayana*, was based on this. The *Bhagavad Gita* is a famous episode of the *Mahabharata* where Krishna relates his philosophies to Arjuna.

Hinduism postulates that we will all go through a series of rebirths or reincarnations that eventually lead to *moksha*, the spiritual salvation which frees one from the cycle of rebirths. With each rebirth you can move closer to or further from eventual moksha; the deciding factor is your *karma*, which is literally a law of cause and effect. Bad actions during your life result in bad karma, which ends in a lower reincarnation. Conversely, if your deeds and actions have been good you will reincarnate on a higher level and be a step closer to eventual freedom from rebirth.

Dharma is the natural law which defines the total social, ethical and spiritual harmony of your life. There are three categories of dharma, the first being the eternal harmony which involves the whole universe. The second category is the dharma that controls castes and the relations between castes. The third dharma is the moral code which an individual should follow.

The Hindu religion has three basic practices. They are *puja* or worship, the cremation of the dead, and the rules and regulations of the caste system. There are four main castes: the Brahmin, or priest caste; the Kshatriya, or soldiers and governors; the Vaisyas, or tradespeople and farmers; and the Sudras or menial workers and craftspeople. These castes are then subdivided, although this is not taken to the same extreme in Nepal as in India. Beneath all the castes are the Harijans, or untouchables, the lowest, casteless class for whom all the most menial and degrading tasks are reserved.

Westerners may have trouble understanding Hinduism principally because of its vast pantheon of gods. In fact you can look upon all these different gods simply as pictorial representations of the many attributes of a god. The one omnipresent god usually has three physical representations: Brahma is the creator, Vishnu is the preserver and Shiva is the destroyer and reproducer. All three gods are usually shown with four arms, but Brahma has the added advantage of four heads.

Each god has an associated animal known as the 'vehicle' on which they ride, as well as a consort with certain attributes and abilities. Generally each god also holds symbols. You can often pick out which god is represented by identifying either the vehicle or the symbols.

Most temples are dedicated to one or other of the gods, but most Hindus profess to be either Vaishnavites (followers of Vishnu) or Shaivites (followers of Shiva). A variety of lesser gods and goddesses also crowd the scene. The cow is, of course, the holy animal of Hinduism.

Hinduism is not a proselytising religion since you cannot be converted. You're either born a Hindu or you are not; you can never become one. Similarly, once you are a Hindu you cannot change your caste – you're born into it and are stuck with your lot in life for the rest of that lifetime. Nevertheless the concepts of Hinduism have a great attraction for many westerners and India's 'export gurus' are numerous and successful.

A guru is not so much a teacher as a spiritual guide, somebody who by example or simply by their presence indicates what path you should follow. In a spiritual search one always needs a guru. A sadhu is an individual on a spiritual search. They're an easily recognised group, usually wandering around half-naked, smeared in dust with their hair and beard matted.

See the Gods of Nepal colour section for an illustrated guide to some of the more popular of Nepal's Hindu pantheon.

Hanuman & Medicine

Hanuman the monkey god has an important medicinal connection in Nepal and other Hindu countries. The *Ramayana* recounts how Rama desperately needed a rare herb grown only in the Himalaya and sent Hanuman to procure it for him. Unfortunately by the time he arrived in the mountains Hanuman had forgotten specifically which herb he had been requested to bring back, but got around the problem by simply grabbing a whole mountain, confident that somewhere on the mountain would be the required plant.

On the walls of the Bir Hospital in Kathmandu you can see a large illustration of Hanuman flying through the air, tightly clasping a whole mountain. It's said that he paused for a rest on the banks of the Hanumante River in Bhaktapur and a picture of this event can also be seen there.

Buddhism

Strictly speaking, Buddhism is not a religion, since it is not centred on a god, but a system of philosophy and a code of morality. Buddhism was founded in northern India about 500 BCE when Siddhartha Gautama, born a prince, achieved enlightenment. According to some, Gautama Buddha was not the first Buddha but the fourth, and neither is he expected to be the last 'enlightened one'. Buddhists believe that the achievement of enlightenment is the goal of every being so eventually we will all reach buddhahood.

The Buddha never wrote down his dharma or teachings, and a schism later developed so that today there are two major Buddhist schools. The Theravada (doctrine of the elders) or Hinayana holds that the path to nirvana, the eventual aim of all Buddhists, is an individual pursuit. In contrast, the Mahayana school holds that the combined belief of its followers will eventually be great enough to encompass all of humanity and bear it to salvation. To some, the less austere and ascetic Mahayana school is considered a 'soft option'. Today it is chiefly practised in Vietnam, Japan and China, while the Hinayana school is followed in Sri Lanka, Myanmar and Thailand. There are still other, sometimes more esoteric, divisions of Buddhism, including the Hindu/Tantric Buddhism of Tibet, which is the version found in Nepal.

The Buddha renounced his material life to search for enlightenment but, unlike other prophets, found that starvation did not lead to discovery. Therefore he developed his rule of the 'middle way', meaning moderation in all things. The Buddha taught that all life is suffering, but that suffering comes from our

Sadhus

Sadhus are often people who have decided that their business and family life have reached their natural conclusions and that it is time to throw everything aside and go out on a spiritual search. They may have been anything from the village postal worker, to a wealthy businessperson. While many sadhus are, of course, completely genuine in their search, others are simply beggars and con men following a more sophisticated approach to gathering in the *paisa*.

Sadhus perform various feats of self-mortification and wander all over the subcontinent, occasionally coming together in pilgrimages and other religious gatherings *(melas)*. Most sadhus follow Shiva and are known as Shaivas, but there are also those who follow Vishnu and are known as Vaishnavas.

The sadhus you see around Pashupatinath are Shaivas, and can be further recognised by Shiva's symbol, the trident, which they carry. Shaivas apply lines *(tilaka)* to their foreheads in horizontal stripes. Vaishnavas are numerous at Janakpur. They don't carry a symbol but the tika on their forehead consists of vertical lines – sometimes three vertical lines that look confusingly like a trident.

sensual desires and the illusion that they are important. By following the 'eightfold path' these desires will be extinguished and a state of nirvana, where they are extinct and we are free from their delusions, will be reached. Following this process requires going through a series of rebirths until the goal is eventually reached and no more rebirths into the world of suffering are necessary. The path that takes you through this cycle of births is karma, but this is not simply fate. Karma is a law of cause and effect; your actions in one life determine the role you will play and what you will have to go through in your next life.

In India, Buddhism developed rapidly when it was embraced by the great emperor Ashoka. As his empire extended over much of the subcontinent, so Buddhism was carried forth. Later, however, Buddhism began to contract in India because it had never really taken a hold on the great mass of people. As Hinduism revived, Buddhism in India was gradually reabsorbed into the older religion.

Tibetan Buddhism There are four major schools of Tibetan Buddhism and all of them are represented in the Kathmandu Valley: Nyingmapa, Kargyupa, Sakyapa and Gelugpa. The differences are quite esoteric with their roots often in political as well as major theological disputes.

The Indian sage Padmasambhava (also known as Guru Rimpoche) is credited with establishing Buddhism in Tibet in the 8th century, when he helped build a gompa at Samye. The Nyingmapa order, sometimes referred to as the Old One, traces its origins back to Padmasambhava. The Kargyupa (whispered transmission) order was established by Marpa in the 11th century and has a strong Tantric influence. Marpa's most famous disciple was Milarepa, Tibet's most revered poet.

The Sakyapa was also founded in the 11th century and rose to a position where it ruled Tibet (with the support of the Mongols) until it came into conflict with the Gelugpa (virtuous) order, which had been founded in the 14th century by Tsongkhapa.

The Gelugpa were celibate and advocated monastic discipline. The school introduced the system of reincarnated spiritual leaders and ultimately came to power – again with the support of the Mongols – in the late 17th century. It was a Mongol ruler who conferred the title Dalai Lama (ocean of wisdom) on its leader. The Gelugpa completely isolated Tibet and maintained a strict theocratic state.

In some texts, Tibetan Buddhism may be referred to as Lamaism, and the Gelugpa are known (for obvious reasons) as the Yellow Hats, while the other schools are sometimes collectively identified as the Red Hats.

Islam

Nepal's small population of Muslims (around 750,000 people, or 3.5% of the total population) originated from different parts of Asia, and today are mainly found close to the border with India and in a handful of isolated villages.

The first Muslims, who were mostly Kashmiri traders, arrived in the Kathmandu Valley in the 15th century. A second group arrived in the 17th century from northern India, and they primarily manufactured armaments for the small hill states. The descendants of these early immigrants today speak Nepali and are indistinguishable from upper-caste Hindus.

The largest Muslim group are the Terai Muslims, many of whom had arrived before unification. Others gradually drifted north from India, especially following the War of Independence in 1857. Many of them still have strong ties with the Muslim communities in the Indian states of Bihar and Uttar Pradesh.

A number of Tibetan Muslims arrived in the country along with their Buddhist counterparts following the 1959 Chinese overthrow of Tibet.

Unlike in India, where communal tension is a major problem, Nepal's Hindu and Muslim communities seem able to co-exist peacefully.

Facts for the Visitor

HIGHLIGHTS

While many people come to Nepal just for trekking in the Himalaya, there is indeed a great deal more to the country. The Kathmandu Valley is worth at least a week in itself, although most people seem to fly in and get out as quickly as possible. The temples at Patan, Bhaktapur, Swayambhunath, Pashupatinath and Bodhnath should not be missed.

The Terai, that lowland strip which runs the breadth of the country, is a fascinating area usually completely overlooked by foreign visitors but one which has a great deal to offer. Visiting the Royal Chitwan and Royal Bardia national parks in the Terai offers visitors a chance to see an incredible variety of bird and animal life, including the royal Bengal tiger and the rhinoceros. Other Terai towns, such as Janakpur and Lumbini, are significant religious sites and are also worth a visit.

SUGGESTED ITINERARIES
One Week

With so much to see and do in Nepal there's not a lot of point coming just for a week, but if that's all you have available you could have a good look around the highlights of the Kathmandu Valley in that time. The cities of Kathmandu, Bhaktapur and Patan are the major attractions, with their evocative city squares and ancient architecture.

Two Weeks

With two weeks there's more scope to look around a bit, but it's not enough time to do any serious exploration. In addition to the Kathmandu Valley, you could take up one of a number of other options: a short trek into the Himalayan foothills, a visit to the beautiful lakeside city of Pokhara, or head for Royal Chitwan National Park in the Terai and hopefully catch sight of a rhino and a royal Bengal tiger.

One Month

One month is really the minimum needed to get a good feel for Nepal. The Kathmandu Valley is worth a week (although many people give it just a day or two at either end of their trip). You could then do an extended trek (such as the Everest base camp) or a shorter trek (say, two weeks) and slot in a visit to Pokhara and Royal Chitwan National Park.

Two Months

Those lucky souls with two months at their disposal should have no difficulty in spending that time in Nepal, particularly if trekking is on the agenda. The longer treks, such as the Annapurna Circuit, take a good three weeks, and with the juggling around to and from the trail head it's best to put aside four weeks. This still leaves another four weeks for Kathmandu and Pokhara, and also gives you the chance to explore the Terai, a fascinating area which is overlooked by most visitors. The main attractions of the Terai are the national parks and wildlife reserves – Royal Chitwan, Royal Bardia and Koshi Tappu are all well worth visiting.

PLANNING
When to Go

Climatic factors are very important in planning when to visit Nepal. October-November, the start of the dry season, is in many ways the best time. With the monsoon only recently finished the countryside is green and lush and Nepal is at its most beautiful. Rice is harvested and there are some important and colourful festivals to enjoy. Bear in mind, however, that these festivals can be disruptive (see the Public Holidays & Special Events section later in this chapter for more details). At this time of year the air is sparkling clean, visibility is unexcelled and the Himalayan views are as near perfect as you can ask. Furthermore, the weather is still balmy, neither too hot (as it can be towards the end of the dry season or during the monsoon) nor too cold (as it can be at the height of winter). For obvious reasons, this is also the peak tourist season.

In December-January the climate and visibility are still good, though it can get very cold. Trekkers need to be well prepared, as snow can be encountered on high-altitude treks. Heading for the Everest base camp at this time of year can be a real feat of endurance and the Annapurna Circuit trek is often closed by snow on the Thorung La. Down in Kathmandu the cheaper hotels, where heating is nonexistent, are often chilly and gloomy in the evenings.

February-March-April, the tail end of the dry season, is a good second-best time. The weather gets warmer so high-altitude treks are no longer as arduous, although by the end of the dry season, before the monsoon breaks, it starts to get too hot for comfort. Visibility is not as good as earlier in the dry season since the country is now very dry, and dust in the air reduces that crystal Himalayan clarity. In compensation, Nepal's wonderful rhododendrons and many other flowers are in bloom so there's plenty of colour to be seen along the trekking trails.

May and the early part of June are not the best months as it is extremely hot and dusty and the coming monsoon hangs over you like a threat. Mid-June to September, when the monsoon finally arrives, is the least popular time to visit Nepal. The rains wash the dust out of the air, but the clouds obscure the mountains so you're unlikely to enjoy more than a rare glimpse of the Himalaya. Although it doesn't rain all day it usually does rain every day and the trails (and the roads in most towns) will be muddy and plagued by leeches.

Despite this, it is possible to trek during the monsoon, although high rivers may further complicate matters and it's certainly not as pleasant as other times of year. Landslides sometimes block roads during the monsoon but many visitors still come to Nepal from India as the weather is even less pleasant down on the plains. The latter part of the monsoon, the months of August-September, are a time of festivals which will certainly enliven a visit to Kathmandu.

Maps

An interesting account of the history of mapping in Nepal is found in Harka Gurung's *Maps of Nepal* which covers historic maps right up to the trekking maps of the early 1980s.

The Research Scheme *Nepal Himalaya* maps are better known as Schneider Maps, after their cartographer. These are the best trekking maps available although their price is as high as their quality. The series covers the routes into the Everest region in six separate maps, and the Langtang and Annapurna areas.

There are many locally produced maps available in Nepal which are much cheaper and for most trekkers prove quite adequate. Most of these are produced by Mandala Trekking Maps, and although they are generally only in blueprint form they have recently produced coloured versions for the most popular trekking routes.

Topographic map sheets at 1:25,000 scale are available for large areas of the country, mainly the east. This is an ongoing Finnish-Nepali joint program and is the result of aerial photographs taken in the past few years. As a result the maps are very accurate, but are unsuitable for trekking as the trails aren't always marked. The maps are available in Kathmandu from the Topography Department of the Survey Ministry, at New Baneshwar on the Bhaktapur road, for Rs 80 per sheet.

The problem with most of the detailed maps of Nepal is that villages often have widely diverse names and their actual position is often equally open to question. Reality, when you're there on foot, is often very different from what the map says. Even the Schneider maps often have highly original versions of common place names.

What to Bring

Nepal's climatic variations due to altitude mean that at certain times of year you'll have to come prepared for almost anything.

If you're in Nepal during the winter you'll find it's T-shirt weather in the Terai, but up at the Everest base camp you'll want the best thermal or duck-down gear money can buy!

In the Kathmandu Valley the daytime weather is pleasant year round, but in winter the temperature drops as soon as the sun sets, or even goes behind a cloud. It never reaches freezing in the valley, however, so it's sweater or warm-jacket weather, nothing worse. Climb higher to the valley edge at Nagarkot and you will find it gets much colder. If you plan to ride a bike, or have a respiratory problem, Kathmandu's air pollution is sufficiently bad to justify a mask.

During the monsoon you'll need an umbrella or raincoat, particularly in Pokhara where the rainfall is much heavier than in Kathmandu. In the first month after the monsoon it can be pleasantly warm, even on treks, as long as you're sticking to lower altitudes. Sunglasses, a hat and covering for unprotected skin are all necessary on high-altitude treks or for prolonged exposure in the Terai. (See the Trekking chapter for more details on clothing recommendations for trekking.)

Most clothing is easily and cheaply available in Nepal so if there's a question about a particular item, leave it behind – you can always get one if you need it.

Most toiletries are readily available, including toilet paper. Women should, however, bring tampons if needed. Ear plugs can be more than a luxury if you sleep lightly – cheap hotels and lodges are often very noisy. If you're staying in cheap hotels a padlock can be useful as hotels in this category often lock the doors with a latch and padlock. If you're visiting Royal Chitwan National Park or other places in the Terai a good insect repellent is a near necessity. Bring a torch (flashlight) for trekking and for power cuts.

TOURIST OFFICES

The Ministry of Tourism does not overdo things; there is very little printed informa-tion available and the handful of tourist offices around the country are of extremely limited use.

Local Tourist Offices

There are tourist offices in Kathmandu, Pokhara, Bhairawa, Birganj, Janakpur and Kakarbhitta. Again, these are virtually useless unless you have a specific inquiry. See the relevant sections for contact details.

VISAS & DOCUMENTS
Visas

Visas are required by most nationalities (Indians are an exception) and they are available from embassies and consulates abroad, at the border with India or on arrival at Kathmandu's Tribhuvan airport.

Single entry tourist visas are valid for 60 days and cost US$30. Single re-entry visas cost US$55, double re-entry visas cost US$70, while multiple entry visas are US$90.

At the airport, and sometimes at border crossings, officials insist on payment in US cash dollars. One passport photo is also required. It is possible to get US dollars at the airport currency exchange counter (no credit cards), but US dollars in cash will almost certainly be unavailable at the land borders (bring your own!).

There are inevitably queues at the immigration counter at Tribhuvan airport, and there can be hassles at the land crossings, so it is preferable to get your visa before arrival. Outside your home country, they are most conveniently obtained in Bangkok (Thailand), and Calcutta and Delhi (India). You must, however, use your visa within three months of the date it is issued.

Visa Extensions Tourist visas can be extended for 30 days at a cost of US$50, and one photo is required. The maximum stay period is 150 days in any calendar year. If a visitor has previously entered Nepal within the last 150 days, they can obtain a 30-day visa at a cost of US$50. Again this visa can be obtained from a Royal Nepalese Embassy abroad or upon arrival at the international airport.

The Department of Immigration's Kathmandu office is inconveniently located south-east of the centre.

See the Government Offices section in the Kathmandu, Patan & Bhaktapur chapter for details of opening hours. In Pokhara the immigration office is near the lake.

Trekking Permits

Trekking Permits have been abolished for the main trekking areas of Everest, Annapurna and Langtang. The National Park and Conservation fees have not been abolished. Permit requirements for all remote regions are still in effect.

Trekking permits are only issued at the immigration offices in Kathmandu and Pokhara, and can only be extended at those cities.

See the Permits section in the Trekking chapter for more details.

Other Documents

If it is possible you might drive a car or ride a motorbike while in Nepal then it is worth having an international driving permit.

When travelling in Asia it's a good idea to keep a number of passport photos with your passport so they are immediately handy for trekking permits, visa applications and other official documents. Passport photos are easily and cheaply obtained in Kath-

mandu – around Rs 100 for four in B&W or Rs 150 for four in colour.

EMBASSIES & CONSULATES
Nepali Embassies & Consulates

Australia
(☎ 02-9233 6161, fax 9223 6144)
Level 1, 17 Castlereagh St, Sydney, NSW 2000
(☎/fax 03-9650 6683)
Suite 1, Level 3, 277 Flinders Lane, PO Box 6, Melbourne, Vic 8009
(☎ 08-9386 2102, fax 9386 3087)
Suite 2, 16 Robinson St, Nedlands, WA 6009
(☎ 07-3230 2007)
Level 7, 127 Creek St, Brisbane, Qld 4000

Bangladesh
(☎ 601890, fax 886401, email rnedhaka@bdmail.com)
United Nations Rd, Road 2, Baridhara, Dhaka

Belgium
(☎ 02-346 2658, fax 344 1361, email rne.bru@skynet.be)
Ave Winston Churchill 68, 1180 Brussels

Canada
(☎ 416-226 8722, fax 226 8878)
2 Sheppard Ave, East, Sulte 1700, Toronto, Ontario M2N 5Y7

China
(☎ 6532 1795, fax 6532 3251)
No 1, Sanlitun Xi Liu Jie, Sanlitun Lu, Beijing
(☎ 682 2881, fax 683 6890)
Norbulingka Rd 13, Lhasa, Tibet Autonomous Region

Denmark
(☎ 3312 4166, fax 3315 1045)
2 Teglgaardstraede, 1452 Copenhagen K

Finland
(☎ 115 1333, fax 680 1024)
Kanavaranta 9, 00160 Helsinki

Travel Insurance

A travel insurance policy to cover theft, loss and medical problems is a good idea. There is a wide variety of policies available, so check the small print. Some policies specifically exclude 'dangerous activities', which can include trekking.

You may prefer a policy which pays doctors or hospitals directly rather than you having to pay on the spot and claim later. If you have to claim later make sure you keep all documentation. Some policies ask you to call back (reverse charges) to a centre in your home country where an immediate assessment of your problem is made.

Check that the policy covers an emergency flight home.

France
(☎ 01 46 22 48 67, fax 01 42 27 08 65)
45 bis Rue des Acacias, 75017 Paris
Germany
(☎ 0228-343097, fax 856747, email
nepal.cmb@mail.k.mcs.de)
Im Hag 15, 53179 Bonn
India
(☎ 011-332 9969, fax 332 6857, email
ramjanaki@hotmail.com)
1 Barakhamba Rd, New Delhi 110002
(☎ 033-479 1117, fax 479 1410)
1 National Library Ave, Alipore, Calcutta
700027
Italy
(☎ 06-3545 0656, fax 3542 0720)
Piazzale Medaglie d'Oro 20, Rome 00136
Japan
(☎ 3705 5558, fax 3705 8264, email
nepembjp@big.or.jp)
14-9 Tokoroki 7-chomeSetagaya-ku,
Tokyo 158
Myanmar (Burma)
(☎ 550633, fax 549803)
16 Natmauk Yeiktha (Park Ave), PO Box 84,
Yangon (Rangoon)
Pakistan
(☎ 051-828838, fax 828839)
House 506, Street 84, Attaturk Ave, Ramna G-
6/4, Islamabad
Russia
(☎ 095-244 7356, fax 244 0000)
2nd Neopalimovsky Pereulok 14/7, Moscow
Singapore
(☎ 336 1677, fax 337 1737)
1 North Bridge Rd, #18-05 High St Centre,
Singapore 0617
Spain
(☎ 451 1221, fax 451 2148)
Mallorca 194 Pral 2, 08036 Barcelona
Switzerland
(☎ 01-201 4515, fax 201 4435)
Bleicherweg 33, Zurich
Thailand
(☎ 391 7240, fax 381 2406)
189 Sukhumvit 71 Rd, Bangkok 10110
Tibet
(☎ 682 2881, fax 683 6890)
Norbulingka Rd 13, Lhasa
UK
(☎ 020-7229 1594, fax 7792 9861, email
101642.43@compuserve.com)
12A Kensington Palace Gardens, London W8
4QU
USA
(☎ 415-434 1111, fax 434 3130)
Suite 400, 909 Montgomery St, San Francisco,

California 94133
(☎ 202-667 4550, fax 667 5534, email
nepali@erols.com)
2131 Leroy Place NW, Washington, DC 20008

Embassies in Nepal

Travellers continuing beyond Nepal may
need visas for Bangladesh, China, India,
Myanmar (Burma) or Thailand. The only
visas for Tibet/China dished out in Kathmandu are for organised groups; individuals
wishing to travel to Tibet should get a visa
before arriving in Nepal (Delhi is a good
place to get them). See the Tibet section in
the Getting There & Away chapter for advice
about travelling independently in Tibet. Foreign embassies in Kathmandu include:

Australia
(☎ 371678, fax 371533)
Bansbari, just beyond the Ring Rd in Maharajganj
Bangladesh
(☎ 372843, fax 373265)
Maharajganj. Open Sunday to Thursday from
9 am to 1 pm and 1.30 to 5 pm, visa applications up to 11 am only; no charge, two photos,
24 hours
China
(☎ 411740, fax 414045)
Baluwatar. Open Monday to Friday from 9 am
to noon and from 3 to 5 pm; visa applications
Monday, Wednesday and Friday from 10 to
11.30 am; passports will be returned the next
working day
France
(☎ 412332, fax 419968, email ambafr@mos
.com.np)
Lazimpat
Germany
(☎ 412786, fax 416899)
Gyaneshwar
India
(☎ 410900, fax 413132, email indemb@mos
.com.np)
Lainchaur. Open Monday to Friday from 9 am
to 1 pm and 1.30 to 5.30 pm; visa applications
Monday to Friday from 9.30 am to 12.30 pm,
collect from 4.45 to 5.30 pm – allow at least
seven days for processing; 15-day to six-month
(multiple entry possible) visas available, cost
varies according to nationality
Israel
(☎ 411811, fax 413920, email israelm@mos
.com.np)
Bishramalaya House, Lazimpat

Italy
   (☎ 412743, fax 413879)
   Baluwatar (Lalita Niwas Rd)
Japan
   (☎ 426680, fax 414101)
   Pani Pokhari
Myanmar (Burma)
   (☎ 521788, fax 523402)
   Chakupat, Patan City Gate, Patan. Open Monday to Friday from 9.30 am to 1 pm and 2 to 4.30 pm; visa applications morning only, 14 day visas available, three photos, 24 hours
Pakistan
   (☎ 374024, fax 374012)
   Ring Road, Maharajganj. Open Monday to Friday from 9 am to 5.30 pm
Russia
   (☎ 412155, fax 416571)
   Baluwatar
Thailand
   (☎ 371410, fax 371408)
   Maharajganj; open Monday to Friday from 8.30 am to 12.30 pm and 1.30 to 4.30 pm; visa applications Monday to Friday from 9.30 am to 12.30 pm, about US$10, two photos, 24 hours
UK
   (☎ 410583, fax 411789)
   Lainchaur
USA
   (☎ 411179, fax 419963)
   Panipokhari

Your Own Embassy It's important to realise what your own embassy – the embassy of the country of which you are a citizen - can and can't do to help you if you get into trouble.

Generally speaking, it won't be much help in emergencies if the trouble you're in is remotely your own fault. Remember that you are bound by the laws of the country you are in. Your embassy will not be sympathetic if you end up in jail after committing a crime locally, even if such actions are legal in your own country.

In genuine emergencies you might get some assistance, but only if other channels have been exhausted. For example, if you need to get home urgently, a free ticket home is exceedingly unlikely – the embassy would expect you to have insurance. If you have all your money and documents stolen, it might assist with getting a new passport, but a loan for onward travel is out of the question.

CUSTOMS

All baggage is X-rayed on arrival and departure. In addition to import and export of drugs, customs is concerned with the illegal export of antiques. Visitors are permitted to import the following articles for their personal use (and we quote):

Cigarettes, 200 sticks; cigars, 50 sticks; alcoholic liquor, one bottle not exceeding 1.15 litre; one binocular; one movie camera with 12 rolls of film; one video camera; one ordinary camera with 15 rolls of film; one tape recorder with 15 tape reels or cassettes; one perambulator; one bicycle; and one stick.

Antiques

Customs' main concern is preventing the export of antique works of art – with good reason since Nepal has a great many treasures, many kept under conditions of very light security. It would be a great shame if international art thieves and 'collectors' forced more of it to be kept under lock and key. Unfortunately a lucrative international market has led to the theft of a staggering amount of irreplaceable art.

It is very unlikely that souvenirs sold to travellers will be antique (despite the claims of the vendors), but if there is any doubt, they should be cleared and a certificate obtained from the Department of Archaeology (☎ 215358) in the National Archives building on Ram Shah Path, Kathmandu. These controls also apply to the export of precious and semiprecious stones.

Animal Furs & Trophies

Unfortunately, there is still a thriving trade in animal furs and trophies, despite the fact that this is also officially prohibited. Many seriously endangered species, including the beautiful snow leopard, are still being hunted for valuable parts of their corpses.

While there's a market this will continue – the argument that because the animal is already dead there is no further harm caused by having its skin made into a coat is entirely spurious. If there is any cosmic justice, those that encourage the trade will be reincarnated as rabbits on fur farms in Siberia!

MONEY
Currency
The Nepali rupee (Rs) is divided into 100 paisa (p). There are coins for five, 10, 25 and 50 paisa, and for one, two, five and 10 rupees, although as the rupee coins are not in wide circulation and prices are generally rounded to the nearest rupee, you often don't come across any coins at all. This is a great contrast to a time not long ago, when once outside the Kathmandu Valley, it was rare to see any paper money. Mountaineering books from the 1950s often comment on the porters whose sole duty was to carry the expedition's money – in cold, hard cash!

Bank notes are for one, two, five, 10, 20, 50, 100, 500 and 1000 rupees. Away from major centres changing a Rs 1000 note can be very difficult, so it is always wise to have at least some of your money in small denomination notes. Even in Kathmandu, many small businesses, especially rickshaw and taxi drivers, simply don't have sufficient spare money to allow them the luxury of carrying a wad of change.

Note that dollar prices quoted in this book are US dollars.

Exchange Rates

country	unit		rupee
Australia	A$1	=	Rs 43
euro	€1	=	Rs 71
France	1FF	=	Rs 11
Germany	DM1	=	Rs 36
India	IRs 100	=	Rs 160
Japan	¥100	=	Rs 55
UK	UK£1	=	Rs 110
USA	US$1	=	Rs 67

Exchanging Money
Major international currencies including the US dollar and pounds sterling, are readily accepted, and in Nepal the Indian rupee is also like a hard currency – the Nepali rupee is pegged to the Indian rupee at the rate of IRs 100 = NRs 160. Beware that Indian Rs 500 notes are not accepted anywhere in Nepal, apparently due to the presence of forgeries.

Official exchange rates are set by the government's Nepal Rastra Bank. Rates at the private banks vary, but are generally not far from the official rate. The daily *Rising Nepal* and *Kathmandu Post* newspapers list the Nepal Rastra Bank's rate, providing a useful reference point.

There are exchange counters at the international terminal at Kathmandu's airport and banks and/or moneychangers at the various border crossings. Pokhara and the major border towns also have official money-changing facilities, but changing travellers cheques can be difficult elsewhere in the country, even in some quite large towns. If you're trekking take enough small denomination cash with you to last the whole trek.

The usual banking hours are Sunday to Thursday, 10 am to 2 pm, and until noon on Friday.

Legal Exchange When you change money officially, you are required to show your passport, and you are issued with a Foreign Exchange Encashment Receipt showing your identity and the amount of hard currency you have changed. Hang onto the receipts as they have a number of potential uses.

Many upmarket hotels and businesses are obliged by the government to demand payment in hard currency; they will also accept rupees, but only if you can show a Foreign Exchange Encashment Receipt that covers the amount you owe them. In practice this regulation seems to be widely disregarded and you are not asked to prove the source of your rupees.

Airlines are also required to charge tourists in hard currency, but most seem unwilling to accept anything other than cash, travellers cheques or credit cards. Budget hotels, bus companies and most small businesses are usually only too happy to get rupees and do not muck around with encashment receipts.

If you leave Nepal via Kathmandu's airport the downstairs exchange counter will re-exchange up to 15% of the amount shown on 'unused' exchange certificates. The receipts used for re-exchange are kept by the bank, so make sure you have photocopies if you need them for other purposes. Be warned that official re-exchange is not possible at any bank branches at the border crossings.

The best private banks are the Nepal Bank Ltd, Nepal Grindlays Bank, Rastriya Banijya Bank and the Nepal Indo-Suez Bank. Some hotels and resorts are also licensed to change money, and while their rates are usually OK it's best to check first.

Rates and commissions charged vary from bank to bank, so it pays to shop around.

In addition to the banks there are licensed moneychangers in Kathmandu, Pokhara, Birganj, Kakarbhitta and Sunauli/Bhairawa. The rates are often marginally better than the banks, but the commissions are higher, so check before changing. The big advantages of the moneychangers over the banks is that they open much longer hours (typically 9 am to 7 pm) and often seven days a week, and they are also much quicker, the whole process often taking no more than a few minutes.

Black Market Exchange The once thriving black market is pretty subdued these days. Touts around Thamel in Kathmandu and Lakeside in Pokhara still offer to change money, but the premium over the bank rate is usually less than 5%, so it's hardly worth the (small) risk. It is of course illegal, and the money is often used in the drug trade.

Credit Cards Major credit cards are widely accepted at mid-range and better hotels, restaurants and fancy shops in the Kathmandu Valley and at Pokhara. Elsewhere it's safer to assume that credit cards won't be accepted, and so you will need to carry enough cash or travellers cheques to cover your costs.

Branches of Nepal Grindlays bank will make cash advances against Visa and MasterCard in Nepali rupees (no charge), and will also sell foreign currency travellers cheques against the cards with a 2% commission.

The American Express agent is Yeti Travels (☎ 01-227635, fax 226153) which has its office off the forecourt of the Hotel Mayalu on Jamal Tol just around the corner from Durbar Marg in Kathmandu. They advance travellers cheques to card holders. There's a standard 1% commission. The office is open Monday to Friday from 10 am to 1 pm and 2 to 5 pm.

International Transfers If you do not follow the right steps money transfers from overseas can be very time-consuming. Make any transfer by fax because transfers by mail can take forever. Pin down every possible detail, ensure that you know which bank the money is going to, make sure they have your name exactly right and if possible ensure that you are notified at the same time as the bank. It's important to choose the right bank as well – check that your bank has links with a bank in Nepal and does not have to operate through an intermediary. See the Kathmandu chapter for addresses of international banks with offices in Kathmandu.

Western Union claim they can transfer money from many countries to Nepal in 24 hours. The agent in Kathmandu is Sita World Travel in Thamel (☎ 418363, fax 227557, email sitaktm@sitanep.mos.com.np).

Costs

If you stay in rock-bottom accommodation and survive on a predominantly Nepali diet you could live in Nepal for less than $5 a day. On an independent 'village inn' or 'teahouse' trek your living costs are likely to be around that level.

On the other hand if you stay in comfortable mid-range hotels (say $10 to $20 a double), eat in popular tourist-oriented restaurants, rent bicycles and take taxis from time to time your living costs could be around $20 to $30 a day.

At the top end it is possible to spend $100 a night for a five-star double room in Kathmandu; a meal for two in one of Nepal's very best restaurants can cost $30 to $40; and a deluxe trek booked from overseas can cost $100 a day.

Residents should bear in mind that most of the major upmarket tour and trekking operators offer significant discounts, so make your status clear when you ask for prices and make bookings.

Tipping & Bargaining

Tipping is prevalent in Kathmandu. In expensive establishments you should tip up to 10% whereas in smaller places some loose change or Rs 10 will be most appreciated. Do not worry about it in the really cheap restaurants. Taxi drivers don't expect to be tipped.

Before bargaining, try to establish a fair price by talking to local people and other travellers. Paying too much feeds inflation, while paying too little denies the locals a reasonable return for their efforts and investments. Not everything is subject to bargaining: respect standard food, accommodation and entry charges, and follow the going rate for services.

Bargaining should never be treated as a matter of life and death importance – it's usually regarded as an integral part of a transaction and is, ideally, an enjoyable social exchange. Nepalis do not ever appreciate aggressive behaviour. A good deal is when both parties are happy. Try to remember that Rs 10 might quite a difference to the seller, but in US hard currency it amounts to less than 20 cents.

Taxes

Most hotels in the mid to upper range charge a 10% to 12% tax, on top of which is slapped a 2% Tourism Service Charge.

POST & COMMUNICATIONS
Post

The postal service to and from Nepal is, at best, erratic and can be extremely slow, but just to surprise you, things can also be amazingly efficient – we received two separate letters from Australia which both arrived within three days! Most articles do finally arrive, but they can take weeks.

Poste restante services are reasonably well organised, but as with any other Asian country you should ask people writing to you to print your family name clearly and to underline it. Misfiled mail often results from confusion between family names and given names.

Postal Rates At the Kathmandu main post office, stamps are sold from 8 am to 7 pm from Sunday to Friday, and from 11 am to 3 pm on Saturday. Most bookshops in Thamel, including Pilgrims, also sell stamps and deliver postcards to the post office, which is much easier than making a special trip to the post office yourself.

Airmail rates (in Rs) for the first 20gm are:

Destination	Letter	Postcard
USA, Canada, Australia	20	15
Africa, Europe, Japan, Korea	18	12
Asia (excluding SAARC)	15	10
SAARC (excluding Nepal & India)	10	8
Nepal, India	1	1

Parcel Post Having stocked up on souvenirs and gifts in Nepal, many people take the opportunity to send them home from Kathmandu. Parcel post is not cheap or quick, but the service is reliable.

The contents of a parcel must be inspected by officials before it is wrapped so do not take it to the post office already wrapped. There are packers at the Kathmandu foreign post office who will package it for a small fee. The maximum weight for sea mail is 20kg; for air mail it's 10kg.

See also the Shopping section at the end of this chapter for details on sending things home by courier, which is even more expensive.

Parcel post rates (in Rs) from Nepal are:

Sea Mail	1kg	5kg	10kg	20kg
Australia	864	1410	2027	3388
UK/EU	1006	1720	2364	3952
USA	672	1593	2664	5598

Air Mail	First 250gm	Each additional 250gm
Australia	1056	156
UK/EU	1075	185
USA	898	230

Telephone & Fax

Thankfully the telephone system works pretty well, and it's easy to make local, STD and international calls. Reverse-charge (collect) calls can only be made to Canada, Japan and the UK.

So-called 'communications centres' (often with fax machines) have mushroomed in Nepal and although rates do vary, they're pretty competitive. It's really only worth using the government telegraph offices to make a lengthy international call.

Domestic STD Area Codes

Bhairawa	☎ 071
Biratnagar	☎ 021
Birganj	☎ 051
Butwal	☎ 071
Chitwan (Sauraha)	☎ 056
Dhangadhi	☎ 091
Dhankuta	☎ 026
Dharan	☎ 027
Gorkha	☎ 064
Hetauda	☎ 057
Hile	☎ 026
Ilam	☎ 027
Janakpur	☎ 041
Kakarbhitta	☎ 023
Kathmandu	☎ 01
Mahendranagar	☎ 099
Narayanghat	☎ 056
Nepalganj	☎ 081
Pokhara	☎ 061
Tansen	☎ 075

With the private operators, expect to pay around Rs 170 per minute to Australia, France, the UK and USA, around Rs 185 to New Zealand and Germany, and around Rs 215 to Israel. Many of the hotels also have direct-dial facilities, but always check their charges before you phone. International faxes to anywhere cost Rs 185 per page to send, and around Rs 20 per page to receive.

At the government telegraph offices, there is a minimum charge for the first three minutes (whether you use all the time or not), then a per-minute rate. For Australia, Canada, France, Germany, New Zealand, the UK and the USA, the first three minutes is Rs 432 and additional minutes are Rs 144. For southern Africa, Denmark, Israel and Italy, the first three minutes cost Rs 540, followed by Rs 180 per minute. Faxes are charged at the 'additional minute' rate.

STD calls usually cost Rs 15 per minute regardless of destination.

Email & Internet Access

Consider opening a free email account such as eKno (www.ekno.lonelyplanet.com), HotMail (www.hotmail.com) or Yahoo! Mail (mail.yahoo.com). You can then access your mail from any net-connected computer world-wide. Email and Internet services are offered by dozens of places in Kathmandu and Pokhara – Rs 8 to Rs 10 per minute. See the relevant sections for locations.

INTERNET RESOURCES

The World Wide Web is a rich resource for travellers. You can research your trip, hunt down bargain airfares, book hotels, check on weather conditions or chat with locals and other travellers about the best places to visit (or avoid).

There's no better place to start your Web explorations than the Lonely Planet Web site (www.lonelyplanet.com). Here you'll find succinct summaries on travelling to most places on earth, postcards from other travellers and the Thorn Tree bulletin board, where you can ask questions before you go or dispense advice when you get back. You can also find travel news and updates to many of our most popular guidebooks, and the subWWWay section links you to the most useful travel resources elsewhere on the Web.

There are a number of interesting sites which carry a great deal of information about Nepal. The following sites also have excellent links:
www.catmando.com/wwwvlnp.htm
www.info-nepal.com

BOOKS

There is no shortage of books about Nepal – the Himalaya and heroic mountaineers, the colourful religions and exotic temples, the reclusive history and brave Gurkhas have all inspired writers and photographers, and the results are piled high in numerous bookshops in Nepal, of which there is a surprisingly good selection. Most are in Kathmandu, although there are a number in Pokhara.

Most books are published in different editions by different publishers in different countries. As a result, a book might be a hardcover rarity in one country while it's readily available in paperback in another. Fortunately, bookshops and libraries search by title or author, so your local bookshop or library is best placed to advise you on the availability of the following recommendations. These are only some of the more interesting titles and include books that are long out of print and others which may only be available in Nepal.

Lonely Planet

There are a number of Lonely Planet books that are of interest to visitors to Nepal. *Read this first: Asia* is invaluable for first-time travellers to the region. *Shopping for Buddhas* by Jeff Greenwald, part of the Journeys travel literature series, is an acute and funny book about the author's travels in Nepal, motivated by the obsessive pursuit of a perfect Buddha statue. The *Nepali phrasebook* is a valuable introduction to the language, and travellers who want to take the kids will find *Travel with Children* by Maureen Wheeler a handy reference.

Trekking in the Nepal Himalaya by Stan Armington covers everything you need to know before setting out on a trek in Nepal. The book includes day-by-day coverage of all the main trekking routes, with an excellent medical section covering the problems likely to be encountered in the mountains.

Guidebooks

Other guidebooks to Nepal include APA's *Nepal*, one of the Insight series of photographic coffee table guides. APA also publishes a useful pocket guide, *Nepal* by Lisa Choegyal, which gives some good day-trip itineraries and plenty of tips. *Nepal Namaste* by Robert Rieffel is an excellent locally produced book with all sorts of odd titbits of information.

The Himalaya Experience by Jonathan Chester is an interesting, colourful appetite-whetter for the entire Himalayan region. It has a great deal of interesting information about trekking and climbing and some wonderful photographs.

An Introduction to the Hanuman Dhoka is no longer readily available, but it gives a good short description of the buildings around the Durbar Square area of Kathmandu.

Kathmandu – The Hidden City by Annick Holle is a small, locally produced book which takes you on a number of walks around Kathmandu, revealing some of the lesser known back streets where tourists rarely get to. It is definitely for the dedicated sightseer.

Trekking, Biking & Rafting Guides

A Guide to Trekking in Nepal by Stephen Bezruchka covers all the main trekking routes with detailed descriptions, and is probably the best all-round reference for the individual trekker.

Other excellent guides are the Trailblazer series, with separate guides to the Annapurna and Everest regions.

If you're interested in treks close to Kathmandu, *Treks on the Kathmandu Valley Rim* by Alton C Byers III details a number of one day and overnight treks near Kathmandu.

James Giambrone's *Kathmandu: Bikes & Hikes* gives details on 10 hikes and 11 mountain-bike rides around the valley; it also has a decent fold-out map, although it's now somewhat dated.

Anyone who is seriously interested in rafting and kayaking, and especially anyone contemplating a private expedition, should get hold of Peter Knowles & David Allardice's *White Water Nepal*, which is available in Kathmandu. It has detailed information on river trips, 60 maps, river profiles and hydrographs, plus advice on equipment and health – in short all the information a prospective river runner could want.

History & Politics

Although browsing through a good Kathmandu bookshop will reveal plenty of histories of Nepal there is no definitive book which tells it all in a readable fashion. In particular there has been little accounting of recent events in Nepal, especially the push for greater democracy and the underlying political unrest.

Fatalism & Development – Nepal's Struggle for Modernization by Dor Bahadur Bista is an often controversial analysis of Nepali society and its dynamics. It has a very good historical introduction, and the author looks especially critically at the role of the caste system.

The Political History of Nepal by Margaret W Fisher is now more than 35 years old and even *Nepal in Crisis* by Blaikie, Cameron & Seddon is rather dated.

Charlie Pye-Smith's *Travels in Nepal* is a travel account on one level, but the author's travels around the country are highly directed: he was there to study the impacts and benefits of foreign aid to Nepal and his conclusions are incisive and interesting. In between the aid projects he chain-smokes his way around quite a few interesting places and appears to finish up as much in love with the country as many less single-minded visitors! See Foreign Aid under Economy in the Facts about Nepal chapter for more about this book.

Heroes & Builders of Nepal by Rishikesh Shaha is a brief volume detailing the lives of some of Nepal's early historical figures.

The Challenge to Democracy by T Louise Brown is an excellent reference on the political history up until around 1996, but with a price tag of $85 it's for the dedicated.

General

Toni Hagen's *Nepal – the Kingdom in the Himalaya* (1998) is one of the most complete studies of Nepal's people, geography and geology. Hagen has travelled extensively through Nepal since the 1950s and the book refleets his intimate knowledge of the country and also has fine colour plates. This book is now in its fourth edition, and is one of the best and most up to date references available.

A rather dated account of Nepal is Jeremy Bernstein's *The Wildest Dreams of Kew* (1970) which covers the country's history in a very readable style and includes an interesting trek to the Everest base camp.

Michel Peissel takes a trip to the fabled region of Mustang, close to the border with Tibet and to the north of Jomsom, in *Mustang – A Lost Tibetan Kingdom*, but again, it's pretty old, having been published in the late 1960s.

A more recent saunter around Nepal and Tibet is recounted in the amusingly written *To the Navel of the World* by Peter Somerville-Large. The author also does some deep-winter trekking, using yaks, in the Solu Khumbu and up to the Everest base camp. His encounters with tourism in remote locations are very funny.

Although Pico Iyer's best seller *Video Night in Kathmandu* gallivants all around Asia, the chapter on Nepal has some astute and amusing observations on the collision between Nepali tradition and western culture, particularly video culture.

The Waiting Land: A Spell in Nepal by Dervla Murphy is an interesting account of a visit to Nepal at a time when great changes were at hand. She tells of her time spent in a Tibetan refugee camp near Pokhara, and of her travels in the Langtang region. In *Mister Raja's Neighbourhood*, Jeff Greenwald gives an amusing account of his travels in Nepal.

Helping a captured yeti *Escape from Kathmandu* is only one adventure in Kim Stanley Robinson's off-the-wall romp around Nepal. There's also an illegal ascent of Everest with a reincarnate lama, an attempt to kidnap King Birendra, a visit to Shambhala, a very logical explanation for why Prince Charles is the way he is, and the best ever description of what they do to Kathmandu while you're away trekking.

Misery Behind the Looms is a sobering account of the plight of the young children who are forced to work in almost slave-like conditions in the carpet factories of the Kathmandu Valley.

Travelers' Tales Nepal, one of a series published by Travelers' Tales Inc, is a collection of 37 interesting and wide ranging stories from a variety of writers, including people such as Peter Matthiessen and Jimmy Carter.

Culture, People & Festivals

Festivals of Nepal by Mary Anderson is an excellent rundown on Nepal's many festivals and includes interesting accounts of many of the legends and tales behind them. There is also a great deal of background information about the Hindu religion. Jim Goodman's *Nepalese Festivals* is another worthwhile reference. Mary Rubel's *The Gods of Nepal* is a detailed description of Hindu and Buddhist deities.

People of Nepal, by the Nepali anthropologist Dor Bahadur Bista, describes the many and diverse ethnic groupings found in the country, as does the *Ethnic Groups of Nepal*, by DB Shrestha & CB Singh.

Sherpas of Nepal by C Von Furer Haimendorf focuses on the Sherpas of the Everest region in a rather dry and academic manner. From the same author *Himalayan Traders* is a rather more readable follow-up, concentrating on the changes in trading patterns and cultures among Nepal's Himalayan people.

Michel Peissel's *Tiger for Breakfast* is a biography of the colourful gentleman who was probably the best known resident expatriate in the kingdom – Boris Lissanevitch of the Royal Hotel and Yak & Yeti Restaurant.

The lives of a number of Nepali village women are depicted in *Bending Bamboo Changing Winds* by Eva Kipps. Also giving an interesting insight into Nepali women is *Nepali Aama* by Broughton Coburn, a book which details the life of a remarkable Gurung woman. *The Violet Shyness of Their Eyes: Notes from Nepal* by Barbara J Scot gives a fascinating insight into the lives and roles of women in Nepal.

Natural History

The Royal Chitwan National Park's wildlife is detailed in KK Gurung's *The Heart of the Jungle*. *Indian Wildlife* covers all the national parks on the subcontinent, including Chitwan and Bardia in Nepal with APA's usual high standards of photography.

Birds of Nepal by Robert Fleming Sr, Robert Fleming Jr & Lain Singh Bangdel is a field guide to Nepal's many hundreds of birds. *Himalayan Flowers & Trees* by Dorothy Mierow & Tirtha Bahadur Shrestha is the best available field guide to the plants of Nepal.

Other recommended titles are:

A Popular Guide to the Birds & Mammals of the Annapurna Conservation Area by Carol Inskipp
Birdwatchers' Guide to Nepal by Carol Inskipp
Flowers of the Himalaya by Oleg Polunin & Adam Stainton
Forests of Nepal by Adam Stainton
Mount Everest National Park: Sagarmatha, Mother of the Universe by Margaret Jefferies
Nepal's Forest Birds: Their Status and Conservation by Carol Inskipp
Royal Chitwan National Park: Wildlife Heritage of Nepal by Hemanta R Mishra & Margaret Jefferies
The Book of Indian Animals by SH Prater
Trees & Shrubs of Nepal & the Himalaya by Adrian & Jimmie Storrs.

Architecture & the Arts

Lydia Aran's *The Art of Nepal* is readily available in Nepal and concentrates on the art that can actually be seen in the country. See Arts in the Facts about Nepal chapter for more on this book.

The Austrian publisher Anton Schroll has published two exhaustive studies of the architecture of the Kathmandu Valley. *Kathmandu Valley I* covers the most important temples and buildings in great detail while *Kathmandu Valley II* has individual plans of a great many temples and buildings. This is strictly for the academics but it's amusing to see how many other guidebooks have used these titles in their research. Often they've even copied the mistakes!

The Traditional Architecture of Kathmandu Valley by Wolfgang Korn has some superb line drawings showing the most important architectural forms, along with an interesting text describing their historical development.

Nepal by Michael Hutt is an excellent guide to the art and architecture of the Kathmandu Valley. The book outlines in some depth the main forms of art and architecture, and then goes on to describe specific sites within the valley, often with layout plans. It also features excellent colour plates, as well as black and white photos.

Mary Shepherd Sluiser's *Nepal Mandala – A Cultural Study of the Kathmandu Valley* is another two volume academic study of the valley. Volume II is full of excellent photographs.

Nepal – Art Treasures from the Himalaya by Waldschmidt describes and illustrates many Nepali works of art. The art of the whole Himalayan region is covered in Madanjeet Singh's *Himalayan Art*, again with excellent photographs.

In *Kathmandu Valley Towns,* Fran Hosken writes about the temples, people, history and festivals of the towns of the Kathmandu Valley. The book is illustrated with a great many colour photographs and halftones.

Erotic Themes of Nepal by Trilok Chandra Majupuria & Indra Majupuria is an interesting locally produced book on the erotic art seen on some temples, although it has to work hard to make a book-length study of the subject!

Hallvard Kåre Kuloøy's *Tibetan Rugs* is a fascinating and well illustrated introduction to the subject. If you enjoy the Tibetan rugs made in Nepal you may be disappointed to find that the author summarily dismisses modern rugs as doing 'very little justice to a very splendid tradition'.

Himalayan Voices by Michael Hutt is subtitled *An Introduction to Modern Nepali Literature*, and it includes work by contemporary poets and short-story writers.

Trekking Accounts

John Morris' *A Winter in Nepal* recounts in a very readable fashion a trek from Kathmandu to Pokhara. Like other accounts of the time it's interesting to compare it with the situation today – there was no Kathmandu to Pokhara road in those days. Morris was a retired British army Gurkha

officer and his ability to speak Nepali gave him an excellent insight into Nepali life.

Peter Matthiessen's *The Snow Leopard* is, on one level, an account of a trek from Pokhara up to Dolpo in the west of Nepal, keeping an eye open for snow leopards on the way. On other levels, however, it's clear the author is searching for much more than rare wildlife and this widely acclaimed book doggedly pursues the big questions with the Himalaya as a background.

George Schaller, Matthiessen's companion on this trek, includes this same journey in *Stones of Silence*, an account of various journeys in the Himalaya.

Mountains & Mountaineering

There can be few activities that so inspire people to write about them as that of mountaineering. Every first ascent of a Himalayan peak seems to have resulted in a book about it, together with the numerous other books about the mountains written simply because it seemed a good idea. *The Ascent of Rum Doodle* by WE Bowman is a classic spoof of these often all-too-serious tomes.

Some mountaineering books, however, are excellent reads. If you can find HW Tilman's *Nepal Himalaya* in a library it gives an often amusing account of some early trekking expeditions together with the odd mountain assault which had, by today's standards, an amazing lack of advance planning. Although Tilman was a Himalayan mountaineering pioneer he probably contributed even more to the current popularity of trekking. His book has been republished together with other Tilman classics in *The Seven Mountain-Travel Books*. Tilman's dry wit is quite delightful.

Maurice Herzog's *Annapurna* is a mountaineering classic. Herzog led the first group to reach the top of an 8000m peak, but the descent turned into a frostbitten nightmare taking them to the very outer edges of human endurance.

Naturally there have been numerous books about climbing Everest, including *Forerunners to Everest* by Rene Dittert, Gabriel Chevalley & Raymond Lambert. It describes the two Swiss expeditions to Everest in 1952 and includes a good description of the old expedition route march. Sir John Hunt's *The Conquest of Everest* is the official account of the first successful climb of the world's highest mountain. *Everest* by Walt Unsworth is probably the best history of Everest mountaineering.

In the 1970s unconquered peaks were few and far between so attention turned to climbing by more difficult or spectacular routes. This was technical climbing of a high order and Englishman Chris Bonnington's various expeditions were the best known examples of the craft. His book *Annapurna South Face* describes in detail the planning that goes into making a major expedition, the complicated logistics of the actual climb, and makes an authoritative account of a highly technical assault on a difficult face.

Bonnington also wrote *Everest the Hard Way*, describing his expedition's first ascent of the south-western face in 1975. This climb was a perfectly planned and executed race to the top, and the book is illustrated with superb mountain photography. Despite his record of leading some of the most acclaimed mountaineering expeditions of the time, Bonnington did not reach the top of Everest until 1985, when he set a record as the oldest Everest summiteer. He was 50 years old at the time but just nine days later his record fell to 55-year-old American climber Dick Bass.

Galen Rowell, the renowned mountain photographer, has written *Many people come, looking, looking*. It is a thought provoking study of the impact of trekking and mountaineering on the Himalayan region. There's a good description of the Annapurna Circuit trek and a quick sidetrip to knock off a little 6000m peak!

Other mountaineering books include *Annapurna to Dhaulagiri* by Harka Gurung, which covers the period between 1950 and 1960, when most of Nepal's major peaks 'fell' to mountaineering expeditions. Herbert Tichy's *Himalaya* describes the author's journeys in the region from the 1930s, including

his ascent of Cho Oyu, the third highest peak climbed at that time.

Into Thin Air by Jon Krakauer recounts the disastrous Everest expedition of 1996 in which eight climbers died. This was a controversial expedition as there were a number of inexperienced, paying climbers.

Finally, for the most keen do-it-yourself mountaineers Bill O'Connor's *The Trekking Peaks of Nepal* is a complete description of the climbing routes up Nepal's 18 'trekking peaks'.

FILMS

Despite its stunning scenery, Nepal is surprisingly little used as a film location. Recently the film *Everest*, shot in the impressive Imax format, has proved very popular and is credited by some as having significantly boosted the number of people wanting to trek in the Everest region in recent years.

NEWSPAPERS & MAGAZINES

Nepal's main English-language daily paper, *Rising Nepal*, is basically a government mouthpiece. It covers most important international news while events in Nepal are reported in a very individual style!

For a more balanced view of local issues there's the daily *Kathmandu Post*, which is not too bad. The international news is patchy and it mostly reports on regional issues.

The paper that really tackles the main issues in depth is the weekly *Independent*, which gives some interesting insights into the local political scene. *Spotlight* is a local weekly current affairs magazine which is also worth a look.

For international news you'll have to look farther afield. The *International Herald Tribune* is widely available in Kathmandu – at a price. *Time* and *Newsweek* are readily available and Indian dailies such as the *Statesman* or the *Times of India* can also be found.

Traveller's Nepal is a useful free monthly tourist magazine distributed at many hotels, including the Kathmandu Guest House. It often has very interesting articles about sightseeing, festivals, trekking and other activities in Nepal.

Himal is a bimonthly magazine mainly devoted to development and environment issues. Unfortunately its recent shift to focus on south Asia rather than simply Nepal and the Himalaya means that there will no doubt be a lot less coverage of Nepal issues. It's an excellent publication with top-class contributors.

There are also a number of Nepali newspapers and magazines online, including:

Himal
    www.himalmag.com
Links to a variety of news services, including
    Kathmandu Post & Independent
    www.nepalnews.com

RADIO & TV

Radio Nepal has news bulletins in English at 8 am and 8 pm daily. There's one local television station, but in most places people also watch the Indian Doordarshan channel. Satellite TV is widespread. Most upmarket hotels have dishes, and you can watch everything from the BBC world service to MTV and American wrestling.

In the Kathmandu Valley, two popular FM radio stations playing contemporary music are Kantipur FM (96.1 MHz) and Hits FM (100.0 MHz).

PHOTOGRAPHY & VIDEO
Film & Equipment

In Kathmandu and Pokhara there are numerous camera and film shops and good-quality film is readily available. Do check, however, that the packaging has not been tampered with, and that the expiry date has not been exceeded. There have been cases where people have bought exposed film that has been wound back on the spool.

If in doubt, open the cardboard packaging and check, but you are extremely unlikely to be ripped off in the larger shops. Out in the smaller cities and towns, film is also available, but there is little choice and even greater chance of coming across expired film.

Colour-print film can be processed rapidly, competently and economically in Kathmandu and Pokhara, and there are numerous places offering a same-day service for print film. The developing charge is typically Rs 40 plus around Rs 5 for each print. Colour slides can be developed in Kathmandu, but it's risky and you're better off taking undeveloped films with you and having them processed elsewhere. Prepaid Kodachrome and Fujichrome has to go overseas.

Typically, Fujicolor 100 colour-print film costs about Rs 155 (36 exposures), Fujichrome 36 exposure slide film about Rs 345 and Ektachrome 200 36 exposure slide film about Rs 475.

Technical Tips

Nepal is an exceptionally scenic country so bring plenty of film. It can also provide you with some challenging photo opportunities. For great shots you need a variety of lenses, from a wide-angle lens if you're shooting inside compact temple compounds to a long telephoto lens if you're after perfect mountain shots or close-ups of wildlife. A polarising filter is useful to increase contrast and bring out the blue of the sky.

Remember to allow for the exceptional intensity of mountain light when setting exposures at high altitude. At the other extreme it's surprising how often in Nepal you find the light is insufficient. Early in the morning, in dense jungle in Royal Chitwan National Park, or in gloomy temples and narrow streets you may often find yourself wishing you had high-speed film. A flash is often necessary for shots inside temples or to fill in shots of sculptures and reliefs.

Restrictions

It is not uncommon for temple guardians to disallow photos of their temple, and these wishes should be respected.

Video

Bringing a video camera to Nepal poses no real problem, and there are few camera fees to worry about.

Photographing People

Most Nepalis are content to have their photograph taken but always get permission first. Sherpa people are an exception and can be very camera shy. Bear in mind that if someone poses for you (especially those saintly sadhus), they may insist on being given some baksheesh for doing so.

Respect people's privacy and bear in mind that most Nepalis are extremely modest. Although people carry out many activities in public (they have no choice), it does not follow that passers-by have the right to watch or take photographs. Riverbanks and village wells, for example, are often used as bathrooms, but the users expect as much consideration and privacy as you would in your own house.

Religious ceremonies are also often private affairs, so first ask yourself whether it would be acceptable for a tourist to intrude and to take photographs at a corresponding ceremony in your home country, and then get explicit permission from the senior participants. The behaviour of many would-be National Geographic photographers at places like Pashupatinath (the most holy cremation site in Nepal) is horrendous. Imagine the outrage a busload of scantily clad, camera toting tourists would create if they invaded a family funeral in the west.

Airport Security

All luggage (including carry-on cabin baggage) is X-rayed at Kathmandu airport on the way in and the way out of the country, and while the X-ray equipment is supposedly film-safe, there have been instances where exposed film has been damaged. To be on the safe side, have exposed film inspected manually when leaving the country.

TIME

Nepal is five hours and 45 minutes ahead of GMT; this curious time differential is intended to make it very clear that Nepal is a separate place to India, where the time is five hours and 30 minutes ahead of GMT!

When it's noon in Nepal it's 1.15 pm in Bangkok, 6.15 am in London, 1.15 am in New York, 10.15 pm the previous day in Los Angeles or San Francisco, and 4.15 pm in Sydney or Melbourne, not allowing for daylight saving time or other local variations.

ELECTRICITY
Voltage & Cycles

Electricity is only found in major towns and some odd outposts like Namche Bazaar in the Solu Khumbu. When available it is 220V/50 cycles and 120V appliances from the USA need a transformer.

Plugs & Sockets

Sockets usually take three round pin plugs, sometimes the small variety, sometimes the large. Some sockets take plugs with two round pins.

Reliability of Supply

Outside Kathmandu blackouts are a fact of life and can be random, or regular. In winter, power shortages are endemic, especially if there has been low rainfall in the previous monsoon (which means water flow is reduced and the hydroelectric resources have to be rationed).

Power surges are also likely. If you are using expensive equipment (computers, TVs, fridges etc) it is worth buying a volt guard with spike suppressor (meaning an automatic cut-off switch). These are widely available from most electronic shops for around Rs 1000.

LAUNDRY

There are no public laundrettes in Nepal. Hotels generally discourage guests from doing their own laundry, especially in Kathmandu where water shortages are common. Most hotels have a laundry service, and this is generally very reasonably priced.

TOILETS

Throughout the country, the 'squat toilet' is the norm except in hotels and guesthouses geared toward tourists and international business travellers.

Next to the typical squat toilet is a bucket and/or tap. This water supply has a two-fold function; flushing the toilet and cleaning the nether regions while still squatting over the toilet. More rustic toilets in rural areas may simply consist of a few planks over a hole in the ground.

Public toilets are rare, but can usually be found in bus stations, larger hotel lobbies and airports, although the cleanliness may leave a bit to be desired. While on the road between towns and villages it is acceptable to go discreetly behind a tree or bush.

HEALTH
Travel health depends on your predeparture preparations, your daily health care while travelling and how you handle any medical problem that does develop. While the potential dangers can seem quite frightening, in reality few travellers experience anything more than an upset stomach.

Predeparture Planning
Immunisations Plan ahead for getting your vaccinations: some of them require more than one injection, while some vaccinations should not be given together. Note that some vaccinations should not be given during pregnancy or to people with allergies – discuss with your doctor.

It is recommended you seek medical advice at least six weeks before travel. Be aware that there is often a greater risk of disease with children and during pregnancy.

Discuss your requirements with your doctor, but vaccinations you should consider for this trip include the following (for more details about the diseases themselves, see the individual disease entries later in this section).

Diphtheria & Tetanus Vaccinations for these two diseases are usually combined and are recommended for everyone. After an initial course of three injections (usually given in childhood), boosters are necessary every 10 years.

Polio Although virtually nonexistent in the west these days, polio is still prevalent in Nepal. Keep up to date with this vaccination, normally given in childhood, with a booster every 10 years.

Hepatitis A Hepatitis A vaccine (eg Avaxim, Havrix 1440 or VAQTA) provides long-term im-

munity (possibly more than 10 years) after an initial injection and a booster at six to 12 months.

Alternatively, an injection of gamma globulin can provide short-term protection against hepatitis A – two to six months, depending on the dose given. It is not a vaccine, but is ready-made antibody collected from blood donations. It is reasonably effective and, unlike the vaccine, it is protective immediately, but because it is a blood product, there are current concerns about its long-term safety.

Hepatitis A vaccine is also available in a combined form, Twinrix, with hepatitis B vaccine. Three injections over a six-month period are required, the first two providing substantial protection against hepatitis A.

Typhoid Vaccination against typhoid is never 100% effective but offers good protection. It is advisable for travel to Nepal, and is available either as an injection or as capsules to be taken orally.

Cholera Despite the existence of cholera in Asia, cholera vaccination is not required and the chance of actually catching the disease as a traveller is virtually nil.

The current injectable vaccine against cholera is poorly protective and has many side effects, so it is not generally recommended for travellers.

Hepatitis B Travellers who should consider vaccination against hepatitis B include those on a long trip, as well as those visiting countries where there are high levels of hepatitis B infection, where blood transfusions may not be adequately screened or where sexual contact or needle sharing is a possibility. Vaccination involves three injections, with a booster at 12 months. More rapid courses are available if necessary.

Yellow Fever A yellow fever vaccine is the only vaccine that is a legal requirement for entry into many countries, including Nepal, but this only applies when coming from an infected area (parts of Africa and South America).

Rabies Rabies is a viral brain infection transmitted to humans from animals, usually dogs. Vaccination should be considered by those who will spend a month or longer in a country where rabies is common, especially if they are cycling, handling animals, caving or travelling to remote areas, and for children (who may not report a bite). Pre-travel rabies vaccination involves having three injections over 21 to 28 days. If

Medical Kit Check List

Following is a list of items you should consider including in your medical kit – consult your pharmacist for brands available in your country.

☐ **Aspirin** or **paracetamol** (acetaminophen in the US) – for pain or fever.

☐ **Antihistamine** – for allergies, eg hay fever; to ease the itch from insect bites or stings; and to prevent motion sickness.

☐ **Antibiotics** – consider including these if you're travelling well off the beaten track; see your doctor, as they must be prescribed, and carry the prescription with you.

☐ **Loperamide** or **diphenoxylate** – 'blockers' for diarrhoea; **prochlorperazine** or **metaclopramide** for nausea and vomiting.

☐ **Rehydration mixture** – to prevent dehydration, eg due to severe diarrhoea; particularly important when travelling with children.

☐ **Insect repellent, sunscreen, lip balm** and **eye drops.**

☐ **Calamine lotion, sting relief spray** or **aloe vera** – to ease irritation from sunburn and insect bites or stings.

☐ **Antifungal cream** or **powder** – for fungal skin infections and thrush.

☐ **Antiseptic** (such as povidone-iodine) – for cuts and grazes.

☐ **Bandages, Band-Aids (plasters)** and other wound dressings.

☐ **Water purification tablets** or **iodine.**

☐ **Scissors, tweezers** and a **thermometer** (note that mercury thermometers are prohibited by airlines).

☐ **Syringes** and **needles** – in case you need injections in a country with medical hygiene problems. Ask your doctor for a note explaining why you have them.

☐ **Cold** and **flu tablets, throat lozenges** and **nasal decongestant.**

☐ **Multivitamins** – consider for long trips, when dietary vitamin intake may be inadequate.

someone who has been vaccinated is bitten or scratched by an animal, they will require two booster injections of vaccine; those not vaccinated require more. The human rabies immune globulin (HRIG) is available in Kathmandu.

Japanese B Encephalitis Consider vaccination against this mosquito-borne disease if spending a month or longer in the Terai during the monsoon. Vaccination involves three injections over 30 days.

Tuberculosis (TB) Although tuberculosis is endemic in Nepal, the risk to travellers is very low, unless you will be living with or closely associated with local people. Vaccination against TB is not recommended for casual visitors to Nepal.

Malaria Medication Antimalarial drugs do not prevent you from being infected but kill the malaria parasites during a stage in their development and significantly reduce the risk of becoming very ill or dying. Expert advice on medication should be sought, as there are many factors to consider, including the area to be visited, the risk of exposure to malaria-carrying mosquitoes, the side effects of medication, your medical history and whether you are a child or an adult or pregnant. Travellers to isolated areas in the Terai may like to carry a treatment dose of medication for use if symptoms occur.

Health Insurance Make sure that you have adequate health insurance. See the Travel Insurance boxed text under Visas & Documents in this chapter for details.

Travel Health Guides If you are planning to be away or travelling in remote areas for a long period of time, you may like to consider taking a more detailed health guide.

CDC's Complete Guide to Healthy Travel, Open Road Publishing, 1997. The US Centers for Disease Control & Prevention recommendations for international travel.

Staying Healthy in Asia, Africa & Latin America, Dirk Schroeder, Moon Publications, 1994. Probably the best all-round guide to carry; it's detailed and well organised.

Travellers' Health, Dr Richard Dawood, Oxford University Press, 1995. Comprehensive, easy to read, authoritative and highly recommended, although it's rather large to lug around.

Where There Is No Doctor, David Werner, Macmillan, 1994. A very detailed guide intended for someone, such as a Peace Corps worker, going to work in an underdeveloped country.

Travel with Children, Maureen Wheeler, Lonely Planet Publications, 1995. Includes advice on travel health for younger children.

Healthy Travel, Asia & India, Dr Isabelle Young, Lonely Planet Publications, 2000. Packed with answers to all the common health questions.

There are also a number of excellent travel health sites on the Internet. From the Lonely Planet Web site there are links at www.lonelyplanet.com/weblinks/wlprep.htm#heal to the World Health Organization and the US Centers for Disease Control & Prevention.

Other Preparations Make sure you're healthy before you start travelling. If you are going on a long trip make sure your teeth are OK. If you wear glasses take a spare pair and your prescription.

If you require a particular medication take an adequate supply, as it may not be available locally. Take part of the packaging showing the generic name rather than the brand, which will make getting replacements easier. Have a legible prescription or letter from your doctor to show that you legally use the medication to avoid any problems.

Basic Rules

Food There is an old colonial adage which says: 'If you can cook it, boil it or peel it you can eat it ... otherwise forget it.' Vegetables and fruit should be washed with purified water or peeled where possible. Beware of ice cream which is sold in the street or anywhere it might have been melted and refrozen; if there's any doubt (eg a power cut in the last day or two), steer well clear.

Meat in Nepal can be dodgy, especially beef and pork as much of it is imported from India. The same applies to seafood. Chicken is usually OK.

If a place looks clean and well run and the vendor also looks clean and healthy, then the food is probably safe. In general, places that are packed with travellers or locals will be fine, while empty restaurants are questionable. The food in busy restaurants is cooked and eaten quite quickly with little standing around and is probably not reheated.

Water The number one rule is *be careful of the water* and especially ice. It is not safe to drink tap water in Nepal.

Nutrition

If your food is poor or limited in availability, if you're travelling hard and fast and therefore missing meals or if you simply lose your appetite, you can soon start to lose weight and place your health at risk.

Make sure your diet is well balanced. Cooked eggs, tofu, beans, lentils (dhal in India) and nuts are all safe ways to get protein. Fruit you can peel (bananas, oranges or mandarins for example) is usually safe (melons can harbour bacteria in their flesh and are best avoided) and a good source of vitamins. Try to eat plenty of grains (including rice) and bread. Remember that although food is generally safer if it is cooked well, overcooked food loses much of its nutritional value. If your diet isn't well balanced or if your food intake is insufficient, it's a good idea to take vitamin and iron pills.

In hot climates make sure you drink enough – don't rely on feeling thirsty to indicate when you should drink. Not needing to urinate or small amounts of very dark yellow urine is a danger sign. Always carry a water bottle with you on long trips. Excessive sweating can lead to loss of salt and therefore muscle cramping. Salt tablets are not a good idea as a preventative, but in places where salt is not used much, adding salt to food can help.

If you don't know for certain that the water is safe, assume the worst. Bottled water is available everywhere, but the unrecyclable plastic bottles are creating a huge litter problem. The best way not to contribute to this is to purify the tap water yourself using iodine.

Take care with fruit juice, particularly if water may have been added. Milk should be treated with suspicion as it is often unpasteurised, though boiled milk is fine if it is kept hygienically. Tea or coffee should also be OK, since the water should have been boiled.

Water Purification The simplest way of purifying water is to boil it thoroughly. Vigorous boiling should be satisfactory; however, at high altitude water boils at a lower temperature, so germs are less likely to be killed. Take care to boil it for longer in these environments.

Consider purchasing a water filter for a long trip. There are two main kinds of filter. Total filters take out all parasites, bacteria and viruses and make water safe to drink. They are often expensive, but they can be more cost effective than buying bottled water. Simple filters (which can even be a nylon mesh bag) take out dirt and larger foreign bodies from the water so that chemical solutions work much more effectively; if water is dirty, chemical solutions may not work at all. It's very important when buying a filter to read the specifications, so that you know exactly what it removes from the water and what it doesn't. Simple filtering will not remove all dangerous organisms, so if you cannot boil water it should be treated chemically. Chlorine tablets will kill many pathogens, but not some parasites like giardia and amoebic cysts. Iodine is more effective in purifying water and is available in tablet form. Follow the directions carefully and remember that too much iodine can be harmful.

Environmental Hazards

Altitude Sickness Lack of oxygen at high altitudes (over 2500m) affects most people to some extent. The effect may be mild or severe and occurs because less oxygen reaches the muscles and the brain at high altitude, requiring the heart and lungs to compensate by working harder. Symptoms of Acute Mountain Sickness (AMS) usually develop during the first 24 hours at altitude but may be delayed by up to three weeks. Mild symptoms include headache, lethargy, dizziness, difficulty sleeping and loss of appetite. AMS may become more severe without warning and can be fatal. Severe symptoms include breathlessness, a dry, irritative cough (which may progress to the production of pink, frothy sputum), severe headache, lack of coordination and balance, confusion, irrational behaviour, vomiting, drowsiness and unconsciousness. There is no hard-and-fast rule as to what is too high: AMS has been fatal at 3000m, although 3500 to 4500m is the usual range.

Treat mild symptoms by resting at the same altitude until recovery, usually a day or two. Paracetamol or aspirin can be taken for headaches. If symptoms persist or become worse, however, *immediate descent is necessary*; even 500m can help. Drug treatments should never be used to avoid descent or to enable further ascent.

The drugs acetazolamide and dexamethasone can be useful in helping to prevent and treat AMS. Acetazolamide (Diamox) can be used to treat mild symptoms of AMS (headaches and nausea) and can also prevent mild symptoms of AMS if taken prior to ascending. It is only recommended you do this if you have had previous experience of AMS and know you are susceptible. Dexamethasone is a powerful steroid which can drastically reduce symptoms but, unlike Diamox, it does not alleviate the actual acclimatisation problems and can lead to a false sense of improved health.

To help prevent acute mountain sickness:

- Ascend slowly – have frequent rest days, spending two to three nights at each rise of 1000m. If you reach a high altitude by trekking, acclimatisation takes place gradually and you are less likely to be affected than if you fly directly to high altitude.

- It is always wise to sleep at a lower altitude than the greatest height reached during the day if possible. Also, once above 3000m, care should be taken not to increase the sleeping altitude by more than 300m per day.
- Drink extra fluids. The mountain air is dry and cold, and moisture is lost as you breathe. Evaporation of sweat may occur unnoticed and result in dehydration.
- Eat light, high-carbohydrate meals for more energy.
- Avoid alcohol as it may increase the risk of dehydration.
- Avoid sedatives.

Heat Exhaustion Dehydration and salt deficiency can cause heat exhaustion. Take time to acclimatise to high temperatures, drink sufficient liquids and do not do anything too physically demanding.

Salt deficiency is characterised by fatigue, lethargy, headaches, giddiness and muscle cramps; salt tablets may help, but adding extra salt to your food is better.

Anhidrotic heat exhaustion is a rare form of heat exhaustion that is caused by an inability to sweat. It tends to affect people who have been in a hot climate for some time, rather than newcomers. It can progress to heatstroke. Treatment involves removal to a cooler climate.

Heatstroke This serious, occasionally fatal, condition can occur if the body's heat-regulating mechanism breaks down and the body temperature rises to dangerous levels. Long, continuous periods of exposure to high temperatures and insufficient fluids can leave you vulnerable to heatstroke.

The symptoms are feeling unwell, not sweating very much (or at all) and a high body temperature (39° to 41°C or 102° to 106°F). Where sweating has ceased, the skin becomes flushed and red. Severe, throbbing headaches and lack of coordination will also occur, and the sufferer may be confused or aggressive. Eventually the victim will become delirious or convulse. Hospitalisation is essential, but in the interim get victims out of the sun, remove their clothing, cover them with a wet sheet or towel and then fan continually. Give fluids if they are conscious.

Hypothermia Too much cold can be just as dangerous as too much heat. If you are trekking at high altitudes or simply taking a long bus trip over mountains, particularly at night, be prepared. In Nepal's mountain regions you should always be prepared for cold, wet or windy conditions even if you're just out walking or hitching.

Hypothermia occurs when the body loses heat faster than it can produce it and the core temperature of the body falls. It is surprisingly easy to progress from very cold to dangerously cold due to a combination of wind, wet clothing, fatigue and hunger, even if the air temperature is above freezing. It is best to dress in layers; silk, wool and some of the new artificial fibres are all good insulating materials. A hat is important, as a lot of heat is lost through the head. A strong, waterproof outer layer (and a 'space' blanket for emergencies) is essential. Carry basic supplies, including fluid and food containing simple sugars to generate heat quickly.

Symptoms of hypothermia are exhaustion, numb skin (particularly toes and fingers), shivering, slurred speech, irrational or violent behaviour, lethargy, stumbling, dizzy spells, muscle cramps and violent bursts of energy. Irrationality may take the form of sufferers claiming they are warm and trying to take off their clothes.

To treat mild hypothermia, first get the person out of the wind and/or rain, remove their clothing if it's wet and replace it with dry, warm clothing. Give them hot liquids (not alcohol) and some high-kilojoule, easily digestible food. Do not rub victims: instead, allow them to slowly warm themselves. This should be enough to treat the early stages of hypothermia. The early recognition and treatment of mild hypothermia is the only way to prevent severe hypothermia, which is a critical condition.

Motion Sickness Eating lightly before and during a trip will reduce the chances of motion sickness. If you are prone to motion sickness try to find a place that minimises movement – near the wing on aircraft, near

Everyday Health

Normal body temperature is up to 37°C (98.6°F); more than 2°C (4°F) higher indicates a high fever. The normal adult pulse rate is 60 to 100 per minute (children 80 to 100, babies 100 to 140). As a general rule the pulse increases about 20 beats per minute for each 1°C (2°F) rise in fever.

Respiration (breathing) rate is also an indicator of illness. Count the number of breaths per minute: between 12 and 20 is normal for adults and older children (up to 30 for younger children, 40 for babies). People with a high fever or serious respiratory illness breathe more quickly than normal. More than 40 shallow breaths a minute may indicate pneumonia.

the centre on buses. Fresh air usually helps; reading and cigarette smoke don't. Commercial motion-sickness preparations, which can cause drowsiness, have to be taken before the trip commences. Ginger (available in capsule form) and peppermint (including mint-flavoured sweets) are natural preventatives.

Prickly Heat Prickly heat is an itchy rash caused by excessive perspiration trapped under the skin. It usually strikes people who have just arrived in a hot climate. Keeping cool, bathing often, drying the skin and using a mild talcum or prickly heat powder or resorting to air-conditioning may help.

Sunburn In the tropics, the desert or at high altitude you can get sunburnt surprisingly quickly, even through cloud. Use a sunscreen, a hat, and a barrier cream for your nose and lips. Calamine lotion or a commercial after sun preparation are good for mild sunburn. Protect your eyes with good quality sunglasses, particularly if you will be near water, sand or snow.

Medical Problems & Treatment

Self-diagnosis and treatment can be risky, so you should always seek medical help. An embassy, consulate or five-star hotel can usually recommend a local doctor or clinic. Although we do give drug dosages in this section, they are for emergency use only. Correct diagnosis is vital. In this section we have used the generic names for medications

– check with a pharmacist for brands available locally.

Note that antibiotics should ideally be administered only under medical supervision. Take only the recommended dose at the prescribed intervals and use the whole course, even if the illness seems to be cured earlier. Stop immediately if there are any serious reactions and don't use the antibiotic at all if you are unsure that you have the correct one. Some people are allergic to commonly prescribed antibiotics such as penicillin; carry this information (eg on a bracelet) when travelling.

Diarrhoea Simple things like a change of water, food or climate can all cause a mild bout of diarrhoea, but a few rushed toilet trips with no other symptoms is not indicative of a major problem.

Dehydration is the main danger with any diarrhoea, particularly in children or the elderly as dehydration can occur quite quickly. Under all circumstances *fluid replacement* (at least equal to the volume being lost) is the most important thing to remember. Weak black tea with a little sugar, soda water, or soft drinks allowed to go flat and diluted 50% with clean water are all good. With severe diarrhoea a rehydrating solution is preferable to replace minerals and salts lost. Commercially available oral rehydration salts (ORS) are very useful; add them to boiled or bottled water. In an emergency you can make up a solution of six teaspoons of sugar and a half teaspoon of salt to a litre of boiled or bottled water. You need to drink at least the same volume of fluid that you are losing in bowel movements and vomiting. Urine is the best guide to the adequacy of replacement – if you have small amounts of concentrated urine, you need to drink more. Keep drinking small amounts often. Stick to a bland diet as you recover.

Antibiotics can often rapidly and dramatically limit a bout of diarrhoea, allowing you to get on with your trip. Whether or not you take antibiotics should depend largely on how severe it is and whether or not you have the time to wait for the symptoms (if relatively mild) to abate of their own accord. In certain situations antibiotics are definitely required: diarrhoea with blood or mucus (dysentery), any diarrhoea with fever, profuse watery diarrhoea, persistent diarrhoea not improving after 48 hours and severe diarrhoea. These suggest a more serious cause of diarrhoea and in these situations gut-paralysing drugs should be avoided. In these situations, a stool test may be necessary to diagnose what bug is causing your diarrhoea, so you should seek medical help urgently.

Where this is not possible the recommended drugs for bacterial diarrhoea (the most likely cause of severe diarrhoea in travellers) are norfloxacin 400mg twice daily for three days or ciprofloxacin 500mg twice daily for five days. However, these are not recommended for children or pregnant women. The drug of choice for children would be co-trimoxazole with dosage dependent on weight. A five day course is given. Ampicillin or amoxycillin may be given in pregnancy, but medical care is necessary.

Gut-paralysing drugs such as loperamide or diphenoxylate can be used to bring relief from the symptoms, although they do not actually cure the problem. Only use these drugs if you do not have access to toilets, eg if you *must* travel. Note that these drugs are not recommended for children under 12 years.

Two other causes of persistent diarrhoea in travellers are giardiasis and amoebic dysentery. You should seek medical advice if you think you have giardiasis or amoebic dysentery, but where this is not possible, tinidazole or metronidazole are the recommended drugs. Treatment is a 2g single dose of tinidazole or 250mg of metronidazole three times daily for five to 10 days.

Giardiasis This is caused by a common parasite, Giardia lamblia. Symptoms include stomach cramps, nausea, a bloated stomach, watery, foul-smelling diarrhoea and frequent gas. Giardiasis can appear several weeks after you have been exposed to the parasite. The symptoms may disappear for a few days and then return; this can go on for several weeks.

Amoebic Dysentery This is caused by the protozoan Entamoeba histolytica and is characterised by a gradual onset of low-grade diarrhoea, often with blood and mucus. Cramping abdominal pain and vomiting are less likely than in other types of diarrhoea, and fever may not be present. It will persist until treated and can recur and cause other health problems.

Fungal Infections Fungal infections occur more commonly in hot weather and are usually found on the scalp, between the toes (athlete's foot) or fingers, in the groin and on the body (ringworm). You get ringworm (which is a fungal infection, not a worm) from infected animals or other people. Moisture encourages these infections.

To prevent fungal infections wear loose, comfortable clothes, avoid artificial fibres, wash frequently and dry yourself carefully. If you do get an infection, wash the infected area at least daily with a disinfectant or medicated soap and water, and rinse and dry well. Apply an antifungal cream or powder like tolnaftate. Try to expose the infected area to air or sunlight as much as possible and wash all towels and underwear in hot water, change them often and let them dry in the sun.

Hepatitis Hepatitis is a general term for inflammation of the liver. It's common worldwide. There are several different viruses that cause hepatitis, and they differ in the way that they are transmitted. The symptoms are similar in all forms of the illness, and include fever, chills, headache, fatigue, feelings of weakness and aches and pains, followed by loss of appetite, nausea, vomiting, abdominal pain, dark urine, light-coloured faeces, jaundiced (yellow) skin and yellowing of the whites of the eyes. People who have had hepatitis should avoid alcohol for some time after the illness, as the liver needs time to recover.

Hepatitis A is transmitted by contaminated food and drinking water. You should seek medical advice, but there is not much you can do apart from resting, drinking lots of fluids, eating lightly and avoiding fatty foods. Hepatitis E is transmitted in the same way as hepatitis A; it can be particularly serious in pregnant women, but is rare in Nepal.

There are almost 300 million chronic carriers of **hepatitis B** in the world. It is spread through contact with infected blood, blood products or body fluids, for example through sexual contact, unsterilised needles and blood transfusions, or contact with blood via small breaks in the skin. Other risk situations include having a shave, tattoo or body piercing with contaminated equipment. The symptoms of hepatitis B may be more severe than type A and the disease can lead to long term problems such as chronic liver damage, liver cancer or a long term carrier state. Hepatitis C and D are spread in the same way as hepatitis B and can also lead to long term complications.

There are vaccines against hepatitis A and B, but there are currently no vaccines against the other types of hepatitis. Following the basic rules about food and water (hepatitis A and E) and avoiding risk situations (hepatitis B, C and D) are important preventative measures.

HIV & AIDS Infection with the human immunodeficiency virus (HIV) may lead to acquired immune deficiency syndrome (AIDS), which is a fatal disease. Any exposure to blood, blood products or body fluids may put the individual at risk. The disease is often transmitted through sexual contact or dirty needles – vaccinations, acupuncture, tattooing and body piercing can be potentially as dangerous as intravenous drug use. HIV/AIDS can also be spread through infected blood transfusions; some developing countries cannot afford to screen blood used for transfusions.

If you do need an injection, ask to see the syringe unwrapped in front of you, or take a needle and syringe pack with you (available from pharmacies in Nepal).

Fear of HIV infection should never preclude treatment for serious medical conditions.

Intestinal Worms These parasites are most common in rural, tropical areas. The different worms have different ways of infecting people. Some may be ingested on food such as undercooked meat (eg tapeworms) and some enter through your skin (eg hookworms). Infestations may not show up for some time, and although they are generally not serious, if left untreated some can cause severe health problems later. Consider having a stool test when you return home to check for these and determine the appropriate treatment.

Meningococcal Meningitis This serious disease can be fatal. There are rare epidemics in Nepal.

A fever, severe headache, sensitivity to light and neck stiffness which prevents forward bending of the head are the first symptoms. There may also be purple patches on the skin. Death can occur within a few hours, so urgent medical treatment is required.

Trekkers to rural areas of Nepal should be particularly careful, as the disease is spread by close contact with people who carry it in their throats and noses and spread it through coughs and sneezes; they may not be aware that they are carriers. Lodges in the hills where travellers spend the night are prime spots for the spread of infection.

Treatment is large doses of penicillin given intravenously, or chloramphenicol injections.

AIDS in Nepal

Prostitution does exist in Nepal, particularly in the border towns and along the main truck routes, but it is virtually invisible to western visitors. In addition, it is believed that over 100,000 Nepali women work in Indian brothels, often in conditions little different to slavery, and over 30,000 of these are estimated to be HIV positive. When obvious AIDS symptoms force these women to retire, some do manage to return to Nepal. Sadly, they are shunned by their families and there is virtually no assistance available to them or their children.

Up to half a million Nepali men seek seasonal work in Indian cities, and in common with migrant workers elsewhere it is likely that many patronise brothels while they are away. Finally, there are estimated to be 10,000 intravenous drug users in Nepal who are at risk. No official figures are available, but it is clear that AIDS has the potential to become a major problem.

Sexually Transmitted Diseases HIV/AIDS and hepatitis B can be transmitted through sexual contact – see the relevant sections earlier for more details. Other STDs include gonorrhoea, herpes and syphilis; sores, blisters or rashes around the genitals and discharges or pain when urinating are common symptoms. In some STDs, such as wart virus or chlamydia, symptoms may be less marked or not observed at all, especially in women. Chlamydia infection can cause infertility in men and women before any symptoms have been noticed. Syphilis symptoms eventually disappear completely but the disease continues and can cause severe problems in later years.

While abstinence from sexual contact is the only 100% effective prevention, using condoms is also effective. The treatment of gonorrhoea and syphilis is with antibiotics. The different sexually transmitted diseases each require specific antibiotics.

Typhoid Typhoid fever is a dangerous gut infection caused by contaminated water and food. Medical help must be sought.

In its early stages sufferers may feel they have a bad cold or flu on the way, as early symptoms are a headache, body aches and a fever which rises a little each day until it is around 40°C (104°F) or more. The victim's pulse is often slow relative to the degree of fever present – unlike a normal fever where the pulse increases. There may

also be vomiting, abdominal pain, diarrhoea or constipation.

In the second week the high fever and slow pulse continue and a few pink spots may appear on the body; trembling, delirium, weakness, weight loss and dehydration may occur. Complications such as pneumonia, perforated bowel or meningitis may occur.

Insect-Borne Diseases
Malaria This serious and potentially fatal disease is spread by mosquito bites. It is not found in the tourist areas of Nepal – the Kathmandu Valley, Pokhara, and the Himalaya – but is known to exist in the lowland Terai region throughout the year. If you are travelling in endemic areas it is extremely important to avoid mosquito bites and to take tablets to prevent this disease. Symptoms range from fever, chills and sweating, headache, diarrhoea and abdominal pains to a vague feeling of ill-health. Seek medical help immediately if malaria is suspected. Without treatment malaria can rapidly become more serious and can be fatal.

If medical care is not available, malaria tablets can be used for treatment. You need to use a malaria tablet which is different from the one you were taking when you contracted malaria. The standard treatment dose of mefloquine is two 250mg tablets and a further two six hours later. For Fansidar, it's a single dose of three tablets. If you were previously taking mefloquine and cannot obtain Fansidar, then other alternatives are Malarone (atovaquone-proguanil; four tablets once daily for three days), halofantrine (three doses of two 250mg tablets every six hours) or quinine sulphate (600mg every six hours). There is a greater risk of side effects with these dosages than in normal use if used with mefloquine, so medical advice is preferable. Be aware also that halofantrine is no longer recommended by the WHO as emergency standby treatment, because of side effects, and should only be used if no other drugs are available.

Travellers are advised to prevent mosquito bites at all times. The main messages are:

- wear light-coloured clothing
- wear long trousers and long-sleeved shirts
- use mosquito repellents containing the compound DEET on exposed areas (prolonged overuse of DEET may be harmful, especially to children, but its use is considered preferable to being bitten by disease-transmitting mosquitoes)
- avoid perfumes or aftershave
- use a mosquito net impregnated with mosquito repellent (permethrin) – it may be worth taking your own
- impregnating clothes with permethrin effectively deters mosquitoes and other insects

Dengue Fever This viral disease is transmitted by mosquitoes and is fast becoming one of the top public health problems in the tropical world. It is not known whether there is a risk of contracting the disease in Nepal, although it certainly does exist in northern India. Unlike the malaria mosquito, the *Aedes aegypti* mosquito, which transmits the dengue virus, is most active during the day, and is found mainly in urban areas, in and around human dwellings.

Signs and symptoms of dengue fever include a sudden onset of high fever, headache, joint and muscle pains (hence its old name, 'breakbone fever') and nausea and vomiting. A rash of small red spots sometimes appears three to four days after the onset of fever. In the early phase of illness, dengue may be mistaken for other infectious diseases, including malaria and influenza. Minor bleeding such as nose bleeds may occur in the course of the

illness, but this does not necessarily mean that you have progressed to the potentially fatal dengue haemorrhagic fever (DHF). This is a severe illness, characterised by heavy bleeding, which is thought to be a result of second infection due to a different strain (there are four major strains) and usually affects residents of the country rather than travellers. Recovery even from simple dengue fever may be prolonged, with tiredness lasting for several weeks.

You should seek medical attention as soon as possible if you think you may be infected. A blood test can exclude malaria and indicate the possibility of dengue fever. There is no specific treatment for dengue. Aspirin should be avoided, as it increases the risk of haemorrhaging. There is no vaccine against dengue fever. The best prevention is to avoid mosquito bites at all times by covering up, using insect repellents containing the compound DEET and mosquito nets – see the Malaria section earlier for more advice on avoiding mosquito bites.

Cuts, Bites & Stings
See Less Common Diseases for details of rabies, which is passed through animal bites.

Cuts & Scratches Wash well and treat any cut with an antiseptic such as povidone-iodine. Where possible avoid bandages and Band-Aids, which can keep wounds wet.

Bedbugs & Lice Bedbugs live in various places, but particularly in dirty mattresses and bedding, evidenced by spots of blood on bedclothes or on the wall. Bedbugs leave itchy bites in neat rows. Calamine lotion or a sting relief spray may help.

All lice cause itching and discomfort. They make themselves at home in your hair (head lice), your clothing (body lice) or in your pubic hair (crabs). You catch lice through direct contact with infected people or by sharing combs, clothing and the like. Powder or shampoo treatment will kill the lice and infected clothing should then be washed in very hot, soapy water and left in the sun to dry.

Bites & Stings Bee and wasp stings are usually painful rather than dangerous. However, in people who are allergic to them severe breathing difficulties may occur and require urgent medical care. Calamine lotion or a sting relief spray will give relief and ice packs will reduce the pain and swelling.

Leeches Leeches may be present in damp conditions; they attach themselves to your skin to suck your blood. During the monsoon trekkers often get them on their legs or in their boots. Salt or a lighted cigarette end will make them fall off. Do not pull them off, as the bite is then more likely to become infected. Clean and apply pressure if the point of attachment is bleeding. An insect repellent may keep them away.

Snakes To minimise your chances of being bitten always wear boots, socks and long trousers when walking through undergrowth where snakes may be present. Don't put your hands into holes and crevices.

Snake bites do not cause instantaneous death. Immediately wrap the bitten limb tightly, as you would for a sprained ankle, and then attach a splint to immobilise it. Keep the victim still and seek medical help, if possible with the dead snake for identification. Don't attempt to catch the snake if there is a possibility of being bitten again. Tourniquets and sucking out the poison are now comprehensively discredited.

Women's Health
Gynaecological Problems Antibiotic use, synthetic underwear, sweating and contraceptive pills can lead to fungal vaginal infections, especially when travelling in hot climates. Yeast infections (thrush) are characterised by a rash, itch and discharge and can be treated with a vinegar or lemon-juice douche, or with yoghurt. Nystatin, miconazole or clotrimazole pessaries or vaginal cream are the usual treatment. Maintaining good personal hygiene and wearing loose-fitting clothes and cotton underwear may help prevent these infections.

Sexually transmitted diseases are a major cause of vaginal problems. Symptoms include a smelly discharge, painful intercourse and sometimes a burning sensation when urinating. Medical attention should be sought and sexual partners must also be treated. For more details see the section on Sexually Transmitted Diseases earlier. Besides abstinence, the best thing is to practise safer sex using condoms.

Pregnancy It is not advisable to travel to some places while pregnant as some vaccinations normally used to prevent serious diseases are not advisable during pregnancy. In addition, some diseases are much more serious for the mother (and may increase the risk of a stillborn child) in pregnancy (eg malaria).

It is generally considered inadvisable to travel to altitude (above around 3650m) when pregnant, so any treks going over this height should be avoided.

Most miscarriages occur during the first three months of pregnancy. Miscarriage is not uncommon and can occasionally lead to severe bleeding. The last three months should also be spent within reasonable distance of good medical care. A baby born as early as 24 weeks stands a chance of survival, but only in a good modern hospital.

Pregnant women should avoid all unnecessary medication, although vaccinations and malarial prophylactics should still be taken where needed. Additional care should be taken to prevent illness and particular attention should be paid to diet and nutrition. Alcohol and nicotine, for example, should be avoided.

Less Common Diseases
The following diseases pose a small risk to travellers, and so are only mentioned in passing. Seek medical advice if you think you may have any of these diseases.

Cholera This is the worst of the watery diarrhoeas and medical help should be sought. Outbreaks of cholera are generally widely reported, so you can avoid such problem areas. *Fluid replacement is the most vital* *treatment* – the risk of dehydration is severe as you may lose up to 20L a day. If there is a delay in getting to hospital, then begin taking tetracycline. The adult dose is 250mg four times daily. It is not recommended for children under nine years nor for pregnant women. Tetracycline may help shorten the illness, but adequate fluids are required to save lives.

Rabies This fatal viral infection is found in many countries, including Nepal. Many animals can be infected (such as dogs, cats, bats and monkeys) and it is their saliva which is infectious. Any bite, scratch or even lick from an animal should be cleaned immediately and thoroughly. Scrub with soap and running water, and then apply alcohol or iodine solution. Medical help should be sought promptly to receive a course of injections to prevent the onset of symptoms and death.

Tetanus This disease is caused by a germ which lives in soil and in the faeces of horses and other animals. It enters the body via breaks in the skin. The first symptom may be discomfort in swallowing, or stiffening of the jaw and neck; this is followed by painful convulsions of the jaw and whole body. The disease can be fatal. It can be prevented by vaccination.

Tuberculosis (TB) TB is a bacterial infection usually transmitted from person to person by coughing but which may be transmitted through consumption of unpasteurised milk. Milk that has been boiled is safe to drink, and the souring of milk to make yoghurt or cheese also kills the bacilli. Travellers are usually not at great risk as close household contact with the infected person is usually required before the disease is passed on. You may need to have a TB test before you travel as this can help diagnose the disease later if you become ill.

WOMEN TRAVELLERS
Nepal is perhaps among the safest countries in the world for women travellers. However, as is the case in most countries, women should still be cautious, especially when trekking. Never trek alone, and only trek with companies that have been recommended by trustworthy friends.

It's a good idea to bear in mind that some Nepali men have peculiar ideas about the morality of western women, given their exposure to western films, 'immodest' clothing, and inter-racial holiday flings. Dress modestly, and avoid situations where you cannot call for help should a situation get out of hand.

GAY & LESBIAN TRAVELLERS
There's no gay scene to speak of in Nepal (it's illegal). Gay couples holding hands in public will experience no difficulties, as this is socially acceptable, but displays of intimacy *by anyone* are frowned upon.

DISABLED TRAVELLERS
Travellers with a physical disability may find it tough going in Nepal. Trying to get around in a wheelchair would be well-nigh impossible: facilities such as access ramps and wheelchair-friendly hotel rooms simply don't exist.

SENIOR TRAVELLERS
Older travellers will find that their age will probably command them a certain amount of respect, but on a practical level there are no discounts or other concessions available.

TRAVEL WITH CHILDREN
Surprisingly few people travel with children in Nepal, yet with a bit of planning it is remarkably hassle free. Certainly it's hard work, but then staying home with kids is hard work too, so why not get out and enjoy it? As always, children are great ice-breakers, and the local hospitality and friendliness shines through even more.

In the main tourist centres (Kathmandu and Pokhara), most hotels will have triple rooms, and quite often rooms with four beds, which are ideal for families with young children. Finding a room with a bathtub can be a problem, however, especially at the bottom end of the market. Garden space is at a premium in Kathmandu hotels, but many places have a roof garden, and some of these can be good play areas for kids. Check thoroughly, however, as some are definitely not safe.

One of the hardest parts about life on the road with kids in Nepal is eating out at restaurants. While the food is excellent and there's always something on the menu which will appeal to kids – even if it's only chips or banana porridge – service is usually quite slow and things take quite a while to arrive. By the time the food arrives your kids (especially if they are really young) will be bored stiff and ready to leave. You can minimise the hassles by eating breakfast at your hotel, having lunch at a place with a garden (there's plenty of these) where the children can let off steam, and in the evening going to the restaurant armed with pencils, colouring books, stories and other distractions to keep them busy for half an hour. High chairs are virtually nonexistent.

Walking the crowded and narrow streets of Kathmandu can be a hassle with young kids unless you can get them up off the ground – a backpack is ideal, but a pusher or stroller would be more trouble than it's worth.

One of the most rewarding things to do with kids is to take them trekking in the mountains. Once again, very few people seem to do this yet the experience for everyone is well worth the effort. The main consideration is that to have an easy trip you need to hire enough porters to carry not only your gear but also any young children. This is not as expensive as it sounds, with porters costing around $5 per day. See the Trekking chapter for more details.

If your child needs disposable nappies, these are available in Kathmandu and Pokhara – for a price. Better to bring them with you if possible. Even better would be to use cloth ones, but this can be a headache and you may well decide the convenience of disposable ones worth it. Bear in mind, however, that disposable nappies are far from disposable – they are in fact almost indestructible – and waste disposal in Nepal is already a major problem.

DANGERS & ANNOYANCES
Trekking

Surrounded by western comforts in Kathmandu, it is easy to forget that Nepal is, in terms of many physical resources, an undeveloped country. This means that people are extremely poor, hygiene is often bad, transport (particularly of the road variety) is dangerous, rescue facilities are limited, and medical facilities are often primitive or nonexistent.

Fired up by the gung-ho stories of adventurous travellers, it is also easy to forget that mountainous terrain is always potentially dangerous. Nepal, of course, is a continuous series of the most spectacular mountains in the world. And the risks are correspondingly real.

Only a tiny minority of people do finally end up in trouble, but the tragedy is that accidents and their consequences can often be avoided or minimised if people have a realistic understanding of where they are and what they are doing, and if they observe common sense rules and take a few basic precautions. See the Trekking chapter for more details.

The Kathmandu Environment Education Project (KEEP) and the Himalayan Rescue Association (HRA) offices, both in Thamel, can give up-to-date information on trekking conditions and health risks. A visit to either or both is strongly recommended. Several embassies and consulates have registration forms at the centres; if they don't, you can register at the actual embassy or consulate. The forms record your name, rough itinerary, insurance details and next of kin, and can obviously speed up a search or medical evacuation.

Theft

Things do get stolen in Nepal, just like anywhere else in the world, but theft is still extremely rare. There are pickpockets in crowded areas of old Kathmandu; backpacks can disappear from bus roofs and from hotel storage rooms; possessions get stolen from camp sites; and on rare occasions lone trekkers have even been mugged and robbed.

There's little chance of ever retrieving your gear if it is stolen, and even getting a police report for an insurance claim can be difficult. Try the local police station, but if you aren't getting anywhere, go straight to Interpol (☎ 412602) at the Police Headquarters in Naxal, Kathmandu; the postal address is PO Box 407. There is a local Interpol office just off Durbar Square but it will only handle your case if the theft actually took place in Kathmandu. The documentation requires a passport photo, and photocopies of your passport and visa; the process takes two days.

BUSINESS HOURS

Most government offices in Kathmandu are open from 10 am to 5 pm from Sunday to Thursday during summer and from 9 am to 4 pm during the winter months (roughly mid-November to mid-February since the winter starting date for the change of hours varies with the Nepali calendar). Offices close at 3 pm on Friday. Saturday is the weekly holiday and most shops and all offices and banks will be closed, but Sunday is a regular working day.

PUBLIC HOLIDAYS & SPECIAL EVENTS

Many holidays and festivals affect the working hours of government offices and banks. These will be closed for, among others, Shivaratri, the Nepali New Year, Teej, Indra Jatra, Dasain, Tihar, the queen's birthday on 7 November and the king's birthday on 29 December.

Nepal's colourful holidays and festivals occur virtually year round and a visit to Nepal is almost certain to coincide with at least one, particularly in the Kathmandu Valley. Certain times of year, particularly August and September towards the end of the monsoon, are packed with festivals. They go a long way towards compensating for the less-than-ideal weather at this time of year.

Dasain is the most important of all Nepali celebrations, perhaps most closely approximated by Christmas and New Year in the west. Tens of thousands of Nepalis hit the road to return home to celebrate with their families. This means the villages are full of life if you are trekking, but it also means that all the buses and planes are fully booked and overflowing, that porters may be hard to find (or more expensive than usual), and that cars are hard to hire. Many hotels and restaurants in regional towns close down completely, and doing business in Kathmandu, outside of Thamel, becomes almost impossible.

The most important days, when everything comes to a total halt, are the ninth day, when thousands of animals are sacrificed, and the 10th day when blessings are received from elder relatives and superiors. Banks and government offices are generally closed from the eighth day to the 12th. The final day of Dasain is on the full moon in September or October.

For interesting accounts of many of the festivals and the legends behind them read Mary M Anderson's *The Festivals of Nepal*, or *Nepalese Festivals* by Jim Goodman.

Nepali holidays and festivals are principally dated by the lunar calendar, falling on days relating to new or full moons. The Nepali new year starts on 13 April with the month of Baisakh and is 57 years ahead of the Gregorian calendar used in the west. The year 2000 in the west is 2057 in Nepal. The Newars, on the other hand, start their new year from the day after Deepawali, which falls on the night of the new moon in late October or early November. Their calendar is 880 years behind the Gregorian calendar so 2000 in the west is 1120 to the Newars of the Kathmandu Valley.

Predicting the exact dates for Nepali holidays and festivals is not always easy. In Nepal the lunar calendar is divided into bright and dark fortnights. The bright fortnight is the two weeks of the waxing moon, as it grows to become the full moon (*purnima*). The dark fortnight is the two weeks of the waning moon, as the full moon shrinks to become the new moon (*aunsi*). Therefore a festival might fall 'on the 11th day of the bright fortnight of Falgun'.

What sometimes seems like a cavalier attitude towards numbering days actually has a logical explanation. The sun rises every 24 hours but the period between successive moonrises can vary from 22 to 27 hours. Thus several times each year there can be a 'moon day' (the period from one moonrise to the next) which has no sunrise within it, and several others that have two sunrises. Thus the lunar calendar will sometimes jump a day, and on other occasions it will hiccup and repeat a day. Predicting a date far in advance is additionally complicated by the periodic adjustments which have to be made to bring the shorter lunar year back into line with the solar year which the Gregorian calendar follows. See the Nepali Calender for the corresponding Gregorian months in the Nepali year.

The Festival Calendar covers dates through to the end of 2001, hopefully with reasonable accuracy. Check the dates when you're in Kathmandu.

January-February
Magh Sankranti
The end of the coldest winter months is marked by this festival and ritual bathing, despite the cold, during the Nepali month of Magh. The festival is dated by the movement north of the winter sun and is one of the few festivals not timed by the lunar calendar. Soon after, on the new-moon day, the Tribeni Mela (a mela is a fair) is held at various places including Devghat, on the banks of the Narayani River near the town of Narayanghat in the Terai.

Basant Panchami
The beginning of spring is celebrated by honouring Saraswati and since she is the goddess of learning this festival has special importance for students and scholars. The shrine to Saraswati just below the platform at the top of Swayambhunath is the most popular locale for the festivities. This is also a particularly auspicious occasion for weddings.

February
Losar
The new year for the Tibetan and Bhotiya people commences with the new moon in February and is welcomed with particular fervour at the great Bodhnath stupa. Colourfully dressed lamas parade around the stupa carrying banners and portraits of the Dalai Lama. Ceremonies are also performed at Swayambhunath and in the Tibetan community at Jawlakhel near Patan. Crowds of Tibetans dressed in their most traditional costumes and furiously twirling their prayer wheels, watch the proceedings. The Sherpa people of the Solo-Khumbu region also celebrate at this time.

February-March
Maha Shivaratri
Shiva's birthday falls on the new-moon day of the month of Falgun. Festivities take place at all Shiva temples but most particularly at the great Pashupatinath Temple, and devotees flock there not only from all over Nepal but also from all over India.

Many sadhus make the long trek to Nepal for this festival and the king of Nepal will also appear late in the day since Shiva, as Lord Pashupati, is asked to protect Nepal at the conclusion of any official message. The crowds bathing in the Bagmati's holy waters at this time are a colourful and wonderful sight. The sadhus, meanwhile, will be up to all their usual fun and games whether it's rolling in the ashes, performing impossible feats of yoga or sticking thorns through their tongues. Overall, however, Maha Shivaratri is a serene and peaceful festival, reflecting the deep devotion which Hindus hold for their religion.

Holi/Fagu
This exciting festival is closely related to the water festivals of Thailand and Myanmar and takes place on the full-moon day in the month of Falgun. By this time, late in the dry season, it is beginning to get rather hot and the water which is sprayed around so liberally during the

Nepali Calendar

January-February	Magh
February-March	Falgun
March-April	Chaitra
April-May	Baisakh
May-June	Jeth
June-July	Asaar
July-August	Saaun
August-September	Bhadra
September-October	Ashwin
October-November	Kartik
November-December	Mangsir
December-January	Pus

festival is a reminder of the cooling monsoon days to come. Holi is also known as the Festival of Colours and as well as spraying water on everything and everyone, coloured powder (particularly red) and coloured water are also dispensed. Foreigners get special attention, so if you venture out on Holi leave your camera behind (or keep it well protected) and wear old clothes which can get colour-stained.

At one time Holi used to take place on the eight days leading up to the full moon; these days activities are usually restricted to one day.

The festival is said to be inspired by the exploits of Krishna, particularly an incident when he caught his favourite milkmaids sporting in the Jamuna River. A pole supporting a three tiered umbrella is set up in front of the Basantapur Tower in the centre of Kathmandu and on the final day the umbrella is taken down and burnt.

Other activities also take place during Holi. Guru Mapa, the demon of the Yitum Bahal in Kathmandu (see Walking Tour 1 in the Kathmandu section), has his annual feed on Holi night. The inhabitants of Yitum Bahal sacrifice a buffalo on the banks of the Vishnumati River, cook it in the afternoon in their great courtyard and in the middle of the night carry it in huge cauldrons to the Tundikhel where the demon is said to live to this day.

More peacefully, singing and dancing continues until late at night during another cheerful festival in Tarke Gyang on the Helambu trek.

March-April
Chaitra Dasain

Also known as Small Dasain, in contrast with the Big Dasain in the month of Kartik, this festival takes place exactly six months prior to the more important one. Like the other Dasain it's dedicated to Durga and once again it's a bad day for goats and buffaloes who do their unwilling bit for the goddess early in the morning in Kot Square.

Seto Machhendranath

The Chaitra Dasain sacrifices also signal the start of the Seto (White) Machhendranath festival, a month prior to the much larger and more important Rato (Red) Machhendranath festival in Patan. The festival starts with removing the image of Seto Machhendranath from the temple at Kel Tole and placing it on a towering and creaky wooden temple chariot or rath. For the next four evenings the chariot proceeds from one historic location to another eventually arriving at Lagankhel in the south of Kathmandu. There the image is taken down from the chariot and carried back to its starting point in a palanquin while the chariot is disassembled and put away until next year.

April
Bisket Jatra

Nepali new year starts in mid-April, beginning of the month of Baisakh, and the Bisket festival in Bhaktapur is the most spectacular welcome for the new year and one of the most exciting annual events in the valley. Magh Sankranti is the only other important religious festival set by the solar rather than the lunar calendar.

Bisket is Bhaktapur's great chariot festival but whereas in Kathmandu and Patan it is Machhendranath who gets taken for a ride, here it is Bhairab, accompanied by Betal and, in a second chariot, the goddess Bhadrakali. The ponderous chariots of the gods always appear shaky and unsafe and moving them requires enormous amounts of energy.

From Taumadhi Tole, outside Bhairab's temple, the huge temple chariot proceeds around the town, pausing for a huge tug of war between the eastern and western sides of town. The winning side is charged with looking after the images of the gods during their week-long riverside sojourn. After the battle the chariots slither down the steep road leading to the river, where a huge 25m-high lingam is erected. In the evening of the following day, new year's day, the pole is pulled down, again in an often violent tug of war. As the pole crashes to the ground the new year officially commences.

As is usual in Nepal, legend is piled upon legend, and far in the past there's a tale of a beautiful princess and a valiant prince behind the Bisket festival:

The king of Bhaktapur had an insatiable daughter who not only required a new lover each night but left him dead each morning! Finally a brave prince showed up and despite an exhausting session with the princess forced himself to stay awake afterwards. Late that night two threadlike wisps emerged from the beautiful princess's nostrils, and grew into venomous snakes in the night air. Before they could strike and consign the prince to the scrap heap of discarded lovers he drew his sword and killed them both. Of course the prince and princess married and lived happily ever after and from the top of the towering Bisket lingam stream two banners, symbolic of those two deadly snakes.

Other events also take place around Bhaktapur for a week preceding the new year and for some days after. Members of the potters' caste put up and haul down their own lingam, and processions also carry images of Ganesh, Lakshmi and Mahakali around town. The new year is also an important time in the valley for ritual bathing, and crowds of hill people visit the Buddhist stupas of Swayambhunath and Bodhnath.

Balkumari Jatra

Thimi, the smaller town near Bhaktapur, also welcomes the new year with an exciting festival. This event was instituted by King Jagat Jyoti Malla in the early 1600s but here it is Balkumari, another of Bhairab's consorts, who is honoured. All through new year's day devotees crowd around her temple in Thimi and as dusk falls hundreds of ceremonial oil lamps (chirags) are lit. Some devotees lie motionless around the temple all night with burning oil lamps balanced on their legs, arms, chests and foreheads.

The next morning men come from the various toles or quarters of Thimi and from surrounding villages, each team carrying a palanquin known as a khat with images of different gods. As the 32 khats whirl around the temple red powder is hurled at them and the ceremony reaches fever pitch as the khat bearing Ganesh arrives from the village of Nagadish. The crowds parade up and down the main street until late in the morning when Ganesh, borne by hundreds of men, makes a break for home, pursued by the other khats. If they can catch Ganesh the activities are prolonged but eventually Ganesh departs and the festival moves on to the Taleju Temple.

Sacrifices are now made to Balkumari and in the small village of Bode another khat festival, with just seven khats rather than 32, takes place. Here a volunteer spends the whole day with an iron spike piercing his tongue. Successful completion of this painful rite brings merit to the whole village as well as the devotee.

Festival Calendar

As the actual holidays aren't declared more than a year in advance, many of the following dates are estimates only, but should be correct to within a day or so. Check in Nepal for exact dates.

Name of Festival	Place	1999	2000	2001
Magh Sankranti	Narayanghat	mid-Jan	mid-Jan	mid-Jan
Basant Panchami	Swayambhunath	22 Jan	10 Feb	29 Jan
Losar	Bodhnath & others	16 Feb	5 Feb	23 Feb
Maha Shivaratri	Pashupatinath	15 Feb	4 Feb	22 Feb
Holi	all over Nepal	1 Mar	19 Feb	9 Mar
Chaitra Dasain	all over Nepal	25 Mar	12 Apr	2 Apr
Bisket Jatra	Bhaktapur	14 Apr	14 Apr	14 Apr
Buddha Jayanti	Swayambhunath	30 Apr	18 Apr	7 May
Naga Panchami	all over Nepal	16 Aug	5 Aug	25 Jul
Gai Jatra	Kathmandu	27 Aug	16 Aug	5 Aug
Krishna Jayanti	Patan	2 Sep	22 Aug	9 Sep
Teej	Pashupatinath	12 Sep	1 Sep	22 Aug
Dasain				
Fulpati	all over Nepal	16 Oct	4 Oct	24 Sep
Vijaya Dashami	all over Nepal	19 Oct	7 Oct	27 Sep
Kartika Purnima	all over Nepal	24 Oct	13 Oct	2 Oct
Tihar				
Deepawali	all over Nepal	7 Nov	26 Oct	14 Nov
Bhai Tika	all over Nepal	9 Nov	28 Oct	16 Nov
Haribodhini Ekadashi	Kathmandu	19 Nov	7 Nov	27 Oct
Bala Chaturdashi	Pashupatinath	7 Dec	25 Nov	14 Dec
Sita Bibaha Panchami	Janakpur	12 Dec	30 Nov	20 Nov
Mani Rimdu	Solo Khumbu	Nov	Nov	Nov

April-May
Rato Machhendranath

Although Seto and Rato Machhendranath may well be the same deity, the Rato or Red Machhendranath festival of Patan is a much more important occasion than the Kathmandu event. Machhendranath is considered to have great powers over rain and, since the monsoon is approaching at this time, this festival is a plea for good rain.

As in Kathmandu the festival consists of a day-by-day temple chariot procession through the streets of the town, but here it takes a full month to move from the Pulchowk area, where the image is installed in the chariot, to Jawlakhel where the chariot is dismantled.

Along the way the main chariot is accompanied for most of its journey by a second smaller chariot containing the image of Rato Machhendranath's Bodhisattva companion from the Minanath Temple, near the Rato Machhendranath Temple south of Patan's Durbar Square.

The highlight of the festival is the Bhoto Jatra, or showing of the sacred vest. Machhendranath was entrusted with the jewelled vest as there was some dispute as to who owned it. The vest is displayed three times in order to give the owner the chance to claim it – although this doesn't actually happen. The king of Nepal attends this ceremony, which is also a national holiday.

From Jawlakhel, Rato Machhendranath does not return to his Patan temple, however. He has a second home in the village of Bungamati and he spends six months of each year at this temple, to where he is now conveyed on a khat. Every 12 years, however, the Rato Machhendranath festival becomes an even more important and time-consuming event when the chariot continues all the way to Bungamati. The next enactment of the complete Patan to Bungamati procession will be in 2003.

The temple chariots (raths) used in these processions are immense wooden affairs with wheels metres in diameter and a towering but often rather ramshackle edifice constructed on top. It takes hundreds of devotees to tow the main chariot and the Nepali army is often called in to help in the Patan Rato Machhendranath festival, despite the intense local enthusiasm to take part in pulling the chariot. The long procession is often halted to await an auspicious occasion for the next leg, or to make important roadside repairs to the chariot.

Similar temple chariot processions take place in India including the largest of them all, the great Jagannath procession at Puri in the state of Orissa.

Buddha Jayanti (Buddha's Birthday)

Siddhartha Gautama (Buddha) was born at Lumbini, so it is fitting that his birthday should be celebrated in Nepal. Swayambhunath is the centre for the celebrations although events also take place at Bodhnath and in Patan.

A constant procession of pilgrims makes its way around the stupa at Swayambhunath. The stupa's collection of rare thangkas and mandalas is shown on the southern wall of the stupa courtyard on this single day each year. The stupa's lamas dress in colourful silk robes and dance around the stupa with accompaniment provided by musicians.

Mata Tirtha Puja

The last day of the dark fortnight of Baisakh is Mata Tirtha Puja. It's the Nepali equivalent of Mother's Day and every Nepali should go to 'look upon their mother's face'. Those whose mothers have died in the past year are supposed to bathe at the Mata Tirtha pond, about 10km south-west of Kathmandu near Thankot road.

May-June
Kumar Sasthi

The birthday of Shiva's son Kumar or Kartikkaya, the god of war and brother of Ganesh, is also known as Sithinakha. The festival also marks the start of the rice planting season and is an annual occasion for cleaning wells. Once the god of war's birthday was commemorated by stone-throwing contests. Since these often turned into strictly local, but often decidedly real, 'wars' they're now confined to young boys.

July-August
Naga Panchami

On the fifth day after the new moon in the month of Saaun, snakes (nagas) are honoured. Numerous legends are told about snakes and they are said to have all sorts of magical powers including special powers over the monsoon rains. Pictures of the nagas are hung over the doorways of houses and this not only propitiates the snakes but also keeps harm from the household. Various foods are put out for the snakes and there are interesting legends behind the offerings of milk and boiled rice:

A farmer inadvertently killed three baby snakes with his plough and the enraged mother snake chased the farmer back to his house and killed the farmer, his wife and his two sons. The daughter was about to get the same treatment when she offered the serpent a bowl of milk. The snake was so taken by this act of kindness that it spared the daughter and offered her any wish. 'Bring my parents and brothers back to life', replied the daughter and the snake duly did so. Ever since then snakes are offered a bowl of milk on Naga Panchami.

The bowl of rice is offered because of an incident at the Siddha Pokhari pond just outside Bhaktapur which, the legend relates, was once inhabited by an evil naga. A holy man determined to kill the naga himself by taking the form of a snake, and told his companion to be ready with a bowl of magic rice. If, after he entered the pond, the water turned white then the naga had won and it was all over. If, on the other hand, the water turned red then he had defeated the naga and although he would emerge from the pond in the form of a snake, the magical rice would restore his original form.

Sure enough the water turned red but when the holy man in the form of a hideous serpent emerged from the water his horrified companion simply turned tail and ran, taking the rice with him. The holy man tried to catch him but failed and eventually decided to return to the pond and remain there. To this day the inhabitants of Bhaktapur keep well clear of the Siddha Pokhari pond and on the day of Naga Panchami a bowl of rice is put out – just in case the holy man/snake turns up.

Janai Purnima

On the day prior to and on the day of the full moon in the month of Saaun all high-caste men (Chhetri and Brahman) must change the janai (sacred thread) which they wear looped over their left shoulder and tied under their right arm. The three cords of the sacred thread symbolise body, speech and mind, and young men first put on the thread in an important ritual that officially welcomes them into their religion. From that date they wear the sacred thread for the rest of their lives, changing it on this one occasion each year as well as any time it has been damaged or defiled, such as coming into contact with a woman while she is menstruating.

Although only men wear the thread, anybody, including curious foreigners, can wear a yellow thread or raksha bandhan around their wrist – right for men, left for women. Wearing this thread on your wrist is said to bring good fortune and on this day priests tie the threads on all comers. You are supposed to wear it for at least a week, but preferably for three months until the Festival of Lights (during Tihar) in October-November.

Janai Purnima also brings crowds of pilgrims to the sacred Gosainkund Lake, across the mountains to the north of Kathmandu. There they garland a statue of Shiva and throw coins at the sacred lingam which rises up from the lake. A direct channel is said to lead from the lake to the pond in the Kumbeshwar Temple in Patan and a silver lingam is installed in the pond for the occasion. The rituals at the temple attract jhankris, faith healers who perform in a trance while beating drums.

Gai Jatra

The Gai Jatra (Cow Festival) takes place immediately after Janai Purnima on the day after the Saaun full moon, and is dedicated to those who died during the preceding year. Newars believe that after death, cows will guide them to Yama, the god of the underworld, and finding your way on this important journey will be much easier if by chance you should be holding onto a cow's tail at the moment of death! Therefore on this day cows are lead through the streets of the valley's towns or, if a cow is not available, small boys dress up as cows.

The festival also celebrates an event during the reign of King Pratap Malla (1641-74). The king's youngest son died and the queen was grief-stricken. Nothing could cheer her up and eventually the king offered rewards to anybody who could bring a smile to her face. Crowds of people appeared before the royal palace and danced and clowned, dressed in outlandish costumes. The queen could not help laughing at this mass outbreak of merry madness and the king proclaimed that henceforward Gai Jatra would be a day for costumes and games. So it is that many other peculiar outfits appear on the streets, apart from boys dressed up as cows, and the festival is celebrated with maximum energy on the streets of Bhaktapur.

Ghanta Karna

Ghanta Karna falls on the 14th day of the dark fortnight of Saaun. Ghanta Karna, which means 'bell ears', was a horrible demon who was so named because he wore bell earrings to drown out the name of Vishnu, his sworn enemy. The festival celebrates his destruction when a god, disguised as a frog, lured him into a deep well where the people stoned and clubbed him to death. Ghanta Karna is burnt in effigy on this night and evil is cleansed from the land for another year.

August-September
Krishna Jayanti (Krishna's Birthday)

The seventh day after the full moon in the month of Bhadra is celebrated as Krishna's birthday, sometimes also known as Krishnasthami. Krishna is an incarnation of Vishnu and his daring exploits, good nature and general love of a good time endear him to many people. The Krishna Mandir in Patan is the centre for the celebrations and an all-night vigil is kept at the temple on the night before his birthday. Oil lamps light the temple and singing continues through the night.

Teej

The Festival of Women lasts three days, from the second to the fifth day after the Bhadra new moon. It is based in Pashupatinath and women celebrate Teej in honour of their husbands and in hope of a long and happy married life.

The festival starts with a sumptuous meal and the women gather together and spend the rest of the day feasting and talking, right through until midnight when they must commence 24 hours of fasting. During the day of the fast women from all over the valley converge on Pashupatinath, traditionally dressed in red and gold saris, usually the ones in which they were married. At Pashupatinath the women take ritual dips in the river and call on the gods to protect their husbands.

The following morning the women must offer their husbands small items of food which have previously been offered to the gods. The day-long fast can then be broken although in some years the festival continues for an extra day in which case this is a day of partial fasting. Another ritual bathing ceremony takes place on this day, preferably at a river confluence, such as where the Bagmati and Vishnumati rivers meet, just south of Kathmandu. Completion of these ceremonies washes away all female sin, including the sin of a woman touching her husband during her period!

Gunla

The 15 days before and after the full moon in August or early September is celebrated as a full month of Buddhist ceremonies, penance and fasting. Activities are centred on Swayambhunath. Pancha Dan, the Festival of Five Offerings, is held in Patan during Gunla but there are various other festivals and ceremonies during the month.

Gokarna Aunsi

The Nepali equivalent of Father's Day is celebrated by visiting living fathers at their homes and honouring deceased fathers at the Shiva Temple in Gokarna.

September
Indra Jatra

This important festival runs from the end of the month of Bhadra into the beginning of Ashwin.

Indra Jatra is a colourful and exciting festival which manages to combine homage to Indra with an important annual appearance by Kumari (the living goddess), respects to Bhairab and commemoration of the conquest of the valley by Prithvi Narayan Shah. The festival also marks the end of the monsoon and the start of the fine months which follow.

Indra is the ancient Aryan god of rain and he once paid a visit to the Kathmandu Valley to pick a certain flower which his mother Dagini needed for the festival of Teej. Unfortunately for Indra he was captured in the act of stealing the flowers and imprisoned until his mother came down to rescue him. When she revealed whom they had imprisoned, his captors gladly released him but the festival continues to celebrate this remarkable achievement – villagers don't capture a real god every day of the week! In return for his release Dagini promised to spread morning moisture and dew over the crops for the coming months and to take back with her to heaven all those who had died in the past year.

The festival therefore honours the recently deceased and pays homage to Indra and Dagini for the coming harvests. It starts with the erection of a huge pole outside the Hanuman Dhoka, Kathmandu. The carefully selected pole has first been brought to the Tundikhel and then carried to the square. The pole is set up while images and representations of Indra, usually as a captive, are displayed and sacrifices of goats and roosters are made. At the same time the screened doors obscuring the horrific face of White Bhairab are opened and for the next three days his gruesome visage will stare out at the proceedings.

The day before all this activity, three golden temple chariots have been assembled in Basantapur Square, outside the home of the Kumari, the living goddess. In the afternoon, with the Durbar Square packed with colourful and cheerful crowds, two boys emerge from the Kumari's house. They play the roles of Ganesh and Bhairab and will each ride in a chariot as an attendant to the goddess. Finally, the Kumari herself appears either walking on a rolled-out carpet or carried by attendants so that her feet do not touch the ground.

The chariots move off and the Kumari is greeted from the balcony of the old palace by the king. The procession then continues out of Durbar Square towards Hanuman Dhoka where it stops in front of the huge White Bhairab mask. The Kumari greets the image of Bhairab and then, with loud musical accompa-

Shiva in his fierce manifestation as Bhairab – the destroyer of human ignorance and evil.

niment, beer starts to pour from Bhairab's mouth! Grabbing a sip of this beer is guaranteed to bring good fortune, but one lucky individual will also get the small fish which has been put to swim in the beer – this brings especially good luck!

The procession moves off again and for the remaining days of the festival it moves from place to place around the town, to the accompaniment of ceremonies, dances and other activities. Numerous other processions also take place around the town until the final day when the great pole is lowered and carried down to the river. It was during the Indra Jatra festival back in 1768 that Prithvi Narayan Shah conquered the valley and unified Nepal so this important event is also commemorated in this most spectacular of Kathmandu occasions.

Ganesh Chata

On Ganesh Chata, the fourth day of the bright fortnight in September, offerings are made to Ganesh. The festival celebrates a bitter dispute between Ganesh and the moon goddess, and the Nepalis try to stay indoors on this night and shut out all signs of moonlight.

September-October
Pachali Bhairab Jatra

The fearsome form of Bhairab, as Pachali Bhairab, is honoured on the fourth day of the bright fortnight in September or early October. The festivities are in line with Bhairab's bloodthirsty nature as there are numerous sacrifices.

October-November
Dasain

The pleasant post-monsoon period when the sky is clearest, the air is cleanest and the rice is ready for harvesting is also the time for Nepal's biggest annual festival. Dasain lasts for 15 days, finishing on the full-moon day of late September or early October, and there are a number of important days right through the festival. Although much of Dasain is a quiet family affair there are colourful events for visitors to see both in Kathmandu and in the country. Dasain is also known as Durga Puja since the festival celebrates the victory of the goddess Durga over the forces of evil in the guise of the buffalo demon Mahisasura. Since Durga is a bloodthirsty goddess, the festival is marked by wholesale bloodletting and features the biggest animal sacrifice of the year. Dasain also celebrates Rama's victory over the 10-headed demon Ravana.

Even before Dasain commences Nepalis spring-clean their houses, while in the country, swings and primitive hand-powered Ferris wheels are erected at the entrance to villages or in their main square. For trekkers, Dasain is very much 'the festival of swings'! On the first day of the festival, a sacred jar of water is prepared in each house and barley seeds are planted in carefully prepared soil. Getting the seeds to sprout a few centimetres during Dasain ensures a good harvest.

Fulpati is the first really important day of Dasain and is called 'the seventh day' although it may not actually fall on the seventh day. Fulpati means 'sacred flowers' and a jar containing flowers is carried from Gorkha to Kathmandu and presented to the king at the Tundikhel parade ground. The flowers symbolise Taleju, the goddess of the royal family, whose most important image is in the Gorkha palace. From the parade ground the flowers are transported on a palanquin to the old Royal Palace on Durbar Square where they are inspected again by the king and his entourage.

Maha Astami or the 'great eighth day' and Kala Ratri the 'black night' follow Fulpati and this is the start of the sacrifices and offerings to Durga. The hundreds of goats you may see contentedly grazing in the Tundikhel parkland prior to Maha Astami are destined to die for the goddess. At midnight, in a temple courtyard near Durbar Square, eight buffaloes and 108 goats are beheaded with a single stroke of the sword or knife.

The next day is Navami and the Kot Square near Durbar Square, scene of the great massacre of noblemen which led to the Rana period of

Nepali history, is the scene for another great massacre. Visitors can witness the bloodshed but you need to arrive early to secure a place on the foreigners' balcony. Sacrifices continue through the day and blood is sprinkled on the wheels of cars and other vehicles to ensure a safe year on the road. At the airport each Royal Nepal Airlines aircraft will have a goat sacrificed to it! The average Nepali does not eat much meat, but on this day almost everybody in the country will find that goat is on the menu for dinner.

The 10th day of the festival, Vijaya Dashami, is again a family affair as cards and greetings are exchanged, family visits are made and parents place a red tika mark on their children's foreheads. In the evening, the conclusion of Dasain is marked by processions and masked dances in the towns of the Kathmandu Valley. The Kharga Jatra or sword processions feature priests dressed up as the various gods and carrying wooden swords, symbolic of the weapon with which Durga slew the buffalo demon. This day also celebrates the victory of Lord Rama over the evil King Ravana in the Ramayana. The barley sprouts which were planted on the first day are picked and worn as small bouquets in the hair.

Kartika Purnima, the full-moon day marking the end of the festival, is celebrated with gambling in many households and you will see even small children avidly putting a few coins down on various local games of chance. Women fast and many of them make a pilgrimage to Pashupatinath near Kathmandu. Although Dasain is principally a Hindu festival it has also been adopted by Buddhists, and activities also take place at Buddhist shrines in Patan and Bhaktapur. In the country the swings and Ferris wheels will be busier than ever, before finally being dismantled for another year.

Tihar

With its colourful Festival of Lights, Tihar (also called Deepawali or Diwali) is the most important Hindu festival in India, and in Nepal it ranks second only to Dasain. The five days of activities take place in late October or early November.

The festival honours certain animals on successive days, starting with offerings of rice to the crows which are sent by Yama, the god of death, as his 'messengers of death'. On the second day, dogs are honoured with garlands of flowers and tikas. This must be a considerable surprise to most Nepali dogs, who are usually honoured with no more than the occasional kick, but the fact that, in the afterworld, it is dogs who guide departed souls across the river of the dead must not be forgotten. Bhairab's vehicle also happens to be a dog. On the third day it is cows who are remembered and on this day you will often see cows with one horn painted silver, one gold. On the fourth day bullocks are honoured.

The third day, Deepawali, is the most important day of the festival when Lakshmi (Vishnu's consort and the goddess of wealth) comes to visit every home which has been suitably lit for her presence. Since one can hardly turn down a surprise visit from the goddess of wealth, homes throughout the country will be brightly lit with candles and lamps for the Festival of Lights. The effect is highlighted because Deepawali falls on the new-moon day.

The fourth day is also the start of the new year for the Newar people of the Kathmandu Valley. The fifth day is known as Bhai Tika and on this day brothers and sisters are supposed to meet and place tikas on each others' foreheads. Sisters offer small gifts of fruit and sweets to their brothers while the brothers give

The Ages of Brahma

Each universe has a Brahma who lives for 100 years, Brahma years, that is, which are much longer than our earth years. Each day in a Brahma year is a Kalpa, and each Kalpa or Brahma day is in turn divided into 1000 Mahayugas or Great Ages.

In a single Great Age there are four Yugas which follow a prescribed pattern. In the first Yuga everything is fine, but in the second Yuga evil makes its appearance and the eternal struggle between good and evil commences. In the third Yuga good is in serious trouble and in the fourth Yuga, the Kaliyuga, evil comes out on top and it's time for Vishnu to take on his 10th incarnation as Kalki the destroyer and bring the whole mess to a quick end. And where are we currently in this cycle of existence? About halfway through the fourth Yuga.

their sisters money in return. The markets and bazaars of Kathmandu will be busy supplying the appropriate gifts.

Haribodhini Ekadashi

Ekadashi falls twice in each lunar month, on the 11th day after each new and full moon. Each Ekadashi is celebrated with ceremonies and activities but the Haribodhini Ekadashi, falling in late October or early November on the 11th day after the new moon, is the most important. On this day Vishnu awakens from his four month monsoonal slumber and the best place to see the associated festivities is at Budhanilkantha, the temple of the sleeping Vishnu. Activities also take place at other Vishnu temples and many Vishnu devotees make a circuit of the important ones from Ichangu Narayan to Changu Narayan, Bishankhu Narayan and Sekh Narayan.

Mahalakshmi Puja

Lakshmi is the goddess of wealth, but to farmers wealth is rice so this harvest festival, following immediately after Haribodhini Ekadashi, honours the goddess with sacrifices and colourful dances.

November-December
Bala Chaturdashi

Like Ekadashi there are two Chaturdashis each month and Bala Chaturdashi falls on the new-moon day in late November or early December. Pilgrims flock to Pashupatinath for this festival, burning oil lamps at night and bathing in the holy river on the following morning. A pilgrimage is then made along a traditional route through the woods overlooking Pashupatinath, and as they walk the devotees scatter sweets and seeds for their deceased relatives to enjoy in the afterlife. The festival is at its most colourful during the first evening and is best observed from the other side of the Bagmati River, looking down towards the temple with its singing and dancing lamp-lit pilgrims.

Bala, incidentally, once worked at Pashupatinath where he cremated corpses until an unfortunate incident transformed him into a demon. He then haunted the area around the temple until a means was found to dispose of him. Various legends relate how the demon was killed by one of poor Bala's former friends and the festival of Bala Chaturdashi was then instituted.

Sita Bibaha Panchami

On the fifth day of the bright fortnight in late November or early December, pilgrims from all over Nepal and India flock to Janakpur to celebrate the marriage of Sita to Rama. It was in Janakpur that Sita was born and she and Rama have temples in the town. The wedding is re-enacted with a procession carrying Rama's image to Sita's temple by elephant. Rama's birthday is celebrated in March in Janakpur and Kathmandu.

Mani Rimdu

The Sherpa festival of Mani Rimdu takes place at the monastery of Thyangboche in the Solu Khumbu region. The three day festival features masked dances and dramas performed by the monastery's monks and celebrates the victory of Buddhism over the older Bön religion. Another Mani Rimdu takes place six months later in May-June at the Thami Monastery, a day's walk west of Namche Bazaar.

Other Festivals & Ceremonies

Ekadashi Ekadashi falls twice in each lunar month, 11 days after the full moon and the new moon. The annual Haribodhini Ekadashi is a major festival, but other Ekadashis are also celebrated, often with music and singing.

Marriage Ceremonies It's important that weddings take place on an auspicious date and cartain months of the year (Pus in particular) are extremely ill-starred for marriages. Only five months of a year – namely Magh, Falgun, Baisakh, Jeth and Mangsir – are ideal, although if pressed, a talented astrologer can find an auspicious date at even the most inconvenient time. Spring is the favourite time of year and on ideal days in Baisakh there will be numerous wedding bands marching around town at the same time.

A traditional Newari wedding is a complicated affair lasting up to a week. The various stages of the ceremony move back and forth between the bride and groom's homes and include a procession led by a band. The religious ceremony, where a fire 'witnesses' the marriage, is held at the bride's house and the festivities conclude with a wedding banquet. Although more couples are making their own choice of partners many marriages are still arranged.

Very different forms of marriage take place in the hills. For example, polyandry (where a woman takes more than one husband) is still practised in parts of the Sherpa country.

In Nepal, as in a number of other Asian countries, the bride never wears white. White is the colour of death and funerals, red is a much happier and more auspicious colour. Married women wear vermilion in the parting of their hair.

ACTIVITIES
Trekking
Nepal is one of the world's top destinations for trekkers. Trekking gives you a chance to get out into the countryside to places accessible only on foot, meet some of the people from the many diverse ethnic groups and view some of the most spectacular scenery on earth.

There are many destinations, and almost as many ways of getting to them, so some planning is required, although this can easily be done once you arrive in Nepal. See the Trekking chapter for more details.

Rafting & Kayaking
With the Himalaya in the backyard it should come as no surprise that Nepal has some of the world's best white-water rafting.

There are literally dozens of companies, most based in Kathmandu, which run white-water trips of all standards and cater to all budgets to the many rivers of Nepal. See the Rafting & Kayaking chapter for full details.

Mountain Biking
Mountain biking is becoming an increasingly popular recreational pursuit in Nepal. The Kathmandu Valley offers some superb routes, and on most of these you are rewarded with breathtaking Himalayan views. See the Mountain Biking chapter for more details.

Hot-Air Ballooning
For a different view of the Himalaya and the Kathmandu Valley, try viewing it from a basket suspended 2000m above the floor of the valley! One company in Kathmandu operates balloon flights every morning during the season, and while not cheap they are undeniably spectacular. See the Kathmandu chapter for details.

COURSES
Yoga & Meditation
Nepal is a popular place for people to take up spiritual pursuits. Activity is centred around the Kathmandu Valley, and there are a number of places and options.

Check the notice boards in Thamel for up-to-date information about yoga and Buddhism courses, and shop around before you commit yourself. A number of courses are regularly advertised.

The Arogya Ashram (☎ 470776) near the Pashupatinath Temple teaches yoga. Arogya also has a branch in Kathmandu.

The Himalayan Yogic Institute & Buddhist Meditation Centre (☎ 413094, fax 410992, PO Box 817, Kathmandu) has talks, retreats and courses. To find the centre, head away from Thamel on Lazimpat until you get to the Hotel Kathmandu; turn right after the hotel and the centre is on the right after about 200m. This centre is affiliated with the monastery at Kopan (☎ 226717), north of Bodhnath, which offers very reasonably priced courses which run from seven to 28 days. (See the Around the Kathmandu Valley chapter for details.) For more information on Kopan write to the Nepal Mahayana Centre, PO Box 817, Kathmandu, Nepal.

Yoga Studio (☎ 417900, PO Box 5098, Kathmandu) has been highly recommended for Hatha Yoga lessons for all levels. It's at Tangal Pokhari, a 10 minute bicycle ride east of the palace. Buddhist prayer flags are festooned across the roof.

In Maharajganj in Kathmandu, the Kathmandu Centre of Healing (☎ 413094, PO Box 8975) offers courses for a veritable smorgasbord of healing practices including Reiki, yoga, meditation, Thai massage and Aikido.

A recommended place for yoga is the Shakti Healing Yoga Centre (☎ 222875, fax 225184, PO Box 12184), which offers courses for beginners at $15. The centre is mid-way between Durbar Square and Swayambhunath.

Language

Nepali is not a difficult language to learn, and there are a number of courses available. You will often see signs and notices around Kathmandu advertising language courses, many of them conducted by ex-Peace Corps workers. Embassies should be able to recommend somewhere that they themselves use.

Most schools offer courses (often around two weeks long) or individual tuition. Places to try in Kathmandu include the Speed Language Institute (☎ 220999) in Bagh Bazaar; Insight Nepal (☎ 418963); the Bud Language Institute (☎ 249576); or the School of International Languages (☎ 211713) at the university. Expect to pay about US$50 for a two week course, around US$3 for private hourly tuition.

WORK

For a western visitor, working in Nepal is very difficult, although it is not impossible. The easiest work to find is teaching English as there are many private schools and a great demand for English-language lessons. At less than $100 a month the pay is very low. Other possibilities include work with airline offices, travel and trekking agencies, consultants or aid groups but the prospects are remote.

Officially you need a work permit if you intend to find employment in Nepal and you are supposed to have this before you arrive in the country. Changing from a tourist visa once you are in the country is rarely permissible. The work permit has to be applied for by your employer and you are supposed to leave the country while the paperwork is negotiated. The process can take months.

ACCOMMODATION

In Kathmandu there is a very wide variety of accommodation from rock-bottom flea pits to five-star international hotels. The intense competition between the many cheaper places keeps prices down and standards up – Kathmandu has many fine places with pleasant gardens and rooms for less than $10 a night including private bathroom and hot water. At peak times, on the other hand, rooms in the four and five-star places can be in short supply.

Pokhara also has a variety of accommodation. The choice is concentrated more at the budget end of the market, although there are a couple of luxury hotels.

The main towns of the Terai all have accommodation ranging from hotels of reasonable standard, where rooms with fans and mosquito nets are around Rs 250, to grimy, basic places catering to local demand for around Rs 30. Some of the cheap places will only have tattered mosquito nets, if any at all, so if you're on a tight budget and want to sleep at night, bring one with you.

Elsewhere in the country the choice of hotels can be very limited but there are places to stay along most of the major trekking trails. It's quite possible to trek from lodge to lodge rather than camp site to camp site. On some trails the standards may be spartan – the accommodation may be dormitory-style or simply an open room to unroll your sleeping bag. Smoke can be a real problem in places where the chimney has yet to make an appearance. At the other extreme some trails, like the popular Pokhara to Jomsom route, have excellent lodges and guesthouses at every stopping place.

FOOD & DRINK

Real Nepali food is distinctly dull. Most of the time it consists of a dish called *dal bhat tarakari* which is made up of lentil soup, rice and curried vegetables. The occasional dal bhat tarakari, prepared to tourist tastes in Kathmandu restaurants, can be just fine. Strictly local versions, eaten day in and day out while trekking, can get very boring indeed. Of course Indian cuisine has had a major influence on Nepal and many Tibetan dishes have come over the border, along with the many Tibetan refugees. Other popular local food and drink includes:

beer – the locally produced beer is quite good, especially after a hard day's walking or bicycling around the valley. Beer is usually found in the hills as well, carried there by porters especially for thirsty trekkers, but is unlikely to be cold. There are a number of locally produced brands that theoretically replicate the original recipes – Tuborg (Danish), Star (German), Iceberg (Indian), San Miguel (Filipino). Star and Iceberg are generally the cheapest, and cost around Rs 90 to Rs 130 in Kathmandu restaurants.

buff – water buffalo, casually abbreviated to buff, is the usual substitute for beef since cows are sacred and (officially at least) cannot be eaten. You may come across anything from buff burgers to buff steaks. Increasingly, 'real' beef is imported from India.

chang – the home brew of the Himalaya, a mildly alcoholic concoction made from barley, millet or rice.

curd – yoghurt is known throughout the subcontinent as curd and the buffalo milk curd of Nepal can be very good.

gundruk – dried vegetables are used in this traditional Nepali soup.

gurr – potatoes are the staple food of the Sherpas and although they are a relatively recent introduction, have come to assume the same importance in the Solu Khumbu as they do in Ireland. Gurr is made from raw potatoes ground and mixed with spices and then grilled like a large pancake and eaten with cheese.

lassi – refreshing drink of curd mixed with water; make sure the water is safe.

momo or *kothe* – typical Tibetan dish made by steaming or frying meat or vegetables wrapped in dough; similar to dim sum or ravioli.

sikarni – a sweet curd dessert that may include nuts and dried fruit.

tama – traditional Nepali soup made from dried bamboo shoots.

thugpa – traditional Tibetan meat soup.

tsampa – ground grain, usually barley, mixed with tea, water or milk and eaten dry either instead of rice or mixed with it; the staple dish in the hill country.

Although the real local food is often limited in its scope and is heavily influenced by Indian cuisine, Kathmandu's restaurants offer an amazing variety of dishes. In the days of 'Asia overlanding', when many travellers arrived in Kathmandu having made a long and often wearisome trip through Asia from Europe, Kathmandu's restaurants had a near mythical appeal. Ecstatic reports filtered back along the trail of superb restaurants and fine cuisine.

These days, when most travellers jet straight in from abroad, the food doesn't seem quite so amazing, but Kathmandu's many restaurants still do give international cuisine a damn good try and they will attempt almost anything. There's a special appeal to being high in the Himalaya and being able to choose between not just European and Asian dishes but also almost anything else from Mexican tacos to Japanese sukiyaki. Of course Nepali interpretations of foreign dishes often arrive a little off target but Nepal is a great place to try Tibetan dishes and the Indian food can also be very good.

Such a variety of restaurants is particularly amazing when you consider that in 1955 Kathmandu had just one restaurant. Leave Kathmandu (and Pokhara) behind, however, and you're soon back to dal bhat tarakari.

Many of the 'international' restaurants use large quantities of imported food. Cows, for instance, are theoretically not killed in Hindu Nepal, so beef is imported frozen from Calcutta or Delhi. By ordering with a little care, and especially avoiding beef steaks, it is possible to eat local ingredients and prevent the vital foreign currency you are contributing to the economy heading straight out of the country to pay for your luxuries.

Care in Eating & Drinking

Don't drink the water is the prime health rule on the subcontinent and it certainly applies to Nepal. Diarrhoea, dysentery or even hepatitis can all result from indulging in contaminated drinking water.

In actual fact the relative safety of the water varies with the season. Drinking tap water is never a good idea, but during the dry season from around November to April you would probably get away with it, in Kathmandu at least. During the monsoon, however, when the heavy rains wash all sorts of stuff into the water supply, don't even consider it. Drinking boiled and filtered water is a better idea at any time of year and absolutely imperative in the wet season.

Most good restaurants do boil and filter their water, and although there's no way of telling if it has been boiled or not, tea will be safe, because boiling water is essential for its preparation. Plastic bottles of mineral water are ubiquitous. Although these seem to be safe (mostly anyway), the empty bottles are creating a major litter problem. The best alternative is to have your own water bottle and to treat the water with iodine. This is 100% safe and has the added benefit of not requiring a fire. See the Health section earlier in this chapter for information on iodine treatment.

At higher altitudes the water is generally safer than it is lower down and in more densely populated areas. Nevertheless, trekkers should never drink water from springs or streams unless they are absolutely positive they are at a higher level than any villages or cattle. In Nepal that is a very hard thing to guarantee and it is always wiser to prepare your drinking water carefully. Chang, the popular Tibetan beer, is generally safe and is found along many trekking routes.

Food stalls on the street should be approached with extreme caution and ice cream from street vendors should be completely avoided. In good restaurants the ice cream is usually fine. Meat is more likely to be unhealthy than vegetable or egg dishes; a glance at most Nepali butchers will soon show you why! If you're in doubt about the quality of meat dishes stick to vegetarian.

Beware of salads except in places you know take special care with their food preparation. Salads rinsed in untreated water are notorious for causing stomach problems. Sandwiches can also be risky.

Many travellers do develop some sort of stomach upset while in Nepal although fortunately it's usually just travellers' diarrhoea. See the Health section for more details.

ENTERTAINMENT
Nepal is not the place to come if you're after the highlife. Nightlife is pretty much restricted to Kathmandu and to a lesser extent Pokhara; in other regional towns and cities it's very much early to bed territory.

Kathmandu has an increasing number of bars, mainly in the Thamel area, which stay open late, and there's a couple of low-key nightclubs. There's only one cinema showing western films, and there are four casinos, all of them attached to five-star hotels.

Cultural dance performances are also held in Kathmandu, and as tourist entertainment at some of the resorts in Chitwan.

SHOPPING
Nepal is a shopper's paradise whether you are looking for a cheap souvenir or a real work of art. Although you can find almost anything in the tourist areas of Kathmandu

Chang Recipe

If you develop a taste for chang and would like to brew some at home here's the recipe. Get a 25L or 50L fermenting vessel from a brewery supply shop. For the smaller vessel boil about 2kg of millet for several hours. Millet swells considerably so make sure there is plenty of water and it doesn't stick. When it cools, stick it in the fermenting vessel and fill it with water. (You can pass the millet through a blender to smooth it out first, if desired.) Then add burgundy yeast and the juice of a lemon and leave to ferment. This can take several weeks or a couple of months depending on taste. If you like a little extra kick to your chang add sugar, a kilogram or two, to the fermenting brew – this is really cheating since in Nepal sugar would be too expensive to be used in this way.

The final product will have to be strained through a cloth and racked to remove the yeasty taste. This should not be taken as the only way to produce chang – experiment with it; in Bhutan for example they drink a chang made from half millet and half rice.

Karel Tiller

there are specific specialities in different parts of the valley. Wherever you shop remember to bargain, although with the increasing number of totally tourist-oriented shops more fixed-price establishments are beginning to appear.

One place you could start is the Amrita Craft Collection, south of the Kathmandu Guest House in Thamel. They have quite a broad collection of crafts and clothing, all priced. (Subtract 20% and you get a good benchmark for what you should pay on the street if you are an excellent bargainer.)

Antiquities cannot be taken out of the country, and baggage is inspected by Nepali customs with greater thoroughness on departure than on arrival. If you've bought something which is possibly antique, you should get a receipt and a description of the object from the shop where you bought it. Art theft is a real problem in Nepal and it would be a great shame if some of the superb museum pieces which currently stand in the open, where they may have been for over 1000 years, have to be moved into protected museums.

A permit is required from the Department of Archaeology (☎ 215358) in order to take out of the country any object which looks as if it could be more than 100 years old. The office is in the National Archives building on Ram Shah Path and if you visit between 10 am and 1 pm you should be able to pick up a permit by 5 pm the same day. The customs office (☎ 215525) at Tripureshwar can also provide information.

Thangkas

Thangkas are the traditional Tibetan Buddhist paintings of religious and ceremonial subjects. The subject may be a mandala, the wheel of life, aspects of Buddha or the various Bodhisattvas, fierce protector deities or historical figures. Thangkas are usually colourful and packed with detail to every corner of the painting.

Although there are genuine antique thangkas to be found it's highly unlikely that anything offered to the average visitor will date from much beyond last week. Judicious use of a smoky fire can add the odd century in no time at all. Thangkas do vary considerably in quality but buy one because you like it, not as a valuable investment.

Thangkas are available in many locations including the Tibetan shops around Bodhnath. There are good thangka shops in Thamel in Kathmandu and in the Durbar Square shops in Bhaktapur. There's also an outlet near the Pujari Math monastery. Thangkas cost anything from Rs 200 to Rs 2000 and beyond, and like many other crafts the more you see the more you will appreciate the difference between those of average and those of superior quality. Size also plays a part in the final price of course. Traditionally thangkas are framed in silk brocade.

Block Prints

Locally produced rice paper is used for the block prints of Nepali, Tibetan and Chinese deities. They are sold as pictures or are used for calendars, cards, lanterns and other uses. A print typically costs from Rs 50 to Rs 100. There's a good selection in the Print Shop near the Kathmandu Guest House.

Tibetan Carpets

Carpet-weaving is a major trade in Nepal, brought from Tibet by the refugees who now carry on the craft with great success in their new homes. There are carpet-weavers around the Kathmandu Valley and also in Pokhara. Some of their output is now exported to Tibet, where the Chinese have unfortunately managed to totally stamp out the archaic craft. A genuine Tibetan carpet purchased in Tibet is probably indeed made by genuine Tibetans, but in Nepal. The Tamang people also make carpets.

Jawlakhel, on the southern outskirts of Patan, is the carpet-weaving centre in the valley and there are numerous carpet shops as you enter the area. You can see carpets being woven here and also in other places around the valley, including around the Bodhnath Stupa. There are larger and smaller sizes available, but the traditional size for a Tibetan carpet is 1.8m by 90cm. They're sturdily woven with colourful designs featuring Tibetan Buddhist symbols and dragons. These days it is more difficult to find the brilliant reds and blues produced by chemical dyes; more often carpets will be in the pale pastel shades which come from vegetable dyes. Small square carpets are often used to make seat cushions.

Clothing & Embroidery

Tibetan and Nepali clothes have always been a popular buy but recently western fashions made strictly for the tourist market have also become an important industry. You can buy handmade shirts at outlets in Thamel and there are also shops in Kathmandu (see the Kathmandu Shopping section) selling superb hand-painted silk dresses at a fraction of what they would cost in the west.

There is still a demand for traditional styles such as the Tibetan wool jackets which are popularly known as *yakets*. Nepali coats, crossing over at the front, closed with four ties and traditionally made in purple velvet material, are a popular buy.

Embroidery has always been popular in Nepal and there are lots of little tailor shops around Kathmandu where the sewing machines rattle on until late at night adding colourful dragons and Tibetan symbols to customers' jackets and jeans. Mountaineers like to return from Nepal with jackets carrying the message that this was the Country X, Year Y expedition to Peak Z. You can take your own clothes to be embroidered or buy T-shirts

and other items already embroidered. Badges embroidered with suitable messages are another good buy – you can add a badge to your backpack saying that you walked to the Everest base camp or completed the Annapurna Circuit.

A Nepali cap or *topi* is part of Nepali formal wear for a man and they are traditionally made in Bhaktapur. There's a cap shop right beside the Bhairabnath Temple in Bhaktapur as well as a group of cap specialists between Indra Chowk and Asan Tole in the old part of Kathmandu. Caps typically cost from Rs 50 to Rs 300.

Pottery

Terracotta pottery is made in a number of sites but particularly in Thimi and Bhaktapur. The Potters' Square, just south of Durbar Square in Bhaktapur, is a wonderful sight. Thousands of pots are neatly lined up across the square while in the shelters around the sides of the square, potters busily turn out more and more.

In Thimi they specialise in making attractive little flowerpots, often in the shape of dragons, elephants or mythical beasts. You can buy them in Thimi or from stalls near Indra Chowk in Kathmandu or Taumadhi Tole in Bhaktapur.

Jewellery

Kathmandu's many small jewellery manufacturers turn out a wide variety of designs with an equally wide range of standards.

Antiques

Treat the word 'antique' with great caution in Nepal. Maureen and I were sitting on the top platform of the Shiva Temple in Kathmandu's Durbar Square watching life pass by one afternoon, when one of Kathmandu's numerous young wheelers and dealers came by to practise his English with us. We talked about this and that, and then noticed another young man several steps below us busily working away on something with a variety of tools and a small blowtorch.

'Do you know what he's making?' said our companion.

'No,' we replied, 'what is he making?'

'He's making it very old,' was the reply.

Tony Wheeler

You can buy jewellery ready-made; ask them to create a design for you or bring in something you would like copied. There are several good shops around Thamel, particularly down towards Chhetrapati.

These outlets mainly cater to western tastes but there are also many shops for the local market as Nepali women, like Indian women, traditionally wear their wealth in jewellery. Cheap ornaments can also be fun; you can buy an armful of glass bangles for a few rupees or colourful beads by the handful.

Masks & Puppets

Papier-mâché masks and colourful puppets are sold at shops in Kathmandu, Patan and Bhaktapur. Thimi is the centre for manufacturing masks which are used in the traditional masked dances in September and it's interesting to see them being made there. Ganesh, Bhairab and the Kumari are the most popular subjects for the mask and they make good wall decorations. Prices typically range from around Rs 50 to Rs 300.

Puppets make good buys as gifts for children and are made in Bhaktapur as well as other centres. They're often of multi-armed deities clutching little wooden weapons in each hand. The puppet heads may be made of easily broken clay or more durable papier-mâché. Smaller puppets cost from around Rs 100 to Rs 400 but you can also pay Rs 500 to Rs 850 for a larger figure. As usual, quality does vary and the more puppets you inspect the more you will begin to appreciate the differences.

Metalwork

Patan is the valley centre for bronze casting and the best variety of metalwork is found in the shops around Patan's Durbar Square. (See the Patan Shopping section for more details.) Often, beautifully made figures featuring the full range of Tantric Buddhist deities can be bought at costs ranging from Rs 2000 to Rs 5000 for good-quality smaller figures. Of course simpler work can be found much more cheaply. The metal game boards and pieces for the traditional Nepali game *bagh chal* make a good buy.

Other Nepali Crafts

A khukuri, the traditional knife of the Gurkhas, can cost from Rs 300 to Rs 2000. Khukuri House, near the Rum Doodle Bar in Thamel is a good place to start looking.

Bhaktapur is the centre for woodcarving and you can find good objects in and around Tachupal Tole. Cassettes and CDs of Nepali, Indian and general Himalayan music are a fine souvenir of a visit to Nepal. There are lots of music shops in Kathmandu selling local music as well as bootlegged western tapes.

For all sorts of small souvenirs the huge market area in Basantapur Square in Kathmandu is a good place to browse. Wandering the crowded and bustling market street from Indra Chowk to Asan Tole is always likely to turn up some interesting bargain.

Other Tibetan Crafts

Tibetan crafts include a variety of religious items such as the *dorje* (thunderbolt symbol) and the popular prayer wheels. Tibetans are keen traders and prices at Bodhnath and Swayambhunath are often very high.

Tea

Tea is grown in the east of Nepal, close to the border with India near Darjeeling where the finest Indian tea is grown. Ilam and Mai Valley are the best Nepali brands, but they are not cheap. Expect to pay around Rs 600 per kilogram for good Ilam tea, which is not much cheaper than Darjeeling tea.

Sending Purchases Home

By far the best way of getting something back home is to take it with you. Shipping or mailing objects can be fraught with dangers and hidden expenses. For a start there's no guarantee that it will be sent at all. If you leave your purchase for a shop to mail to you and it never turns up what can you prove? They will say they mailed it and the post office has lost it somewhere along the line, and you have no idea whether they have or not (nor any way of proving your suspicions!).

If an object is shipped to you, you may find that customs charges for clearance and collection at your end add up to more than the initial cost of sending it. Often it would have been worth paying extra to bring it with you in the first place.

Unless you are very sure about the reliability of the shop, do not ask the shop where you made the purchase to send it for you. There are a number of packing companies in Kathmandu but some of them are no more reliable than a shop might be. Diki Continental Exports (☎ 417681, fax 414997, email dikicont@mos.com.np), opposite the Hotel Mandap in Thamel, and Sharmasons Movers (☎ 249565, fax 249449, email pacmov@ mos.com.np) are two that have been recommended. The international courier company DHL (☎ 222358, fax 220215) has an office on Durbar Marg and in Thamel.

Air freight costs are punitive – around $40 per kilogram to Europe or Australia, $50 to the USA. Sea freight is much cheaper than air, but it is also much slower and less reliable – packages are sent overland to Calcutta or Bombay, and then wait until a full container has been consolidated.

Getting There & Away

AIR
Airports
Kathmandu is the site for Nepal's only international airport, Tribhuvan airport.

Airlines
The notoriously unreliable Royal Nepal Airlines Corporation (RNAC) has a London-Frankfurt-Kathmandu service. However, it is worth flying with any airline other than RNAC if at all possible, as their services are frequently subject to inconveniences such as delays and cancellations.

Austrian Airlines and the Dutch company Transavia have direct flights between Europe and Nepal, and Aeroflot also connects Nepal with Europe via Moscow. Two Middle Eastern airlines, Gulf Air and Qatar Airways, have connections between Europe and Nepal, although these involve a change of aircraft in the Middle East. Travellers arriving from Europe or from the east coast of North America with other airlines transfer to RNAC or Indian Airlines in New Delhi for the final short flight from New Delhi to Kathmandu.

From the west coast of North America or from Australasia, Bangkok is the usual transfer point, although there are also flights to Kathmandu from Hong Kong and Singapore. Thai International and RNAC share the Bangkok to Kathmandu route.

Where to Sit
If you want to see the mountains as you fly into Kathmandu you must sit on the correct side. Flying in from the east – Bangkok, Calcutta, Hong Kong, Yangon (Rangoon) or Singapore – you want the right side. Flying in from the west – New Delhi or Varanasi – you want the left side.

Arriving in Nepal by Air
The international terminal is a modern building and everything operates reasonably smoothly. Touts are excluded from the building, so everything is fairly calm until you hit the outside world.

There's a branch of the Arab Bank prior to clearing immigration on the 1st floor. There's another branch on the ground floor of the departure section; both are open for flights, which normally means till around 8 pm, and both have decent exchange rates.

There's a duty-free shop with a limited range of liquor and cigarettes available for sale in US dollars to arriving and departing passengers.

Warning

The information in this chapter is particularly vulnerable to change: prices for international travel are volatile, routes are introduced and cancelled, schedules change, special deals come and go, and rules and visa requirements are amended. Airlines and governments seem to take a perverse pleasure in making price structures and regulations as complicated as possible. You should check directly with the airline or a travel agency to make sure you understand how a fare (and ticket you may buy) works. In addition, the travel industry is highly competitive and there are many lurks and perks.

The upshot of this is that you should get opinions, quotes and advice from as many airlines and travel agents as possible before you part with your hard-earned cash. The details given in this chapter should be regarded as pointers and are not a substitute for your own careful, up-to-date research.

Leaving Nepal by Air

Check in at least two hours early; for some airlines in the high season (those that have a reputation for overbooking) it is worth getting there even earlier. Also, don't forget to confirm and reconfirm your flight at least 72 hours before departure. At the airport, it is possible to re-exchange up to 15% of the Nepali rupees you have officially changed, but you must be able to show unused Foreign Exchange Encashment Receipts. If you are leaving for India, you can get between Indian Rs 500 and Rs 2000 on presentation of your ticket.

Make sure you have clearance for anything that might be construed as an antique – metal statues show up on the baggage x-ray and are often checked. The x-ray machines that screen cargo baggage are definitely not film safe. Those that screen hand luggage are meant to be film safe, but to be on the safe side, insist that the security officers physically inspect your precious film.

There is a pleasant restaurant on the top (2nd) floor, which is open to all, or go through immigration on the 1st floor, where there is a restaurant, open to passengers only. On the ground floor is a post office.

The small duty-free shop has a limited range of liquor and cigarettes available for purchase with US dollars.

Travellers with Special Needs

If you have special needs of any sort – you've broken a leg or you're vegetarian, travelling in a wheelchair, taking the baby, terrified of flying - you should let the airline know as soon as possible so that they can make arrangements accordingly. You should remind them when you reconfirm your booking (at least 72 hours before departure) and again when you check in at the airport. It may also be worth ringing round the airlines before you make your booking to find out how they can handle your particular needs.

Airports and airlines can be surprisingly helpful, but they do need advance warning. Guide dogs for the blind will often have to travel in a specially pressurised baggage compartment with other animals, away from their owner; smaller guide dogs may be admitted to the cabin. All guide dogs will be subject to the same quarantine laws (six months in isolation etc) as any other animal when entering or returning to countries currently free of rabies such as Australia.

Deaf travellers can ask for airport and in-flight announcements to be written down for them.

Children under two travel for 10% of the standard fare (or free, on some airlines), as long as they don't occupy a seat. They don't get a baggage allowance either. Children between two and 12 can usually occupy a seat for half to two-thirds of the full fare and do get a baggage allowance. Push chairs can often be taken as hand luggage.

Departure Tax

A departure tax of Rs 1000 is payable in Nepalese rupees at the Arab Bank counter in the departures terminal.

The UK & Europe

Ticket discounting has long been established in the UK and it's wide open – the various agencies advertise their fares and there's nothing under the counter about it at all.

Trailfinders, in West London, produces a lavishly illustrated brochure which includes air fare details. STA Travel also has branches in the UK. Look for ads in the Sunday papers and *Exchange & Mart*. Also look out for free magazines which are widely available in London. Start by looking outside the main railway stations.

Most British travel agencies are registered with Association of British Travel Agents (ABTA). If you have paid for you flight to an ABTA-registered agent which then goes out of business, ABTA will guarantee a refund or an alternative. Unregistered bucket shops are riskier but also sometimes cheaper.

The Globetrotters Club (BCM Roving, London WC1N 3XX) publishes a newsletter called *Globe* which covers obscure destinations and can help in finding travelling companions.

Air Travel Glossary

Baggage Allowance This will be written on your ticket and usually includes one 20kg item to go in the hold, plus one item of hand luggage.

Bucket Shops These are unbonded travel agencies specialising in discounted airline tickets.

Bumped Just because you have a confirmed seat doesn't mean you're going to get on the plane (see Overbooking).

Cancellation Penalties If you have to cancel or change a discounted ticket, there are often heavy penalties involved; insurance can sometimes be taken out against these penalties. Some airlines impose penalties on regular tickets as well, particularly against 'no-show' passengers.

Check-In Airlines ask you to check in a certain time ahead of the flight departure (usually one to two hours on international flights). If you fail to check in on time and the flight is overbooked, the airline can cancel your booking and give your seat to somebody else.

Confirmation Having a ticket written out with the flight and date you want doesn't mean you have a seat until the agent has checked with the airline that your status is 'OK' or confirmed. Meanwhile you could just be 'on request'.

Courier Fares Businesses often need to send urgent documents or freight securely and quickly. Courier companies hire people to accompany the package through customs and, in return, offer a discount ticket which is sometimes a phenomenal bargain. In effect, what the companies do is ship their freight as your luggage on regular commercial flights. This is a legitimate operation, but there are two shortcomings – the short turnaround time of the ticket (usually not longer than a month) and the limitation on your luggage allowance. You may have to surrender all your allowance and take only carry-on luggage.

Full Fares Airlines traditionally offer 1st class (coded F), business class (coded J) and economy class (coded Y) tickets. These days there are so many promotional and discounted fares available that few passengers pay full economy fare.

ITX An ITX, or 'independent inclusive tour excursion', is often available on tickets to popular holiday destinations. Officially it's a package deal combined with hotel accommodation, but many agents will sell you one of these for the flight only and give you phoney hotel vouchers in the unlikely event that you're challenged at the airport.

Lost Tickets If you lose your airline ticket an airline will usually treat it like a travellers cheque and, after inquiries, issue you with another one. Legally, however, an airline is entitled to treat it like cash and if you lose it then it's gone forever. Take good care of your tickets.

MCO An MCO, or 'miscellaneous charge order', is a voucher that looks like an airline ticket but carries no destination or date. It can be exchanged through any International Association of Travel Agents (IATA) airline for a ticket on a specific flight. It's a useful alternative to an onward ticket in those countries that demand one, and is more flexible than an ordinary ticket if you're unsure of your route.

No-Shows No-shows are passengers who fail to show up for their flight. Full-fare passengers who fail to turn up are sometimes entitled to travel on a later flight. The rest are penalised (see Cancellation Penalties).

On Request This is an unconfirmed booking for a flight.

Air Travel Glossary

Onward Tickets An entry requirement for many countries is that you have a ticket out of the country. If you're unsure of your next move, the easiest solution is to buy the cheapest onward ticket to a neighbouring country or a ticket from a reliable airline which can later be refunded if you do not use it.

Open Jaw Tickets These are return tickets where you fly out to one place but return from another. If available, this can save you backtracking to your arrival point.

Overbooking Airlines hate to fly empty seats and since every flight has some passengers who fail to show up, airlines often book more passengers than they have seats. Usually excess passengers make up for the no-shows, but occasionally somebody gets bumped. Guess who it is most likely to be? The passengers who check in late.

Point-to-Point Tickets These are discount tickets that can be bought on some routes in return for passengers waiving their rights to a stopover.

Promotional Fares These are officially discounted fares, available from travel agencies or direct from the airline.

Reconfirmation At least 72 hours prior to departure time of an onward or return flight, you must contact the airline and 'reconfirm' that you intend to be on the flight. If you don't do this the airline can delete your name from the passenger list and you could lose your seat.

Restrictions Discounted tickets often have various restrictions on them – such as needing to be paid for in advance and incurring a penalty to be altered. Others are restrictions on the minimum and maximum period you must be away, such as a minimum of 14 days or a maximum of one year.

Round-the-World Tickets RTW tickets give you a limited period (usually a year) in which to circumnavigate the globe. You can go anywhere the carrying airlines go, as long as you don't backtrack. The number of stopovers or total number of separate flights is decided before you set off and they usually cost a bit more than a basic return flight.

Stand-By This is a discounted ticket where you only fly if there is a seat free at the last moment. Stand-by fares are usually available only on domestic routes.

Transferred Tickets Airline tickets cannot be transferred from one person to another. Travellers sometimes try to sell the return half of their ticket, but officials can ask you to prove that you are the person named on the ticket. This is less likely to happen on domestic flights, but on an international flight tickets are compared with passports.

Travel Agencies Travel agencies vary widely and you should choose one that suits your needs. Some simply handle tours, while full-services agencies handle everything from tours and tickets to car rental and hotel bookings. If all you want is a ticket at the lowest possible price, then go to an agency specialising in discounted tickets.

Travel Periods Ticket prices vary with the time of year. There is a low (off-peak) season and a high (peak) season, and often a low-shoulder season and a high-shoulder season as well. Usually the fare depends on your outward flight – if you depart in the high season and return in the low season, you pay the high-season fare.

London to Kathmandu on RNAC's flights costs £650 return; Gulf Air, charges £799 return. Austrian Airlines charges $899 for the return flight from Vienna to Kathmandu.

The USA

Intense competition between Asian airlines on the US west coast and Vancouver has resulted in ticket discounting.

The *New York Times*, the *Chicago Tribune*, the *LA Times* and the *San Francisco Examiner* all produce weekly travel sections in which you'll find any number of travel agency ads. Student travel specialists Council Travel and STA Travel have offices in major US cities. The magazine *Travel Unlimited* (PO Box 1058, Allston, Mass 02134, USA) publishes details of the cheapest air fares and courier possibilities for destinations all over the world from the USA.

Fares to Kathmandu will often be about the same from the east or west coast – it's about as far away as you can get in either direction! Typical return fares are from around US$1575.

Australia & New Zealand

STA Travel and Flight Centres International are major dealers in cheap air fares. Check the travel agency ads in the *Yellow Pages* or the travel section in the Saturday newspapers and phone around.

Fares from Australia depend on the season and typically cost around A$1500 return. Bangkok is the most popular transit point although you can also fly via Singapore or Hong Kong.

From Kathmandu to east coast Australia, a one-way ticket with Singapore Airlines costs US$650.

India

Royal Nepal Airlines Corporation (RNAC) and Indian Airlines share the main routes between India and Kathmandu. Both airlines give a 25% discount to those under 30 years of age on flights between Kathmandu and India; no student card is needed. The Nepali airline Necon Air has recently started flying from Kathmandu to Patna,

and may by now also be operating to Lucknow. Buddha Air was also planning to start flights to India.

New Delhi is the main departure point for flights between India and Kathmandu. The one hour New Delhi to Kathmandu flight costs US$142 one way. RNAC has two flights daily, Indian Airlines has one.

Other cities in India with direct air connections with Kathmandu are Calcutta (US$96), Varanasi (US$71) and Patna (US$75).

Elsewhere in Asia

Other departure points for Kathmandu and approximate one-way fares include:

Bangkok, Thailand	US$318
Dhaka, Bangladesh	US$114
Karachi, Pakistan	US$272
Lhasa, Tibet	US$228
Singapore	US$300

There are also some interesting through fares; one to consider is with Biman Bangladesh Airlines' Kathmandu-Dhaka-Yangon-Bangkok ticket which sells for US$311. A direct Kathmandu to Bangkok ticket costs US$220.

LAND

Political and weather conditions permitting there are four main entry points into Nepal by land: three from India, one from Tibet.

A steady trickle of people drive their own motorbikes or vehicles overland from Europe – there are some interesting, though difficult, routes to the subcontinent through Eastern Europe and the republics that were once a part of the USSR. An international carnet is required. If you want to abandon your transport in Nepal, you must either pay a prohibitive import duty or surrender it to customs. It is not possible to import cars more than five years old.

India

The most popular crossing points from India are Sunauli/Bhairawa (south of Pokhara), Raxaul Bazaar/Birganj (south of Kathmandu) and Kakarbhitta (near Siliguri and Darjeeling in the far east). There are other less popular, but still viable, options.

Through Tickets Many travellers have complained about scams involving ticket packages to India. The package usually involves coordination between at least three different companies so the potential for an honest cock-up is at least as high as the potential for a deliberate rip-off. (See the Ticket Scams to India boxed text below.)

Two long-standing and reliable Nepali companies handling through tickets are Wayfarers Travel Service (☎ 417176, fax 245875, email wayfarer@mos.com.np) in Thamel, Kathmandu; and Yeti Travels (☎ 221234, fax 226152) in Durbar Marg, Kathmandu. Bear in mind, however, that everyone has to change buses at the border whether they book a through ticket or not, and that despite claims to the contrary, there are no 'tourist' buses on either side of the border. Buses through to Varanasi cost from Rs 500, and to Darjeeling Rs 650. Bus/train packages to Agra cost Rs 3250 including an air-con sleeper on the train, or Rs 1150 in

2nd class. Bus/train to Delhi costs Rs 3650 with air-con, Rs 1250 in 2nd class.

It is worth considering making advance bookings if you are in a major hurry, or plan to use the Indian railway system. Some trains, and especially sleeping compartments, can be heavily booked (this is apparently the case for Gorakhpur to Delhi trains). A Nepali agency will need a week to organise a booking. Beware – there's always a chance that what you pay for and what you get will be two different things. Make sure you get a receipt clearly specifying what you think you have paid for, and hang on to it.

To/From Delhi If you are travelling to or from Delhi or elsewhere in western India the route through Sunauli/Bhairawa is the most convenient, but you can also enter at Mahendranagar in the far west of Nepal, although this is a much more difficult route.

Via Sunauli Delhi to Gorakhpur involves an overnight rail journey, from where frequent buses make the three-hour run to the border.

Ticket Scams to India

Many people have written complaining about scams involving through tickets to India, especially out of Pokhara. Mind you, there's always plenty of scope for disaster when travelling on the subcontinent. That's why it's such good fun! The following extract is a classic example:

I paid Rs 2000 ($40) for a bus to the Indian border, a bus from there to Gorakhpur and an air-con sleeper on a train to Delhi. The bus to the border ran out of fuel three times and was four hours late. The bus to Gorakhpur broke down 5km into the 100km trip and was abandoned, forcing me to catch a taxi for the remainder of the journey.

Once in Gorakhpur, I was to take a receipt to a travel agency to have my air-con sleeper ticket to Delhi issued. The receipt was issued by the travel agent in Pokhara, but the travel agent in Gorakhpur denied any knowledge of air-con on this particular train and refused to issue me with anything other than a 2nd-class ticket. I spoke to the station master about my problem and he was extremely unhelpful, arousing my suspicion that he may have been in with the travel agent.

While I was in the middle of a heated argument with the Gorakhpur travel agent, two English guys stormed into the shop screaming 'Liar, I'll kill you!' The three of us bombarded the agent with facts, asking for our money back, but he just laughed, closed up his shop for the night and walked off.

Buses to Kathmandu from Sunauli travel north along the beautiful Siddhartha Hwy to Mugling before joining the Kathmandu-Pokhara (Prithvi) Hwy. The journey takes around nine hours, and there are both day and night buses. Buses to Pokhara also travel via Mugling, and the trip also takes nine hours.

See the Sunauli/Bhairawa section in the Terai chapter.

Via Mahendranagar The border crossing at Mahendranagar is the most interesting option. It will take a while for things to start operating smoothly, but when they do, this will present an interesting alternative route from Delhi or some of the hill stations in northern Uttar Pradesh. When the Mahendra Hwy is finally completed (some time in the next five years would be nothing short of a miracle) the route will be open all year, but until then it is a dry-season-only proposition, and strictly for the hardy.

There are daily buses from Delhi to Banbassa, the nearest Indian village to the border (11 hours). Banbassa is also connected by rail to Bareilly, and by bus with the hill station Almora in India.

There are direct buses from Mahendranagar to Kathmandu (at 2 pm), but they take a gruelling 22 hours. The countryside is beautiful and fascinating, so it's much better to do the whole trip during daylight and to break the journey at Nepalganj. There are plenty of night and day buses from Nepalganj to Kathmandu (14 hours) and night buses to Pokhara (15 hours).

See the Mahendranagar section in the Terai chapter for details of the border crossing.

To/From Varanasi Once again, the Sunauli/Bhairawa crossing is the most convenient. There are direct buses from Varanasi and the journey takes about nine hours.

From Sunauli it's another nine hours to Kathmandu or Pokhara (day and night buses on both routes).

Some private companies make bookings all the way through to Kathmandu and Pokhara for around Indian Rs 300, includ-ing spartan accommodation at Sunauli. However, if you organise things yourself as you go, it will be cheaper, plus you will have more flexibility, including a choice of bus within Nepal and also of accommodation in Sunauli. Catch a bus to Sunauli, stay overnight on the Nepal side of the border (there are several reasonable hotels in Sunauli and Bhairawa), then catch a Nepali bus the next morning.

To/From Calcutta & Patna The Raxaul Bazaar/Birganj entry point is the most convenient option in the east of India.

Calcutta to Patna takes about 10 hours, and you can do this by overnight train. It's then a five hour journey from Patna to Raxaul Bazaar (the Indian border town).

Raxaul Bazaar is virtually a twin town with Birganj in Nepal. Both towns are dirty, unattractive transit points strung along the highway and are full of heavy traffic. The border is open from 7 am to 7 pm every day.

All direct buses between Birganj and Kathmandu or Pokhara turn west at Hetauda, then at Narayanghat turn north to Mugling which is on the Kathmandu-Pokhara (Prithvi) Hwy. Although it is not as spectacular as the Tribhuvan Hwy, this is nonetheless an interesting route with some beautiful views. It also means that all buses go through Tadi Bazaar, the jumping-off point for Sauraha and Royal Chitwan National Park.

Between Birganj and Kathmandu direct buses take around 11 hours; between Birganj and Pokhara they are marginally quicker. There are numerous night and day buses.

See the Birganj section in the Terai chapter for border crossing details.

To/From Darjeeling Kakarbhitta is the obvious entry point, but the Mahendra Hwy can be blocked by floods during the monsoon, in which case it would be necessary to travel by train from Siliguri to Patna before entering Nepal at Birganj.

There are many companies that handle bookings between Darjeeling and Kathmandu, although with all of them you have to change buses at the border and Siliguri.

It's almost as easy to get from Darjeeling to Kathmandu on your own though this involves four changes – a bus from Darjeeling to Siliguri, then a minibus from Siliguri to Raniganj at the border, a rickshaw across the border to Kakarbhitta and a bus from Kakarbhitta to Kathmandu. This is cheaper than the package deal, you have a choice of buses from the border, plus you have the option of travelling during the day and overnighting along the way.

Buses to Kathmandu travel west along the Mahendra Hwy to the Tribhuvan Hwy between Birganj and Hetauda, then head briefly north to Hetauda. They then travel west again until Narayanghat where they turn north to Mugling, on the Kathmandu-Pokhara (Prithvi) Hwy.

It's more than 600km between Kakarbhitta and Kathmandu, which means direct buses can take an exhausting 15 hours to complete the trip, and the direct buses all travel at night.

If you have time it is worth considering breaking your journey at Janakpur, which is roughly halfway, and an interesting place in its own right. This will enable you to travel during the day and get a feel for the Terai; the flood plain of the Sapt Kosi is particularly interesting. There are day buses from Kakarbhitta that go to a number of towns on the Terai including Janakpur, and night buses direct to Pokhara. See the Kakarbhitta section in the Terai chapter for details.

Tibet

Currently the route to Tibet from Nepal (via Kodari) is closed to individual travellers, but independent travellers are entering Tibet through China and continuing, without problems, to Nepal. Only organised groups are allowed to cross from Nepal into Tibet, but this option is expensive.

On the face of it, it doesn't make much sense to allow individuals into Tibet from China, but not from Nepal. However, the package business is so lucrative and Nepal is so full of seditious Tibetans, that the Chinese must see little incentive to change. Bear in mind the road is of poor quality and is regularly closed by landslides during the monsoon.

Political disasters are even more likely than natural ones. Tibet is a volatile region with regular violent protests against Chinese rule and these upheavals are often followed by restrictions on visitors to the region. Usually these restrictions are applied more stringently to independent visitors than to people on organised tours. The baseline is that if you intend to enter or leave Nepal via Tibet you should come prepared with alternative plans in case travel along this route proves impossible.

Organised Tours A number of agencies in Kathmandu organise fully inclusive return trips to Lhasa, with prices around US$100 per day for eight to 12-day trips.

Most tours from Kathmandu take eight days and involve a flight to Lhasa and an overland return trip (or vice versa). The flights stop from the end of November to the end of March because of the weather. China International Travel Service (CITS), the state travel agency, operates the tours within China.

Travel agencies in Nepal specialising in trips to Tibet include:

Green Hill Tours
(☎ 414968, fax 424065, email ghill@wlink.com.np)
PO Box 5072, Thamel
Kathmandu Travels & Tours
(☎ 471577, fax 225131)
PO Box 459, Ganga Path, Kathmandu
Natraj Tours & Travels
(☎ 222014, fax 227372, email natraj@vishnu.ccsl.com.np)
PO Box 495, Durbar Marg, Kathmandu
Nepal Travel Agency
(☎ 430188, fax 431861, email nta@vishnu.ccsl.com.np)
PO Box 1501, Ram Shah Path, Kathmandu
Tibet Travels & Tours
(☎ 249140, fax 249986, email kalden@tibet.wlink.com.np)
PO Box 7246, Tridevi Marg, Thamel, Kathmandu
Yeti Travels
(☎ 221234, fax 226152, email yeti@vishnu.ccsl.com.np)
PO Box 5376, Durbar Marg, Kathmandu

Independent Travel If independent travel into Tibet is permitted you must first get a Chinese visa (see the Embassies & Consulates section in the Facts for the Visitor chapter for more details).

From Khasa (Zhangmu), the Tibetan town just over the border, there are just two buses a week to Lhasa, so you must plan carefully or you may be stranded for several days. Take food and drink on this trip, as there's not much available along the way. It's also possible to get rides on trucks to Shigatse, but the 15 hour trip in the back of a truck is strictly for the hardy. From Shigatse there are local buses to Gyantse and from there to Lhasa.

This is not an easy trip by any means. Altitude sickness is a real danger as the maximum altitude along the road is 5140m and there have been reports of deaths.

It is not possible to catch a bus direct from Kathmandu to Kodari, but daily buses run to Barabise. They take around five agonising hours. From Barabise there are buses that take two hours to get to Kodari. Since there's nothing much to see from Kodari, travelling out here by bus is a little pointless unless you are actually going on to Tibet. See the Around the Kathmandu Valley chapter for more information on the Arniko Hwy.

Getting Around

Getting around Nepal can be a challenging business. The impossible terrain and extreme weather conditions, plus incompetence and disorganisation, mean that trips rarely go exactly according to plan. On the other hand, Nepali ingenuity will usually get you to your destination in the end. Although travel can be frustrating, it also creates memorable moments by the score. Good humour and patience are essential prerequisites. Losing your cool will get you nowhere fast.

The whole gamut of transport options is available, with the possible exceptions of submarine and monorail. Most of the others can be found together on the average road, simultaneously competing with ducks, dogs, chickens, pigs and invincible pedestrians, and none of them has the vaguest traffic sense.

Walking is still the most important, and the most reliable, method of getting from A to B and for moving cargo; more is carried by people and porters than by every other form of transport combined.

Biking is popular with visitors – local buses are so slow and uncomfortable that bikes are often almost as quick, over short distances at least, and have the added advantage of allowing you to travel at your own speed and to stop whenever you like. There are a number of other human-powered contraptions ranging from barrows to bicycle rickshaws, canoes, kayaks and rafts.

There are numerous forms of animal transport. Bullocks, oxen, buffaloes and ponies are all attached to carts. Elephants, donkeys and yaks are all ridden or used to carry loads.

The 'infernal' combustion engine is making an increasingly obnoxious impact on the environment. There are two-stroke auto-rickshaws, three wheeled *tempos* and motorbikes, petrol-driven cars and motorbikes, and smoke-belching diesel buses and trucks. The buses range from lumbering dinosaurs held together by bits of wire and the combined hopes of the passengers, to brand-new Tatas from India, the kings of the road.

Then there are planes (of ranging sizes) and there's a train at Janakpur, a cableway (a kind of ski lift that carries cargo) at Hetauda, and even a new cable car which carries passengers up to the temple of Manakamana near Mugling.

One of the major considerations when using any form of public transport is to avoid travelling during festival times, especially major ones such as Dasain and Deepawali. Buses and planes are booked solid for days either side of these festivals and it can be extremely difficult to get about – you will probably end up on the roof of buses, and can forget about plane travel unless you have booked weeks in advance.

AIR

There are a number of private companies operating alongside the long-running, government-owned Royal Nepal Airlines Corporation (RNAC). These are Necon Air, Buddha Air, Lumbini Airways, Cosmic Air and Gorkha Airlines. So far at least, these airlines only operate on the more popular (ie economically viable) routes. The prices are the same as RNAC, but the private companies offer better service, and are more reliable. Necon Air is very efficient and highly recommended, as is Buddha Air.

The main air travel hubs are Kathmandu, Pokhara, Nepalganj in the west and Biratnagar in the east.

RNAC operates by far the most comprehensive range of scheduled flights around the country, with flights to Bajhang, Bajura, Bhairawa, Bharatpur, Bhojpur, Biratnagar, Chaurjhari, Dhangadhi, Dolpo, Janakpur, Jomsom, Jumla, Kathmandu, Lamidanda, Lukla, Manang, Nepalganj, Phaplu, Pokhara, Ramechhap, Rumjatar, Rukum, Sanfebagar, Simara (Birganj), Simikot, Surkhet, Taplejung and Tumlingtar.

Necon Air is the next-biggest, servicing Kathmandu, Pokhara, Bhairawa, Biratnagar, Janakpur and Nepalganj.

Buddha Air has the fastest and most modern aircraft – the trip to Pokhara takes just 20 minutes, compared with up to 40 minutes with other airlines. Buddha Air has daily flights servicing Kathmandu, Pokhara, Biratnagar, Bhairawa and Nepalganj.

Lumbini Airways has a fairly comprehensive schedule, servicing Kathmandu, Bajura, Bhairawa, Bharatpur, Jomsom, Lukla, Simikot, Jumla, Dolpo, Nepalganj, Surkhet, Phaplu and Simara (Birganj).

Other airlines tend to come and go, but currently there is also Gorkha Airlines and Cosmic Air, both of which have pretty limited services.

Some flights, such as Kathmandu to Lukla, are used mainly by trekkers. These flights are frequent during the trekking season, but the schedules can be extremely variable. Kathmandu to Jomsom flights, for example, are plagued by bad weather at both ends. Early-morning departures from Kathmandu are often delayed by fog, but if they don't arrive in Jomsom by around 11 am landing may be impossible due to high winds! The end result is regular cancellations. Flights out of Lukla are equally unreliable – the airport can easily be closed for a week by bad weather – and there are often enormous backlogs of frustrated trekkers waiting for flights, both in Kathmandu and Lukla.

It is advisable to book domestic flights a week in advance and, just as for flights out of Nepal, the most important rule is to reconfirm and reconfirm again. Names can easily 'fall off' the passenger list, particularly where there is pressure for seats.

Air Fares

Residents and Nepali citizens pay approximately 75% of the tourist price for domestic airfares. Airlines will only accept payment in hard currency from visitors. See the Nepal Air Fares chart for details.

All the airlines also have daily mountain flights which costs $99. See the Mountain Flights boxed text in The Himalaya & Mountaineering chapter for details.

NEPAL AIR FARES

All prices US$ one way

Mountain Flights $99

Domestic Airport

The domestic terminal is the old Kathmandu airport, and its age shows. It can be a nasty and chaotic spot, particularly when flights are cancelled and crowds of stressed tourists generate an atmosphere of fear and loathing. You can escape the worst of the crush in the restaurant on the 1st floor; it's allegedly run by the Hotel de l'Annapurna, so you are unlikely to be poisoned although it is very shabby.

Check in an hour early for domestic flights; there is a Rs 100 airport tax payable at check in. Once through security, the waiting lounge is reasonably comfortable and you can also get drinks. Remember not to carry pocket knives or gas cigarette lighters in your carry-on luggage.

It can be difficult finding a taxi into Kathmandu if you arrive late. If the worst comes to the worst, it's a 10 minute walk to the international terminal, where you are certain to find something.

See Kathmandu's Getting Around section in the Kathmandu, Patan & Bhaktapur chapter for information on transport to/from the airport.

BUS

Buses are the main form of public transport in Nepal and in relative terms they're incredibly cheap. Very often they're also incredibly uncomfortable. It's always best to book a couple of days in advance.

There are numerous services with buses and smaller minibuses around the Kathmandu Valley, out from Kathmandu towards the Tibetan border, down to the Indian border or to Pokhara. Buses also run from Pokhara to the Indian border as well as along the length of the country from near Darjeeling in the east to Mahendranagar in the west. This road, called the Mahendra Hwy, runs through the Inner Terai, parallel to the Indian border. As well as the regular public buses between Kathmandu and Pokhara there are a number of services aimed particularly at the western-tourist market.

Many people – locals and westerners – prefer to ride on bus roofs. The arguments in favour are that you get an exhilarating ride with great views, the opportunity to watch your bags and, sometimes, room to stretch your legs. Some people argue it is also safer, because you can jump off before

Crowded and uncomfortable, bus travel is an experience in itself – but what an experience!

the bus goes over the side into a gorge! This latter point is debatable. If you are on top, make sure you're well wedged in, so you don't catapult off when the bus swerves, brakes, or lurches (see the Bus Ride boxed text on the opposite page for a first-hand account). It's also best to sit facing forwards – that way you can see low-hanging wires and branches before you get swatted. Make sure you have sunscreen and appropriate clothing too.

Types of Buses & Services

There are both government and private buses. The government bus company, known as Sajha Yatayat, has distinctive blue and white Japanese buses which service all the main routes except the far east and far west. These buses are generally scheduled to run only during the day, except on the longest routes. A few years ago these were the preferred buses to take as they were reliable and relatively uncrowded. These days however the buses are very shabby, poorly maintained and rarely run to schedule. Each major town has a Sajha office where you can make advance reservations.

There are literally dozens of private bus companies – it seems all you need is one bus and you've got yourself a company. The vehicles are all Indian Tata buses, and range from new and reasonably comfortable to

Bus Ride – A traveller's account

Ah! The Kathmandu to Kakarbhitta bus trip. I remember it as if it were yesterday. It was. I'm sitting in Darjeeling eating buffalo curd and reflecting on how nice it is to be alive.

As we climbed out of the Kathmandu Valley at 4.30 pm we were 'shaking down' – trying to contort ourselves into the tight spaces we had rented and attempting to find some semblance of comfort. Then we reached the rim of the valley and began hurtling down that *awesome* series of hairpin bends and switchbacks. As we thundered suicidally down this impossible road I mused whimsically on the average life expectancy of Nepali bus drivers, that is until the rather obvious realisation dawned that, given my present position, a much more pertinent question might be the life expectancy of the average passenger!

I gave up such dark thoughts to think about the love of my life, far off in England, but the moment was rudely interrupted as, lurching into yet another precipice-edged corner, the driver braked violently to avoid another bus lying on its side diagonally across the road. Not a sight calculated to inspire confidence, but one has to look on the bright side. Firstly, it had toppled *onto* the road rather than *off* into the chasm. Secondly, it wasn't my bus.

The road steadily deteriorated, as roads are wont to do in Nepal. A little over an hour later I found my face pressed against the window, a gravel embankment flying towards me, inches from ruining my complexion. Looking on the bright side seemed rather more difficult. I am convinced it was only my slender 54 kg frame catapulting across the lap of my Nepali travelling companion that tipped the balance – literally – in favour of the bus returning to the point at which any good bus should be: extremely horizontal.

Things returned to normal – or as normal as they could be. Several hellish hours later, the road surface suddenly changed from obscene to impeccable. But the cruel hoax was soon revealed when the road quickly reverted to type. This stretch on the Terai is the worst road I've ever travelled, worse even than one memorable track into the Australian outback.

All in all it was a great trip, but don't forget to pack your stoicism and humour, and get some extra fat on your bum in Kathmandu to absorb the bumps!

Lloyd Donaldson, New Zealand

unbelievably shabby, poorly maintained death-traps. As with the Sajha buses, there is a booking office in each town where you can buy tickets in advance on the long-distance routes.

Private buses run on all routes, and on the longer routes there are 'express' buses scheduled both by day and night. Fares are ridiculously cheap, but day buses are marginally cheaper than night buses. Day travel is generally preferable because you get to see the countryside (and there are some spectacular roads) and it's safer. Express bus drivers have mastered the art of maniacal driving, and accidents are not at all uncommon. Daylight travel is slower than at night simply because there are more people getting on and off, however, the danger posed by express night buses should not be underestimated.

There's nothing very express about the express buses, but they are lightning fast in comparison to local buses which run shorter routes, carry people, their luggage and often animals, and seem to stop more than they go. Travelling by local bus is no fun and should be kept to a minimum, although to get to many of the trekking road-heads there is little alternative.

NEPAL'S HIGHWAYS

There are just two main highways in Nepal, and their conditions vary from new and well-engineered to bone-jarring and pot-holed – more of the latter than the former, unfortunately.

The main highway is the busy Mahendra Hwy, which runs the length of the country from the Indian border at Kakarbhitta in the east to the Indian border at Mahendranagar in the west.

The busy Prithvi Hwy links Kathmandu with Pokhara. Between Kathmandu and Mugling the road parallels the Trisuli River, the most popular rafting river in the country. It then follows the Marsyangdi (which joins the Trisuli at Mugling) as far as Dumre, and from Damauli to Pokhara it follows the Seti Gandaki River. See the Kathmandu to Pokhara section in the Pokhara chapter for a full description of this route.

There are two minor highways, although they're hardly deserving of the title. Both offer spectacular views and are well worth travelling on. The Tribhuvan Hwy (or Rajpath) branches off the Prithvi Hwy at Naubise, about 30km from Kathmandu, and heads south over the mountains to Hetauda, and on to the Indian border at Birganj. The other is the Siddhartha Hwy, which joins Pokhara with Butwal on the Mahendra Hwy, going via the interesting town of Tansen (Palpa).

Mahendra Highway
East – Kakarbhitta to Narayanghat

This section of the highway is sealed, is in excellent condition and carries relatively little traffic.

Fifteen minutes from Kakarbhitta, past several tea plantations, is the town of Birtamod. A good bitumen road from here goes to Ilam, a starting point for treks in the Kanchenjunga region.

The first town of real consequence that you come to is Itahari, 100km from Kakarbhitta. There's nothing much to be said for it, however, apart from the fact that it is at the intersection of the road that runs south to Biratnagar, Nepal's second largest city, and north to Hile and Basantapur, starting points for Kanchenjunga, Makalu and Arun Valley treks.

After Itahari the road enters the flood plain of the Sapt Kosi, one of the Ganges' largest tributaries. This mighty river is now partially controlled by the impressive Kosi Barrage and its surrounding earthworks. Even so, the low-lying region seems at times to be more water than land. Metres of silt have obviously made the fields extremely fertile and there is a high population density.

Mud and thatch villages are built on small areas of high ground, and the people are closely related to their Indian neighbours. Emerald green paddies stretch to the horizon and the villages are surrounded by water lilies and hyacinths. Often, the houses are overgrown with pumpkin plants, which are trained onto the roofs. Fish is a vital part of the local diet, and wherever you look you'll see children and women fishing in the canals and ponds. The birdlife is prolific, with Brahmani kites, greater and lesser egrets, and cranes and ducks of every description.

On either side of the barrage the road is built on a raised levy. After Mohanpur you begin a long stretch of the Terai proper, skirting the Chure Hills, which seem to jump from the plains.

Since the eradication of malaria in the 1950s, much of this land has been settled. Many of the settlers have come from the hills, but have swiftly adapted to their new environment and have prospered. Frequently, houses have been built on stilts to cope with the annual floods.

Nearly 110km past the Kosi Barrage you reach Lalbiti: the turn-off to Janakpur (25km from the highway), one of the Terai's most attractive cities. The countryside is intensively cultivated and densely populated. As you travel farther west, however, there are fewer people, fewer of the bright Indian saris and more trees. Between Dalkebar and Amlekhganj there is an almost unbroken stretch of magnificent sal forest.

At Amlekhganj the Mahendra Hwy briefly joins the Tribhuvan Hwy to Hetauda. From Hetauda, the road runs along the edge of the Mahabharat Range and the Rapti River. There are some rich, cultivated fields, but a great deal of forest remains. On the other side of the Rapti lies the Royal Chitwan National Park, famous for its tigers and rhinos.

After Belva, the valley begins to broaden and the reason it is called the Inner Terai becomes clear – it's flat, fertile and heavily populated. There are some Tharu villages as well as many Gurung and other hill peoples. About 77km after Hetauda, you come to the small roadside town of Tadi Bazaar, the departure point for Royal Chitwan National Park.

The road from Tadi to Narayanghat is not particularly interesting; there's a lot of development and Narayanghat and Bharatpur run together and sprawl a long way. All buses travel west to Narayanghat and then turn north, following the Narayani River through the hills to Mugling on the Kathmandu-Pokhara (Prithvi) Hwy.

West – Mahendranagar to Narayanghat

The far west is the least developed and most traditional part of the Terai. It's inhabited by Tharus, Bajis (Abadhi speakers from India), Muslims and more recent migrants from the hills.

The 45km stretch from Mahendranagar to Ataria is a diabolical mess. It was single lane bitumen at one stage, but these days there are more potholes than black-top, and vehicles travel at a crawl.

Between Ataria and Chisopani (on the western bank of the Karnali River) there are a number of bridges still to be completed, and the last 10km stretch into Chisopani is basically a winding dirt track along the bank of the Karnali. This section from Mahendranagar should gradually improve as the bridges are completed; things happen slowly in this part of the world. Travel is often severely disrupted during the monsoon due to the lack of bridges.

The Karnali is one of the largest rivers in Nepal, draining the western third of the country. Thanks to the World Bank an enormous single-span suspension bridge has been built at Chisopani, at the point where the river flows through its last gorge and spills out onto the plains. There is no formal accommodation at Chisopani, but travellers have stayed with families and at chai shops (around Rs 30).

After the Karnali River the road is excellent black-top. It runs through the sal forest of the Royal Bardia National Park; keep your eyes peeled for monkeys, deer and peacocks. After you leave the forest you enter an agricultural zone inhabited by Tharus and a growing number of migrants from the hills. As you approach Kohalpur, 71km from Chisopani and the turn-off for Nepalganj, there are increasing numbers of Muslims – the white spires of mosques can be seen in the villages.

Nepalganj is 16km south of Kohalpur, and lies on the flat, hot Gangetic plain at the western end of the Rapti Valley. The Rapti Valley, like the Chitwan Valley, is described as the Inner Terai, and lies along the Rapti River between the Duduwa Hills to the south and the Chure Hills and Mahabharat Range to the north. The valley is attractive and intensively cultivated and seems to become more fertile the farther east you travel. There are endless fields of mustard, interspersed with small Tharu settlements and the much grander Newari-style houses of their landlords *(zamindars)*. There are a number of grubby and depressing roadside villages with the usual chai shops – the largest being Kusum (71km from Nepalganj) and Lamahi (52km from Kusum).

About 25km from Lamahi, the road crosses the Rapti River and climbs over the foothills before dropping down to the Terai proper. Butwal, where buses turn north to Pokhara along the Siddhartha Hwy, is the next major town, 97km from the bridge over the Rapti and 245km from Nepalganj.

The road from Butwal to Narayanghat (93km) is not particularly interesting. There are a couple of places where there are quite steep climbs over ridges of the Chure Hills, but most of the countryside is flat and monotonous sal forest. The soil is too sandy to be farmed. There are some unattractive strips of roadside development, inhabited mainly by relatively recent migrants from the hills. From Narayanghat there is a link to Mugling on the Kathmandu-Pokhara (Prithvi) Hwy; see the Kathmandu to Pokhara section in the Pokhara chapter.

Hitching

Hitching is never entirely safe in any country in the world, and we don't recommend it. Travellers who decide to hitch should understand that they are taking a small but potentially serious risk. People who do choose to hitch will be safer if they travel in pairs and let someone know where they are planning to go.

Tribhuvan Highway

The Tribhuvan Hwy (or Rajpath) was the first road to link the Kathmandu Valley with the outside world; it was built by the Indian government and completed in 1956. If you have time and feel energetic, consider catching a Sajha Yatayat bus over the mountains from Hetauda to Kathmandu.

If you are travelling in a group or have the funds, consider hiring a car. It won't be cheap, partly because you'll have to pay for the driver's return trip whether or not you return yourself. Think in terms of $150. Alternatively, if you're fit and have a mountain bike, this is regarded as one of the most spectacular cycling routes in the country; see the Mountain Biking chapter.

You begin to climb into the Mahabharat Range the moment you leave Hetauda. The road is in good condition, but it's very narrow, so it's a case of drivers leaning almost constantly on their horns and hoping they won't meet an out-of-control Tata truck around the next blind corner.

The change from the Terai is remarkably sudden; you're soon among forested hills and it is almost impossible to believe the plains are so close. As you gain altitude you enter magnificent rhododendron forests. The highest point on the road is 2400m, just before you reach Daman. Daman is famous as a viewpoint with one of the most complete panoramas of the Himalaya that you can find. The view – from Dhaulagiri to Everest – is simply awe-inspiring.

After Daman you travel through the intensely cultivated Palung Valley. From here to Kathmandu, every possible inch of the hills is farmed. There are more good views of the Himalaya before you reach Naubise on the Kathmandu-Pokhara (Prithvi) Hwy. Daman is about three hours from Kathmandu and Hetauda by car, four hours by bus.

Siddhartha Highway

From Butwal, the Siddhartha snakes up through the picturesque Mahabharat Range to the historic town of Tansen (Palpa). It is a narrow, winding road which is generally in pretty poor condition, and is subject to landslides during the monsoon.

Between Tansen and Pokhara there are some superb views as the road winds down to cross the Kali Gandaki at Ramdhighat, a popular take-out for rafting trips coming down from the upper stretches of the river. The hills all through this area are heavily cultivated and the road passes though many small villages. The condition of the road improves as you get closer to Pokhara, the last 30km or so being good bitumen.

CAR & MOTORCYCLE

There are no drive-yourself rental cars available in Nepal but you can easily hire cars with drivers. Expect to pay around $40 a day, plus fuel, which at the time of research, was set at Rs 39 per litre across the country.

It is quite popular to hire cars for return trips to both Pokhara and Royal Chitwan National Park. A car from Kathmandu to Pokhara should cost around $30 one way, although this can rise at peak times. A car to Chitwan should cost around $60, but could also rise at peak times.

Motorbikes can be rented in Kathmandu. See Kathmandu's Getting Around section in the Kathmandu, Patan & Bhaktapur chapter for more details about car and motorbike rental.

BICYCLE

In Kathmandu and Pokhara there are many bicycle-rental outlets and this is a cheap and convenient way of getting around. Virtually the entire valley is accessible by bike, though if you are venturing far outside the Kathmandu and Patan area, a mountain bike is definitely worthwhile. A regular bicycle only costs around Rs 50 per day, and a mountain bike costs from Rs 150 to Rs 200. Children's bicycles can also be hired. See the Mountain Biking chapter for more information on cycling in Nepal.

LOCAL TRANSPORT
Taxi

Larger towns such as Kathmandu and Pokhara have taxis which, between a group of people, can be a good way to explore the Kathmandu Valley. Metered taxis have black

Bicycle rickshaws are a great (and cheap!) way to see the world go by over short distances.

licence plates; private cars often operate as taxis, particularly on long-distance routes or for extended periods, and have red plates.

Fuel prices and therefore taxi rates often rise faster than meters can be recalibrated, so frequently there is a surcharge on top of the meter reading. If the meters are out of date (at the time of research they were OK) tourists will be hard pushed to convince drivers to use their meters (with or without a surcharge) and will almost certainly have to negotiate the fare in advance.

Rickshaw

Auto-rickshaws, those curious and noxious three wheeled motorcycle-engined devices, are also found in Kathmandu.

Bicycle rickshaws are common in the old part of Kathmandu and can be a good way of making short trips through the crowded and narrow streets. They are also the most common form of short-distance public transport in towns throughout the Terai.

Note that auto-rickshaws and bicycle rickshaws operate much like taxis, and that the three wheeled tempos are more like minibuses – leaving when full and having fixed fares.

ORGANISED TOURS

Most travel agencies in Kathmandu run organised tours (public and private) by car or bus to places of interest around the valley and farther afield. If your stay in Nepal is too short to permit any decent exploration on your own, then you will do well to join a conducted or private tour. For more information, see Organised Tours under the Kathmandu section of the Kathmandu, Patan & Bhaktapur chapter.

Kathmandu, Patan & Bhaktapur

For most visitors to Nepal, the Kathmandu Valley is their arrival point and the epicentre of their visit. This small mountain-sheltered valley is the historical centre of Nepal, the place where kingdoms rose and fell, palaces and temples were built, destroyed and rebuilt, and Nepali art and culture were developed and refined.

The three major towns – Kathmandu, Patan and Bhaktapur – each have an artistic and architectural tradition that rivals anything you'll find in the great cities of Europe. Kathmandu is the capital and the largest city in the country; it also has the international airport and is where most visitors stay. Patan, the second largest, is separated from Kathmandu by a river, but in other respects the two cities are virtually continuous. Bhaktapur, the third largest, is towards the eastern end of the valley and its relative isolation is reflected in its slower pace and more distinctly medieval atmosphere.

Scattered around the valley are hundreds of temples and shrines, traditional villages and agricultural scenes of timeless beauty (see the Around the Kathmandu Valley chapter for more details). A great deal is easily accessible by foot, bicycle, bus or taxi, but the more time you have the better. You will be hard-pressed to do any justice to the place in less than a week.

HISTORY

The Newars are regarded as the original inhabitants of the valley, but their origins are shrouded in mystery. They speak a Tibeto-Burmese language, which indicates they originated in the east, but their physical features range from distinctively Mongoloid, again suggesting the east, to Indo-Aryan, which of course points to India.

In balance, it seems most likely that the Kathmandu Valley has long been a cultural and racial melting pot, with people coming from both east and west. This fusion has resulted in the unique Newari culture that is

---

HIGHLIGHTS

- Strolling around and soaking up the atmosphere of the history-rich capital city and nearby towns

- Spending an hour on the steps of the Maju Deval in Kathmandu, just watching the world go by and following up with an evening meal at one of the city's many varied restaurants

- Visiting the glorious Pulchowki rhododendron forest, in bloom from February to April

- Viewing the stunning Newari architecture of Patan, and visiting the Tibetan carpet-making workshops there

- Visiting the famous Golden Gate and Peacock Windows in Bhaktapur, where many of the oldest buildings have been fully restored

---

responsible for the valley's superb art and architecture.

The Newari golden age peaked in the 17th century when the valley consisted of small city-states, and Nepal was a vitally important trading link between Tibet and the north Indian plains. The valley's visible history is inextricably entangled with the Malla kings. It was during their reign, particularly in the 17th and 18th centuries, that many of the valley's finest temples and palaces were built. Competition between the cities was intense and an architectural innovation in one place, such as the erection of a column bearing a statue of the ruling king, would inevitably be copied in the other cities.

Sorting out who built what and when is considerably complicated by the fact that at any one time there was not just one Malla king. Each of the three city-states in the valley – Kathmandu, Patan and Bhaktapur – had its own. Some of the most important

Malla kings are listed in the introduction to the relevant cities.

The unification of Nepal in 1768 by Gorkha's King Prithvi Narayan Shah signalled the end of the Kathmandu Valley's fragmentation. Nepali, an Indo-European language spoken by the Khas of western Nepal, replaced Newari as the country's language of administration.

GEOGRAPHY

The bowl-like Kathmandu Valley is about 25km from east to west, perhaps 20km from north to south. Kathmandu lies at a height of around 1300m, while the surrounding hills range from 1500m to 2800m in height. If you fly in, you clearly see how isolated and unusual the valley is – embedded like a jewel among endless rugged mountains.

A large and growing population is posing numerous problems. Due to the surrounding mountains, Kathmandu is particularly vulnerable to air and water pollution, and both problems are already serious. The mountains also make transport extremely difficult: the valley has only three fragile overland lifelines. There's one two-lane road out of the valley to the south and on to India, and another road north-east to Tibet that washes away every year.

The valley is very fertile, capable of growing grain (rice, corn, wheat) and a wide range of fruit (from bananas to oranges) and vegetables. However, urban development is rapidly encroaching on valuable agricultural land, so the valley is increasingly dependent on imported food and fossil fuels.

A number of rivers drain towards the centre of the valley and join the holy Bagmati River, which then flows south through the Chobar Gorge to finally reach the Ganges. Geologists have confirmed ancient myths that claim the valley once lay under water.

CLIMATE

The Kathmandu Valley has a temperate climate that is pleasant most of the year. Snow is almost unheard of, although there are frosts. Monsoons are nowhere near as severe as they are on the plains.

Between October and March it can become quite cold at night (0°C) and the days become short, although it's sunny and warm between mid-morning and mid-afternoon (say 20°C). Visibility is good from October to early February, although there are two impediments: thick early morning fog which doesn't clear until mid-morning and wreaks havoc with airline schedules; and the temperature inversion which often traps a thick layer of warm smog under a layer of colder air.

By April things start to heat up and there are often storms in the afternoon. The real heat and humidity coincide with the monsoon proper, which usually commences in mid-June. Expect daytime temperatures around the low to mid-30°Cs, and nighttime temperatures between 15°C and 20°C. Fortunately, much of the rain falls during the night or on the surrounding hills.

FLORA & FAUNA

Most of the valley has been converted to highly productive farmland, but several pockets of uncleared land remain: Gokarna, just past Bodhnath; Nagarjun just past Balaju; and others on several of the surrounding hills, notably Pulchowki.

The native forests consisted of oak and other broad-leafed trees, pines and rhododendrons (laliguras) that grow over 15m high. Pulchowki, the highest point overlooking the valley, has a magnificent rhododendron forest and shouldn't be missed if you're in the valley in spring (February to April). Australians will recognise the eucalyptus, grevillea and bottlebrush that line many of the valley's roads.

Once upon a time the valley probably had populations of leopards, jungle cats, wolves, black bears, sloth bears, otters and jackals. Unfortunately these are long gone.

No visitor to Swayambhunath will avoid the rhesus macaque monkeys that infest the hillside. Nor, if you walk past the Royal Palace in Kathmandu, will you miss the colonies of fruit bats that spend their days chattering in the trees before they take to the sky each evening.

ECONOMY

Today the valley is the most developed part of Nepal, with a network of roads and electricity linking most of the villages. Despite rapid development, however, much of the valley is still devoted to small-scale farming. The availability of improved seeds, fertilisers and extensive irrigation has increased productivity and made it possible to grow wheat as well as the traditional rice.

Nepal's small industrial base is mainly concentrated in the lowland towns of the Terai, although the factories in the valley (including cement, brick, light engineering, food and beverage) contribute more than 20% of the country's industrial output.

The Kathmandu Valley is the centre for many traditional crafts. Newari artisans have long exported pottery, brassware and bronze religious artefacts. The tradition continues, only these days the buyer is often a tourist. The 'Tibetan' carpet industry is now the valley's largest private employer, and carpets are among the country's major export earners.

Kathmandu is the administrative and educational centre for the country. Many of the Ranas' grand palaces are now home to bureaucracies that are, arguably, of greater benefit to the general populace. Kathmandu is also the main focus for visiting tourists, so there has been a large investment in the necessary infrastructure and many people are dependent on the tourist dollar.

PEOPLE

The Newars still form the largest single group in the valley and there are some smaller towns and villages, such as Thimi, Chapagaon or Sankhu, which remain Newari strongholds. Many of the people living on the surrounding hills are Tamangs, Bahuns and Chhetris, who can generally be distinguished from the Newars by their solitary households.

In recent years many immigrants from throughout the country have come to the valley in search of jobs and education. There are, therefore, significant minorities of almost every Nepali ethnic group. Since the Chinese invasion of Tibet in 1959, thousands of Tibetan refugees have settled in the valley; there is also a large community of Indian traders and business people and significant communities of other foreigners.

The latest census (1991) found that Kathmandu had a population of 419,000 (235,000 in 1981), Patan had 117,000 (110,000) and Bhaktapur had 61,000 (60,000). The combined population of the valley was 1,099,000 (617,000) meaning the valley is home to nearly 6% of Nepal's people and that the population density is about 1800 per sq km. Current estimates put the valley's population at around 1.5 million.

Newars

It is not surprising that the Newar people were influenced by Tibet and India. What is surprising is their creative response to this stimulus, which actually led to a genuine exchange with their giant neighbours. Medieval Newari society has left a religious, architectural and artistic legacy that is unique, and spectacular by any standard.

Although most Newars have Mongoloid physical characteristics, some don't, so their origins are shrouded in mystery. It is now generally accepted that they are a mixture of many different peoples who were attracted to the valley, possibly originating with the Kiratis, or an even earlier group. (See History in the Facts about Nepal chapter for more details.)

Perhaps the Newars' most striking characteristic is their love of communal life; Newari houses are invariably clustered together, usually around sites of religious significance. Although their economy was centred on agriculture and trade, they created sophisticated urban communities which catered to a breadth of human needs in an integrated way that has rarely been matched.

Today there are around 1,000,000 Newars, largely centred in the Kathmandu Valley. Always traders and merchants, the Newars continue to fill this role throughout the kingdom. Their proximity to the centre of power has also led to them having a disproportionate influence in the bureaucracies of Kathmandu. Many now live in depressingly ugly bungalows on the outskirts of the city proper, and many of their traditions are on the wane.

Architecture The most important social unit was the family and the family house was the starting point for urban planning. Rich Newars built handsomely proportioned brick houses with tiled roofs that were up to five storeys high. In the country, the ground floor was often used for stabling animals, while in the city it was used for commerce.

A community developed when a series of houses was built in a rectangle around a courtyard/square, or *chowk*. The chowk, often with running water and a temple or shrine, was the centre of day-to-day life, and still is today. Here, the markets buzz, children play, women work (weaving, washing, drying grain) and chat, old people doze in the sun, men talk over the community's business and religious ceremonies take place.

The cities and towns of the valley were made up of a compact network of these interlocking squares, courtyards, twisting alleyways, ponds and temples, often centred around a main square. Fortunately, much of this tradition remains. Decorated with carved windows and doorways, statues and shrines, and humming with gregarious people, a Newari town is a remarkable synthesis of art and everyday life.

Religion The vast majority of Newars are Hindu and fall under a caste system, although there is still a significant minority of Buddhists. This simplistic description, however, masks an incredibly diverse and complex system of beliefs.

Since the 5th century, kings and aristocrats have been Hindu and their influence gradually led to Buddhists adopting castes and a hereditary priesthood (the Banrhas). The many collapsing *bahals* (monasteries) testify to a long-gone Buddhist golden age.

The end result is that a purist from either religion would not recognise many of the Newari gods or the practices that go into their worship. For not only have aspects of both religions combined, they have been added to by a Tantric tradition, Tibetan Buddhism and even older local deities and beliefs.

This has led to a confusing proliferation of gods who are often hybrids unashamedly shuffled from one pantheon to another. There are literally hundreds of these divinities, and over 150 days of festivals a year to celebrate them. From a functional point of view, most people are free to follow whatever gods and goddesses particularly appeal to them, so theological consistency (including the distinction between Hinduism and Buddhism) is irrelevant, certainly to the people themselves. (See Religion in the Facts about Nepal chapter for more details.)

Customs The Newars are divided into castes, whether they nominally consider themselves Hindu or Buddhist, and these include untouchables (tinkers, butchers and some others). Caste rules are not quite as rigid as in some parts of India, but intermarriage is still rare and untouchables are still grossly disadvantaged.

The usual dress for a Newari woman is a sari and blouse, often with a shawl. The men wear trousers with a baggy seat that are tighter around the calves (like jodhpurs), a long untucked double-breasted shirt, a vest (waistcoat) or coat and the traditional Nepali cap *(topi)*. The most distinctive caste is the Jyapu (farmers), and many of them still lead highly traditional lives. Jyapu women wear black saris with a red border, while the men often wear the traditional trousers and shirt with a long piece of cotton wrapped around the waist. They prefer to carry goods and vegetables on a shoulder pole.

Newari children are welcomed into their community and caste at the age of seven when boys' heads are shaved leaving only a topknot, and girls are symbolically married to the soul of their future husband. Most Newars have arranged marriages and on auspicious dates, wedding processions are a common sight. The procession starts at nightfall and is led by a band, often in ragtag uniforms making a cacophony of noise with clarinets, trumpets and drums.

Traditionally, men were members of a unique cooperative institution known as a *guthi*. This is a religious and social group based on family and other local links. Guthis may own land and are often responsible for the upkeep of particular temples and financing particular rites, as well as the welfare of their members.

Tamangs

The Tamangs are closely related to Tibetans. Their name apparently means 'horse trader', although most are now sedentary farmers or labourers. Their appearance, language and Lamaist Buddhist beliefs all bear testimony to their origins. Indeed, many of the 'Tibetan' souvenirs for sale in Kathmandu are actually made by Tamangs. Tamangs can be found throughout the central Himalaya, and especially around the Kathmandu Valley. (See People in the Facts about Nepal chapter for more details.)

Bahuns (Brahmins) & Chhetris (Kshatriyas)

In Hindu theory Bahuns and Chhetris are the two highest castes (respectively the priests and warriors). In Nepal, however, most are descended from the Khas kingdoms that flourished in western Nepal and were home to Indo-Aryans who migrated to Nepal over the centuries. The Bahuns and Chhetris played an important role in the court and armies of Prithvi Narayan Shah, and after unification many were rewarded with lands in and around the Kathmandu Valley.

They continue to dominate the processes of government in Kathmandu. See People in the Facts about Nepal chapter for more details.

Kathmandu

☎ 01

Kathmandu is the capital of Nepal, the largest city in the country and the main centre for hotels and restaurants. This amazing city can seem, in places, to be a huge intricate sculpture unchanged since the Middle Ages. At other times it can be just another Third World capital rushing into the modern era.

For many people, arriving in Kathmandu is as shocking as stepping out of a time machine – the sights, sounds and smells can lead to sensory overload. There are narrow streets and lanes with carved wooden balconies above tiny hole-in-the-wall shops, plus town squares packed with extraordinary temples and monuments and markets bright with fruit and vegetables as well as a constant throng of humanity. Then there's the choking dust and fumes, stinking gutters, concrete monstrosities, touts, Coca-Cola billboards and maimed beggars.

The gap between rich and poor is a chasm, but despite the pressures of extreme overcrowding and poverty, people retain a good-humoured self-respect and integrity. It is probably safer to walk the streets here than it is in your home town – and certainly much more interesting.

Like Patan and Bhaktapur (the other major towns of the valley), Kathmandu's historic centre is concentrated around Durbar Square (*durbar* is Nepali for palace). There's a distinct difference between the tightly packed old city area and the more spacious newer parts of town.

Malla Kings

Malla kings of particular importance in Kathmandu included:

Ratna Malla	1482-1528
Mahendra Malla	1560-1574
Sadasiva Malla	1574-1583
Shiva Singh Malla	1578-1620
Pratap Malla	1641-1674
Prithvibendra Malla	1680-1687
Bhaskara Malla	1687-1714
Jagat Jaya Malla	1722-1736
Jaya Prakash Malla	1736-1768

ORIENTATION

Most of the interesting things to see in Kathmandu are clustered in the old part of town from Kantipath (the main north-south road) west towards the Vishnumati River.

New Rd, constructed after the great earthquake of 1934, starts from the ornamental entrance by Kantipath and goes straight into the heart of old Kathmandu, changing its name to Ganga Path before it comes to Durbar Square.

The office of Royal Nepal Airlines (RNAC) is at the Kantipath end of New Rd and along this road are banks, shops and the modern shopping heart of the city. Continue farther along New Rd to Ganga Path and you reach the large Basantapur Square, then Durbar Square where the old Royal Palace is located. Freak St, Kathmandu's famous street from the hippie/overland era, runs south off Basantapur Square.

Running north-east from Durbar Square is the thoroughfare that was once the main trading artery of the city and is still the busiest street in old Kathmandu. This narrow road, usually thronged with people, cuts through the heart of old Kathmandu from Indra Chowk through Kel Tole to Asan Tole.

Kantipath forms the boundary between the older and newer parts of the city. Just south of the New Rd junction is the main post office, easily located by the nearby Bhimsen Tower (or Sundhara). On the east side of Kantipath is the large open parade ground known as Tundikhel, and on the eastern edge of this is the City bus station, for buses around the Kathmandu Valley.

Continuing north along Kantipath from New Rd takes you past the government-run Bir Hospital on the left – look for Hanuman on the wall carrying a Himalayan mountain complete with medicinal herbs. On the right is Ratna Park and then Rani Pokhari. Kantipath crosses Tridevi Marg at the corner of the new Royal Palace compound and continues into Maharajganj, the embassy sector.

Running parallel to and east of Kantipath is Durbar Marg, a wide street flanked by travel agencies, airline offices and a number of restaurants and expensive hotels. It ends at the main entrance to the new Royal Palace. Turn left from Durbar Marg in front of the palace, cross Kantipath, and Tridevi Marg will take you past the South Asian Association for Regional Cooperation (SAARC) and

after a couple of blocks will bring you into the Thamel area, the popular cheap tourist accommodation and restaurant centre of the city. Thamel is a 15 to 20 minute walk north from the centre of Kathmandu.

The city is encircled by the Ring Road, and on it in the north of the city is the main Kathmandu bus station, and on the eastern edge Tribhuvan international airport.

Addresses

In old Kathmandu, streets were not given names, and although some of the major thoroughfares now do have names, most still don't. Smaller streets and laneways never do. Kathmandu grew as a series of interlocking squares that gradually swallowed neighbouring villages. The names of these squares, villages, and other landmarks (perhaps a monastery or temple) came to be used as addresses of sorts.

For example, the address of everyone living within a 100m radius of Thahiti Tole is Thahiti Tole and if you want to find them you go to Thahiti Tole and ask around – simple if you can speak Nepali and can find your way around the warren of laneways and courtyards. Thamel is now used to describe a sprawling area with at least a dozen roads and several hundred hotels and restaurants. They all have the same one-word address – Thamel.

Given this anarchic approach it is amazing that any mail gets delivered – it does, but slowly. Most businesses have post office box numbers. If you're trying to find a particular house, shop or business, make sure you get detailed directions (unless, of course, you have a foolproof Lonely Planet map!).

INFORMATION
Tourist Offices

The government tourist office (☎ 220818) is on Ganga Path diagonally opposite Basantapur Square, and it may or may not have some brochures and maps. It's open Sunday to Thursday, 9 am to 6 pm, and until 4 pm on Friday.

The Tourist Service Centre (☎ 247041) on Bhrikutimandap Marg, on the eastern side of Tundikhel, is a new government centre

KATHMANDU

KATHMANDU

To Budhanilkantha (15km), Maharajgan (3km), Lazimpat & Embassies

To Naxal (500m), Pashupatinath (5km), Airport (6km) & Bodhnath (6km)

Nag Pokhari

Royal Palace

Kamaladi

Bagh Bazaar

Durbar Marg

See Durbar Marg Map p180

Rani Pokhari

Ratna Park

Lekhnath Marg

Bhagwan Bahal

Kantipath

Tridevi Marg

Jyatha

See Walking Tour 2 Map p157

Thahiti Tole

Asan Tole

Kel Tole

New Road

Thamel

Chhetrapati

Paknajol

See Greater Thamel Map pp166-67

Kilagal

Indra Chowk

Siddha Path

Ganga Path

To Balaju (3km) & Kathmandu BusPark (3km)

See Walking Tour 1 Map p154

Old Royal Palace

See Durbar Square (Kathmandu) Map p142

Durbar Square

Basantapur Square

To Swayambhunath (1km)

Footbridge

To National
& Art Gallery (3km)

To Soaltree Holiday:
Inn (1km) & Pokhara
(206km)

See Walking Tour 3 Map p159

See Freak Street
Map p170

eak St

31

32

33
34

Tundikhel

35

36

37

26

Bhrikutimandap Marg

Exhibition
Ground

Prithvi Path

Tukucha Khola

Ram Shah Path

Singh
Durbar

38

39

40

To Hotel Everest
(1km), Bhaktapur
(10km), Airport
(6km) & Arniko
Highway

Thapathali

54

53

48

49

52

50

51

47

41

46

Tripureshwar Marg

Teku

44

43

45

Bagmati River

Footbridge

Vishnumati River

42

To Kirtipur (5km) &
Dakshinkali (21km)

To Patan (2km)

500 m

250

0

KATHMANDU

PLACES TO STAY
1   Hotel Ambassador
4   Hotel Vajra
10 Yak & Yeti Hotel

PLACES TO EAT
17 Bhanchha Ghar Restaurant

OTHER
2   Shobabaghwati Temple
3   Bijeshwari Temple
5   Indrani Temple
6   Nepal International Clinic
7   Temple
8   Gulf Air
9   Bangladesh Biman
11 China Airlines; Qatar Airways
12 Buddha Air
13 Air India; Indian Airlines
14 Kathmandu Plaza
15 Heritage Plaza; Moon Sun Disco; Transavia

16 Mosque
18 Himalayan Buddhist Meditation Centre
19 DHL; Himalayan Express; Aeroflot
20 Austrian Airlines
21 Clocktower
22 French Cultural Centre
23 Bir Hospital
24 Mahakala Temple
25 City Bus Station
26 Tourist Service Centre
27 RNAC (International & Domestic Tourist Flights)
28 RNAC (Other Domestic Flights)
29 US Library; Information Service
30 Nepal Bank
31 Vegetable Market
32 Bhimsen Tower
33 Tempos to Patan & Bodhnath
34 Main Post Office

35 Buses for Pharping & Dakshinkali
36 Martyr's Memorial Gate
37 Bhadrakali Temple
38 Supreme Court
39 National Archives
40 Babar Mahal Revisited
41 Army Headquarters
42 Cableway Station
43 Pachali Bhairab
44 Tindeval Temple
45 Raj Ghat
46 Central Telegraph Office
47 National Stadium
48 Swimming Pool
49 Ministry of Tourism
50 Bhaktapur Trolley-Bus Terminus
51 Tripureshwar Mahadev Temple
52 Kalmochan Temple
53 Bluebird Supermarket
54 Nepal Rastra Bank

which exists supposedly to provide information and service to tourists. It doesn't seem to do much of either.

There's also a tourist office at the international terminal at the airport (☎ 470537), where they usually dish out a handy free map to arriving passengers.

Other Tourist Information There are a number of good notice boards in Thamel that are worth consulting if you are looking for information on such diverse things as apartments, travel and trekking partners, yoga and meditation courses, language courses and cultural events. The Kathmandu Guest House has a good board (to the left in the front courtyard), as do the Pumpernickel Bakery and the Fire & Ice restaurant.

Other particularly useful boards are found at the Trekkers' Information Centre (run by HRA, ☎ 262746, email hra@aidpost.mos .com.np) in Thamel opposite the Shree Guest House; and at the Travellers' Information Centre (run by KEEP, ☎ 259275, email tours@keep.wlink.com.np), in the same street less than 100m away. The peo-

ple in the information centres are happy to answer general queries, and there are some useful notebooks with up-to-date information from other trekkers. KEEP also has a good collection of reference books. The centres are open from 10 am to 5 pm Sunday to Friday. KEEP also provides a mineral water refill service for Rs 10 per litre.

Another good source of independent trekking information and advice is the slide shows held regularly during the season at the Kathmandu Guest House. See Information in the Trekking chapter for details.

Most travel agents are happy to answer queries, but swing into a pretty hard sell making it hard to get impartial information. The people in the office of Green Hill Tours (in the compound next to the Kathmandu Guest House) are tuned into independent budget travellers' needs, and Wayfarers Travel Services close by are also reliable.

Nepal Travellers is a good-quality, free monthly magazine that covers a broad range of interesting topics and has a good section of practical information, with addresses and phone numbers.

Money

See the Facts for the Visitor chapter for a discussion on exchange rates and commissions. In brief, it is worth checking the rate that banks and moneychangers offer and the commission they charge – both vary. Note that prices are quoted in US dollars.

The most convenient bank for travellers staying in the Thamel region is the small branch of the Nepal Grindlays Bank south of the Kathmandu Guest House. It is open Sunday to Thursday from 9.45 am to 3.30 pm, and closes at 12.45 pm on Friday. The main Nepal Bank (☎ 221185, fax 222381) in Dharmapath near New Rd is handy if you're staying in Freak St and has the important advantage of being open from 7 am to 7 pm seven days a week. There are several banks on Durbar Marg; the Nepal Indo-Suez Bank (☎ 228229, fax 226349) is convenient and efficient.

Kathmandu also has a Nepal Grindlays Bank at the Thamel end of Kantipath (☎ 233128); Citibank (☎ 228884), GPO Box 2826, with an office in the Yak & Yeti Hotel; and the Nepal Arab Bank (☎ 227181, fax 226905), GPO Box 3729, Kantipath. Grindlays will make advances on Visa and Master-Card in Nepali rupees and travellers cheques.

The American Express agent is Yeti Travels (☎ 227635, fax 226153) which has its office off the forecourt of the Hotel Mayalu on Jamal Tole, just around the corner from Durbar Marg. It will make cash advances between 10 am and 1 pm. Sita World Travel (☎ 418363), up the laneway opposite the Three Goddesses Temple in Thamel, is the agent for Western Union money transfers. See Money in Facts for the Visitor.

There are also a number of licensed moneychangers in Thamel. Their hours are much longer than the banks, but rates vary considerably so shop around. Some charge commission, others don't.

Kathmandu also has a great number of 'change money' men and although this black market is officially illegal it is widely accepted. A popular T-shirt worn by many visitors announces that, among other things, they don't want to change money!

Post

The main Kathmandu post office is on the corner of Kantipath and Khichapokhari, close to Bhimsen Tower. The stamp counter is theoretically open from 8 am to 7 pm, Sunday to Thursday, and from 11 am to 3 pm on Saturday, but it can provide a classic dose of queuing and frustration. Unless you have a *lot* of mail, you are best off taking advantage of the hotels, bookshops and communication centres who will tackle the bureaucracy for you for a nominal charge. See the Facts for the Visitor chapter for postal charges.

The poste restante section at the main post office is quite efficient: the staff sort letters into alphabetically arranged boxes and you simply sit down and go through them yourself. You are required to show your passport before you take anything away. Make sure your correspondents print and underline your surname; if in doubt check under your first name as well. The section (inside to the left, behind the main counter) is open from 10.15 am to 4 pm Sunday to Thursday (closing one hour earlier mid-November to mid-February), and from 10.15 am to 2 pm on Friday, closed Saturday.

Parcels may be sent from the separate foreign post office just north of the main post office. It's open Sunday to Thursday from 10 am to 5 pm until 2 pm on Friday. Parcels have to be examined and sealed by a customs officer and then packed in an approved manner. It's something of a procedure, so if you're short of time you're best off using one of the many cargo agencies. Diki Continental Exports (☎ 417681, fax 414997), opposite the Hotel Mandap in Thamel, and Sharmasons Movers (☎ 222709, fax 222026) are two that have been recommended.

American Express has a clients' mail service at its offices off the forecourt of the Hotel Mayalu in Jamal Tol. Address letters to American Express, Yeti Travels Pty Ltd, Hotel Mayalu, Jamal Tole, PO Box 5376, Durbar Marg, Kathmandu.

Telephone & Fax

International phone calls can be made and faxes can be sent from the central telegraph

KATHMANDU

office about 500m south of the post office, opposite the National Stadium. The service is open 24 hours and the process is quick and painless.

The dozens of 'communication centres' in Thamel and elsewhere offering fax, telephone and mailing services are more convenient, although somewhat more expensive. Phone calls and faxes cost around $3 per minute to pretty well anywhere. If a phone call is short, the convenience of the private operators far outweighs the comparative expense, but if you talk for any length of time you may be better off catching a taxi or tempo to the central telegraph office (around Rs 30). See the Facts for the Visitor chapter for more information on rates.

For domestic information dial ☎ 197.

Email
Email services are widely available in Thamel. Providers range from a hotel or travel agent with one computer to cybercafes with a dozen or more terminals. The network is often congested and you may have to spend quite a while online for even simple matters like checking email.

Rates are fairly standard at Rs 8 to Rs 10 per minute online, or Rs 10 per kb if you are sending email and don't actually need to go online.

Cybercafes One of the most sophisticated places is K@mandu Cybermatha on Kantipath just east of Thamel. It's air-conditioned and probably has the most reliable network connections. It's also among the more expensive places.

Also professional is the EasyLink Cybercafe, in Thamel north of the main Thamel Chowk.

Travel Agencies
Kathmandu has a great number of travel agencies, particularly along Durbar Marg, Kantipath and in Thamel. See the Trekking chapter for details of trekking agencies.

For straightforward travel and ticketing matters, try Wayfarers Travel Service (☎ 417176, fax 245875, email wayfarer@

mos.com.np) in Thamel, not far from the Kathmandu Guest House.

Bookshops
Kathmandu has a large number of very good bookshops. Many have particularly interesting selections of books on Nepal including books that are not usually available outside the country. Prices for British and US books are surprisingly competitive with their home-market prices.

As well as shops with new books there are many shops with second-hand books for sale and trade. Most dealers will buy back books for 50% of what you paid.

Tiwari's Pilgrims Book House is a couple of doors north of the Kathmandu Guest House and has an extensive collection of books on Nepal and other Himalayan regions. There's another even better shop owned by the same company, on the road from Durbar Marg to the Yak & Yeti Hotel. Known as the Kailash Bookshop, it also has an antiquarian section. There's also a branch of Pilgrims opposite the Himalaya Hotel near Patan.

Walden Book House at Chhetrapati is another place with a very good range, as is the Barnes & Noble shop just south of the Kathmandu Guest House.

There are many other good bookshops around Thamel, including Bookland on Tridevi Marg. Mandala Book Point on Kantipath has an excellent selection of books, with a good range in French and German.

Libraries
There are a number of libraries and cultural centres in Kathmandu. The British Council Library (☎ 222698) on Kantipath has a good selection of books on Nepal as well as British newspapers and magazines. It's open Monday and Friday from 11 am to 6 pm, Tuesday to Thursday from 11 am to 5 pm, and is closed on weekends.

Only Nepalis and foreign residents in Nepal are allowed to use the American Library (☎ 410041) in Gyaneshwar, east of the city centre. It's open Monday to Friday from 11 am to 6 pm.

The French Cultural Centre (☎ 224326) is in Bagh Bazaar and has French publications and organises French film nights (small admission charge). The Goethe Institute (☎ 250871) in Ganabahal, near Bhimsen Tower, has German film nights and occasional exhibitions as well as a library.

Rastriya Pustakalaya, the Nepal National Library (☎ 521132), is at Pulchowk in Patan and has books in English and Hindi. The Tribhuvan University Library of Kirtipur has a good collection and is open Sunday to Friday from 9 am to 6 pm.

The Kaiser or Kesar Library (☎ 411318) is worth a visit just to see the building and gardens. It's part of the Department of Education compound on the corner of Kantipath and Tridevi Marg, and has an incredible collection of books on Buddhism, Tibet and Nepal. Kaiser Shamsher Jung Bahadur Rana was a Rana aristocrat, scholar, scientist and gourmet. He built up a superb collection of books all of which, it is said, he read in their original language. Most of his palace is now used for government offices, but his library is kept as he left it and can be visited.

Government Offices

Most government offices in Kathmandu are open Sunday to Thursday 10 am to 5 pm, and until 4 pm during the winter months (mid-November to mid-February). Offices close at 3 pm on Friday and all day Saturday.

The immigration office, where trekking permits are also issued, is way out halfway to the airport along the Bhaktapur road, which is a real chore as you have to visit the place twice on the same day to get a trekking permit or visa extension. To get there, take the airport road past the Hotel Everest and turn left (north) by the huge new Convention Centre. The immigration office is exactly 1km down the road on the left. Any transaction with the immigration office requires two trips or a wait of several hours. There is nothing of interest in the vicinity except the small *Friends Restaurant* opposite the office. Taxis charge about Rs 100 each way from Thamel. It's open from 10 am to 1 pm Sunday to Thursday and 10 am to noon on Friday for applications, although you have to go back between 4 and 5 pm (2 to 3 pm on Friday) to retrieve your passport. It's wise to start the process early as renewing a visa or obtaining a trekking permit can be time-consuming. See Visas in the Facts for the Visitor chapter for more details.

Medical Services

The centrally located, government-operated Bir Hospital (☎ 221119) cannot be recommended. The best bet in the Kathmandu Valley is the Patan Hospital (☎ 522278), which is partially staffed by western missionaries and is in the Lagankhel district of Patan, close to the last stop of the Lagankhel bus. Bear in mind that they have to give reasonable care to as many people as possible. The hospital also has an ambulance service (☎ 527003). Also reasonably well equipped is the Teaching Hospital (☎ 412404) in Maharajganj (they have a ventilator).

The CIWEC clinic (☎ 228531, fax 241732, email advice@ciwecpc.mos.com.np) just off Durbar Marg is used by many foreign residants of Kathmandu. It has operated since 1982 and has developed an international reputation for research into travellers' medical problems. It's open from 9 am to noon and 1 to 4 pm weekdays and is staffed by westerners. With a single visit costing around $30, it is hardly surprising the clientele is almost exclusively western as well.

The Nepal International Clinic (☎ 412842, email nic@naxal.wlink.com.np) is near the Jaya Nepal cinema, close to Thamel. It has an excellent reputation and is cheaper than the CIWEC clinic. It's open from 9 am to 5 pm every day; a consultation costs about $25.

If you need an optometrist, Mr Kaiser Malla (☎ 222504) in Bagh Bazaar near the French Cultural Centre, is recommended. For dental work, the American dental clinic (☎ 249517), in front of the American Club (part of the US embassy) on Kantipath, or the Belgian-Nepali joint venture HOPE Dental Centre (☎ 423411, afternoon only) in Lazimpat are both reliable.

continued on page 150

DURBAR SQUARE (Kathmandu)

Durbar in Nepali means 'palace' and in Patan and Bhaktapur, as well as Kathmandu, there are durbar squares in front of the old palaces. The king no longer lives in the old Royal Palace in Kathmandu: the palace was moved north to Narayanhiti about a century ago. At that time it was on the edge of the city, now it's close to the popular tourist area of Thamel.

Clustered around the central Durbar Square are the old Royal Palace (Hanuman Dhoka), numerous interesting temples, the Kumari Chowk or Kumari Bahal (House of the Living Goddess) and the Kasthamandap (House of Wood).

It's easy to spend hours wandering around Durbar Square and the adjoining Basantapur Square. This is very much the centre of old Kathmandu and watching the world go by from the terraced platforms of the towering Maju Deval is a wonderful way to get a feel for the city. Although many of the buildings around the square are very old, a great deal of damage was caused by the great earthquake of 1934 and many were rebuilt, not always in their original form.

The Durbar Square area is actually made up of three loosely linked squares. To the south is the open Basantapur Square area, off which runs Freak St. The main Durbar Square area, with its popular watch-the-world-go-by temples, is to the west. Running north-east is a second part of Durbar Square which contains the entrance to the old Royal Palace and an assortment of temples. From this open area Makhan Tole, at one time the main road in Kathmandu and still the most interesting street to walk down, continues north-east.

A good place to start an exploration of the square is with what may well be the oldest building in the valley, the unprepossessing Kasthamandap. (Note: the numbers in the following sections correspond to item numbers on the key for the Durbar Square (Kathmandu) map.)

Kasthamandap (36)

In the south-western corner of the square the Kasthamandap, or House of Wood, is the building which gave Kathmandu its name. Although its history is uncertain, it was possibly constructed around the 12th century. A legend relates that the whole building was made with the wood from a single sal tree. At first it was a community centre where visitors gathered before major ceremonies, but later it was converted to a temple to Gorakhnath.

A small wooden enclosure in the centre of the building houses the image of the god. Images of Ganesh can be found at each corner of the building and there are also shrines to a number of other gods. Bronze lions guard the entrance, and Hindu epics are illustrated around the 1st-floor cornices of the three-storey building.

The squat, medieval-looking building is busy in the early-morning hours when porters sit here waiting for customers.

Kasthamandap

Ashok Binayak (34)

On the northern side of the Kasthamandap, at the top of Maru Tole (the laneway down to the river), stands the tiny Ashok Binayak, or Maru Ganesh Shrine. The small size of this shrine belies its importance, as this is one of the four most important Ganesh shrines in the valley. Ganesh is a much-loved god and there is a constant stream of visitors here. A visit to this shrine is highly recommended by Hindus to ensure safety on a forthcoming journey. It's uncertain how old the temple is, although its gilded roof was added in the 19th century.

Shiva Temple (35)

The Shiva Temple near the Kasthamandap and the Ashok Binayak is used by vegetable sellers, and occasionally by barbers who can generally be seen squatting on the temple platform, administering 'short back and sides'.

Maru Tole

Maru Tole leads down to the Vishnumati River where a footbridge meets the pathway to Swayambhunath on the other side. This was a busy street in the days of hippies and flower power, but today there's little sign of why it should have been called either Pie or Pig Alley – not only are the pie shops gone but it's also much cleaner. One thing Maru Tole does have is Maru Hiti, one of the finest sunken water conduits in the city.

Maju Deval (32)

A pleasant hour can easily be spent sitting on the platform steps of the Shiva temple known as the Maju Deval. From here you can watch the constant activity of fruit and vegetable hawkers, the comings and goings of taxis and rickshaws, and the flute and other souvenir sellers importuning tourists. The nine stage platform of the Maju Deval is probably the most popular meeting place in the city. The large, triple roofed temple has erotic carvings on its roof struts and offers great views over the square and across the roofs of the city.

The temple dates from 1690 and was built by the mother of Bhaktapur's King Bhupatindra Malla. Although the temple has a well known Shiva lingam inside, the roof is topped by a pinnacle shaped like a Buddhist stupa. At the bottom of the temple stairway is a small temple to Kam Dev, a 'companion' of Shiva. It was built in the Indian *shikhara* style, with a tall corncob-like spire.

Maju Deval

Trailokya Mohan Narayan Temple (41)

The other temple standing in the open area of the square is the smaller five tiered, three roofed Trailokya Mohan Narayan. The temple was built by Prithvibendra Malla in 1680 and is easily identified as a temple to Narayan or Vishnu by the fine Garuda kneeling before it. The Garuda figure was a later addition, erected by the king's widow soon after his death. Look for the Vaishnavite images on the carved roof struts and the window screens with their decoratively carved medallions.

DURBAR SQUARE (KATHMANDU)

To Thamel • To Kot Square • To Indra Chowk

Police Headquarters

0   250   500 m

Makhan Tole

Sundari Chowk

Mohan Chowk

Hanuman Dhoka

Nasal Chowk

Mul Chowk

Dahk Chowk

Durbar Square

Lohan Chowk

HANUMAN DHOKA (Old Royal Palace)

Hnuluche Chowk

Lam Chowk

Maru Tole

Kumari Chowk

Basantapur Durbar

Ganga Path

Basantapur Square

Surkha Path

New Road

Dharma Path

See Freak Street Map p170

Shiva-Parvati Temple (30)

From the steps of the Maju Deval you can look across the square to the Shiva-Parvati Temple, where images of Shiva and his consort look out from the upstairs window on the comings and goings below them. The temple was built in the late 1700s by Bahadur Shah, son of Prithvi Narayan Shah. Although the temple is not very old by Kathmandu standards, it stands on a two stage platform which may have been an open dancing stage hundreds of years earlier. A Narayan (Vishnu) Temple stands to one side of it.

Kumari Bahal (42)

At the junction of Durbar and Basantapur squares is a white three storey building with intricately carved windows. The Kumari Bahal (House of the Living Goddess) faces Durbar Square, its door guarded by stone lions. The building, in the style of the courtyarded Buddhist *viharas* (abodes) of the valley, was built in 1757 by Jaya Prakash Malla. Inside lives the young girl (the Kumari) who is selected to be the town's living goddess, until she reaches puberty and reverts to being a normal mortal!

Inside the building the three storey courtyard, or Kumari Chowk, is enclosed by magnificently carved wooden balconies

Kumari Bahal

PLACES TO STAY
8 Kathmandu Lodge
39 Kumari Guest House
50 Hotel Classic

PLACES TO EAT
2 Festive Fare Restaurant

OTHER
1 Mahendreshwar Temple
3 Tana Deval Temple
4 Taleju Temple
5 Mahavishnu Temple
6 Kotilingeshwar Mahadev Temple
7 Kakeshwar Temple
9 Great Drums
10 Krishna Temple
11 Saraswati Temple
12 Stone Vishnu Temple

13 Great Bell
14 King Pratap Malla's Column
15 Jagannath Temple
16 Kala (Black) Bhairab
17 Indrapur Temple
18 Vishnu Temple
19 Stone Inscription
20 Mohan Tower
21 Hanuman Statue
22 Audience Chamber
23 Narsingha Statue
24 Panch Mukhi Hanuman Temple
25 Dancing Shiva Statue
26 Tribhuvan Museum
27 Degutaleju Temple
28 Seto (White) Bhairab
29 Bhagwati Temple
30 Shiva-Parvati Temple
31 Narayan Temple

32 Maju Deval
33 Lakshmi Narayan Temple
34 Ashok Binayak (Maru Ganesh Shrine)
35 Shiva Temple
36 Kasthamandap (House of Wood)
37 Singh Sattal
38 Kabindrapur Temple
40 Garuda Statue
41 Trailokya Mohan Narayan Temple
42 Kumari Bahal
43 Gaddhi Baithak
44 Coronation Platform
45 Kirtipur Tower
46 Basantapur Tower
47 Patan (Lalitpur) Tower
48 Bhaktapur Tower (Lakshmi Bilas)
49 Tourist Office

and windows. Photographing the goddess is forbidden, but you are quite free to photograph the courtyard when she is not present. Westerners are not allowed to go beyond this area. The courtyard contains a miniature stupa carrying the symbols of Saraswati, the goddess of learning.

The big gate beside the Kumari Bahal conceals the huge chariot which takes the Kumari around the city of Kathmandu once a year, a festival begun during the rule of Jaya Prakash Malla.

Gaddi Baithak (43)
The eastern side of Durbar Square is closed off by this white neoclassical building. The Gaddi Baithak with its imported European style was built as part of the palace during the Rana period and makes a strange contrast to the traditional Nepali architecture that dominates the square.

Bhagwati Temple (29)
Next to the Gaddi Baithak, this triple storey, triple roofed temple is easily missed since it surmounts the building below it, which has *thangka* (religious Tibetan painting in cloth) shops along its front. The best view of the temple with its golden roofs is probably from the Maju Deval across the square. The temple was built by Jagat Jaya Malla and originally had an image of Narayan. This image was stolen in 1766, so when Prithvi Narayan Shah conquered the valley two years later he simply substituted it with an image of the goddess Bhagwati, which he just happened to be toting around with him. In April each year the image of the goddess is conveyed to the village of Nuwakot, 65km to the north, then returned a few days later.

A succession of interesting buildings and statues stand to the northeast of the Bhagwati Temple.

Great Bell (13)

On your left as you leave the main square along Makhan Tole is the Great Bell erected by Rana Bahadur Shah (son of Prithvi Narayan Shah) in 1797. During the Malla era a novel addition to one of the valley's Durbar squares would almost immediately be imitated in another. Curiously, Patan and Bhaktapur got their bells in 1736, while the Kathmandu version did not follow until long after the fall of the Mallas. The bell's ring will drive off evil spirits, but it is only rung during *puja* (worship) at the Degutaleju Temple (27).

Stone Vishnu Temple (12)

Next to the bell is a small stone Vishnu Temple about which very little is known. It was badly damaged by the earthquake of 1934 and has only recently been restored.

Saraswati Temple (11)

Next is the Saraswati Temple which also suffered badly from the great earthquake. Prior to the quake it was over 14m high, but now is only half that height. Like the adjoining Vishnu Temple, little is known about its history.

Krishna Temple (10)

The history of the octagonal Krishna Temple is well documented. It was built in 1648 by Pratap Malla, perhaps as a reply to Siddhinarsingh's magnificent Krishna Mandir in Patan. Inside there are images of Krishna and two goddesses which, according to a Sanskrit inscription, are modelled on the king and his two wives! The temple also has a Newari inscription but this neglects to mention the king's little act of vanity.

Krishna Temple

Just beyond the temple are the **Great Drums** (9) to which a goat and a buffalo must be sacrificed twice a year. Then there is the police headquarters building, beyond which is **Kot Square.** It was here that Jung Bahadur Rana perpetrated the famous 1846 massacre which led to a hundred years of Rana rule. *Kot* means 'armoury' or 'fort'. During the Durga Puja festival each year, blood again flows in Kot Square as hundreds of buffaloes and goats are sacrificed. Young soldiers are supposed to lop each head off with a single blow.

King Pratap Malla's Column (14)

Across from the Krishna Temple is a host of smaller temples and other structures, all standing on a huge raised platform in front of the old Royal Palace and the towering Taleju Temple (4). The square stone pillar, known as the Pratap Dhvaja, is topped by a statue of the famous King Pratap Malla, seated with folded hands and surrounded by his two wives, his four sons and another, infant, son. He looks towards his private prayer room on the 3rd floor of the Degutaleju Temple (27). The column was erected in 1670 by Pratap Malla and preceded the similar columns in Patan and Bhaktapur.

This area and its monuments are usually covered in hundreds if not thousands of pigeons, and you can buy packets of grain to feed them.

Seto Bhairab (28)

Seto (White) Bhairab's horrible face is hidden away behind a grille opposite the Pratap Malla column. The huge mask dates from 1794 during the reign of Rana Bahadur Shah, the third Shah dynasty king. Each September during the Indra Jatra festival the gates are swung back to reveal the mask for a few days. At that time the face is covered in flowers and rice and at the start of the festivities beer is poured through the horrific mouth. Crowds of men fight to get a drink of this blessed beer! At other times of year you can peek through the lattice to see the mask, which is used as the symbol of Royal Nepal Airlines.

Jagannath Temple (15)

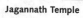

This temple, noted for the erotic carvings on its roof struts, is the oldest structure in this part of the square. Pratap Malla claimed to have constructed the temple during his reign but it may actually be much older, dating back to 1563 during the rule of Mahendra Malla. The temple has a three tiered platform and two storeys. There are three doors on each side of the temple but only the centre door opens.

Jagannath Temple

Kala Bhairab (16)

Behind the Jagannath Temple is the large figure of Kala (Black) Bhairab. Bhairab is Shiva in his most fearsome aspect and this huge stone image of the terrifying Kala Bhairab has six arms, wears a garland of skulls and tramples a corpse, symbolic of mankind's ignorance. The figure was said to have been brought here by Pratap Malla, having been found in a field to the north of the city. The image was originally cut from a single stone although the upper right-hand side has been repaired with another stone, and the sun and moon to the left and the lions at the top are later additions. It is said that telling a lie while standing before Kala Bhairab will bring instant death and it was once used as a form of trial by ordeal!

Indrapur Temple (17)

Immediately to the east of horrific Bhairab stands the mysterious Indrapur Temple. This curious temple may be of great antiquity but little is known of its history. Even the god to which it is dedicated is controversial – inside there is a lingam indicating that it is a Shiva temple. But half-buried on the southern side of the temple is a Garuda image, indicating that the temple is to Vishnu. And to compound the puzzle the temple's name clearly indicates it is dedicated to Indra! The temple's simple design and plain roof struts together with the lack of an identifying *torana* (the space above temple doors indicating the deity to which the temple is dedicated) give no further clues.

Vishnu Temple (18)

Little is known about the adjoining Vishnu Temple either. This triple roofed temple stands on a four-level base. The roof strut carvings and the golden image of Vishnu inside show that it is a Vishnu temple, but it is not known how old it is, although it was in existence during Pratap Malla's reign.

Kakeshwar Temple (7)

Kakeshwar Temple

North of the Vishnu Temple, this temple was originally built in 1681 but rebuilt after it was badly damaged in the 1934 earthquake. It may have been considerably altered at that time as the temple is a strange combination of styles, starting with a two level base from which rises a lower floor in typical Nepali style. Above the 1st floor, however, the temple is in Indian shikhara style, topped by a spire shaped like a water vase or *kalasa*, indicative of a female deity.

Stone Inscription (19)

On the outside of the palace wall, opposite the Vishnu Temple (18) is a stone inscription to the goddess Kalika written in 15 languages, including French. King Pratap Malla, renowned for his scholastic abilities, set up this inscription in 1664 and a Nepali legend relates that milk will flow from the spout in the middle if somebody is able to read all the languages!

Kotilingeshwar Mahadev Temple (6)

This early Malla temple dates from the reign of Mahendra Malla in the 16th century. The three stage plinth is topped by a temple in the *gumbhaj* style, which basically means a square structure topped by a dome. The bull facing the temple indicates that it is a Shiva temple.

Mahavishnu Temple (5)

Built by Jagat Jaya Malla, this double roofed temple on a four level plinth was badly damaged in the 1934 earthquake and was not restored. Only the golden spire on the roof, topped by a golden umbrella, hints at its prior appearance.

Mahendreshwar Temple (1)

At the extreme northern end of the square, this temple dates from 1561, during Mahendra Malla's reign. The temple was restored in 1963 and is dedicated to Shiva. A small image of Shiva's bull Nandi fronts the temple and at the north-eastern corner there is an image of Kam Dev. The temple has a wide, two level plinth and a spire topped by a golden umbrella.

Taleju Temple (4)

The square's most magnificent temple stands at its north-eastern extremity but is not open to the public. Even Nepalis can only visit the temple during the annual Dasain festival.

The Taleju Temple was built in 1564 by Mahendra Malla. Taleju Bhawani was originally a goddess from the south of India, but she became the titular deity or royal goddess of the Malla kings in the 14th century. Taleju temples were erected in her honour in Patan and Bhaktapur as well as in Kathmandu.

Taleju Temple

The temple stands on a 12 stage plinth and reaches over 35m high, dominating the Durbar Square area. The eighth stage of the plinth has a wall around the temple, in front of which are 12 miniature temples; four more miniature temples stand inside the wall which has four wide and beautifully carved gates. If entry to the temple were permitted it could be reached from within the palace or from the Singh Dhoka (Lion Gate) from the square.

HANUMAN DHOKA (OLD ROYAL PALACE)

Hanuman's brave assistance to noble Rama during the exciting events of the *Ramayana* has led to the monkey god's appearance guarding many important entrances. Here, cloaked in red and sheltered by an umbrella, a **Hanuman statue** (21) marks the entrance, or *dhoka*, to Kathmandu's old Royal Palace and has even given the palace its name. The statue dates from 1672, but the face has disappeared under a coating of red paste applied by faithful visitors.

Standards bearing the double-triangle flag of Nepal flank the statue while on each side of the palace gate are stone lions, one ridden by Shiva, the other by his wife Parvati. Above the gate a brightly painted niche is illustrated, with a figure of a ferocious Tantric version of Krishna in the centre. On one side is the gentler Hindu Krishna in his traditional blue colour accompanied by two of his comely *gopis* (milk-maids). On the other side is King Pratap Malla and his queen.

The palace was originally founded during the Licchavi period, but as it stands today most of it was constructed by King Pratap Malla in the 17th century. The palace was renovated many times in later years. The oldest parts are the smaller Sundari Chowk and Mohan Chowk at the northern part of the palace (both closed). From here construction moved south and in all there are 10 courtyards, or chowks, in the palace.

Entrance to the palace costs Rs 250 and it is open daily (except Tuesday) from 10.30 am to 3 pm (4 pm in summer).

Nasal Chowk

From the entrance gate you immediately enter the most famous chowk. *Nasal* means 'dancing one', and the courtyard takes its name from a small figure of the **Dancing Shiva** (25) inside the whitewashed chamber on the eastern side of the square. Although the courtyard was constructed in the Malla period many of the buildings around the square were Rana constructions. During that time the Nasal Chowk became the square used for coronations, a practice which continues to this day. King Birendra was crowned in the 1975 ceremony on the platform (44) in the centre of the courtyard. The nine storey Basantapur Tower (46) looms over the southern end of the courtyard.

The rectangular courtyard is aligned north-south and the entrance is at the north-western corner. Near the entrance there is a surprisingly small but beautifully carved doorway which once led to the Malla kings' private quarters. The panels have images of four gods.

Beyond the door is a large **statue of Narsingha** (23), Vishnu in his man-lion incarnation in the act of killing a demon. The stone image was erected by Pratap Malla in 1673 and the inscription on the pedestal explains that he placed it here in fear that he had offended Vishnu by dancing in a Narsingha costume. The **Kabindrapur Temple** (38) in Durbar Square was built for the same reason.

Next there is the **Audience Chamber** (22) of the Malla kings. The open veranda houses the Malla throne and portraits of the Shah kings. A golden image of Mahavishnu is set into an open veranda on the eastern wall. This image was originally in the **Mahavishnu Temple** (5) in the square, but was moved here after the 1934 earthquake.

Panch Mukhi Hanuman Temple (24)

At the north-eastern corner of the Nasal Chowk stands the Panch Mukhi Hanuman with its five circular roofs. Each of the valley towns has a five storey temple, although it is the great Nyatapola Temple of Bhaktapur which is by far the best known. Hanuman is worshipped in the temple in Kathmandu but only the priests of the temple may enter it.

Basantapur Tower (46)

King Prithvi Narayan Shah was involved in the construction of the four red-coloured towers around the Lohan Chowk. The towers represent the four ancient cities of the valley: the Kathmandu or Basantapur Tower, the Kirtipur Tower (45), the Bhaktapur Tower or Lakshmi Bilas (48) and the Patan or Lalitpur Tower (47).

The dominant nine storey Basantapur Tower was extensively restored prior to King Birendra's coronation. A series of steep stairways climbs to the top from where there are superb views over the palace and the city. The struts along the facade of the Basantapur Tower, particularly those facing out to Basantapur Square, are decorated with erotic carvings.

Mul Chowk

This courtyard was completely dedicated to religious functions within the palace and is configured like a vihara (a dwelling place for Buddhist monks), with a two storey building surrounding the courtyard. Mul Chowk is dedicated to Taleju Bhawani, the royal goddess of the Mallas, and sacrifices are made to her in the centre of the courtyard during the Dasain festival. A smaller Taleju temple stands in the southern wing of the square and the image of the goddess is moved here from the main Taleju Temple during the Dasain festival. Images of the river goddesses Ganga and Jamuna guard the golden temple doorway which is topped by a golden torana. Unfortunately, from the **Bhaktapur Tower** (48), where visitors normally observe the courtyard, the view is less than inspiring and the temple itself cannot be seen at all.

Degutaleju Temple (27)

Degutaleju is another manifestation of the Malla's personal goddess Taleju and this temple was built by Shiva Singh Malla and is integrated into the palace structure itself. The triple roofed temple actually starts from above the common buildings it surmounts.

Mohan Chowk

North of the Nasal Chowk is the residential courtyard of the Malla kings. It dates from 1649 and at one time a Malla king had to be born here to be eligible to wear the crown. The last Malla king, Jaya Prakash Malla, had great difficulties during his reign, even though he was the legitimate heir, because he was born elsewhere. The golden water-spout, known as Sun Dhara, in the centre of the courtyard delivers water from Budhanilkantha in the north of the valley. The richly sculptured spout is actually several metres below the courtyard level. The Malla kings would ritually bathe here each morning.

The courtyard is surrounded by towers at its four corners and north of the Mohan Chowk is the small Sundari Chowk.

Rana Additions & Tribhuvan Museum (26)

The part of the palace west of Nasal Chowk, overlooking the main Durbar Square area, was principally constructed by the Ranas in the mid to late part of the 19th century. Ironically, it is now home to an interesting museum that celebrates King Tribhuvan's successful revolt against their regime. If you are interested in Nepal's modern history a visit is a must. There are some fascinating re-creations of the king's bedroom and study with genuine personal effects that give quite an eerie insight into his life. There are also lots of photos and newspaper clippings that catch the drama of his escape and triumphant return. And there are several magnificent thrones, some superb stone carvings and, oddly, a coin collection.

Entry is from Nasal Chowk, and cameras have to be deposited in lockers at the door.

Mythological lions guard the entrance to Kumari Bahal, Durbar Square, Kathmandu.

PAUL BENSSEN

Marijuana

In Kathmandu's flower-power era in the 1960s and early 70s, the easy availability of marijuana and hashish was undoubtedly a major attraction. In its hippie heyday Kathmandu had hash shops and hash calendars, and hash cookies appeared on every hip restaurant menu. Many of the 'freaks' who congregated in Nepal in those days were high in places other than the Himalaya!

The drug had always been easily available, but its users were mainly sadhus, for whom it has religious importance. Then, in the run-up to King Birendra's coronation, hashish was banned and, possibly in protest, the huge Singh Durbar building, a palace from the Rana period, burnt down the next night.

Hashish is still banned, but illegal or not, it's readily available in Nepal, although potential smokers should keep the less than five star condition of Nepali jails firmly in mind. Don't try taking any out of the country either – travellers have been arrested at the airport on departure.

continued from page 139

Emergency

Red Cross Ambulance	☎ 228094
Police, Durbar Square	☎ 100, 223011
Fire Brigade	☎ 101, 221177

FREAK ST

Kathmandu's famous street from the old hippie days of the late 1960s and early 70s runs south from Basantapur Square. Its real name is still Jochne but since the early 70s it has been far better known as Freak St. In its hippie prime this was the place for cheap hotels, colourful restaurants, hashish shops, moneychangers and, of course, the weird and wonderful 'freaks' who gave the street its name. In those days Freak St was one of the great gathering places on the road east.

Times change and Freak St today is a pale shadow of its former self and, while there are still cheap hotels and restaurants, it's the Thamel area in the north of the town which is the main gathering place. However, for those people who find Thamel altogether too much of a scene, Freak St offers a quiet and interesting alternative. Its recent historical connections are interesting and you are right in the heart of old Kathmandu where real life continues.

WALKING TOURS

A stroll around Kathmandu will lead the casual wanderer to many intriguing sights, especially in the crowded maze of streets, courtyards and alleys in the market area north of Durbar Square. There are temples, shrines and many individual statues and sculptures hidden away in the most unlikely places. You really appreciate Kathmandu's museum-like quality when you stumble upon a 1000-year-old statue, something which would be a prize possession in many western museums, that here is being used as a children's plaything or a washing line. The walks described later can be made whenever you have an hour or two to spare. Walking Tour 1 and Walking Tour 2 can be used as routes from the accommodation centre of Thamel to the central Durbar Square area.

All the walks take you to a number of markets, temples and chowks, which are the centre of Nepali life. A number of chowks are surrounded by bahals or bahils, dwellings for monastic Buddhist communities, although none are used for that purpose today – they have been taken over by families and sometimes schools.

The courtyards may be large and open, dotted with *chaityas* (small stupas) and shrines, or they may be tightly enclosed within a single building. A bahil is distinguished from a bahal because it also includes accommodation for nonmonastic visitors, it is generally simpler, and the main shrine may not necessarily be in the centre of the courtyard.

The walks can be made as individual strolls or linked together into one longer walk. Walking Tour 1 gives you a taste of the crowded and fascinating shopping streets in the oldest part of Kathmandu and also takes you to some of the city's most important temples. Walking Tour 2 visits some very old bahals, an important Buddhist stupa, passes by a number of ancient and important stoneworks and introduces you to a toothache god. Walking Tour 3 takes you to a lesser known section of Kathmandu, without spectacular attractions but where the normal life of the city goes on and tourists are fairly rare.

Walking Tour 1 – North from Durbar Square

The road angling across the city from Durbar Square to the artificial lake of Rani Pokhari is the most interesting street in old Kathmandu. Modern roads like Durbar Marg are no match for this narrow artery's varied and colourful shops, temples and people. The road was at one time the main street in Kathmandu and the start of the route to Tibet. It was not replaced as Kathmandu's most important street until the construction of New Rd, after the great earthquake of 1934, and it was not paved until the 1960s.

Makhan Tole The crowded street known as Makhan Tole (*makhan* is Nepali for 'butter') starts from the north-eastern corner of Durbar Square, by the Taleju Temple, and runs towards the busy marketplace of Indra Chowk. Many worthwhile shops along this stretch of the street sell *thangkas*, paintings and clothes.

Directly across from the Taleju Temple, at the start of the street, is a kneeling 10th century **Garuda statue** (1). It faces a small Vishnu Temple. To your right, in a walled courtyard just past the long row of stalls, is the **Tana Deval Temple** (2) with three carved doorways and struts showing the multi-armed Ashta Matrikas (mother goddesses).

Indra Chowk The busy shopping street of Makhan Tole soon spills into Indra Chowk, the courtyard named after the ancient Vedic

deity, Indra. On the left of the square is a notable building which is covered in brightly coloured modern ceramic tiles. From the balcony four metal lions rear out over the street. This is the **Akash Bhairab Temple** (3) or Bhairab of the Sky Temple, which is actually upstairs; the ground floor is occupied by shop stalls.

To get to the temple you have to climb a flight of steps at the right-hand end of the building, guarded by two more metal lions. At the entrance a sign announces that non-Hindus may not enter, and in any case there's not much to see. The silver image is visible through the open windows from out in the street, and during important festivals, particularly Indra Jatra (August/September), the image is displayed in the square. A large lingam is also erected in the centre of the square at that time.

In a small niche just before the Akash Bhairab Temple is a very small but much visited brass **Ganesh shrine** (4). Indra Chowk is traditionally a centre for the sale of blankets and cloth and there are often many sellers and buyers on the platforms of the Mahadev Temple. Shawls and woollen rugs are sold from the platform of the **Shiva Temple** (5), which is a smaller and simplified version of Patan's Krishna Mandir.

From the south of the square Surkha Path leads to New Rd; the shops along this road sell consumer goods imported from Hong Kong and Singapore and many of them end up in India. The road heading directly north from Indra Chowk leads to Thamel. Before you leave Indra Chowk look for the narrow alley to the right, crowded with stalls selling the glass bangles and beads which are so popular with Nepali women.

Kel Tole It's only a short stroll from Indra Chowk to the next square, Kel Tole, where you'll find one of the most important and ornate temples in Kathmandu, the **Seto (White) Machhendranath Temple** (6). The arched entrance to the temple is guarded by a small Buddha figure on a high stone pillar, facing two metal lions. The temple attracts both Buddhists and Hindus as the

Buddhists consider Seto Machhendranath to be a form of Avalokiteshvara while to the Hindus he is an incarnation of Shiva who can bring rain. Although the temple's age is not known, it was restored during the 17th century.

In the courtyard there are numerous small shrines, chaityas and statues, including a mysteriously European-looking figure facing the temple. It may well have been an import from Europe, which has simply been accepted into the pantheon of gods. Facing the other way, just in front of the temple, are two graceful bronze figures of the Taras seated on top of tall pillars.

Inside the temple you can see the white-faced image of the god, sitting rather like a seated Buddha image. The image is taken out of the temple during the Seto Machhendranath festival in March/April each year and paraded around the city in a chariot. The procession finally ends at the Machhendranath Temple in the south of the city (visited on Walking Tour 3).

During the day Kel Tole is busy with worshippers, children playing and the people whose homes surround it.

As you leave the temple, to the right the small triple roofed **Lunchun Lunbun Ajima** (7) is a Tantric temple, white-tiled around the lower level and with some erotic carvings on the struts at the back. The diagonal street continues to Asan Tole, the busiest of the junctions along the old street (covered on Walking Tour 2). Walk partway towards Asan Tole to see the three, four and five

---

Erotic Art

The most interesting woodcarving on Nepali temples is on the roof struts, and on many temples these carvings include erotic scenes. These scenes are rarely the central carving on the strut, usually they're the smaller carving at the bottom of the strut, like a footnote to the larger image. Nor are they sensuous and finely sculptured like those at Khajuraho and Konark in India. In Nepal the figures are often smaller, cruder, even quite cartoon-like.

The themes have a Tantric element, a clear connection to the intermingling of Tibetan Buddhist and Hindu beliefs in Nepal, but their real purpose is unclear. Are they simply a celebration of an important part of the cycle of life? A more explicit reference to Shiva's and Parvati's creative roles than the enigmatic lingams and yonis scattered around so many temples? Or are they supposed to play some sort of protective role for the temple? It's popularly rumoured that the goddess of lightning is a shy virgin who wouldn't dream of striking a temple with such goings-on, although that's probably more a tourist-guide tale than anything else.

Whatever the reason for their existence the Tantric elements can be found on temples in all three of the major towns of the valley. On some temples it may just be the odd depiction here and there while on others something will be happening on every roof strut. The activities range from straightforward exhibitionism to the *mithuna* scenes of couples engaged in often quite athletic acts of intercourse. More exotic carvings include ménages à trois scenes of oral or anal intercourse or couplings with demons or animals. Temples with some of the more interesting erotic carvings include:

Kathmandu

In Durbar Square there are carvings on many of the roof struts of the Jagannath Temple just outside the Hanuman Dhoka palace entrance. The lofty Basantapur Tower of the old palace, overlooking Basantapur Square, has some of the finest erotic carvings on its roof struts. The large Shiva Temple in the middle of the square, also known as the Mahadev Temple or the Maju Deval Temple, is a popular place to watch the activity in the square and also has some erotic struts.

storey houses, tightly squeezed together on the right hand side of this stretch of the street. On the left, the polygonal **Krishna Temple** (8) is jammed between other buildings with the ground floor occupied by shops. The woodcarvings on this temple are very elaborate.

Return to Kel Tole and turn west. The shops along this stretch specialise in Nepali caps. At the next junction the large **Jana Bahal Temple** (9) is on your left. The domed temple is of little interest; it was probably hastily constructed after an earlier temple was destroyed, perhaps by an earthquake.

A Child-Eating Demon Continue across the junction and on your left you pass the small **Kilgal Tole** beside the road. It's a grubby little square with a decaying pagoda temple (10) and, in the middle, a fine chaitya with faces on each side.

An opening on your left leads into the long, rectangular **Yitum Bahal** court-yard (11). A small white-painted stupa (12) stands in the centre of the courtyard. Opposite it, on the western side of the courtyard, is one of the oldest bahals in the city, its entrance flanked by the usual stone lions. This is the **Kichandra Bahal** (13), dating from 1381. A chaitya (14) in front of the entrance is completely shattered by a *bodhi* tree which has grown right up through its centre.

Inside the Kichandra Bahal there is a pagoda-like sanctuary in the centre and to the south is a small chaitya decorated with

Erotic Art

North of the centre, near the restaurant and guesthouse centre of Thamel, the Three Goddesses Temples dedicated to Dakshinkali, Mankamna and Jawalamai have a number of interesting roof struts. The Indrani Temple, on the east bank of the Vishnumati River where you cross it going from Thamel to Swayambhunath, is another temple with interesting scenes. South of Durbar Square the small Ram Chandra Mandir has some tiny carvings on each of its roof struts.

Patan

In Patan's Durbar Square the Jagannarayan or Charnarayan Temple is the most interesting temple in the town for erotic carvings.

Bhaktapur

Several temples in Bhaktapur have erotic scenes including the Pashupatinath Temple in Durbar Square. There are also some carvings in the Cafe Nyatapola in Taumadhi Tole where the soaring five storey Nyatapola Temple is located. The Dattatraya Temple near the Pujari Math monastery in the eastern part of town also has low-relief figures around its base.

Elsewhere in the Valley

There are many other temples with erotic artwork around the valley. The Jal Binayak Temple dedicated to Ganesh at Chobar Gorge, just south of Patan, has many interesting roof struts as does the Mahadev Temple at Gokarna, east of Bodhnath. Other temples worth inspecting include the small Ajima or Shitala Devi Temple in the Mahendra park, near the sleeping Vishnu figure, and the Bagh Bhairab Temple in Kirtipur.

Several temples in and around Pashupatinath have erotic scenes but non-Hindus aren't permitted to enter the temple courtyards to see them. En route to Pashupatinath, however, you can visit the Mahadev Gyaneshwar in Deopatan, the village by Pashupatinath.

Bodhisattvas in a standing, rather than the usual sitting, position. On the northern side of the courtyard are four brass plaques mounted on the upper storey wall. The one on the extreme left shows a demon known as Guru Mapa taking a child from a woman and stuffing it greedily into his mouth. The demon had an appetite for bad children and the two central plaques show two more children, presumably lining up to be consumed! Eventually the demon was bought off with the promise of an annual feast of buffalo meat, and the plaque to the right shows him sitting down and dipping into a pot of food.

To this day Guru Mapa is said to live in a tree in the Tundikhel field and a buffalo is sacrificed to him every year. With such a clear warning on the end result of juvenile misbehaviour it's probably fitting that the courtyard houses a primary school, right under the Guru Mapa plaques!

Nara Devi Temple From Kichandra Bahal go back into the large courtyard, exit at the north and turn left. On your right at the next junction is the **Nara Devi Temple** (15) which gives the street its name. The temple is dedicated to Kali, Shiva's consort in her destructive incarnation, and is also known as the Seto Kali (White Kali) Temple.

Although the temple, with its three tiers, glowing golden roof and red and white guardian lions, is quite old, some of the decorations (including the black and white chequerboard paint) are clearly much later additions. Kali's powers protected the temple from the 1934 earthquake which destroyed so many other temples in the valley. A Malla king once stipulated that a dancing ceremony should be held for the goddess every 12 years and dances are still performed on the small platform (16) across the road. Hidden away across the road is a three roofed **Narsingha**

WALKING TOUR 1

To Thamel

To Thamel

0   50   100 m

Kilgal Tole

To Asan Tole

Kel Tole

Glass-Bead Shops

Makhan Tole

Sukha Path

Indra Chowk

Kot Square

Thangka Shops

Shops

FINISH

START

Durbar Square

Hanuman Dhoka (Old Royal Palace)

To New Road

1   Garuda Statue
2   Tana Deval Temple
3   Akash Bhairab Temple
4   Ganesh Shrine
5   Shiva Temple
6   Seto (White) Machhendranath Temple
7   Lunchun Lunbun Ajima
8   Krishna Temple
9   Jana Bahal Temple
10 Pagoda Temple Platform
11 Yitum Bahal
12 Stupa
13 Kichandra Bahal
14 Chaitya
15 Nara Devi Temple
16 Dance Platform
17 Wooden Window
18 Yatkha Bahal
19 Kathmandu Lodge

Temple to Vishnu as the demon-destroying man-lion. You have to find your way to it through a maze of small courtyards.

Postage Stamp Window At the Nara Devi corner turn left (south) and you soon come to a nondescript modern building on your left with an utterly magnificent wooden window (17). It has been called *deshay madu* in Nepali, which means 'there is not another one like it'. An Rs 0.50 postage stamp issued in 1978 showed the window. Next to the building is a recently restored triple roofed pagoda which serves as a locater.

A little farther south and on your right is the entrance to the **Yatkha Bahal** (18), a huge open courtyard with an unremarkable stupa in the centre. Directly behind it is an old building which used to have its projecting upper storey supported by four superb carved wooden struts. Dating from the 14th century, they were carved in the form of *yakshis*, or nymphs, one of them gracefully balancing a baby on her hip. Unfortunately they have been removed, hopefully just for refurbishment and replacement.

Back on the road and heading south you soon pass Kot Square, scene of the great massacre that brought the Ranas to power in 1846. The Kathmandu Lodge (19) is on your right and you soon see Durbar Square ahead.

Walking Tour 2 – South of Thamel

The second walk can be started from the southern end of Thamel or can easily be linked to Walking Tour 1 to make a figure eight either from Thamel or Durbar Square. This walk can be started from Thahiti Tole or, if that's hard to find, from the Hotel Gautam on Kantipath. To get to Thahiti Tole walk south from Thamel on the road from the main Thamel Chowk; the first open square is Thahiti.

Thahiti Tole In the stupa (1) in the centre of the square is a stone inscription indicating it was constructed in the 15th century. Legends relate that it was built over a pond

which was plated with gold and the stupa served to keep thieves at bay. Or perhaps the pond was full of dangerous snakes and the stupa kept the snakes in their place – these legends vary!

The **Nateshwar Temple** (2), on the northern side of the square, is dedicated to Shiva and the metal plates on the doors show creatures busily playing a variety of musical instruments. Above the door are somewhat crudely painted pictures of Shiva's *ganas*, or companions, in this case a skeleton-like creature and what looks like a yeti.

Two Ancient Bahals Leave the north-eastern corner of the square taking the narrow road running east. You soon come to the entrance of the **Musya Bahal** (3) on your right, with a modern facade but guarded by white lions. The road continues east and then takes a right-left bend at the corner of which is a second, and much better preserved, old monastery, the **Chusya Bahal** (4).

This stretch of street is popular with potters and you often see them working in the road outside the bahals, or see their products piled up inside. Often it's just the simple little disposable cups used by *chia* sellers.

Beyond the second bahal there's a string of upper-level budget hotels and, right at the Kantipath intersection, the Hotel Gautam (5). Turn south and cross the road to the Rani Pokhari.

Rani Pokhari The large fenced lake called Rani Pokhari (Queen's Pond) was built by King Pratap Malla in 1667 to console his queen over the death of their son. Various legends and tales are connected with the tank and it's believed that it may actually have been built by Pratap Malla at an earlier date and only renamed for his queen after their son died; according to records the son was trampled by an elephant.

Unfortunately the gate to the tank is kept locked except on one day each year during the festival of Deepawali; you will have to be content with peering through the fence. A causeway leads across the tank to a small and undistinguished **Shiva Temple** (7).

Across Kantipath from the tank is the long building originally known as the Durbar School, which was the first school in Nepal. It has been renamed the **Bhanubhakta School** after the Nepali poet of that name. Retrace your steps north to the junction at the north-western corner of the Rani Pokhari and cross Kantipath to Bhothahiti, and then walk south-west past the bicycle and clothing shops to Asan Tole.

Asan Tole From dawn until late at night, Asan Tole is jammed with buyers, sellers and passers-by. The six roads meeting at this junction make it the busiest junction in Kathmandu. Every day produce is carried to this popular marketplace from all over the valley so it is fitting that the three storey

Annapurna Temple (8) is dedicated to the goddess of abundance, Annapurna. The smaller two storey pagoda (9) is dedicated to Ganesh. On the left-hand (western) side of the square are shops which sell spices and dried fruit. Near the centre of the square is a small Narayan or Vishnu Temple (10).

Sore Eyes & Toothache Take the road leading directly west out of Asan Tole and after a short distance, on your left, an anonymous entrance leads into **Haku Bahal** (11). Look for the sign advertising 'The Optic House'. This tiny bahal has a finely carved wooden window overlooking the courtyard.

A few strides farther you come to the triple roofed **Ugratara Temple** (12), directly across from a small lane which heads off

Asan's Fish

A few steps in front of the Annapurna Temple in Asan Tole is a paving stone with a foot-shaped depression which is said to be of a fish. Since the square is almost always crowded it can be difficult see – but don't worry, it is there, and an interesting little legend relates how this 'fish' fell out of the sky one day.

Once upon a time a famous astrologer named Barami was about to become a father. A bell would be rung to announce the birth of his child so he waited expectantly in his study. At the instant that he heard the sound of the bell across the rooftops, he cast his newborn son's horoscope, and discovered to his horror that he was not the father. In anger and disgust he abandoned his wife and new child and fled from the kingdom. Not until many years later did he return to Kathmandu where he became the pupil of a younger but even more brilliant astrologer named Dak.

As a final test Dak asked Barami to foretell what miraculous event would shortly occur in Asan Tole. Barami correctly predicted that a fish would fall from the heavens, and he correctly predicted the exact time this strange event would occur, but he missed by several steps the exact place where it would crash to earth. His teacher suggested that he had forgotten to take account of the wind. Sure enough this was found to be the case.

Barami realised he had forgotten to take account of the wind once before: on the occasion that the sound of a bell carried to his ears the news of his son's birth. Correcting for the wind factor Barami once again cast his son's horoscope. To his delight he discovered that it was indeed his own son, and to his amazement that the boy's name was Dak!

This left Dak and Barami with a peculiar problem: a son must revere his father and a pupil must revere his teacher yet here the son had been teaching the father. Eventually the decision was reached that father and son should jointly erect a monument to the event that had brought them together again. And there it is in Asan Tole, a small memorial to a fish that fell out of the sky.

north. Come here if your eyes are sore: a prayer at the shrine is said to work wonders for the eyes. A few steps farther along is a small sunken shrine (13) and you then arrive at a crossroads with an open square to the north. Turn left (south) and on your left you will see a lump of wood (14) into which thousands coins have been nailed. A coin and nail embedded in the wood is supposed to cure toothache, and the deity who looks after this ailment is represented by a tiny image in the ugly lump of wood. The square at the junction here is known as Bangemudha, which means 'twisted wood'.

Ancient Buddha Turn north again to the open square where the small double roofed **Ikha Narayan Temple** (15) is easily identified by the kneeling Garuda figure in front of it. The temple houses a beautiful 10th or 11th century four-armed Vishnu figure. The square also has a fine image of the goddess Saraswati (16) playing her lute.

The northern side of the square is closed off by a modern building with shops shut by roller doors on the ground floor. In the middle of this nondescript frontage, directly beneath an upper storey sign announcing 'Photo Copy' is a standing Buddha figure (17), framed by modern blue and white tilework. The image is only about 60cm high but it dates from the 5th or 6th century. A very similar Buddha figure stands on the riverbank near the temple of Pashupatinath.

If the toothache god hasn't done his duty you now pass a string of dentists' shops, proclaimed by the standard signs showing a smiling mouthful of teeth. On the right there's a small open area surrounded by concrete with a red-coloured Ganesh head and then a small but intricate stone relief (18) dating from the 9th century. It shows Shiva sitting with Parvati on Mt Kailash, her hand resting proprietorially on his knee in the pose known as *Uma Maheshwar*. Various deities and creatures, including Shiva's bull Nandi, stand around them.

There's an impressive wooden balcony across the road which is said to have had the first glass windows in Kathmandu. Nearby is a rather worn out, and bricked-in, stone trough. A little farther on your left a single

WALKING TOUR 2

1 Stupa
2 Nateshwar Temple
3 Musya Bahal
4 Chusya Bahal
5 Hotel Gautam
6 Aroma Restaurant
7 Shiva Temple
8 Annapurna Temple
9 Ganesh Pagoda
10 Narayan Temple
11 Haku Bahal
12 Ugratara Temple
13 Sunken Shrine
14 Wood With Coins
15 Ikha Narayan Temple
16 Saraswati Shrine
17 Buddha Statue
18 Stone Relief
19 Nag Bahal
20 Kathesimbhu Stupa
21 Avalokiteshvara Statue

broken stone lion (his partner has disappeared) guards a passageway above which hangs a carved wooden torana. Inside is the small enclosed courtyard of the **Nag Bahal** (19), with painted murals above the shrine, which is flanked by banners with double-triangle flags.

Mini Swayambhunath Just a couple of steps beyond the Nag Bahal entranceway is a wider entrance to the **Kathesimbhu Stupa** (20), just south of Thahiti Tole. The entrance is flanked by stone lions which have been beheaded, and more-recent metal lions atop tall concrete pillars.

In the courtyard is a copy, dating from around 1650, of the great Swayambhunath complex outside Kathmandu. If a devotee is unable to make the ascent to Swayambhunath then a circuit of this miniature replica is said to be a good substitute. Just as at Swayambhunath, there is a small pagoda to Harti, the goddess of smallpox, right behind the main stupa.

Various statues and smaller chaityas stand around the temple including, off the north-east of the stupa, a fine standing image of Avalokiteshvara (21) enclosed in a glass case and protective metal cage. He carries a lotus flower in his left hand, and the Dhyani Buddha Amitabha is seen in the centre of his crown with downcast eyes.

From Kathesimbhu it's only a short walk north to Thahiti Tole, the starting point of Walking Tour 2.

Walking Tour 3 – South from Durbar Square

Starting from beside the Kasthamandap in Durbar Square another circular walk can be made to the older parts in the south of the city. This area is not as packed with historical interest as the walks north of Durbar Square, but the streets are less crowded and you are far less likely to run into other tourists.

Bhimsen Temple Starting from the Kasthamandap (1) in the south-western corner of Durbar Square, the road out of the square forks almost immediately around the

Singh Sattal (2), a squat building with small shop stalls around the ground floor and golden-winged lions guarding each corner of the upper floor. Take the road running to the right of this building and you soon come to a square tank-like *hiti* (3), or water conduit, where men will usually be washing clothes.

Immediately beyond this is the highly decorated Bhimsen Temple (4) which is fronted by a brass lion on a pillar and has white-painted lions guarding the two front corners. Bhimsen is supposed to watch over traders and artisans so it's quite appropriate that the ground floor of this well-kept temple should be devoted to shop stalls. Immediately beyond the Bhimsen Temple a road branches off down to the river and across to the National Museum and Swayambhunath.

Jaisi Deval Temple Continue south beyond the Bhimsen Temple then turn sharp left (uphill) where the road ends. At the top of the hill you'll come out by the tall, triple roofed, 17th century Jaisi Deval Temple (5), which stands on a seven level base. This is a Shiva Temple, as shown by the bull on the first few steps and the mildly erotic carvings on some of the temple struts. Right across the road from the temple is a stone lingam (6) rising a good 2m from a yoni. This is definitely a god-sized phallic symbol and a prayer here is said to aid fertility.

In its procession around the town during the Indra Jatra festival, the Kumari Devi's chariot pauses here. During its stop, dances are held on the small platform (7) across the road from the temple.

Ram Chandra Mandir Cross the road from the broken chaitya (8) and enter the courtyard of the Ram Chandra Mandir (9). This small temple is notable for the tiny erotic scenes on its roof struts. This is straightforward sex and no funny business; it looks as if the carver set out to illustrate 16 different positions, starting with the missionary position, and just about made it before running out of ideas.

Bahals & Machhendranath Temple
There are a series of bahals on the next stretch of the walk but most of them are of little interest. Cross the road from the Ram Chandra Mandir and enter the small courtyard of the **Takan Bahal** (10). The surprisingly large 14th century stupa in the centre has recently been restored and is now in fine condition.

The road continues with a few slight bends then turns sharply back at Wonde junction marked by several temples, including a taller shikhara-style temple (11).

WALKING TOUR 3

1 Kasthamandap	10 Takan Bahal
2 Singh Sattal	11 Shikhara Temple
3 Hiti (Water Conduit)	12 Musum Bahal
4 Bhimsen Temple	13 Bahal & Many Chaityas
5 Jaisi Deval Temple	14 Machhendranath
6 Stone Lingam	Temple
7 Dance Platform	15 Hari Shankar Temple
8 Shattered Chaitya	16 Vishnu Temple
9 Ram Chandra Mandir	17 Adko Narayan Temple

If you take the downhill road leading from this junction you merge on to Tripureshwar Marg, just beyond the Vishnumati River bridge. Across this busy road another road continues down to the river and to the starting point of the cableway used to transport cement over the foothills from the Terai. Ignoring this possible diversion, the walk continues past Bramha Tol to the **Musum Bahal** (12) with four ancient Licchavi chaityas and a caged-in well. Turn sharp left (north) at the next main junction and look out for a large, open bahal (13) packed with numerous chaityas.

The road opens into Lagankhel, an open square with a Machhendranath Temple (14) standing about 5m high. During the annual Seto Machhendranath festival the image of the god is transported here from the Seto Machhendranath Temple in Kel Tole (see Walking Tour 1). The final stage of the procession is to pull the god's chariot three times around the temple, after which the image is taken back to its starting point on a palanquin while the chariot is dismantled here.

Turn left out of Lagankhel and walk back to the tall Jaisi Deval Temple (5), then turn right (north) back towards Durbar Square.

Shiva & Vishnu Temples At the next crossroads the small, relatively slender **Hari Shankar Temple** (15) stands to the left of the road. The narrow brick-paved laneway beside this combination Shiva and Vishnu Temple runs down to the Bhimsen Temple (4) passed earlier on.

Continue north past a Vishnu Temple (16) to a second Vishnu Temple, the **Adko Narayan Temple** (17). Although this may not look impressive, it is said to be one of the four most important Vishnu temples in Kathmandu. A Garuda figure fronts the temple, lions guard each corner, tiny ceramic tiles decorate the ground floor and there are mildly erotic scenes on some of the upper roof struts.

Beyond the temple you pass the Singh Sattal building (2) once again and arrive back at the starting point.

Kumari Devi

Not only does Nepal have countless gods, goddesses, deities, Bodhisattvas, *avataars* (incarnations of deities living on earth) and manifestations, which are worshipped and revered as statues, images, paintings and symbols, the country also has a real living goddess. The Kumari Devi is a young girl who lives in the building known as the Kumari Bahal, right beside Kathmandu's Durbar Square.

The practice of having a living goddess probably came about during the reign of Jaya Prakash Malla, the last of the Malla kings of Kathmandu, whose reign abruptly ended with the conquest of the valley by Prithvi Narayan Shah in 1768. As usual in Nepal, where there is never one simple answer to any question, there are a number of legends about the Kumari.

One is that the Malla king had intercourse with a pre-pubescent girl, that she died as a result and that he started the practice of venerating a young girl as a living goddess in penance. Another tells of a Malla king who regularly played dice with the goddess Taleju, the protective deity of the valley. When he made an unseemly advance she threatened to withdraw her protection, but relented and promised to return in the form of a young girl. Still another tells of a young girl possessed by the goddess Durga and banished from the kingdom. When the furious queen heard of this she ordered her husband to bring the young girl back and keep her as a real goddess.

Whatever the background, in reality there are a number of living goddesses around the Kathmandu Valley, although the Kumari Devi or Royal Kumari is the most important. The Kumari is selected from a particular caste of Newari gold and silversmiths. She is customarily somewhere between the age of four and puberty and must meet 32 strict physical requirements ranging from the colour of her eyes and the shape of her teeth to the sound of her voice. Her horoscope must also be appropriate, of course.

Once suitable candidates have been found they are gathered together in a darkened room where terrifying noises are made, men dance by in horrific masks and gruesome buffalo heads are on display. Naturally these goings-on are unlikely to frighten a real goddess, particularly one who is an incarnation of Durga, so the young girl who remains calm and collected throughout this ordeal is clearly the new Kumari. In a process similar to the selection of the Dalai Lama, the Kumari then chooses items of clothing and decoration worn by her predecessor as a final test.

Once chosen as the Kumari the young girl moves in to the Kumari Bahal with her family and lives there, apart from a half-dozen ceremonial forays into the outside world each year. The most spectacular of these occasions is the August-September Indra Jatra festival, when she travels through the city on a huge temple chariot over a three day period. During this festival the Kumari customarily blesses the king of Nepal and it is curious that Prithvi Narayan Shah's defeat of the Malla kingdoms took place at this time, just as if the goddess Taleju had indeed withdrawn her protection over the valley. The new king was blessed by the Kumari and the custom continued without skipping a beat!

The Kumari's reign ends with her first period, or any serious accidental loss of blood. Once this first sign of puberty is reached she reverts to being a normal mortal, and the search must start for a new Kumari. During her time as a goddess the Kumari is supported by the temple income and on retirement she is paid a handsome dowry. It is said that marrying an ex-Kumari is unlucky, but it's more likely a natural belief that taking on a spoilt ex-goddess is likely to be hard work!

HUGH FINLAY

RICHARD I'ANSON

RICHARD I'ANSON

Durbar Squares

The images and gods of the squares watch on, while the aspects of life they represent are played out daily. As a reminder of human ignorance, Kala Bhairab (bottom left), tramples a corpse.

Durbar Squares
Clockwise from top left: Offerings to ensure a good monsoon – Naga shrine, Patan; flute seller in Kathmandu – music is a big part of Nepali life; Ganesh, the god of prosperity, is a popular element of Patan's Durbar Square; bronze gilded shrew at Kathmandu's Durbar Square – a good clue that this is a temple to Ganesh.

OTHER TEMPLES & BUILDINGS
Three Goddesses Temples
Next to the modern Sanchaya Kosh Bhawan Shopping Centre and across the road from the immigration office in Thamel are the temples of the three goddesses. The street here is named Tridevi Marg – *tri* means 'three' and *devi* means 'goddesses'. The goddesses are Dakshinkali, Mankamna and Jawalamai and the temples are chiefly interesting for the roof struts, some with erotic carvings illustrating rather interesting positions.

Mahakala Temple
This temple, on the Tundikhel (east) side of Kantipath just north of New Rd, was very badly damaged in the 1934 earthquake and is of little architectural merit following its reconstruction. If you can see inside the darkened shrine you may be able to make out the 1.5m high figure of Mahakala, the Great Black One, a particularly ferocious form of Shiva. Kal means 'death' as well as 'black' in Nepali so it can also be described as the Temple of Great Death. The Tantric god has Buddhist as well as Hindu followers. You can climb to the top of one of the buildings around the courtyard to look over the Tundikhel field.

Bhimsen Tower
This white, minaret-like watchtower, also known as Sundhara, is a useful landmark although it's of no importance. It stands near the main post office and was built by a Rana

prime minister and rebuilt after being severely damaged by the 1934 earthquake.

Pachali Bhairab
Between Tripureshwar Marg and the Bagmati River is a huge and ancient *pipal* tree. The tree forms a sanctuary over the image of Pachali, which is surrounded by tridents. Nearby lies what some believe to be the brass body of Baital, another of Shiva's manifestations. Others believe it is Surya, the sun god. Worshippers gather here on Tuesday and Saturday, and it is particularly busy here during the festival of Pachali Bhairab Jatra, which falls on the fourth day after the bright fortnight in September or early October.

NATIONAL MUSEUM & ART GALLERY
Not far from Swayambhunath, the National Museum is a bit disappointing, but the art gallery (when it is open) has a fine collection of religious art. A visit can easily be combined with a trip to Swayambhunath.

The museum has a rather eccentric collection that includes some moon rock, a number of moth-eaten stuffed animals, a vast number of uniforms and military decorations, swords and guns, and a portrait gallery. The most interesting exhibit is a leather Tibetan cannon.

The gallery displays a number of treasures. There's a superb collection of statues and carvings (stone, wood, bronze, terracotta) – some pieces date to the 1st century BCE. If you have an interest in this area of art a visit is a must.

The museum is closed on Tuesday and is open from 10 am to 2.30 pm on Friday. The rest of the week it opens from 10 am to 5 pm in summer and until 4 pm in winter. Ticket sales stop an hour before closing time; entry is Rs 10.

THINGS TO DO
Swimming Pools & Sauna
Generally, pools in the major hotels can be used by friends of hotel guests or, at some hotels, by outsiders for a $2 to $3 charge. The

---

Visiting Hindu Temples

Non-Hindus are barred from entering a number of temples in Nepal although Nathalie Nellens, a Belgian visitor, commented 'non-Hindu is rather meaningless when it is much more your colour than your religious beliefs that count'. She's probably right: a Nepali Christian or Muslim would probably find it easy to gain entrance!

biggest hotel pool is at the Hotel de l'Annapurna but, reflecting its popularity, it charges $5 for one day membership. Longer membership charges are a bit more reasonable.

There are public pools at Balaju and at the National Stadium although they close during the October to February winter months. The National Stadium pool in the south of Kathmandu costs Rs 15 and is open from 10 am to 5 pm; Monday is reserved for women. The Balaju pool costs Rs 10 but it can get very crowded.

The Kathmandu Physical Fitness Centre (☎ 413638) in Lazimpat, has weight-training equipment, a jacuzzi and a sauna. Short and long-term membership is available. There's also an excellent sauna, open to visitors, at the Vajra Hotel on the way to Swayambhunath.

Hot-Air Ballooning

On a clear day it's a superb way to view the vast expanse of the Himalaya – from over 6000m up – and it's also a chance to get some clean air! The view of Kathmandu and the valley is equally breathtaking.

The flights take place daily during the season and, depending on the wind, fly either east to west or vice versa over the city. It's an amazing experience, although crossing right over the international airport is a little unnerving, and the landing in a rice field usually attracts a huge, excited and curious crowd of local villagers – a real 'The Day the Balloon Landed' experience.

The cost of the one hour flight is $195 per person, which includes transport to and from your hotel, and a full buffet breakfast at a Thamel restaurant. For bookings contact Balloon Sunrise Nepal (☎ 418214, fax 424157, email nepal@intrek.wlink.com.np).

ORGANISED TOURS

There are limited organised tours of Kathmandu and these are mostly geared to group tours. Grayline (☎ 413188), with a desk at the Yak & Yeti Hotel, is the only operator with scheduled trips, and even these only operate on certain days of the week, and only during the tourist season. A three-hour tour of Bhaktapur, Bodhnath and Pashupatinath operates on Monday (Rs 250); to Patan and Swayambhunath tours go daily (Rs 350); and if there's a group of four or more people they operate four-hour afternoon tours to Nagarkot (Rs 400 per person) and Dhulikhel (Rs 300).

If there's a group of you, it's just as easy to hire a taxi for half a day.

PLACES TO STAY

Kathmandu has an excellent range of places to stay, from expensive international-style hotels to cheap and comfortable lodges.

This section is divided by price into budget, mid-range and top end, and then by location. A budget hotel or guesthouse is a place where you can get a double room for less than Rs 500, say $8. There are quite a few where you can get a room for less than Rs 200 ($3) and some where you can pay less than Rs 120 ($2). Mid-range means from $10 to $50 a night and the top end is from $50 up. A double room in the most expensive hotels in Kathmandu costs more than $150 a night, getting close to the nation's average annual per capita income! Quite a few hotels bridge the budget and mid-range categories by having a range of room standards and charging accordingly – these places have been grouped according to their lowest price.

All mid-range and top-end hotels charge a VAT tax of 10% plus a Tourism Service Charge of 2%. Almost all quote their prices in US dollars, however, at all but the most expensive places you can pay the equivalent in local currency. Where you are required to pay foreign currency (see Money in the Facts for the Visitor chapter), it means payment by either cash, travellers cheques, credit cards, or rupees accompanied by a Foreign Exchange Encashment Receipt. Budget places usually quote prices in rupees and rarely bung on a tax.

It is definitely worth looking around if you plan to stay for any length of time. It's difficult to recommend particular hotels, especially in the budget and middle brackets, because particular rooms in each hotel can vary widely. Many of these hotels have additions to additions, and while some rooms may be very gloomy and run-down others might be very pleasant. A friendly crowd of fellow travellers can also make all the difference.

For budget and mid-range places the Thamel area is the main locale, and it is something of a tourist ghetto. Its development has been rapid and uncontrolled, with ugly multi-storey hotels and signboards taking the place of beautiful Newari houses. The introduction of a one-way traffic system and daily garbage collection have gone a long way to halting what seemed like an unstoppable slide into chaos and squalor, but it's still a very busy place during the peak season.

The Thamel area is where the largest number of independent travellers stay, and there are dozens and dozens of lodges, restaurants, travel agencies and shops, and a bustling cosmopolitan atmosphere. It's still a convenient and enjoyable area to stay for a short time, however, especially if you want to meet fellow travellers. It can also be a welcome relief to find western menus, people who speak English and hot showers at budget prices.

The name Thamel is used to describe a sprawling area with at least a dozen roads and several hundred hotels and restaurants. It is so well known and has such cachet that many places now claim Thamel as their address, even though they are in bordering areas that have traditionally had different names. The problem is partly due to the fact that these areas never had strictly defined limits anyway.

Despite what the hotel owners might think, many people prefer to be a bit removed from the crowded centre of Thamel. There are several places on its periphery that are close enough to be reasonably convenient but aren't absolutely in the centre of the maelstrom.

In a megalomaniacal attempt to establish some order, we have somewhat arbitrarily divided the greater Thamel area (see the Greater Thamel map) into: Thamel, around the two main intersections; Paknajol, to the north; Bhagwan Bahal, to the north-east; Jyatha, to the south-east; and Chhetrapati, to the south-west.

There is still a scattering of really rock-bottom places along Freak St, close to Durbar Square, and these offer the impecunious an escape from the Thamel crowds. The Freak St location is also excellent, and real Newari city life continues in the surrounding side streets. Most of the accommodation possibilities are *very* basic, but they are also among the cheapest in Kathmandu.

Mid-range places are more widely scattered, with a majority in and around Thamel. Kathmandu's limited number of international-standard hotels are also widely spread, some of them quite a distance from the city centre. There's also an increasing number of mostly top-end resorts springing up around the valley, and these usually offer views, a peaceful rural atmosphere and are less than an hour from the centre of Kathmandu. For those with the funds, they offer an alternative to being right in the city.

There is a hotel reservations counter as soon as you get out of customs at the airport. Most of the hotels it represents are reasonably expensive, but it has a few in the $5 to $10 bracket, and the staff arrange free transport. If you don't feel like tackling the touts and taxis outside the main doors, this service can be useful.

Taxi drivers and hotel touts (they are often one and the same) lie in wait outside the airport terminal and around bus stations. If you ask to be taken to one of the hotels recommended in this book, you may well be told that the place in question has closed or become ridiculously expensive. Though this may be possible, it is considerably more likely that they want you to go to the hotel where they get the best commission – often more than 50% of the room price. The best solution is to take a taxi to Thamel or Freak St (Rs 200, about $3.50, from the airport) and look for yourself. If you are travelling as a group or couple, leave one person in a restaurant to look after heavy bags while a search is made.

During the peak times (October to November, February to April) rooms in the most popular hotels can be in short supply. Otherwise, there are so many fiercely competitive mid-range and budget places that only the really popular hotels are likely to be full. The prices given here are the high-season prices shown on hotel tariff cards. At all but the top-end hotels these are pure fiction, shown to you more in the hope that you might be silly enough to pay them. In reality prices are highly negotiable; 50% discounts are par for the course.

PLACES TO STAY – BUDGET

Intense competition between Kathmandu's enormous number of low-priced hostelries means that you can find hot showers in even the cheapest places, although they are usually solar-heated and is only hot in the late afternoon.

Hotels in this category do not have heating and Kathmandu in winter is a rather chilly place. In winter you'll appreciate places with a garden as it's always pleasant to sit outside during the cool, but invariably sunny, autumn and winter days. A south-facing room will mean you get some sunlight in your room. In general, the top-floor rooms are the best, as you stand a chance of getting a view and having easy access to the roof (often a nice place to relax).

Thamel

Any mention of Thamel has to start with the **Kathmandu Guest House** (☎ 413632, fax 417133, email kgh@thamel.mos.com.np) the first hotel to open in the area, and still one of the most popular. It also serves as the central landmark – everything is 'near the Kathmandu Guest House', 'five minutes from the Kathmandu Guest House' or whatever. It's not the best value for money in town, but most people enjoy the atmosphere and it's usually booked out weeks in advance during the peak months. The position is excellent and you definitely feel you're at the nerve centre with various expeditions coming and going, trekkers looking for partners and a constant hum of activity. There's parking space for cars out the front, a very pleasant garden, a money-change desk

(guests only), a storage facility for luggage and valuables, a travel desk, a hairdresser and even an art gallery upstairs – this is budget travel in the deluxe category! The cheapest rooms form part of the original 13-room guesthouse. They are large although pretty worn and cost $6/8 with washbasin. In the newer wing pleasant, small rooms with bath are $17/20 a single/double. At the top of the scale are very large, modern rooms with air-con at $50/60. Cots are available for $3. There's a 12% tax on top of all these prices, and discounts are available for longer stays.

If this is too luxe for your budget you don't have to go far for something cheaper – there are a dozen or more places within a stone's throw. Turning south from the Kathmandu Guest House there's a cluster of hotels, starting with the **Hotel Star** (☎ 414000), right next door, which features prominently in Kim Stanley Robinson's *Escape from Kathmandu*. It has long been a popular alternative to the Kathmandu Guest House. The rooms are nothing special but it is quiet and quite OK. Rooms start at Rs 150/200 with common bath, and Rs 250/350 with attached bathroom.

The basic but good value **Cosy Corner Lodge** (☎ 428025, email stupa@wlink.com .np) is adjacent to the Hotel Star, and has OK singles/doubles, all with common bath at Rs 100/150.

Pheasant Lodge (☎ 417415) is tucked farther around the laneway so it feels quite removed from the Thamel bustle, although it is as central as you can get. There's an atmospheric courtyard and although the rooms are basic, they're good value – which is why it's often full. Rooms are Rs 100/150.

Continue south a bit farther along the main street (sometimes known as JP Rd) and you come to **Mom's House Lodge** (☎ 417184), which aside from the awful name, is run by very helpful people and has basic but clean rooms from Rs 100/120, or Rs 200/250 with private bath. The only drawback is the noise from the surrounding restaurants and bars, although this does stop around 10 pm.

Gorkha Lodge (☎ *221279*), further south again, is one of the cheapest around, with rooms at Rs 100/200 with common bath.

Hotel Horizon (☎ *220904, fax 252999*) is a good choice off the main street, down near the bank of tapestry shops, and has a range of rooms at reasonable prices. They start at $4/6 for fairly spartan rooms with bathroom and go to $12/15 for larger rooms, and $20 for luxury rooms which are good.

Tucked away in the lane behind the Pumpernickel Bakery, the *Memorable Guest House* (☎ *419288*) hardly lives up to the name, but it's clean and convenient. Singles/doubles are a bargain at Rs 100/125 with common bath, Rs 150/200 with bath.

In this same quiet back lane is the *Hotel Pacifist* (☎ *258320*), which has good sized rooms at Rs 165/220, or Rs 250 for something slightly bigger. All have attached bath.

The main road from the centre of Kathmandu to Thamel runs into the main Thamel chowk. Cheapies in this area include the *Hotel Puska* (☎ *228997, fax 250200*), which is not great but decent value at $3/4 with common bath, $4/6 attached; and the nearby *Visit Nepal Guest House* (☎ *251465*) which is OK at Rs 200/300 with bath.

Closer to the centre of Thamel on the traffic-choked extension of Tridevi Marg, the *Marco Polo Guest House* (☎ *251914, fax 250513*) is popular. The rooms at the back are particularly good and there are some surprisingly pleasant rooftop patios. Doubles cost $4, or $6 with bath.

Right next door is the quiet and clean *Student Guest House* (☎ *251551, fax 413155, email krishna@student.wlink.com .np*), with decent sized but somewhat dark rooms at $5/8.

Paknajol

This area lies to the north of Thamel and can be reached by continuing north from the Kathmandu Guest House, or by approaching on Lekhnath Marg.

Tucked down an inconspicuous laneway, the *Mustang Guest House* (☎ *426053, fax 221344, email chitaure@mos.com.np*) is good value, with pleasant, quiet rooms.

Rooms are Rs 140/180 with shared bath, or Rs 200/250 with private bath.

Down a lane to the west is *Hotel Florid* (☎ *416155, fax 412747, email florid@ wlink.com.np*). There is a small garden at the rear, and no buildings behind so there's a feeling of space which is often lacking in Thamel. The rooms are small but OK, and cost $4/5 with common bath, or $6/8 with attached bath.

Farther north again and also down a laneway is the *Lonely Planet Guest House* (☎ *412715*), but we should point out that it is absolutely no relation! The rooms, though spartan, are quite good. Singles/doubles are from $8/10.

Not far from the steep Paknajol intersection (north-west of Thamel) there are a couple of pleasant guesthouses. They're away from traffic, a short walk from Thamel (but it could be a million miles), and they have beautiful views across the valley towards Balaju and Swayambhunath. The small and friendly *Tibet Peace Guest House* (☎ *415026, fax 420165*) has well equipped rooms with lockers, bathrooms and telephones; singles/doubles cost from $4 to $8, and there's a small restaurant. At the end of the road the *Kathmandu Peace Guest House* (☎ *415239, fax 411932*) offers singles/doubles from $3/4 with shared bath or from $6/8 with private bath, TV, fan and phone – great value in this range.

Turn left at the T-junction after the Hotel Garuda and you come to several reasonable cheapies. Neat and clean rooms at the *Holy Lodge* (☎ *416265*) cost from $3/5 without bath to $7/10 with bath. Almost next door is the *Capital Guest House* (☎ *414150*), a reasonably modern place with single/double rooms with attached bath at $8/12, or with common bath at $5/8.

Across the road is the *Prince Guest House* (☎ *414456, fax 220143*), which is a very decent budget place, and the rooftop and rear gardens are pleasant. Rooms cost $6/8 with bath and phone.

There's a small group of hotels built around a cul de sac off Lekhnath Marg. *Hotel Pilgrims* (☎ *416910, fax 424943, email*

GREATER THAMEL

GREATER THAMEL

GREATER THAMEL

PLACES TO STAY

1 Kathmandu Peace Guest House
2 Tibet Peace Guest House
3 Hotel Manang; Hotel Marshyangdi
4 Lonely Planet Guest House
5 Hotel Gauri Shankar
6 Hotel Greeting Palace
7 Hotel Pilgrims
8 Jhigu Thayabhu
9 Hotel Malla
10 Hotel Norbhu Linka
11 Hotel Buddha
13 Hotel Florid
14 Hotel Shree Tibet
15 Hotel Vaishali
16 Hotel Thamel
18 Souvenir Guest House
19 Hotel Yeti
21 Hotel Karma
22 Hotel Tashi Dhargey
23 Mustang Guest House
25 Hotel Mandap
28 Holy Lodge
29 Capital Guest House
31 Prince Guest House
32 International Guest House

33 Hotel Garuda
35 Acme Guest House
42 Panda Hotel
43 Kathmandu Guest House; Las Kus Restaurant
47 Hotel Star; Pub Maya
48 Cosy Corner Lodge
49 Pheasant Lodge
54 Hotel The Earth
56 Mom's House Lodge
64 Hotel Excelsior
65 Memorable Guest House
66 Hotel Swoniga
67 Hotel Pacifist
73 Marco Polo Guest House; Student Guest House
75 Hotel Earth House
76 Tibet Holiday Inn
80 Hotel Tilicho
90 Mustang Holiday Inn
91 Hotel White Lotus
92 Shangrila Guest House
94 Shree Guest House
98 Hotel Puska
102 Hotel Tashi Dhelek
103 Thorong Peak Guest House
104 Gorkha Lodge
105 Hotel Horizon

106 Hotel Lai Lai
108 Tibet Guest House
109 Nirvana Hotel
115 Potala Guest House
122 Hotel Blue Diamond
123 Hotel Norling
124 Hotel Dynasty
125 Fuji Guest House
127 Hotel Utse
129 Lhasa Guest House
130 Siddhartha Guest House
132 Hotel Mountain
134 Kantipur Temple House
135 Hotel New Gujar
136 Hotel Jagat

PLACES TO EAT

17 Thamel House Restaurant
24 Krua Thai Restaurant
26 Thama Fuji Restaurant
27 San Francisco Pizza Palace
30 Rum Doodle Restaurant & Bar
36 Pizza Hut
37 Northfield Cafe; Ultimate Descents
44 Brezel Bakery

hotel@pilgrims.wlink.com.np) is undistinguished (especially some of the dark singles), but the place is clean, well managed and provides pretty good value for money. Singles/doubles are $8/10 with shared facilities; doubles with bath are $15. As always, the prices are highly negotiable.

In the same group is the popular *Hotel Greeting Palace* (☎ 417212, fax 417197), which offers good-sized carpeted rooms at $10/15, or deluxe (meaning with TV and slightly larger) at $15/25, but nobody pays that much. *Hotel Gauri Shankar* (☎ 417181, fax 411605) has smallish rooms, but is otherwise OK at $15/20, or $2 more with breakfast.

Bhagwan Bahal

This area to the north-east of Thamel takes its name from a Buddhist monastery. Some travellers like the area because it is much quieter than Thamel proper, and has not yet been completely taken over by restaurants, souvenir shops and travel agencies.

Hotel Earth House (☎ 418197, fax 41635), just off Tridevi Marg, is a good budget hotel which is already starting to show its age. But it does have friendly staff, a nice rooftop garden and a variety of clean and decent rooms. Singles/doubles start at $4/6 but can go as high as $10/16. The rooms at the back are best.

Panda Hotel (☎ 424683, fax 425657) is a little beyond the Earth House. The front rooms with balcony are good value; others can be dark so check first. Singles/doubles with common bath are $4/8, $8/10 attached.

Farther again is the small *Souvenir Guest House* (☎ 410277) on the way north to the Hotel Malla, and it has a nice garden. Singles/doubles are Rs 200/300 with shared bath, or Rs 300/400 with private bath, but in the high season the prices are $5/8 and $8/15 respectively.

GREATER THAMEL

45 La Dolce Vita
46 Le Bistro Restaurant
50 Restaurant Casa Della Pasta; Ultimate Planet Bar; Barnes & Noble Bookhouse
52 Yin Yang Restaurant
55 Khana Ghar Restaurant
57 Third Eye Restaurant
58 Alice's Restaurant
60 Helena's Restaurant
61 KC's Restaurant
62 Pumpernickel Bakery
71 Old Vienna Inn; Gourmet Delicatessen
79 Fire & Ice; Dechenling Restaurant
88 Fuji Restaurant
93 City Garden Restaurant
96 Omei Japanese Restaurant
97 Les Yeux Restaurant; Maples
99 Cinderella Restaurant
100 Wiesel Bakery
101 Green Leaves Restaurant
107 Everest Steak House
110 Nepalese Kitchen
111 Tibet's Canteena
112 Rimini Pizzeria

117 Narayan's Restaurant
118 Ajima Silk Road Restaurant
119 Al Pollo Restaurant
121 La Menagerie Bar & Restaurant
128 Dolma Momo Restaurant
141 Delicatessen Center

OTHER
12 Moneychanger
20 EasyLink Cybercafe
34 Thamel 66 Bar
38 Tom & Jerry Pub; Nargila Restaurant
39 Pilgrims Book House; Pilgrims Feed N Read; G's Terrace
40 New Orleans Bar
41 Bhagwan Bahal
51 Wayfarers Travel Services
53 Nepal Grindlays Bank
59 Namche Bazaar Building
63 Garden Cafe
68 Bicycle Hire
69 Himalayan Holistic Healing Centre
70 Underground Bar
72 Best Shopping Centre

74 Taxi & Auto-Rickshaw Stand
77 Sanchaya Kosh Bhawan Shopping Centre
78 Bookworld
81 Sita World Travel; Western Union
82 Immigration Office
83 Three Goddesses Temple
84 Kaiser Library
85 Bus Stop for Pokhara Tourist Buses
86 US Embassy; American Club
87 Nepal Grindlays Bank
89 British Council
95 KEEP; Himalayan Rescue Association
113 Amrita Craft Collection
114 Walden Book House
116 Nepal Colour Lab
120 Silk Road Bar
126 Raja Yoga Centre
131 K@mandu Cybermatha
133 Nepal Arab Bank
137 Lucky Traveller Service
138 Nateshwar Temple
139 Kathesimbhu Stupa
140 Chusya Bahal

Turn right just before the Souvenir (as you head north) and you come to the *Hotel Yeti* (☎ 414858, fax 252115, email adventure@ mos.com.np) which is a reasonable place with a garden and sunny rooms. Singles/doubles with shared bath are $8/10, or $12/16 with private facilities, but you should get it for less unless things are really busy.

Jyatha

The neighbourhood to the south-east of Thamel has traditionally been known as Jyatha, but increasingly the word is used to describe the main north-south road that runs into the western end of Tridevi Marg.

South along Jyatha Rd you reach the basic, cheap and friendly *Shree Guest House* (☎ 256105, email joshi@vishnu.ccsl .com.np). Rooms here cost Rs 150/250 for a room with attached bath.

Farther south is the *Hotel Blue Diamond* (☎ 226320, fax 226392), which has rooms with fan and bath at $12/15 or $18/22 with air-con. It's a fairly modern place, set well back from the street. It's popular with tour groups.

New Tibet Rest House (☎ 225319, fax 226945, sunny@sunnytrv.mos.com.np) is run by the same people as the popular Tibet Guest House in Chhetrapati and has singles/doubles at $6/10; $10/15 with bath.

A bit farther south is the *Siddhartha Guest House* (☎ 227119), with a small garden with fruit trees. Rooms are pretty standard for Thamel, and cost $5 for a double with common bath, $8/12 attached. Next door is the *Lhasa Guest House* (☎ 226147, fax 228019) a good place with rooms at Rs 200/250 with common bath, Rs 250/350 attached.

Chhetrapati

This area is named after the important five-way intersection (notable by the distinctive bandstand) to the south-west of Thamel. The farther you are from Thamel, the more traditional the surroundings become.

South of the Kathmandu Guest House and left at the junction (Narayan's Restaurant is a good landmark) you'll see the very popular *Potala Guest House (☎ 220467, fax 223256)* where singles/doubles are from $10/15. There's hot water and a small, quiet garden.

Freak St & Durbar Square Area

Although Freak St's glory days have passed, a few determined restaurants and lodges have hung on. Staying here offers two big pluses – you won't find anything cheaper, and you're right in the heart of the old city. Thamel is so crowded and hectic that Freak St offers a good alternative, although the choices are much fewer.

Freak St's real name is Jochne (although no-one uses it) and it runs south from Basantapur Square, the open square full of souvenir-sellers adjoining Durbar Square.

Hotel Sugat (☎ 245824, fax 221824, email maryman@mos.com.np) actually overlooks the square and is one of the best options in the area. Rooms tend to be dark, but they're large and decent. Singles/doubles with shared bath start at $2/5; or $5/6 with private bath.

Almost next door to the Sugat is the *Park Guest House (☎ 247487)* which has small rooms with fan and TV, and some overlook Basantapur Square. It's modern and consequently a bit more expensive than some in this area, at $4/8 with common bath, $8/9 with attached.

Just off Freak St proper is the excellent *Annapurna Lodge & Diyalo Restaurant (☎ 24784)*. The place is well kept and cheerful, in contrast to some of the Freak St dives. A single/double is Rs 125/150 with shared bath, or Rs 200/250 with private bath.

Century Lodge (☎ 247641) is one of Freak St's long-term survivors and remains a popular, atmospheric place offering excellent value for money. Rooms cost just Rs 85/165 with common bath, or there are small doubles with attached bath at Rs 250.

Pagoda Lodge (☎ 247629) is reached from the same courtyard in the heart of Freak St. It's about as basic as they get, and rooms cost just Rs 75/150, all with common bath, although even this is negotiable.

Monumental Lodge (☎ 247864) is across the road with rooms for Rs 55/100, or Rs 200 with private bath. Conditions are as spartan and straightforward as the price would indicate, but if you're travelling on a very tight budget they offer all you can expect!

Himalaya's Guest House (☎ 246555), a couple of short blocks west of Freak St is excellent. This modern place has clean and comfortable rooms from Rs 150/250 with common bath and Rs 300 for a double with attached bath. There's a good cafe here, and the rooftop views are great.

Hotel Pokhara View (☎ 241773) is a modern place which, while comfortable, lacks the atmosphere of some places in this

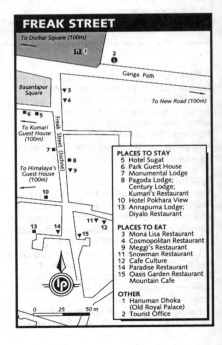

FREAK STREET

To Durbar Square (100m)

Ganga Path

Basantapur Square

To New Road (100m)

Freak Street (Jochne)

To Kumari Guest House (100m)

To Himalaya's Guest House (100m)

PLACES TO STAY
5 Hotel Sugat
6 Park Guest House
7 Monumental Lodge
8 Pagoda Lodge;
   Century Lodge;
   Kuman's Restaurant
10 Hotel Pokhara View
13 Annapurna Lodge;
   Diyalo Restaurant

PLACES TO EAT
3 Mona Lisa Restaurant
4 Cosmopolitan Restaurant
9 Meggi's Restaurant
11 Snowman Restaurant
12 Cafe Culture
14 Paradise Restaurant
15 Oasis Garden Restaurant
   Mountain Cafe

OTHER
1 Hanuman Dhoka
   (Old Royal Palace)
2 Tourist Office

0   25   50 m

area. The double rooms are OK at Rs 120, but the singles are little more than glorified cupboards.

Kumari Guest House, run by the friendly Mrs Bhagawati Joshi, is an old-style building (mind your head) with great views over Durbar Square. The rooms are basic, but clean. Rooms with shared bath are good value at Rs 150/200.

Only a few steps north of Durbar Square, then to your left on Pyaphal Tole, the **Kathmandu Lodge** (☎ 254173, fax 242390, email wave@hppc.mos.com.np) is a popular choice, offering a little more comfort than the Freak St places. It's clean and well kept, although the sickly green paintwork doesn't help. Rooms with fan cost Rs 150/200 with shared bath, and Rs 200/300 with private bath.

PLACES TO STAY – MID-RANGE
Mid-range in Kathmandu means from around $10 to $50 for a double. The borderlines are fuzzy. The Kathmandu Guest House is partly a mid-range hotel as many of its rooms are over $10, but it does offer cheaper ones as well.

Thamel
Thorong Peak Guest House (☎ 253458, fax 251008) has a good location in the centre of things, but off the main street in a small cul de sac. The hotel has a rather garish Tibetan-moderne decor and some of the rooms are a bit dark, although most are large and airy. Full single/double prices are $14/18 with private bath, or $8/12 with shared bath, but the discounted rates are 30% less.

Hotel Tashi Dhelek (☎ 217446), next door, is a comfortable, modern hotel with rooms at $18/25, or with TV at $22/30 (discounted to $12/18 in the low season).

Close to the Kathmandu Guest House is the **Hotel The Earth** (☎ 229039, fax 223194), another modern and rather nondescript place charging $12/15 for rooms with attached bath. Also in the thick of things is the **Hotel Excelsior** (☎ 41566, fax 410853, email excel@wlink.com.np), a large place with standard rooms at $18/23, or deluxe

rooms with TV at $22/30. There's even a lift in case you can't stagger to the 4th floor.

A little farther along the same lane is the new and unexciting **Hotel Swoniga** (☎ 253253, fax 260855). The rooms are quite well furnished, and have TV, fan and a balcony. The discounted rate is $15/25, otherwise you're looking at $25/35.

Hotel Garuda (☎ 416340, fax 413614, garuda@mos.com.np) is in a cramped area of Thamel about 100m north of the Kathmandu Guest House. The hotel is well run, clean, and good value. There's a great view over the Thamel area from the rooftop. Singles/doubles are from $9/13, up to $29/36 for a heated room with TV and balcony.

Acme Guest House (☎ 414811, email amc@wlink.com.np) is tucked away close by. The rooms are quite large, and there is an open lawn area, which is something of a rarity in crowded Thamel. It's not bad value at $14/18 with bath, up to $20/25 with balcony and heating. Discounts are available.

Paknajol
Hotel Mandap (☎ 413321, fax 419734), just around the double bend north of the Kathmandu Guest House, is a bit rough around the edges these days, and is only good value if you get their discounted rates of $10/12; the full rate is $20/25.

Hotel Buddha (☎ 413366, fax 413194, email rhinotvl@ccsl.com.np), farther on, is another modern place with a pleasant garden. The rooms tend to be on the small side, but are comfortable with attached bath, telephones and wall-to-wall carpeting. Rooms are $35/40, but discounts of 25% are possible.

Hotel Karma (☎ 417897, fax 418547) is a good, straightforward hotel in a quiet lane running between two main thoroughfares. Standard, airy rooms cost $12/18, or slightly larger rooms are $16/26. Expect a discount of around 20%.

Farther around the same lane is the **Hotel Shree Tibet** (☎ 419902, fax 425938), a clean place with good rooms, although many are dark due to the buildings being very close together. Singles/doubles go for

$10/15, although there is room to negotiate here. The small restaurant serves decent food.

Hotel Tashi Dhargey, (☎ 417030, fax 423543) has good rooms at $10/12 with fan and phone, or $15/18 with air-con and TV.

Follow the double bend north of the Kathmandu Guest House and turn left towards the Holy Lodge, continuing through several more sharp bends, and you'll find the *International Guest House* (☎ 252299, fax 252999, email igh@wlink.com.np). It's in an area known as Kaldhara and has singles/doubles for $13/18 with shared bath, or $20/25 with private bath, but discounts up to 50% are offered. It's a pleasant hotel with one of the best rooftop views in the city. This area is quieter and less of a scene than Thamel but not too far away from the restaurants.

Hotel Thamel (☎ 417643, fax 418547, email hotelthamel@visitnepal.com) is down the first lane on the left as you head due north from the EasyLink Cybercafe. It's one of the modern breed of comfortable concrete monstrosities, with deluxe air-con rooms from $45/55, and rooms with private balconies looking back to the city for $30/40, all with TV and phone. A discount of 50% is offered outside the high season.

Bhagwan Bahal

Hotel Tilicho (☎ 416828, fax 424144), on Tridevi Marg, is a clean rather characterless place, but offers pretty high standards. Singles/doubles are from $15/20, but it's worth negotiating the price and checking a number of rooms before you pick one.

Almost next door is the *Tibet Holiday Inn* (☎ 411453, fax 222223), a similar place but set back from the somewhat noisy street. Large, clean rooms here cost $20/25, or deluxe from $30/45, but discounts are a matter of course.

Hotel Norbhu Linka (☎ 414799, fax 419005, email ggclama@vishnu.ccsl.com .np) is a large, modern place with good rooftop views. At the discounted rates of $20/27, this place is good value as the rooms are large and have TV and attached bath. The full tariff is $40/55, plus 10% tax.

Jyatha

Turn left (east) only a short distance down the Jyatha Rd and a couple of twists and turns will bring you to a neat little cluster of modern guesthouses, directly behind the Sanchaya Kosh Bhawan Shopping Centre on Tridevi Marg. This is a central, but quiet location.

Mustang Holiday Inn (☎ 249041, fax 249016, email ntb@mhi.wlink.com.np) has pleasant rooms and is well run. Rooms are $8/10 with shared bath, or $15/20 with private bath, though these are negotiable, even in the high season.

Also in this quiet little enclave are the *Shangrila Guest House* (☎ 250188), with rooms at Rs 200/300 with common bath, Rs 300/400 attached; and the popular *Imperial Guest House* (☎ 249339, fax 249733), which charges $9/12.

Hotel White Lotus (☎ 249842) is another here, and it is good value at Rs 150/200 with common bath, Rs 200/300 attached.

Hotel Utse (☎ 226946, fax 257615, email utse@wlink.com.np) is a comfortable Tibetan hotel owned by Ugen Tsering, who is one of the original Thamel pioneers with his long-running and popular Utse Restaurant. The rooms are spotlessly clean and very comfortable – putting some of the more expensive hotels to shame. Singles/doubles cost from $13/20, or there are deluxe rooms with carpet and TV for $17/24. It's a very well run hotel, with a good rooftop area, and is often full in the peak months. Right next door, *Hotel Norling* (☎ 240734, fax 226735), also Tibetan- run, has good-sized rooms at $10/18, or $18/20 with a bit more comfort.

Tucked away in a quiet lane behind the Utse, the new *Hotel Dynasty* (☎ 263172, fax 250793, email dynasty@mos.com.np) is a good find. It's a modern, upmarket place which even has a lift. The rooms are a good size and have air-con, TV and phone, and cost $45/55; without air-con it's $35/45.

In the same lane is the *Fuji Guest House* (☎ 250435, fax 229234), with straightforward, carpeted rooms with attached bath and balcony at $15/20, or with common bath at $6/10; discounts are available.

Farther south along Jyatha is another modern place, the **Hotel Jagat** (☎ 250732, fax 227701), which is small, clean and comfortable, and costs $10/14 with TV and attached bath, and $20 for a room with three beds. Very close by and set well back from the street is the large **Hotel New Gujar** (☎ 226623, fax 228621), which is characterless and somewhat shabby, but remains popular with tour groups. It's reasonable value at $12/16, it's just a pity they haven't made better use of the large forecourt, which is currently concrete.

One of the more interesting places in this category is the **Kantipur Temple House** (☎ 250131, fax 250078, email kantipur@ templhouse.wlink.com.np), along a short alley at the southern end of Jyatha. It's actually a new hotel, but has been built in old Newari temple style, and is very well done. The tastefully decorated rooms cost $40/50.

Chhetrapati

Two popular mid-range hotels can be found in Chhetrapati. Coming from the Kathmandu Guest House in Thamel turn right at the junction by Narayan's Restaurant and you pass a string of restaurants, bookshops and guesthouses on your way to Chhetrapati Square. The **Tibet Guest House** (☎ 251763, fax 260518, email tibet@guesths.mos.com .np) is in the lower-middle bracket. It has good sized and well maintained rooms with bath from $15/17, and others with shared bath for $10/11, all plus 10% tax. There's a restaurant, a pleasant garden and good views from the rooftop garden.

Nirvana Hotel (☎ 227421, fax 222668, email hotel@nirvana.wlink.com.np) has smallish but pleasant rooms, each with balcony, TV, phone and attached bath. There's a small garden and at the discounted rate of $15/20 is good value. High season rates are $30/40.

Farther west beyond Chhetrapati Square, the **Hotel Lai Lai** (☎ 254419, fax 255338) has a number of rooms with good views across the river to Swayambhunath. The rooftop views are also excellent. The rooms themselves are nothing special, but at the discount rate of $12/15 are good value. High season prices are $25/30.

Central Kathmandu

There are several older mid-range hotels right in the centre of old Kathmandu. The **Hotel Panorama** (☎ 221502) is a larger hotel near New Rd with singles/doubles from $10/15.

On Surkha Path only a minute's walk from Durbar Square is the **Hotel Classic** (☎ 223636, fax 223611), which has excellent views over the square from the rooms on the 6th floor. Although the quoted prices are $65/75 for air-con singles/doubles, a discount of 50% seems to be offered as a matter of course. This is not bad value, given the location. The hotel also boasts a 'telescopic tower' for viewing the mountains.

Elsewhere

North of Thamel, in the Lazimpat embassy area, the **Hotel Ambassador** (☎ 410432, fax 413641, email rajan@mos.com.np) is run by the same people as the Kathmandu Guest House. There's a good restaurant and a small garden, but it is on a rather noisy intersection. The hotel is within walking distance of Thamel or Durbar Marg. Rooms cost from $30/40 for a single/double, or $40/50 with air-con.

A few hundred metres farther north, and just off the road to the right, is the **Hotel Manaslu** (☎ 410071, fax 416516, email postfax@mos.com.np), a very nice modern hotel with a pleasant garden area. The slightly inconvenient location explains the cheap price of $28/32.

Across the river in the Bijeshwari area, on the way from Thamel to Swayambhunath, the **Hotel Vajra** (☎ 272719, fax 271695) is one of Kathmandu's most interesting hotels in any price category. It has a distinct style and a superb location looking across the river to Kathmandu. The hotel has an art gallery, its own theatre where classical Nepali dances are performed, a library with books on Tibet and Buddhism, a rooftop garden and the Explorer's Restaurant. Rooms cost $33/38 with attached bath, or

$53/61 in the much swankier new wing, all plus 12% tax. The one catch to staying at the Hotel Vajra is its location, which makes it terrible for getting a taxi. If you're staying here it's wise to have a bicycle at the ready.

Closer again to Swayambhunath is the **Hotel Manjushree Swayambhu Peace** (☎ 275540, fax 275440), not far from the eastern steps. It's a large, modern place and many of the rooms have views of either Swayambhunath or the city. Straightforward rooms cost $15/20.

Increasingly, people are looking to escape the pollution and bustle of central Kathmandu, and one of the nicest alternatives, which is not too far removed, is the **Hotel Sunset View** (☎ 480057, fax 482219, email sunset@wlink.com.np) at New Baneswar – continue along the Arniko Highway and take the first right past the Hotel Everest, opposite the huge conference centre. There's a beautiful garden with great views, 12 comfortable rooms and an excellent restaurant that serves good Nepali food. Rooms are $48/66 with garden views, or $58/70 with valley views. A 15% discount is usually available.

PLACES TO STAY – TOP END

Top-end hotels in Kathmandu cost from $50 for a double room; the most expensive hotels are around $200 for a double. Only a handful of these hotels are centrally located although the less conveniently positioned hotels usually offer a free bus service into town. All offer 24 hour room service, 24 hour satellite television and the best available communications. You can also pay by credit card.

The rates below are the standard individual rates for the high season; they're certainly negotiable for groups and are also likely to be flexible during the monsoon.

Thamel

Hotel Manang (☎ 410993, fax 415821, email htlmnang@vishnu.ccsl.com.np) in Paknajol is a modern three-star hotel with everything you could possibly need. Many of the rooms have magnificent views and all

have TV, air-con, phone and mini-bar. Facilities include a restaurant, room service and a parking area. Standard singles/doubles are $55/65 (discounted to $40/55), and deluxe rooms are $80/90, plus 10% tax.

Hotel Marshyangdi (☎ 414105, fax 410008, email htlgold@mos.com.np), next door, has been established longer and offers a similarly high standard. The rooms are large and well furnished with writing desks and chairs. Singles/doubles cost $55/65 in standard rooms, $70/80 in deluxe rooms, plus 10% tax, but discounts of up to 40% are available depending on occupancy levels.

Hotel Vaishali (☎ 413968, fax 414510, email vaishali@vishnu.ccsl.com.np) has pleasantly furnished but small rooms with air-con, TV and minibar for $90/110, but they seem to be on offer at a more realistic $45/55 much of the time. A bonus here in summer is the small swimming pool.

Hotel Mountain (☎ 246744, fax 249736), on busy Kantipath, has small but pleasant rooms with air-con, TV and phone at $80/90, but discounts of 40% shouldn't be too hard to get.

Central Kathmandu

Entered from Durbar Marg, but set well back from the road, the **Yak & Yeti Hotel** (☎ 248999, fax 227781) boasts probably the best known hotel name in Nepal, due to its connections with the legendary Boris Lissanevitch, its original owner. It is also the hotel that, more than any other in Kathmandu, actually achieves five-star standards without abandoning all references to the country it happens to be in. The oldest part of the hotel is part of a Rana palace, and it houses the hotel's restaurants and casino that retain an overblown but spectacular Rana-baroque decor. The rooms are in two modern wings: the Newari Wing is the older of the two and the rooms incorporate elements of carved wood and local textiles without being kitsch. They're very comfortable and well maintained, and cost $160/170. The newer Durbar Wing has conventional 'international standard' rooms at $170/180. There are also executive rooms in this wing, complete with fax machine, at $225. Business people will find a well equipped business centre with secretarial, translation and interpretation facilities.

Hotel de l'Annapurna (☎ *221711, fax 225236, email a'purna@taj.mos.com.np)* is one of Kathmandu's longest established 'new' hotels, and is architecturally an undistinguished example of a 1960s international hotel. Its central location on Durbar Marg is convenient, and apart from the usual five-star facilities, including bars and restaurants, there's a casino and nightly dance shows (see Entertainment), plus the largest hotel swimming pool in Kathmandu (about 25m). The rooms are comfortable, and standard singles/doubles are $120/130, or there are much plusher deluxe rooms for $140/150, all plus 12% tax.

Hotel Sherpa (☎ *227000, fax 222026)*, opposite the Hotel de l'Annapurna on Durbar Marg, is cheaper, and rates four stars, although it is a bit gloomy and dull. It also lacks a swimming pool, or even a nice garden (a garden oasis can be a much-appreciated escape in Kathmandu). The rooms are well equipped and quite pleasant. Singles/doubles are $105/115.

Just south of the Hotel de l'Annapurna on Durbar Marg, the *Hotel Woodlands Dynasty Plaza* (☎ *222683, fax 225650)* is a four-star hotel that has decent facilities, including a swimming pool and a good vegetarian restaurant. It's much better than its unprepossessing exterior suggests, although the better Thamel hotels certainly give it tough competition. Rooms are large and comfortable but overpriced at $105/115.

The *Hotel Malla* (☎ *418383, fax 418382, email malla@htlgrp.mos.com.np)* is on the northern edge of Thamel, near the new Royal Palace – a five minute walk to all the Thamel restaurants. The rooms are air-con, and have TV, phone and minibar. There's a restaurant and bar and a superb garden, complete with a mini-stupa topping a mini-hill in the centre. Singles/doubles are $122/146, or there are deluxe rooms for $120/150, all plus 14% tax. In the low season a 20% discount is offered.

Elsewhere

Kathmandu's original luxury hotel, the *Soaltee Holiday Inn Crowne Plaza* (☎ *273999, fax 272205, email hdayinn@shicp.com.np)*, is on the western edge of town but operates a bus service into town for its guests. It's one of the largest hotels in Nepal and apart from good restaurants, bars, swimming pool and other facilities it also has a casino. Singles/doubles are $160/170; deluxe rooms are $180/190.

The *Hotel Everest* (☎ *488100, fax 490288)* is on the eastern edge of town, beside the main road to the airport and Bhaktapur. The modern building is eight storeys high, making it one of the tallest buildings in Nepal, and the views, especially on the northern side, are spectacular. The standards are reasonably high and the facilities are good, but it's still probably overpriced at $150/160.

North of the city in the Lazimpat embassy area, the *Hotel Shanker* (☎ *410151, fax 412691)* is an atmospheric place in a converted Rana palace. The exterior of the building is grandly baroque, but the decor in the rooms is not the best and the whole place is in serious need of a revamp – the potential is huge. The main restaurant has retained its grandeur and has good food and service, and the palace itself has a fine lawn and gardens. Rooms are $90/105.

Close by is the new *Radisson Hotel* (☎ *419358, fax 411720, email radkat@mos .com.np)*, a very modern, well maintained and pleasantly decorated hotel with excellent facilities. Standard rooms are $175, while larger deluxe rooms, complete with nice touches such as data ports for laptop computers, are $185.

Farther north again, the *Hotel Shangri-La* (☎ *412999, fax 414184, email hosang@ mos.com.np)* is one of Kathmandu's best hotels. The rooms are attractive and well maintained, the service is swift and professional, and best of all, there's a beautiful garden with an adjoining restaurant, and a swimming pool. Rooms are not cheap at $120/130, but very good value in this range.

Dwarika Village Hotel (☎ *470770, fax 471379, email dwarika@mos.com.np)*, built in traditional style and featuring superb examples of antique woodwork, is an outstanding and unusual hotel. The owners have rescued thousands of carvings from around the valley (from buildings facing demolition or collapse) and many have been incorporated into the complex, which consists of a small cluster of buildings separated by pleasant brick-paved courtyards. A large workshop is funded by the hotel and craftspeople patiently repair and restore lattice windows and carvings that would otherwise almost certainly be lost in Kathmandu's rush to survive and modernise. The end result is a beautiful hybrid – a cross between a museum and a boutique hotel.

The hotel is near the airport and Pashupatinath, and its only disadvantage is that it's a bit of a distance to the eating places in Thamel or Durbar Marg; taxis are not a problem, however. The hotel has won a Heritage Award from the Pacific Asia Travel Association (PATA), and has excellent rooms at $135/155, $40 more for deluxe rooms. The rooms are large, atmospheric and very comfortable, but do not have air-con or TV.

PLACES TO EAT

Kathmandu's restaurants attempt an amazing variety of international cuisines with a reasonable degree of success. There are few places in south Asia where your choice of restaurants is so varied. After long months on the road in India or long weeks trekking in Nepal most travellers find Kathmandu a culinary paradise. Recent arrivals from the west may not be quite so impressed, but some places are great value by any standards.

If you eat in the really rock-bottom restaurants around Kathmandu, be cautious about hygiene. Few travellers spend long in Nepal without coming across something which disagrees with them even if they're very fastidious about where they eat. Eating 'street food' from stalls and pavement kitchens in Kathmandu is likely to wreak havoc on all but the strongest of stomachs. Health standards have definitely improved in Kathmandu over the years, however, and you are highly unlikely to have serious problems if you eat in the popular tourist-oriented restaurants. In these places it's even safe to try a salad, drink a glass of water and eat the ice cream – although some would argue that this is living dangerously.

In the budget range, Kathmandu has numerous tea stalls and shops. Many may not even have a name but at these stalls dal bhat tarakari – the lentil soup, rice and vegetable everyday meal of most Nepalis – will be the main dish on offer. By up-country standards these places aren't cheap – dal bhat tarakari will probably set you back Rs 50.

In Thamel, if you stay away from beer, you can eat until you burst for less than Rs 200. A bottle of beer can cost anything from Rs 90 to Rs 130 and nearly double your bill.

As you might expect, the top restaurants have prices to match, but they're still reasonable by western standards. More expensive restaurants slap a 10% to 15% government tax on top of their bill, but you'll still probably only pay less than $20 per person.

Tipping is becoming more accepted (and appreciated) in Nepal but your loose change or 5% is fine in cheaper places; a bit more will be expected in the expensive restaurants.

This section is divided geographically, with final sections on expensive places and places specialising in Nepali food.

Thamel

Thamel restaurants spill into Paknajol, Jyatha and Chhetrapati, just like Thamel hotels. The junction outside the Kathmandu Guest House is the centre of Thamel dining and you can find numerous budget-priced restaurants within a minute's walk in either direction.

While there are literally dozens of budget restaurants in Thamel, there is often little to choose between them in what they offer – a standard menu has a go at pretty well everything, and after eating in a few you may well come to the conclusion that all the chefs were taught by the same person, or perhaps there is only one chef who runs around and cooks at all of them! The food tends to be remarkably similar, and often very bland. What marks the difference between these places more than anything is the atmosphere, music, service and who happens to be there on the night. There are exceptions, however, and these days there are some restaurants in Thamel serving really top class food at affordable prices.

The central Thamel restaurants include the best known of the lot, *KC's Restaurant*. Kaysee himself no longer presides, but he hit the magic travellers' restaurant formula spot-on. Although the food is still good, the restaurant has become a bit expensive by Thamel standards. A delicious breakfast starts at around Rs 100 (which isn't bad), but a vegetarian lasagne is Rs 190, and one of KC's famous steaks (Kathmandu's sizzle plate mania started right here) is around Rs 200.

On this same stretch of Thamel's restaurant centre you can try the *Pumpernickel Bakery* for freshly baked bread. In the morning, overland travellers crowd in for croissants and filter coffee in the pleasant garden area at the back.

Also across the road from KC's is *Helena's Restaurant*, another of the long-running places with the standard Kathmandu menu ranging from vegetarian dishes and soups through pastas and burgers to steaks, with a great selection of cakes and pies to follow at around Rs 50. Nearby, the easily missed *Garden Cafe* is a pleasant spot for an alfresco breakfast, without the crowds.

Alice's Restaurant, in the Namche Bazaar building south of the Kathmandu Guest House, is a decent place, a cut above the cheapies, but still very reasonable. Pizza is Rs 110, vegetable moussaka Rs 100 and pancakes Rs 45.

Around the intersection near the Kathmandu Guest House are a couple of *Hot Bread* outlets which do a roaring trade in sandwiches, bread rolls, pizza slices (Rs 50) and pastries. These are really popular at lunchtime, and the ham and cheese rolls (Rs 65) make a great lunch on the run. One of these places has an upstairs terrace; the other is purely for take-aways.

Restaurant Casa Della Pasta is a flash new place near the Kathmandu Guest House, with excellent Italian food, good service and a big movie screen. This place is part of the plush Ultimate Planet Bar (see Entertainment).

Third Eye is a long-running favourite that retains something of the old Kathmandu atmosphere. There's a sit-down section at the front, and a more informal section with low tables and cushions at the back. Indian food is the speciality, but there are also a small number of continental offerings, such as excellent chateaubriand using real beef flown in from India. The tandoori dishes here are especially good. It's wise to book a table at this popular place in the high season.

Yin Yang, across the street from the Third Eye, is one of the new breed of Thamel restaurants. It serves authentic Thai food cooked by an authentic Thai chef. It's not particularly cheap, with starters around Rs 90 and main meals from Rs 200 to Rs 300, but the food is a definite cut above the imitation Thai food found elsewhere. You won't get in here without a booking in the high season.

Down the road from the Yin Yang, *Wiesel Bakery* serves good vegetarian food. It has a pleasant garden and is a nice quiet place for breakfast, with newspapers to read and music playing in the background. This is another place with a good range of cakes, breads and pastries.

Another place on this street worth mentioning is the *Green Leaves Restaurant*, which is mostly outdoor and has Nepali musicians performing each evening. If you sit inside you can watch the kitchen activity through the large window. The pasta dishes are great, and good value at Rs 70 to Rs 90.

Many Thamel restaurants have a go at some Italian dishes, but *La Dolce Vita*, with the movie motifs, makes the best attempt at true Italian cuisine and the menu is a bit more imaginative than the standard Thamel offering, with delights such as tiramisu. There are both indoor and open-air sections, and the food is pretty good. Prices are a little higher than the rock-bottom Thamel average – vegetarian dishes Rs 130 to Rs 160, pizzas Rs 180 to Rs 200, pasta Rs 150 to 190 – but so is the quality.

Continue a little north and you come to Pilgrims Book House. Out through the rear of the shop is *Pilgrims Feed N Read*, but it is also accessible from the compound next to the Kathmandu Guest House. It's a relaxed place, with indoor and outdoor areas, and Tibetan beer *(thumpa)* is available on request.

Above Pilgrims Book House is the efficiently run *G's Terrace*. It's a pleasant spot for an evening drink and has a good music selection. The menu features a number of authentic German dishes, and there's draught beer and German newspapers. It's a bit more expensive than some places, but the standards are correspondingly high and the prices include tax. Fillet steak is Rs 210, Bavarian potato soup with sausage is Rs 155, and chicken chilli is Rs 155.

Next door again is the compound with the Ultimate Descents office and the open-air *Northfield Cafe*, run by the same Mike as the famous Mike's Breakfast in Naxal. This is the place for serious breakfast devotees – eggs any way you like (sensational eggs florentine) – and the Mexican lunch dishes are also good, although prices are a bit higher than elsewhere.

Several other popular restaurants cluster near the landmark Kathmandu Guest House corner. The name may be French, but *Le Bistro Restaurant* has the familiar international menu with lots of pasta dishes. A prime attraction here is the large open courtyard, ideal for pleasant outdoor dining. The good-value breakfasts are particularly popular; two eggs, toast and tea costs around Rs 80. There are a number of decent vegetarian dishes like pizza and enchiladas for around Rs 100, but steaks jump to Rs 180.

The Kathmandu Guest House's *Las Kus Restaurant* serves straightforward, well prepared food and is another popular breakfast spot. This is a good place to try traditional Tibetan dishes like *momo* (pasta stuffed with meat and/or vegetables, a bit like large ravioli). Directly across the road and upstairs is the *Brezel Bakery*, a pleasant rooftop spot overlooking the Thamel activity below. This is another good breakfast place, with fresh brown bread.

A few doors along on the 1st floor is the *Nargila Restaurant*, one of the very few places to offer Middle Eastern food. They do a pretty reasonable job of it too. Felafel and pitta is Rs 95, or there's couscous (Rs 75) and dips such as *baba ghanoush* or hummus served with pitta for Rs 60.

The *Rum Doodle Restaurant* was named, of course, after the world's highest mountain, the 40,000½-foot Mt Rum Doodle. The heroic conquest of Rum Doodle was dramatically described in that spoof on heroic mountaineering books, *The Ascent of Rum Doodle* (Dark Peak, Sheffield, 1979). The restaurant is in the same side street as the Holy Lodge, and specialises in steak and pasta. It's a favourite meeting place for mountaineering expeditions, particularly in the upstairs 40,000½ Foot Bar.

Farther north, opposite the Hotel Mandap, is another good open-air Thai place, the new *Krua Thai*. The food is reasonably authentic (ie, spicy) although not that cheap: soups are Rs 180 to Rs 210, main courses Rs 210 to Rs 440.

Also in this area is the *Tama Fuji*, one of a number of Japanese restaurants in Thamel. The food is pretty decent and reasonably priced.

In the modern Sanchaya Kosh Bhawan Shopping Centre on Tridevi Marg there are a couple of places worth mentioning. *Fire and Ice* is an excellent open-air Italian place serving some of the best pizzas in Kathmandu (Rs 180 to Rs 270), imported Italian soft-serve ice cream, seriously good coffee and rousing opera – Italian, of course. It's deservedly popular and you'll need a reservation in the high season, or eat early. Next door is the *Dechenling Restaurant*, a good little Tibetan place with very reasonable prices.

The *Utse Restaurant*, in the hotel of the same name in Jyatha, is one of the longest-running restaurants in Thamel and turns out excellent Tibetan dishes, such as momo and *kothe* (fried pasta stuffed with meat/vegetables). Talumein soup costs Rs 55, and the traditional Tibetan-style meals are also worth a try: *kadug dhayshey* for four is Rs 1320, gacok is Rs 1220. Gacok (also spelt gyakok) is a meal named after the brass tureen which is heated at the table and from which various meats and vegetables are served.

An excellent spot for momos is the tiny *Dolma Restaurant*, just a few doors along from the Utse. This place is typical of the Tibetan eateries dotted around town – it's just a hole in the wall, and momos are the only thing on the menu, but they are excellent and at Rs 15 for a plate, top value.

In this same street, the *Omei Restaurant* is not a bad Japanese place, and the *Chikusa* is a Japanese coffee shop.

Across from the Marco Polo Guest House is the *Old Vienna Inn* which is the place to come if you're after Wiener schnitzel, goulash etc. Unfortunately it is one of the old Thamel places which is very tired these days. Most mains are around Rs 200 to Rs 250. The *Gourmet Delicatessen* in front of the restaurant is good, with all sorts of unlikely food – from sausages and salami, to apple strudel and ice cream.

Other good places for deli items are the *Tit Bits* deli in the Hotel Garuda, and the glossy *Delicatessen Center*, prominently signposted on Kantipath and with a mind-boggling array of imported cheeses.

Overlooking Thamel chowk itself are the rooftop *Maples* and *Les Yeux*, which both have a standard Thamel menu and a good view.

Head south from Thamel into Chhetrapati to find more popular travellers' restaurants including *Narayan's Steak House Restaurant*, another of the long-term survivors in this area. It's very popular, competent and low-priced with a wide range of breakfast dishes, pasta (Rs 90 to Rs 110) and pizza (Rs 100 to Rs 125). Narayan's also produces delicious ice cream in half a dozen different flavours, and offers a great selection of pies and cakes.

Close by is the *Everest Steak House*, which is very popular, especially with returned trekkers suffering from protein deficiency. The steaks are excellent and range from Rs 175 to Rs 200, although chateaubriand is a dazzling Rs 650. There are also

some vegetarian alternatives, including pizza (Rs 110 to 170) and pasta (Rs 150).

Freak St

Freak St has a number of restaurants where you can find good food at low prices, although the choice is fairly limited. Even if you're staying in other areas of the city it's nice to know there are some good places for lunch if you're sightseeing around Durbar Square.

The popular *Diyalo Restaurant* at the Annapurna Lodge is a good little place with a large menu, including crepes (Rs 85), burgers (Rs 85), and a few Chinese and Indian dishes, all for less than Rs 90.

The *Paradise Restaurant* is a good vegetarian place, with dishes such as lasagne (Rs 80) and vegetarian schnitzel burgers (Rs 85).

Cafe Culture is a cosy place to hang out with a good atmosphere, good music and board games to help while away the time. The menu features vegetarian dishes (Rs 70 to Rs 85) and there's a great range of lassis and juices.

Next door, the long-running *Snowman* is a bit old hat these days but it still has the best range of cakes in this area.

Up at the Basantapur Square end of Freak St, the *Mona Lisa* is a pleasant place with friendly staff. Right next door and also overlooking the square is the *Cosmopolitan Restaurant*.

At the other end of Durbar Square, *Festive Fare* is a reasonable rooftop place right opposite the Taleju Temple. There are great views over the Hanuman Dhoka rooftops, and the food and service aren't too bad either.

Central Kathmandu

The restaurants in the glossier Kantipath and Durbar Marg areas are generally more expensive than around Thamel although there are a few lower-priced exceptions. See Expensive Restaurants later for some of Kathmandu's real night-out possibilities.

Several places on Durbar Marg have good food from the subcontinent. The *Mangalore Coffee House*, just around the corner from Durbar Marg, serves good south Indian vegetarian dishes like *masala dosa* (curried vegetables wrapped in a crisp, lentil-flour pancake) for Rs 30, and is a popular local gathering place.

Nanglo Cafe & Pub has a popular open-air terrace dining area and an international menu. There's quite a lively atmosphere and there's a 'cybercorner' for surfers. A large pizza costs Rs 180, burgers Rs 65 to Rs 90, pasta Rs 85 to Rs 105, and a fixed Nepali lunch with rice, dal, meat, vegetable curry, pickle and green salad is Rs 165.

Nirula's, near the Hotel de l'Annapurna on Durbar Marg, is an outlet of the well known Indian chain, with a range of pizzas and burgers. However, the air in here is stale and the whole place – staff included – looks thoroughly tired. The only things worth bothering with are the ice creams (Rs 30). Much better is the *Wimpy* outlet, also on Durbar Marg. Also close by is another *Hot Breads* outlet, with good bakery items.

Beside the entrance to the Hotel de l'Annapurna, the *Annapurna Coffee Shop* offers a standard 'big hotel' style menu with burgers from Rs 225, pizza from Rs 250, Nepali dishes from Rs 100 to Rs 250 and milkshakes or lassi (yoghurt with sugar and fruit) at Rs 100. It's popular but the food is only average.

DURBAR MARG

PLACES TO STAY
14 Hotel de l'Annapurna
19 Hotel Sherpa
25 Hotel Woodlands Dynasty Plaza
28 Hotel Mayalu; Yeti Travels (American Express)

PLACES TO EAT
3 Seoul A-ir-ring
5 Kushi Fuji Restaurant; Tukche Takali Kitchen
8 Hot Breads Bakery
10 Baan Thai Restaurant; Wimpy
11 Koto Restaurant
12 Ghar-e-Kebab Restaurant
13 Annapurna Coffee Shop
20 Nirula's
22 Nanglo Chinese Room; Nanglo Cafe & Pub
23 Amber Restaurant
24 Moti Mahal Restaurant; Godavari; Tansen Restaurant
27 Mangalore Coffee House

OTHER
1 Royal Palace
2 Pakistan International Airways
4 Curio Arts
6 Singapore Airlines
7 Noor Gems; Ritual Art Gallery
9 Potala Art Gallery
15 CIWEC Clinic
16 CIWEC Clinic
17 Thai International & British Airways
18 Lufthansa & Air France
21 Dawa Arts
26 Taxi & Auto-Rickshaw Stand

Other Durbar Marg possibilities include the moderately priced *Koto Restaurant*, which some say prepares the best Japanese food in town. A set menu is Rs 300, but there are plenty of dishes for around Rs 150. The *Baan Thai* serves excellent Thai food, and the service is very attentive. Expect to pay around Rs 400, plus service and drinks.

Close by is the *Kushi Fuji Restaurant*, a Japanese place with both traditional and table seating. You can order a la carte from the extensive menu, or there is a variety of set meals from Rs 530 to Rs 580.

Moti Mahal serves pretty decent Indian food. Most main dishes are around Rs 150 to Rs 200. Upstairs is the vegetarian section, the *Godavari*, with dosas at Rs 60, and a thali lunch for Rs 150 or dinner at Rs 180. Just a few doors along is the more expensive *Tansen*, which has a very good reputation for Indian food.

At the opposite end of Durbar Marg the *Seoul A-ri-ring* has a pleasant rooftop area and serves dishes barbecued at your table for Rs 400. Other main dishes are Rs 200 to Rs 400, or there's a set meal at Rs 500 (Rs 700 seafood). It's open daily for lunch and dinner.

Elsewhere

You can start the day at one of the best and most popular breakfast places in the city. As the name suggests, *Mike's Breakfast* specialises in breakfasts and they do them well. The restaurant is in the suburb of Naxal, opposite the police headquarters about a 15 minute walk from the top end of Durbar Marg, and Mike presides over the whole operation. Meals are served in the attractive, leafy garden of an old Rana house, and are accompanied by soothing classical music.

Mike's is open daily from 7 am to 9 pm, and does pizza on Tuesday and Friday nights only. It's not cheap, but is certainly a laid-back way to start the day. The breakfast menu includes excellent waffles with yoghurt, fruit and syrup at Rs 170, or a smoked trout omelette at Rs 230. Lunch is also good, with dishes like quiche and salad costing around Rs 160. While you're here take a look at the excellent Indigo Gallery.

Nepali Restaurants

There is a growing number of restaurants around town which specialise in Nepali food. These run the gamut from unobtrusive little places in Thamel where Rs 100 will get you a good meal, up to fancy places with cultural shows which cost 10 times that, but are still good value. Most places offer a set meal, either veg or nonveg, and you sit on cushions at low tables.

One of the cheapest is the *Jhigu Thayabhu* in Paknajol, north of Thamel Chowk. Meat dishes cost Rs 50 to Rs 100, vegetarian Rs 30 to Rs 70, or there is a set lunch for $8.

The *Thamel House* (☎ 410388) is set in a traditional old Newari building, and so has bags of atmosphere. The food is also traditional Nepali, although they may try to lumber you with the set menu at Rs 550. Ask for the a la carte menu and choose individual dishes (Rs 60 to Rs 150); there are a few unusual ones, such as wild boar. It's a good night out, although the service can be patchy.

On Durbar Marg there's the small *Tukche Thakali Kitchen*, which also includes Tibetan dishes. The interior is a bit gloomy, but the food is good and reasonably priced at Rs 125 for a veg set lunch, or Rs 155 with meat. In the evenings it's Rs 400 for a fixed menu of around 10 dishes.

The *Kathmandu Kitchen* near the southern end of Durbar Marg is a straightforward place with both floor and table seating areas. The set menu features a dozen or so dishes, and is not bad value at $11, although the atmosphere is lacking.

Bhanchha Ghar is in a traditional three storey Newari house in Kamaladi, just east of Durbar Marg from the turn-off by the clocktower. There's an upstairs loft where you stretch out on handmade carpets and cushions for a drink, snacks and a brief 'cultural show' featuring the various ethnic costumes of Nepal. You then move downstairs to take advantage of an excellent menu of traditional Nepali dishes and delicacies. Musicians stroll between the tables playing traditional Nepali folk songs. It's not cheap ($12 per person, plus drinks and tax) but the food is very good, and the range is probably the best of any of the Nepali restaurants. It's open daily from 11 am to 10.30 pm.

In the same vein, but perhaps more ambitious, is the *Bhojan Griha*, in a recently restored 150-year-old mansion in Dilli Bazaar, east of the city centre. It's worth eating here just to see the imaginative renovation of this beautiful old building. Again, dancers and musicians stroll through the various rooms throughout the evening. Although most of the seating is traditional (ie on the floor), there are a couple of rooms with conventional tables if your knees or back can't hack it! The set menu is Rs 997, plus tax and drinks, but it's a worthwhile night out.

One of the best places for Nepali food is the *Krishnarpan* restaurant at Dwarika's Village Hotel on the Ring Rd. It possibly lacks some of the atmosphere of other places, but the food gets consistent praise from diners. Prices range from $18 for a six course meal up to $29 for a full 16 course extravaganza.

Expensive Restaurants

Kathmandu's big hotels have some interesting restaurant possibilities and although the prices are sky-high by Nepali standards, they're remarkably cheap compared to the cost of similar restaurants in the west. One thing you will consistently find in these more expensive places is heating, which is rare in the cheaper places.

One of the most famous possibilities is the Yak & Yeti's *Chimney Room* (☎ 248999). It retains a tenuous historical link with Russian-born Boris Lissanevitch, who was the founder of the Royal Hotel, Kathmandu's first hotel for western visitors. The central, open fireplace gives it plenty of atmosphere, but unfortunately apart from the borsch, which is still excellent, there are few reminders of Boris' days. Nevertheless, the food is well prepared, if somewhat bland. The borsch is Rs 130, and chicken stroganoff is Rs 405. Other main dishes are from Rs 550 to Rs 1000.

Also in the Yak & Yeti is the *Naachghar Restaurant* (☎ 248999). It's a grand, baroque room with high ceilings, gilt mirrors, marble, and ornate plasterwork. Performances of Nepali music and dance are given, but ring ahead to check what nights they are on. The menu is strong on both Indian and Nepali dishes – those from the tandoor are said to be good – but there are also some continental options. Vegetarian dishes are around Rs 170 to Rs 350, nonveg from Rs 370 to Rs 400.

The *Ghar-e-Kebab*, on Durbar Marg outside the Hotel de l'Annapurna, has some of the best Indian and tandoori food in the city. Indian miniatures hang on the walls and in the evenings classical Indian music is played and traditional Urdu *ghazals* (love songs) are sung. A complete meal for two including drinks costs about Rs 2000.

At the Royal Palace end of Kantipath, the *Fuji Restaurant* (☎ 225272) serves quality Japanese food. It's away from the road in an atmospheric pavilion that was built in 1905 in the grounds of the nearby Bahadur Bhawan Palace (now government offices). The tempura set menu is Rs 450 to Rs 650 or you can choose from the a la carte menu and probably get away with, around Rs 500 per person, including a beer. It's open daily except Monday for lunch and dinner.

The trek out to the Soaltee Holiday Inn Crowne Plaza on the western side of town may be worthwhile to try the excellent Indian and Nepali dishes at the *Himalchuli Restaurant*. It features woodcarvings from Bhaktapur and traditional Nepali music plays in the background, but it's only open in the evenings. Local dishes cost around Rs 300, while Indian dishes are Rs 130 to Rs 300. Many say the Soaltee's misnamed *Al Fresco Italian Restaurant* (it's actually indoors) serves the best Italian food in Nepal; soups are around Rs 120, pizzas Rs 225 to Rs 325, pasta Rs 275 to Rs 315 and veal scaloppine Rs 500.

Also out of town, the *Far Pavilions Restaurant* at the Hotel Everest offers great views over Kathmandu from its 7th-floor vantage point and serves tandoori (Rs 340 to Rs 700) and other Indian dishes. Main courses are around Rs 350, or there's a set thali meal at Rs 550 nonveg or Rs 500 veg. It's a good place, but is open in the evenings only.

Out at the Babar Mahal Revisited complex (see Shopping later) near Singh Durbar, the **Simply Shutters Bistrot** offers excellent French influenced food in very pleasant surroundings, particularly in the evenings when the courtyard is illuminated. Entrees are Rs 120 to Rs 200, main courses are Rs 300 to Rs 380. The restaurant is open daily from noon to 11 pm.

ENTERTAINMENT

Nepal is an early-to-bed country and even in Kathmandu you'll find few people on the streets after 10 pm. This is gradually changing, particularly in Thamel, as a number of places are now licensed to stay open a bit later – there's even a high-tech disco due to open soon. Of course the crowded restaurants and bars are great places to meet and talk with people and the big hotels do offer some traditional nightlife for those who positively cannot live without it. Kathmandu also has cultural shows, cinemas and four of west Asia's very few casinos.

Bars

There are half a dozen bars scattered around Thamel, all within a short walk of each other. Each has quite a distinctive atmosphere, so it's worth poking your nose in each to see which has the crowd and the style that appeals to you. Closing time is officially 10 pm, although every so often one or other of them will get a live band and a midnight licence, and things really hop.

Tom & Jerry's, upstairs opposite Pilgrims, is a rowdy place with pool tables. Close by is the **New Orleans**, a popular place which often has live music. It's also not a bad place to eat.

The **Pub Maya** near the Kathmandu Guest House is a long-running place which remains popular, as does the associated **Maya Cocktail Bar**. At the end of the Kathmandu Guest House street, the **Thamel 66 Bar** is another possibility.

One of the most well known places is the **Rum Doodle**, which attracts an interesting crowd of adventurers (see Places to Eat).

Close to Thamel Chowk is the **Underground Bar**, which seems to stay open later than most, and always has the music cranked up pretty high. On Tridevi Marg the **Jolly Blues Bar** is also currently popular.

In the new building between the Kathmandu Guest House and the Yin Yang Restaurant is the **Ultimate Planet Bar**. It's a very plush place with leather seating and a sophisticated sound and light system. There's a small dance floor, and dances are held on a regular basis, with entry including a buffet dinner. Beer is reasonably priced at around Rs 150.

Disco

Kathmandu has just one disco – the **Moon Sun Disco** at the Heritage Plaza in Kamaladi. It's open nightly until late and is popular among well-to-do Nepalis.

Casinos

Kathmandu has four casinos, all at the up-market hotels – the Soaltee, Everest, de l'Annapurna and the Yak & Yeti.

If you turn up at any of them within a week of arrival with your onward airline ticket and your passport you can get Indian Rs 200 of free coupons. You can play in either Indian rupees (almost a hard currency in Nepali terms) or US dollars, and winnings (in the same currency) can be taken out of the country when you leave. The casinos are open 24 hours a day, and they'll ply you with free beer if you're actually playing at the tables. The main games offered are roulette and blackjack, the main clients are Indian. Nepalis are forbidden from entering altogether.

Nepali Music & Dance

There are regular performances of Nepali music and dancing in Kathmandu, including at the **National Theatre**. All the big hotels have nightly 'cultural shows', usually in their main restaurant around 7 pm, and these typically cost around Rs 200.

The Himalchuli Cultural Group is a dance troupe which performs nightly at the *Cultural Hall* attached to the Hotel Shankar in Lazimpat, north of the Royal Palace. The hour-long show costs Rs 300 and starts at 7 pm in summer, 6.30 pm in winter.

Cinemas

Video Night in Kathmandu (see Books in the Facts for the Visitor chapter) has certainly had an impact on the city – there are video shops everywhere and cinemas are having a hard time of it. Indian films, usually not subtitled, are the usual cinematic fare, although there are occasional English-language films. Admission charges are minimal and catching a Hindi movie is well worthwhile since not understanding the language is not a real obstacle to enjoying these comedy-musical spectaculars. The Indians call them 'masala' movies as they have a little bit of everything in them.

In the small video parlours – and a number of the restaurants in Thamel – popular western movies appear on pirated videos or laser discs almost as soon as they hit the cinemas in the west. You'll see the movies chalked up on pavement blackboards on the streets.

In the Kathmandu Plaza in Kamaladi is the Kathmandu Minivision, the only cinema in Kathmandu showing western films. Programs and screening times are usually published in the *Kathmandu Post*.

SHOPPING

Everything turned out in the various centres around the valley can be found in Kathmandu although you may often find a better choice or more unusual items in the real centres – eg head for Jawlakhel, south of Patan, for Tibetan carpets; to Patan for cast metal statues and other craftwork; to Bhaktapur for the finest woodcarvings and pottery; and to Thimi for more pottery and masks. See Shopping in the Patan and Bhaktapur sections for more details.

Crafts of various kinds are on sale all around Kathmandu, and the money that tourists spend on craft items makes an important contribution to Nepal's economy, as has been the case for hundreds of years.

The most important rules when buying anything worth a reasonable amount of money are firstly, to put in some legwork and secondly, buy just before you leave, not just after you arrive. Prices vary hugely and until you have done some research, you'll have no idea whether you're being ripped off (to an acceptable degree) or not.

Lastly, all serious shoppers should read Jeff Greenwald's humorous *Shopping for Buddhas* (a title in Lonely Planet's Journeys series), which gives fair warning of the fate that can befall obsessive types.

Bronze Statues

The best place to start is on Durbar Marg, but there are also some shops worth visiting on New Rd. This is one area where research is vitally important, as quality and prices do not necessarily have any direct correlation. Curio Arts on Durbar Marg is a good place to start.

Curios

An endless supply of curios, stuff, knick-knacks, pieces, thingos and plain junk is

---

Babar Mahal Revisited

This shopping complex at Babar Mahal, near the Singh Durbar government offices, is an example of what can be done with a bit of imagination – oh, and plenty of money. The building consists of old Rana palace outbuildings, and they have been redeveloped to house a dozen or so upmarket shops and a couple of good restaurants. Although aimed at the tour groups, it's worth coming for a look as the shops sell top quality merchandise.

turned out for tourists. Most does not come from Tibet (but from the local Tamang community) and most are not more than six weeks old, but none of this matters. If you shop around you can find creations that are beautifully made by craftspeople whose time is obviously not worth a lot of money. Basantapur Square is the headquarters for this trade, but before you match wits with these operators, visit the Amrita Craft Collection in Thamel. This relatively small shop has a wide collection, all with marked prices that are reasonably fair.

Thangkas
The main centre for thangkas is just off Durbar Square, and this is where you'll find the best salespeople (not necessarily the best thangkas). For modern work in Thamel, visit the Tibetan Thangka Treasure, near KC's restaurant. The Indigo Gallery, at Mike's Breakfast in Naxal, has some excellent pieces.

Clothing
Kathmandu is the best place in the valley for clothes and many places have good-quality ready-to-wear western fashions, particularly shirts. Amusing embroidered T-shirts are a popular speciality. There are lots of good tailors around Thamel and, apart from embroidered T-shirts, they'll also embroider just about anything you want on your own jacket or jeans. Tara Boutique, with shops on Tridevi Marg near Thamel and on Durbar Marg, makes wonderful hand-painted pure silk women's fashions at prices very favourable with what you'd pay at home.

Handicrafts
For general handicrafts such as handmade paper, ceramics and woodwork, much of it made by disadvantaged or minority groups, one of the best places to start looking is Kopundol, the road which runs from Bagmati Bridge up to Patan. Here there are a number of shops, such as Dhukuti, Mahaguthi (also with an outlet in Lazimpat) and WEAN (Women Entrepreneurs Association

of Nepal), with a wide range of goods at reasonable prices.

Gems & Jewellery
Buying gems is always a risky business unless you know what you're doing. Be immediately suspicious of anyone who tells you that you will be able to make an enormous profit – if it was possible and legal they would do it themselves. Noor Gems on Durbar Marg is a long-running and reputable place.

There are dozens of jewellery shops in Thamel and elsewhere in the city including New Rd and Durbar Marg. Much of the merchandise comes from India, but a lot is also produced locally. When walking between Thamel and Durbar Square you'll often come across small shops with a few craftspeople working with silver.

The prices for silver jewellery are very low compared with what you'd pay at home, and many people have jewellery made to order. You buy the stones or draw the design and they'll have it made up usually in just a day or two. The quality is usually excellent, but be sure to agree on a price before giving the go-ahead to have anything made.

Tibetan Antiques
Kathmandu seems to be the world clearing house for a continual stream of antiques being brought out of Tibet. These include everything from thangkas to carpets, jewellery, storage chests, carvings, religious objects, saddles and clothing. Since the Chinese have done their utmost to destroy Tibetan culture, removing some of what remains to safety is perhaps more morally acceptable than some other 'collecting' that goes on in Nepal. There are a number of good shops on Durbar Marg, but don't go without a very healthy wallet. The Ritual Art Gallery and Potala Art Gallery are both worth a look.

Kashmiri Goods
Since the war in Kashmir killed the tourist trade there, many Kashmiris have migrated to Nepal to sell traditional crafts such as carpets,

tapestry, woollen shawls and papier-mâché. These guys are excellent salespeople, so buy with caution. Prices are pretty good; they would be cheaper in Kashmir of course, but might well come with a bonus bullet. Cottage Crafts on the ground floor of the Sanchaya Kosh Bhawan Shopping Centre (across the road from the immigration office) has a good selection and reliable prices.

Indian Goods
With the resurgence of popularity for Gujarat and Rajasthan's embroidered clothing and manchester, a number of shops have opened in Kathmandu. Prices are, needless to say, considerably higher than if you buy in India, but considerably less than if you buy in the west.

Trekking Supplies
The Bluebird supermarkets have a wide variety of goods. There's a branch near the Blue Star Hotel near the main bridge across the Bagmati to Patan, and another in Lazimpat on the continuation of Kantipath (on the right-hand side about 1km from Thamel).

In Thamel, for trekking food like noodles, nuts, dried fruit and cheese, there's a number of small supermarkets, such as the Best Shopping Centre at the end of Tridevi Marg, at the corner where it narrows and enters Thamel proper.

GETTING THERE & AWAY
See the Getting There & Away chapter for details of getting to Kathmandu by air or land.

Air
Kathmandu is the only international arrival point for flights to Nepal and is also the main centre for domestic flights.

International Airlines International airlines with offices in Kathmandu include:

Aeroflot
   (☎ 227399) Kamaladi
Air India
   (☎ 415637) Hattisar
Austrian Airlines
   (☎ 241506) Kamaladi
Bangladesh Biman
   (☎ 434740) Naxal
British Airways
   (☎ 222266) Durbar Marg
Cathay Pacific
   (☎ 248944) Kamaladi
China Southwest Airlines
   (☎ 411302) Hattisar
Druk Air
   (☎ 225166) Durbar Marg
Gulf Air
   (☎ 430456) Hattisar
Indian Airlines
   (☎ 410906) Hattisar
Lufthansa
   (☎ 223052) Durbar Marg
Myanmar (Burma) Airways
   (☎ 224839) Durbar Marg
Necon Air
   (☎ 473860) Sina Mangal
   (☎ 258664, reservation@necon.mos.com.np)
   Tridevi Marg, Thamel
Pakistan International Airlines
   (☎ 223102) Durbar Marg
Qatar Airlines
   (☎ 422961) Hattisar
Royal Nepal Airlines
   (☎ 220757) Kantipath
Singapore Airlines
   (☎ 220759) Durbar Marg
Thai International
   (☎ 223565) Durbar Marg
Transavia
   (☎ 414192) Kamaladi

Numerous other airlines are represented in Kathmandu. There are three important rules with flights out of Kathmandu – reconfirm, reconfirm and reconfirm! This particularly applies to Royal Nepal Airlines, and at peak times when flights are heavily booked you should reconfirm when you first arrive in Nepal and reconfirm again towards the end of your stay. Even this may not guarantee you a seat – make sure you get to the airport very early as people at the end of the queue can still be left behind.

Domestic Airlines The various domestic airlines have offices around the city. However, these companies, their offices and their phone numbers seem to change with the weather; it is far less hassle to buy tickets through a travel agent or your hotel.

Domestic airlines that are currently operating include:

Buddha Air
(☎ 417802, buddha_air@wlink.com.np)
Hattisar
Cosmic Air
(☎ 427150, soi@wlink.com.np) Maharajganj
Gorkha Airlines
(☎ 423137, gorkha@mos.com.np) Hattisar
Lumbini Airways
(☎ 483381, lumbiniair@wlink.com.np)
Kamaladi
Necon Air
(☎ 473860) Sina Mangal
(☎ 258664, reservation@necon.mos.com.np)
Tridevi Marg, Thamel
Royal Nepal Airlines Corporation (RNAC)
(☎ 225347, fax 225348)
RNAC Building, corner New Rd and Kantipath.
Computer reservations for flights to Pokhara,
Meghauli (for Chitwan), mountain flights,
Jomsom, Lukla and Bharatpur only. Open daily
9 am to 4 pm.

RNAC has computerised booking only on
six routes (see earlier), and these are booked
at the main RNAC office; all other domestic flights are booked in an utterly haphazard
manner at a small office just around the corner. Here it seems the booking clerk keeps
issuing tickets as long as people keep
fronting up with money. There appear to be
no reservation charts to speak of, so the potential for overbooking is high. Confirm
more than once, and get to the airport early.
The other domestic carriers seem to be well
organised.

Bus

The main bus station is on the Ring Rd at
Balaju, north-west of the city centre. It is
officially called the Gongbu Bus Park, but
is generally known as the Kathmandu Bus
Terminal, or simply 'bus park'. This bus
station is basically for all long-distance
buses to Pokhara and destinations in the
Terai. It's a huge and busy place, and there
are no signs in English so unless you read
Nepali it can be thoroughly confusing.
There's at least one reservation counter for
each destination, and bookings for long
trips should be made a day in advance.

Buses for destinations within the Kathmandu Valley, and for those on the Arniko
Highway (Jiri, Barabise and the Tibetan

Buses from Kathmandu Bus Terminal

Destination	Duration (hrs)	Cost (Rs)	Ticket Window
Bhairawa	12	159 n, 128 d	13
Biratnagar	11½	299 n, 265 d	6
Birganj	8	145 n, 114 d	13
Butwal	8	132 d	13
Dharan	12	285 n	5
Gorkha	5	85 d	18
Hetauda	8	66	23, 24
Hile	overnight	335 n	5
Janakpur	8	206 n, 206 d	10
Kakarbhitta	14	339 n	1, 2
Mahendranagar	18	383 n	13
Narayanghat	3	82 n, 70 d	13
Nepalganj	14	280 n, 224 d	13
Pokhara	8	114 d	17

d = day; n = night

border), operate from the City bus station, in the centre of the city on the eastern edge of Tundikhel.

The exceptions to this are the more expensive tourist buses – heavily promoted in Thamel – which depart from the Thamel end of Kantipath. See the Pokhara chapter and Chitwan in the Terai chapter for more details.

See the table for a list of destinations served from Kathmandu.

GETTING AROUND

The best way to see Kathmandu and the valley is to walk or ride a bike. Most of the sights in Kathmandu can easily be covered on foot, and this is by far the best way to appreciate the city. When and if you run out of steam, there are plenty of reasonably priced taxis and auto-rickshaws. There are also limitless opportunities for short walks around the valley. A number are described in the Around the Kathmandu Valley chapter.

The valley is the perfect size and shape for bicycling. A single-speed bike is fine around the three main cities, but if you want to get into the countryside consider hiring a multi-geared machine. Since the furthest point in the valley is never more than about 20km from Kathmandu you can ride out (uphill) and return (downhill) easily within a day. Bike speed allows you to appreciate your surroundings and stop whenever you like.

To/From the Airport

Kathmandu's international airport is named Tribhuvan airport after the late king, though it used to rejoice in the name Gaucher (literally cow pasture!).

Getting into town is quite straightforward. There is an organised taxi service on the ground-floor foyer immediately after you leave the arrivals baggage collection and customs section. The taxis, called Down Town Services, have a fixed fare of Rs 250 to Thamel or Durbar Marg.

Once outside the international terminal you are confronted by hordes of hotel touts, who are often taxi drivers making commission on taking you to a particular hotel. Many hold up a signboard of the particular

hotel they are connected with, and if the one you want is there, you can get a free lift. The only drawback is that the hotel is then much less likely to offer you a discount as they will be paying a hefty commission to the taxi driver.

If you don't want to be taken to a hotel of their choice, a ride to Thamel or the city centre should cost no more than Rs 200, although in the opposite direction you should be able to get one for Rs 100.

There are public buses which leave from the main road – about 300m from the terminal – but they're only really useable if you have very little luggage and know exactly how to get to where you want to go.

Bus

While bus travel is very cheap, it is often unbelievably crowded. The primary disadvantage, apart from severe discomfort, is that you cannot see the views or stop when you want. Still, if you're short of cash and want to get from point A to B *reasonably* quickly, they'll do. Over a short distance – say from Thamel to Bodhnath – you'll probably be just as quick on a bicycle. The smaller minibuses and curious little three wheeled tempos are generally quicker than the full-sized buses and are slightly more expensive.

Nearly all buses to points around the valley operate from the City bus station. As with anything in Nepal, however, there are exceptions to the rule.

The incredibly dilapidated electric trolley buses to Bhaktapur leave from the southern end of Kantipath near the National Stadium. These cost Rs 4 and drop you off a 10 minute walk from the centre of Bhaktapur. Buses to Pharping (Dakshinkali) leave from Martyr's Gate.

Buses to Bungamati, Godavari and Chapagaon leave from Patan. See the Patan section for more details.

Taxi

Taxis are quite reasonably priced. The current charge for a metered taxi is Rs 7 flagfall and Rs 2 for every 200m, and drivers don't usually take too much convincing to use the meter for short trips, although in the evenings you may have to negotiate. Shorter rides around town rarely come to more than Rs 50.

Many so-called taxis are in fact private vehicles operating as taxis. Consequently they don't have meters, in which case it's a matter of negotiating the fare in advance. Licensed taxis have black licence plates while private cars have red plates. Taxis can be booked on ☎ 420987, or at night call ☎ 224374.

Between several people, longer trips around the valley, or even outside it, are also affordable. A half-day sightseeing trip within the valley should cost around Rs 800, and a full-day trip, Rs 1500.

Other approximate taxi fares (from Thamel) include:

Pashupatinath	Rs 50
Bodhnath	Rs 80
Patan	Rs 100
Bhaktapur	Rs 200
Changu Narayan	Rs 500
Dhulikhel/Nagarkot	Rs 800

For longer journeys outside the valley count on about Rs 2500 per day plus fuel, for which prices are set by the government. At the time of research, it was around Rs 40 per litre.

Auto & Cycle-Rickshaw

Three-wheeled metered auto-rickshaws are quite common in Kathmandu and cost as little as half of what you would pay for a cab. Flagfall is Rs 1.50, plus Rs 6 per kilometre. They're still a bit of a lottery – most will blankly refuse to use the meter and if this is the case make sure you establish a price. Most rides around town should cost less than Rs 40.

Bicycle rickshaws cost Rs 30 to Rs 50 for most rides around town – they can be more expensive than going by auto-rickshaw or taxi. The tourist rate from Thamel to Durbar Square is Rs 40, from Thamel to the Hotel de l'Annapurna Rs 25. You must be certain to agree on a price before you start.

Car

Although you cannot rent cars on a drive-yourself basis they can readily be rented with a driver from a number of operators. Try Gorkha Travels (☎ 224896) or Yeti Travels (☎ 221234), or one of the many travel agents in Thamel.

The rental cost is fairly high both in terms of the initial hiring charge and fuel. Full-day charges are as high as Rs 3000 a day, although they can be lower, especially if you are not covering a huge distance. Around the valley expect to pay about Rs 2500 plus fuel.

Motorbike

There are a number of motorbike rental operators around Freak St and Thamel. Officially you need an international driver's licence, but no-one ever checks. You are also required to leave a substantial deposit or your passport. For Rs 400 per day you'll get a 100cc Indian-made Honda road bike, and will basically be restricted to the Kathmandu Valley (but also including Daman, Kakani, Nagarkot and Dhulikhel). A 250cc trail bike costs around Rs 1000 per day.

Motorbikes can be great fun, once you master the traffic. However, think carefully before you do hire, as you will be encouraging the proliferation of noisy, polluting machines and adding to Nepal's trade imbalance. Most reasonably fit people will find that a mountain bike is a better option, especially as you can get to more places.

Bicycle

Once you get away from the crowded streets of central Kathmandu, cycling is a pleasure, and if you're in reasonable shape this is the ideal way to explore the valley. It costs around Rs 50 a day for a regular single-speed Indian or Chinese-made bicycle. Check the brakes before taking it out and be certain to lock it whenever you leave it.

Multi-geared mountain bikes have become the rage in Kathmandu and many places around Thamel rent them out. Most are Chinese or Indian made bikes which are not all that strong, but should be fine for light use around the valley. Imported bikes are available for rent but these cost considerably more. Count on Rs 200 a day, which, if you are planning to really explore the valley, is money well spent. It's a real pleasure to surge up the long hill into Patan, sweeping by all the riders of regular bikes who have to get off and push.

For rental of high quality equipment, check out Dawn Till Dusk in the Kathmandu Guest House compound.

Patan

☎ 01

Patan is separated from Kathmandu only by the Bagmati River and is the second largest town in the valley. It is often referred to as Lalitpur, which means 'city of beauty'. Patan has a long Buddhist history and the four corners of the city are marked by stupas said to have been erected by the great Buddhist emperor Ashoka around 250 BCE. Later inscriptions refer to palaces in the city in the 5th century CE although Patan's great building boom took place under the Mallas in the 16th, 17th and 18th centuries.

Patan's central Durbar Square is absolutely packed with temples; it's an architectural feast with a far greater concentration of temples per square metre than in Kathmandu or Bhaktapur. Numerous other temples of widely diverse style as well as many bahals (Buddhist monasteries) are scattered around this fascinating town.

Malla Kings

The Malla kings of Patan were responsible for most of the city's great buildings. The Malla kings included:

Jayasthiti Malla	1372-1395
Siddhinarsingh Malla	1620-1661
Srinivasa Malla	1661-1684
Yoganarendra Malla	1684-1705
Vishnu Malla	1729-1745
Rajya Prakash Malla	1745-1758
Visvajita Malla	1758-1760

ORIENTATION & INFORMATION

Durbar (Palace) Square is the centre of Patan. From here, four main roads lead to the four Ashoka stupas while the city radiates out in concentric circles. Jawlakhel, to the south of the city, has a major Tibetan population and is the centre for carpet-weaving in the valley.

It is possible to stay in Patan, although it's so close to Kathmandu that it scarcely seems worthwhile and the choice of accommodation and restaurants is far more limited.

Buses from Kathmandu drop you at the Patan Dhoka city gate, about a 15 minute walk from Durbar Square. There's another, larger bus stop directly south of Durbar Square, near the Southern (Lagan) Stupa. Taxis normally drop you at Patan Dhoka, the original entrance to the city and also about a 15 minute walk from Durbar Square. If you come to Patan by bicycle an interesting route from Kathmandu is to take the track down to the river from opposite the big convention centre on the Bhaktapur road. A footbridge crosses the river here and you enter Patan by the Northern Stupa near the Kumbeshwar Temple.

GOLDEN TEMPLE

Also known as the Kwa Bahal, Hiranya Varna Mahavihar, or the Suwarna Mahavihara (Golden Temple), this unique Buddhist monastery is a few minutes north of Durbar Square. Legends relate that the monastery was founded in the 12th century, although the earliest record of its existence is 1409. From the street a sign points to the monastery, entered through a doorway flanked by painted guardian lion figures, giving no hint of the magnificent structure within.

The large rectangular building has three roofs and a copper-gilded facade. Inside the shrine are images of the Buddha and Avalokiteshvara and a stairway leads to the 1st floor where monks will show you the various Buddha images and frescoes which illustrate the walls. The life of the Buddha is illustrated in a frieze in front of the main shrine.

The inner courtyard has a railed walkway around three sides. Shoes and other leather

PATAN

To Kathmandu (2km)

Bagmati River

PLACES TO STAY
1 Summit Hotel;
  Garden Restaurant
2 Hotel Greenwich Village
7 Hotel Himalaya
8 Hotel Narayani
34 Aloha Inn; Nepal
  Grindlays Bank
35 Hong Kong Guest House
36 Hotel Clarion
37 Mountain View Guest House
46 Mahabuddha Guest House

PLACES TO EAT
30 Roast Chicken
  Take-Aways
31 German Bakery; Tasty Bite
38 Cafe de Patan
39 Taleju Restaurant & Bar

OTHER
3 Janakpur Women's
  Development Centre
  Craft Shop
4 Clay & Crafts (Crafts Shop)
5 Kalamandir (Crafts Shop)
6 Mahaguthi (Crafts Shop)
9 Western (Pulchok) Stupa
10 Bus Stop (Patan City Gate)
11 Patan Dhoka (City Gate)
12 Ganesh Mandir

13 Chandeswari Temple
14 Nag Bahal
15 Chaityas
16 Pim Bahal
17 Lokarkirti Mahavihar
18 Nyakachuka
19 Naga Baha
20 Golden Temple
  (Kwa Bahal)
21 Megaliths
22 Northern Stupa
23 Kumbeshwar Technical
  School
24 Kumbeshwar Temple
25 Dhum Bahal
26 Uma Maheshwar Temple
27 Om Bahal
28 Rada Krishna Temple
29 Haka Bahal
32 Zoo
33 Palmists
40 Bishwakarma Temple
41 Educational Wooden Toys
42 I Baha Bahal
43 Rato (Red) Machhendranath
  Temple
44 Minanath Temple
45 Mahabouddha Temple
47 Uku Bahal
48 Lagankhel Bus Stop
49 Southern (Lagan) Stupa

Kopundol

To Footbridge

To Balkumari
Temple

Durbar
Square

See Durbar Square
(Patan) Map p19E

Royal
Palace

To Chobar
(3km)

Haugal

Jawlakhel

To Eastern
(Teta) Stupa (500m)

Ring Road

0   125   250 m

Lagankhel

To Godavari (18km)

articles must be removed if you leave the walkway and enter the inner courtyard itself. In the centre of the courtyard is a small but very richly decorated three storey temple crowned by a golden roof with an extremely ornate *gajur* (a bell-shaped top). Look for the sacred tortoises which potter around in the courtyard – they are temple guardians. The monastery was dedicated by a Patan merchant grown rich from trade with Tibet. Entry to the temple is Rs 25.

KUMBESHWAR TEMPLE

Directly north of Durbar Square is one of the valley's three five-storey temples. The others are the towering Nyatapola Temple of Bhaktapur and the smaller Panch Mukhi Hanuman of the old Royal Palace in Kathmandu.

The Kumbeshwar Temple dominates the streets around it and is said to date from 1392, when it was completed by Jayasthiti Malla, making it the oldest extant temple in Patan. The temple is noted for its fine proportions and elegant woodcarvings. There are numerous statues and sculptures around the courtyard dating from a number of Nepali dynasties, from the Licchavis to the Mallas, including a particularly fine Ganesh figure. The temple is, however, dedicated to Shiva, as indicated by the large Nandi, or bull, facing the temple inside the main entrance.

The temple platform has two ponds whose water is said to come straight from the holy lake at Gosainkund, a long trek north of the valley (see the Trekking chapter). An annual ritual bath in the Kumbeshwar Temple's tank is claimed to be as meritorious as making the arduous walk to Gosainkund.

South of the courtyard is an important **Bhairab Temple** with a life-size wooden image of the god. Also on the southern side of the Kumbeshwar Temple is the single storey **Baglamukhi Temple** where the goddess is represented by the small temple's gilded archway with its canopy of snakes. On the western side of the Kumbeshwar Temple courtyard is the large **Konti Hiti**, a popular gathering place for local women.

Also on the northern side, the Kumbeshwar Technical School, which was established to train local untouchables, sells very good-value carpets and woollen jumpers and has a small display area on the ground floor (see Shopping).

Thousands of pilgrims visit the temple during the Janai Purnima festival in July and August each year to worship the silver and gold lingam which is set up in the tank. It's a colourful occasion with bathers immersing themselves in the tank while members of the Brahmin and Chhetri castes replace the sacred thread they wear looped over their left shoulder. *Jhankris* (sorcerers) beating drums and wearing colourful headdresses and skirts dance around the temple to complete the dramatic scene.

UMA MAHESHWAR TEMPLE

There are a number of other interesting temples and bahals in this northern area of Patan. Returning from the Kumbeshwar Temple to Durbar Square the small and inconspicuous double roofed Uma Maheshwar Temple is set back from the road on its eastern side. Peer inside the temple where you can see (a light will help) a very beautiful black-stone relief of Shiva and Parvati in the pose known as Uma Maheshwar – the god sitting cross-legged with his shakti leaning against him rather seductively.

BISHWAKARMA TEMPLE

Walk south from Durbar Square through the Hauga area with its many brassware shops and workshops. There is a small bahal almost immediately on your right (west) and then a laneway also leading west. A short distance down this lane is the brick Bishwakarma Temple, with its entire facade covered in sheets of embossed copper. Directly above the doorway is what looks like a Star of David. The temple is dedicated to carpenters and craftspeople and, as if in proof, you can often hear the steady clump and clang of metalworkers' hammers from nearby workshops.

Returning to the main road running south from Durbar Square you soon come to a chaitya shrine of Lakshmi Narayan on the eastern side of the road and the **I Baha Bahal**

Kathmandu

Clockwise from top: A rare glimpse of Kathmandu's Seto Bhairab – imagine beer pouring out of his mouth during Indra Jatra; traditional metalwork flourishes in Nepal; wooden masks and puppets in all shapes and sizes; Buddhist stupas symbolise the five elements: earth, water, fire, air and ether.

Mountains of fruit in the Kathmandu Valley.

Nepali woman.

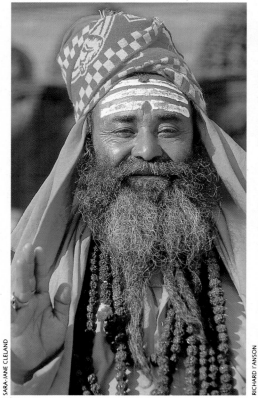

A sadhu with *tilaka* on his forehead.

Colourful market dyes.

on the western side. The monastery dates from 1427 but is now rather run-down and decrepit; part of it is being used as a school. A little farther south is the old but recently restored **Chakba Lunhiti** with three water-spouts.

RATO MACHHENDRANATH TEMPLE

Continue south from Durbar Square for a few more minutes to the Rato (Red) Machhendranath Temple, on the western side of the road. Rato Machhendranath, the god of rain and plenty, comes in a variety of incarnations. To Buddhists he is the Tantric edition of Avalokiteshvara while to Hindus he is another version of Shiva.

Standing in a large, spacious courtyard the three storey temple dates from 1673, although an earlier temple may have existed on the site since 1408. The temple's four elaborately carved doorways are each guarded by lion figures and at ground level on the four corners of the temple plinth are reliefs of a curious yeti-like creature. A diverse collection of animals (including peacocks, horses, bulls, lions, elephants and fish) top the pillars facing the northern side of the temple; they are the Tibetan symbols for the months of the year. The metal roof is supported by struts, each showing Avalokiteshvara standing above figures being tortured in hell. Prayer wheels are set into the base of the temple.

The Machhendranath image is just a crudely carved piece of red-painted wood, but each year during the Rato Machhendranath celebrations it is paraded around the town on a temple chariot. The complex celebration moves the image from place to place over a period of several weeks in the month of Baisakh (April/May), finally ending at Jawlakhel where the chariot is disassembled.

Occurring on a 12 year cycle (the next time will be in 2003) the procession continues out of Patan to the village of Bungamati, 5km to the south. Dragging the heavy chariot along this bumpy and often uphill track is no easy feat. In the village the god has another temple where, since 1593, it has been the custom for the image to spend six months of each year.

MINANATH TEMPLE

To the eastern side of the main road from Durbar Square is a two storey temple dedicated to a Buddhist Bodhisattva who is considered to be the brother of Rato Machhendranath. The Minanath image is also towed around town during the Rato Machhendranath festival, but in a much smaller chariot. The temple originally dates from the Licchavi period but has undergone several recent restorations and 'improvements' and has roof struts carved with figures of multi-armed goddesses, all extraordinarily brightly painted. A large prayer wheel stands in a cage beside the temple.

MAHABOUDDHA TEMPLE

Despite its height, the Temple of the Thousand Buddhas (Mahabouddha Temple) is not clearly visible because it is surrounded by other buildings. It's a shikhara-style temple, modelled after the Mahabouddha Temple at Bodhgaya in India, where the Buddha gained enlightenment.

The temple takes its name from the terracotta tiles with which it is covered, each bearing an image of the Buddha. It is believed to have originally been built in 1585 although some sources suggest an earlier date. It suffered severe damage in the 1934 earthquake and was totally rebuilt. Unfortunately, without plans to work from, the builders ended up with a different-looking temple and there were enough bricks left over to construct a smaller shikhara-style shrine to Maya Devi, the Buddha's mother, which stands to the south-west of the Mahabouddha.

The Mahabouddha Temple is about 10 minutes walk south-east of Durbar Square. A signpost points down a lane full of curio shops leading to the temple, if you have trouble finding it simply ask directions. The roof terrace of the shops at the back of the courtyard has a good view of the temple.

continued on page 199

DURBAR SQUARE (Patan)

As in Kathmandu, the ancient Royal Palace of Patan faces on to the square, but it is a concentrated mass of temples, undoubtedly the most visually stunning display of Newari architecture to be seen in Nepal. The rectangular square has its longer axis running north-south and the palace forms the eastern side of the square. A continuous row of temples in widely diverse styles faces the palace on the western side.

The square rose to its full glory during the Malla period, and particularly during the reign of King Siddhinarsingh Malla. Patan's major market, the **Mangal Bazaar,** is beside the square.

Bhimsen Temple (6)

At the northern end of Durbar Square the Bhimsen Temple is dedicated to the god of trade and business, which possibly explains its well-kept and prosperous look. Bhimsen, a hero of the *Mahabharata*, was said to be extraordinarily strong.

The three-storey temple has had a chequered history. Although it is not known when it was first built, an inscription records that it was rebuilt in 1682 after a fire. Restorations also took place after the great 1934 earthquake, and again in 1967. A lion tops a pillar in front of the temple, while the brick building has an artificial marble facade and a gilded facade on the 1st floor.

Bhimsen Temple

Manga Hiti (11)

Immediately north of the palace is the sunken Manga Hiti, one of the water conduits with which Patan, and even more so Bhaktapur, are so liberally endowed. This one has a lotus-shaped pool and three wonderfully carved stone crocodile-head waterspouts. Next to it is the **Mani Mandap** (10), a pavilion built in 1700 and used for royal crownings.

Vishwanath Temple (7)

Next to the Bhimsen Temple stands the Vishwanath (Shiva) Temple. This elaborately decorated two storey temple was built in 1627 and has two large stone elephants guarding the front entrance. Shiva's vehicle, the bull, is on the other side of the temple while inside is a large lingam. As yet further proof of Shiva's influence, the roof struts are decorated with erotic themes. The temple has been restored in recent years.

Krishna Mandir (8)

Continuing into the square, the third temple you reach is the Krishna Mandir, which is dedicated to Krishna and was built by King Siddhinarsingh Malla. Records indicate that the temple was completed with the installation of the image on the 1st floor in 1637. With its strong Mughal influences, this stone temple is clearly of Indian design, unlike the nearby brick and timber, multi-roofed Nepali temples. The 1st and 2nd floors are made up of a line of pavilions from the top of which rises a corncob-like shikhara. Musicians can often be heard playing upstairs.

Krishna Mandir

Krishna is an incarnation of Vishnu so the god's vehicle, the man-bird Garuda, kneels with folded arms on top of a column (9) facing the temple. The stone carvings along the beam above the 1st-floor pillars recount events of the *Mahabharata* while on the 2nd floor there are scenes from the *Ramayana*. These fine friezes are accompanied by explanations in Newari of the narrative scenes.

A major festival is held here in August/September on the occasion of Krishna's birthday, Krishnasthami.

Jagannarayan Temple (14)
The two storey brick Jagannarayan or Charnarayan Temple is dedicated to Narayan, one of Vishnu's incarnations. It is reputed to be the oldest temple in the square, dating from 1565, although an alternative date in the late 1600s has also been suggested. The temple stands on a brick plinth with large stone lions, above which are two guardian figures. The roof struts are carved with erotic figures.

King Yoganarendra Malla's Statue (18)
Immediately north of the Hari Shankar Temple is a tall column topped by a figure of King Yoganarendra Malla. The golden figure of the kneeling king, protected by the hood of a cobra, has been facing towards his palace since the year 1700. On top of the cobra's head is the figure of a bird; legends say that as long as the bird remains there the king may still return to his palace. Accordingly a door and window of the palace are always kept open and a hookah (a water pipe used for smoking) is kept ready for the king should he return. A rider to the legend adds that when the bird flies off, the elephants in front of the Vishwanath Temple will stroll over to the Manga Hiti for a drink!

Other Vishnu Temples
Behind the statue of the king are three smaller Vishnu temples. The small plastered shikhara-style temple was built in 1590 and is dedicated to Narsingha, Vishnu's man-lion incarnation. To one side is a small Narayan temple and behind it another Vishnu temple.

Hari Shankar Temple

Hari Shankar Temple (21)
This three storey temple to Hari Shankar, the half Vishnu, half Shiva deity, has roof struts carved with scenes of the tortures of the damned, a strange change from the erotic scenes on the Jagannarayan. It was built in 1704-05 by the daughter of King Yoganarendra Malla.

Taleju Bell (23)
Diagonally opposite the Taleju Temple (20) in the palace complex, the large bell, hanging between two stout pillars, was erected by King Vishnu Malla in 1736. An earlier bell, erected in 1703, was moved to the Rato Machhendranath Temple at that time. Petitioners could ring the bell to alert the king to their grievances. Shop stalls are in the building under the bell platform, and behind it is a lotus-shaped pool with a bridge over it.

Krishna Temple (27)

This attractive octagonal stone temple, also known as the Chyasim Deval, completes the 'front line' of temples in the square. The stairway to the temple, which faces the palace's Sundari Chowk, is guarded by two stone lions. The temple was built in 1723 and, like the square's Krishna Mandir mentioned earlier, makes a clear contrast with the usual Nepali pagoda temple designs.

Bhai Dega Temple (22)

Behind the Krishna Temple stands the squat Bhai Dega, or Biseshvar, dedicated to Shiva. It's a singularly unattractive temple although it is said to contain an impressive lingam. A few steps back from the square

DURBAR SQUARE (PATAN)

To Bus Stop
To Golden Temple (100m)
To Kumbeshwar Temple (200m)

PLACES TO STAY
15 Third World Guest House & Restaurant

PLACES TO EAT
4 Cafe de Temple
31 Taleju Restaurant & Bar

To Cafe de Patan

Mani Keshar Chowk

Royal Palace

Mul Chowk

Sundari Chowk

0   20   40 m
Approximate Scale

To Rato Machhendranath Temple (300m)

To Mahabouddha Temple (400m)

9 Garuda Statue on Column
10 Mani Mandap
11 Manga Hiti
12 Cafe Pagoda
13 Golden Gate (Sun Dhoka); Museum
14 Jagannarayan Temple
16 Vishnu Temples
17 Narsingha Statue
18 King Yoganarendra Malla's Statue
19 Mahaguthi Crafts Shop
20 Taleju Temple
21 Hari Shankar Temple
22 Bhai Dega Temple
23 Taleju Bell
24 Degutalle Temple
25 Statue of Jamuna
26 Statue of Ganga
27 Krishna Temple (Chyasim Deval)
28 Narsingha Statue
29 Ganesh Statue
30 Hanuman Statue
32 Taxi Stand

OTHER
1 Metalwork Shops
2 Art Galleries
3 Watercolour Paintings
5 Ganesh Temple
6 Bhimsen Temple
7 Vishwanath Temple
8 Krishna Mandir

is another stone shikhara-style temple, clearly owing inspiration to the important Krishna Mandir of the square. This same design pops up in several other temples around Patan. The popular Cafe de Patan is just behind this temple.

ROYAL PALACE

Forming the whole eastern side of the Durbar Square is the Royal Palace of Patan. Parts of the palace were built in the 14th century, but the main construction was during the 17th and 18th centuries by Siddhinarsingh Malla, Srinivasa Malla and Vishnu Malla. The Patan palace predates the palaces of Kathmandu and Bhaktapur. It was severely damaged during the conquest of the valley by Prithvi Narayan Shah in 1768 and also by the great earthquake of 1934, but it remains one of the architectural highlights of the valley with a series of connecting courtyards and three temples dedicated to the valley's main deity, the goddess Taleju.

Mani Keshar Chowk & Patan Museum

The northern courtyard and museum are entered from the square by the Golden Gate, or Sun Dhoka (13). This is the newest part of the palace, completed in 1734. The courtyard is entered through a magnificent gilded door topped by a golden torana showing Shiva, Parvati, Ganesh and Kumar. Directly above the golden door is a golden window, at which the king would make public appearances.

The rear courtyard here is reached by a passage between the Mani Keshar Chowk and the Taleju Temple. It was used for dance and drama performances during the Malla period and one wall is decorated with erotic figures. Today it houses the excellent Museum Cafe (see Places to Eat).

Patan Museum (13) This part of the palace has been superbly renovated and houses one of the finest museums on the subcontinent. There have been some modern elements added to the building as part of the renovations, and the result is a beautiful synthesis of old and new.

The main feature of the museum is an outstanding collection of cast bronze and gilt copper work, mostly of Hindu and Buddhist deities. Three galleries are devoted to Hinduism, and two to Buddhism. Another gallery shows the stages involved in the production of hammered sheet metal relief designs (known as repoussé) and the 'lost wax' method of casting. In yet another there are also some fascinating photos of Patan at the turn of the century. The museum is open daily (except Tuesday) from 10.30 am to 4.30 pm; entry is Rs 120, and you need at least an hour or so. For a sneak preview of the museum check out its Web page at www.asianart.com/patan-museum.

Mul Chowk & the Taleju Temples

The central courtyard is the largest and oldest of the palace's three main chowks. Two stone lions guard the entrance to the courtyard which was built by Siddhinarsingh Malla, destroyed in a fire in 1662 and rebuilt by Srinivasa Malla in 1665-66. At the centre of the court-yard stands the small gilded **Bidya Temple.**

The palace's three Taleju temples stand around the courtyard. The doorway to the Shrine of Taleju or **Taleju Bhawani,** on the southern side of the courtyard, is flanked by the river goddesses Ganga on a tortoise (26) and Jamuna on a mythical crocodile or *makara* (25).

The five storey **Degutalle Temple** (24), topped by its circular triple roofed tower, is on the north-eastern corner. The larger, square, triple roofed **Taleju Temple** (20) is directly north, looking out over Durbar Square. It was built by Siddhinarsingh Malla in 1640, rebuilt after a fire and rebuilt after the 1934 earthquake which completely demolished it. The goddess Taleju was the personal deity of the Malla kings from the 14th century, and Tantric rites were performed to her in this temple.

Taleju Bhawani

Sundari Chowk & Tusha Hiti

South of the larger Mul Chowk is the Sundari Chowk with its sunken tank known as the Tusha Hiti. The superbly carved stonework in the tank depicts the eight Ashta Matrikas, the eight Bhairabs and the eight Nagas. The tank was originally built in about 1670 and restored in 1960. A toy-size replica of the Krishna Mandir in the main square sits above the tank.

The courtyard is surrounded by a three storey building with finely carved struts and windows. The entrance to the courtyard from the main square is guarded by stone statues of Hanuman (30), Ganesh (29), and Vishnu as Narsingha, the man-lion (28). The gilded metal window over the entrance from the square is flanked by windows of carved ivory. Behind the Sundari Chowk, but unfortunately not open to the public, is the Royal Garden with a water tank known as the Kamal Pokhari.

PAUL BEINSSEN

People exiting the Krishna Mandir at Durbar Square, Patan

continued from page 193

RUDRA VARNA MAHAVIHARA

Also known as Uku Bahal, this Buddhist monastery near the Mahabouddha Temple is one of the best known in Patan. A large rectangular structure with two storey gilded roofs encloses a courtyard absolutely packed with interesting bits and pieces. There are dorjes, bells, banners, peacocks, elephants, Garudas, rampant goats, kneeling devotees and a regal-looking statue of a Rana general. The lions are particularly curious – apart from regular Nepali ones, seated on pillars with one paw raised in salute, there are also a couple with a decidedly British appearance, looking as if they should be guarding a statue of Queen Victoria in her 'not amused' incarnation rather than a colourful Nepali monastery.

As you enter the courtyard look for the finely carved wooden struts on the right. They are said to be among the oldest of this type in the valley and prior to restoration they were actually behind the monastery, but were moved to this safer location inside the courtyard. The monastery in its present form probably dates from the 19th century, but certain features and the actual site are much older.

HAKA BAHAL

Take the road west from the southern end of Durbar Square, past the Cafe de Patan, and you soon come to the Haka Bahal, a typical rectangular building with an internal courtyard. Traditionally, Patan's Kumari (living goddess) is a daughter of one of the priests of this monastery.

ASHOKAN STUPAS

The four stupas marking the boundaries of Patan are said to have been built when the great Buddhist emperor Ashoka visited the valley 2500 years ago. Although remains of all four can still be seen today they probably bear little similarity to the original stupas. The Northern Stupa is just beyond the Kumbeshwar Temple, not far from Durbar Square. It's well preserved and whitewashed.

The other three are all grassed over. The Southern, or Lagan, Stupa is just south of the bus stand and is the largest of the four. The smaller western, or Pulchok, Stupa is beside the main road from Kathmandu through to Jawlakhel and directly opposite the Hotel Narayani. Finally, the small Eastern, or Teta, Stupa is well to the east of centre, across the Ring Road and just beyond a small river.

ZOO

Nepal's only zoo is in the south-western part of Patan, just north of Jawlakhel. It includes a reasonably extensive collection of Nepali wildlife, including rhinos, tigers, leopards, monkeys and birds. It is yet another depressing animal prison, although there are plans afoot to give it a major revamp.

Keen naturalists, students of the grotesque and young kids may still enjoy a visit. Admission is Rs 60; Rs 30 for children. It is open daily except Monday from 10 am to 6 pm (last entry 5 pm).

JAWLAKHEL

The 'Tibetan Refugee Camp' is no longer really a camp at all, but a large centre for carpet production. It was established in 1960 with help from the International Red Cross and the Swiss government and employs 1000 refugees in the production of Tibetan carpets. This is where the enormous carpet industry of today got its start; it's still the place to begin if you want to buy a carpet.

You may well be able to buy cheaper carpets outside the camp, but those in the shops by the entrance have marked prices so you can get a good idea of values (other Tibetan crafts are also on sale). You can go inside to the workshop area and see the carpets being made (see also Shopping).

KOTESHWAR MAHADEV TEMPLE

Outside the Patan city limits, the important temple of Koteshwar Mahadev is just north of the confluence of the Manohara and Hanumante rivers, which in turn joins the Bagmati River. Mahadev means 'great god', the usual term for Shiva, but Koteshwar can

Patan Walk

The Patan Tourist Development Organisation has developed a fascinating walk that traverses some of the most interesting sections of the old city. Unnoticed by many visitors, much of the traditional heart of the city still survives and a complex structure of interlinked courtyards, laneways and squares can be explored.

While exploring at random is quite feasible, the walk which has been developed (and is erratically signposted throughout) takes you through the northern and north-western parts of the city, from Patan Dhoka to Durbar Square. It offers a fascinating insight into the traditional rules, regulations and cultural institutions that lay behind the creation of Newari towns and the way in which modern developments are bringing change.

The walk is described in a small booklet entitled *Patan Walkabout*, which is available from the bookstore at Patan Dhoka.

also be translated as 'millions of gods' so this is a temple of Shiva with many faces, a particularly powerful form of Lord Shiva. The shrine's Shiva lingam is said to date from the 8th century.

A little south of the temple is the **Kuti Bahal** where travellers bound for Tibet were customarily farewelled. The monastery has a 15th century chaitya.

PLACES TO STAY

Patan's accommodation consists mainly of mid-range and top-end places. Some overseas aid agencies are in Patan, particularly around Jawlakhel, and many long-term foreign residents live here.

PLACES TO STAY – BUDGET

Right in the centre of Patan, a short walk from Durbar Square, the popular *Cafe de Patan* (☎ 537599) also has rooms. The position is excellent and the rooms are pleasant, although a little overpriced. Clean doubles with shared bath are Rs 300; with attached bath it's Rs 500.

Third World Guest House (☎ 522187) has a better location, with all rooms having views over the square. It's a privilege you pay for, however, as the rooms cost $15 with common bath, and $20 with attached bath, although there appears to be some room to negotiate.

Close to the Mahabouddha Temple south-east of Durbar Square, the *Mahabud-*

dha Guest House (☎ 540575) is a comfortable little place. The rooms all have common bath, but there is one bathroom for every three rooms. The cost is Rs 250 for a double.

Farther away in Jawlakhel, the *Hong Kong Guest House* (☎ 527067) is noisy as hell at the front but quieter at the rear. Rooms range from Rs 150/350 with common bath up to Rs 600 for a double with attached bath, TV and phone.

Between Jawlakhel and Durbar Square is the district of Kumaripati, and here you'll find the *Mountain View Guest House* (☎ 538168), down a side street off the main road. It's nothing flash, but is clean and comfortable. Single/doubles with common bath cost Rs 200/300, or there are a few double-bed rooms with bath for Rs 350.

PLACES TO STAY – MID-RANGE

Patan has a popular mid-range hotel if you'd like a complete break from Kathmandu. The *Aloha Inn* (☎ 522796, fax 524571, email aloha@ati.mos.com.np) is in the Jawlakhel area, not too far from the southern edge of the old city. Rooms here are $30/40 plus 11% tax. It's a friendly place, clean, well kept and quiet, and there's a very pleasant garden.

Close by and a little closer to the old city is the *Hotel Clarion* (☎ 524512, fax 224464), which is set in a pleasant garden but is still uncomfortably close to the noisy road – ask for a room at the back. Comfortable, well kept rooms with attached bath, TV and phone cost $45/50, but try for 30% less.

PLACES TO STAY – TOP END

Patan also has a number of top-end hotels although none of them are close enough to the interesting centre of the old city to be really convenient.

Summit Hotel (☎ 521894, fax 523737, email summit@wlink.com.np) tops a hillock in the Kopundol area and has great views across the river to Kathmandu and the distant mountains. There's a very beautiful garden with a swimming pool – a real pleasure in hot weather. The Summit Hotel's inconvenient location is its only drawback; finding taxis can sometimes be difficult. Standard rooms cost $75/85, or $10 more with mountain views, dropping to $55/70 in summer. There are some budget rooms with common bath and no views for $25/35 ($15/25 in summer). There's a pleasant bar and the Garden Restaurant turns out superb food.

Also topping the Kopundol hill is the nearby *Hotel Greenwich Village* (☎ 521780, 526683) with singles/doubles at $60/70, but discounts of up to 40% are offered. There's also a swimming pool, and a top-floor restaurant to take advantage of the view.

Two other Patan hotels are more distinctly in the top-end price bracket. The *Hotel Narayani* (☎ 525015, fax 521291, email info@nbe.mox.com.np) has a garden, a swimming pool and rooms at $70/85, plus 10% tax, although discounts of 30% seem to be par for the course. The modern *Hotel Himalaya* (☎ 523900, fax 523909) has terrific views, a swimming pool, tennis and badminton courts and is at the top of the Kathmandu price range with rooms from $110/120. The hotel has a shuttle bus to the city centre.

PLACES TO EAT

Just a few steps from the south-western corner of Durbar Square, the small *Cafe de Patan* is a long-running favourite with two pleasant open-air dining areas – a small courtyard and a rooftop garden. It's a good place for a drink, snack or even a meal. It turns out a superb lassi and a number of good-value dishes, such as pizza and chicken, from Rs 50 to Rs 135.

Overlooking the square, the nicely decorated *Third World Restaurant* has a brilliant rooftop area with views over Patan and on a clear day, pagodas with a Himalayan backdrop. Snacks are around Rs 80, burgers, pastas and sandwiches around Rs 90.

Cafe de Temple on the northern edge of the square has excellent views from the roof, and an ambitious menu, with snacks for Rs 50 to Rs 150 and main meals (continental, Indian and Chinese) for Rs 80 to Rs 180. The *Cafe Pagoda* also looks directly onto this northern part of the square and has a similar menu, but is tucked off the least interesting corner.

In the rear courtyard of the museum is the excellent open-air *Museum Cafe*, which is operated by the Summit Hotel. Light meals cost Rs 100 to Rs 190, which is a bit more than elsewhere, but the setting more than compensates.

At the opposite end of the square is the *Taleju Restaurant & Bar*. Head for the 5th-floor terrace, as the views from here are outstanding, especially on a clear day when you have the snow-capped Ganesh Himal as a backdrop. The food comes a distant second.

Near the zoo roundabout at Jawlakhel the *German Bakery* does cakes, pastries, cold drinks and sandwiches. Close by is the *Tasty Bite*, with a large Nepali and Chinese menu mostly in the Rs 50 to Rs 150 range. There are also a number of chicken tandoori and take-away places here.

SHOPPING

Patan has many small handicraft shops and for certain crafts it is the best place in the valley. The Tibetan Jawlakhel area in the south of Patan is the place for Tibetan crafts and carpets. There is a string of carpet shops as you enter Jawlakhel, and a shop front, Khukuri House, is the official supplier of khukuri knives to the renown British Gurkha regiments.

Those interested in crafts should definitely visit the string of interesting shops at Kopundol, just to the south of the main Patan bridge. A number are run as part of nonprofit development organisations, so their prices are fair, and the money actually goes to the craftspeople, sometimes as training and product development.

One of the best of these organisations is Mahaguthi, which was established with the help of Oxfam. It has three shops and it sells a wide range of crafts produced by thousands of people. Among other things they sell beautiful handwoven cotton cloth (*dhaki*), rice paper, pottery, block prints, woven bamboo, woodcrafts, jewellery, knitwear, embroidery and Mithila paintings. The Kopundol shop is on the right as you go up the hill, but there are also shops on Durbar Square, Patan, and in Lazimpat, north of the Royal Palace.

Near the Kumbeshwar Temple, the Kumbeshwar Technical School provides the untouchable community of Patan with skills and they produce excellent carpets, jumpers and woodwork. You can buy direct, and they have a small showroom and shop on the ground floor of the school.

Metalwork

Patan is the centre for bronze-casting and other metalwork. The statues you see on sale in Kathmandu will most probably have been made in Patan and there are a number of excellent metalwork shops just north of Durbar Square. They have fine images of Buddha, the Green and White Taras and other figures from the Tantric Buddhist pantheon. Good-quality gold-plated and painted bronze figures will cost Rs 2000 to Rs 5000 for smaller ones, up to more than Rs 10,000 for large images.

Paintings

Immediately north of Durbar Square, just beyond the Bhimsen Temple, are a number of interesting shops selling paintings. The Arjun Art Gallery has Sherpa-style paintings rather like the naive art of the Balinese 'young artist'. It's clearly something developed for the tourist trade but never mind, they're nicely done and you can have all of the Kathmandu Valley, or even all of Nepal, in one painting. Prices start at Rs 2000.

A couple of doors down is the Madhu Chandra Art Gallery which has excellent paintings of Nepali birds by CBS Dangol. The prices range from Rs 300 or Rs 400 and up.

Carpets

Those interested in carpets must visit Jawlakhel and Bodhnath. The Tibetan 'Refugee

---

Tigers & Goats

Nepal's national board game is *bagh chal*, which literally means move (chal) the tigers (bagh). The game is played on a lined board with 25 intersecting points. One player has four tigers, the other has 20 goats and the aim is for the tiger player to 'eat' five goats by jumping over them before the goat player can encircle a single tiger and prevent it moving.

The game starts with the four tigers at the four corners of the board. Play alternates between the goats and the tigers and the goat player brings his goats on to the board one at a time. No goat can be moved from its initial position until every goat has been brought on to the board. By backing up one goat with another so that the tiger cannot jump them the goats can soon clutter up the board so effectively that the tigers cannot move. That is if the tigers haven't done a good job of eating the goats!

All you need to play is a board scratched out on the dirt and 24 bottle caps or stones as markers, but you can also buy attractive brass bagh chal sets in Kathmandu, or in Patan where they are made.

Camp' at Jawlakhel has numerous shops on the approach road, past the zoo. The carpets at the Kumbeshwar Technical School are fairly priced, and this is possibly the only place where you can buy carpets made from 100% pure Tibetan wool.

Toys

Just south of Durbar Square is Educational Wooden Toys, which sells wonderful wooden toys including authentic Nepali trucks from Rs 285 to Rs 600, with auto-rickshaws for Rs 500 and rickshaws for Rs 375. You can find these toys on sale in Kathmandu (including at some of the craft shops), but they're cheaper here where they're made. The factory is only a stone's throw from the shop and it's fascinating to see the parts being cut out with pedal operated jigsaws.

GETTING THERE & AWAY

You can easily get to Patan from Kathmandu whether by bicycle, taxi, bus or tempo. It's an easy 5km ride from Thamel to Patan's Durbar Square. The same trip costs around Rs 100 by taxi. Buses leave regularly from the City bus station and drop you at the Patan city gate, a short walk from Durbar Square (Rs 2). Tempos (route 14) also operate from the Kathmandu main post office as soon as they have 10 passengers (Rs 4). Some buses for more distant destinations leave from Patan: to Godavari and Chapagaon they leave from Lagankhel and to Bungamati from Jawlakhel.

Bhaktapur

☎ 01

Bhaktapur, also known as Bhadgaon (pronounced 'bud-gown') or the City of Devotees, is the third major town of the valley and in many ways the most medieval. Since the major German-funded Bhaktapur Development Project in the 1970s, it has been a much cleaner and tidier town, but there's still a distinctly timeless air to the place. The project restored buildings, paved dirt streets and established sewerage facilities.

The oldest part of the town is around Tachupal Tole (Dattatraya Square), to the east. Bhaktapur was the capital of the whole valley during the 14th to 16th centuries and during that time the focus of the town shifted west, to the Durbar Square area. Much of the town's great architecture dates from the end of the 17th century during the rule of King Bhupatindra Malla.

Malla Kings

As in Kathmandu and Patan, Bhaktapur's important buildings date from the Malla period. Notable Malla kings include:

Yaksha Malla	1428-1482
Raya Malla	1482-1505
Eksha Mal Malla	1505-1568
Jagat Jyoti Malla	1613-1637
Jagat Prakash Malla	1644-1673
Jitamitra Malla	1673-1696
Bhupatindra Malla	1696-1722
Jaya Ranjit Malla	1722-1769

Ranjit Malla enjoyed a relationship with King Prithvi Narayan Shah which saved his city from destruction and also resulted in the deposed Malla kings of Kathmandu and Patan taking shelter here.

ORIENTATION & INFORMATION

Bhaktapur rises up on the northern bank of the Hanumante River. It's basically a pedestrian's city and much better for it. Taxis and tour buses stop at the tour bus park on the northern edge of Bhaktapur, a short walk from the heart of the city; public buses stop at Navpokhu Pokhari on the western edge of town. If you come to Bhaktapur by trolley bus the stop is on the main road bypassing Bhaktapur, a 10 to 15 minute walk south of Taumadhi Tole.

For the visitor Bhaktapur is really a town of one curving road, punctuated by squares. From the bus stop at Navpokhu Pokhari you come first to the Durbar Square, then Taumadhi Tole with the famous five storey Nyatapola Temple, then to Tachupal Tole, or Dattatraya Square. Keep walking in that

BHAKTAPUR

BHAKTAPUR

Places to Stay
30 Namaste Guest House
31 Traditional Guest House

13 Mahakali Temple
14 Bus Stop to Changu Narayan
15 Mahalakshmi Temple
16 Nagarkot Bus Stop
17 Minibus Stop
18 Nava Durga Temple
19 Temple
20 Shikhara Temple
21 Temple
22 Three Storey Temple
23 Wakupati Narayan Temple
24 City Ticket Booth
25 Inacho Bahal
26 White Chaitya
27 Small Three Roofed Temple
28 Lun Bahal
29 Sukul Dhoka
32 Moneychanger
33 Bhagwati Temple
34 Kumari Temple
35 Chaityas, Statues & Shrines
36 Shiva-Parvati Shrine; Hanuman Statue
37 Hilltop Ganesh Shrine
38 Jeth Ganesh Temple
39 Vishnu Temple
40 City Ticket Booth
41 Trolley Bus Terminus

OTHER
1 Bhaktapur Hospital
2 Post Office
3 Kathmandu & Patan Minibuses
4 Lion Gate
5 Ni Bahal
6 Jaya Varahi Temple
7 Ganesh Shrine
8 Cinema
9 Taxi Stand
10 Minibus & Taxi Park
11 City Ticket Booth
12 Vishnu Temple

direction and you'll eventually reach Nagarkot, high up on the edge of the valley.

All foreigners visiting Bhaktapur are charged a fee of Rs 300. This is collected at the various entrances to the city; on the larger streets there is a ticket booth; smaller streets have roaming ticket collectors who pop up out of the woodwork when someone tries to enter by this way. If you are staying overnight (or longer) in Bhaktapur, you only need to pay the entrance fee once.

Bhaktapur has several cheap guesthouses around the centre of town and it's a fascinating place to stay overnight.

NAVPOKHU POKHARI TO TOWN

Approaching Bhaktapur the road skirts an open field (also known as the Tundikhel) and the **Siddha Pokhari**. If you're staying overnight in Bhaktapur you'll probably want to go straight to Durbar Square to drop off your bags, otherwise, the southern route into town is much more interesting since it is the main road through Bhaktapur connecting Taumadhi Tole and Tachupal Tole.

For the southern route, turn south from the corner of Navpokhu Pokhari and then left on the road, immediately before the town's Lion Gate. You pass a small tank on your right and then the much larger **Teka Pokhari**. Just before the next major road junction, to your left, is the constricted, tunnel-like entrance to the tiny **Ni Bahal**, dedicated to the Maitreya Buddha, the Buddha yet to come.

Cross the junction, where the road runs downhill to the **Mangal Tirtha Ghat**, and on your left is the red-brick **Jaya Varahi Temple**. There are elaborately carved wooden toranas over the central door and the window above it. At the western end of the temple is the entrance to the upper floor, flanked by stone lions and banners. Two ornate windows, on either side of the upper torana, were at one time coloured gold and some traces remain.

A few more steps brings you to a small Ganesh shrine that is jutting into the street. Continue to **Nasamana Square**, which is somewhat decrepit but has a Garuda statue without a temple. Almost immediately after

this is a second square with the Jyotirlingeshwar, a shikhara-style temple which houses an important lingam. Behind the shrine is an attractive hiti, one of the many sunken water conduits in Bhaktapur. A few more steps brings you to the turn-off to Potters' Square while a little farther on you come to Taumadhi Tole.

POTTERS' SQUARE

Potters' Square can be approached from Durbar Square, Taumadhi Tole or along the southern road into town from Siddha Pokhari and Navpokhu Pokhari. You also pass right by the square when walking into town from the trolley bus stop.

On the northern side of the square a small hillock is topped by a Ganesh shrine and a shady pipal tree. There are fine views from here over the river to the hills south of Bhaktapur. The square itself has two small temples, a solid-brick **Vishnu Temple** and the double roofed **Jeth Ganesh Temple**. The latter is an indicator of how long the activity all around the square has been going on – the temple was donated by a wealthy potter in 1646 and to this day its priest is a potter. Pottery is very clearly what this square is all about. Under the shady open verandas or tin-roofed sheds all around the square, the potters' wheels spin and clay is thrown. In the square itself, literally thousands of finished pots sit out in the sun to dry, and are sold in the stalls around the square and between the square and Taumadhi Tole.

TAUMADHI TOLE TO TACHUPAL TOLE

The curving main road through Bhaktapur runs from beside the Bhairabnath Temple in Taumadhi Tole to Tachupal Tole, the old centre of town. The first stretch of the street is a busy shopping thoroughfare with a constant hum of activity and everything is on sale, from brass pots to video cassettes, from porters' tumplines (the leather or cloth strips across the forehead or chest used to support a load carried on the back) to mineral water.

continued on page 212

DURBAR SQUARE (Bhaktapur)

Bhaktapur's Durbar Square is much larger and more spacious than Kathmandu's and much less crowded with temples than Patan's. It wasn't planned that way: Victorian illustrations show the square packed with temples and buildings, but the disastrous earthquake of 1934 destroyed many of them and today empty plinths show where some once stood.

Erotic Elephants Temple (2)

Just before you enter the square, coming from the bus stop, pause for a little bit of Newari humour. On your left just before the entrance-way to the square is a hiti. A few steps before that, but on the south side of the road, perhaps 100m before the entranceway, is a tiny double roofed Shiva-Parvati temple with some erotic carvings on its temple struts. One of these shows a pair of copulating elephants, in the missionary position! It's a *hathi* (elephant) Kamasutra.

Ugrachandi & Bhairab Statues

The square is entered from the western end, passing by an entry gate (to a school) with two large stone lions built by King Bhupatindra Malla. On the northern wall are statues (6) of the terrible Bhairab and the equally terrible Ugrachandi, or Durga, the fearsome manifestation of Shiva's consort Parvati. The statues date from 1701 and it's said that the unfortunate sculptor had his hands cut off afterwards, to prevent him from duplicating his masterpieces.

Ugrachandi has 18 arms holding various weapons and symbols and she is in the act of very casually killing a demon with a trident. Bhairab has to make do with just 12 arms but the god and goddess are both garlanded with necklaces of human heads! The gates and courtyard which these powerful figures guard are of no particular importance.

Western End Temples

A number of less significant temples crowd the western end of Durbar Square. They include the **Rameshwar Temple** (7) to Shiva and the **Bhadri Temple** (8) to Vishnu as Narayan. In front of them is an impressive larger **Krishna Temple** (9) and just beyond that is a shikhara-style **Shiva Temple** (11) erected by King Jitamitra Malla in 1674.

King Bhupatindra Malla's Column (22)

King Bhupatindra Malla was the best known of the Malla kings of Bhaktapur and had a great influence on the art and architecture of the town. Like the similar column in Patan's Durbar Square this one was a copy of the original in Kathmandu. The king sits with folded arms, studying the magnificent entrance gate to his palace.

Vatsala Durga Temple (23) & Taleju Bell (21)

Beside the king's statue and directly in front of the palace is the stone Vatsala Durga Temple, built by King Jagat Prakash Malla in 1672. The

Vatsala Durga Temple

shikhara-style temple has some similarities to the Krishna Mandir in Patan. In front of the temple is the large Taleju Bell which was erected by King Jaya Ranjit Malla in 1737 to call the faithful to prayer at the Taleju Temple.

A second, smaller bell stands on the temple's plinth and is popularly known as the 'barking bell'. It was erected by King Bhupatindra Malla in 1721, supposedly to counteract a vision he had in a dream, and to this day dogs are said to bark and whine if the bell is rung.

Chyasilin Mandapa (20)
Beside the Vatsala Durga Temple is an attractive water tank (24) and in front of that is the Chyasilin Mandapa. This octagonal temple was one of the finest in the square until it was destroyed by the 1934 earthquake. Using some of the temple's original components it has been totally rebuilt. There's a good view over the square from inside – note the metal construction inside this outwardly authentic building.

Siddhi Lakshmi Temple (19)
By the south-eastern corner of the palace stands the stone Siddhi Lakshmi Temple. The steps up to the temple are flanked by male and female attendants each leading a rather reluctant child and a rather eager-looking dog. On successive levels the stairs are flanked by horses, rhinos, man-lions and camels.

The 17th century temple marks the dividing line between the main Durbar Square and its secondary part, at the eastern end of the Royal Palace. Behind the temple is another **Vatsala Temple** (16) while to one side of it are two rather lost-looking large stone lions (18), standing by themselves out in the middle of the square.

Pashupatinath Temple (25)
Behind the Vatsala Durga Temple is the Pashupatinath Temple, dedicated to Shiva as Pashupati. The temple dates from the 17th century and is a replica of the main shrine at Pashupatinath. It's notable for the erotic carvings on the roof struts which show some exhausting looking positions.

Siddhi Lakshmi Temple

Pashupatinath Temple

Fasidega Temple (17)

The large, white, rather ugly Fasidega Temple is dedicated to Shiva and stands in the centre of the secondary part of Durbar Square. There are various viewpoints around the valley – the Changu Narayan Temple is one of them – from where you can study Bhaktapur at a distance. In each case the white bulk of the Fasidega is always an easy landmark to pick out. The temple sits on a six level plinth with elephant guardians at the bottom of the steps, lions and cows above them.

Fasidega Temple

Tadhunchen Bahal (28)

The southern and eastern side of the secondary part of the square is made up of double storey *dharamsalas* (rest houses for pilgrims), now

DURBAR SQUARE & TAUMADHI TOLE (BHAKTAPUR)

To Minibus Stop (150m)

Royal Palace

Taleju Chowk

Sundari Chowk

START

To Tachupal Tole (500m) & Traditional Guest House (50m)

Durbar Square

To Tachupal Tole (500m)

To Potters' Square (300m)

Taumadhi Tole

FINISH

To Potters' Square (300m) & Trolley Bus Stop (1km)

PLACES TO STAY
26 Shiva Guest House
27 Golden Gate Guest House
29 Nyatapola Guest House
30 Pagoda Guest House
32 New Nyatapola Inn
39 Bhadgaon Guest House

PLACES TO EAT
10 Cafe de Temple Town
31 Marco Polo Restaurant
34 Sunny Restaurant
35 Cafe Nyatapola

OTHER
1 Shiva Parvati Temple
2 Erotic Elephants Temple
3 Shiva Temple
4 House of a Malla Prince
5 Old Town Entrance Gate
6 Ugrachandi & Bhairab Statues
7 Rameshwar Temple
8 Bhadri Temple
9 Krishna Temple

11 Shiva Temple
12 Police
13 Art Gallery
14 Golden Gate (Sun Dhoka)
15 55 Window Palace
16 Vatsala Temple
17 Fasidega Temple
18 Stone Lions
19 Siddhi Lakshmi Temple
20 Chayasilin Mandapa
21 Taleju Bell
22 King Bhupatindra Malla's Clownm
23 Vatsala Durga Temple
24 Water Tank
25 Pashupatinath Temple
28 Tadhunchen Bahal
33 Nyatapola Temple
36 Dabu (Dance Platform)
37 Bhairabnath Temple
38 Lun Hiti
40 Jagannath Temple
41 Shiva Shrine
42 Til Mahadev Narayan Temple

used as shops. As you enter the street leading east from the square, the Tadhunchen Bahal or Chatur Varna Mahavihara is an ancient-looking monastery on the southern side. In the inner courtyard the roof struts on the eastern side have some highly unusual carvings showing the tortures of the damned. In one a snake is wrapped around a man, another shows two rams butting an unfortunate's head from opposite sides, while a third strut shows a nasty tooth extraction being performed with a large pair of pliers! The monastery dates from the 15th century.

ROYAL PALACE

Bhaktapur's Royal Palace was founded by Yaksha Malla and added to by successive kings, particularly Bhupatindra Malla. As with the old palaces of Kathmandu and Patan, visitors are restricted to certain areas, but only seven courtyards remain of the 99 the palace was once claimed to have. Unfortunately the palace suffered great damage in the 1934 earthquake and its subsequent reconstruction did not match its original artistry.

Art Gallery (13)

The western end of the palace has been made into an art gallery. The entrance to the gallery is flanked by figures of Hanuman the monkey god and Vishnu as Narsingha, his man-lion incarnation. These guardian figures date from 1698 and Hanuman appears in Tantric form as the four armed Hanuman-Bhairab. This part of the palace was once known as the Malati Chowk.

The gallery has a fine collection of Hindu and Buddhist paintings, palm-leaf manuscripts, thangkas and metal, stone and woodcrafts. Admission to the gallery is Rs 20 and it is open daily, except Tuesday, from 10.15 am to 4 pm (2.30 pm on Friday).

Golden Gate (14) & 55 Window Palace (15)

Adjoining the gallery the magnificent Golden Gate, or Sun Dhoka, is the entrance to the 55 Window Palace. The Golden Gate is generally agreed to be the single most important piece of art in the whole valley. The gate and palace were built by King Bhupatindra Malla but not completed until 1754 during the reign of Jaya Ranjit Malla.

A Garuda, the vehicle of Vishnu, tops the gate and is shown disposing of a number of serpents, the Garuda's sworn enemies. The four headed and 16 armed figure of the goddess Taleju Bhawani is below the Garuda and directly over the door. She is the family deity of the Malla dynasty and there are temples to her in the royal palaces in Kathmandu, Patan and Bhaktapur.

The Golden Gate opens to the inner courtyards of the palace. First you enter a small entrance courtyard then the larger **Mul Chowk** which leads round to the **Taleju Chowk** entrance. Unfortunately only Hindus can enter Taleju Chowk, although non-Hindus can peer in from the doorway. Beyond Taleju Chowk is **Kumari Chowk** and **Sundari Chowk** with its bathing tank, the Kamal Pokhari.

TAUMADHI TOLE

A short street, lined with tourist shops, leads downhill from behind the Pashupatinath Temple in Durbar Square to the second great square of Bhaktapur, the Taumadhi Tole. Here you find the highest temple in the valley and also the Cafe Nyatapola whose balconies provide a great view over the square. The building was renovated for its new purpose in 1977 and even has some finely carved roof struts with erotic themes.

Nyatapola Temple (33)

The five storey, 30m high Nyatapola Temple is not only the highest temple in the whole Kathmandu Valley, but also one of the best examples of traditional Nepali temple architecture. The towering temple is visible from Durbar Square, but some of the finest views of the temple are from farther away. If you take the road running out of the valley to Banepa and Dhulikhel or walk up towards the Surjya Binayak Temple south of Bhaktapur you can see the temple soaring up above the other buildings, with the hills at the edge of the valley as a background.

The temple was built during the reign of King Bhupatindra Malla in 1702 and its design was so elegant and its construction so well done that the 1934 earthquake caused only minor damage. The stairway leading up to the temple is flanked by guardian figures at each plinth level. The bottom plinth has the legendary wrestlers Jayamel and Phattu, said to have the strength of 10 normal men. On the plinths above are two elephants, then two lions, two griffins and finally two goddesses, Baghini in the form of a tiger and Singhini in the form of a lion. Each figure is said to be 10 times as strong as the figure on the level below and presiding over all of them, but hidden away inside the temple, is the mysterious Tantric goddess Siddhi Lakshmi to whom the temple is dedicated.

Only the temple's priests can see the image of the goddess, but the temple's 108 carved and painted roof struts depict her in her various forms. Various legends and tales relate to the temple and its enigmatic inhabitant. One is that she maintains a balance with the powers of the terrifying Bhairab, comfortably ensconced in his own temple just across the square.

Bhairabnath Temple (37)

The recently restored triple roofed Bhairabnath Temple (also known as the Kasi Vishwanath or Akash Bhairab) has an unusual rectangular plan and has had a somewhat chequered history. It was originally built as a one storey temple in the early 17th century but was rebuilt with two storeys by King Bhupatindra Malla in 1717. The 1934 earthquake caused great damage to the temple and it was completely rebuilt and the 3rd floor added.

Casually stacked beside the temple you can see the enormous wheels and other parts of the temple chariot on which the image of Bhairab is conveyed around town during the Bisket festival. Curiously,

Bhairabnath Temple

despite Bhairab's fearsome powers and his massive temple, his image is only about 30cm high! A small hole in the central door is used to push offerings into the temple's interior, but the actual entrance to the Bhairabnath Temple is through the small **Betal Temple,** behind the main temple. The temple is guarded by two brass lions and there's a host of interesting details on the front.

Til Mahadev Narayan Temple (42)

It's easy to miss the square's third interesting temple, the Til Mahadev Narayan, as it is hidden away behind the buildings on the southern side of the square. You can enter the temple's courtyard through a narrow entrance through those buildings, or through an arched entrance facing west, just to the south of the square.

This double roofed Vishnu Temple has a Garuda kneeling on a high pillar in front, flanked by pillars bearing Vishnu's conch and chakra symbols. Some of the temple's struts also have Garudas. A lingam in a yoni stands in a wooden cage in front and to one side of the temple. Despite the temple's neglected setting it is actually an important place of pilgrimage and one of the oldest temple sites in the town: an inscription indicates that the site has been in use since 1080. Another inscription states that the image of Til Mahadev installed inside the temple dates from 1170.

Til Mahadev Narayan Temple

A statue of 'Narsinga' or Vishnu in his man-lion incarnation in the act of killing a demon. Durbar Square, Bhaktapur

PAUL BENSSEN

continued from page 205

At the first bend there are two interesting old buildings on the right-hand (southern) side. The **Sukul Dhoka** is a *math* (priest's house), with superb woodcarving both on its facade and inside in the courtyard. Almost next door is the **Lun Bahal**, originally a 16th century Buddhist monastery that was converted into a Hindu shrine with the addition of a stone statue of Bhimsen. If you look into the sanctum, in the inner courtyard, you can see the statue, dating from 1592, complete with a ferocious-looking brass mask.

A little farther along, the road opens into the **Golmadhi Square** with a deep hiti, the small, triple roofed Golmadhi Ganesh Temple and adjacent to it a white chaitya. Another short stretch of road brings you to another small open area with a *path* or pilgrim's shelter on your right. Behind it is a tank and the Inacho Bahal (described in the later Walking Tour section). A few more steps brings you to Tachupal Tole.

TACHUPAL TOLE

It's only about a 10 minute walk from the Nyatapola Temple to the square containing the Dattatraya Temple and the Pujari Math monastery. Today you stroll down a well paved street, a result of the major 'renovation' Bhaktapur underwent in the late 1970s. These brick-paved streets are a real contrast to some of the muddy, potholed alleys reminiscent of the past, which you can still find in the back blocks of town.

South from this square a maze of narrow laneways, passageways and courtyards runs down to the ghats on the river. Tachupal Tole, which is also called Dattatraya Square, was probably the original central square of Bhaktapur so this is most likely the oldest part of the town.

Dattatraya Temple

This tall, square temple was originally built in 1427 but alterations were made in 1458. Like some other important structures in the valley it was said to have been built using the timber from a single tree. The temple is dedicated to Dattatraya although the Garuda-topped pillar and the traditional weapons of Vishnu indicate that Dattatraya is actually another of Vishnu's many incarnations. He is also said to have been Shiva's teacher and is even claimed to have been a cousin of Buddha so the temple is important to Shaivites, Vishnaivites and Buddhists.

The three storey temple is raised well above the ground on its base, around which are carved some erotic scenes. The front section, which was a later addition to the temple, stands almost separate and the temple entrance is guarded by the same two Malla wrestlers who watch over the first plinth of the Nyatapola Temple.

Bhimsen Temple

At the other end of the square is the two storey Bhimsen Temple, variously dated to 1605, 1645 or 1655. The temple is squat, rectangular and open on the ground floor. It's fronted by a platform with a small double roofed Vishnu Temple and a pillar topped by a brass lion. Behind it is the deeply sunken and rather pretty Bhimsen Pokhari.

Pujari Math & Museums

There are 10 buildings around the square which were originally used as maths. The best known was the Pujari Math, which has been restored by the same German aid project which has done so much work in Bhaktapur. The Pujari Math was originally constructed in the 15th century during the reign of King Yaksha Malla, but restored in 1763. Until this century an annual caravan brought tributes to the monastery from Tibet.

The Pujari Math is principally famed for the superb peacock window, in the small alley beside the monastery, on its left-hand side if you face it from the square. The window is reputed to be the finest carved window in the valley and is the subject of countless postcards and photographs. There are some extraordinarily rich woodcarvings inside the building's courtyard.

The building now houses a **Woodcarving Museum** which is open daily from 10 am to 5 pm, except Friday when it closes at 3 pm, and Tuesday when it is closed all day. Admission is Rs 20 plus Rs 20 to use a camera. The museum has some fine examples of the woodcarving for which Bhaktapur, and indeed the whole Kathmandu Valley, has long been famous.

Directly across the square from the Pujari Math is the **Brass & Bronze Museum** with fine examples of metalwork from the valley. Its opening hours and admission price are the same as those for the Woodcarving Museum. At the other end of the square,

near the Bhimsen Temple, is a **Handicrafts Centre** selling woodcarvings and other examples of Bhaktapur crafts.

Salan Ganesh Temple

Just north of Tachupal Tole is another open area with the small Salan Ganesh Temple, dating from 1654. The open temple is ornately decorated, but the image is just a rock with only the vaguest elephant-head shape. To one side of the temple is the Ganesh Pokhari, a large tank.

TACHUPAL TOLE (BHAKTAPUR)

WALKING TOUR

Bhaktapur is a fascinating town to wander in, and the lack of traffic makes walking a real pleasure, particularly in comparison to Kathmandu where walking would be so much more enjoyable without motor vehicles to dodge.

This circular walk takes you by a number of interesting temples and shrines, but in Bhaktapur it's simply observing the timeless and seemingly unchanging rituals of life which is most interesting. Look for grain laid out to dry in the sun, people collecting water or washing under the communal taps, dyed yarns hung out to dry, children's games, fascinating shops, potters at work or women pounding grain: there's plenty to see. Perhaps most entrancing of all is Bhaktapur's medieval atmosphere.

North of Town

Starting from the north-eastern corner of Durbar Square (see main Bhaktapur map) walk to the east of the high Fasidega Temple, and continue a little farther up the road to a walled-in Vishnu Temple (12). Cross the junction and walk uphill past a large tank surrounded by fine old houses. Turn right towards Nagarkot and you soon come to the **Mahakali Temple** (13), where the shrine tops a small hill and is reached by a steep flight of steps.

Just beyond this temple turn right, walk downhill and then turn left and continue until you reach the tiny, open, double roofed **Mahalakshmi Temple** (15). Turn right (south) here and continue down to another large tank, the Naga (Snake) Pokhari. Here the typically green water contrasts nicely with the dyed yarns hung out to dry alongside the tank. On the western side of the tank two temples flank a central white shikhara while a cobra rears up from a small island in the middle of the tank.

Nava Durga Temple (18)

Turn left around the tank, continue to a second tank and then to the Salan Ganesh Temple, described in the Tachupal Tole section. A little farther on take a short detour north to the Nava Durga Temple. This Tantric temple is said to be the site for strange sacrificial rites. The golden door is surmounted by a golden window and is guarded by metal lions. It all contrasts nicely with the red-painted brick frontage. There's another large tank, the **Quathandau Pokhari**, just north of the temple.

Wakupati Narayan Temple (23)

Back on the route you soon come back to the main east-west road which runs through Taumadhi Tole and Tachupal Tole. Around this area there are more potters at work. Turn right and immediately on your left is the entrance to the Wakupati Narayan Temple. The ornate, golden temple is double roofed and is fronted by a line-up of no less than four Garudas.

South of Town

Continue on to Tachupal Tole and turn left down the side of the Pujari Math; directions to its famous peacock window are well signposted. Jog right, left, right and left again then immediately on your left is the ornate little **Inacho Bahal** (25) with prayer wheels, Buddha figures and a strange miniature pagoda roof rising up on a pillar above the courtyard.

Riverside Ghats

From here the road drops down to the Hanumante River, leaving urban surroundings for rural ones and passing by a curious collection of shrines, chaityas, statues and lingams (35), including a bas-relief of a well endowed nude Shiva. Just to the left of the bridge on the **Hanuman Ghat** is a shrine with a bas-relief of Rama and Sita, guarded by a statue of their faithful ally Hanuman (36). On the nearby building are four paintings including one showing Hanuman returning to Rama from his Himalayan medicinal herb foray, clutching a whole mountain in his hand. It's said that he paused here for a rest.

Cross the bridge and then take a hairpin turn back from the road onto a pleasant paved footpath. This rural stroll ends by another temple complex where you cross the river by the **Chuping Ghat**. Here, as at the Hanuman Ghat or the Ram Ghat by the bridge to the trolley bus stop, there are areas for ritual bathing and cremations.

Khalna Tole

Above the river is the open area of Khalna Tole, the centre for the spectacular activities during the annual mid-April Bisket Jatra. Bhairab's huge triple roofed chariot is assembled from the parts scattered beside the Bhairabnath Temple and behind the Nyatapola Temple in Taumadhi Tole. The chariot is hauled here with Betal, his sidekick the tiny temple behind the Bhairabnath Temple, riding out front like a ship's figurehead while Bhadrakali, his consort, accompanies them in her own chariot. The images of the gods shelter in the octagonal *path* during the festival and a towering 25m high lingam is erected in the stone yoni base. Bisket ends and the Nepali New Year starts when the lingam is taken down. Bhairab and Betal return to Taumadhi Tole while Bhadrakali goes back to her shrine by the river.

The circular walk ends with a gentle climb back into the town, emerging at the southern side of Taumadhi Tole.

SURJYA BINAYAK TEMPLE

About 1km out of town this 17th century Ganesh Temple is said to be a good place to visit if you're worried about your children being late speakers! It's also popular with Nepali marriage parties. To get there take the road down past the Potters' Square to Ram Ghat, cross the river and continue to the main road by the trolley bus stop. The road continues across the other side and rises gently uphill with some fine views back over the rice paddies to Bhaktapur.

Where the road turns sharp right, a steep stairway climbs up to the temple on a forested hilltop. As you step inside the temple enclosure the very realistic-looking long-tailed rat, sitting on top of a tall pillar, immediately indicates that this temple belongs to Ganesh. The image of the god sits in an enclosure in the bottom of a shikhara

and there's a second golden image on the shikhara spire. Statues of kneeling devotees face the image and the shikhara is flanked by large bells.

PLACES TO STAY

A growing number of visitors to Bhaktapur are staying overnight. There's plenty to see and one of the pleasures is that once evening falls all the day-trippers from Kathmandu disappear, and don't return until after breakfast the next day. There are a number of small guesthouses, all close to Durbar Square.

Golden Gate Guest House (☎ 610534) is entered by a passageway from Durbar Square or from the laneway between Durbar Square and Taumadhi Tole. The owners are friendly, there are fine views from the roof and rooms cost Rs 200/300, all with common bath, or there's doubles at a steep Rs 600 with bath. Some of the rooms have balconies and there's also a restaurant downstairs.

Entered from behind the Pashupatinath Temple on Durbar Square, the *Shiva Guest House* (☎ 610946) has singles/doubles at Rs 250/500, some of which have good views over Durbar Square, but even this hardly justifies the price. This is again simple and spartan with a restaurant on the top floor and rooftop.

Off the same laneway is the *New Nyatapola Inn* (☎ 611852, email dhaubel@craft .mos.com.np), which is not bad value at Rs 400 for a double with attached bath, although some of the rooms are a bit spartan.

Just off Durbar Square, the *Traditional Guest House* (☎ 611057) has plain, but adequate rooms. The position is excellent and the views from the rooftop of this nice old building are simply stupendous. Doubles (all with bath) cost from Rs 200 to Rs 300, depending on size.

There are a couple of newer places just off Taumadhi Tole. The *Bhadgaon Guest House* (☎ 610488, fax 610481) is just off the south-western corner of the square, and again, has excellent rooftop views. The rooms are large, clean and comfortable, and cost Rs 400/600 with bath.

On the lane which heads off from the north-western edge of the square is the squeaky clean *Pagoda Guest House* (☎ 613248). This place has very comfortable rooms and pleasant management. There's a variety of rooms, all clean and well maintained, which cost from $5/6 with common bath up to $15/20 with attached bath. There's also a roof-top restaurant here, but the views are pretty limited.

For some real shoestring accommodation there's the *Nyatapola Guest House* (☎ 612415) close by, which has basic rooms with common bath at Rs 100/150, and a nice terrace restaurant.

Close by, the *Namaste Guest House* (☎ 610500) is modern but characterless with small rooms at Rs 200/250 with common bath, and doubles with bath from Rs 300 to Rs 500.

A really pleasant option out of Bhaktapur itself is the *Bhaktapur Guest House* (☎ 610670), perched on the edge of the valley with great views back to Kathmandu. The setting is very peaceful and quiet, and it offers an excellent retreat from Kathmandu. The rooms are comfortable, and cost $20/25, although at quiet times this can come down as low as $10/15. There's also a restaurant and bar. The guesthouse is signposted off to the south of the Arniko Highway, about 1km before the trolleybus terminus, and is then a steep 10 minute walk (or short drive) up a rocky path.

PLACES TO EAT

Bhaktapur is certainly no competition for Kathmandu when it comes to restaurants, but don't worry, you won't starve. Right in Taumadhi Tole the *Cafe Nyatapola* is in a building which was once a traditional pagoda temple – it even has erotic carvings on some of the roof struts. From upstairs there are good views over the square but it is very cramped and often dominated by large groups of tourists. Prices are also comparatively high.

On the corner of the square, beside the Nyatapola Temple, the *Marco Polo Restaurant* is a better bet than Cafe Nyatapola if you want a substantial meal. Pizzas are Rs 100, and there's a range of Chinese, Indian and continental dishes from around Rs 80 to Rs 100. There's a small balcony with limited views over Taumadhi Tole.

In the opposite corner of the square is the small *Sunny Restaurant*, which has a terrace, great views over the square and no crowds.

On Tachupal Tole, opposite the Dattatraya Temple, the *Cafe de Peacock & Soma Bar* is one of the best spots in the valley to while away an afternoon. The food is good and the views of the beautiful square mesmerising. The best tables are often reserved by tour groups at lunchtime. The full international menu includes pizza and pasta for around Rs 130 to Rs 150, Mexican and western dishes at Rs 150 to Rs 180, and there is also a set Nepali meal for Rs 200 vegetarian, or Rs 300 nonveg. The cafe is open from 9 am to 9 pm.

Don't forget to try Bhaktapur's famous speciality – *jujudhau*, the 'king of curds' – while you are here. You can have it at the three main restaurants, and there are several places selling curd near the Navpokhu Pokhari bus stop.

SHOPPING

As in Patan there are a number of crafts for which Bhaktapur is the centre. You'll find all the Kathmandu Valley crafts on sale in Kathmandu itself, but it's often fun to shop for them close to their point of origin and you may well find better examples or unusual pieces. There are plenty of shops and stalls catering to visitors around Durbar Square and Taumadhi Tole.

Pottery

Bhaktapur is the pottery centre of the valley and a visit to Potters' Square is a must. There are many stalls around the square or just below Taumadhi Tole selling pottery. Much of the work is traditional pots for use in Nepali households (nice but not very transportable), but there are also items catering to tourist tastes, such as attractive elephant or dragon planters.

Woodcarving & Puppets

Bhaktapur is renowned for its woodcarving and you'll see good examples in the Handicrafts Centre on Tachupal Tole. There are other shops around the squares and you will find unusual pieces in the alley beside the Pujari Math, right under the Peacock Window in fact. If you buy anything which looks like it might be old, make sure you get a descriptive receipt for it as it's likely to be checked on departure from Kathmandu. If it really is very old you will not be allowed to take it out of the country.

Some of the best puppets, on sale in their thousands in all the valley towns, come from Bhaktapur.

GETTING THERE & AWAY
Bus

Travelling by public bus or minibus to Bhaktapur you disembark near the walled water tank called Navpokhu Pokhari, just beyond the even larger Siddha Pokhari and a short walk from Durbar Square. The minibuses from Kathmandu's City bus station are strictly for masochists and the poverty stricken – they are nearly always crowded and can take over an hour, although they only cost Rs 4.

The Chinese-built trolley buses are preferable, even though they are in an advanced state of decay and also get crowded (usually only around peak hour, though). At the Bhaktapur end, you have to walk 10 minutes to get to the town centre (by Ram Ghat and up into the town by Potters' Square).

The trolley buses leave Kathmandu from Tripureshwar Marg, cost Rs 4, and take around 35 minutes, unless you get caught in a traffic jam. The last minibus back to Kathmandu leaves about 6 pm, the trolley buses run until about 9 pm.

Buses for Nagarkot leave regularly from the north-eastern corner of the city and cost Rs 10. Buses from Changu Narayan leave from the northern edge of the city where the road to Changu Narayan leaves the main road.

Bicycle

The main road to Bhaktapur runs through to Dhulikhel, Barabise and finally to Tibet, so it carries a lot of bellowing, belching buses and trucks. Avoid peak hours. A better alternative for cyclists is to ride via Thimi. Take the Thimi turn-off – which is left at a T-junction after the Bhaktapur road crosses the Manohara River.

Taxi

Taxis cost around Rs 250, one way, and they drop you at the tour bus park on the northern edge of the city, but still just a short walk from Durbar Square.

Around the Kathmandu Valley

Apart from the three major cities of the valley, Kathmandu, Patan and Bhaktapur, there are countless villages, temples and stupas around the valley and on the surrounding hills. The crowds, traffic and modern trappings of Kathmandu can quickly be left behind for quiet villages and lush, terraced hills.

The valley beyond the cities has certainly changed over the years, and not always for the better, especially along the roads. Fortunately, however, aspects of traditional life are maintained as the people of the valley coax their livelihood from the land, and temples continue to provide a focal point for their lives. The seasons roll on, and the timeless demands of the fields, the family and the gods are still major priorities.

You can even find good treks in the valley, ranging from day walks to more ambitious hikes. Some of the possibilities are described in this chapter.

The ancient Buddhist stupa of **Swayambhunath**, a dramatic spot within walking distance of central Kathmandu, is probably the best known site in Nepal and attracts a constant stream of worshippers. The hilltop site offers a fine view over the valley that is helpful for orienting yourself if you've just arrived.

The most important Hindu temple is **Pashupatinath**, on the eastern side of Kathmandu near the airport. It's a centre for pilgrims from all over the subcontinent. A visit here can be combined with Bodhnath, another Buddhist stupa and the centre for a thriving Tibetan community.

If you will not have the opportunity to trek elsewhere, it is especially worth visiting one of the famous viewpoints on the rim of the valley, from where you can see the snow peaks of the Himalaya. There are numerous lodges and hotels at Nagarkot, Dhulikhel and Kakani.

If you have more time, there are less well-known, although important, temples such as: Changu Narayan, north of Bhaktapur and a treasure house of Nepali art; Dakshinkali, in the south-western corner of the valley and the site for animal sacrifices to Kali; or Budhanilkantha north of Kathmandu, with a massive 1400-year-old statue of Vishnu. There are many more.

The smaller towns and villages have tended to retain a more traditional Newari lifestyle, and if you find Bhaktapur interesting consider visiting Kirtipur (south-west of Kathmandu), Sankhu (north-east of Bhaktapur) or Panauti (outside the valley near Banepa, south-east of Bhaktapur). There are many more alternatives.

Daman, a viewpoint that overlooks the entire Himalaya from Dhaulagiri to Mt Everest, is a day trip from Kathmandu which is worth considering (see the Terai chapter).

CULTURAL CONSIDERATIONS

You do not have to go far to escape the hordes of camera-clutching tourists, but you will nonetheless be unable to escape their legacy: suspicious people and the cries of 'One rupee, one rupee' from children. If

---

HIGHLIGHTS

- Visiting the ancient Buddhist stupa of Swayambhunath, and Nepal's most important Hindu temple, Pashupatinath

- Taking one of the many short treks around the valley, with the opportunity to visit temples and to view the snow peaks of the Himalaya

- Enjoying the traditional Newari lifestyle of many of the smaller towns and villages

- Heading to the centuries-old Bodhnath Stupa, north of Kathmandu, with its influential Tibetan population

---

KATHMANDU VALLEY

you do venture off the beaten track, your responsibility as a visitor is greater than ever.

Whatever the temptation, do not give gifts to begging children. Do not intrude with a camera, unless it is clearly OK with the people you are photographing. Ask before entering a temple compound, although unless otherwise noted it is permissible to enter and photograph the temples described in this chapter. See Society & Conduct in the Facts about Nepal chapter for further details on cultural considerations.

ACCOMMODATION

In recent years there's been an increase in the number of accommodation options outside Kathmandu. If you don't need the bright lights and bustle of Thamel or the city, staying elsewhere in the valley can make a lot of sense. Unfortunately most of the options are not all that cheap, although places such as Dhulikhel and Nagarkot have a fair range. Some of the other options include Pharping, Dakshinkali, Lele, Godavari and Kakani – see the relevant sections for details.

GETTING AROUND

Swayambhunath and Pashupatinath can be reached on foot, but by far the easiest and most economical way of getting around the valley is by bicycle. If you are aiming for somewhere on the rim of the valley, make sure you have a mountain bike. It's possible for a reasonably fit person to go anywhere in the valley and return to Kathmandu within daylight on such a bike.

Buses and minibuses service all of the roads, but although cheap, they are uncomfortable and limiting. If you are part of a group or if the budget allows, you could consider hiring a car or taxi for the day. Motorbikes also offer a way of accessing most parts of the valley.

There is one company in Kathmandu which offers limited tours around the valley for around Rs 400 for half a day. (See Organised Tours in the Kathmandu chapter for details.) If you have limited time or want a speedy introduction to the area, they're worth considering. On the other hand, taxis can be hired for Rs 800 per half day, Rs 1500 per full day. With a taxi you aren't stuck to a schedule, and if you have this book who needs a guide?

Valley Walks

There are many interesting walks around the valley and many of them make pleasant alternatives to vehicles or bicycles. You can, for example, follow a trail from Kirtipur to Chobar and from there into Patan, or walk from the Gokarna Mahadev Temple to Bodhnath. These walks, and others, are detailed under Getting There & Away in the appropriate sections.

In addition, there are a number of interesting walks down from Nagarkot on the valley rim to various points in and outside the valley, including a pleasant short stroll down to the beautiful temple of Changu Narayan.

For more details on walks on the edge of the Kathmandu Valley, look for Alton C Byers' *Treks on the Kathmandu Valley Rim*, or James Giambrone's *Kathmandu: Bikes & Hikes*, which are available in Kathmandu bookshops.

Routes

This chapter has been organised following the roads that radiate out from Kathmandu.

Distances quoted are from the centre of Kathmandu. Each route has been named for the most important sites along the route, which are given clockwise from the Swayambhunath route. In most cases there is no alternative to going and returning on the same route unless you walk or mountain-bike cross-country.

Swayambhunath Route

SWAYAMBHUNATH (2KM)

The Buddhist temple of Swayambhunath, situated on the top of a hill west of the city, is one of the most popular and instantly recognisable symbols of Nepal. The temple is colloquially known as the 'monkey temple' after the large tribe of handsome monkeys which guards the hill and amuses visitors and devotees with tricks, including sliding gracefully down the double banisters of the main stairway to the temple. The roving monkeys quickly snatch up any offerings of food made by devotees and will just as quickly grab anything you may be carrying.

Geologists believe that the Kathmandu Valley was once a lake, and legends relate that the hill on which Swayambhunath stands was an island in that lake. It is said that Emperor Ashoka paid a visit to the site over 2000 years ago. An inscription indicates that King Manadeva ordered work done on the site in 460 CE and by the 13th century it was an important Buddhist centre. In 1346 Mughal invaders from Bengal broke open the stupa to search for gold. Under the Mallas, various improvements were made and the great stairway to the stupa was constructed by King Pratap Malla in the 17th century.

An entry fee of Rs 50 is payable if you enter the site from the car park on the western side, but not if you climb the stairway from the east – maybe the thinking is that if you've slogged it up the steps you have already earned your admission!

Eastern Stairway

Although you can get to the temple by vehicle, and save yourself the long climb up the stairs, the eastern stairway is by far the best way of approaching Swayambhunath. Look for the yellow and red stone seated Buddha figures at the base of the hill. The bottom end of the steps is guarded by figures of Ganesh and Kumar on their animals. Near the start of the steps is a huge 'footprint' on a stone, said to be either that of the Buddha

SWAYAMBHUNATH

1 Shantipura Building
2 Avalokiteshvara with Four Arms
3 Dhyani Buddha Aksobhya
4 Shantipura (Sky Symbol)
5 Agnipura (Fire Symbol)
6 Ancient Stone Inscription
7 Gompa Prayer Wheel
8 Buddha of Light
9 Hariti (Ajima) Temple
10 Nagpura (Water Symbol)
11 Path (Pilgrims' Shelter) & Gompa
12 Jamuna & Ganga Images
13 Swayambhunath Stupa
14 Pratapura Shikhara
15 Dorje (Thunderbolt Symbol)
16 Buddhist Museum
17 Vayupura (Air Symbol)
18 Vasupura (Earth Symbol)
19 Anantapura Shikhara

Dhyani Buddhas & Shaktis
A Amoghasiddhi
B Locana (Shakti of Aksobhya)
C Aksobhya
D Vairocana
E Mamki (Shakti of Ratnasambhava)
F Ratnasambhava
G Pandara (Shakti of Amitabha)
H Amitabha
I Tara (Shakti of Amoghasiddhi)

or of Manjushri. Halfway up the steps there is another small collection of stonework including a scene showing the birth of the Buddha, his mother holding a tree branch and the Buddha taking seven miraculous steps immediately after his birth.

As you climb the final stretch look for the pairs of animals – Garudas, lions, elephants, horses and peacocks – the 'vehicles' of the Dhyani Buddhas. If you tire on the ascent, pause to watch the monkeys' antics, or check out the trinkets on sale with the numerous hawkers, and when you reach the top remember that you should always walk around a stupa in a clockwise direction.

Great Thunderbolt

As well as building the great stairway, Pratap Malla also added a pair of *shikharas* (Indian-style temples) and the stone lions and *dorje* which visitors see immediately upon reaching the top of the stairs. Dorje is the Tibetan word for this thunderbolt symbol, in Sanskrit it is called a *vajra*. Dorjes are often accompanied by a bell; the thunderbolt symbolises male force and the bell symbolises female wisdom. Around the pedestal supporting Swayambhunath's mighty dorje are the animals of the Tibetan calendar.

A dorje, the thunderbolt symbol of Buddhist power.

Stupa

From the flattened top of the hill, the soaring central stupa is topped by a gold-coloured square block from which the watchful eyes of the Buddha gaze out across the valley in each direction. The question mark-like 'nose' is actually the Nepali number *ek* (or one) and is a symbol of unity. Between and

above the two eyes is a third eye, symbolising the Buddha's clairvoyant powers.

Set around the base of the central stupa is a continuous series of prayer wheels which pilgrims, circumambulating the stupa, spin as they pass by. Each carries the sacred mantra *om mani padme hum*. The prayer flags fluttering from the lines leading to the stupa's spire also carry mantras and each wave in the breeze carries the words away. The stupa's white-painted base represents the four elements – earth, fire, air and water – while the 13 concentric rings on the spire symbolise the 13 degrees of knowledge and the 13 steps that must be taken towards nirvana, which in turn is represented by the umbrella at the top.

Stupa Platform

The great stupa is only one of many points of interest at Swayambhunath. Starting from the massive dorje at the top of the stairs turn right to the monastery or *gompa* where, with a great deal of crashing, chanting and trumpeting, a service takes place every day at around 4 pm. Inside the gompa there's a huge prayer wheel and a 6m-high figure of Avalokiteshvara. Behind the stupa, adjacent to the International Buddhist Library, is a *path* or resthouse for pilgrims with an open ground floor and a gompa above it.

The dorje at the top of the stairs is flanked by two white temples in the Indian shikhara style, both dating from 1646. The one to the right, in front of the gompa, is the Pratapura shikhara while to the left is the identical Anantapura shikhara. Behind the stupa is the pagoda-style Hariti Temple with a beautiful image of Hariti, the goddess of smallpox. This Hindu goddess (to the Newars she is Ajima), who is also responsible for fertility, indicates again the constant interweaving of Hinduism and Buddhism in Nepal.

Near the Hariti Temple there are pillars on which figures of various gods and goddesses are seated. Look for the figure of Tara making the gesture of charity. Actually, there are two Taras, Green Tara and White Tara, who are sometimes believed to be the two wives of King Songtsen Gampo, the first royal patron of Buddhism in Tibet. The Taras are two of the female consorts to the Dhyani Buddhas.

Behind the stupa, bronze images of the river goddesses Jamuna and Ganga guard an eternal flame in a cage.

The symbols for the four elements – earth, air, water and fire – can be found around the hilltop. Behind the Anantapura shikhara are Vasupura, the earth symbol, and Vayupura, the symbol for air. Nagpura, the symbol for water, is just north of the stupa while Agnipura, the symbol for fire, is at the north-western corner of the platform. Shantipura, the symbol for the sky, is at the extreme north of the platform, in front of the Shantipura building.

In this same northern area of the platform you will find an ancient stone inscription,

dating from 1372, and a large image of the Buddha, next to the Agnipura symbol. There are numerous little shops and stalls around the stupa that sell jewellery and curios.

From its hilltop setting, Swayambhunath offers fine views over Kathmandu and the valley. It's particularly striking in the early evening when the city is illuminated, and the site is also very attractive under the soft glow of moonlight.

Getting There & Away

You can approach Swayambhunath by taxi or under your own power – either on foot or by bicycle. Unless you ask to be taken to the stairway on the eastern side, taxis will take you on the road via the National Museum & Art Gallery and deposit you at the car park on the western side, from where it's an easy

---

The Dhyani Buddhas

There are five Dhyani Buddhas or 'Buddhas in Meditation' who represent various aspects of Buddhahood, unlike the mortal flesh-and-blood Buddha, Gautama Buddha. Around many stupas the figures of the five Dhyani Buddhas in different meditative postures face out from the stupa in niches, four of them facing the four cardinal directions. Once you know the hand positions you can use a stupa like a compass. The Swayambhunath stupa is a good place to study the Dhyani Buddhas, and the description that follows is from that stupa.

Amoghasiddhi faces north and raises his right hand, palm out to shoulder height in what is known as a protective position. His animal or 'vehicle' is the Garuda. You can see the animals in niches below the Buddhas' shrines. As you move round the stupa clockwise you'll come to Aksobhya, the lord of the east; one of his hands touches the earth. This is known as the position of subduing the devil, Mara. The Buddha reaches down to touch the earth in order that it witness his resistance to temptation. His vehicle is the elephant.

Facing south is Ratnasambhava who rides a horse and turns his palm outwards. Amitabha faces the west and his hands rest on his lap, palm up in a meditative position. His vehicle is the peacock. The fifth of the Buddhas is Vairocana who usually appears in the centre of the stupa and therefore is not so easily seen. If he is shown he normally faces the south-east, and at Swayambhunath you can see his figure standing beside Aksobhya in the eastern niche. His animal is the lion; his hands are held up to his chest and he makes two circles with his fingers, rather like a scuba diver's 'OK' sign!

Each Dhyani Buddha is identifiable by his colour, his hand positions, his direction and his vehicle but each also has a shakti or female companion and a Bodhisattva or spiritual follower. Their shaktis or consorts are shown at the subcardinal points around the stupa. Amitabha is the Dhyani Buddha of our era and his Bodhisattva is none other than Avalokiteshvara or, as he is often known in the valley, Manjushri or Machhendranath.

climb to the top of the hill. The other routes end with the long steep climb up the eastern stairway to the stupa, and this is a far more interesting way to approach Swayambhunath and the easy stroll from Kathmandu is a pleasure in itself. From Thamel, taxis to the car park cost around Rs 50, or Rs 40 to the bottom of the stairway.

There are two popular foot or bicycle routes to Swayambhunath and using both makes the trip into a pleasant circuit. Starting from Durbar Square take Maru Tole (Pie Alley) down to the river where a footbridge crosses to the western side. Flat, stone cremation ghats can be seen by the riverside. From there the path passes houses and shops to the open green at the base of the hill. Along the way you'll see people working in vegetable gardens and preparing wool for Tibetan carpets. There's quite a large Tibetan community in this area.

If you go there by bicycle you are likely to find a number of small boys offering to 'look after' your bicycle. It's probably wise to pay a rupee or two of 'protection money', otherwise you may find your tyres have gone mysteriously flat and a pump will then have to be rented from one of the nearby shops!

The alternative route starts from Chhetrapati, near Thamel. From the Chhetrapati Tole junction the road descends to the river, with the Swayambhunath Stupa clearly visible in the distance, and passes the three riverside temples mentioned earlier.

AROUND SWAYAMBHUNATH

There are many small buildings and shrines down the hillside behind Swayambhunath. A smaller stupa stands on a hillock, with an adjacent gompa and an important shrine to Saraswati, the goddess of learning. At exam time, many scholars come here to improve

PAUL BEINSSEN

PAUL BEINSSEN

HUGH FINLAY

PAUL BEINSSEN

atan

his 'city of beauty', packed with temples and crowded with markets, is a feast for the senses.

Bhaktapur
Clockwise from top: Potters' Square; Nyatapola Temple dominates the Bhaktapur skyline, while life continues below; a sadhu studying scriptures; carrying bales of hay Newari-style.

Narayan, the sleeping Vishnu, lies peacefully in a pond in Budhanilkantha.

RICHARD I'ANSON

Buddha, with third eye.

GREG ELMS

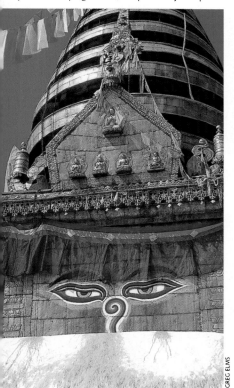

Buddha's eyes gaze over the valley at Swayambhunath.

GREG ELMS

A sadhu holds his begging bowl.

RICHARD I'ANSON

Kathmandu Valley
Believed to have once been a lake, the Kathmandu Valley today is rich with ancient architecture and traditional life.

their chances and schoolchildren come here during Basant Panchami, the Festival of Knowledge.

There are various Tibetan settlements and gompas around the base of the Swayambhunath hill. The 2km or 3km-walk north-west of Swayambhunath will take you to Ichangu Narayan, an interesting Hindu temple (see the section later). The National Museum & Art Gallery (see the Kathmandu, Patan & Bhaktapur chapter) is on the road from Kathmandu to the stupa.

The **Natural History Museum**, west of Swayambhunath, has a large collection of butterflies, fish, reptiles, birds and animals. It's open daily from 10 am to 5 pm except Saturday and government holidays, and admission is free.

There are several routes to Swayambhunath from Kathmandu and if you take the route from Thamel, via the Chhetrapati Square and down to the Vishnumati River, there are three interesting temples to look at. The **Indrani Temple** is just beside the river on the Kathmandu side and is chiefly notable for the brightly coloured erotic scenes on its roof struts. There are cremation ghats beside the river; in 1989 the bridge here collapsed during a heavy monsoon. Across the river and just upstream is the **Shobabaghwati Temple**. A footpath runs from here up the steep hill to the **Bijeshwari Temple**, from where the road continues to the Swayambhunath hill.

Ichangu Narayan Temple (5km)

At the edge of the valley floor, about 3km north-west of Swayambhunath, the shrine of Ichangu Narayan (not to be confused with Changu Narayan east of Kathmandu) is one of the Kathmandu Valley's important Vishnu shrines. The two-storey, 18th century temple is fronted by two square stone pillars bearing Vishnu's conch shell and chakra symbols. Various statuary can be found around the courtyard. The site of the temple was actually consecrated in 1200 and an earlier temple was built here after a famine in 1512. There's a small temple to Bhagwati on a hill overlooking Ichangu Narayan.

Getting There & Away The road to Ichangu Narayan starts beyond the Ring Rd, on the western side of the Swayambhunath hill. It quickly changes from a road to a track and as it climbs a steep hill (look back for the views over the valley), the track soon becomes a footpath. From the top of the hill, marked by a small temple, the trail descends slightly and then continues to climb gradually, leaving the valley proper. Finally, at the end of a little village is the temple compound. Going back to Kathmandu by bicycle is one long downhill breeze but you'll certainly work up a sweat getting to the temple.

An alternative route to Ichangu Narayan is a day walk from Balaju, to the north of Kathmandu. The trail climbs from Balaju to the top of Nagarjun hill and skirts around the valley edge through the Jamacho Forest Reserve and the Nagarjun Forest, descending to the Ichangu Narayan trail to the west of the village and temple.

Kakani & Trisuli Bazaar Route

Kakani is a viewpoint with spectacular views of the Ganesh Himal. A narrow, winding tarmac road, in reasonable though not great condition, continues to Trisuli Bazaar. From Trisuli Bazaar to Dhunche the road deteriorates to very rough gravel, but the views are spectacular. Dhunche is the starting point for a number of treks in the Langtang region. From Dhunche, a military road continues along the Langtang Valley before crossing the Trisuli River and heading westwards to Samdang (at 3600m). 4WD is essential.

Just before Malekhu, on the Kathmandu-Pokhara (Prithvi) Hwy, there's a bridge over the Trisuli River. This is the new road to Trisuli Bazaar, superseding the road that leaves the valley at Kakani. This makes an interesting circular bike ride a possibility, taking in Kakani, Trisuli, Dhading and Malekhu.

BALAJU (3KM)

The industrial centre of Balaju is less than 2km north of Thamel, just beyond the Ring Rd, and the expansion of the capital has virtually swallowed up this nearby suburb. Despite this, the Balaju park is still a peaceful retreat and its image of the sleeping Vishnu makes an interesting contrast with the larger Vishnu image at Budhanilkantha.

The gardens at Balaju were originally constructed in the 18th century and are now known as **Mahendra Park**. They are something of a disappointment – there's a lot of concrete and litter, and numerous ineffectual gardeners. Apart from the Vishnu image, there are a couple of small temples, an interesting group of *chörtens* (shrines) and lingams (for the aficionado) and the 22 waterspouts from which the park takes its name, 'Bais Dhara Balaju'.

Officially, the Balaju Vishnu image is said to be a copy of the older image at Budhanilkantha but there is no positive proof of which one is actually older. Certainly the Balaju image is in more pleasant surroundings than its better known relation. Although the king of Nepal cannot visit Budhanilkantha (since he is an incarnation of Vishnu and to gaze on his own image could be disastrous) no such injunction applies to Balaju, where the Vishnu image is just a copy of the real thing! Admission costs Rs 3, plus another Rs 2 if you take in a camera, and the park is open daily 7 am to 7.30 pm. The pool, which can often be very crowded, is open between March and September, and the admission fee is Rs 35.

Shitala Mai Temple

The double roofed 19th century Shitala Mai Temple stands in front of the Vishnu image and around it is a curious assembly of gods. They include a 16th century image of Hari Shankar – the half-Shiva, half-Vishnu deity – and a 14th century figure of the multi-armed goddess of smallpox, Shitala Mai. Others include Bhagwati, Ganesh and, in the usual clash of Hindu and Buddhist imagery, a statue of the Buddha protected by the hood of a snake.

Getting There & Away

You can get to Balaju by tempo from the National Theatre corner of the Rani Pokhari or walk there from Thamel. It's an interesting day walk from Balaju to Ichangu Narayan, west of Swayambhunath, skirting the edge of the valley.

NAGARJUN FOREST RESERVE

On the hill behind Balaju is the walled Nagarjun Forest Reserve with pheasants, deer and other animals. This, along with the former Gokarna Safari Park and Pulchowki, is one of the last significant areas of untouched forest in the valley.

You can continue up the hill to Jamacho, a popular Buddhist pilgrimage site. There are excellent views to the north stretching, on a clear day, all the way from the Annapurnas to Langtang Lirung, while the whole of the Kathmandu Valley is laid at your feet to the south.

There is a steep, 30km unpaved road to Nagarjun at the top, or you can walk up a wide, easy-to-follow and considerably shorter trail in about two hours. There are a number of picnic shelters around a stupa and a viewing tower.

The reserve is officially open daily from 7 am to 10 pm, but the gatekeeper has been known to refuse entry until 10 am. Admission is Rs 5 per person, plus Rs 50 per car and Rs 15 for a motorbike.

Getting There & Away

The main entrance to the reserve is about a 20 minute bike ride from Thamel. The walking trail to the top begins just past the gate on the right. It's steep for the first hour, and there is no water along the way or at the top. There are several routes you can take on the way down. Don't take the road if you're on foot – it's 30km long.

KAKANI (23KM)

Standing at 2073m on a ridge north-west of Kathmandu, Kakani is nowhere near as popular as Nagarkot, but does offer magnificent views of Ganesh Himal and the central and western Himalaya.

Apart from looking at the view (one could argue this is enough) there's not much to do. There is a century-old summer villa used by the UK embassy and a large police training college, although this does not seriously impinge on the tranquillity of the surroundings.

The road to Kakani also offers beautiful views. Once you're through the pass and out of the valley, Kathmandu seems light years away. Although the valley is terraced 1000m from top to bottom, many trees have been left behind and prosperous-looking houses dot the hillsides.

Although it's easy to get to Kakani on a day trip, it's worth staying overnight if you want to see the view (you stand a much better chance if you are there early in the morning before the clouds roll in).

Place to Stay & Eat

There's only two accommodation options in Kakani. The government-owned *Tara Gaon Kakani Hotel* (☎ 290812) is an old-fashioned place with wonderful views. Although small, it's also quite comfortable, and on a clear day the views from the front lawn are superb. Rooms with bath and some with views, cost $20/25. The hotel also serves reasonably priced meals.

Kakani Guest House, just before the Tara Gaon Kakani Hotel, is a typical village lodge, and is as basic as they come. It's friendly, however, and doubles cost Rs 250. Dal bhat is available, but there's very little else. With advance notice you may be able to eat at the Tara Gaon Hotel.

Getting There & Away

Kakani is an hour by car or motorbike from Kathmandu, so it would be a long, though rewarding, bike trip. There are a number of restaurants along the way so drinks or food are not a problem. The road is sealed almost all the way and it is a fairly gentle climb – although consistent. It is downhill all the way home! See the Mountain Biking chapter for details of a route that takes in Kakani.

Kakani is 3km from the main Dhunche road. Turn onto the broken bitumen road just before the Kaulithana police checkpoint

(the first outside Kathmandu) and there is a signpost for the Tara Gaon Kakani Hotel and the police training college.

Buses for Kakani, Trisuli and Dhunche leave from the Kathmandu bus park on the Ring Rd. You can catch a Trisuli or Dhunche bus, get off at Kaulithana (about Rs 20) and walk the 3km to Kakani.

TRISULI BAZAAR (68KM)

Trisuli Bazaar is a classically unattractive roadside town that owes its development to a large hydroelectric project on the Trisuli River, and the fact that it was once a trail head for treks into the Langtang region. These days trekkers head straight through to Dhunche, and there are very few persuasive reasons to stop. There's nothing to see, and the only oddity is the proliferation of hairdressers.

Nawakot, a small village a few kilometres south-east of Trisuli, has the ruins of a fortress that was built by Prithvi Narayan Shah when he was planning his campaign to take the Kathmandu Valley. It can be reached by bike or foot and is an interesting spot.

Places to Stay

There are several thoroughly unimpressive places on the eastern side of the bridge, which you reach when you enter town, before the turn-off to Dhunche. If you continue over the bridge, there are a few dal bhat restaurants and a couple of reasonable options. The *Trishuli Rest House* is the best of a bad lot, although the *Ranjit Hotel* is also OK.

Getting There & Away

It is a spectacular drive from Kakani along a narrow, twisting road with great views, and would be an excellent long descent by bike. Buses leave from the Kathmandu bus park between 6.30 am and about 2.30 pm (Rs 42, five hours).

DHUNCHE (119KM)

By the time you reach Dhunche you have been inspected by countless redundant police and army checkpoints, plus paid Rs 1000 to enter the Langtang National Park. Irritation evaporates quickly, however, because there are great views of the Langtang Valley, and although the modern section of Dhunche is pretty tacky, it's definitely a Tamang town, and the old section is virtually unchanged. Many people start trekking from Dhunche, although there is a bus to Syabru as well. (See the Trekking chapter.)

Places to Stay & Eat
There are a number of decent trekking-style hotel restaurants. The *Hotel Namaste* is clean, serves good food, and costs Rs 50 a double, or Rs 20 for a dorm bed. The *Hotel Langtang View* has similar prices and is also OK.

Getting There & Away
The road to Dhunche is bad, but it deteriorates further if you continue to Syabru. The views on both stretches are spectacular. A bus leaves from the Kathmandu bus park at 7 am, and arrives in Dhunche at about 3.30 pm.

SAMDANG (153KM)
The road becomes increasingly steep and spectacular after Dhunche. It drops down to cross the Trisuli River, then climbs steeply up the other side, continuing to Samdang, at 3600m, where there is the pleasant *Ganesh Himal Resort* (☎ 227929). Rooms cost $35, and advance bookings are essential. This would be a great base for day walks, and the views are stupendous.

Budhanilkantha Route

DHUM VARAHI (5KM)
Lying in an unprepossessing schoolyard just inside the Ring Rd to the north-east of the city proper, a huge pipal tree encloses a small shrine and a dramatic 5th century sculpture of Vishnu. Vishnu is shown reincarnated as a wild boar with a stocky human body, holding Prithvi, the earth goddess, on his left elbow.

From a historical point of view, the statue is interesting because it is an original depiction of an animal-human, created before iconographic rules were established, which perhaps contributes to the unusual sense of movement and vitality that the statue possesses. The statue shows Vishnu rescuing Prithvi from the clutches of a demon.

Getting There & Away
A visit to Dhum Varahi could be combined with a visit to Budhanilkantha, especially if you are approaching the Budhanilkantha intersection on the Ring Rd from Pashupatinath (see the Around Pashupatinath map later). If you are coming from Pashupatinath take the third dirt road on your left after crossing the Dhobi River. The statue lies under a huge pipal tree in the grounds of the Shridhumrabarah Primary School.

If you are coming from the intersection of the Budhanilkantha road with Ring Rd take the second dirt road on the right after the Panchayat Silver Jubilee Garden, which features a square, black-marble column topped with a conch shell. Continue until you see the pipal tree after about a kilometre.

BUDHANILKANTHA (15KM)
Vishnu has many incarnations and in Nepal he often appears as Narayan, the creator of all life, the god who reclines on the cosmic sea. From his navel grew a lotus and from the lotus came Brahma, who in turn created the world. So in the end everything comes from Vishnu and at Budhanilkantha the legend is made real. Here, a stone image of Vishnu lies serenely in a pond – the most impressive, if not the most important, Vishnu shrine in the country.

The 5m long image of Vishnu as Narayan is believed to have been created in the 7th or 8th century. It was sculpted during the Licchavi period, probably somewhere outside the valley and laboriously dragged here. Two other similar figures of the reclining Vishnu were also carved out of stone and all three were subsequently lost for many centuries. The image here at Budhanilkantha was the first found and is also the largest, but whether it was also the original (from which the others were copied) remains unresolved.

Narayan lies back peacefully on a most unusual bed – the coils of the multi-headed snake, Ananta. The snake's 11 hooded heads rise protectively around Narayan's head. Narayan's four hands hold the four symbols of Vishnu – a chakra (representing the mind), a mace (primeval knowledge), a conch shell (the four elements) and a lotus seed (the moving universe). A legend relates that the lost image was discovered when a horrified farmer saw blood coming from the ground when his plough struck the huge buried image.

During the early Malla period, Vishnuism had gone into decline as Shiva became more popular. King Jayasthiti Malla is credited with reviving the popularity of Vishnu, in part by claiming to be an incarnation of the multi-incarnated god.

To this day, the kings of Nepal make the same claim and because of this they are forbidden, on pain of death, from seeing the image at Budhanilkantha. They are allowed to look at the valley's other two reclining Vishnu images, which are said to be simply copies of the Budhanilkantha figure. One of these 'replicas' is at Balaju, the other, not on view to tourists, is in the old Royal Palace in Kathmandu.

The sleeping Vishnu image, which lies in a small sunken pond enclosure, attracts a constant stream of pilgrims, and prayers take place every morning at 9 am. Vishnu is supposed to sleep through the four monsoon months, waking at the end of the monsoon. A great festival takes place at Budhanilkantha each November, on the day Vishnu is supposed to awaken from his long annual slumber.

Non-Hindus are not permitted to enter the enclosure, but there are good unobstructed views from outside the fence surrounding it.

Getting There & Away

Buses (Rs 4) and tempos (Rs 6, route 5) leave from the Kathmandu City bus station and take around an hour. A taxi costs around Rs 150. The shrine is at the top of a flight of stone steps, about 100m beyond the bus and tempo terminus.

By bicycle it's a long, gradual, uphill haul – hard, sweaty work rewarded with a very pleasant return trip. You could pause at Dhum Varahi on one leg of your trip.

Pashupatinath & Bodhnath Route

PASHUPATINATH (5KM)

Nepal's most important Hindu temple stands on the banks of the Bagmati River, between Kathmandu and the airport and slightly south-west of Bodhnath. You can visit Pashupatinath en route to Bodhnath, as the two sites are an interesting short walk apart.

Pashupatinath Temple

Not only is Pashupatinath the most important Hindu temple in Nepal, it's one of the most important Shiva temples on the subcontinent and draws numerous devotees from all over India, including many colourful sadhus, those wandering ascetic Hindu holy men.

Shiva is the destroyer and creator of the Hindu pantheon and appears in many forms. His 'terrible' forms are probably best known, particularly his appearances in Nepal as the cruel and destructive Bhairabs, but he also has peaceful incarnations including those of Mahadev and Pashupati, the lord of the beasts. As the shepherd of both animals and humans, Shiva as Pashupati shows his most pleasant and creative side.

Pashupati is considered to have a special concern for Nepal and accordingly he features in any message from the king. Before commencing an important journey the king will always pay a visit to Pashupatinath to seek the god's blessing. Although Shiva is often a bloodthirsty god he is not so in his incarnation as Pashupati so no animal sacrifices are made here, although they are made at the nearby Guhyeshwari Temple. Nor is leather (since it comes from cows) allowed inside the temple and you will see Hindus removing their shoes before entering.

Near the entrance to the temple there are people selling flowers, incense and other offerings. Although non-Hindus are not allowed inside the temple you may catch a glimpse inside of the mighty figure of Nandi, Shiva's bull. It dates from the last century but the small bull in front of the temple is about 300 years old. The black, four headed image of Pashupati inside the temple is said to be even older and an even earlier image was destroyed by Mughal invaders in the 14th century.

There is plenty to be seen along the riverbanks and you can look down into the temple from the terraced hillside on the opposite bank.

The Riverbanks

The Bagmati is a holy river and, as at Varanasi on the Ganges, Pashupatinath is a popular place to be cremated. The burning ghats immediately in front of the temple,

PASHUPATINATH

1 Pashupatinath Temple
2 Huge Golden Trident
3 Hermits' Cave
4 11 Chaityas
5 Lingam with Shiva Face
6 Guhyeshwari Temple
7 Gorakhnath Temple Complex
8 Vishwarup Temple
9 Rajrajeshwari Temple
10 Cremation Ghats
11 Bachhareshwari Temple
12 Standing Buddha Image
13 Ram Temple

To Bodhnath (1km)

Bagmati River

(dry weather only)

Footbridge

Footbridge

To Ring Road (330m)

To Ring Road (330m)

To Ring Road (330m)

0   75   150 m

north of the footbridges, are reserved for the cremation of royalty although you will often see ritual bathing taking place in the river here.

The four square, cremation ghats just south of the bridges are for the common people and there is almost always a cremation going on. The log fires are laid, the shrouded body lifted on top and the fire lit with remarkably little ceremony.

There's often a crowd of tourists – cameras and video cameras at the ready – watching like vultures from the opposite bank. Photography is permitted, but be discreet – many tourists behave with an amazingly insensitive disregard for the funeral parties. However extraordinary the sights might seem, this is a religious ceremony, often marking a family tragedy, and the participants should be accorded respect. Behave as you would wish people to behave at a funeral in your home town.

Farther south of these cremation ghats, but still on the western bank of the river, is the ancient 6th century **Bachhareshwari Temple** with Tantric figures and erotic scenes. It is said that at one time Shivaratri festival activities included human sacrifices at this temple. Just outside the temple entrance, right at the end of the western embankment, is a half-buried, but quite beautiful, 7th century standing Buddha image.

Two footbridges cross the Bagmati River, and facing the temple from across the river are 11 stone *chaityas* (small stupas), each containing a lingam. From this bank you can watch the activities on the other bank, in front of the temple. Offerings and flowers are on sale, devotees dip in the river and there's a constant coming and going. From the northern end of the embankment you can see the cave-like shelters which were used at one time by hermits and sadhus. These days the yogis and sadhus head for the **Ram Temple**, farther down the river, especially during the great festival of Shivaratri.

The Terraces

Climb up the steps from the eastern riverbank to the terrace where you can look down into the Pashupatinath Temple. It's not a very inspiring sight: the golden roof of the central two tiered pagoda, which dates from 1696, is surrounded by ugly corrugated-iron roofs. Look for the enormous golden trident rising up on the right (northern) side of the temple and the golden figure of the king kneeling in prayer on the left side. Behind the temple, you can see a brightly coloured illustration of Shiva and his *shakti* (consort) looking out over the temple.

At the northern end of this terrace is a Shiva lingam on a circular pedestal. A finely featured face of the god has been sculptured on one side of the lingam. It's an indication of the richness of Nepal's artistic heritage that this piece of sculpture, so casually standing on the grassy terrace, is a masterpiece dating from the 5th or 6th century!

Gorakhnath & Vishwarup Temples

The steps continue up the hill and, as with the steps to Swayambhunath, are a popular playground for monkeys. The Gorakhnath complex is at the top of the hill. A *shikhara* fronted by a towering Shiva trident is the main structure, but there's a positive jungle of temples, images, sculptures and chaityas with Shiva imagery everywhere. Images of the bull Nandi stand guard, tridents are dotted around and lingams rise up on every side.

You can turn right from the path and head to the Vishwarup Temple but there's no point since, again, non-Hindus are denied entry to the temple precinct and from outside there's nothing to see. Instead, continue beyond the Gorakhnath Temple where the pathway turns steeply downhill to the river.

Guhyeshwari Temple

The Guhyeshwari Temple is dedicated to Shiva's shakti in her terrible manifestation as Kali. Like the Pashupatinath Temple, entry is banned to all but Hindus, and the high wall around the temple prevents you from seeing inside. Guhyeshwari was built by King Pratap Malla in the 17th century and the temple, standing in a paved courtyard surrounded by *dharamsalas* (pilgrims' resthouses), is topped by an open roof with four gilded snakes arching up to support the roof finial. You can see the snakes from outside. The temple's main entrance gate by the river is an imposing and colourful affair. To the west of the main temple building is a series of white, stupa-like temples.

The temple's curious name comes from *guhya* (vagina) and *ishwari* (goddess) – it's the temple of the goddess' vagina!

When Shiva was insulted by his father-in-law, Parvati was so incensed that she burst into flames and it was this act of self-immolation which gave rise to the practice of *sati* or suttee, where a widow was consigned to the same funeral pyre as her deceased husband. The grieving Shiva carried off his shakti's corpse but as he wandered aimlessly, the body disintegrated and this is where her yoni fell.

Special Events

Activities take place at Pashupatinath almost all the time, but it is generally busiest (with genuine pilgrims, not tourists) from 6 to 10 am and again from 6 to 7.30 pm. The best time to visit the temple is on Ekadashi – 11 days after the full and new moon each month. On those days there will be many pilgrims and in the evening the ringing of bells will indicate that the *arati* (light) ceremony is to take place.

In February/March each year, the festival of Shivaratri celebrates Shiva's birthday with a great fair at the temple. Pilgrims come from all over Nepal and India for this festival, and if you're in Kathmandu at the time don't miss it. Another fair takes place in November.

Getting There & Away

Buses to Bodhnath go via Pashupatinath from the City bus station, and the stop for Pashupatinath is called Gosala. Pashupatinath is an easy bicycle ride from Kathmandu: ride east from Thamel along Tridevi Marg, passing in front of the Royal Palace. It gets more complicated after that, but you can't go wrong as long as you keep heading east. The airport is very close to Pashupatinath, so some of the roads carry a lot of traffic.

It's a pleasant, short walk between Pashupatinath and Bodhnath. From the Guhyeshwari Temple, the dome of Bodhnath is clearly visible to the north. Take the footbridge across the river right in front of Guhyeshwari and head north for a few minutes, and turn right at the first track you come across. You eventually come out on the main road, right across from the main entrance to the stupa enclosure.

CHABAHIL (6KM)

The **Chabahil Stupa** is like a small replica of Bodhnath, about 1.5km west of Bodhnath, back towards Kathmandu. The small village of Chabahil has been virtually swallowed up by the expansion of Kathmandu but the site is very old and the original stupa was said to have been built by Ashoka's daughter Charumati. It certainly predates Bodhnath and around the main stupa are a number of small chaityas from the Licchavi period, dating back to between the 5th and 8th centuries. The site includes a 1m high, 9th century statue of a Bodhisattva, which is claimed to be one of the finest pieces of sculpture in the valley.

Nearby is the small **Chandra Binayak Ganesh Temple** with a double roof in brass. Ganesh's shrew stands on a pillar in front of the shrine, waiting for the tiny image of the god inside. A short distance south, but still on the Kathmandu side of the main road, is the well designed **Jayabageshwari Temple** dating from the late 17th century.

BODHNATH (6KM)

On the eastern side of Kathmandu, just north of the airport and an interesting walk from Pashupatinath, is the huge stupa of Bodhnath, the largest stupa in Nepal and one of the largest in the world. It is the religious centre for Nepal's considerable population of Tibetans and there are a number of thriving monasteries and many small shops selling Tibetan artefacts (beware, prices are high and bargaining is essential).

Many of these Tibetans are refugees who fled their country following the unsuccessful uprising against the Chinese invaders in

1959. They have been energetic and successful in the intervening years, as the large houses surrounding Bodhnath testify. While political and religious oppression continues in Tibet, this is one of the few places in the world where Tibetan culture is both accessible and unhindered.

Late afternoon is a good time to visit, when the group tours depart and the place once again becomes a Tibetan town. Prayer services are held in the surrounding gompas and as the sun sets the community turns out

to circumambulate the stupa – a ritual that combines religious observance with a social event. Do not forget to walk around the stupa in a clockwise direction.

Bodhnath has always been associated with Lhasa and Tibetan Buddhism. One of the major trade routes from Lhasa came through Sankhu, and Bodhnath therefore lies at the Tibetan traders' entry to Kathmandu. One can easily imagine the traders giving thanks for their successful journey across the Himalaya, or praying for a safe return. People

AROUND PASHUPATINATH

Dhum Varahi

To Budhanilkantha (9km)

To Kopan Monastery (1km)

Dhobi River

Ring Road

0   250   500 m

Bodhnath

Hyatt Hotel

Chabahil

Chandra Binayak Ganesh Temple

Chabahil Stupa

To Gokarna (4km), Sundarijal (9km) & Sankhu (14km)

To Kathmandu

Deopatan

See Pashupatinath Map p230

Footbridges

Guhyeshwari Temple

Gorakhnath Temple

Jayabageshwari Temple

Bagmati River

Pashupatinath

Vishwarup Temple

Dwarika's Village Hotel

To Airport (1km)

Runway

Tribhuvan Airport

still come here to pray before undertaking a journey in the Himalaya.

Gompas

There are a number of gompas surrounding Bodhnath that can be visited as long as you are respectful and discreet.

Do not forget to remove your shoes and hat before you enter a gompa. Ask before taking photos and avoid taking photos during a service. Smoking is not permitted anywhere in the main compounds. Do not step over or sit on the monks' cushions, even if no-one is sitting on them. During cere-

---

Bodhnath Stupa

There does not seem to be any agreement on how old the site is, but it is likely that the first stupa was built some time after 600 CE, after the Tibetan king, Songtsen Gampo, was converted to Buddhism by his two wives – the Nepali princess Bhrikuti (sometimes regarded as an incarnation of the Green Tara) and Wencheng Konjo from China (the White Tara). The current stupa was probably built after the depredation of the Mughal invaders in the 14th century.

Stupas were originally built to house holy relics, or to commemorate an event or place, with a structure that symbolises Buddhist beliefs. They are never hollow. It is not certain if there is anything interred at Bodhnath, but some believe that there is a piece of bone that once belonged to Gautama Buddha.

The base of the stupa takes the shape of a mandala (symbolising earth); on this four tiered base sits the dome (symbolising water); then comes the spire (symbolising fire); the umbrella (symbolising air); and the pinnacle (symbolising ether). The Buddha's watchful eyes gaze out in four directions from the square base of the spire. There is a third eye between and above the two normal eyes and the 'nose' is not a nose at all but the Nepali number one, signifying the unity of all life. The spire is made up of 13 steps, representing the 13 stages on the journey to nirvana.

Around the base of the stupa's circular mound are 108 small images of the Dhyani Buddha Amitabha. A brick wall around the stupa has 147 niches, each with four or five prayer wheels bearing that immortal mantra *om mani padme hum*. On the northern side of the stupa is a small shrine dedicated to Ajima, the goddess of smallpox.

monies enter quietly and stand by the wall near the main entrance; do not walk around in front of the altar, or between the monks, or cross the central area of the temple.

It is appropriate to make an offering to the lama, especially if you do take photographs. A *khata* (white scarf) is traditional, but these days rupees are also appreciated; monasteries depend for their existence on the donations of the faithful.

Decorations All the gompas are decorated with impressive mural paintings depicting mythological scenes, and sometimes *thang-kas* (painted on cotton, framed in brocade and hung), although there is quite a range in quality. The subjects are usually deities, great lamas, ritual diagrams (mandalas which represent the forces of the universe and aid meditation) and the wheel of life. The wheel of life is represented in the porch of every gompa and represents Buddha's knowledge and the way humans can escape their conditioning and achieve nirvana. Extremely complex rules govern these traditional arts; all stress spirituality, order and symmetry, not originality.

You will also see huge statues of various Buddhas (the Tibetans believe Buddha has

been reincarnated many times), prayer wheels, strategically arranged lamps filled with ghee (clarified butter) and sometimes offerings of rice.

To the western eye, the gompas are riots of colour, but awesome nonetheless. Most religious rites involve the recitation of sacred texts and chanting, often punctuated by musical instruments. The instruments dramatise and underline particular passages – usually in a quite unmusical way. Drums and cymbals crash, and trumpets and oboes moan repetitively. The result can be dramatic and moving.

Sakyapa Gompa This is the only gompa that opens directly onto the stupa (on the western side). There are some fine paintings and a magnificent Tara covered in beautiful embroideries. Don't miss the massive prayer wheel on the left of the entrance.

Chinya-Lama Gompa Named after a lama who had trained in China, this gompa is on the right of the path that leaves to the north of the stupa.

Nyingmapa Gompa This is one of the most recently completed (1984) and impressive

AROUND THE KATHMANDU VALLEY

The Tibetan Calendar

Around the base of the great dorje at the top of the stairway to Swayambhunath are the symbols of the 12 animals of the Tibetan calendar. The animals are similar to those of the Chinese calendar:

Snake	1929	1941	1953	1965	1977	1989	2001
Horse	1930	1942	1954	1966	1978	1990	2002
Sheep	1931	1943	1955	1967	1979	1991	2003
Monkey	1932	1944	1956	1968	1980	1992	2004
Goose	1933	1945	1957	1969	1981	1993	2005
Dog	1934	1946	1958	1970	1982	1994	2006
Pig	1935	1947	1959	1971	1983	1995	2007
Rat	1936	1948	1960	1972	1984	1996	2008
Bull	1937	1949	1961	1973	1985	1997	2009
Tiger	1938	1950	1962	1974	1986	1998	2010
Hare	1939	1951	1963	1975	1987	1999	2011
Dragon	1940	1952	1964	1976	1988	2000	2012

gompas. It has a large and thriving community – there are lots of young novices. The gompa is a large, reddish-ochre building (designed after a monastery in Tibet) surrounded by lower, white buildings that form a large courtyard. There are some very fine interior decorations that are the work of artists from Bhutan.

Kargyupa Gompa Known also as Ka-Nying Sheldrup Ling Monastery, this large white gompa is equal to the Nyingmapa

Gompa in size. It has a richly decorated interior with some fine paintings and large thangkas. The entrance is to the left of the main metal gates and westerners are welcome; the lama speaks English. The gompa hosts an annual seminar on Vajrayana training, usually in October for two weeks.

Sakyapa Gompa This gompa, to the north-east of the stupa, does not have the imposing architectural unity of the previous two – it has obviously been built in stages

BODHNATH

over a number of years – but it is no less interesting. There are some high-quality frescoes (inside the vestibule) and the main room is richly gilded and atmospheric.

Gelugpa Gompa To the right of the lane that runs north-east from the stupa, the Gelugpa Gompa is the least imposing gompa in appearance, but it nonetheless attracts large crowds of worshippers and has many young monks.

Special Events
The Tibetan new year (*losar*) in February is celebrated by large crowds of pilgrims, who come to watch the lamas perform their rites. Long copper horns are blown, a portrait of the Dalai Lama is paraded around, and masked dances are performed.

Places to Stay
There are a number of guesthouses in the tangle of lanes north and east of the stupa, but prices are marginally higher than in Kathmandu.

At the bottom of the scale is the *Peace Guest House*, just inside the main entrance to the stupa compound from the main road. It's about as basic as they come, but you can't beat the price of Rs 80 for a bed in a five-share room.

A small step up the scale is the *Kailash Guest House* (☎ 480741), on the road leading north from the Sakyapa Gompa. It's quite basic, but the management is friendly, and the rooms not bad at Rs 150/200 with common bath, or Rs 250 for a double with bath.

Lotus Guest House (☎ 472320) provides a very pleasant option if you want to escape the madness of Kathmandu for peace and quiet and if you want to be close to Bodhnath. Rooms are spotlessly clean and there is a nice garden. Singles/doubles with common bath cost Rs 220/300, or Rs 260/350 with attached bath, which is good value for Bodhnath.

Also good, but more expensive, and with excellent rooftop views out over the stupa – and the airport – is the *Happy Valley Guest House* (☎ 471241, fax 471876), a modern hotel near the Sakyapa Gompa. This is a very well appointed hotel with friendly management. Rooms cost $20/35, or there are larger carpeted singles at $35.

The new *Hotel Padma* (☎ 479052, fax 481550) is right by the stupa but doesn't take advantage of this excellent position as all rooms are inside with no views. The rooms are large and comfortable, with phone and bath. The cost is $18/25, but a 20% discount seems fairly usual.

Places to Eat
There are a number of restaurants around the stupa itself. The *Original Stupa View* which really does have a stupendous view, as well as excellent food. Main meals including an interesting range of vegetarian and Italian dishes are around Rs 170 to Rs 200. Right next door is the *SV Terrace Restaurant*, where the food is cheaper and less imaginative.

Also with good rooftop views and worth a try is the *Ristorante la Calabria*, on the eastern edge of the enclosure. Predictably, pasta features heavily on the menu, and main courses are from Rs 120 to Rs 180.

Farther around the stupa enclosure are the *Himalayan* and *Land of Snows* restaurants. Both provide standard and fairly unexciting menus, which are only partially offset by the views.

Om Shanti, also on the stupa enclosure, has a few tables which overlook the stupa. It is otherwise pretty ordinary, although it is cheap. Tibetan dishes are Rs 25 to Rs 30, Indian dishes Rs 35 to Rs 80.

For those on a shoestring budget, there are plenty of small Tibetan eating houses in the streets behind the stupa – any place with a curtain across an open door is probably one. The *Restaurant Boudha* is typical of these places.

Getting There & Away
Buses to Bodhnath run regularly from the City bus station (Rs 3, one hour). Tempos from Kantipath (routes 2 and 28) are slightly quicker and more expensive. Bicycles or taxis are better options. It's an interesting

short walk between Bodhnath and Pashupatinath (see the Pashupatinath section for details).

Grayline includes Bodhnath on their itineraries, and it is usually combined with Pashupatinath, although sometimes combined with Swayambhunath. (See Organised Tours in the Kathmandu chapter for details.)

KOPAN (9KM)

The Kopan Monastery (☎ 481268, fax 481267), a popular centre for courses on Buddhism and other Tibetan-related subjects, stands on a hilltop to the north of Bodhnath. You can visit Kopan on a walk between Bodhnath and the Gokarna Mahadev Temple; locals will point the way.

The centre has short courses on Tibetan medicine, thangka painting and other subjects but the major attraction for westerners is the 10-day residential **course** introducing Buddhist psychology and philosophy. The cost is about $250 including accommodation and food, but the participants must observe strict disciplinary rules.

GOKARNA MAHADEV TEMPLE (10KM)

Only a short distance north-east of Bodhnath the Sundarijal road turns off from the Sankhu road and after a couple of kilometres of twists and turns takes you to the old Newari village of Gokarna. The village is surrounded on three sides by the Gokarna Forest Reserve and is notable for its fine riverside Shiva temple.

Built in 1582 the triple roofed Mahadev (Great God) or Gokarneshwar (Lord of Gokarna) Temple stands on the banks of the Bagmati River and its inner sanctum enshrines a particularly revered Shiva lingam. Over the temple entrance is a golden *torana* (a space for a deity) with Shiva and Parvati making an appearance in the centre in the *Uma Maheshwar* position (Parvati's hand resting on Shiva's knee) with a figure of the Garuda above them.

The temple's great interest is the surprisingly varied collection of sculptures and reliefs all around the site. They even line the pathway down from the road to the temple courtyard, starting with a Buddha figure at the top, and feature a varied collection of gods and goddesses, some dating back over a thousand years.

The sculptures include figures from Hindu mythology including Narad, Surya (sun god), Chandra (moon god) and Kamadeva (god of love). There's a bearded image of Brahma, Ganesh makes his usual cheerful appearance and Vishnu appears as Narsingha, making a particularly thorough job of disembowelling a nasty demon. Shiva's bull, Nandi, stands beside the temple and as well as the inevitable lingams dotted around there's even a nude figure of Shiva, complete with erect lingam. Durga makes three appearances, one of them as Ajima. The finest of the Gokarna statuary is in the small shrine house in the north-western corner of the courtyard. This 8th century sculpture of the beautiful goddess **Parvati** shows her at her radiant best; you can see why Shiva fancied her!

To one side of the main temple, just above the river, is the small, open, single storey **Vishnu Paduka**. This relatively recent addition shelters a metal plate bearing Vishnu's footprint. Outside, and set into the steps above the river, is an image of Shiva reclining on a bed of cobras, just like the reclining Vishnu images at Budhanilkantha and Balaju.

The temple guardians here can be touchy about photos being taken, so ask permission before firing away.

Getting There & Away

You can walk, cycle, take a tempo (route 28 from Kantipath or Bodhnath) or a taxi to Gokarna. Taxis may be reluctant to go as the road is quite rough once you turn off the main road. Expect to pay Rs 300 return.

There's also an interesting walking route between Gokarna and Bodhnath via the monastery at Kopan. The clear trail starts from just beyond the bridge, on the Kathmandu side of Gokarna. It starts off steeply north-west and runs through fields and bamboo groves past teahouses to Kopan on top of a small hill. From Kopan it's an easy walk south-west to Bodhnath.

SUNDARIJAL (15KM)

At the north-eastern edge of the valley, the streams which eventually join the Bagmati River flow over the waterfalls at Sundarijal into a century old reservoir. This is also the starting point for the popular trek to Helambu. The main reservoir which supplies drinking water to the valley is about a two hour walk uphill from here. A smaller trail

forks off before the reservoir to a small **rock cave**, where a 13th century image of Mahadevi (great goddess) can be found.

See the Nagarkot section in this chapter for details of the long valley-rim walk to Sundarijal from Nagarkot.

Getting There & Away

Buses leave from Kathmandu's City bus station and cost Rs 15. Otherwise, it's a pleasant bicycle ride along the quiet roads past Gokarna.

GOKARNA MAHADEV TEMPLE

0   3   6 m

Bagmati River

1 Vishnu Paduka (Vishnu's Footprint)
2 Figure of woman with four arms and a pot on her head
3 Trident with skeleton figure at base
4 Parvati Shrine
5 Well-endowed Shiva
6 Shiva image reclining on a bed of cobras
7 Ganesh
8 Hanuman
9 Golden Torana with Uma-Maheshwar in centre
10 Gokarna Mahadev Temple
11 Nandi (Shiva's bull)
12 Bearded Brahma
13 Narsingha (Vishnu's man-lion incarnation)
14 Buddha
15 Cow

AROUND THE KATHMANDU VALLEY

Sankhu & Vajra Jogini Route

The route to Sankhu follows the old Tibetan trade route past Bodhnath. After Bodhnath the road to Sundarijal turns off to the northeast and the road to Sankhu continues to the east.

GOKARNA SAFARI PARK (10KM)

Continuing east of Bodhnath from Kathmandu, the entrance to the former Royal Game Reserve or King's Forest is off the Sankhu road. A deer park was created here late in the 19th century and the walled reserve has spotted deer (chital), hog deer (laghuna), monkeys and birds.

This is one of the few woodlands left on the valley floor, and used to be a great spot for picnics and a bit of game-spotting. Unfortunately, it has been closed, and a golf course and resort are being developed in the open part of the reserve closest to the road. The golf course should have been completed by now, but entry may be only for golf club members.

Getting There & Away

The reserve is about 2.5km from Bodhnath, so it can be easily reached by bicycle. Buses run quite frequently to Sankhu from the City bus station and you can get off at the entrance.

SANKHU (20KM)

Sankhu was once an important post on the trading route between Kathmandu and Lhasa, and although the town's great days are over, you can still see many signs of its former prosperity. The town was first settled in the Licchavi era and there are many old homes decorated with fine woodcarving. Although many traditional aspects of Newari life continue in the town, the most persuasive reason to visit this place is the beautiful Vajra Jogini Temple complex, an easy walk or bicycle ride about 2km north of town.

Getting There & Away

Buses to Sankhu leave from the City bus station. They take about two hours (Rs 18).

It's easy to reach Sankhu by bike. The road is sealed and flat (with a few minor exceptions), and basically follows the Manohara River. It's an attractive and interesting ride taking about 1½ hours beyond Bodhnath. Rather than backtrack all the way, in the dry season at least it is possible to cross the Manohara and climb to the fascinating Changu Narayan Temple (see the Changu Narayan section for details). See the Nagarkot section for details of the interesting walk down to Sankhu.

VAJRA JOGINI (22KM)

Perched high above the valley, in a grove of huge, old trees, this complex of temples is well worth visiting. The main temple was built in 1655 by Pratap Malla of Kathmandu, but it seems likely the site has been used for much longer than that. The origins of the Tantric goddess who is worshipped in this bewitching spot are hard to determine.

The climb up the stone steps to the temples is steep and hot, but there are a number of waterspouts where you can cool off. About halfway up there's a shelter and some carvings of Kali and Ganesh. A natural stone represents Than Bhairab and sacrifices are made at its foot.

As you enter the main temple compound you will see several fine bells (the Tantric female equivalent to the vajra or thunderbolt) on your right. There are two temples and the one nearest to the entrance is the Vajra Jogini Temple, a pagoda with a three tiered roof of sheet copper. There is some beautiful repoussé work on the southern facade. The struts are carved with protective animals and gods from the Buddhist pantheon. The goddess' image cannot actually be seen through the door.

The two tiered temple furthest from the entrance enshrines a chaitya and commemorates Ugra Tara, or Blue (Nilo) Tara, a Buddhist goddess. The woodcarving around the doors is very fine. There are various chaityas around the platform and a gilt lion on a pillar. In the north-western corner of the courtyard (the far left when you enter) is the entrance to a cave, which is used for Tantric practices, and a Tibetan inscription. Behind the temples and up some stairs are buildings which were once used as pilgrim resthouses and priests' houses.

Getting There & Away

At Sankhu, turn left at the bus stop and walk north through the village (where there is some beautiful woodcarving). Just after the road turns to the right, take the road on the left which runs out of the village (under an ugly concrete archway). There are some fine stone carvings of Vishnu and Ganesh after the arch. The road then forks: the left fork is the traditional approach for pedestrians and follows the small river; the right fork is drivable (though rough) and is OK for bikes.

There's a car park at the foot of the steps to the temple complex. If you get there by bicycle, it will be necessary to pay a few rupees to someone to look after it for you. It's quite a stiff climb to the temples.

Changu Narayan Route

THIMI (10KM)

Thimi is the fourth largest town in the valley, outranked only by Kathmandu, Patan and Bhaktapur. It's a typical Newari town and its 'capable people' (the name of the town is derived from this Newari expression) operate thriving cottage industries producing pottery and papier-mâché masks. They also grow vegetables for the markets of Kathmandu.

The town's main road runs north-south between the old and new Bhaktapur roads which form the northern and southern boundaries of the town. In the centre of the southern square is the 16th century **Balkumari Temple**. Balkumari was one of Bhairab's shaktis and a much less magnificent Bhairab Temple is found nearby (see the Tantric Goddesses boxed text below). Thimi also has a 16th century **Narayan Temple** and a 15th century **Mahadev Temple**.

AROUND THE KATHMANDU VALLEY

Tantric Goddesses

The name Vajra Jogini suggests a close association with Tantric beliefs. A *vajra* (*dorje* in Tibetan) is the Buddhist thunderbolt symbol that looks a bit like a hollow dumb-bell and Vajrayana is the name for the Tantric form of Buddhism. Tantric beliefs developed as a synthesis of ancient pre-Hindu religions and new ideas that rejected many orthodox Hindu and Buddhist beliefs. Tantric believers hold that endless rebirths on the journey to nirvana can be avoided by incorporating magical rites with all the energies of existence – both good and bad – under the strict tutelage of a lama. Sex and sexual imagery play a central role.

Hinduism was initially a patriarchal religion introduced by the Aryan invaders of India, and overriding the existing earth goddesses. The development of *shaktis* or the female consorts of the new male gods allowed the resurgence of the female forces. These goddesses have enjoyed tremendous popularity in the Kathmandu Valley, sometimes completely overshadowing their male counterparts, especially in Tantric belief. A parallel development in Buddhism produced the female counterparts to the Dhyani Buddhas.

A Jogini is the female counterpart to a Bhairab, one of the wrathful forms of Shiva. In other words, a Jogini is the wrathful form of Shiva's partner Mahadevi (great goddess) who is Parvati in a more peaceful manifestation. Among some of Mahadevi's fearsome manifestations are Kali, Durga, Annapurna and Taleju.

So who is Vajra Jogini you ask? A Tantric goddess is the simple answer – a unique Nepali goddess possibly combining elements from Hinduism, Buddhism and perhaps even earlier religions.

Just to the north of Thimi is **Nade** and from here a stone pathway leads up through an archway to the **Ganesh Dyochen**. Nearby is a locally popular triple roofed **Ganesh Temple**. Farther north is Bode, with the interesting 17th century **Mahalakshmi Temple**.

Special Events

In a Nepali new year's day ceremony, 32 deities are carried to the Balkumari Temple in palanquins. The arrival of the Ganesh image from Nade is the high point of the colourful festivities (a great deal of bright red powder gets chucked around). A similar but smaller ceremony also takes place at the Mahalakshmi Temple in Bode.

CHANGU NARAYAN TEMPLE
(22KM)

The beautiful and historic temple of Changu Narayan stands on a hilltop at the eastern end of the valley, about 4km north of Bhaktapur. Although the temple dates from 1702, when it was rebuilt after a fire, its origins go

CHANGU NARAYAN TEMPLE

right back to the 4th century and there are many important stone images and sculptures dating from the Licchavi period.

Despite the temple's beauty and interest it attracts relatively few visitors because of its comparative inaccessibility, although these days you can drive or catch a bus right to the temple via Bhaktapur. Alternatively, it makes a pleasant walk from that town or an interesting destination on the walk down from Nagarkot.

The double roofed temple is dedicated to Vishnu in his incarnation as Narayan and is exceptionally beautiful with quite amazingly intricate roof struts depicting multi-armed goddesses. It is fronted by a figure of Garuda said to date from the 5th century. The man-bird mount of Vishnu has a snake around his neck and kneels with folded hands facing the temple. Stone lions guard the wonderfully gilded door, flanked by equally detailed gilded windows. Two pillars at the front corners carry two traditional symbols of Vishnu, the conch shell and the chakra.

Despite the beauty of the temple itself it is, in Nepali terms, relatively new and the much older images found in the temple courtyard are of equal interest. There are various images of Vishnu, carrying the symbols associated with the god in his four hands. In the north-western corner there is an image of Vishnu astride the Garuda which is illustrated on the Rs 10 banknote. Beside the Garuda figure which faces the front of the temple is one of the oldest Licchavi stone inscriptions in the valley.

Other images include one of Vishnu as Narsingha, his man-lion incarnation, in the act of disembowelling a demon. Another shows him as Vikrantha, the six armed dwarf who transformed into a giant capable of crossing the universe in three gigantic steps. Behind these two images is a small black slab showing Narayan reclining on the serpent Ananta at the bottom and Vishnu with 10 heads and 10 arms in the centre. This beautifully carved image dates from the 5th or 6th century.

Other points of interest include the statues of King Bhupatindra Malla and his queen, kneeling in a gilded cage in front of the temple. Look at the brick paving of the courtyard. In the centre, triangular bricks are used while out towards the edge there are older rounded-corner bricks. The village of Changu stands below the temple hill and has some Licchavi remains.

Places to Stay & Eat
The small *Restaurant Champak* is in the south-western corner of the temple complex. By the car park at the end of the road at the entrance to Changu village, the *Lovely Coffee House* has drinks and snacks, and great views out over the valley to Bhaktapur.

Getting There & Away
Public buses run regularly between Changu Narayan and Bhaktapur. A taxi from Kathmandu costs around Rs 500 return, and from Bhaktapur around Rs 150.

It takes about two hours on foot or about an hour by mountain bike to get to Changu Narayan from Bhaktapur. It's a wonderful

CHANGU NARAYAN TEMPLE

1 Police Post
2 Vishnu & Garuda Image (from Rs 10 note)
3 Krishna Shrine
4 Nriteshwar Shrine
5 Winged Lions
6 Vishnu Image
7 Mahavishnu
8 Mahadev Shiva Lingam
9 Images of Avalokiteshvara & Vishnu
10 Pillar with Chakra Symbol
11 Garuda Image
12 Statue of King Bhupatindra Malla & His Queen
13 Stone Lions
14 Changu Narayan Temple
15 Griffins
16 Pillar with Conch Shell Symbol
17 Pashupatinath Shrine
18 Bhairab Shrine
19 Relief of Vishnu as Narsingha
20 Relief of Vishnu as Vikrantha
21 Lakshmi Narayan Temple
22 Reliefs of Narayan on the Serpent Ananta & 10 Headed Maheshwar
23 Elephants
24 Mahadev Shiva Shrine
25 Ganesh Shrine
26 Restaurant Champak

AROUND THE KATHMANDU VALLEY

Narsingha

The image of Vishnu as Narsingha or Narsimha is a common one in the valley. In his man-lion incarnation the god is traditionally seen with a demon stretched across his legs, in the act of killing the creature by disembowelling it. You can find Narsingha at work at Changu Narayan, in front of the palace in Patan, just inside the Hanuman Dhoka entrance in Kathmandu and at the Gokarna Mahadev Temple.

The demon was supposedly undefeatable as it could not be killed by man or beast, by day or night or by any weapon. Vishnu's appearance as Narsingha neatly overcame the first obstacle for a man-lion is neither a man nor a beast. He then waited until evening to attack the demon, for evening is neither day nor night. And instead of a weapon Narsingha used his own nails to tear the demon apart.

---

downhill run on the way back but quite a steep climb on the way there. A long spur runs down from the eastern edge of the valley and the temple tops the final bump of this lengthy ridge. There is a sealed road from Bhaktapur right to the village of Changu, which is only a short stroll from the temple, and you can easily get a taxi to Changu Narayan from Bhaktapur. A number of walking trails, inconsistently signposted, lead to Changu Narayan from Bhaktapur and once you get out of the town the hill is clearly visible.

If you're on foot or bike, you can continue to Bodhnath, Sankhu, Gokarna or other attractions in the north-east of the valley. From the northern and western entrances of the temple a short, steep path descends to Manohara River – crossed easily by wading or by a temporary bridge during the dry season (impossible in the monsoon). This brings you out to the Sankhu road at Bramhakhel about 3.5km south-east of Gokarna.

If you approach Changu Narayan from the Sankhu road you'll see a small sign for Changu Narayan on a building wall on the south side at the entry to Bramhakhel. It's a five minute walk across the fields to the river and the temporary bridge. It's quite a steep and difficult scramble up the hill that will take at least 45 minutes (especially if you're carrying a bike). You might like to go slower as there are a couple of small Newari hamlets along the way, and great

views. There's quite a labyrinth of paths up the hill and it's not a bad idea to have a guide (and bicycle carrier). You will probably find small boys offering their services – establish a price in advance. From Changu Narayan it's an exhilarating half-hour bike ride to Bhaktapur, another 45 minutes from Kathmandu.

A third way of reaching Changu Narayan is by the pleasant downhill stroll from Nagarkot (see the following Nagarkot section). Walking down from Nagarkot to Changu Narayan and then on to Bhaktapur is a much more interesting walk than the straightforward walk down to Bhaktapur.

Nagarkot Route

The route to Nagarkot goes by Thimi and Bhaktapur before climbing steeply up to the village on the valley rim.

NAGARKOT (30KM)

There are various places around the edge of the Kathmandu Valley which offer great mountain views, but the resort village of Nagarkot is generally held to be the best. Mountain watchers make their way up to the village, stay overnight in one of Nagarkot's lodges, then rise at dawn to see the sun appear over the Himalaya.

Nagarkot is on a ridge on the north-eastern rim of the valley and the view extends all the way from Dhaulagiri in the west past Mt Everest (little more than a dot on the horizon) to Kanchenjunga in the east. An easy hour's walk south from the village will give an even better 360° view from a lookout tower on a ridge. You have to cross an army checkpoint and they will only let you walk through in the morning.

A pilgrimage to Nagarkot will nearly always be rewarded with a view between October and March, but you will be very lucky to catch more than a glimpse through the clouds of some snow-capped mountains in the June to September monsoon period. It can get very cold at Nagarkot in autumn or winter so if you're staying overnight come prepared with warm clothing.

The main centre of Nagarkot, in reality a small cluster of guesthouses, is a 10 minute walk north of the main road that runs through to the army camp. Nagarkot originally owed its existence to the camp, but now it relies on tourism. It was never a traditional village, so while the views can be stunning, and the surrounding countryside is great for walking, the unplanned scatter of lodges is not itself attractive.

Right in the centre of things is a lookout, between the huge Club Himalaya Resort and the Tea House.

There are a number of walks to and from Nagarkot, including fine walks down to Sundarijal, Sankhu, Changu Narayan or Bhaktapur in the valley or south to Banepa (beyond the valley).

Places to Stay & Eat

Nagarkot has a fair selection of lodges, guesthouses and hotels – most of them far from pretty. They usually offer a range of facilities at a range of prices, and most are expensive for the facilities you get – but what price the view? Most people eat at their lodge, and most are unimpressed with the cuisine.

Nagarkot accommodation is spread out along the dirt track which heads north from the bus stop at the town's one and only intersection. Nagarkot is very much a one-night stand, and few visitors stay longer

although you can make some pleasant strolls in the surrounding country.

Accommodation can be in short supply late in the day during the peak season, in which case you may have to settle for whatever you can get, which will probably mean a room without a view. In the low season there are fewer visitors and prices are highly negotiable.

Most places have electricity, but hot water and heating are hard to come by, especially at the budget end of the market. A torch (flashlight) is useful (for an early-morning start to the lookout tower) and warm clothing (even a sleeping bag) can be worthwhile. There's not much to do in the evenings, so bring a book.

The winding road takes a sharp turn at the cluster of shops which mark the Nagarkot bus stop. From here a dirt track veers left and after a few hundred metres comes to a hilltop group of hotels which are the most popular and best situated at Nagarkot. They cluster around the Mahakali shrine, and many have rooms that offer Himalayan views straight from your bed. At the worst you'll just have to take a few steps outside to bring the whole panorama into view.

The first place you come across is the uninspiring *Hotel Snowman* (☎ 290746). Even with discounts of 50% it's overpriced. The full tariff is $18/25 for plain rooms with attached bath. Deluxe rooms with views go for $30/40.

Hotel Sun & Mountain (☎ 290871), the next place along, is a modern and unremarkable place with rooms that all face the wrong direction! It's also way overpriced at $35/40, but discounts are available. Behind it is the similar *Hotel Space Mountain*.

Next is a group of budget hotels around the Mahakali shrine. The *Hotel at the End of the Universe* (☎ 610874) has some standard rooms from $4/6, including a few pleasant bamboo-walled cottages with attached toilet. There are also some modern brick rooms with hot shower at $15. While none of the rooms has a view, the restaurant does. With a carpeted bench around low tables it's a popular gathering place in the evening.

Galaxy Hotel (☎ 290797, fax 259142), just below, has very comfortable rooms with bath for $20/25, although discounts are often available. Most rooms are reasonably pleasant, and have at least partial views, so you may consider the cost worthwhile.

Continue beyond the Mahakali shrine, skirting the bank official's house, and you reach the *View Point Hotel*, which is a more upmarket option, with rooms starting at $14/20 and rising to $24/30 for a combination of comfort and views. All rooms have

private bath with hot water. The restaurant has a fireplace.

Just beyond the View Point Hotel is the *Peaceful Cottage* (☎ 290877) which has rooms of varying standards. The prices start from $5/8 for hardboard partitioned cells with views, and there are also better rooms with private bath and hot water for $10/20. Topping the rise is the *Cafe du Mont* with magnificent views, and average food (you can't have everything!).

Separated from this group of lodges by a couple of hundred metres is the *Niva Niwa Lodge* (☎ 290797, fax 259142), a modern and clean but unremarkable place, with prices that seem hard to justify – $75/95 for rooms with bath. Even with the 20% discount offered they are expensive.

The *Hotel Country Villa* (☎ 221012, fax 290827, email nam@wlink.com.np) a bit farther along the dirt road, has good rooms, most with excellent views, and there's a decent restaurant. Room rates are $30/40, though a 15% discount is offered without much prodding. The *Himalayan Resort* close by and similarly priced is another reasonable place.

A good place farther along still is the relaxed *Nagarkot Naldum Village*, with small bamboo cottages with stunning views – from bed – at $20 with attached toilet (also with views!). This place is a bit of a walk, but if you're after peace and quiet it could be ideal, and the *Greenpeace Restaurant* here turns out consistently good food.

There's another good place about 4km away on the Sankhu road, past Nagarkot Naldum Village. *The Farmhouse* is in an old, beautifully renovated Newari house and is highly recommended. It's run by Kathmandu's Hotel Vajra, and the rates are reasonably high, although meals are included. Singles/doubles are $30/40.

The road which forks off to the right by the Hotel Snowman leads to a few more hotels. Accessed off a steep side track is *The Fort* (☎ 290869, fax 290749, email fort@ mos.com.np), a large place built in Newari style. The front rooms have excellent views and the whole place is geared towards tour

NAGARKOT

PLACES TO STAY
1 Nagarkot Naldum Village
2 Himalayan Resort
3 Hotel Country Villa
4 Hotel Miles Stone
5 Hotel Green Valley
6 Niva Niwa Lodge
7 The Fort
8 Hotel Chautara Keyman
9 View Point Hotel
10 Peaceful Cottage;
   Cafe du Mont
12 Hotel at the end
   of the Universe
13 Galaxy Hotel
14 Hotel Space Mountain
15 Hotel Sun & Mountain
16 Hotel Snowman
20 Club Himalaya Resort

PLACES TO EAT
18 Tea House Restaurant

OTHER
11 Mahakali Shrine
17 Bus Stop
19 Lookout

To Sankhu &
The Farmhouse
(500m)

0   200   400 m

Walking Track
to Changu Narayan

To Bhaktapur
(15km)

Army Camp

Army Checkpost

To Lookout
Tower
(1km)

groups. The rooms cost $57/63, and a 20% discount is offered in the low season.

Farther along is the **Hotel Chautara Keyman** (☎ 290875, fax 225136), which is rather big and ugly, and is expensive at $48/60. The individual cottages are much better, and these also cost $48/60. A discount of 20% may be available if things are slow.

At the end of the dirt road, perched on the edge of a steep slope, is the **Hotel Green Valley** (☎ 290878). It's nothing flash, but it has a couple of cheap rooms with common bath and views at Rs 250. Singles/doubles with attached bath cost Rs 400/600.

The **Hotel Mile Stone** (☎ 290888, fax 260024) next door to the Green Valley is a good little place with just four cottages. These are excellent value at Rs 200 with attached bath, and the cosy restaurant is also good.

South of the bus stop, towards the army camp and perched right on the ridge is **Club Himalaya Resort** (☎ 290883, fax 290868, emial club@mos.com.np), which is run by the Kathmandu Guest House. A large construction like this was probably inevitable in Nagarkot, but it really does nothing for the rural ambience. Having said that, the building has been well thought out and each room has a private balcony with view, and there are also views from the atrium-type lobby with its restaurant and indoor swimming pool and jacuzzi. The rooms are large and well furnished, and cost $75/90 including breakfast.

Above the main intersection is the modern **Tea House**, a restaurant with a nice terrace aimed at day-trippers. It is an attractive building with good views, and it's open from 6 am to 8 pm. Main meals are around Rs 100, and a Coke is Rs 30.

Getting There & Away

There's a road right to Nagarkot from Bhaktapur so you can take a bus or taxi all the way there. Walking to or, preferably, from Nagarkot is, however, an interesting alternative and there are several possible routes, all detailed in the Treks from Nagarkot section that follows.

Buses operate to a somewhat unreliable schedule from Bhaktapur, departing every hour or so and costing Rs 10. The bus can be very slow (taking up to two hours) and extremely crowded. The roof is not only less crowded but also offers fine views. A taxi from Bhaktapur costs about Rs 500 one way or Rs 800 return.

Grayline (☎ 413188), based at the Yak & Yeti Hotel in Kathmandu, offer afternoon tours to Nagarkot if there's four or more people.

TREKS FROM NAGARKOT

There are a number of trekking routes to or from Nagarkot. If you only want to walk one way it's a good idea to take the bus to Nagarkot and walk back down. The following walks are all written heading downhill from Nagarkot.

Nagarkot to Bhaktapur

Until the road from Nagarkot to Bhaktapur was built, this walking trail was the only way to go. Now with buses running back and forth it's neither necessary nor all that enjoyable. You would be better off taking one of the alternative routes, but if you do want to walk back down it's relatively easy to take the wide, easy trail which short-cuts across the road turns. The trail eventually joins the road on its final gradual ascent to Bhaktapur; you can follow this and turn off at the eastern end of the town or simply catch a bus, should one come by. It takes about two hours to walk down, and perhaps twice that walking up.

Going down you leave the main road to descend through a pine forest, then follow a stream to a cluster of bamboo trees near the city reservoir where you rejoin the main road. From here you enter the town at the eastern end and continue to Tachupal Tole.

Nagarkot to Changu Narayan Temple

Walking down to Changu Narayan is a much more interesting alternative to the walk down to Bhaktapur. From Nagarkot it is very easy to see the long spur which extends into the Kathmandu Valley. At the very end of the spur the ridge line gives one final hiccup and then drops down to the valley floor. The beautiful temple of Changu Narayan is on the top of this final bump on the ridge line.

The walking trail from Nagarkot follows the road to Bhaktapur along a ridge, branching off at a sharp hairpin bend. It's easier to take the bus from Nagarkot down to this bend rather than to walk all the way down to Changu Narayan. The short ride saves you the tedious part of the walk, where the walking trail runs close to the road.

From the bend, the trail climbs uphill through a pine forest for about 20 minutes until it reaches the top of the ridge and then it simply follows the ridge line undulating gently down to Changu Narayan. The walking trail passes through small Chhetri villages with wonderful views over the valley to the Himalaya beyond. Finally, the shining roof of Changu Narayan appears above the village of **Changu** itself from where a stone-paved street leads to the temple. From the hairpin bend (where you leave the Nagarkot to Bhaktapur road) it takes about one to 1½ hours to walk to the temple. See the earlier Changu Narayan Temple section for information about this temple.

From Changu Narayan you can descend to the Manohara River to the north and take the road back to Bodhnath and Kathmandu. Alternatively you can continue south to Bhaktapur, either by the direct trail or by the road running slightly to the east.

Nagarkot to Sankhu

Fewer walkers follow the trail to Sankhu, just north of the Nagarkot to Changu Narayan ridge line in the north-east of the valley. The picturesque Newari town is surrounded by rich agricultural land and is easily visible from Nagarkot or from the trail down to Changu Narayan. The trail follows the same ridge line then drops steeply down the hillside in a north-westerly direction, joining the main Helambu to Sankhu trail and passing a group of teahouses where you can ask directions to the important temple of

Vajra Jogini. The temple is to the north of Sankhu and by leaving the main trail you can walk west to this interesting site before completing the descent to Sankhu.

From Sankhu buses run back to Kathmandu via Bodhnath every couple of hours.

Nagarkot to Sundarijal

It takes two easy days or one very long one to reach Sundarijal from Nagarkot on a trail which follows the valley rim. From Sundarijal you can take the road to Gokarna, Bodhnath and Kathmandu or you can continue for another day along the rim to Shivapuri and Budhanilkantha. Some trekking agencies operate treks on this valley-rim walk, but it is also possible to find accommodation in teahouses. There are many confusing trail junctions so ask directions frequently.

The trail starts from the Mahakali shrine heading north-north-east, and passes the village of Kattike (about one hour) and then turns more northerly to Jorsim Pauwa (about one hour). Walk farther down through Bagdhara with its teahouses to Chowki Bhanjyang (about one hour). From Chowki Bhanjyang another hour's walk will take you farther north through Nagle to **Bhotichaur**, which makes a good place to stop overnight in a teahouse.

The walk continues by returning towards Chowki Bhanjyang for a short distance and then taking the fork by a *chautara* (porters' resting place) uphill and then more steeply uphill to cross a ridge line before dropping down on the middle of three trails to Chule. The trail contours around the edge of the valley, crossing several ridge lines running down into the valley, before dropping down to **Mulkarkha** and the trail past the reservoir and along the pipeline to Sundarijal. The last part of this trail to Sundarijal is the first part of the popular Helambu Trek.

Nagarkot to Banepa

The town of Banepa is outside the valley and is the major junction town on the way to Dhulikhel on the Arniko Hwy (the road to the Tibetan border). From Nagarkot, you start this walk near the tower south of Banepa, at the southern part of the ridge and follow a steep descent to the east. Following a precise trail is difficult, but that is no problem since all the trails lead to Banepa. A few kilometres north of Banepa the trail passes through the old Newari town of Nala with its interesting temples.

From Banepa, you can take a bus back to Kathmandu or to Dhulikhel. See the following section for more information on Banepa and Nala.

Dhulikhel & Arniko Highway Route

The Arniko Hwy to Dhulikhel passes by Thimi, skirts the southern side of Bhaktapur and then climbs out of the valley before dropping down to Banepa, continuing on to Dhulikhel, the Tibetan border and to Lhasa. This route is also covered in the Mountain Biking chapter.

BANEPA (29KM)
Just outside the valley, the small town of Banepa is a busy crossroads with a statue of King Tribhuvan marking the centre of town. Dhulikhel is 3km beyond Banepa; the temple town of Panauti is about 7km south; the interesting village of Nala is just to the north-west; and Chandeshwari, with its legendary old temple, is only 1km or so north-east – yet Banepa itself is of very limited interest. Indeed the main road, all that most visitors see, is a dusty, noisy affair and waiting for a change of bus at that busy crossroads is often decidedly unpleasant.

Chandeshwari Temple
Only 1km or so north-east of Banepa the temple to the goddess Chandeshwari perches on the very edge of a gorge. The road out of Banepa runs gently uphill then just as gently downhill through open fields and then a short village street, past an old tank and right to the arched entrance gate to the temple.

The people of this valley were once terrorised by a demon known as Chand and when Parvati, in her demon-slaying mode, got rid of the nuisance she took the name Chandeshwari, 'slayer of Chand', and this temple was built in her honour.

The temple is entered through a doorway topped by a brilliantly coloured relief of Parvati disposing of the demon. The triple roofed temple has roof struts showing the eight Ashta Matrikas and eight Bhairabs, but the temple's most notable feature is on the west wall which is painted with a huge and colourful fresco of Bhairab at his destructive worst.

The temple also has a Shiva shrine complete with lingam, and Nandi and Ganesh also make an appearance. The ghats below the temple, beside the stream, are an auspicious place to die and people come here when their end is nigh.

Other Attractions
Banepa itself has few buildings of interest although there are some pleasant squares and quieter laneways in the older part of town to the north-west. The old town square has two Narayan temples with virtually back-to-back worshipful Garuda statues. Right beside the turn-off to Chandeshwari is an attractive tank with bas reliefs of gods at one end.

Getting There & Away
Regular buses leave from the City bus station and the trip to Banepa costs Rs 15, taking two hours. Buses continue on from Banepa to Dhulikhel and farther towards Kodari on the Tibetan border. There are also a few regular services south from Banepa to Panauti.

NALA (33KM)
The interesting small town of Nala is about 4km north-west of Banepa. Nala's **Bhagwati Temple** dominates the central square of the town and is one of the very few four tiered temples in the Kathmandu Valley. On the edge of the settlement is the Buddhist pagoda temple of **Karunamaya**, dedicated to Avalokiteshvara.

AROUND THE KATHMANDU VALLEY

PANAUTI (36KM)

Standing in a valley about 7km south of Banepa, the small town of Panauti is at the junction of the rivers Roshi Khola and Pungamati Khola. Like Allahabad in India a third 'invisible' river is said to join the other two at the confluence. The town is relatively untouched and has a number of interesting temples, one of which may be the oldest in Nepal. Panauti once stood at the junction of important trading routes and had a royal palace in its main square. Today it's just a quiet backwater, but all the more interesting for that.

Indreshwar Mahadev Temple

The three storey Indreshwar Mahadev Temple in the village centre is a Shiva temple. It was originally built in 1294 over a Shiva lingam and was subsequently rebuilt in the 15th century. In 1988 an earthquake caused serious damage. In its original form it may well have been the oldest temple in Nepal – Kathmandu's Kasthamandap may predate it but Kasthamandap was originally built as a dharamsala, not as a temple.

Around the temple are many shrines including one dedicated to the beautiful wife of a Vedic sage, Ahilya.

Legends relate that she was seduced by the god Indra who tricked her by assuming the shape of her husband. When the sage returned and discovered what had happened he took a bizarre revenge upon Indra by causing Indra's body to become covered in yonis, female sexual organs! Naturally Indra was somewhat put out by this and for many years he and his wife Indrayani repented at this auspicious confluence of rivers. Eventually Parvati, Shiva's consort, took pity upon Indrayani and turned her into the invisible river which joins the two visible ones in Panauti. More years passed and eventually Shiva decided to release Indra from his strange problem. Shiva appeared in Panauti as a great lingam and when Indra bathed in the river the yonis disappeared. The lingam is the one which stands in the temple.

The temple, run-down though it may be, is certainly a fine one and the roof struts depicting the various incarnations of Shiva and some discreetly amorous couples are said to

be masterpieces of Newari woodcarving. The courtyard has numerous smaller shrines apart from the stone pillar to Ahilya.

To one side of the main temple is a rectangular **Bhairab Temple** with faces peering out of the three upstairs windows, rather like the Shiva-Parvati Temple in Kathmandu's Durbar Square. A small double roofed Shiva Temple stands by the north-western corner while a Vishnu shrine with a 2m high image of the god faces the temple from the west. Look for the pots and pans hanging under the roof eaves of the main temple. They're donated to the temple by newlyweds to ensure a happy married life.

Other Temples

Across the Pungamati Khola is the 17th century **Brahmayani Temple**; a suspension bridge crosses the river at this point. Brahmayani is the chief goddess of the village and her image is drawn around the town each year in the chariot festival. This temple was restored with French assistance in 1982-83.

On the town side of the river, actually at the junction where the two rivers meet, is a **Krishna Narayan Temple** with some woodcarvings of similar age and style to the Indreshwar Mahadev Temple. The riverbank stone sculptures are also of interest, but, unfortunately, the late 1980s were cruel to Panauti: apart from the earthquake there were also severe floods which swept away the cremation ghats at the river junction.

Special Events

Panauti celebrates a chariot festival at the end of the monsoon each year when images of the gods from the town's various temples are drawn around the streets in temple carts. The festival starts from the town's old Durbar Square.

There are a number of important religious sites across the subcontinent that play host to huge *melas* (religious fairs that attract enormous crowds of pilgrims, worshippers and sadhus). Every 12 years (next in 2010), the Magh Sankranti festival around mid-January (the Nepali month of Magh), is celebrated with a great mela in Panauti.

Getting There & Away

Buses run regularly from Banepa to Panauti and leave from the *chowk* (marketplace) with the king's statue in the middle of Banepa (Rs 4). See the Treks from Dhulikhel section for information on walking to Panauti.

DHULIKHEL (32KM)

Only 3km south-east of Banepa is the interesting small town of Dhulikhel. It's popular as a Himalayan viewpoint, in part because the road to Dhulikhel is easier than the steep and winding road to Nagarkot, but also because Dhulikhel is real, not just a tourist resort. It's also a good centre for short day treks – many visitors come here to stretch their legs before setting off on longer treks.

Dhulikhel is a district headquarters and has a number of government offices, a high school and even a small jail. Its population is Newar although there are people of many other groups in the surrounding villages. The prime Himalayan viewpoint is the parade ground, on the ridge just east of the centre. In the late 1960s Dhulikhel was a gathering point for hippies who even planned to build their own temple here! An even better view can be found from the hill topped by a Kali Temple, about 30 minutes walk along the Namobuddha trail.

A new highway to the eastern Terai is currently under construction with Japanese assistance. The highway starts in Dhulikhel and when finished will considerably shorten the travelling time between Kathmandu and the towns of the eastern Terai. What the likely huge increase in heavy vehicle traffic will do for the peaceful ambience of Dhulikhel – and the narrow and inadequately engineered Arniko Hwy back to Kathmandu – is unclear.

Temples

The old part of the town, west of the bus stop, is an interesting area to wander around with some fine old Newari buildings and several interesting temples. The town's main square has a tank, the small triple roofed **Harisiddhi Temple** and a **Vishnu Temple** fronted by two worshipful Garudas in quite different styles. One is a kneeling stone

DHULIKHEL

Krishna Temple

Bhagwati Shiva Temple

To Dhulikhel Lodge Resort (300m),
Banepa (3km) & Kathmandu (26km)

Bus Park

Vishnu Temple

Harisiddhi Temple

Tank

Ganesh Temple

Arniko Highway

Silk Road Lodge

Mountain View Guest House

To Dhulikhel Mountain Resort (4km) & Kodari (85km)

To Post Office, Mountain Viewpoint, Kali Temple, Nawa Rangu Guest House, Shiva Temple & Namobuddha

Kings Statue

Tank

To Panauti

0   100   200 m

AROUND THE KATHMANDU VALLEY

Garuda topping a low pillar while the second Garuda is in bright metal, flanked by two kneeling devotees, and is more like the bird-faced Garudas of Indonesia than the conventional Nepali Garudas. The triple roofed temple has been decorated with brightly coloured ceramic tiles. Beyond the square, the western end of the town is marked by a hill topped by a modern **Krishna Temple** and the **Bhagwati Shiva Temple**.

Walking in the other direction you pass the post office and the mountain viewpoint, and reach the junction where the road turns south to Namobuddha. Continue straight on from the junction and dip down to a picturesque little **Shiva Temple** at the bottom of a gorge. Water flows through the site where the main sanctum is a squat, square block decorated with coloured tiles and topped with a metal dome with four *nagas* (snake deities) arching down from the pinnacle. The temple is fronted by figures of Nandi on pillars and kneeling devotees. To one side is a fine image of Ganesh, while in a second small shrine only the feet remain of three images, the result of art thieves' work. Below that is a tank but this is a temple with everything – if you look around you can find images of Hanuman, Saraswati, Shiva and Parvati, lingams, tridents and much more.

Dhulikhel's final temple attraction is the **Kali Temple** high up the hill towards Namobuddha. Climb up here for the excellent view, not for the temple which is of little interest.

Places to Stay & Eat

Dhulikhel has a small number of places to stay, both in and around town, although there's not much choice in the budget range.

Nawa Rangu Guest House & Restaurant (☎ 61226), on the way towards the post office and Shiva Temple, is a curious place with a restaurant hung with interesting naive-style paintings, and basic trekking lodge-style rooms and bathroom facilities. The food is good, especially the lemon pancakes and wheat porridge! Basic rooms are Rs 100/150.

On the main road there are a couple of possibilities, neither of them very attractive.

Mountain View Guest House does indeed have mountain views. The rooms are basic but adequate, and cost Rs 200 a double. *Silk Road Lodge* (☎ 61269) next door is cheaper at Rs 150 for a double with common bath.

Just off the main road, near the Dhulikhel bus stop, is the *Dhulikhel Lodge Resort* (☎ 61114, fax 64001). This is a large, modern place with good rooms and superb views. It is aimed at groups who want to get out of Kathmandu for a day or so, and the cost is $50/58, with discounts of up to 30% making it very good value. The restaurant here is popular with day-tripping groups.

A few hundred metres farther on towards Banepa there are a number of other resort-type places, offering varying degrees of luxury. *Mirabel Resort* (☎ 61972, fax 63225, email sre@vishnu.ccsl.com.np) is a rather out of place Mediterranean style resort, but it is very well done and offers the top accommodation in Dhulikhel. There's two restaurants, a bar, and terrace with excellent views. The rooms have views, a balcony, fridge, TV and phone and cost $90/100.

Farther again is the *Himalayan Horizon Hotel* (☎ 61296, fax 61476). The building is a bit of a monster but it does feature traditional woodcarving and all the rooms face straight out on to the Himalayan peaks. There's a restaurant/terrace area in front of the hotel with equally good views plus a beautiful garden running down the hill. Rooms in this comfortable hotel are $51/55, or there are larger deluxe rooms for $52/66, and a 20% discount applies in the low season. The restaurant is relatively expensive, but has excellent food, including a variety of Nepali dishes.

There's a few other 'resorts' in this area, but they have little to recommend them.

Dhulikhel Mountain Resort (☎ 61466, fax 420778 in Kathmandu), is another up-market place, 4km beyond the village downhill towards Barabise and the Tibetan border. The Himalayan views from here are equally superb and rooms cost $76/78, although a 20% discount is usually offered. Accommodation is in luxurious, thatched cottages, and there's solar-heated hot water.

Just past the Dhulikhel Mountain Resort is the *Himalaya Mountain Resort* (☎ *61158*), a very quiet little place with a garden and great views. The rooms are probably overpriced at $30/34 for a single/double with attached bath, although the 20% discount makes it more acceptable. There's a decent restaurant, serving Newari food. These last two places are probably only a realistic option if you have your own transport.

Getting There & Away

Regular buses to Dhulikhel leave from the City bus station (Rs 18, two hours). The buses skirt Bhaktapur at the eastern end of the valley and then climb over the Sanga pass out of the valley, before dropping down to Banepa then climbing again to Dhulikhel, 32km from Kathmandu. The fare is Rs 5 for the short ride from Banepa to Dhulikhel. A taxi from Kathmandu costs about Rs 700, or from Bhaktapur about Rs 450.

The walk to Dhulikhel from Nagarkot is an interesting alternative. After watching the sunrise at Nagarkot you can walk down through Nala to Banepa, from where you can take a bus the last few kilometres to Dhulikhel. See the Treks from Nagarkot section earlier in this chapter for more information.

TREKS FROM DHULIKHEL
Namobuddha Trek

The trek from Dhulikhel to Namobuddha or Namura is a fine walk in itself and also a good leg-stretcher for longer treks. It takes about three hours each way, so it makes a good day walk. The walk can be made either as a return trip or as a loop to avoid backtracking. If you start early enough you can even continue on from Namobuddha to Panauti and return from there via Banepa by bus.

Namobuddha is a relatively easy trek which can even be made during the monsoon. From Dhulikhel the trail first climbs up to the Kali Temple lookout then drops down through the village of **Kavre** and past a number of teahouses. It then climbs again through pine woods past **Phulbari** and up and down a couple of more hills before reaching the Namobuddha hill. Asking directions is no problem, as any westerner heading in this direction is assumed to be going to Namobuddha!

Surprisingly there is very little known about the stupa at Namobuddha although it is an important destination for Buddhist pilgrims.

A legend relates that a Buddha came across a tigress close to death from starvation and unable to feed her cubs. The sorrowful Buddha allowed the hungry tigress to consume him.

If you climb to the top of the hill from the stupa, you will reach the site where this event is supposed to have taken place – a stone tablet on the hill here depicts it. An important festival is held at this site in November.

From Namobuddha the circuit walk continues downhill through **Sankhu** and past a couple of water mills then climbs for about one hour to **Batase**. Next it passes through another pine wood and drops down to cross a stream before climbing up again to Dhulikhel.

Panauti Trek

Another interesting walk leads from Dhulikhel to the small village of Panauti. The pleasant two hour stroll starts off south from Dhulikhel then turns west, crosses rice fields and runs along the course of a small stream. It eventually meets the Banepa to Panauti road a little north of the town. Panauti is a beautiful little town with numerous temples and magnificent woodcarvings – see the earlier Panauti section.

From Panauti you can take a bus to Banepa, just 7km north, and from there back to Dhulikhel or to Kathmandu. Alternatively, you can keep on walking west to Godavari in the south of the Kathmandu Valley. There are several alternative routes to Godavari. One runs west through Bhaleswar and along the Roshi Khola valley, taking about six hours direct to Godavari.

An alternative to this route runs southwest and climbs up the back of Pulchowki then takes the road down from Pulchowki to Godavari. A third route runs farther south through Kalar, but also climbs the back of Pulchowki before taking the road down to Godavari. Either route via Pulchowki entails a long day's walk from Panauti.

ARNIKO HIGHWAY BEYOND DHULIKHEL

The Arniko Hwy provides Nepal's overland link with Tibet and China. Many people who make the trek into the Solo Khumbu region and the Everest base camp travel out along the highway, taking the turn-off to Jiri, which is the last stop before you have to start walking. Buses to Jiri leave from Kathmandu from 6 am (Rs 120, 10 to 12 hours).

Past Barabise the road is particularly vulnerable to landslides and during the monsoon large sections are swept away; it's very unlikely to be open between May and August. Even when the highway is passable it's of limited use in breaking India's stranglehold on Nepal. It is an enormous distance from Lhasa to the industrial centres of China, so it is, in most cases, still cheaper to ship Chinese goods via Calcutta than to truck them over the mountains.

When roadworkers first tackled the Himalaya, they decided to follow the rivers, which had already done the hard work of cutting through the mountains. They have now realised that the zone just above the rivers is particularly vulnerable to erosion from below and landslides from above – which is why Nepali houses and traditional trails are often built along the top of ridges. As a result, many of the roads that were developed by foreign countries' agencies have turned out to be serious liabilities for the Nepali government, who must fund their ongoing maintenance.

AROUND DHULIKEL

After Dhulikhel the road descends into the beautiful **Panchkhal Valley**, reaching the town of Panchkhal after about 20 minutes drive. About five minutes beyond Panchkhal a dirt road takes off to the left, giving road access to the Helambu region.

About 8km later you arrive at **Dolalghat**, a thriving town at the confluence of the Indrawati River and Sun Kosi (the departure point for many rafting trips). The turn-off to Jiri is another 14km away, on the right.

Lamosangu

Lamosangu is a few kilometres after the Jiri turn-off on the road to Kodari, and is an interesting Sherpa town with some decent trade stores (compared with Barabise, Tatopani and Kodari). There are standard dal bhat shops, but nothing to do. *Silu Lodge* is in the middle of town. It's a five storey building with a shop on the ground floor and the top two floors are the lodge. Three rooms on the top floor have a terrace which is a good spot to sit outside and have a beer after a hard bike-ride. Fairly clean doubles cost Rs 110.

Next you pass a magnesite mine (one of the few mines in the country) which was only developed because of its placement beside a sealed road.

Barabise

Barabise is the next bustling bazaar town, the final stop for buses from Kathmandu, and the largest settlement along the road. ('Hell Hole!' is one way it has been described.) Barabise marks the end of the sealed section of the Arniko Hwy, which continues in the form of an unsurfaced track. In the dry season, passing trucks kick up the top layer of dust causing choking dust storms. In the wet, the dust transforms into mud. Landslides are more frequent as the side of the gorge steepens, especially during or after heavy rain.

There's nothing to do in Barabise but sit and watch street life go past, or perhaps curse the bus drivers for your lack of sleep!

Places to Stay & Eat *Himalaya Hotel* has doubles for Rs 80 and serves reasonable dal bhat. *Barabise Guest House* has doubles for Rs 90, some of which are at the rear of the building, so take one of these if you want to avoid being woken at the crack of dawn by noisy bus drivers. Both places are in the middle of town on the left-hand side heading towards Tibet.

Tatopani

The next point of interest is Tatopani, a small village with a string of small guesthouses which survive by housing visitors to the hot springs. It is in a more picturesque setting and is much quieter than Barabise.

The thing to do here is go to the **hot springs**. Five minutes walk north of the bazaar, look for a sign (with a direction arrow) on a building on the right-hand side. You then descend some steps to the springs which come out as a set of showers (great after a hard bike-ride from Dhulikhel). There is also a small gompa above the town, marked by the usual prayer flags, which has a fine view.

Places to Stay & Eat *Sonam Lodge* has doubles for Rs 80, and dal bhat is available. It's reasonably clean, and the owner is friendly. *Sherpa Lodge* has doubles for Rs 60, and once again, dal bhat is available. Both places are very similar, and both are at the southern end of town, two shops apart.

Kodari (121km)

Kodari is nothing more than a collection of shabby wooden shanties perched perilously on the edge of the gorge on the Nepali side of the **Friendship Bridge**. It is possible to continue past the Nepali checkpoint and across the bridge. Stop in the middle to pose for photos on the red line drawn across the road. You can then continue straight past the Chinese guards and under the barrier into Tibet, which looks just like Nepal. With a bike, you can continue for a steep 8km until you reach Chinese customs, on the edge of Khasa (Zhangmu), the first settlement. A visa is needed to progress farther, but some people have managed to leave their bikes at the barrier and check the town out for a couple of hours. There's not much to see.

Places to Stay & Eat There's one lodge, *Laxmi Lodge & Bhojanalaya*, which is very basic, serves dal bhat, and has beds for Rs 35 per person.

CHARIKOT

If you take the turn-off to Jiri, the first town you come to is Charikot, a pleasant place situated on a ridge with a stunning view. Located just before the town sign, *Sagun Guest House* has friendly staff and good food. A double costs Rs 85. Because of its position on the edge of town, it's quiet, but misses the view. The *Laxmi Lodge & Restaurant* is in the main square and offers excellent views. It's a charming traditional building with spiral staircases leading to wooden balconies. Rooms at the front cost Rs 100 and rooms at the back, with no view, are Rs 60.

JIRI (143KM)

Jiri, also quite a pleasant place, has many lodges to choose from. The bus stops at the far end of town so you walk back up to find somewhere to stay. *Sagarmatha Lodge & Restaurant* is OK with doubles for Rs 50. On the far side of town – farthest from the bus stop – *Sherpa Guide Lodge* has doubles for Rs 40. This is among the cheapest and best places in town.

Godavari & Pulchowki Route

The road to Godavari is sealed and there's quite a bit of traffic, so this is not one of the best bike rides around the valley. There are quite a number of things to see, however.

If you have access to a car it is worth considering a trip to the top of nearby Pulchowki, especially in spring (March, April and May) when the rhododendrons are in bloom.

HARISIDDHI (10KM)

This is a small Newari village with a four tiered pagoda temple to Harisiddhi Bhawani.

BISHANKHU NARAYAN (15KM)

If you're looking for an excuse to get off the beaten track, the shrine of Bishankhu Narayan will do nicely. The shrine itself is something of a disappointment, despite the fact that it is one of the most important Vishnu shrines in the Kathmandu Valley. A steep stairway leads to a tiny cave – more a fissure in the rock – and there's nothing much to see. On the way, however, you pass through an attractive village, and there are some good views from the shrine itself.

Getting There & Away

The unsealed road to Bishankhu Narayan takes off to the north from the undistinguished village of Bandegaon then veers to the south-east and crosses a small stream. After 1km you come to a small village. The road forks at the 'village green'; take the left fork and continue for another 1km to reach the shrine.

GODAVARI (22KM)

Godavari is not really a town, although there are a number of points of interest in the area, such as the Royal Botanical Gardens, St Xavier's College, Godavari Kunda, and Pulchowki Mai, plus a controversial marble quarry. The sealed road from Kathmandu continues to the foot of the hills and to St Xavier's College – the awful scars from the quarry are also clearly visible. Here an unsealed road continues to the south; the sealed road veers left (north-east) to the gardens.

Royal Botanical Gardens

The main entrance to the gardens is flanked by white-painted walls. Though a quiet and peaceful spot, few of the trees and plants are labelled, so unless you already know what you're looking at you won't end up any the wiser. There really aren't many persuasive reasons for visiting unless you're a keen botanist. The gardens are open from 10 am to 5 pm and entry is Rs 2.

Godavari Kunda

A dirt road continues past the entrance to the botanical gardens and after 100m or so you come to the Godavari Kunda – a sacred spring – on your right. It's a curious spot, and although none of the architecture or sculpture is particularly inspiring it is revered by Hindus. Every 12 years – next in 2003 – thousands of pilgrims come here to bathe and gain merit. Clear mountain water collects in a pool in an inner courtyard, then flows through carved stone spouts into a larger pool in the outer courtyard.

Pulchowki Mai

If you return towards the marble quarry and take the dirt road to the south, Pulchowki Mai is a couple of hundred metres past St Xavier's College and virtually opposite the main gates to the quarry. The site is dilapidated and somewhat overshadowed by the quarry. There's a three tiered pagoda to a Tantric mother goddess flanked by a temple to Ganesh. There are two large pools before the temple compound fed by nine spouts that represent the nine streams that flow off Pulchowki.

Places to Stay

Signposted off the road a few kilometres before Godavari is the excellent *Godavari Village Resort* (☎ 533675, fax 290777). This new place consists of a number of attractive buildings which sprawl down a hillside, with idyllic views over rice paddies to the valley and mountains beyond. The rooms are large and well furnished, and have TV, heater, fan and phone. There's also a large restaurant, pool, sauna and jacuzzi. The cost is $150/165, but a discount of 15% is usually possible.

Getting There & Away

There are local minibuses between Lagankhel in Patan and Godavari; the one hour journey costs Rs 6. It would be quite feasible to ride a mountain bike – the road is good – but if you're going to make the effort, there are more interesting rides in the valley.

PULCHOWKI

This 2762m mountain is the highest point around the valley and not surprisingly there

are absolutely magnificent views from the summit. This is also home to one of the last surviving cloud forests in central Nepal. The mountain is famous for its spring flowers, in particular its magnificent red and white rhododendrons.

Unfortunately, there's a telecommunications tower on the summit and an army camp. The open shrine to Pulchowki Mai may once have been a pretty spot, but it's now covered in rubbish. The views and the superb forest, however, make the journey worthwhile.

Getting There & Away

The unsealed road is rough in places but quite OK for a normal car if you take it slowly. It takes about 45 minutes from the bottom. You would need to be very keen to undertake the climb on a mountain bike, although it could certainly be done.

Chapagaon & Lele Route

The road to Lele is an ideal mountain-bike trip. It's sealed to Chapagaon and there are great views and some attractive villages along the way. By bicycle it's quite a stiff climb in places – which is all the better for the return trip. Allow the best part of a day, although it's only an hour from the Ring Rd to Chapagaon.

SUNAKOTHI (10KM) & THECHO (12KM)

The small village of Sunakothi is strung out along the road. There are two temples – one to Jagannath and the other to Bringarshwar Mahadev.

About 2km farther south, Thecho also has two temples, the brightly coloured Balkumari Temple and a two tiered pagoda to Brahmayani.

CHAPAGAON (13KM)

Chapagaon is a prosperous village with a number of shops and temples and shrines strung along the road. Near the entrance to the village is a Ganesh shrine. There are two dilapidated two-tiered temples (one looks as if it has been hit by a truck) dedicated to Narayan and Krishna, and there's also a Bhairab shrine with erotic carvings on its struts.

Vajra Varahi

A small temple complex – an important Tantric site – lies about 500m east of the main road. When you enter Chapagaon take the path on your left after the two-tiered temples. Notice the disused irrigation system, with stone channels and bridges, behind the village. The temple lies in a grove of trees and was built in 1665, but is now surrounded by less-distinguished shelters and an unfortunate amount of litter. Nonetheless, it's an interesting and atmospheric place that has probably been a centre for worship for millennia. Photography is banned.

Getting There & Away

Local minibuses leave from Lagankhel in Patan and the one to 1½ hour journey costs Rs 8. By mountain bike, Chapagaon is about an hour from the Ring Rd (note the comparison with the bus time!). About 10 minutes after Chapagaon the road starts to climb into the foothills. The sealed road continues to the Leprosy Mission and Tika Bhairab in the Lele Valley. If you are running out of enthusiasm, an unsealed road takes off to the left – there's a pipal tree and chautara. The road is in poor condition but you are rewarded with fantastic views across the valley to the Ganesh Himal. If you keep going you cross a saddle and enter the tranquil Lele Valley.

LELE (19KM)

Lele Valley seems a million miles from the hustle and bustle of Kathmandu, and there are few visitors. It's a peaceful, beautiful valley that in many ways seems untouched by the 20th century.

Tika Bhairab

The Tika Bhairab is a huge, multi-coloured painting on a brick wall. The shrine lies at the confluence of two rivers and is marked by a huge sal tree.

Places to Stay

The Malla Hotel in Kathmandu operates the very pleasant *Malla Alpine Resort* (☎ *410966, fax 418382*), well signposted near Lele. The 18 rooms offer great views, and just so you don't have to tough it too much there is also a pool, sauna and a great restaurant. The cost is $61/72, plus tax.

Bungamati Route

The road to Bungamati, one of the most picturesque small towns in the valley, provides yet another ideal mountain-biking expedition. The road to Bungamati is the continuation of the main road that runs through Jawlakhel (the Tibetan refugee camp on the outskirts of Patan), on the other side of the Ring Rd.

KHOKNA

Khokna is not as appealing as Bungamati, partly because it was seriously damaged in the 1934 earthquake, but it has retained many traditional aspects of Newari life. It is famous for producing mustard oil. There is no central square, as in Bungamati, but there's plenty of action in the main street, including women spinning wool. The main temple is a two tiered construction dedicated to Shekali Mai a mother goddess.

Getting There & Away

From Karya Binayak Temple in Bungamati, Khokna is a 10 minute walk across the paddy fields. Take note of the water tank surrounded by a low brick wall on the outskirts of the village, because if you don't want to retrace your steps to Bungamati, the track that returns to the main road takes off from here.

BUNGAMATI (10KM)

Bungamati is a classic Newari village dating from the 16th century. It is perched on a spur of land overlooking the Bagmati River and is shaded by large trees and stands of bamboo. Fortunately, the village streets are too small and hazardous for cars. Visitors are rare, so tread gently.

Rato Machhendranath Temple

Bungamati is the birthplace of Rato Machhendranath, regarded as the patron of the valley, and the large shikhara-style temple in the centre of the village square is his home for six months of the year (he spends the rest of his time in Patan). The process of moving him around Patan and backwards and forwards to Bungamati is central to one of the most important annual festivals in the valley. See the Rato Machhendranath section in the Kathmandu, Patan & Bhaktapur chapter, and Public Holidays & Special Events in the Facts for the Visitor chapter for details.

The chowk around the temple is one of the most beautiful in the valley – here one can see the heart of a functioning Newari town. There are many chörtens (Tibetan Buddhist stupas) and a huge prayer wheel, clearly pointing to the syncretic nature of Newari religion.

Karya Binayak Temple

Between Bungamati and Khokna, the Karya Binayak Temple is dedicated to Ganesh. The temple is not particularly interesting and Ganesh is simply represented by a natural stone but the view is spectacular. From this point, surrounded by trees, you can look over the Bagmati Valley to the foothills, or back to Bungamati, tumbling down the opposite hill.

Getting There & Away

Buses to Bungamati leave from Jawlakhel in Patan (Rs 7, 1½ hours).

By bicycle from Patan, continue over the Ring Rd from the main road through Jawlakhel. After you cross the Niche River, veer left. The right fork takes you through to the Chobar Gorge where you can cross the Bagmati River and return to Kathmandu by a different route. It's a pleasant ride along a gradually climbing ridge to get to Bungamati.

Approximately an hour after leaving the Ring Rd you'll come out at a viewpoint marked by a single, large tree. It's worth pausing here to take in the lie of the land. To the left lies Bungamati, then swinging to the right comes Karya Binayak then about 1km away, Khokna. Follow the road down to Bungamati and take the right fork which passes to the left of a large pond. The footpath then veers to the left and climbs up to the distinctive, white shikhara temple and the town square.

To get to Karya Binayak, retrace your steps to the first pond you came to, follow the path around it and take the right fork. It's a five minute walk across the rice paddies to the temple.

Kirtipur, Chobar & Dakshinkali Route

KIRTIPUR (5KM)

Strung out along a ridge south-west of Kathmandu, the small town of Kirtipur is a relatively neglected and timeless backwater despite its proximity to the capital. At one time it was associated with Patan and then became a mini-kingdom in its own right. During the 1768 conquest of the valley by Prithvi Narayan Shah it was clear that Kirtipur, with its superbly defensible hilltop position, would be the key to defeating the Malla kingdoms so it was here the Gorkha king struck first and hardest. Kirtipur's resistance was strong but eventually, after a bitter siege, the town was taken and the inhabitants paid a terrible price for their courageous resistance. The king, incensed by the long struggle his forces had endured, ordered the nose and lips cut off every male inhabitant in the town. Fortunately, for a small minority, he was practical as well as cruel and those who could play wind instruments were spared. It is said that the news of this barbaric act considerably dampened plans for resistance among the inhabitants of the other valley towns, and Patan, Bhaktapur and Kathmandu quickly fell.

At one time there were 12 gates into the city and traces of the old city wall can still be seen. Today the Kirtipur Cottage Industry Centre is a major industry for the town. As you wander through Kirtipur, you can see dyed yarn hanging from upstairs windows and hear the background clatter of the town's handlooms. Many of the town's 9000 inhabitants are weavers or farmers; the lower-caste people generally live outside the old city wall, lower down the hill. Kirtipur's hilltop position offers fine views over Kathmandu with the Himalaya rising behind.

Tribhuvan University

The campus of Nepal's university, named after King Tribhuvan, stands below the Kirtipur hill and has the best library facilities to be found in Nepal. Many Kirtipur farmers lost their land to the university site and have had to turn to other employment.

Temples

Kirtipur's ridge is actually two hills, with a lower saddle between them. The **Chilanchu Vihara** tops the southern hill and has a central stupa with four smaller stupas, numerous statues and bells and Buddhist monastery buildings around it.

At the bottom of the saddle where the hills meet is the **Bagh Bhairab Temple**, sacred to both Hindus and Buddhists. This famous triple roofed temple is decorated with swords and shields from the Newari troops defeated by King Prithvi Narayan Shah. They can be seen attached to the walls of the temple, sheltered by the upper roof. The temple's principal image is of Bhairab in his tiger form. Look for the temple's torana to the left of the entrance door with an image of Vishnu astride the Garuda and, below him, Bhairab between Ganesh and Kumar. Sacrifices are made early on Tuesday and Saturday mornings.

From the saddle, a long stone stairway, flanked by stone elephants, leads to the triple roofed **Uma Maheshwar Temple**, or Hindu Kvat. The elephants wear spiked saddles to keep children from riding them!

Curiously, the main image of Shiva and Parvati is a standing one, not in the standard Uma Maheshwar pose. To the left of the central image of the god and his consort is a smaller image in the standard pose. The temple was originally built in 1673 and had four roofs until it was badly damaged by the earthquake of 1934. Following its restoration the temple itself is not of great interest – the stairway and the fine views from the top are better. From this hilltop you can see the nearby villages of Panga and Nagaon.

Getting There & Away

Numerous buses and minibuses depart from the City bus station and take around 45 minutes (Rs 5). They terminate at the university from where you can stroll up the hill to the town itself. Alternatively, and much more comfortably, it's a short trip by taxi (around Rs 180).

It takes around 1½ hours to reach Kirtipur by mountain bike, and it's quite a long, steep hill from the Dakshinkali road (first left after the Ring Rd bridge over the Bagmati River). After about 1km from the bridge, turn right at the road flanked by two low, brick gatehouses. Continue up the hill for 1km or so and take the left fork where the minibuses park (right to the university). You'll notice a modern Thai-designed Buddhist temple to the left of Kirtipur's Naya Bajaar (new bazaar), which has grown up at the foot of the Kirtipur hill.

Instead of simply returning the same way you can continue from Kirtipur to Chobar and the Chobar Gorge then back through Patan, which is mostly rideable, but also an interesting walk. From the Chilanchu Vihara at the south-eastern end of Kirtipur, go down the hill by the mound known as the Mazadega (built with the intention of being the foundations of a stupa). At the base of the hill follow the Pharping Rd around and take the trail leading towards Chobar, just past the Thai temple. You can't go wrong, since Chobar tops the prominent hill to the south-east.

A diversion farther south from the trail described above will take you through the small village of Panga which has a number of temples, none of great age or interest. A path continues from Panga to Nagaon, an even smaller village. The trail to Chobar meets Pharping Rd just before the base of the hill, but you can turn off this and follow a narrow footpath straight up the hill until you come into the centre of the interesting small village of Chobar, right on the top of the hill.

After you've visited Chobar's Adinath Lokeshwar Temple (see following) continue down the other side of the hill towards the river. Aim for the large cement works, clearly visible beside the river. The Chobar Gorge and the Jal Binayak Temple are immediately to the north of the cement works. See the Chobar Gorge section for the walk from there to Patan.

CHOBAR (6KM)

The picturesque little village of Chobar tops a hill overlooking the Bagmati River where it flows through the Chobar Gorge. Although the gorge is a regularly visited attraction, far fewer people come to Chobar itself. Perhaps they're put off by the steep hill.

Adinath Lokeshwar Temple

Chobar's main attraction is the temple of Adinath Lokeshwar. The temple was originally built in the 15th century and reconstructed in 1640. Inside the main sanctuary the face of Rato Machhendranath can be seen peering out. The temple is dedicated to this popular valley deity and is sacred to both Hindus and Buddhists. Six Buddha faces are lined up beneath the temple's golden torana but the most interesting feature is the many metal pots, pans and water containers which are fixed to boards hanging all around the temple roofs. These kitchen utensils are donated to the temple by newlyweds in order to ensure a happy married life.

Getting There & Away

Transport to Pharping and Dakshinkali runs by Chobar, but see the Kirtipur and Chobar Gorge sections for details of walking between Kirtipur and Patan via Chobar and the Chobar Gorge.

CHOBAR GORGE (6KM)

Eons ago the Kathmandu Valley was the Kathmandu Lake. In that long-ago time the hill of Swayambhunath was an island; gradually the lake dried up to leave the valley we see today.

Legends relate that the change from lake to valley was a much more dramatic one, for Manjushri is said to have taken his mighty sword and with one blow cut open the valley edge to release the pent-up waters. The place where his sword struck rock was Chobar on the southern edge of the valley and the result was the Chobar Gorge.

Countless snakes were washed out of the valley with the departing waters but Kartotak, 'king of the snakes', is said to still live close to the gorge in the Taudaha pond. Whether or not the great serpent is still there, the pond is certainly a place where ducks pause on their long annual migration from Siberia to India. A hill known as Dinacho (which means 'meditation point') or Champa Devi rises beyond the pond.

The Chobar Gorge is south of Patan where the Bagmati River cuts through the edge of the Chobar hill, the highest hill along this side of the valley. The pretty village of Chobar tops the hill and a stone-paved track runs from the river's edge right to the top of the hill where the Adinath Lokeshwar Temple forms the centre of the settlement. Down by the river, just south of the gorge, is another important temple, the Jal Binayak.

The valley's first cement factory is a more recent and less pleasing addition to the scenery. A neat little suspension bridge spans the river; it was manufactured in Aberdeen in Scotland in 1903. From the bridge there are fine views of the gorge on one side and the Jal Binayak Temple on the other.

Jal Binayak Temple

Just below the gorge on the riverbank stands one of the valley's most important

Ganesh shrines. The triple roofed temple dates from 1602 although there was probably a temple here even earlier. On the temple's platform there is an aged and worn image of Shiva and Parvati in the Uma Maheshwar pose which predates the temple itself by 500 years.

The temple's Ganesh image is simply a huge rock, projecting out the back and bearing very little likeness to an elephant-headed god. The temple's roof struts depict eight Bhairabs and the eight mother goddesses or Ashta Matrikas with whom Ganesh always appears. On the lower roof Ganesh himself appears on some of the struts, with beautiful female figures standing beside him and tiny, brightly painted erotic depictions below. A bronze figure of Ganesh's 'vehicle', in this case a shrew rather than a rat, stands respectfully in the temple courtyard, facing the shrine.

Getting There & Away

The Chobar Gorge is usually visited en route to Pharping and Dakshinkali by road. A more interesting way to reach the gorge is to walk there from Kirtipur via the village of Chobar. See the earlier Kirtipur section for more details.

From the gorge you can cross the bridge and walk up the hill turning north towards Patan. A road suitable for cars ends at a small village at the top of the hill and you can follow this road, past the Nakhu jail and across the Nakhu Khola, finally crossing the Ring Rd and entering Patan at Jawlakhel.

SEKH NARAYAN TEMPLE (18KM)

The Sekh Narayan Temple is the centrepiece of an interesting collection of temples, pools and carvings. The pools are beside the road to Pharping, at a point it makes a sharp left-hand turn (coming from Kathmandu) and they are often used by local women for washing clothes. The main temple is above the pools and is sheltered under a multi-coloured, overhanging cliff. It forms an interesting juxtaposition between the work of man and god. In true Nepali style, a Buddhist monastery has been built next door.

The temples and carvings have suitably diverse ages. The Sekh Narayan Temple, one of the most important Vishnu temples in the valley, was built in the 17th century, but it is believed the cave has been a place of pilgrimage for much longer. Beside the shrine is a bas relief of Vishnu Vikrantha, also known as the dwarf Vamana. This possibly dates from the Licchavi period, or the 5th or 6th century.

Half-submerged in one of the crystal-clear ponds is a **sculpture of Surya**, the sun god, framed by a stone arch and with a lotus flower at each shoulder. This dates from the 12th or 13th century. Finally, the Tibetan gompa is a 20th century addition. Hindus believe that Gautama Buddha was Vishnu's 10th incarnation, but we don't know if this is the connection.

Getting There & Away

Sekh Narayan is close to Pharping and is probably best reached by foot from the village if you haven't got your own transport.

VAJRA JOGINI TEMPLE (18.5KM)

On a hillside overlooking Pharping is the 17th century Vajra Jogini Temple, dedicated to the same goddess as the Vajra Jogini Temple near Sankhu and built at about the same time. See the earlier Vajra Jogini section for a discussion on the goddess' origins. The pagoda-style temple is in a courtyard surrounded by relatively modern two storey, Newari-style living quarters. Vajra Jogini is featured in the temple's toranas.

Getting There & Away

The temple is just a short walk behind Pharping on the hill that overlooks the town. The main gompa at Gorakhnath (see the following section) is only a few hundred metres to the west up a flight of steps. It is possible to walk an interesting circuit from Dakshinkali to Gorakhnath, Vajra Jogini, Pharping and back to Dakshinkali in less than two hours. See Getting There & Away in the Dakshinkali section later in this chapter.

Coming from Kathmandu and after Sekh Narayan, you approach Pharping past a soccer field. The main road swings left around the field, but if you continue straight ahead you will come first to Vajra Jogini (on the side of the hill) then Gorakhnath.

GORAKHNATH (19KM)

Several gompas and temples have sprung up around the Gorakhnath cave behind Pharping. The white Tibetan gompa – perched high on the hill like an eagle's nest, at the centre of a web of prayer flags – is particularly interesting.

There are magnificent views overlooking Pharping, the Bagmati River and the valley. You can even see the Himalaya on a clear day. Somewhere in the complex is a cave which the Tibetans associate with Padmasambhava, the Bodhisattva sometimes credited with introducing Buddhism to Tibet.

Getting There & Away

Gorakhnath is an easy walk from Pharping and Vajra Jogini, and a bit of a scramble from Dakshinkali. It can be combined with an interesting walk that takes in all these places (see the Dakshinkali section) or reached by road.

PHARPING (19KM)

Pharping is a thriving, traditional Newari town, surprisingly untouched by the swarm of tourists that visit Dakshinkali. The main road skirts the village so there are few vehicles in the village proper. Before King Prithvi Narayan Shah unified Nepal this was another tiny city-state.

Places to Stay

Perched on a ridge a few kilometres before Pharping, the **Hattiban Resort** (☎ 371397, fax 371561, email nepal@intrek.wlink.com .np) offers some of the best views in the entire valley. The small resort is set in a pine forest, and is reached by a rough, steep and winding 2km track from the main road, although you can leave your vehicle in the (guarded) car park at the bottom and take the resort 4WD up the track. The resort buildings are pleasant, being timber lined, and the restaurant has an excellent terrace. There are 24 rooms, each with balcony and bath. Rooms cost $66/77; the food is fairly pricey at around $10 for a main meal.

Closer to Pharping is the **Dakshinkali Club Resort**, about 800m off the road along an amazingly bumpy stone-paved track.

Right by the main gate to Dakshinkali, and also with good views, is the quiet **Dakshinkali Village Inn** (☎ 290653, fax 330889), a modest place with decent rooms and a good restaurant. The rooms cost $12/20, although discounts of 15% to 25% are offered, depending on the time of year. The garden setting is very pleasant.

Places to Eat

In Pharping itself there's a couple of small restaurants. The **Snowland** is a good little Tibetan restaurant, but all food is made to order and so it doesn't pay to be in a hurry. The momos with soup (Rs 20) here are excellent. Close by is the **Asura Cave** restaurant.

Getting There & Away

Buses leave throughout the day from the City bus station, Kathmandu, take about two hours and cost Rs 11.

DAKSHINKALI

At the southern edge of the valley, in a dark, somewhat spooky location in the cleft between two hills and at the confluence of two rivers, stands the bloody temple of Dakshinkali. The temple is dedicated to the goddess Kali, Shiva's consort in her most bloodthirsty incarnation, and twice a week faithful Nepalis journey here to satisfy her blood lust. The six armed main image of Kali in the temple is of black stone and she tramples upon a male figure.

Sacrifices are always made to goddesses, and the creatures to be sacrificed must be uncastrated male animals. Saturday is the major sacrificial day of the week when a steady parade of buffaloes, chickens, ducks, goats, sheep and pigs come here to have their throats cut or their heads lopped off. Tuesday is also a sacrificial day, but the blood does not flow quite as freely as on Saturday. During the annual celebrations of

Dasain in October the temple is literally awash with blood and the image of Kali is bathed in it.

After their rapid dispatch the animals are butchered in the stream beside the temple and their carcasses will later be brought home for a feast, otherwise a picnic may be held on the hillside. Non-Hindus are not allowed into the compound where Kali's image resides, but it is OK to take photos from outside. The temple itself is not particularly interesting, although there are some fine brass nagas forming a canopy over the compound.

This is one of the most important sites in the valley so on the sacrificial days it is crowded with Nepali families – and tourists. Most big hotels and the tour companies cart bus loads of camera-laden visitors along. Tours to the 'exciting animal sacrifices' are big business for Kathmandu travel agencies. As a result, there are a number of teahouses, and a good number of hustlers selling souvenirs and goodness knows what else. Be prepared to pay picturesque sadhus for the privilege of taking their photograph.

Despite the carnival spirit, witnessing the sacrifices is a strange and, for some, a confronting experience. The slaughter is surprisingly matter-of-fact, but it creates a powerful atmosphere. Unfortunately, many tourists behave poorly, perching vulture-like from every available vantage point in order to get the most gory possible photos. However extraordinary the sights might seem, this is a religious ceremony, and the participants should be treated with respect, not turned into a sideshow.

Getting There & Away

Buses only operate on Tuesday and Saturday – the most important days for sacrifice – and though there are plenty of them, they are very crowded. If you have a car, allow 45 minutes for the journey. On other days catch a bus to Pharping and it's an easy 1km downhill walk or ride from there.

It is an enjoyable, but exhausting two hour bike ride from Kathmandu. The views are exhilarating, but it is basically uphill all the way – so mountain bikes are the way to go. Tuesday is probably the better day to pick as the traffic is not too heavy. Make sure you get an early start, as the shrine is busiest early in the morning. You're advised to pay someone a couple of rupees to mind your bike in the car park.

Consider making the interesting two hour circuit from Dakshinkali to Gorakhnath, Vajra Jogini, Pharping and back to Dakshinkali. Take the path that runs above the left (southern) side of the sacrificial compound, which brings you out into a cleared part of the gorge with several picnic shelters. There's a steep scramble up a goat track that follows a ridge on the right (north-western) side of the gorge. At the top you come out on a plateau – you'll immediately see the white monastery surrounded by prayer flags on a nearby hill. Make your way through the paddy fields, on the narrow paths between the rice. It takes about 40 minutes to get to Gorakhnath. Vajra Jogini is a few hundred metres down some steps to the east of the gompa, and a short walk to Pharping. From Pharping follow the main road about 1km downhill to Dakshinkali.

Pokhara

Pokhara is the most popular destination in Nepal after Kathmandu. Its fame rests on the natural beauty of its lakeside location and its proximity to the mountains, not on a great historical or cultural endowment. It's the starting point for some of the most famous treks in Nepal, and there are also plenty of short walks and day trips, suitable for children or weary trekkers, that can be made around the valley.

Pokhara has an enormous number of good value hotels and restaurants, and although it is undoubtedly a tourist town, it has a relaxed and peaceful atmosphere, completely removed from the hectic bustle of Kathmandu and even further removed from the outright chaos of many Indian cities. It's an oasis where leisurely meals, good books and short walks can easily fill several days – ideal if you are recovering from (or gearing up for) a trek, or travel in India.

The roads that link Kathmandu and the Indian border with Pokhara are comparatively recent innovations and the region has changed rapidly as a result. The road from Naubise to Pokhara, called the Kathmandu-Pokhara (Prithvi) Hwy, was originally built with Chinese assistance in the early 1970s. The Tribhuvan Hwy (or Tribhuvan Rajpath, sometimes simply referred to as the Rajpath) was the first road link with Kathmandu and was completed by the Indian government in 1956; it joins the Kathmandu-Pokhara (Prithvi) Hwy at Naubise, 29km from Kathmandu. The most direct route between Pokhara and Sunauli on the Indian border is the attractive Siddhartha Hwy, also built by the Indian government.

Most of the heavy traffic from the Terai and India to Kathmandu and Pokhara uses the road between Narayanghat and Mugling, then either turns east to Kathmandu or west to Pokhara. The sections between Narayanghat and Mugling, and Mugling and Kathmandu, are particularly busy. Mountain biking is a great way to get around Nepal,

HIGHLIGHTS

- Spending a few hours at Gorkha's fort, palace and temple complex, where some buildings date from the early 17th century
- Relaxing at Pokhara's peaceful lakeside location, surrounded by the majestic snow-capped mountains of the Himalaya
- Taking the three or four day Annapurna Skyline Trek, which provides fine views of the Annapurnas and the Pokhara Valley; a fine trek to do with children

but it would be worth catching a bus over both these sections.

After travelling in Nepal or India, Pokhara has an almost Disneyland unreality about it. The climate is mild; incredible snow-capped mountains are reflected in a sheltered lake; cool western music drifts from every restaurant; menus offer everything in the world except dal bhat; hotel rooms are clean, and open onto sunny gardens; there's very little traffic; village life persists, but everyone speaks English; and it's very relaxed.

The first tourists to discover Pokhara were hippies in the early 1970s. In Pokhara many discovered the perfect venue for doing the things they were best at – getting stoned, eating, growing their hair, talking, and staring into the middle distance while looking cool. They came for a week and stayed for months. The world has changed since then (and so have the drug laws and visa regulations), but Pokhara retains something of the laid-back, hedonistic style of this time, although rampant Thamel-style development threatens to overwhelm the Lakeside tourist area.

Viewed from Pokhara, the Himalaya is indeed a mighty mountain range, looming over the horizon much closer than it does in Kathmandu. Only foothills separate the town from the full height of the mountains, and the magnificent 8000m peaks of the Annapurna Range utterly dominate the view to the north (weather permitting, of course). In the Kathmandu Valley the high temples are all around you, in the Pokhara Valley the mountains are.

The valley has three large lakes. Two of them, Rupa Tal and Begnas Tal, are slightly to the east of town while the third and largest, Phewa Tal, is the focal point for Pokhara's tourist industry.

Pokhara stands at 884m above sea level, about 700m lower than Kathmandu. The autumn and winter temperatures are generally much more comfortable than in often-chilly Kathmandu, but the monsoon rains are twice as heavy, and the humidity uncomfortably high.

Although the Pokhara Valley is chiefly inhabited by Bahuns and Chhetris, the hills around Pokhara are predominantly inhabited by Gurungs. These sturdy tribal people continue to play an important part in the Gurkha regiments in India and overseas, and their earnings have a major impact on the local economy.

Pokhara's development has been relatively recent and rapid. Only with the eradication of malaria in the 1950s did it become safe to live here. The construction of the airstrip in the 1950s, and of the hydroelectric power dam (with Indian aid) in 1968 plus the building of the roads to Kathmandu and the Indian border in the early 1970s, catapulted Pokhara into the 20th century.

ORIENTATION

Pokhara is a surprisingly sprawling town, stretching in a north-south direction for about 5km. Starting from the north there's the busy bazaar area which also contains the oldest part of Pokhara – the town as it was before electricity, roads and the airport totally transformed it. South of the bazaar is the bus station and south again is the airport.

West of the bus station and airport is Phewa Tal, the Lakeside tourist centre where Pokhara's great and growing number of hotels and restaurants are predominantly located. It's a long walk from place to place in Pokhara and if you go from south to north it's uphill all the way.

Most of Pokhara's local shops and the post office are around the Mahendrapul (or Mahendra Pool) Bridge in the bazaar area. The bazaar is a long, strung-out affair and the campus of the Pokhara University is also found in that area.

The tourist office and three of the town's larger hotels are close to the airport while a number of government buildings, including the immigration office, are between the airport and Phewa Tal.

Starting at the south-eastern end of the lake, near the airport, there's a hydroelectric station. This area is often rather confusingly called Damside (although the dam and the lake are continuous) or Pardi. There are quite a number of hotels in the Damside area although Lakeside has even more.

Finally there's the Lakeside area itself, also known as Baidam, where the majority of foreign visitors to Pokhara stay. Along the Lakeside road there's a continuous and increasingly tawdry stretch of small hotels, restaurants and shops. In this book, Lakeside has rather arbitrarily been divided into three sections: Lakeside East (or Ammat) ending at the Royal Palace; Lakeside West (or Pallo Patan) ending just before the intersection known as Camping Chowk, where the main road returns eastward to town; and Lakeside North (or Khaharey).

INFORMATION
Tourist Office

Pokhara's tourist office (☎ 20028) is near the airport. The office is open approximately mid-February to mid-November, 10 am to 5 pm, and mid-November to mid-February, 9 am to 4 pm; on Friday it closes at 3 pm. It is closed on Saturday and public holidays. The office has virtually no information to offer and it's hard to think of a reason to visit.

There is also a tourist desk in the arrivals area of the airport, but it is equally useless.

Money
For those staying at Lakeside the Nepal Grindlays Bank is convenient. Although it is only open standard banking hours, you can make cash and travellers cheque advances against Visa and MasterCard.

Alternatively there are plenty of private moneychangers strung out the whole length of Lakeside, and these are open seven days a week.

Post & Communications
The area code for Pokhara is ☎ 061.

The post office is a long way from the Lakeside and Damside hotels in the bazaar area near Mahendrapul Bridge. If you want to make overseas phone calls or calls to Kathmandu, there's a telecommunications building east of the post office along the bridge, or any number of private phone centres in Lakeside.

For email and Internet users there are plenty of communication places in Lakeside. The going rate is somewhat higher than in Kathmandu at Rs 10 per minute. The network is often congested resulting in slow connections.

Immigration Office
The immigration office is convenient to the Lakeside and Damside hotels. It can extend visas and issue trekking permits (for the Annapurna region only). It's open 10.30 am to 1 pm, Sunday to Thursday (to noon Friday) for applications and from 3 pm for passport pick-ups.

ACAP Information Office
The Annapurna Conservation Area Project (ACAP) has a small office at the immigration office, and it's here that you pay the Rs 1000 entry fee to the Annapurna Conservation Area. This is also an excellent place for information on trekking in the Annapurna region, including the latest weather and trail conditions. The office is open 9 am to 4 pm Sunday to Friday.

Bookshops
There are numerous bookshops along the Lakeside road offering new and second-hand books and maps. The Bongsor Valley in Han Suyin's *The Mountain is Young* is based on the Pokhara Valley.

PHEWA TAL
Phewa Tal, or Phewa Lake, is the tourist centre of Pokhara and the second largest lake in Nepal. Only Rara Lake in the far west of the country is larger.

From Phewa Tal you can set off on walks or bicycle rides, or take to the lake in one of the numerous boats *(doongas)* available for rent at Lakeside. The boats cost from Rs 100 to Rs 150 an hour, and are most expensive opposite the Varahi Temple, but get cheaper as you head south to Damside. You can simply paddle yourself lazily around or jump overboard for a swim in the pleasant waters. If rowing yourself is too strenuous, a boat plus boatman will cost from around Rs 100 per hour. Sail boats are hired near the Hotel Fewa for Rs 250 per hour, less for half a day.

If you are boating near Damside, keep well away from the dam wall as currents can be strong especially during and immediately after the monsoon; in the past people have had trouble here.

The Lakeside villages are mainly inhabited by Chhetris although these days there is a great deal of outside influence as well.

Along Lakeside are a number of banyan and pipal trees with *chautaras* built around them. These stone platforms were designed to provide a resting place for walkers, and building them was one good way of improving one's karma for future existences.

MOUNTAIN VIEWS
The wonderful Annapurna panorama forms a superb backdrop to Pokhara. You can see the mountains clearly from the lake, while from the other side of Phewa Tal, by the Fish Tail Lodge, you can actually see them twice if you count their reflection in the often placid waters.

Alternatively you can climb to Sarangkot or one of the other viewpoints around the valley and enjoy a closer uninterrupted view. See the Around Pokhara section later.

The incredible Annapurna massif includes the Lamjung Himal, Hiunchuli, Varahashi-khar, Khangsar Kang, Tarke Kang and Gangapurna mountains; but it's the five Annapurna peaks, Annapurna I to IV plus Annapurna South, and the magnificent Machhapuchhare which are best known.

Machhapuchhare means 'fish tail' and if you walk several days west along the Jomsom Trek route (see the Trekking chapter) you will find that the mountain actually has a second peak, and from that side it does indeed look like a fish tail. From Pokhara, however, it's simply a superb pyramid: a Himalayan Matterhorn, only much higher.

Machhapuchhare stands out not only because of its prominent shape and lonely position, but because it is closer to Pokhara than the other peaks. In actual fact, at 6997m, it is lower than the five Annapurnas.

An attempt to climb it in 1957, led by the legendary Mountain Travel founder, the late Colonel Jimmy Roberts (who, incidentally, settled in Pokhara after his retirement), got to within 50m of the top, but turned back when the Sherpas refused to conquer such a holy summit.

Climbing is now not allowed on this mountain. Robert Rieffel in *Nepal Namaste* questions how Machhapuchhare acquired its holy image: if it's so significant, why on earth is it called 'fish tail' when so many other unholy Nepali peaks are named after gods and goddesses?

The other peak with a mountaineering tale to tell is Annapurna I, which, at 8091m, is the highest in the range. It's also part of a long ridge line and because it's farther north appears less conspicuous.

Annapurna I's claim to fame is that when a small French expedition, led by Maurice Herzog, reached the summit in 1950; it was the first time an 8000m peak had been climbed. Herzog's book *Annapurna*, a mountaineering classic, traces the hardships of organising a climb in what was then a remote, inaccessible and little-known area. The harrowing aftermath of the climb, when a severe storm caught the retreating mountaineers, re-sulted in Herzog losing most of his fingers and toes from frostbite.

To the west of the Annapurnas is Dhaulagiri, at 8167m. The Kali Gandaki River, which cuts the deepest gorge in the world, flows between Dhaulagiri and the Annapurnas and actually predates the rise of the Himalaya. For a while, before more precise measuring methods were available, it was thought that Dhaulagiri was the world's highest mountain.

TEMPLES
Pokhara, unlike the towns of the Kathmandu Valley, is not noted for its temples. In fact there are very few of even minor note.

In the lake there's a small island with the double roofed **Varahi Temple** dedicated to Varahi, who is Vishnu in his boar incarnation.

In the northern part of the bazaar area, is the small, double-roofed **Bhimsen Temple** with some small and not very notable erotic carvings on the roof struts. The streets of the bazaar area become steadily more attractive and traditional as you move north from the newer area around the bus station to what was the centre of the original settlement of Pokhara. Bhimsen Temple, very much in the Newari style of the Kathmandu Valley, is right on the main road in the oldest part of town.

Slightly farther north, atop a small hill with a park at its base, is Pokhara's best known temple, the **Binde Basini Temple**. Its pleasant and shady setting is actually more impressive than the white shikhara-style temple itself. The temple is dedicated to Durga (Parvati) in her Binde Basini Bhagwati manifestation, and interestingly the image of the goddess is a *saligram*. These black ammonite fossils of marine animals date from the Jurassic period over 100 million years ago and are found in the Himalaya, north of Pokhara, and at several points along the Kali Gandaki. Saligrams provide clear proof that this region was once under the sea.

MUSEUMS
Pokhara has two museums, neither of them worth bothering with. The **Pokhara Museum**

POKHARA

PLACES TO STAY
12 Hotel New Crystal
14 Hotel Mt Annapurna
18 Fish Tail Lodge
23 Shangri-la Village

OTHER
1 National History
  Museum
2 Binde Basini Temple
3 Local Bus Station
  (Baglung Buses)
4 Bhimsen Temple
5 Telecommunications
  Building
6 Tibetan Buddhist
  Monastery

7 Bhadrakali
  Temple
8 Hospital
9 Pokhara Museum
10 Stadium
11 Bus Park
13 Tourist Office
15 Immigration; ACAP
16 Himalayan Rescue
  Association
17 Moneychanger
19 Bus Arrivals
  From Kathmandu
20 Gorkha Airlines
21 RNAC; Lumbini
  Airways; Buddha Air
22 Airport

POKHARA

is north of the bus station on the main road and has exhibits on local history. Entry is Rs 5, and it's open daily except Tuesday.

At the northern end of town, on the Pokhara University campus, is the **Natural History Museum**, also known as the Annapurna Regional Museum. ACAP has some interesting although somewhat dated exhibits on the environmental problems of the area. The natural history section has cement models of Nepali wildlife (you don't have to feed them) and a large butterfly, moth and insect collection. The museum is open 9 am to 1 pm and 2 to 5 pm; there's no entry charge, but make a donation.

SETI GANDAKI RIVER

The Seti Gandaki River flows right through Pokhara but in places it runs completely underground, sometimes dropping to 50m below ground level. *Seti* means 'white' and the water's milky colour comes from limestone in the soil.

There's a good view of this elusive river from the bridge at the northern end of the bazaar; though an even more dramatic view can be found just beyond the airport runway. From the far side of the airport, follow the trail to the river where a footbridge crosses the canyon. The bridge is only about 10m wide but the river flows past a good 30m below, although it is difficult to actually see.

Another good view of the river can be found at Mahendrapul Bridge in the main bazaar area.

DEVI FALLS

Also known as Patale Chango, Devin's or David's Falls, this waterfall is about 2km south-west of the airport on the main Siddhartha Hwy and just before the Tashiling Tibetan Village.

The Pardi Khola is the outflow from Phewa Tal and at Devi Falls it suddenly drops down into a hole in the ground and disappears. One of its alternative names comes from a tale that a tourist named David disappeared down the hole, taking his girlfriend with him! There's a small admission charge to the falls.

The river emerges from its subterranean hideaway 200m farther on and then joins the Phusre Khola before flowing into the Seti Gandaki River.

TIBETAN SETTLEMENTS & MONASTERY

There are a number of Tibetan settlements around Pokhara and you see many Tibetans around the lake selling their crafts and artefacts. The Tashiling Tibetan Village, where they weave Tibetan carpets, is only a couple of kilometres south-west of the airport.

There's also a larger settlement known as Tashipalkhel at Hyangja, a short drive or an hour or two's walk north-west of Pokhara on the start of the Jomsom Trek route.

The hilltop **Tibetan Buddhist Monastery** is a comparatively recent construction with a large Buddha statue and colourful wall paintings. Cross Mahendrapul Bridge from the bazaar area and follow the road, at first paved, to the monastery.

WALKS

The Pokhara area offers some fine walking possibilities ranging from day walks, such as the climb up to Sarangkot, to short three or four-day treks. See the Around Pokhara section later in this chapter for full details.

PLACES TO STAY

There are four accommodation areas in Pokhara: around the bus station and bazaar, by the airport, Damside (Pardi) and Lakeside (Baidam).

There's really no reason to stay in the bazaar area; it's crowded, dirty and noisy. Several of Pokhara's larger and more expensive hotels are near the airport, but the advantages of comfortable hotels have to be weighed against the disadvantage of being a long walk from Lakeside.

Damside at the south-eastern end of the lake is more popular, and many of the touts who meet the tourist buses from Kathmandu will insist that this is the place to go. They will be at pains to point out that the distinction between Damside and Lakeside is meaningless. In one sense they're right (it is a continuous body of water we're talking about), but in several others they're wrong. Damside has a completely different atmosphere from Lakeside.

Firstly, there is quite a difference between being able to look out across the lake proper, as you can at many places in Lakeside, and looking out on the narrow neck of water by the dam. Damside is a new, rather desolate area, and there are fewer farmhouses, fields and trees interspersed between the hotels. Many of the buildings are of the bleak concrete five storey variety and there is a limited range of restaurants – most people eat in their hotels. Finally, you're a 15 minute walk from the action at Lakeside.

On the other hand, there are a couple of pleasant mid-range hotels in Damside, and some people prefer to escape the Lakeside scene. They are further rewarded by the best mountain views – the farther south you go, the less the mountains are obscured by the intervening foothills.

The major accommodation site is Lakeside, where you'll find an enormous number of budget to mid-range lodges and guesthouses. The Lakeside road is a continuous strip of restaurants, which spill out into the open air, and little shops selling everything a traveller could want: tickets, trekking gear, books, fruit juice, clothes, souvenirs. However, if you take any of the eastward-running roads, you quickly escape to land where the buffalo roam. Within two minutes you can be in a cheap and comfortable guesthouse amongst vegetable gardens and Chhetri farmhouses, although tourist development is rapidly reducing the land available for traditional practices.

It is the combination of the magnificent location, good-value accommodation and food, and (not least) the proximity of local village life that accounts for much of Pokhara's appeal.

There are so many places to stay and they change so quickly, that making individual recommendations (especially among budget and mid-range places) is a chancy game. Listen to other travellers' recommendations, and if you arrive by bus avoid the clutches of the touts. The best thing you can do is grab a taxi to somewhere central on Lakeside, have a drink and a bite to eat at one of the restaurants and then ask to leave your bag somewhere safe (most restaurants will happily do this) while you check out some hotels for yourself. Alternatively, find any place for the first night, and then spend some time the next day looking for something better if need be.

When looking for somewhere to stay – in any price range – the important variables are the quality of the room, the views and the garden; the availability of hot water; and the position. If you're staying in one of the really rock-bottom Lakeside places take care of your valuables, as theft is not unknown.

As is the case in Kathmandu, most places quote prices in US dollars, but these are highly negotiable and very few people would pay the advertised price. Bear this in mind with the prices we quote here.

Bazaar Area

There are numerous cheaper hotels around the bus station and near the Mahendrapul Bridge. It's a much less pleasant place to stay than Lakeside and there's no real reason to do so.

Airport Area

Two of Pokhara's large hotels are directly opposite the airport, and two of the best are on the far side of the airport.

Hotel Mt Annapurna (☎ 20037, fax 20027) is Tibetan owned and decorated in Tibetan style; the murals in the restaurant showing Tibetan traders and other scenes are particularly impressive. There's also a fine view of the Annapurna skyline from the roof, and a pleasant garden area. Unfortunately the whole place is looking a bit tired these days, and it's not great value. All rooms have private bathrooms and cost $30/43 for a single/double, plus 12% government tax.

Hotel New Crystal (☎ 20035, fax 20234) is better, with singles/doubles with air-con for $50/64, but for a room with a view of the mountains it's $65/75. All rooms have baths and there's a 12% government tax. The facilities are good, but it's a big soulless place that could be pretty much anywhere.

Shangri-la Village (☎ 22122, fax 21995, email hosangp@village.mos.com.np), arguably Pokhara's best hotel, is signposted about 1km past the southern end of the airport. This is a very low-key place, with buildings arranged around a pool and garden, and with excellent mountain views. Other facilities include a sauna and health club. The rooms are tastefully decorated, and good use has been made of local furnishings. The tariff is $150 for a single/double with air-con, TV and phone. The food here is also good, and the Rs 450 weekend brunch is excellent value, especially for nonguests as, in addition to a full breakfast spread, it also gives you use of the pool for the day.

Farther south again, but accessed from the Kathmandu road east of the airport, is Pokhara's latest hotel folly, the *Dusit Thani Fulbari* (☎ 23451, email fulbari@dusit .com). The location is dramatic, being perched right on the edge of the Seti River gorge, and the mountain views are superb, but one wonders just how they ever hope to fill this 165-room, five-star place. No expense has been spared in its construction; the lobby area makes extensive use of carved wood, and the effect is stunning. Rooms come with all the mod cons you'd expect in a place charging $200/215. Facilities include a golf-course, pool, health club and tennis courts.

Damside Area (Pardi)

South-west of the airport, at the south-eastern end of Phewa Tal, is the Damside or Pardi area. There are a number of lodges and

POKHARA DAMSIDE

To Lakeside (1km)
To Airport (500m)
To Tansen (110km)

PARDI
Pardi
Pardi Dam
Pardi Khola
Ratnapuri

PLACES TO STAY
1 Hotel Holiday
4 Mona Lisa Guest House
5 Ashok Guest House
7 Hotel Try Star
8 Dragon Hotel
9 Hotel Garland
10 Tibet Resort
11 New Hotel Pagoda
12 Hotel Nascent
14 Hotel Peaceful
15 Hotel Garden
16 Hotel Holiday
17 Friendly Guest House
18 Hotel Himalayan
19 Super Lodge
20 Hotel Green View
21 Puma Guest House

PLACES TO EAT
3 Rodee; Don't Pass Me By
6 Bamboo Garden Restaurant
13 German Bakery

OTHER
2 Wayfarers Travel Service

0   50   100 m

hotels, many of which are run by Thakalis from the Kali Gandaki Valley.

Hotel Holiday (☎ 20189) is an unremarkable two storey place with clean rooms, some of which have excellent mountain views. Singles/doubles with shared bath cost from Rs 300/400, rooms with bath are Rs 500/600.

There is a group of decent mid-range places right by the dam – there's not much to separate them, and the most crucial variable is probably which direction your room happens to face, because the views can be impressive. The *Ashok Guest House* (☎ 20374) is well kept and has singles/doubles with bath for $10/15, or $15/20 if you want the view. There are a few cheaper rooms. This has a good position right by the lake. The *Mona Lisa Guest House* is similar.

Dragon Hotel (☎ 20391) is another reasonable mid-range option. Singles/doubles with air-con and bath are $30/35, plus 12% government tax. There's a restaurant, bar and roof garden.

Tibet Resort (☎ 20853) is a pleasant, modern place with a big garden. Rooms here are excellent value at $6/10 with bath. This is one of the best Damside places, although you can't actually see the lake from here.

New Hotel Pagoda (☎ 21802) is also good value. There are views, and the rooms are very clean. Rooms are $5/6 with shared bath, or $8/12 with private bath.

Hotel Green View is a friendly place with some very basic rooms for $3/5. There's also a comfortable newer building with good views and rooms with bath for $10/15.

Hotel Garden (☎ 20870) and *Hotel Peaceful* (☎ 20861) are both decent. Comfortable rooms are $3/5 with shared bath, $7/10 with private bath. The Hotel Garden also has more expensive deluxe rooms, some with excellent views.

Lakeside Area (Baidam)

The road running alongside Phewa Tal is the real visitors' centre for Pokhara. Not only does it have the largest number of hotels, guesthouses and lodges, it also has the widest selection of shops, bookshops, restaurants, travel agencies, bicycle rental and so on.

Although the majority of the Lakeside places are firmly in the budget range, there's also a fair sprinkling aiming for the mid-range with en suite bathrooms, carpets and comfortable beds.

Many of the budget lodges and guesthouses along the lake have similar facilities and prices. Prices tend to vary with demand, rising and falling with the season and the number of travellers passing through. There's usually hot water available in the bathrooms and many places offer very pleasant garden areas, often right in front of your room. The rooms are usually quite simply furnished, but good Pokhara guesthouses are clean and well kept.

Basic doubles cost around Rs 100 for a room with shared bath, or from Rs 250 with private bath. There are increasing numbers of new concrete hotels with totally uninspiring architecture, but with comfortable rooms. They're relatively expensive with rates starting at about $10, and there's usually room for bargaining, especially if you plan to stay more than a couple of days.

You can stay close to the centre of things, on or near the main Lakeside road, or opt for a quieter location either back from the main road or way down at the northern end of the lake. The price for peace and quiet is a slightly longer walk to get to the restaurants and other activities by the water. The farther north you go (towards the foothills), the more restricted are the views of the mountains.

The following suggestions are just a handful of standard places, plus some of the pricier alternatives.

Lakeside East (Ammat) Pokhara's most expensive lakeside hotel is the beautifully positioned *Fish Tail Lodge* (☎ 22171, fax 225236). It's across the lake from the lakeside development and guests are shuttled over to the hotel by a rope-drawn pontoon. The hotel takes its name from Machhapuchhare. From the hotel there are superb views of the mountains, particularly at dawn when they are reflected in the still waters of the lake. The buildings have been imaginatively

POKHARA

POKHARA LAKESIDE

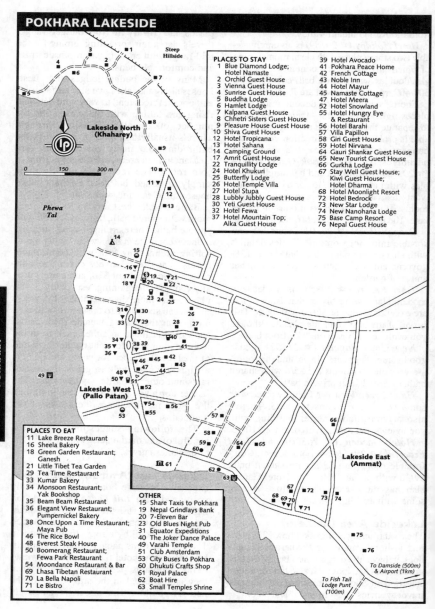

PLACES TO STAY
1 Blue Diamond Lodge;
  Hotel Namaste
2 Orchid Guest House
3 Vienna Guest House
4 Sunrise Guest House
5 Buddha Lodge
6 Hamlet Lodge
7 Kalpana Guest House
8 Chhetri Sisters Guest House
9 Pleasure House Guest House
10 Shiva Guest House
12 Hotel Tropicana
13 Hotel Sahana
14 Camping Ground
17 Amrit Guest House
22 Tranquillity Lodge
24 Hotel Khukuri
25 Butterfly Lodge
26 Hotel Temple Villa
27 Hotel Stupa
28 Lubbly Jubbly Guest House
30 Yeti Guest House
32 Hotel Fewa
37 Hotel Mountain Top;
   Alka Guest House

39 Hotel Avocado
41 Pokhara Peace Home
42 French Cottage
43 Noble Inn
44 Hotel Mayur
45 Namaste Cottage
47 Hotel Meera
52 Hotel Snowland
55 Hotel Hungry Eye
   & Restaurant
56 Hotel Barahi
57 Villa Papillon
58 Giri Guest House
59 Hotel Nirvana
64 Gauri Shankar Guest House
65 New Tourist Guest House
66 Gurkha Lodge
67 Stay Well Guest House;
   Kiwi Guest House;
   Hotel Dharma
68 Hotel Moonlight Resort
72 Hotel Bedrock
73 New Star Lodge
74 New Nanohana Lodge
75 Base Camp Resort
76 Nepal Guest House

Lakeside North (Khaharey)

0   150   300 m

Phewa Tal

Lakeside West (Pallo Patan)

49

PLACES TO EAT
11 Lake Breeze Restaurant
16 Sheela Bakery
18 Green Garden Restaurant;
   Ganesh
21 Little Tibet Tea Garden
29 Tea Time Restaurant
33 Kumar Bakery
34 Monsoon Restaurant;
   Yak Bookshop
35 Beam Beam Restaurant
36 Elegant View Restaurant;
   Pumpernickel Bakery
38 Once Upon a Time Restaurant;
   Maya Pub
46 The Rice Bowl
48 Everest Steak House
50 Boomerang Restaurant;
   Fewa Park Restaurant
54 Moondance Restaurant & Bar
69 Lhasa Tibetan Restaurant
70 La Bella Napoli
71 Le Bistro

OTHER
15 Share Taxis to Pokhara
19 Nepal Grindlays Bank
20 7-Eleven Bar
23 Old Blues Night Pub
31 Equator Expeditions
40 The Joker Dance Palace
49 Varahi Temple
51 Club Amsterdam
53 City Buses to Pokhara
60 Dhukuti Crafts Shop
61 Royal Palace
62 Boat Hire
63 Small Temples Shrine

Lakeside East (Ammat)

To Damside (500m)
& Airport (1km)

To Fish Tail
Lodge Punt
(100m)

Steep
Hillside

POKHARA

designed with references to the local architecture, and sit in attractive gardens. The recently refurbished rooms have all the usual luxury mod cons and cost $85/95, plus 12% tax. There's also a newer wing of deluxe rooms which are more expensive and less attractive, but which do have limited views; these cost $100/110. A 25% discount applies to all rooms in the low season. The hotel is extremely popular, so it is worth booking well in advance if you want to stay. There's a pleasant bar and restaurant and the food is pretty good. Cultural shows are held nightly at 6.30 pm (Rs 150) and these are also open to nonguests.

Nepal Guest House (☎ 22692) is set well back from the road and has large rooms with fan and bath (with tub). The asking price is $20/35, but there's plenty of room for discounting here.

Take the first right after Baba Lodge & Restaurant and you come to the *Base Camp Resort* (☎ 21226, fax 20903, email basecamp@ber.mos.com.np), a good, modern upmarket place. A number of two storey bungalows are grouped around an attractive garden. There's satellite TV, IDD telephones and gas heating. This is a good option if the Fish Tail is booked out. Singles/doubles are $72/75; discounts of up to 35% are possible.

Heading away from the lake's edge you end up in a pleasant village-like area. The first place you come to is the *New Nanohana Lodge*, a modern, fairly undistinguished place with a range of rooms with bath from Rs 250 to $10. Nearby, the *New Star Lodge* has basic rooms for Rs 100/150, and rooms with bath for Rs 350.

Keep going to find the *Gurkha Lodge*, a small, well-kept place with a lovely garden. There are only five double rooms, all with bath, and there has been a real effort to build in sympathy with the local architecture, although rooms are somewhat gloomy. It's worth the price – $12 per room, no bargaining.

The next road leading inland from the lake is lined with places to stay, and though they're convenient, and the mountain views are good, there's not much atmosphere. The

Kiwi Guest House (☎ 22052) is decent. The garden is a bit cramped, but there are good views from the hotel roof. It advertises Kiwi management, which is more literally true than some such claims, since Lal, the owner, did study management in New Zealand. There are a range of rooms from $5 to $20, all of them fair value for what you get. The cheapest have common bath, the most expensive have air-con and TV.

Stay Well Guest House is small with clean and comfortable singles/doubles for $10/20.

Hotel Dharma (☎ 23232) is a decent cheapie although it lacks a garden area. Comfortable rooms cost $10/15 with discounts.

Hotel Bedrock (☎ 21876) is a large and ugly multistorey place with comfortable rooms from $25/45.

Moonlight Resort (☎ 422044, fax 429560) is on the lakeside road, but is set back far enough to offer privacy. Good, basic rooms cost $6 with bath, or there are larger rooms with better facilities at $10/20, although the official price is double this.

There are a number of cheap places down the first north-eastward road past the small temple shrine on the lake's edge. One of these is the *Gauri Shankar* (☎ 20422), with a nice garden and doubles with common bath at Rs 150, and with attached bath at Rs 250.

New Tourist Guest House (☎ 21479) is pleasant with a decent garden and a range of prices depending on the quality of the room and the time of year. Prices start at $2/3, and go up to $10/12 for a luxury room.

The second laneway heading inland has a couple of cheap and decent places, in pleasant surroundings. *Villa Papillon* (☎ 27030), in a leafy, private garden, has doubles for Rs 200, rising to Rs 350 if you want a private bath.

Hotel Nirvana (☎ 23332, fax 23736) on the same lane is well worth checking out. It is immaculately clean and very well maintained, and there are good rooftop views. Some rooms also have views, and the price ranges from $6 to $15.

Giri Guest House (☎ 24955) is almost next door. Big rooms with bath go for Rs 200 on the ground floor, and Rs 300 upstairs.

Lakeside West (Pallo Patan) The real centre of Lakeside activity is beyond the Royal Palace at the point where the road forks around three chautaras and several enormous pipal trees.

Hotel Hungry Eye (☎ 20908, fax 23089, email hungry@eye.mos.com.np) is a popular survivor behind the restaurant of the same name. The rooms are smallish without being cramped, with TV, phone and fan. The official rate is $20/30, but this seems to be permanently discounted to $10/15, which is good value.

Hotel Snowland (☎ 20384, fax 20958, email snowland@mos.com.np) nearby is another long-time favourite. The old rooms in the rear wing are unremarkable, and overpriced at $15/20, although you should be able to pay 20% less than that. The front of the hotel consists of a block of modern deluxe rooms, all with a view of the lake, and these go for $30/35, again with a 20% discount.

There's a good upper mid-range option on the nearby road east. *Hotel Barahi* (☎ 23017, fax 23072) has a huge garden and a wing of very comfortable deluxe rooms at $55/64 with air-con. There are also some older but still comfortable rooms at $25/31 with bath.

The road running eastward from the next chautara (beside the incongruous Cape Cod-style Hotel Meera) has a number of options, but the laneway itself is not as pleasant as some. First there is the very simple, very basic, and cheap *Noble Inn* (☎ 24926). It is modern, with a pleasant garden and OK rooms at Rs 300 with common bath, Rs 400 attached.

Hotel Mayur (☎ 22285, fax 25261) is in the same lane. The top-floor views are excellent, and the modern rooms well kept. The cost is Rs 250/300 on the lower floor, Rs 400/500 upstairs.

Hotel Meera (☎ 21031, fax 24923) is something of an eyesore, and totally inap-

propriate for the setting. Nevertheless, the rooms are good and the front-room views excellent. The cost is $25/35, or there are deluxe rooms with TV and air-con at $35/45. Discounts of up to 30% are offered.

The next eastward lane (just before the next chautara) is very pleasant and retains some of the old Pokhara atmosphere. There are a number of cheapies (around Rs 150), one of the nicer ones being the *Namaste Cottage* set in a secluded garden with rooms around the outside in Indonesian *losmen* style. It's about as basic as they come, but is friendly and popular. Rooms, all with common bath, cost Rs 100 for a double. The *French Cottage* almost next door is similar but lacks the garden and the privacy.

Pokhara Peace Home (☎ 23205) along here is also not a bad place. It has a pleasant garden with a village feel, and rooms cost Rs 150 with common bath, Rs 250/300 with attached bath.

Hotel Avocado (☎ 23617, fax 21565) has good rooftop views, but no garden. Rooms cost Rs 250/300 with bath.

Alka Guest House (☎ 23357, fax 22810) is in a good position right on the main road. The rooms (no singles) are at the back, well away from the road, and are good value at Rs 200 with common bath, Rs 300 with attached.

Nearby, *Hotel Mountain Top* (☎ 20779) is an unmissable four storey monstrosity, and not an uncommon sight these days. Admittedly, the comfortable rooms have superb views and they're not bad value. Singles/doubles with common bath are $12/18, and $20/29 with attached bath, but low-season discounts can bring this down by 50%.

Up the side road beside the Mountain Top there are a few more guesthouses to choose from, including the *Lubbly Jubbly Guest House* (☎ 22881). Despite the absurd name, it's a pleasant little place with a very nice open-air sitting and eating area, although there isn't much garden. Rooms are good value at Rs 100 with common bath, Rs 200 for a larger double with attached bath.

Hotel Stupa (☎ 22608) is another concrete monster, but if that's the sort of place you want, this is as good as any. It's not bad value at $20/35, but be sure to request a discount.

Yeti Guest House (☎ 21423) is set back from the road in a large garden. It's basic, but quite OK at Rs 100 with common bath, Rs 200 attached.

One of the few hotels on the western side of the road is the superbly situated *Hotel Fewa* (☎ 20151), right on the edge of the lake. It is owned and run by Mike of Mike's Breakfast fame in Kathmandu. The rooms are fairly basic but well maintained, and the lakeside location is hard to match. At $19/28 with bath the price is a bit steep.

Back on the eastern side, the *Tranquillity Lodge* (☎ 21030) is a pleasant modern hotel set in a sunny garden. Rooms are large and comfortable, and moderately priced at $15/25. There's certainly room for bargaining, especially out of season – expect to pay around Rs 600 for a double.

The nearby *Butterfly Lodge* (☎ 22892) is similar, and cheaper – Rs 300 for a double, Rs 400 for a larger room.

Farther along is the *Hotel Temple Villa* (☎ 21203), a small and pleasant lodge also in a quiet location. It is clean, and the rooms are large and comfortable. They're reasonable value at $7 for a double with common bath, or $12 with private bath.

Hotel Khukuri (☎ 21540), on the same lane, is a small high-rise with well-appointed rooms at $25/30. There's no garden and unless you absolutely can't survive without a TV and carpet, there's better value elsewhere.

Amrit Guest House (☎ 22862, fax 22201) is near camping chowk, on the west side of the main Lakeside road. It's unremarkable, but good value at Rs 100 for a double with common bath, Rs 250 attached.

Lakeside North (Khaharey)
There are more places to stay beyond the intersection between the lake shore and main roads, both on the lake shore and on the main road itself. Once you get this far north you are tucked in under the foothills and don't get great views of the mountains.

For those with tents the best bet is to make a deal with one of the lodges to camp in their garden. Alternatively, there's the *camping ground*, by the lake near Camping Chowk. The facilities are very basic and there's not much shade, although it is a nice grassy site and is a good option if you have a large vehicle. It costs Rs 40 to pitch a tent and Rs 80 per vehicle.

The places along the main road into Pokhara don't appeal very much. Not surprisingly, the road lacks the peaceful rural atmosphere that the best parts of Lakeside have, and although the traffic is not particularly heavy, there are regular buses and taxis. Most of the hotels are new and are two or three-storey monstrosities with mid-range prices.

Hotel Sahana (☎ 22614, fax 25050) is a modern place with rooms set around a garden. It's quite pleasant, and not bad value when the 15% discount is taken from the official price of $15/25.

Hotel Tropicana (☎ 22118) is a relatively new place with lake views and rooms from $5/8.

As you move farther north, the lake shore becomes much closer, the atmosphere is much more rural, the mountain views are more obscured, and the accommodation generally much more basic.

Pleasure House Lodge is a basic and somewhat characterless concrete building, with upstairs double rooms with common bath at Rs 150, downstairs it's Rs 100.

Chhetri Sisters Guest House (☎ 24066) is a very friendly little place and is indeed run by three sisters. The rooftop views are good, and the rooms OK, although it's a pity they don't have views too. The cost is Rs 200 for a double with common bath, Rs 300 attached.

Kalpana Guest House is slightly back from the road, and being right in amongst the rice fields has a very rural ambience. It's clean, well run and good value at Rs 100/150 with common bath.

Hotel Namaste is farther along, and farther back from the road. It is reached by a foot track, and you'd definitely need a

POKHARA

flashlight if venturing out at night. It's a very basic place, but is certainly quiet and private. Right next door is the similar *Blue Diamond Lodge*.

Hamlet Lodge is a new place right at the foot of the hills, where the track rounds the end of the lake. The facilities are good, and double rooms cost Rs 350.

Vienna Guest House, above and behind the Hamlet Lodge, has excellent lake views because of its elevated position. The rooms are large and spartan but quite OK, and there's a large veranda for relaxing. It's good value at Rs 120 for a double with bath.

Sunrise Guest House, at the end of the small group of tea stalls, is about as close to the lake as you can get. It's another basic place, but is clean and comfortable.

Right out on a point, nestled between the road and the lake shore, is a small, cheap lodge which is basic but popular. *Buddha Lodge* has single and double rooms with common bath, but you would need a bicycle as they are a good 20 minutes' walk from the nearest restaurants.

Elsewhere

Tiger Mountain Pokhara Village (☎ 01-411225, email info@tigermountain.com) is also worth a mention. It is set on a steep ridge about half an hour's drive from Pokhara along the Kathmandu road, and has absolutely amazing views over Pokhara and the mountains. Accommodation consists of cottages made from local stone and slate, each with its own balcony and stunning views. The main lodge building has a bar, eating area and library. The cost is $150 per person per night, which includes all meals and transfers to and from Pokhara.

PLACES TO EAT

Pokhara may not match the variety of food offered in Kathmandu, but you can certainly eat well although, as usual in Nepal, a little caution is always wise. Upset stomachs are as common in Pokhara as anywhere else in the country.

The bazaar area has local restaurants, and other eating possibilities are found in the big

hotels or amongst the numerous cheaper hotels particularly along Lakeside. At most of these travellers' restaurants you'll find the standard 'try anything' menu – which currently means lots of Italian dishes backed up by Indian, Nepali, Mexican, 'Continental' and whatever other possibilities present themselves. The range is certainly an improvement over endless dal bhats or thalis, but despite the apparent variation everything very quickly tastes the same! What differs more is the atmosphere and the crowd at any place on any given evening.

Damside

There is not a great range of restaurants in the Damside area, as most people eat at their hotels. *Don't Pass Me By* and *Rodee* are basic little restaurants right on the edge of the lake, and you can sit outside and enjoy the atmosphere.

There's nothing very German about the *German Bakery* but it's a popular breakfast and snack place. The *Bamboo Garden* completes the Damside restaurant picture.

Lakeside

Most dining possibilities are along the main road skirting Lakeside.

Starting at Lakeside East, one of the first possibilities *Le Bistro*, which has everything from Mexican, Italian, Chinese and Indian to Nepali and they seem to do a pretty good job of all of it. The apple pies are not bad either!

Very close by is the *La Bella Napoli*, with decent pizzas and pastas, and other Italian and western dishes. They also have decent bakery items.

Lhasa Tibetan Restaurant is a big outdoors place with a standard 'try-anything' menu, in addition to a number of Tibetan specialities. The food is very good and the service is fairly fast. *Sha bhakley*, a Tibetan meat pie, is Rs 90, and *momos* (meat/vegetable filled pasta) is Rs 40. Chicken tikka kababs with naan (bread) and salad for Rs 110 is good value, as are the pizzas and vegetable curries.

Hungry Eye, farther along past the Royal Palace, is a long-standing survivor and one of the biggest restaurants on Lakeside. The food is still good (the cakes are excellent), but the service can be chaotic. Pizza ranges from Rs 90 to Rs 150 and a steak is Rs 160.

Moondance Restaurant & Bar, next door, has average prices and food, but a good atmosphere. There's a fireplace inside. The bar here is popular and there's a pool table, darts and other board games to while away the hours.

Boomerang Restaurant is one of a number of outdoor places on the west side of the road. Given that this space should never have been developed, it must also be said that the opportunity has not been wasted. There's a nice garden dotted with chairs, tables and thatched shelters – and great views. It's a great place for breakfast (around Rs 80) or lunch, but dinner is less impressive. They have the normal eclectic menu and prices. The *Fewa Park Restaurant* next door is fairly similar.

Everest Steak House, also with an outlet in Kathmandu, has some of the best views.

Opposite these places is *The Rice Bowl*, a fairly standard place with Tibetan and other dishes, and decent views from the top floor.

Beam Beam is also on the west side of the road, and although the garden is much smaller than the Boomerang's, it is still very pleasant – in some ways cosier. Inside, the big TV/video tends to dominate. The service is excellent, and although the menu is pretty standard, the food is good.

Pumpernickel Bakery, next door, also has a garden. This place has an impressive array of breads and pastries, and is a popular morning spot.

Monsoon Restaurant is a new place with good food and a relaxed atmosphere. It's among the more expensive places, with fish at Rs 190, and other main dishes (steaks, Indian, Nepali) at Rs 150 to Rs 230. The coffee is excellent.

Tea Time Restaurant on the next corner along is a popular place with a cosy front veranda eating area in addition to an indoor section.

Mike's Restaurant at the Hotel Fewa offers the best location and arguably the best food in Lakeside. The open-air terrace is right by the lake (the only place with an actual lake frontage), and the food is excellent. This place is run by Mike of Mike's Breakfast in Kathmandu. The exotic sandwiches with brown bread are well worth the Rs 100 to Rs 140, plus another Rs 40 with soup or salad.

For budget breakfasts try one of the small bakeries, such as the *Sheela* up near Camping Chowk. This is a very popular little place, with excellent chocolate croissants and buns. The *Kumar Bakery* near the Tea Time Restaurant is similar.

Ganesh Bakery is another good breakfast spot, and the views from the amazingly ramshackle upstairs eating area are excellent.

Little Tibetan Tea Garden is a cosy place on the main road into Pokhara from Camping Chowk. Just so no-one feels left out, they not only do excellent Tibetan food (including that traditional favourite, Tibetan pizza!), but also throw in a few Mexican and Italian dishes.

The *Lake Breeze Restaurant*, towards the northern end of the lake, consists of a small elevated building set in a small garden. The lake views and the food are both OK.

At the top end of the spectrum, the bar and restaurant at the *Fish Tail Lodge* is a fine place for a more expensive night out. The fixed breakfast costs Rs 525, or a buffet lunch or dinner is Rs 700, although these are only laid-out when there are sufficient guest numbers. An a la carte dinner for two will probably come to at least Rs 1500. On a clear day it's worth coming over here for a drink in the garden, which has stunning views of Machhapuchhare.

ENTERTAINMENT

The *Fish Tail Lodge* puts on an excellent nightly cultural program featuring Nepali dancing. It runs from 6.30 to 7.30 pm and admission is Rs 150.

There are an increasing number of bars in Pokhara, and the music blares out until 10 or 11 pm each night. There's nothing very bluesy about the *Old Blues Night Pub*, but the sound system is good (and usually cranked up loud) and the pool tables are popular.

Another good bar is the *Maya Pub*, which has a happy hour in the early evening with two cocktails for the price of one.

Club Amsterdam is a new bar with a popular outdoor deck.

The *7-Eleven Bar* near Camping Chowk is a noisy place with live Indian *ghazal* music (Urdu love songs derived from poetry) in the evenings, although purists of that art form would probably be horrified at the mauling the music receives here.

SHOPPING

Pokhara's large Tibetan population sells many crafts and artefacts. Carpet-weaving is a major local industry for these people.

Saligrams, the fossilised sea creatures found north up the Kali Gandaki Valley, are a popular souvenir, but they are often radically overpriced. You shouldn't pay more than about Rs 100.

Trekking Equipment

There are plenty of rental shops in Pokhara, and prices are similar to those in Kathmandu – down sleeping bags and jackets are around Rs 10 to Rs 15 per day. The range of equipment is probably not quite as large however, so if you want anything out of the ordinary you are best off bringing it from home or Kathmandu.

GETTING THERE & AWAY

Some travel agencies in Pokhara offer 'through' tickets or package-deal tickets to cities in India. These are dubious value at the best of times and a number of travellers have written to us complaining of various rip-offs perpetrated by unscrupulous Pokhara agents. These range from promises of tourist buses (there are *no* tourist buses running to/from any of the border crossings), to reserved seats that were definitely not reserved, and air-con train sleepers that turn out to be 2nd class.

See the India section in the Getting There & Away chapter for more information, but if you do decide to buy a package, don't count on everything going smoothly. Make sure you get everything spelt out in a receipt, and hang onto the receipt.

Air

There are many daily services between Kathmandu and Pokhara. As the route is something of a cash cow all the private companies have jumped on the bandwagon; Buddha Air (☎ 21429) and Necon Air (☎ 20256) are recommended. The flight takes less than an hour (closer to 20 minutes with Buddha Air) and costs $61. RNAC (☎ 21021), Lumbini Airways (☎ 27233), Buddha Air and Gorkha Airlines (☎ 25971) are just across the road. It's probably easiest to get one of the many agents at Lakeside to do the running around for the ticket.

There are great Himalayan views if you sit on the right-hand side of the plane from Kathmandu to Pokhara, and vice versa.

Bus

The main Pokhara bus park is a dusty (or during the monsoon, muddy) expanse of chaos, with seemingly little organisation. The booking office for night buses is at the top of the steps that lead into the bus park on its western edge. Day buses can be booked at the small kiosk which sits in the middle rear of the park.

To/From Kathmandu The bus trip between Kathmandu and Pokhara takes seven or eight hours and most departures are early in the morning. The first stretch of road from Kathmandu to Naubise is in average condition, it's excellent from Naubise to Pokhara, with the exception of a 20km stretch around Dumre.

Greenline (☎ 27271) offers daily air-con services to Kathmandu, which is a steep $10 but includes breakfast at Kurintar about halfway.

Public buses (from the bus station) cost Rs 114; tickets for the large tourist buses start from Rs 150 and for the tourist minibuses cost Rs 200. It's a bit dubious whether the extra expense of tourist buses is worthwhile. The minibuses are certainly quicker (often considerably scarier as a result), but the full-sized tourist buses aren't significantly different to the public express buses in terms of time and comfort.

The tourist buses are, however, more convenient when you consider where they pick you up and drop you off. In Kathmandu they pick up and drop off at the Thamel end of Kantipath. In Pokhara, the tourist buses pick up Kathmandu-bound passengers outside their hotels, although all tourist buses coming from Kathmandu terminate at a makeshift terminus at Mustang Chowk, between Damside and the airport.

Taxis await all bus arrivals, and everything is pretty orderly, although there are still plenty of touts. There is absolutely no reason to get sucked in by these characters who will, apart from anything else, get a 50% commission from the hotel they take you to. The best thing you can do is grab a taxi to somewhere central on Lakeside, have a drink and a bite to eat at one of the restaurants and then ask to leave your bag somewhere safe while you check out some hotels for yourself.

To/From Chitwan Public buses between Pokhara and Tadi Bazaar in the eastern Terai cost Rs 85. See the Royal Chitwan National Park section of the Terai chapter for more details.

To/From the Indian Border Buses to Sunauli/Bhairawa near the Indian border depart from the main Pokhara bus park (Rs 128/149, nine hours); buses for Birganj cost Rs 120/149 and take 10 hours; and night buses for Nepalganj take 15 hours and cost Rs 277 via Mugling, Rs 250 via Tansen.

We have received a number of letters complaining that Pokhara agents sell overpriced tickets for alleged tourist buses to the border. There are no tourist buses; so while you do get picked up outside your hotel, you go from there to the bus station where everyone else gets on!

The road to India is called the Siddhartha Hwy because it ends close to Lumbini where the Buddha, Siddhartha Gautama, was born.

See the Getting There & Away chapter for more details on transport to India.

To/From Trekking Routes Pokhara is the base for popular treks such as the Annapurna Sanctuary Trek, Jomsom Trek and the Annapurna Circuit, plus a number of other lesser known alternatives. See the Trekking chapter for details. The road goes all the way to Baglung, so most trekkers take the bus as far as Nayapul (just before Baglung), from where it's just a 20 minute walk to Birethanti. Buses for Baglung leave the local bus station roughly every half hour from early morning until mid-afternoon, and the trip to Nayapul takes about two hours and costs Rs 35.

To Besisahar, for the start of the Annapurna Sanctuary Trek, there is one bus daily at around 7 am from the main Pokhara bus park, and the journey takes around five hours.

GETTING AROUND
It's a long way between the bazaar and Lakeside; a taxi costs around Rs 100. It's a bit of a battle to extract fair prices when catching a taxi from Lakeside to the airport or bus station. Expect to pay as much as Rs 100. Buses shuttle between the lake, airport and bazaar with per-person fares costing around Rs 5.

Share-taxis operate from Camping Chowk in the northern part of Lakeside into the city centre.

There are lots of bicycle rental places along the lake, by the dam or by the airport. Ordinary bikes typically cost around Rs 40 per day, mountain bikes around Rs 100. You can also rent children's bicycles. Pokhara looks deceptively flat but actually slopes steadily uphill as you move north. If you ride a bicycle from the lake to the Binde Basini Temple at the northern end of the bazaar area you'll find it's a wonderfully long freewheel on the way back.

Renting a motorbike costs around Rs 500 per day – a bit more than in Kathmandu. Pokhara and the surrounding roads will not be improved by the growing number of motorbikes.

POKHARA

Around Pokhara

Pokhara is the starting or finishing point for some of Nepal's most popular treks such as the Annapurna Circuit, the Jomsom Trek and the Annapurna Sanctuary Trek. See the Trekking chapter for details.

For those with limited time, less enthusiasm for walking or with small children, the area also has some fine short treks ranging from half-day and day walks to longer treks lasting from two or three days to a week.

DAY WALKS

The following walks can all be made in a day or less.

Sarangkot

This very pleasant walk up to Sarangkot, at an elevation of 1592m, is probably the most popular short excursion from Pokhara. It can be a good, early morning stroll to admire the mountain views, a leg-stretcher before you start out on a longer trek or a place you pass through on the first or last hours of one of the longer treks from Pokhara.

Sarangkot has a number of places to stay or eat – like the *Didi Lodge, Restaurant Sarangkot, Trekking Lodge* or *New Tourist Lodge* – so you can climb up to Sarangkot in the evening, stay overnight and catch the view at dawn, or simply walk up for breakfast. The *View Top Restaurant & Lodge* has the prime views over the lake and pretty good food and it's extensively advertised on the steps up from the lake.

There are a number of routes to Sarangkot, but the easiest way is to walk up from the Binde Basini Temple in Pokhara Bazaar and then head straight down from the top to the lake.

From the temple head directly west and follow the vehicle track which runs most of the way up. You can short-cut many of the sharp corners and from where the vehicle track ends there is virtually a stairway to the top. On the way up you pass several places where women work at handlooms. It takes about two hours to walk to Sarangkot from Binde Basini Temple, versus three or four hours from the Lakeside area *if* you don't get seriously lost!

Sarangkot once had a fort or *kot* and its remains can be seen on the very top of the ridge above Sarangkot. There is a lookout point inside the old fort walls and the view of the Annapurnas to the north is superb.

The view back down over Phewa Tal is equally fine and from the top it takes about two hours to walk down to the lake. It's easy to get lost on the way up from the lake but coming down from Sarangkot is straightfor-ward: you make a very steep descent, stone-staired all the way, down the hillside and through the forest. If you're exhausted when you reach the lake, there are often boatmen waiting to paddle you back to the Lakeside lodge area.

An alternative to the Binde Basini Temple or Phewa Tal routes to the top is the walk from Bhairab Tole in Pokhara via the village of Gyarjati. Another hour's walk be-yond Sarangkot will take you to Kaski or Kaskikot at 1788m. The hill is topped by an unprepossessing Bhagwati temple.

Kahun Danda

To the north-east of the bazaar area of Pokhara is Kahun danda (*danda* means ridge in Nepali). It takes about three hours to walk to this popular viewpoint at 1560m and there's a lookout tower on top of the ridge. The walk starts from the Mahendrapul

AROUND POKHARA

Bridge and continues through Phulbari and up the gradual slope to the top. The remains of the 18th century Kanhu Kot stand on the hilltop.

Mahendra Gufa

The limestone caves at Mahendra Gufa have stalactites and stalagmites and make a good destination for a two hour walk north from Pokhara. The trail to the caves crosses the bridge just north of Bagar at the end of the bazaar and heads toward the village of **Batulechaur**. This village was once an important centre for growing citrus fruit until an epidemic killed all the citrus trees in the Pokhara Valley.

Rupa & Begnas Tals

These two lakes are the second and third largest in the valley, but few travellers visit them even though they're only 15km east of Pokhara.

Buses run regularly from Pokhara to Begnas Bazaar, the small market centre at the very end of the ridge that divides the two lakes. From there it's a pleasant stroll along the ridge to the other end of either lake.

SHORT TREKS
Annapurna Skyline Trek

The three or four day Annapurna Skyline Trek has also been dubbed the 'Royal Trek', as Britain's Prince Charles walked it some years ago. It's a fine trek to do with children; it doesn't reach any great altitudes, doesn't entail any particularly long walking days and there's always plenty to see. It's not a heavily trekked area, however, so there is no village inn accommodation en route.

There are several variations on the route but basically the walk starts from the Kathmandu-Pokhara (Prithvi) Hwy, a few kilometres east of Pokhara, climbs up to a ridge and then for most of the walk follows ridges with fine views of the Annapurnas and then leads back down into the Pokhara Valley.

The walk passes through small villages like Kalikathan, Shaklung and Chisopani before it drops down to the stream which feeds Rupa Tal. The final stretch is along the ridge separating Rupa Tal and Begnas Tal, emerging on the valley floor at Begnas Bazaar from where buses run to Pokhara.

Ghandrung to Ghorapani Trek

This week-long trek to the west of Pokhara also gives fine views of the Annapurnas. The walk starts and finishes at Birethanti, and essentially links the first few days of the Annapurna Sanctuary Trek as far as Ghandrung with the first few days of the Jomsom Trek as far as Ghorapani, then crosses between these two villages.

Near Ghorapani is **Poon Hill**, one of the finest lookout points in the region.

Ghachok Trek

An interesting two-day trek goes north from Pokhara to the interesting Gurung villages around Ghachok. The walk starts from Hyangja, with its Tibetan settlement, and crosses the Mardi Khola to Lhachok, then Ghachok, before turning south and returning to Pokhara through Batulechaur.

Naudanda Trek

This two-day walk, a shorter variation of the Ghandrung to Ghorapani Trek, takes you from Hyangja to Suikhet then to Naudanda and back to Pokhara through Kaski and Sarangkot. Naudanda has a variety of guesthouses and shops.

Kathmandu to Pokhara

For many people, the 206km Kathmandu-Pokhara (Prithvi) Hwy will be their first taste of Nepal's Middle Hills and although for most of the way the road follows rivers at the bottom of deep valleys there are still some magical views – rock gorges and river rapids, precipitous hills, tiered rice terraces and glimpses of the Himalaya.

Migrants from around Nepal (especially the Kathmandu Valley) have been attracted by the minimal economic opportunities offered in the roadside towns that have sprung up. Most towns are the usual unattractive collection of shanties and two storey concrete boxes. There are, however, some interesting places (west of Mugling and off the main road) that are worth visiting, including Gorkha, which was the original capital for the Shah dynasty, and Bandipur, an old Newari trading settlement.

The countryside is inhabited by Bahuns, Chhetris, Magars and Gurungs. The large multistoreyed houses, especially east of Mugling, are most likely owned by Bahuns and Chhetris, but around Mugling the region is dominated by Magars, and to a lesser extent, Gurungs. Historically, the Magars had their own independent kingdoms in western Nepal, and both Magars and Gurungs played a major role in Prithvi Narayan Shah's armies (which unified Nepal), and have since been recruited in large numbers by the British and Indian armies to serve in so-called Gurkha regiments.

Partly thanks to the money that these Gurkhas earn, much of the region seems relatively prosperous, although some Magar families are desperately poor. Land holdings are small, but the region seems to have avoided major problems such as overpopulation, deforestation and land degradation. The intensive, traditional forms of agriculture – based on rice cultivation and a small number of domestic animals – are sophisticated and appear to be sustainable.

KATHMANDU TO NAUBISE

The road leaves from the western end of Tripureshwar Marg and runs through straggling roadside bazaars. About 10km from town, all heavy traffic stops at a police checkpoint to pay a toll, and 4km later the road crosses the rim of the valley. In clear weather there are views (from east to west) of the Ganesh Himal, Himal Chuli, and the twin peaks of Manaslu Himal. You also look down over incredible terracing rising from the Trisuli River and Mahesh Khola.

The road from the rim of the valley to Naubise is in generally good condition, with the occasional bad spot. It snakes down the

hill in a series of switchbacks and is further enlivened by trucks overtaking on blind corners. At Naubise, the Tribhuvan Hwy joins the road after its spectacular journey from Hetauda (see The Terai chapter for details of that route).

NAUBISE TO MUGLING

From Naubise, the road follows the small Mahesh Khola to the point where it joins the Trisuli River just past Baireni (52km from Kathmandu). It then continues along the Trisuli valley through the small town of Gajuritar.

Around Malekhu the gorge is still attractively forested. Just before Malekhu, a bridge over the river leads to Trisuli Bazaar, superseding the old winding one-track road that leaves the valley at Kakani.

Just after Malekhu there are a number of small restaurants, which are good places to break the journey and which also cater to intrepid rafters. The *Hill Top Restaurant* has a great view over the river where most rafting trips start, and has good, reasonably priced food and clean toilets. The *Blue Heaven Restaurant* is virtually on the beach, which is about 75km from Kathmandu and 4km before Benighat.

At Benighat, the large Buri Gandaki River flows into the Trisuli from the north, giving the rafters the volume of water required for plenty of excitement. The road continues to follow the westward-flowing Trisuli to Mugling, where it meets the equally large south-eastward-flowing Marsyangdi Khola.

About 8km before Mugling is Kurintar, and here you'll find the surprisingly sophisticated *River Side Springs Resort* (☎ 056-29429, email nongint@ccsl.com.np). It consists of a number of comfortable cabins, an airy central lodge building and includes facilities such as a swimming pool just a stone's throw from the river. It's rapidly becoming a popular weekend getaway for Kathmandu expats. The cost is $50/60 for the cabins, which have fan and bath and a small veranda. A 50% discount applies to residents of Nepal.

The road from Naubise to Mugling was upgraded in the early 1990s, and is among

POKHARA

the best bits of road in the country – beautifully engineered, smoothly surfaced – and as dangerous as hell. It seems ironic that accidents have increased since the road has been improved from the cratered, axle-busting slalom course that challenged drivers in the late 1980s. The truth is that it's so good that every driver worth his dal bhat goes as fast as his Tata will carry him. In absolute terms this is not very fast, but it is nonetheless about 30km/h faster than is safe.

MUGLING

Mugling is at the junction between the most important road from the plains (from Narayanghat) and the Kathmandu-Pokhara (Prithvi) Hwy, so it is a popular stop for buses and trucks. It's 110km from Kathmandu and 96km from Pokhara, and it lies at an elevation of just 208m, making it the lowest town between Kathmandu and Pokhara.

The town is also at the junction of the westward-flowing Trisuli and the eastward-flowing Marsyangdi rivers, which together form the Narayani, a major tributary of the Ganges. This is the finishing point for most of the serious white-water rafting trips on the Trisuli, and the launching place for the more sedate trips down the Narayani to Narayanghat and the Royal Chitwan National Park.

Places to Stay & Eat

There are literally dozens of restaurants that serve good dal bhat for around Rs 40. Most are owned by Thakalis, and there is little to distinguish one restaurant from another.

Mugling would not be a pleasant place to spend a night. There are plenty of hotels, but few are interested in having a westerner stay, since their main business is prostitution. One that does accommodate the occasional

KATHMANDU TO POKHARA

stranded backpacker is the *Hotel Machhapuchare*, towards the western end of town, near the toll barrier. Avoid the noisy front rooms, and instead take one at the rear, which go for Rs 200 with attached bath. There are also cheaper rooms with common bath, but the management seems reluctant to rent these to tourists. The restaurant downstairs is popular with some of the tourist minibuses that do the Kathmandu to Pokhara run.

For those who are able to afford it, there is a slightly incongruous motel on the Pokhara side of town just over the bridge. The *Motel du Mugling* (☎ *056-29434*) is attractively sited by the confluence of the two rivers. It is very comfortable and has a pleasant terrace with views. The restaurant here does decent food. The rooms are well fitted out, and not bad value at $15/20 for a single/double.

MUGLING TO ABU KHAIRENI

Leaving Mugling, a long suspension bridge crosses the Narayani River just below the junction of the Trisuli and Marsyangdi rivers. About 3km farther on you reach the **Marsyangdi Hydroelectric Powerhouse**, which generates more than a quarter of the country's electricity. Water is diverted to the building you see beside the road from a dam 12km away. The road deteriorates after Mugling, and there are some very rough, very dusty sections until you get past Dumre.

Next you reach Abu Khaireni, 8km from Mugling and another roadside bazaar town. It is at the intersection of the road to Gorkha, and is the starting point for the climb to **Manakamana**, one of the most popular temples in Nepal.

To get to the temple, turn right off the highway on the road to Gorkha; continue for 1km until you see the Manakamana Hotel on

KATHMANDU TO POKHARA

To Ganesh Himal

▲ 18km ▲ Distances between Major towns

Buri Gandaki

Dhading

Trisuli Bazaar

Trisuli River

River Side Springs Resort

Surprise Rapid · Upset Rapid · Twin Rocks Rapid · Teen Devi Rapid · Monkey Rapid · Snell's Nose Rapid · Trisuli

Kurintar · Ladies Delight Rapid · Benighat · Malekhu · Gajuritar · Baireni · Trisuli

38km · 43km

Mahesh Khola

Kathmandu Valley

KATHMANDU

Galchhi Bazaar · Naubise · Thankot (Police Checkpoint)

Tribhuvan Hwy · 29km

To Hetauda (123km)

POKHARA

Bhagwati

It is believed that the goddess Bhagwati will grant wishes in exchange for prayer and animal sacrifices, and she is particularly popular with newlyweds seeking sons. The hereditary role of temple priest is filled by a Magar (not a Brahmin as is usually the case with Hindu temples), suggesting that the goddess is a survivor from the pre-Hindu, shamanistic religion of the Magars.

the right; turn right and cross the river on a suspension bridge; and then climb for three or four hours! The soft alternative is the new Austrian-built chairlift which terminates right by the highway near Mugling. Nepali pilgrims pay a few rupees; foreigners are fleeced Rs 600!

GORKHA
☎ 064

Gorkha, 24km north of the Kathmandu-Pokhara (Prithvi) Hwy, is accessible by a good sealed road that intersects with the highway at Abu Khaireni, 8km west of Mugling. The countryside is spectacular and Gorkha itself is well worth visiting.

Gorkha Durbar

Gorkha Durbar, a fort, palace and temple complex, is the centrepoint and highlight of a visit to Gorkha. Some of the building is believed to date from the reign of King Ram Shah (1606-36), but successive generations have made alterations and additions, often utilising Newari artisans.

The complex is a triumph of Nepali architecture – perched like an eagle's nest high above the town in a perfect defensive position – with superb views of plunging valleys and the soaring Himalaya. It is very easy to imagine an ambitious prince looking out over this dramatic landscape and dreaming of ruling all he could see – and more.

To get to Gorkha Durbar, walk north from the bus station until you come to several small temples (Vishnu, Krishna and Ganesh) surrounding a tank. Head to your right until you come to a square, to the right of which is **Tallo Durbar**, a large, square Newari-style

building that was built in 1835 and housed a Rana who had been banished from Kathmandu for playing a role in one of the never-ending palace intrigues. The building is slowly being renovated and will eventually house a museum.

You pay for the impressive view from the Gorkha Durbar with a steep one hour walk from Tallo Durbar. Return to the square from Tallo Durbar and continue to the north. The old part of town itself is inaccessible to cars, so it's quite pleasant to wander the cobbled, shop-lined streets.

On your left after about 100m you'll see some well-made steps heading directly up to Gorkha Durbar. If you get to the gully where village women wash clothes you've gone too far.

The hillside has a network of paths and retaining walls that must have cost a fortune to build. When you get to the big pipal tree, the path forks and although you can take either path, the gentlest ascent is to the left. After about 200m there is another junction; again head to your left. It's a rewarding walk; when you get to the ridge you are greeted with stupendous views of the Ganesh and Annapurna himal.

From the ridge, you obviously turn right to the palace, but if you turn left you soon come to **Tallokot**, a small, old fort now used as a sacrificial site.

Photography is not permitted once you are inside the Gorkha Durbar complex, and this rule is strictly enforced by soldiers, so you may want to try to capture something on film from here. Officially you are not allowed to wear leather inside the complex, so wear sandshoes or a thick old pair of socks if you are going to do some serious

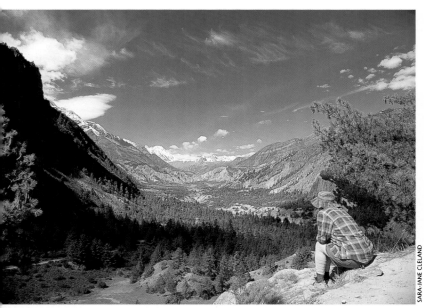
A break on the Annapurna Circuit allows time to ponder the wonder of Brahma's creation.

SARA-JANE CLELAND

Breathtaking backdrop of the Annapurnas.

RICHARD I'ANSON

Tired legs? Spare a thought for the porters.

SARA-JANE CLELAND

Sun, short sleeves and distant snow.

GREG ELMS

Festivals
Colourful, crowded and magical, Nepal's festivals are one of the best ways to witness traditional culture.

exploration, although this rule is not strictly enforced.

If you enter from the west, the first building on your left is the Kalika Temple (note the 'Star of David' window), which has some superb woodcarving. Only a special caste of Brahmin priests and the king can enter, but sacrifices are made outside.

The main palace, called the Dhuni Pati, has latticed windows all around the top floor, but, unfortunately, you're not allowed to enter, so you can only imagine the breezy rooms that lie behind. This was Prithvi Narayan's birthplace and an 'eternal' flame has been burning inside ever since his rule.

Next, go up a few steps. There is a priests' house on the left and two bells on the right. Between the latter are stairs descending to a cave where a reclusive saint named Gorkhanath once lived.

Beyond the priests' house is a four faced Shiva lingam. You can descend to servants' quarters and a temple on the next level, then down again to a crude but dramatic re-painted carving of Hanuman, the monkey god, and six carved stelae.

From here it's another half-hour walk east to **Upkallot**, the highest point on the ridge, with the ruins of a fort, and a telecommunications tower. The views over the palace and across to the Himalaya are stupendous.

Places to Stay

There are some cheap, basic places to stay near the Gorkha bus station. The small *New Amrit Lodge* is very basic, but it's a friendly place and some rooms have sensational views. Rooms (all with common bath) cost Rs 100/150 for a double/triple.

Hotel Gorkha Prince (☎ 20131) is just across the road from the Amrit and is much bigger with a variety of rooms. The inner ones can be gloomy, so ask to see more than

---

The Gurkha King

The ninth Shah king, King Prithvi Narayan Shah, was born in the family's palace that perches over Gorkha. Prithvi Narayan was crowned King of Gorkha in 1743, and proved to be an extraordinary man.

At the time he came to power, Nepal was broken up into numerous small principalities, but by the time he died he had created a unified state that was sufficiently strong to successfully resist the colonial forces that engulfed virtually every other country in Asia.

Although he was a great fighter, he was also an accomplished tactician and administrator. His reputation for religious and cultural tolerance, and for the justice and effectiveness of his administration, was a significant element in his success. He was able to maintain the commitment of his subjects through a process that continued for nearly 30 years – the Kathmandu Valley was not completely conquered until the early 1760s – and he succeeded in convincing a number of states to accept his rule without resorting to direct violence. He had the guile to exploit existing rivalries between states, and where necessary utilised expedient alliances, notably with Palpa (see the Tansen section in The Terai chapter).

Gorkha was the name given to the fearsome soldiers (mostly Bahuns, Thakuris, Chhetris, Magars and Gurungs) under his command. The term Gurkha was later applied to all Nepali soldiers, irrespective of where they were recruited and to what group they belonged. Many have served, and still serve, in the British and Indian armies.

Beautiful and lethal – a Gurkha *khukri* knife.

one. The cost is Rs 100/150 with common bath, Rs 150/200 attached.

Gurkha Inn, close by, has a very pleasant garden setting, and the views from the terrace are excellent. The building itself is a sort of Nepali mock-Tudor, but is also very pleasant and airy. The rooms are comfortably furnished and cost $21/31, although discounts of up to 30% are available, depending on demand.

Hotel Gorkha Bisauni (☎ 20107) is a couple of hundred metres farther down the hill. The recently redecorated rooms, with phone and TV, are quite comfortable, and good value at $10/12 with common bath and $17/22 attached. Discounts are available.

Gorkha Hill Resort (☎ 29325) has a superb site 4km before town (800m down a dirt road to the east of the main road at Laxmi Bazaar). The ageing but well-kept upmarket resort has a very pleasant garden setting, and there are great views across to Gorkha. Though not cheap, the resort is worth the $34/44 charged for singles/doubles. Main meals are $4/8/8 for breakfast/lunch/dinner.

Getting There & Away
The bus park is right in the square at the centre of town, and the booking office for night buses is in the group of shops on the west side of the square. There are two buses a day to and from Pokhara, which cost Rs 60 and take 4½ hours, and seven buses to and from Kathmandu, which cost Rs 85 and take five hours. Buses from Gorkha all leave early in the morning. There are also direct buses from Gorkha to Birganj (Rs 103, six hours, 4 daily), Sunauli (Rs 107, six hours, 1 daily) and Narayanghat (Rs 54, two hours, many daily).

If you are dropped off at Abu Khaireni, 8km from Mugling on the Kathmandu-Pokhara (Prithvi) Hwy, there are local minibuses to Gorkha (Rs 12). It's an enjoyable drive on a good road, but there's a steep climb for cyclists.

DUMRE
Dumre, 18km past Abu Khaireni and a new town which only came into existence after the construction of the road, is a typical, dirty, dusty (or muddy) roadside bazaar. Apart from being the turn-off to Besisahar, the starting point for the Annapurna Circuit Trek, it has nothing at all to recommend it. For Circuit trekkers it's the last place where there is a decent range of supplies at reasonable prices.

Places to Stay & Eat
Trekkers may have to spend the night at Dumre if they arrive late. Try the basic *Mustang Lodge*, opposite the roadside temple in the middle of town, which has singles/doubles for Rs 40/80 with common bath; beware the steep 50m climb to the outside toilet, and keep a torch (flashlight) handy! Another reasonable alternative worth trying is the *Manang Guest House* just off the main road.

GORKHA

Walking Track to Tallokot

Gorkha Durbar

Walking Track to Upkallot

Pipal Tree

0   100   200 m

Tank

1 Temple
2 Ganesh Temple
3 Sobrakhutte Pati
4 Krishna Temple
5 Vishnu Temple
6 Column with Prithvipati Shah Statue
7 Tallo Durbar
8 Bus Booking Office
9 Bus Stand
10 Hotel Gorkha Prince
11 New Amrit Lodge
12 Gurkha Inn
13 Hotel Gorkha Bisauni

To Gorkha Hill Resort (5km),
Prithvi Highway (24km),
Pokhara (112km)
& Kathmandu (142km)

POKHARA

Getting There & Away

By bus, Dumre is about five hours from Kathmandu and 2½ hours from Pokhara. Public buses leave from the Kathmandu bus terminal, cost Rs 60 and could take longer; from Pokhara it costs Rs 40. The tourist buses that travel between Pokhara and Kathmandu will cost around Rs 150.

Many people start their trek by catching shared jeeps or trucks to Besisahar. Expect to pay around Rs 350, although porters and local people pay less. The road is very rough and the journey can take up to five hours, although three hours is more common.

BANDIPUR

Overlooking Dumre, Bandipur is a beautiful Newari hilltop town just south of the Kathmandu-Pokhara (Prithvi) Hwy. Before the construction of the road, Bandipur was a major Newari trading centre, and its bazaars still hint of those days. Stone-paved roads pass between temples and multistoreyed houses, and along the way there are excellent views of the Annapurnas and Machhapuchhare. It takes about two hours to walk up to Bandipur from Dumre, or there's a rough 4WD road which heads off the highway a few kilometres west of Dumre. It takes about 45 minutes to drive.

Bandipur is currently being pushed as a tourist destination, but it is severely hampered by lack of a decent access road and limited accommodation.

The **Bandipur Mountain resort** is a new place with decent facilities, or there are a number of basic local lodges.

DAMAULI

From Dumre it's just 16km to the district headquarters of Damauli which has a bustling bazaar. The main road in the town leads to the panchayat building, while a path to the left drops down to the junction of the Madi Khola and Seti Gandaki rivers. If you walk upstream about 100m you will find a beach which is good for swimming.

DAMAULI TO POKHARA

Soon after Damauli the road crosses the Madi Khola, via a large bridge, and follows the Seti Gandaki River for the remaining 54km to Pokhara. The next town is Khaireni, where a German-assisted agricultural project is based.

After Khaireni, the road passes the turn-off to Rupa Tal and Begnas Tal, which are the second and third largest lakes of the Pokhara Valley. Sisuwa, only 12km from Pokhara, is the last place before you arrive in Pokhara.

POKHARA

The Terai

When people think of Nepal they think of soaring snow-clad mountains, not hot subtropical plains. Despite this, nearly half the country's population lives on a narrow strip of flat and fertile land that lies wedged between the Indian border and the mountains. This is known as the Terai (sometimes spelt Tarai).

With the Kathmandu Valley and the world's highest mountains a few hours away by bus, it is not surprising that the Terai is often just a transit zone for those travelling overland to and from India. Nonetheless, although there is nothing quite as startling as 8000m mountains, the region has a beauty of its own and some fascinating possibilities for travellers. The most well known are the magnificent Royal Chitwan National Park, famous for its elephant safaris and wildlife; Lumbini, the birthplace of Buddha; and Janakpur, the birthplace of Sita (Rama's wife, from the *Ramayana*).

Nobody could forget a dawn ride on an elephant through forests where you might come across tigers, rhinos, crocodiles and peacocks. Nor could anyone forget the neat mud-walled huts and brilliant saris amid the vivid green rice paddies that stretch the length of the Terai, nor the strange waterlogged world of the Sapt Kosi's flood plain, with its birds, thatched villages, hyacinths and lilies.

Large sections of the Terai are still forested, and the land is cut by numerous rivers, often grey and turbulent with snowmelt and silt. These rivers burst from the hills onto the plains, a mere 100m above sea level yet over 1000km from the Bay of Bengal. In most parts of the Terai, western visitors are rare and in the farmlands outside towns there is little to disturb the ancient routines of ploughing, planting and harvesting.

While many hill people have settled in the region (every ethnic group in Nepal is represented) there are also indigenous peoples and large groups that are culturally a part of

HIGHLIGHTS

- Soaking up the unforgettable beauty of the waterlogged Sapt Kosi flood plain, dotted with thatched villages, rice paddies and water lilies, and partly protected in the Koshi Tappu Wildlife Reserve

- Going on an elephant safari and spotting wildlife, which includes the royal Bengal tiger and the Gangetic dolphin, at the magnificent Royal Chitwan National Park

- Visiting peaceful Lumbini, the birthplace of Siddhartha Gautama, known as Buddha, the founder of Buddhism

- Enjoying the good-humoured and courteous hospitality of the varied ethnic groups and the indigenous people of the Gangetic plain

the great Indian civilisations of the Gangetic plain. Despite this extraordinary diversity, the people of the Terai remain distinctively Nepali – unhurried, good-humoured, courteous and friendly.

Unfortunately, most of the border towns are new and unattractive, with Dickensian-looking industries on their outskirts, streets choked with buses and trucks, and little in the way of history or culture. The exceptions are the pilgrim centres of ancient Janakpur, with its sadhus and temples, and Lumbini, which remains more significant for what it was than what it is.

Chitwan should not be missed, and in the cool season (November to February) it is definitely worth travelling during the day and seeing the country, even if you have to suffer a crowded bus and stay in a scruffy border town overnight. The western area of the Terai (west of Sunauli/Bhairawa) is one of the least visited, least developed and most interesting

The magnificent peacock, one of the Terai's many bird species.

parts of the country. The completion of the Mahendra Hwy, which will run the entire length of the Terai from Mahendranagar to Kakarbhitta, will link the region with the rest of Nepal and with India, so when this finally happens, rapid change is likely.

HISTORY

Over the centuries, parts of the Terai have been under the sway of both the Nepali and Indian empires. Some regions were inhabited by sophisticated agricultural and urban communities as early as 800 BCE, but the empires have come and gone, and at times the countryside has been completely reclaimed by forest. The stories of decline are largely unknown, but disease and war certainly played a role – some areas were most recently depopulated as a result of the Muslim invasions of the 14th century, and malaria was a major problem until the 1960s.

Without doubt the Terai's most famous son is Siddhartha Gautama – Buddha – who was born in 563 BCE at Lumbini. Siddhartha was the son of Suddhodana who ruled a small state from Kapilavastu. The ruins near Taulihawa, west of Lumbini, are believed to be his capital. Archaeologists have identified 13 successive levels of human habitation at the site. (See the Taulihawa section later in this chapter.)

The Terai's most famous daughter is Sita, who is believed to have been born where present-day Janakpur stands. The daughter of Janak, the king of Mithila (also known as Videha), Sita is famous for her faithful marriage to Rama, the hero of the Hindu epic the *Ramayana*, which was first written in the 1st or 2nd century BCE. The kingdom of Mithila lives on in the rich culture and language of Nepal's eastern Terai and India's northern Bihar region.

By 321 BCE the Mauryan empire based at Patna, India was on the rise, swallowing the small principalities around it. Under the great Ashoka, the empire controlled more of the subcontinent than any subsequent ruler until the British. Ashoka was one of Buddhism's greatest followers and missionaries, so it was perhaps inevitable that he would visit nearby Lumbini, then a thriving religious centre. In 245 BCE he erected a stone pillar at Lumbini that can still be seen today. Some believe he travelled as far as Kathmandu.

The next great empire to rise in the region was the Gupta empire, again originally based in Patna, which flourished between 300 and 600 CE. The empire extended its influence to Kathmandu and beyond. In the early 13th century invading Mughals occupied large parts of northern India, driving many Hindu refugees towards Nepal and the Kathmandu Valley. It is believed that one of these groups founded the Malla dynasty, which by the 15th century under King Yaksha Malla had extended its power from Kathmandu south to the Ganges River.

The next (and current) Kathmandu-based dynasty, the Shah, won power in 1768 and continued to expand Nepali borders until the kingdom was twice the size it is now – extending south into the Gangetic plain and east and west along the Himalaya. Eventually the Shahs and their famous Gurkha soldiers ran

THE TERAI

up against the British East India Company. In 1816, after two years of relatively inconclusive war, the Nepalis were forced to sign a treaty that considerably reduced their territory. Some land (including the city of Nepalganj) was actually returned to Nepal as a reward for its support for the British during the 1857 Indian Uprising (or War of Independence as it is known in India today).

Most of the Terai was heavily forested until the 1960s, although limited areas were settled, and indigenous Tharu groups were widely dispersed through the region. However, the drainage and spraying programs begun in 1954 markedly reduced the incidence of malaria and this allowed mass migration both south from the hills and north from India. Fertile soils and easy accessibility led to rapid development. The Terai is now the most important region for agricultural and industrial production in Nepal, and the fastest growing.

GEOGRAPHY

The Nepali Terai lies at the northern rim of the great Gangetic plain, ranges from 60m to 300m above sea level and never exceeds more than 40km in width. The Gangetic plain runs table-flat from deep in India to the foothills of the Himalaya, the Chure Hills (known as the Siwalik Hills in India), which abruptly jump 1000m.

Several flat, wide 'valleys' known as the Inner Terai lie behind the first range of hills. These include the valley along the Narayani River (including part of Royal Chitwan National Park) and the Rapti River (east of Nepalganj).

The border with India, being a political creation, does not conform to any particular geographic barrier. To further blur the demarcation, the inhabitants on both sides come and go as they please.

The Terai accounts for 17% of Nepal's total area, but it is, in effect, the country's granary. In general, the soils are highly fertile and this, in addition to abundant water resources, permits the intensive cultivation of a wide variety of crops.

Unfortunately, outside the national parks the native forests are rapidly disappearing and suitable land is heavily exploited. Crop yields are already declining in some areas. The consequences of rapid population increase, deforestation and overworking the land are likely to be disastrous.

During the monsoon, parts of the Terai are subject to serious flooding. The relationship between deforestation in the hills and increased siltation and flooding on the plains is controversial, but there is no doubt that population growth in the hills and industrial development in the Kathmandu Valley are having a serious impact on downstream water quality. This is most critical in the dry season when many streams become mere trickles or dry up completely, and water flows are much reduced on even the major rivers.

CLIMATE

The Terai has a humid, subtropical climate with well over 1500mm of rainfall in most places. The most pleasant time to visit is November to February when you can expect daytime temperatures to average in the mid to high 20°Cs, with cool nights. From April to September temperatures in the 40°Cs are common and this combines with the additional discomfort of the monsoon from June to September.

ECONOMY

Agriculture, as elsewhere in Nepal, is the major contributor to the economy, although the Terai is also home to most of the country's manufacturing industries (with the exception of the carpet industry). More than half the gross domestic product is produced in the Terai.

Many of the Terai's advantages come back to a single fact: it's flat! Development has been assisted by the relative ease with which roads and services can be established. Roads are crucial for industry, but they also enable health and education services, as well as fertilisers and improved seeds to be delivered more efficiently.

Cash crops like sugar cane, jute, tobacco and tea are grown alongside staples like rice, wheat and maize. Land-holdings are much larger than in the hills, but the average size is still under two hectares – hardly a Texan cattle ranch – and they are shrinking as the population grows. Many families work on a share-cropping basis for large landowners and *zamindars* (moneylenders) who take at least 50% of the crop and charge crippling rates of interest. Surplus food is sold to markets in the Kathmandu Valley, although a considerable amount is also given directly to less-fortunate relatives in the hills.

Mechanised transport, proximity to Indian raw materials and the Indian market, and the availability of hydroelectric power has allowed the development of some industry. This is largely concentrated between Birganj and Hetauda, and around Biratnagar. Among other things there are jute mills, a sugar refinery, tanneries and leather factories, biscuit and cigarette factories, and drug manufacturers.

POPULATION

The population has increased rapidly since the 1950s. In 1991 (the date of the most recent census), 46.6% of the population, or over 8.6 million people, lived in the Terai. Due to migration from the mountains and hills plus a high birth rate, the population is increasing rapidly and will probably overtake that of the hills. Unfortunately, it is now clear that the Terai will not be able to absorb excess population from the hills indefinitely, yet the hill population has continued to grow. Population pressures are mounting at an alarming rate.

PEOPLE

Internal migration has meant that the indigenous people of the Terai have been joined by representatives of every ethnic group in the country. However, and not surprisingly, many people are closely related to Indian groups in Bihar and Uttar Pradesh: Indo-Aryan subsistence farmers with dark skin, and Hindu beliefs that are sometimes combined with forms of animism.

Although the common language throughout Nepal is usually Nepali, in the Terai, people are just as likely to speak Maithili, Bhojpuri or Hindi.

Maithili

The most widely spoken language of the Terai (excluding Nepali) is Maithili, a language and culture shared with people on the Bihar side of the border. It is spoken by around two million Nepalis, especially around Janakpur and Biratnagar. Maithili is the language of old Mithila and has its own script, Tirhuta, and a celebrated literature. Most of its speakers are farmers and orthodox Hindus.

Bhojpuri & Abadhi

The next most common language, Bhojpuri, is also used on both sides of the border and is spoken by around 1.5 million people in Nepal, especially around Birganj, though it mingles with Maithili.

Abadhi is another Indian-based language, spoken by around 250,000 Nepalis especially around Bhairawa and Nepalganj.

Tharu

One of the most visible groups in the Terai is the Tharu, a race who are believed to be the earliest inhabitants of the Terai (and they're even thought to be immune to malaria!). About 700,000 Tharu speakers inhabit the length of the Terai, including the Inner Terai around Chitwan, although they primarily live in the west. There are caste-like distinctions between different Tharu groups or tribes. Most have Mongoloid physical features.

Nobody is sure where they came from, although some believe they are the descendants of the Rajputs (from Rajasthan) who sent their women and children away to escape Mughal invaders in the 16th century. The women later married into local tribes. Another belief is that they are descended from the royal Sakya clan, Buddha's family, although they cannot be described as Buddhist.

Customarily the women were heavily tattooed, although these days this is unusual and tattoos are rarely seen on young women. Some groups wear simple white saris, others colourful calf-length dresses and a short blouse or bodice that exposes their belly. Tharu houses have mud-rendered walls and thatched roofs; they are high, dark and cool, with few if any windows. Reliefs of domestic animals are often moulded on the mud walls.

EASTERN TERAI

THE TERAI

Apart from farming, the Tharu are also enthusiastic hunting and fishing people. In particular, groups of young women and children will often be seen heading off on fishing expeditions. Their beliefs are largely animistic, although increasingly influenced by Hinduism, and they live a life that is cleverly adapted to their environment.

Many Tharu are heavily exploited by newly arrived hill people or zamindars. Large numbers have fallen into debt and have as a result entered into a form of bonded labour (known as the *kamaiya* system), little different from slavery.

Other Peoples

There are quite a number of smaller ethnic groups, none exceeding 40,000 people. They include the Danuwar, Darai, Djanghar, Koche, Majhi, Rajbansi, Satar and Tajpuri.

INFORMATION

There are tourist information centres at the borders at Kakarbhitta (☎ 023-20208), Birganj (☎ 051-22083), Bhairawa (☎ 071-20304) and Janakpur (☎ 041-20755), but they are of little practical help.

Most services, including post, telephone and electricity are more widely and efficiently available in the Terai than in the rest of the country.

Malaria is the main worry. Make sure you take preventative medication, especially during the monsoon. If you're coming from westernised Kathmandu you may have been lulled into a false sense of security. Don't drink water or use ice unless you know it has been boiled or properly treated. Skip the dairy products (with the exception of curd) and salads, and peel the fruit. Wash your hands before eating. (See the Health section in the Facts for the Visitor chapter for more details.)

GETTING THERE & AWAY

The Terai is easily accessible from West Bengal, Bihar and Uttar Pradesh in India and from Kathmandu and Pokhara. Bus and plane services are frequent and relatively cheap. The long-distance express buses are even reasonably comfortable, if not entirely safe. The Indian railway system runs close to the border at several points, but most people use the buses because they are much quicker.

Air

Royal Nepal Airlines, Buddha Air, Necon Air, Cosmic Air and Gorkha Airlines all fly to a number of towns in the Terai from Kathmandu. Royal Nepal services from Kathmandu include Bharatpur ($55, daily), Biratnagar ($77, daily), Janakpur ($55, six times weekly), Simara (for those going to Birganj, $44, daily) and Nepalganj ($99, daily). There are also services from the Terai regional hub of Nepalganj to Dhangadhi and Mahendranagar.

See the Getting There & Away sections in each town for more details.

Land

Roads enter the Terai at numerous border crossings in the south. Most travellers going to or from Nepal cross the border at Nautanwa (India) to Sunauli/Bhairawa (Nepal), but other crossings used regularly include: Raxaul Bazaar (India) to Birganj (Nepal); and in the extreme east of the country, from Siliguri (India, near Darjeeling) to Kakarbhitta (Nepal).

See the Getting There & Away chapter for travel on these routes.

GETTING AROUND
Bus

Although airlines service all the major centres, buses are the way most normal mortals travel. This can be a serious penance, for although the price is not high when measured in rupees, it can be in terms of comfort and sanity! The express buses (often running at night only) are usually OK, although wherever possible you should check with a local as to which are the best companies.

Unfortunately, most day buses are of the stopping-all-stations variety and they can be horrifically crowded. Bodies occupy or cling to every possible centimetre. Under these circumstances, the most comfortable place to be is the roof, although you will need to protect yourself from the elements. The problem is that if you don't travel by day, you miss the views and if you do travel by day you run the risk of missing the views (because you are jammed inside a bus) and suffering extreme discomfort.

Whether you travel by day or night, you'll get plenty of excitement. Combine high speeds with poorly maintained vehicles, suicidal overtaking manoeuvres, animals, trucks, children, rickshaws, unmarked roadworks, invincible pedestrians and the potential is obvious – and usually graphically illustrated by wrecked trucks and buses alongside the road. Although buses can't plummet over cliffs on the Terai, they can wind up to impressive speeds ...

See the Getting Around chapter for more details on bus travel.

Car

If you are travelling in a group, or if you have the necessary funds, it is worth considering hiring a car and driver in Kathmandu to explore the Terai. When shared among a group, this is reasonably priced at around $40 per day, plus petrol, for a Toyota Corolla (which would seat three passengers), and it has obvious advantages.

Bicycle

Another alternative is to ride a bike, preferably a mountain bike that is sufficiently sturdy to deal with rough roads. Cycling conditions are ideal: motorised traffic is relatively sparse on the Mahendra Hwy, there are villages at regular intervals, the climate during winter is mild and dry, and the countryside is beautiful and mostly flat.

Getting to the Terai from Kathmandu you either have to tackle the daunting Tribhuvan Hwy via Daman (2322m!), or the section of the Kathmandu-Pokhara (Prithvi) Hwy between Kathmandu and Mugling, which is very busy and dangerous. Consider catching buses over these sections.

See the Mountain Biking chapter for more details.

Royal Chitwan National Park

☎ 056

From the 19th century on, the Chitwan Valley was a centre for the hunting trips that British and Nepali aristocrats found so entertaining. King George V and his son the Prince of Wales, later Edward VIII, never made it to Kathmandu, but they did find time to slaughter wildlife in the Chitwan forests. In 11 fun-packed days during one safari in 1911 they killed 39 tigers and 18 rhinos.

Yet occasional hunting forays into the park did not seriously jeopardise the Terai's wildlife. In fact, the region's status as a hunting reserve probably helped protect it. However, after the success of the malaria eradication program that began in 1954, the survival of tigers and rhinos was soon threatened.

Until the late 1950s, the only settlements in the Chitwan Valley were scattered Tharu villages inhabited by people whose apparent immunity to malaria was rumoured to be the result of their heavy drinking! After malaria was largely controlled by liberal applications of DDT, land-hungry people from the hills were quick to see the potential wealth of the region and the jungle was rapidly transformed into farmland.

As their habitat disappeared so did the tigers and rhinos. By 1973 the rhino population of Chitwan was estimated to have fallen to 100 and there were only 20 tigers left. (Compare those numbers with the British royals' epic hunting trip 60 years earlier!) Fortunately, this disastrous slide was halted when a sanctuary was established in 1964, although this was at the expense of 22,000 people who were forcibly removed from within its boundaries. The national park was proclaimed in 1973 and since that time the animal population has rebounded. Chitwan now contains an estimated 465-plus rhinos and 80 tigers, quite apart from 50 other species of mammals and over 450 different types of bird.

Today the park offers one of the finest wildlife experiences in Asia, although it cannot be compared to the great game reserves of Africa. The wildlife is not as varied or great in number and the high grass and often dense forest mean the animals are much more difficult than those in Africa to find and observe. You have to be extremely lucky to see one of the park's elusive tigers or leopards. On the other hand, an elephant safari is an unforgettable experience, and you are almost certain to see rhinos, various species of deer, monkeys and numerous species of birds.

As with many other national parks throughout the world the park authorities have to tread a careful line between keeping the local people content and protecting the animals of the park. An often heavy-handed army presence, which involves over 1000 men, has kept poaching and woodcutting to a minimum. This no doubt contributes to local resentment, but the two most significant problems are that the park ties up

ROYAL CHITWAN NATIONAL PARK

potential farming land and timber resources, and that surrounding crops are frequently damaged by the park's animals.

The animals do not respect the park's boundaries. Rhinos wander out in November to wreak havoc on rice crops, and then again in February and March when they attack mustard, lentils and wheat. Deer, monkeys and wild pigs also cause a great deal of damage. The little lookout towers (*machan*) you see in many fields outside the park are used by watchers who spend their nights in the

fields waiting to scare off encroaching animals. Fortunately, tiger and crocodile attacks are rare, but there have been fatalities.

On the positive side, in February each year neighbouring villagers are allowed into the park to harvest a number of grass species. Grass has numerous traditional uses, including roof thatching, and provides a valuable cash crop. Working for the park lodges also provides local employment. In contrast to the expensive lodges inside the park, where much of the money goes to

ROYAL CHITWAN NATIONAL PARK

owners in Kathmandu or overseas, many of the budget Sauraha lodges funnel money straight into the pockets of local families (although canny Kathmandu entrepreneurs are also heavily present).

The park is easily accessible from Kathmandu or Pokhara and is actually en route for those heading to/from the Indian border at Birganj and points east, and only a short detour if coming to/from western Nepal or the border at Sunauli. There is something for every budget: at one extreme you can spend $350 a night to stay at the famous Tiger Tops Lodge, while at the other extreme a simple double room in one of the many small lodges in Sauraha, right on the edge of the park in a prime game-viewing area, costs less than $2 a night.

Numerous travel agents in western countries, as well as in Pokhara and Kathmandu, offer package tours to the park. This is the best approach if you plan to stay at one of the expensive lodges inside the park as you can book directly at the lodges' Kathmandu head offices and the package deals usually work out to be better value than the nightly rack rate.

However, packages are both unnecessary and relatively expensive if you plan to stay in the budget lodges at Sauraha. The booking agent obviously has to make money on the deal (which adds to the cost), and although you save a little effort, you pay for this by committing yourself to a particular lodge (which you may or may not like) and to a limited time frame.

Many people find the two night, three day packages too short, because by the time you subtract travelling time (between six and seven hours by bus from Kathmandu or Pokhara) you only have one full day to explore. For most, a visit of two full days is sufficient, although the peaceful atmosphere, good-value accommodation in Sauraha, and the range of available activities can easily tempt you into staying longer.

GEOGRAPHY

Along most of the Terai the Gangetic plain runs to the foot of the Chure Hills (which then merge with the higher Mahabharat Range), but here the Someshwar Hills form the Chitwan Valley, also described as the Inner Terai, which lies between the two.

To the north the park comprises a narrow strip of floodplain along the Narayani and Rapti rivers, a part of the Chitwan Valley and the most visited section of the park. South of this the bulk of the park encompasses the Someshwar Hills, which reach a maximum height of 738m, and are largely inaccessible to visitors. In the east the national park is adjoined by the Parsa Wildlife Reserve, which is not developed for visitors, but provides important additional territory for wildlife.

The park includes a number of small lakes or *tal*. The most interesting, particularly for viewing water birds, are Devi Tal near Tiger Tops, Lami Tal near Kasara, and Bis Hajaar Tal (literally '20,000 lakes') north-west of Sauraha.

The park covers 932 sq km, while the adjoining Parsa Wildlife Reserve covers 499 sq km.

FLORA & FAUNA
Flora
The park has three basic vegetation types – open grassland (which constitutes 20% of the park area); riverine forest (7%); and hardwood forest (73%) that is dominated by sal trees (*Shorea ribusta*). The forests also have *shisham*, kapok, *palash* (or flame-of-the-forest), pipal, strangler fig and the scarlet-flowered *kusum* trees.

Fauna
Chitwan has over 43 different species of mammals; birdwatchers can search for 450 different bird types; and in 1987-88 butterfly spotters identified 67 different types of butterflies at the Machan Resort. Some of the most interesting creatures to be seen in Chitwan include elephants, rhinos and tigers.

Elephant Although you're likely to see more elephants (*hathi*) than any other Chitwan animal, there are no wild elephants in

Flora

The Terai is subtropical, and the flora reflects this. Rapid development has led to large-scale deforestation but fortunately, a surprising amount of forest remains.

Substantial areas are still cloaked in sal *(Shorea robusta)* forests. These forests characteristically grow on well-drained soils and form relatively homogeneous communities. Sal is a magnificent, highly valued hardwood. It grows straight and true (averaging 30m when mature), and has long been used by builders and woodcarvers. The longevity of the buildings and the carvings in the Kathmandu Valley is due to the strength and durability of this wood.

On swampier ground there are scrubby forests of khair *(Acacia catechu)* and shisham *(Dalbergia sissoo)*. Simal trees *(Bombax ceiba)* stand out above the others. They are notable for their spring display of large red flowers and when they are old they develop huge buttresses at their base.

There are also grasslands that form a diverse and complex community of over 50 species. Elephant grasses (the saccharum family) can grow up to 8m high, but there are also shorter species like khar that are vital for thatching.

the park. Chitwan's elephants are all trained Asian, or Indian, elephants.

Training an elephant takes about two years and the Chitwan elephants are usually acquired when they're eight to 20 years old, and can be expected to work until they are 40 or 50. Even elephants born in Nepal (not that there are many) have to go to India to be trained. A trained elephant is not cheap to purchase or to maintain. Typically they cost at least $3000 to buy and then have to be provided with 270kg to 300kg of food a day.

When you're out on an elephant safari you'll see how even that isn't enough; they're constantly pulling up clumps of grass or other tasty vegetation, and shaking it around to dislodge insects and dirt before stuffing it into their mouths. Their drinking capacity is just as impressive – an elephant needs more than 200L a day.

Keeping each elephant happy requires a support team of two or three people. The elephant's rider or master, most commonly known as a mahout, is a *pahit* in Nepali. A pahit comes from India with the elephant and stays for three years while a local pahit is trained. The local pahit then stays with the elephant for life. He is backed up by one or two assistants (*patchouas*) whose main task is gathering the fodder to cater for an elephant's healthy appetite. They also assist the pahit when he saddles up the elephant with its howdah, the riding platform for passengers.

Notice the different ways elephants are ridden. At some lodges the howdah will be a square railed-in platform carrying one passenger at each corner, while at Sauraha the elephants often carry the pahit and two passengers, all three sitting astride the elephant's back.

The elephant has one of nature's most versatile appendages, a combination of nose and upper lip. The trunk has 100,000 muscles and can hold over 9L of water.

It is not simply ear size that distinguishes Indian (Asian) and African elephants; scientifically speaking, the two species are not as closely related as you might think.

Feature	Asian Elephant	African Elephant
toes	five front	four front
	four rear	three rear
ears	fold forward	fold back
	India shaped	
tail		bristly
trunk	one finger	two fingers
trunk	white patches	white stripes

THE TERAI

The Indian elephant is noticeably smaller (males reach an average height of 2.75m and females grow to 2.45m), has smaller ears, a bulbous head and convex back. Only the males, but not all of them, have tusks. The African elephant has enormous ears, a sloping head and a concave back; both the male and female have tusks. The Indian elephant has four nails on each hind foot where the African has only three.

Another major difference, as far as humans are concerned, is the domestication of these huge creatures. Indian elephants are easily trained, African elephants are not; though some people say that any elephant can be trained, and it is simply that in Africa training elephants has not been widely attempted.

Elephants have a gestation period of 22 months and the mother is always assisted by another female in looking after the young calf. The calf is fed for three years and there is usually about seven years between pregnancies, although the elephants are in musth once a year. In the wild, the elephants live in a basically matriarchal society; the bulls do not travel with the herd. Elephants have four teeth and grow six sets during their life. Once the sixth set is worn out the elephant dies of starvation.

Elephant Commands

If you have aspirations of becoming a pahit you'll first have to learn some elephant commands, although each pahit will have his own particular words and ways of saying them:

sit	*baith*
lie down	*sut*
stand up	*maile*
hold your trunk out for me to climb up	*utha*
stop	*rhaa*
go	*agat*
shower me	*chhop*

The numerous rivers in the parks have some fine swimming holes and if you're staying at one of the park lodges you'll kick yourself if you pass up the opportunity to lend a hand at elephant bath time. On a hot day in the Terai there's no better way of cooling off than to sit on an elephant's back in a river and shout *chhop*. If your accent is right you'll be rewarded with a refreshing cold shower!

Rhinoceros While elephants are the creatures you see most often in Chitwan, it's the rhinoceros *(gaida)* you spend most time looking for, and with most hope of success. There are two types of rhino in Africa and three in Asia. The great Indian one-horned rhino, found in Chitwan, is larger than the African black rhino although smaller than the African white. A fully grown Indian rhino can reach 180cm at the shoulder and weigh more than two tonnes.

Rhinos are generally solitary creatures although several may occupy the same area. Their diet is chiefly grass and they have very poor eyesight although their senses of smell and hearing are good. It's their poor sight which leads to the rhino's reputation for bad temper. As they cannot see very well, rhinoceroses are prone to assume almost any shape might be dangerous, so they charge it just in case.

Fortunately for the Indian rhino, its horn is not as large as the African variety and therefore not so valuable to the poachers. Nevertheless, there are many superstitions about rhinos and almost every part of the creature is of value – the urine is considered a charm against disease and ghosts, a rhino-skin bracelet wards off evil spirits, rhino blood cures menstrual problems, and the horn is used for medicinal purposes and is famed as a sexual stimulant. Its value for Arab dagger handles has led to the disastrous decline in rhino numbers in Africa. Along the riverbanks in Chitwan a rhino would mark its territory by dropping excreta in mounds. Since they walked backwards to approach these mounds a waiting poacher had easy prey.

Wildlife Watch

The fauna of the Terai is striking although, as always, shy. From the road, the most obvious species are the handsome black-faced, grey langur monkeys *(bandar)* and the common, brownish-red rhesus monkeys. You may also catch a glimpse of some of the many species of deer – including the spotted (chital), barking *(mirga)*, sambar *(jarayo)*, hog *(laghuna)* and swamp deer. The blue cow *(nilgai)*, Asia's largest antelope, is also quite common, but you won't see this unless you make an effort.

The largest mammal is the Asian elephant, although it is likely there are now only a few individuals surviving in the wild at Royal Bardia National Park and Sukla Phanta Wildlife Reserve. Not far behind in scale and impressiveness is the great Indian one-horned rhinoceros, which can be seen at Chitwan.

There are a number of carnivores, the most magnificent being the royal Bengal tiger *(bagh)* that, thanks to the Terai's national parks, seems to have escaped extinction. There are also leopards *(chituwa)*, wild dogs, jackals, civets, various species of mongoose and cats.

You might also find sloth bears *(bhalu)*, wild boars, porcupines, hares, bats, squirrels and snakes *(sarpa)* – some of which are poisonous (cobra, krait and viper).

The rivers and lakes are home to small numbers of mugger and gharial crocodiles, and the extraordinary Gangetic dolphin.

The Terai is also a birdwatcher's delight with more than 450 migrant and local species recorded. There are cormorants, herons, egrets, storks, cranes, ibis, ducks, kites, goshawks, hawks, eagles, osprey, falcons, kestrels, quail curlews, sandpipers, snipes, gulls, terns, pigeons, parakeets, cuckoos, owls, kingfishers, woodpeckers, swallows, orioles, drongos, babblers, flycatchers, warblers ...

The invertebrates range from butterflies to mosquitoes!

Tiger Chitwan's tigers are probably the most elusive of the park's wildlife. Without artificial assistance, such as staking a young buffalo calf out as live bait, you would be very lucky to see a tiger *(bagh)* in Chitwan. Though their numbers have increased considerably since the park was opened, tigers are solitary creatures and they mainly hunt by night.

Tigers require an enormous amount of space. A male commands a territory of about 60 sq km, and a female about 16 or 17 sq km. Both sexes occupy an exclusive territory although a male's territory may overlap with several females. Chitwan is simply not big enough to support the 50 breeding adults which is felt to be the minimum number to prevent interbreeding. This is part of the reason the adjoining Parsa Wildlife Reserve was proclaimed.

Some Nepalis believe that tigers are the unsettled souls of the dead.

Other Mammals Chitwan is also known for more than 50 other mammals. Leopards *(chituwa)* are as elusive as tigers and the night prowling sloth bears *(bhalu)* are also rarely seen.

Chitwan has four types of deer and you will often catch a fleeting glimpse of them as they dash through the undergrowth. There's the tiny barking deer *(mirga)*, the attractive spotted deer *(chital)*, the hog deer *(laghuna)* and the big sambar deer *(jarayo)*. Gaur, the world's largest wild cattle, are also found in the park.

Langur monkeys *(bandar)* are a common sight, chattering noisily in the tree tops or scattering vegetation down below. The spotted deer often follow the langurs around, taking advantage of their profligate feeding habits. The smaller macaque monkeys are the monkeys commonly found at temples in Nepal and all over the subcontinent. Freshwater or Gangetic dolphins are found in some river stretches in the park, but they are rarely seen.

Reptiles Chitwan has snakes *(sarpa)* of course, including some impressive pythons, plus turtles and two types of crocodiles. The marsh muggers are found in marshes, lakes and occasionally in rivers while the rarer gharial crocodile is exclusively found in rivers. The gharial, which grows to 7m in length and is a harmless fish eater, was in danger of extinction and is still very rare. The gharial breeding centre near Kasara, the park headquarters, has had considerable success, hatching eggs and raising the youngsters to a reasonable size before releasing them into Terai rivers.

WHEN TO GO

Many of the park lodges are closed during the May to August monsoon months when visibility is very poor, the ground is muddy and the flooding rivers make large parts of the park inaccessible. In September the lodges begin to reopen, although at first the rivers are still too high for 4WDs and transfers to the lodges can only be made by elephant.

The best time to visit Chitwan is from October to February when the average daily temperature is 25°C. There are still cold, misty mornings, however, so a warm jacket is recommended. The Terai can be extremely hot and sticky, and even in October the humidity leaves everything feeling permanently damp.

From mid-January to the end of February the local villagers are allowed into the park to cut grass, which is an important part of the local economy. The grasslands are then burnt. While the villagers are crashing about, game is understandably scarce, but February through May is a prime time for game viewing, thanks to the fact that the grass cover has been removed. Sporadic thunderstorms begin in April and the weather becomes unpleasantly hot.

WHAT TO BRING

Park visitors should come prepared for every eventuality. At times the Terai can be stiflingly hot so cool clothes are essential. However, the sun can be fierce and there's not much shade when sitting on an elephant's back, so long sleeves, a shady hat and a good sunscreen are necessary. At the other extreme, winter months can be surprisingly chilly, particularly if you're out on foot or on elephant back at dawn. So, from November to February you should come prepared for the cold with sweaters and a jacket. Good walking shoes (that you don't mind getting wet) are essential at any time of year and you'll want a swimsuit for the rivers.

Neutral colours are best to ensure you blend into the background and are less likely to alert the wildlife. Reds, yellows and whites are particularly conspicuous.

Insect repellent is another Terai necessity. There is still a risk of malaria, and there are plenty of mosquitoes and a wide variety of other voracious insects. Even people who are normally immune to insect attack may discover later that while they were propping up the bar in the evening a full-scale attack was being mounted on their ankles.

In addition to camera gear, preferably with a telephoto lens, binoculars are invaluable.

Warning

Come prepared for Nepal's famous *jukha* (leeches). These operate in force during the monsoon and will still be waiting for unwary jungle walkers during the first month or two of the dry season. See the Health section in the Facts for the Visitor chapter for tips on how to deal with these pests.

There is also a small risk of contracting typhus fever from a tick bite. Check with your guide whether they are a problem, and inspect exposed skin after walking.

INFORMATION

The park entry fee is Rs 1000 and is valid for two days. If you're staying at a lodge in the park this will usually be included in your overall charge, but if you stay outside the park in Sauraha you have to pay the fee yourself. This can be arranged by most Sauraha guesthouses, or you can easily get it yourself from the ranger's office next to the park visitor centre, where you also book rides on government-owned elephants.

The ticket office and visitor centre in Sauraha are open from 6 to 9.30 am and 1.30 to 4.30 pm daily. The visitor centre has an interesting, small museum with exhibits about the park, its creation, the problems it faces and its wildlife. The park headquarters are farther west at Kasara where there is a small museum of skulls and a gharial crocodile breeding project.

There's no bank in Sauraha, but there are a couple of private moneychangers which accept major currencies (cash and cheques).

See the Books section in the Facts for the Visitor chapter for books on wildlife and the park.

There's only one STD phone service in the village, and it has a shared line with poor connections. The best bet for important communication is to try Hello World Communication Service in Tadi Bazaar.

The telephone STD area code is 056.

THINGS TO SEE & DO
Elephant Rides

The greatest thrill at Chitwan is the traditional elephant safari in search of wildlife;

THE TERAI

seeing a rhino from atop an elephant is an experience not to be missed. You won't want to spend your entire visit aboard an elephant, however. It is not a comfortable mode of travel and your first ride is likely to leave you with aches in muscles you didn't know you had, not to mention an interesting selection of bruises!

The lodges inside the park have their own elephants and safaris are a standard activity; two, three or sometimes four passengers ride on a wooden-railed howdah.

At Sauraha, government-owned elephants are available for one to 1½-hour excursions into the park costing Rs 650. Howdahs are not used and two or three passengers sit astride the elephant's back. At peak times the number of visitors exceeds the supply of elephants so it's wise to book your elephant ahead of time; the lodges will generally offer to do this for you. It's easy to make a booking yourself at the ranger's office near the visitor centre, although there can sometimes be a queue. Elephant safaris usually start in the early morning or late afternoon, prime game-viewing times; the government elephants leave at 7.30 am and 4 pm.

Several Sauraha lodges have elephants of their own. The going rate for a two hour safari varies from Rs 400 to Rs 550, but they are restricted to the Baghmara Community Forest, a buffer zone a few kilometres west of the park. While there are still plenty of

trees, the zone is heavily utilised by local villagers grazing animals and collecting fodder and firewood, so it is by no means a wilderness. Some people have seen rhinos and leopards here, and the operators (naturally) claim that game-watching here is as good as in the park. This is extremely unlikely, however, given the proximity of villages and the presence of so many people. If you only have time and money for one ride you are much better off going into the park proper.

When booking a package tour in Kathmandu, or an elephant ride through a lodge, make sure you check whether your ride will take you inside or outside the park. People have been charged Rs 650 for a ride on one of the private elephants and have been misled into thinking that the buffer zone is actually part of the park proper. Ask to see your park entry ticket if you are being taken inside the park.

Jungle Walks

Visitors are allowed to enter the park on foot, but in order to get the most out of the experience, and for reasons of safety, it is best to go with a guide. Most lodges (including some in Sauraha) have their own naturalists, but there are also a number of independent guides. These young locals may not have much formal training, but they're often very knowledgeable about the park's wildlife and where to find it.

Walking is the ideal way to see the park's prolific butterflies and birds, and to see the flora close up. Walks, often nothing more than a pleasant stroll through the jungle, can be exhilarating, but dangerous (see warning following), if you meet a rhino.

Jungle walks from Sauraha usually cost around Rs 60 per person for two hours, Rs 250 for half a day, and Rs 400 for a full day. Short walks will generally cover grassland and riverine forest; you need a day to get into the jungle. Walks can also be combined with canoe trips (see the Canoeing section). Some lodges and guides organise longer overnight treks into remote parts of the park.

Warning

! ● Tourists and guides have been fatally injured by rhinos. Tigers and sloth bears can also be dangerous. Guides should brief you on safety procedures at the beginning of the walk. Many locals regard these walks as dangerous but offer themselves as guides to remain employed. If they refuse to take tourists on guided walks they risk losing their jobs. It's a potentially risky activity (for both guides and tourists) which is perhaps best avoided.

Canoeing

A canoe trip along the Rapti or Narayani rivers is the most restful way of seeing the wildlife, particularly water birds, and with a bit of luck you may also see mugger and gharial crocodiles. With a great deal of luck you might catch a glimpse of a freshwater Gangetic dolphin, although they are as rare a sight as tigers.

Canoe trips from Saraha cost around Rs 100 per person, but trips are normally combined with a walk. The standard program is a one hour float downriver, followed by a three hour guided walk back to the village (costing around Rs 300 in total).

Jeep Safaris

Animals are surprisingly unconcerned by vehicles, so a jeep safari can be more productive than you might expect. It also gives you a chance to get beyond the immediate Saraha area. Most jeep rides take three or four hours and include a visit to the park headquarters at Kasara, about 20km west of Saraha, and the nearby gharial breeding centre. The cost is around Rs 600 per person. Bear in mind that jeeps may not be able to get across the river into the park until the water levels drop sufficiently (maybe from January to April).

Terai Culture

Staying in Saraha gives you an excellent opportunity to explore the surrounding countryside, either on foot or bicycle. Originally, the area was dominated by Tharu, but over the last decade increasing numbers of hill people have bought up the land. Many villages are now a multicultural mixture. They're full of life (and hordes of children) and give a vivid insight into the rigours and pleasures of subsistence farming. The nearest Tharu village is **Bachauli**, east of Saraha towards the Gaida Wildlife Camp.

Some lodges arrange visits to nearby villages and a number organise displays of traditional Tharu dances. The stick dance, with a great circle of men whacking their sticks together, is quite a sight. In Saraha it's usually easy enough to find a lodge

where there will be a performance. Non-guest visitors are charged around Rs 50.

Wildlife Breeding

There are two important breeding projects associated with the national park: the elephant breeding camp 3km west of Saraha is worth visiting, as is the gharial breeding centre near Kasara.

Cycling

Unfortunately, bicycles are not allowed into the park proper – apparently nothing infuriates a rhino more than a bike – but the surrounding countryside is ideal for touring. You can hire standard Indian-made single-speed bicycles in Tadi Bazaar and Saraha for around Rs 60 per day, and these are adequate for negotiating the dusty tracks as long as you are not too ambitious about the distance you want to cover.

Just wandering along the tracks east and west of Saraha is good fun, but if you like to have a specific destination, consider a trip to Bis Hajaar Tal (20,000 lakes) about 1½ hours north-west of Saraha. The lake is famous for its prolific birdlife. To get there, ride to Tadi, turn left (west) onto the Mahendra Hwy at Tadi and continue for about 3km until you reach a signposted bridge over the Khageri Khola. Cross the bridge and take the dirt road on the left (south). After another small bridge the road forks; take the right fork and continue for about 5km. The lake is on the right.

PLACES TO STAY

Basically you can stay inside the park, or at Saraha, and the division between cheap and expensive places to stay is almost equally straightforward – most of the expensive places are inside, and the cheap ones are at Saraha.

For those who can afford it, the lodges inside the park offer considerable luxury, well organised game-watching activities, and an all-encompassing safari atmosphere. Although they can be pretty basic, the Saraha lodges often have an interesting clientele, are scattered around an attractive, partly

THE TERAI

traditional village, and the full range of game-watching activities can be easily organised. When it comes to seeing the wildlife there's little difference between the two options. You've got just as much chance of seeing a rhino whether your room costs $2 or $200 a night.

Inside the Park

Most visitors to the park lodges arrive on package tours from Kathmandu, often as part of a larger tour of Nepal or the region. Advance bookings are necessary. Most of the lodges have attractive individual cottages dotted around a central dining room and bar area. Some have 'tented camps' with luxurious, semi-permanent tents – usually you won't have a private bathroom, but you certainly won't be uncomfortable.

The lodges generally quote either daily charge, which covers activities (including rides on their privately owned elephants) and all meals, but not park entry or the park's camping fee if you stay in a tented camp; or an all-inclusive two or three day package that includes transport from Kathmandu. The only additional expenses will be for drinks and tips.

Tiger Tops (☎ 01-411225, fax 414075, PO Box 242, Durbar Marg, Kathmandu, email info@tigermountain.com) is the best known and easily the most expensive of the lodges. This pioneer Chitwan jungle lodge is operated under the umbrella of Tiger Mountain, a very professional organisation, and enjoys a deservedly high reputation, particularly for its excellent guides and environmentally conscious approach. Whether you think it is worth the amount of money charged probably depends on how much money you have. (Children under 12 receive a 50% discount.) Although the accommodation is comfortable and the food good, those expecting to be pandered to with extravagant five star luxury could be disappointed. Tiger Tops has chosen neither to expand, nor to compromise the safari experience with unnecessary technological and consumerist trappings.

There are actually three Tiger Tops operations in the park. The well known *Jungle Lodge* ($450/600 a night including tax), is the original tree-top hotel. The buildings are on stilts and are constructed from local materials. Rooms are comfortable, the water is solar-heated, but there is no electricity. Open 1 Sept to mid-June, closed for the monsoon.

The *Tented Camp* ($225/300 a night) is 3km east of the lodge in the beautiful Surung Valley. There are 12 safari tents with twin beds and modern toilet and shower amenities. Open 1 October to 30 April.

Tharu Village Safari Resort ($150/200 a night) is the newest addition, and is open all year round. It is built in traditional Tharu style: the long houses are constructed from timber, grass reeds and mud, and decorated with wall paintings. The rooms are attractive and comfortable; each has a queen-size and single bed, and a private bath, and there's a swimming pool. The village is actually just outside the park on the northern bank of the Narayani River.

Temple Tiger (☎ 01-221585, fax 220178, PO Box 3968, Kantipath, Kathmandu) is at the western end of the park, not far from Tiger Tops. Accommodation consists of comfortable elevated individual cabins built largely from local materials, and each with a private viewing area over the grasslands. Minimal forest clearance has taken place here, so the atmosphere is really one of a jungle camp. The daily rate is an excessive $300/400, plus the park entry fee. Children aged three to 12 are charged 50%.

Island Jungle Resort (☎ 01-220162, fax 225615, email island@mos.com.np, PO Box 2154, Durbar Marg, Kathmandu) is also at the western end of the park on a large island in the middle of the Narayani River. The site is superb, one of the best in the park. Accommodation consists of cottages which, although comfortable, are not particularly attractive. The cost is $160/220 a day, although packages can be considerably cheaper, and very good value. There's also tented camp accommodation, which costs $130/200. Children aged three to 10 are charged 50%.

Farther east is *Gaida Wildlife Camp* (☎ 01-220940, fax 227292, PO Box 2056, Durbar Marg, Kathmandu, email gaida@

mos.com.np) which is not far from Sauraha in the only section of park north of the Narayani River. The *Gaida Wildlife Jungle Camp* is 8km south at the base of the Someshwar Hills. The main camp has comfortable thatched huts ($170/220), and the jungle camp has safari tents ($120/160). The wildlife is not particularly prolific immediately around the main camp, but is very good around the jungle camp, which is open October to May.

At the eastern end of the park the *Chitwan Jungle Lodge* (☎ 01-228458, fax 228439, email wildlife@resort.wlink.com.np, PO Box 1281, Durbar Marg, Kathmandu) has rooms constructed in traditional Tharu style with mud walls and thatched roofs. There's no electricity but otherwise the rustic lodge has all mod cons including a restaurant, private baths, and a very pleasant open-air bar. The forest is relatively undisturbed in this part of the park and a river with a terrific swimming (and elephant-bathing) hole runs very close by. A package is $255/400 for a stay of two nights and includes land transport from Kathmandu. If you want to get there by raft then the cost increases by about $100 per person.

Finally, at the eastern end of the park, close to the boundary of the adjoining Parsa Wildlife Reserve, is *Machan Wildlife Resort* (☎ 01-225001, fax 240681, PO Box 78, Durbar Marg, Kathmandu, email wildlife @machan.mos.com.np). This is a particularly attractive resort, but the wildlife is said to be scarcer at this end of the park. Machan compensates by offering excellent facilities including an attractive natural swimming pool and a video library of wildlife films. The accommodation is in well designed timber-frame bungalows with baths, and is decorated with superb Mithila murals. The cost is $205/250 for the first night, with additional nights at $180/200. Return transfers from Kathmandu cost $110 by air and $60 by car.

Sauraha

Sauraha is just outside the park on the northern bank of the Rapti River, which forms the park's boundary. It lies 6km south of Tadi Bazaar (on the Mahendra Hwy).

Sauraha is a simple, quiet little village, accessible only on foot, by jeep or bicycle. It's the sort of place nobody would usually visit – so it provides a good opportunity to observe rural life. There are verdant rice fields, neat mud-walled houses, barns and a village well in the 'centre' of town. Ox carts rumble by and there's a constant background scene of ducks, chickens and children.

Progress is, however, making its inexorable mark and although it is still a very pleasant place to spend a few days, it is showing signs that it could degenerate into a Terai Thamel. Unfortunately, as elsewhere, there appears to be a complete absence of planning and little or no control over new developments.

The welcome given by the touts at the footbridge across the river at Chitrasali between Tadi Bazaar and Sauraha is the worst part of a visit to Sauraha, although it's usually pretty low-key. Treat all their claims with scepticism and definitely do not pay them for any tickets or tours until you have shopped around.

Normally, jeeps from Chitrasali to Sauraha cost Rs 30, so the touts' first gambit is to offer you a cheap, or even free, ride to a lodge. In theory this places you under no obligation, but in practice it's not easy to avoid staying. You are much better off to pay the Rs 30 (hardly a king's ransom) and make it absolutely clear that you intend to check a few different places before you commit yourself.

There are so many lodges and competition is so intense that prices are ridiculously low. Many lodges have therefore come to depend on 'invisible' add-on charges (commissions or service charges for organising bus tickets and game-watching activities) to make a profit. While there is nothing wrong with a charge for services rendered, they can get completely out of hand in Sauraha. Prices are sometimes inflated by ridiculous amounts – particularly since in almost all cases it's easy and straightforward to organise tickets and activities yourself.

THE TERAI

With literally dozens of places, it is impossible to mention them all here. There's a certain lack of originality when it comes to naming these places; it seems they almost all have a three word name taken from a list of about half a dozen words – jungle, safari, Chitwan, tiger, camp, wildlife and river all feature prominently. Although most places have a telephone number, in the smaller places this is often just a nearby private STD phone office.

The most important variable is the quality of the staff and your fellow travellers, both of which change, so ask other travellers for recommendations and check places for yourself. The main north-south road is busier and more developed than the east-west roads.

Budget The budget lodges at Sauraha are all very much out of the same mould: clean and simple mud-and-thatch cottages that sleep two and cost around Rs 100 for doubles. Most have a small veranda, and those with a nice garden can be very pleasant places to stay. The mud-wall architecture keeps things surprisingly cool, and the rooms have insect screens on the windows and/or mosquito nets on the beds. Toilet and bath facilities are shared; hot water is unlikely, but this is not a major problem given the climate.

Chitwan Safari Camp (☎ 23453) has a pleasant garden and a quiet, but central position. It's old-fashioned and simple, and although it is a fraction more expensive than some of the other budget places (Rs 100 to Rs 300 for doubles) you really can't quibble at the price.

Annapurna View Lodge (☎ 29363) is another decent budget place with a nice atmosphere. Cottages cost Rs 100, or with bath it's Rs 150/300. Next door, the *Crocodile Safari Camp* is busy and friendly with standard rooms for Rs 100 and double rooms with private bath for Rs 300. The restaurant is good, but the garden is only ordinary.

Also in this area is the *Skyline Jungle Camp* (☎ 60172), a new place with standard brick cottages at Rs 100, and doubles with bath for Rs 300. The rooms have a shady, verdant veranda.

Nature Safari Camp, farther along the same track, is a modern concrete construction, but the rooms and bathroom facilities are good. Standard rooms are good value at Rs 80 with common bath, and there are also a few with agreeable outlooks and private baths for the bargain rate of Rs 200.

Rainforest Guest House, at the northern end of town, is a quiet and shady budget place with mud and thatch cottages for Rs 100/150, or brick cottages at Rs 300 with bath. This place has a large garden but little shade.

Travellers' Jungle Camp (☎ 29363) is a friendly place with mud-and-thatch cottages at Rs 100, or brick cottages with attached bath at Rs 300 and Rs 400. This is a good family-run place with helpful owners.

Chitwan Resort Camp has clean and decent rooms with private bath for Rs 400, and the restaurant is quite good.

Hotel Wildlife Camp (☎ 29363) has good small cottages with attached bath at Rs 150, and larger rooms for Rs 250 and Rs 400.

Tharu Lodge is a mellow little place close to the river with a nice garden. It's just off the track leading to the elephant breeding centre. Standard mud-and-thatch cottages cost Rs 100, or brick cottages with bath cost Rs 300.

Mid-Range An increasing number of lodges are moving upmarket, or at the very least adding some brick cottages with baths and more-or-less guaranteed hot water.

There are also a number of mid-range places dependent on the package trade which are happy to take on individuals if there are vacancies. Some are pretty good value with slightly more comfortable rooms and private bath from around $7/10 a single/double. Many of these places, eg the Rhino Lodge, Chitwan Tiger Camp, Jungle Nepal Resort Camp among others, have offices in Kathmandu and Pokhara.

The standard tour offered is three days and two nights, including transport, food, accommodation, entry fees, jungle walks, a canoe trip, an elephant ride, a performance of Tharu folk dancing and a tour of a Tharu village. Typically, the packages cost around $85 if you travel to the park by bus, or around $140 if you travel by private car – it is possible to spend considerably less by yourself. They also have combined rafting/Chitwan trips. These are competitively priced and can be as low as $150 for two nights and three days rafting on the Trisuli followed by two nights at Chitwan.

Rhino Lodge (☎ 60161), a reputable mid-range package-oriented place, has a range of double rooms for Rs 500 with bath. The food is pretty ordinary, but the lodge is well geared for safari activities.

Riverview Jungle Camp (☎ 60164) is a decent place, and although central, is not in any way spoilt. It's worth a look, with much larger than usual double cottages for Rs 250, or more substantial brick cottages at Rs 600 with bath.

Jungle Nepal Resort Camp has good facilities, though it's a bit overpriced for individuals at Rs 500.

Terai Resort, close by, has a good garden and river views. Modern cottage rooms with fan, bath and mosquito nets cost Rs 400.

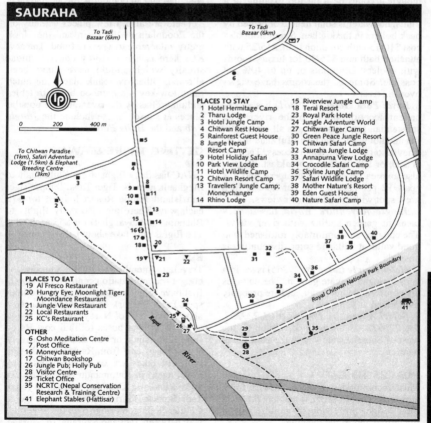

SAURAHA

To Tadi Bazaar (6km)

To Tadi Bazaar (6km)

To Chitwan Paradise (1km), Safari Adventure Lodge (1.5km) & Elephant Breeding Centre (3km)

0   200   400 m

PLACES TO STAY
1 Hotel Hermitage Camp
2 Tharu Lodge
3 Hotel Jungle Camp
4 Chitwan Rest House
5 Rainforest Guest House
8 Jungle Nepal Resort Camp
9 Hotel Holiday Safari
10 Park View Lodge
11 Hotel Wildlife Camp
12 Chitwan Resort Camp
13 Travellers' Jungle Camp; Moneychanger
14 Rhino Lodge
15 Riverview Jungle Camp
18 Terai Resort
23 Royal Park Hotel
24 Jungle Adventure World
27 Chitwan Tiger Camp
30 Green Peace Jungle Resort
31 Chitwan Safari Camp
32 Sauraha Jungle Lodge
33 Annapurna View Lodge
34 Crocodile Safari Camp
36 Skyline Jungle Camp
37 Safari Wildlife Lodge
38 Mother Nature's Resort
39 Eden Guest House
40 Nature Safari Camp

PLACES TO EAT
19 Al Fresco Restaurant
20 Hungry Eye; Moonlight Tiger; Moondance Restaurant
21 Jungle View Restaurant
22 Local Restaurants
25 KC's Restaurant

OTHER
6 Osho Meditation Centre
7 Post Office
16 Moneychanger
17 Chitwan Bookshop
26 Jungle Pub; Holly Pub
28 Visitor Centre
29 Ticket Office
35 NCRTC (Nepal Conservation Research & Training Centre)
41 Elephant Stables (Hattisar)

Royal Chitwan National Park Boundary

Rapti River

THE TERAI

Hotel Hermitage has a river frontage, and ugly but unobtrusive brick cottages at Rs 600.

Chitwan Paradise, farther along the road to the elephant breeding centre, is nicely secluded, and has cottages with common bath at Rs 400, or with attached bath at Rs 800. A bike would be very handy if you're staying here.

Chitwan Tiger Camp (☎ 29369) has an excellent position overlooking the river. There is a bamboo machan (platform) on stilts with the best views in Sauraha, although it could be a bit too exciting in a high wind. Although this place has electric lights, hot water is solar heated or heated by back boilers in the kitchen. Singles/doubles cost $10/15 with common bath, $15/25 with attached bath and $25/40 for luxury rooms with coolers. Discounts of up to 40% are possible. Some of the rooms have views over the river.

Royal Park Hotel (☎ 29361) has an excellent location close to the river. The substantial, spacious cottages all have bath, fan and hot water, and beautiful slate floors. They also have wheelchair access. The cost is $20, or $25 including breakfast. There's also an area set aside for campers, and this costs $2 per person. The bar here is in a great spot with excellent river views.

Jungle Adventure World has a very pleasant garden setting with river views. The cottages are comfortably furnished, and good value at $20, and some discounting is possible.

Hotel Jungle Camp (☎ 29366) is set in a very lush and private garden. The cottages are comfortable but small, and are probably overpriced at $18.

Safari Adventure Lodge (☎ 01-223763, fax 226912) is an upmarket camp to the west of Sauraha, midway to the park headquarters.

PLACES TO EAT

Most accommodation places also do food, and most people seem to eat breakfast at their lodge, preferring to venture out at lunchtime and in the evening.

In Sauraha eating activity is centred around the main intersection. There's a handful of small restaurants here, and a couple have shaded upstairs terraces with excellent views over the river, especially at sunset. The food is generally standard travellers' fare, and the quality is average. Restaurants here include the *Jungle View*, *Moonlight*, *Moondance*, *Tiger* and *Hungry Eye*.

Al Fresco is a flash new two-storey place and is a sign of the Kathmandu money moving in. It's well set up and serves continental, Chinese and Indian food. There's also a separate bar, and an outdoor barbecue garden is planned.

There are also a few places actually on the floodplain of the river, and they look pretty vulnerable to a severe flood. The new *KCs* here is a two-storey concrete monstrosity which should never have been allowed. Other riverbank places are much more low-key – a bamboo hut with tables and umbrellas by the river, and are popular places at sunset. These include the *Jungle Pub* and the *Holly Pub*.

GETTING THERE & AWAY

Air

RNAC has daily flights from Kathmandu to Meghauli, near the Tiger Tops, Temple Tiger and Island Jungle Resort lodges, for $72 each way. There are also daily flights to Bharatpur (Narayanghat) for $55 each way. The flights only take about half an hour.

Bus

Travellers intending to stay at Sauraha, the budget accommodation centre for Chitwan, first have to get to Tadi Bazaar (sometimes spelt Tandi Bazaar), on the Mahendra Hwy, about 15km east of Narayanghat.

Sajha Yatayat buses to Tadi cost Rs 80 from Kathmandu or Pokhara. Alternatively, tourist buses cost from Rs 150 and the trip typically takes six or seven hours. Any travel agent in Kathmandu or Pokhara can make a booking. Ordinary buses drop you in Tadi Bazaar; tourist buses actually go to Chitrasali, the footbridge over the river midway between Tadi and Sauraha. In Sauraha,

THE TERAI

lodges will book tickets (but beware of in-flated prices) or you can book in Tadi at booking stalls near the main intersection.

Greenline has a daily air-con service in each direction for Rs 480, leaving Kath-mandu and Sauraha (Chitrasali) at 8 am.

To Sunauli on the Indian border, buses take about five hours and cost Rs 110; to Birganj buses take about three hours and cost Rs 65. Minibuses run from Tadi Bazaar to Narayanghat, take 30 minutes and cost Rs 6.

There are a couple of possible methods of covering the 6km from Tadi Bazaar to Sauraha. You can walk in a couple of hours – which is pleasant and interesting if it's not too warm. You can take an ox cart (about Rs 15), which is only marginally more com-fortable and certainly no quicker than walking, although if you're not in a hurry it's an interesting ride. The easiest and quickest method, however, is by jeep (Rs 30 from Tadi or Chitrasali); jeeps and touts meet all incoming buses.

Car
Visitors to the park lodges usually get there by car from Kathmandu or Pokhara and this is usually arranged by the lodge operators. A car typically costs around $70 and the 160 to 180km trip (depending where you're going) takes four to five hours.

If you are coming or going from Kath-mandu, you should try to convince your driver to take you one way via the Tribhu-van Hwy passing through Daman and Hetauda. This route will cost extra as the narrow, winding road will add at least an hour to your travel time. See the Daman sec-tion for details of this spectacular route.

The cars usually drop you at the turn-offs from the main road, from where your lodge vehicle will pick you up for the final trip into the park and across the river. This short trip is usually made by 4WD, although in the first month or two after the monsoon ends (September and October) the river may still be too high for vehicles and the transfer may be made by elephant. It's quite a surprise to arrive at the Chitwan Jungle Lodge turn-off, for example, and find an elephant waiting for the final 7km amble to the lodge!

Raft
Numerous Kathmandu rafting operators offer trips down the Trisuli River to Chitwan. Most park lodges will organise a rafting trip in conjunction with your stay in the park.

The rafting trips start from Mugling, where the road to Narayanghat and Chitwan turns off from the Kathmandu-Pokhara (Prithvi) Hwy, or from farther up the Trisuli. It takes two or three days to raft down to Chitwan. Don't expect white-water thrills; this section of the river is more a gentle drift, although there are some fine views and the sandy beaches along the riverside offer great camping spots.

Prices range from around $30 to $75 per day for rafting only, while rafting/Chitwan trips (four nights, five days) can be as low as $150. Shop around and establish details before you hand over your money: where does the rafting trip begin? What size are the groups? What activities are included at Chitwan? What transport is there from the river to your accommodation at Chitwan? See the Rafting & Kayaking chapter for more information.

The Terai from East to West

There are a number of choices that trav-ellers can make travelling to and from India and Kathmandu, so it is not possible to pre-sent the information in this chapter in an order that will suit everyone. Places are de-scribed from east to west, from Kakarbhitta to Mahendranagar.

The main east-west link is the Mahendra Hwy, which for the most part is in excellent condition. From Kakarbhitta in the east to the Karnali River at the western end of Bar-dia National Park in the west, the road is in good condition. Farther west as far as Ataria it is in reasonable condition, although there are as yet no bridges across the many small rivers. The last 45km from Ataria to Mahendranagar out to the far west are without doubt the worst on the Terai.

A number of attractive hill towns are accessible from the Mahendra Hwy and for the sake of convenience they have been included in this chapter. They are Ilam (accessible from Birtamod); Hile, Dharan Bazaar and Dhankuta (accessible from Itahari); Daman, which is between Hetauda and Naubise; and Tansen (Palpa), which is between Bhairawa and Pokhara.

KAKARBHITTA
☎ 023

The sole reason for the existence of Kakarbhitta is its proximity to India. This is the border post for road traffic going to or from Siliguri and Darjeeling. In fact, it's not much more than a glorified bus stop and it's difficult to imagine that anyone would want to stay longer than to make a bus connection.

The surrounding countryside is attractive, however, and you can tell you're not far from Darjeeling when you see the tea plantations on the outskirts of town.

Orientation & Information

There's a tourist office (☎ 20208) just inside Nepal, past customs on the northern side of the road (on the right if you're coming from India). The Nepal Rastra Bank isn't signposted, but it's the unmistakable pink monstrosity on the left (south) side of the road.

The border is open to tourists from 7 am to 7 pm. There are two banks on the Nepali side, but only the Nepal Rastra Bank changes money; it's also open from 7 am to 7 pm every day. There is one moneychanger in the far corner of the bus park, although it only accepts cash.

As you continue away from the border the main bus parking area is a dusty (or muddy) quadrangle on your right, followed by the bazaar and village.

Places to Stay & Eat

There are plenty of places to stay around the bazaar, but the quality is pretty variable. If you want to get a decent night's sleep steer clear of the places that front onto the bus park.

Kanchan Hotel (☎ 70015) is not a bad choice. The rooms are clean, and the restaurant serves decent food. The cost is Rs 150 for a double with common bath, or Rs 250 with attached bath. Bigger rooms with TV and phone cost Rs 450.

Hotel Deurali close by is typical of the bazaar cheapies, and has double rooms with common bath at Rs 120.

Hotel Rajat (☎ 70033), one block behind the rear of the bus park, is without doubt the best on offer. There's a few doubles with common bath at $4, large rooms with TV and phone go for $13, or deluxe rooms are $20. These prices are highly negotiable, however. The hotel also has a bright and airy restaurant on the ground floor.

Getting There & Away

There are plenty of land connections to destinations both in Nepal and India. Many people buy through tickets between Kathmandu and Darjeeling, but this is relatively expensive, and unnecessary. With a through ticket you travel the Kakarbhitta to Kathmandu section at night and miss the sights.

Many travellers are ripped off buying through tickets between India and Nepal – bookings fail to materialise or are for lower quality services than were paid for. Admittedly, these problems are not nearly as common on this route as they are on some others. See the Getting There & Away chapter for more information.

To/From India It's a 10 minute walk from Kakarbhitta to the Indian border post of Raniganj; rickshaws cost about Rs 10 (Indian Rs 6). From Raniganj you take a minibus 36km to Siliguri; this takes around one hour and costs around Indian Rs 5. From Siliguri you take a bus 78km to Darjeeling; buses leave between 6 am and 6 pm, take around 3½ hours (make sure you catch an express) and cost Indian Rs 40. Depending on how quickly you made connections the total trip would not take more than six hours.

It's possible to speed the process by an hour or two by catching a taxi from Raniganj to Siliguri (Indian Rs 50), or from Siliguri to Darjeeling (Indian Rs 120). The overnight buses from Kathmandu all arrive in Kakarbhitta before 10 am; they leave Kakarbhitta for Kathmandu between 3 and 5 pm.

To/From Kathmandu There is plenty of competition for your business if you plan to buy a bus ticket, so it's worth shopping around. The prices won't vary, but the departure times and the quality of the buses can. Night buses can be booked at the office in the front of the bus park.

Night buses for Kathmandu and Pokhara generally leave between 3 and 5 pm (Rs 339, 15 hours). Not only would this be an epic and unpleasant experience, but you'd miss the views. If time and weather allow, consider catching a day bus to Janakpur and stopping over there; they leave between 6.30 and 9 am, take around six hours and cost Rs 153. The road is particularly interesting between Itahari and Janakpur; it runs across the flood plain of the massive Sapt Kosi. See the Getting Around chapter for more details.

There is one night bus for Birganj (Rs 213, 11 hours) plus day buses to Biratnagar (Rs 65, 3½ hours).

Buses for Kakarbhitta leave from the Kathmandu Bus Terminal at 4 and 5 pm. Book a day in advance.

The nearest airport is at Bhadrapur, 10km south of Birtamod, which itself is 13km west of Kakarbhitta. From Bhadrapur there are daily flights ($99) with Cosmic Air and Gorkha Airlines (☎ 023-20549) to Kathmandu.

ILAM
☎ 027

Ilam is an attractive small town at the centre of Nepal's tea industry; the climate of the surrounding hills is similar to Darjeeling's. Few westerners visit, but there is some reasonable accommodation available, and there are good walks, and tea plantations to see.

Places to Stay & Eat
The cheapest places are around the bus park at the bottom end of the town. These can be noisy however, as buses start around 4 am. Of these places, the *Maivalley Guest House* is among the better ones. The *Deurali Lodge* (☎ 20228) is another bus park cheapie.

Tamu Guest House is a bit farther away and so escapes the noise. The rooms are OK and cost Rs 150 for a double.

Danfe Guest House is set right in among the tea plantations, and offers real peace and quiet. Rooms are basic but clean, and good value at Rs 100/200. The guesthouse is a few minutes walk from the bus park: take the stairs up at the rear corner of the bus park, turn right onto the track, then left at the T-junction.

Green View Guest House (☎ 21030) is the best on offer. The rooms are large, clean and modern; most do indeed have a green view – tea plantations. Large doubles with common bath are Rs 250, with attached bath Rs 350.

There's not much in the restaurant stakes. There are a few basic Nepali eateries along the road between the bus park and the main square.

Getting There & Away
The road from the Terai is in good condition and is sealed all the way; it's also very steep and the views are spectacular. Buses leave from Birtamod on the Mahendra Hwy 13km west of Kakarbhitta. They depart from 7 am to 1 pm, take five hours and cost Rs 85.

The road is being pushed farther into the hills beyond Ilam, and currently goes as far as Taplejung. Buses run regularly between Birtamod and Taplejung.

BIRATNAGAR
☎ 021

The observation that Biratnagar is the second largest city in Nepal, and an industrial centre, actually makes it sound worse than it is. It's an energetic, bustling place with the crowds and shops you would expect of a city with several hundred thousand inhabitants. However, there's just nothing much

THE TERAI

to attract the visitor unless you are particularly interested in Nepal's somewhat shaky industrial development, or the strongest, most politicised unions in the country. The border is not open to tourists.

The countryside and surrounding villages are interesting, but difficult to explore without private transport. One possibility is to continue north along Main Rd (with the Hotel Namaskar and Rastriya Banjiya Bank) – this veers left when you leave town; continue westwards until you reach a T-junction; turn right (north) along a dirt road that parallels the sealed road and continue through Sigraha and Haraincha until you reach the Mahendra Hwy to the west of Itahari.

Jute used to be grown in large quantities, and can still be seen, but the industry has been in decline for years. There are numerous groups of people in the region, but the most distinctive are the local Tharu and Danuwars. The Danuwars are very similar in culture and appearance to the Tharu, but the women wear a distinctive embroidered sari.

Places to Stay & Eat
There's quite a range of places at varying prices. Bear in mind, however, that anywhere on Main Rd or near the bus park will be pretty noisy.

Dhankuta Lodge, opposite the bus park, is clean and reasonable with singles/doubles at Rs 100/120, or Rs 150/200 with abath. Avoid the front rooms, which cop the bus park noise.

Hotel Geetanjali (☎ 27335) is also close to the bus park on Malaya Rd. Set in a pleasant garden, the hotel charges Rs 200/250 for doubles without/with bath. There's no restaurant, but decent Indian food is available.

Kathmandu Guest House near Traffic Chowk has gloomy if quiet rooms at Rs 120/180 with bath. It's good value. The *Kohinoor Restaurant* in the same building is worth a try.

Up the scale somewhat is the *Hotel Namaskar* (☎ 21199, fax 25988) on Main Rd near Traffic Chowk, a 15 minute walk from the bus station, which has a range of rooms from Rs 380 to 990. At the top price you get air-con and a private sitting room, but the cheaper rooms are clean and quite adequate, and all rooms have attached bath. There's a good, reasonably priced restaurant.

Getting There & Away
There are daily RNAC (☎ 25576) flights, twice daily Necon Air (☎ 25987) flights, and four times daily Buddha Air (☎ 24693) flights to Kathmandu for $77.

There are plenty of buses to Kathmandu, Kakarbhitta and Janakpur. Night buses to Kathmandu leave at 4.30 pm (Rs 299, 11½ hours), or there are day buses at 4.30 am (Rs 265). There are day buses to Kakarbhitta (Rs 65, 3½ hours, 5.30 am), Janakpur (Rs 114, 4.30 to 11.50 am), Birganj (Rs 178, 8 hours), Dhankuta (Rs 74, 5.30 am and 2.30 pm) and Dharan Bazaar (Rs 23, many daily up to 6 pm).

BIRATNAGAR

To Airport (2.5km) & Itahari (22km)

0   125   250 m

Malaya Road

Main Road

To Indian Border (6km)

1 Rastriya Banjiya Bank
2 Police
3 Traffic Chowk
4 Hotel Namaskar
5 Kathmandu Guest House;
   Kohinoor Restaurant
6 Necon Air Agent
7 Everest Air
8 Mahendra Chowk
9 Milan Hotel & Restaurant
10 RNAC Office
11 Hotel Geetanjali
12 Post Office
13 Dhankuta Lodge
14 Bus Park

THE TERAI

ITAHARI

Itahari is an undistinguished town at the intersection of the Mahendra Hwy and the Biratnagar to Dhankuta road. There is an interesting market held along the dusty lanes south-east of the main intersection.

The hotel pickings are extremely slim. Best of a bad lot perhaps is the *Jaya Nepal Hotel* near the traffic roundabout. Doubles with shared bath go for Rs 150, singles/doubles with attached bath are Rs 250/350. The restaurant here serves passable food.

Getting There & Away

All the long-distance, east-west buses stop in Itahari. There are also plenty of local buses which go to Biratnagar (Rs 12, one hour) and Dharan (Rs 8, 30 minutes). One bus a day leaves at 6 am for Dhankuta (Rs 44, five hours).

DHARAN BAZAAR

☎ 021

Dharan lies right at the foot of the Chure Hills, but the transformation from the Terai is dramatic. It's a bustling bazaar town catering to the hill people of eastern Nepal. It has grown rapidly despite suffering a major earthquake in 1988.

There are no sights of note, but if you're heading into the mountains this will be your best chance for final purchases. A small number of trekkers bound for Hile and Basantapur come through town, and **Chatara**, the finishing point for raft trips on the Sun Kosi, is only 15km to the west. Baraha Chhetra, 5km north of Chatara, is the site for an annual religious festival in late October/early November.

Places to Stay & Eat

There are a few possibilities, but none of them are all that flash.

Hotel Family Inn (☎ 20848) is close to busy Bhanu Chowk, in the centre of town where the buses stop. Reasonable double rooms with common bath cost Rs 200, or so-called deluxe rooms are Rs 350 with attached bath. Avoid the *Hotel Navayug* next door.

Hotel Aangan, about 300m from Bhanu Chowk, is a clean and decent hotel; double rooms with bath cost Rs 350. There are also more expensive air-con rooms.

Getting There & Away

Dharan Bazaar is 50km from the attractive hill town of Dhankuta. Hile, the starting point for a number of treks in eastern Nepal, is 12km past Dhankuta. The spectacular road is sealed as far as Hile, but continues on to Therathum, and is being pushed even farther. Buses to Dhankuta take three hours and cost Rs 44; buses to Basantapur and Therathum (via Hile) leave from 5 am to 2 pm, take five hours and cost Rs 92.

There's also one direct nightly bus in each direction to/from Kathmandu. The trip takes 12 hours, costs Rs 285 and departs at 3.30 pm from Kathmandu.

DHANKUTA

☎ 026

Although Dhankuta is only 50km by excellent road from the Terai, it seems more like a million miles. The largest, flattest spot in the nearby vicinity is the bus station – it soon becomes hard to remember that expanses of water-logged plains exist.

The town is strung along a ridge that basically runs north-south; the bus station is below the ridge. The sad remnants of the forest that once covered the hill are at the northern end of town. There is a collection of small, but decent, lodges which cater to a largely Nepali clientele, but there's no real reason to stay here, unless you want to catch the colourful *haat bajar* (weekly bazaar) on Thursday. Hile is more interesting and has better walking possibilities.

As you walk downhill (south) along the main street the road forks: the right fork goes down to the bus station; the left fork to a spur where there are fine views of the Himalaya. The latter is a pleasant 45 minute walk. After about 15 minutes the main track veers to the left and there is a stile over a barbed wire fence. Climb the stile and follow the ridge line up to the left. Eventually you'll come to a small shrine. There are

THE TERAI

plenty of flowers and birds along the way and, of course, good views.

Places to Stay & Eat

There are some small, clean, basic lodges on the main street.

Shaha Lodge (☎ 20281) is very basic. *Naulo Lodge* (☎ 20481) is much the same.

A good option – and it would be a pleasant place to stay while you explored the surrounding hills – is the *Hotel Parchaya* (☎ 20425). It's clean and bright and there are superb views. To find it, walk north up the ridge until you get to a large pipal tree in the middle of an intersection. The hotel is on the right; two-bed rooms are Rs 60, four-bed rooms cost Rs 120, all with common bath.

Hotel Suravi (☎ 20204) is about as flash as it gets around here. Rooms with common bath cost Rs 75/150, or with attached bath it's Rs 150/300. The restaurant here is quite decent.

Puchhae Cafe next door to the Hotel Parchaya is a good little place with decent music and a relaxing atmosphere.

Getting There & Away

Plenty of buses travel the spectacular road from Dhankuta to Dharan Bazaar (Rs 44, three hours). From Dhankuta the sealed road continues to Hile, then continues unsealed to Therathum. Buses for Basantapur depart from 7.30 am to 2.30 pm, take three hours and cost Rs 58; to Hile it's Rs 12. The road is being pushed farther into the hills, but there are no buses beyond Therathum.

HILE
☎ 026

Hile, a scruffy, bustling, one-street bazaar town strung out along a ridge, is the starting point for Arun Valley treks (possible for individuals) and for treks to Makalu (groups only). Kanchenjunga trekkers (also groups only) usually start at Basantapur. Hile would be a good base for day walks in the region.

Nepal's ethnic map is always complicated, but at Hile it's about as complicated as it gets, with Tibetans, Bahuns, Chhetris, Magars, Tamangs, Rais, Limbus and Indians.

There are fantastic views of the Himalaya, especially of the Makalu massif, from the ridge above the town. Walk along the Basantapur road past the army base and a few hundred metres past the army checkpoint (there's a boom across the road) you can cut up to the left onto a grassy ridge.

Places to Stay & Eat

There are several decent, but basic lodges, with not much to separate them.

Doma Lodge (☎ 20574) is as basic as they come, but it's clean and friendly. Dorm beds cost Rs 20, doubles with bath are Rs 70.

Hotel Himali (☎ 20340) is similar, with dorm beds at Rs 30, and rooms with common bath at Rs 60/100.

Hotel Hillstone near the bus stand is Hile's Hilton. Don't expect too much, but it's clean and the rooms are a decent size. The cost is Rs 250 for a double with bath.

Getting There & Away

Buses to Basantapur and Therathum (about 20km beyond Basantapur and the current roadhead), depart every 45 minutes or so, take around two hours and cost Rs 38.

There's one daily bus to Kathmandu. It leaves at 1.30 pm, arriving early the next morning, and costs Rs 335.

KOSHI TAPPU WILDLIFE RESERVE

The Koshi Tappu Wildlife Reserve protects a section of the Sapt Kosi's flood plain that lies behind the Kosi Barrage. The Sapt Kosi is one of the Ganges' largest tributaries, and the Kosi Barrage is designed to minimise destructive annual floods. Most of the reserve is surrounded by high embankments that control the spread of the river and funnel it towards the barrage.

The main highway skirts the reserve and crosses the river at the barrage. It's a beautiful, fascinating water world. Small thatched villages perch on what little high ground there is and wherever you look there are water birds, and ponds full of flowering plants, all overwhelmed by fields of rice stretching to the horizon.

RICHARD I'ANSON

GREG ELMS

KRAIG LIEB

National Parks

These elephants and rhinos of Chitwan National Park depend on baths to keep themselves cool. Water, dust or mud – any type of bath will do!

Weighing potatoes for sale at Biratnagar market.

Bamboo swings for the Dasain festival.

Selling religious offerings at the Bageshwari Mandir, Nepalganj.

Colourful Biratnagar market.

Behind the embankments the river continuously changes course, and regularly floods during the monsoon, although only to shallow depths. The vegetation is mainly tall grass (*phanta*), with some scrub and riverine forest. Local villagers are allowed to collect grass for thatching every January, which also clears the way for easier wildlife viewing.

The reserve is home to the last surviving population of wild water buffalo (*arna*), various deer, blue cow (*nilgai*), gharial crocodiles and Gangetic dolphins. It is also either a permanent or temporary home to more than 400 species of water birds (migratory and otherwise). These include 20 species of ducks, ibises, storks, egrets, cranes and herons. The migratory species, including the sarus crane from Siberia and the ruddy shelduck from Tibet, take up residence from November to February.

The reserve occasionally hosts birdwatchers between November and February, but very few people visit and the arrival of a tourist out of the blue gives everyone quite a shock. There's one deluxe safari camp, but there's no other formal accommodation, although there is an area where you could camp, and the helpful staff are happy to give visitors the use of a kitchen. The reserve has five elephants, which can be ridden for Rs 650 for one hour. Canoes can also be arranged.

Orientation & Information

The reserve headquarters are at Kusaha, where all visitors must pay a Rs 1000 entrance fee. Kusaha is a 3km walk from the highway, just outside the eastern embankment, on the eastern side of the barrage.

The turn-off to the reserve (signposted) is about 11km north-east of the Kosi Barrage, and about 2km before the village of Laukhi. Coming from Itahari, it's about 46km to Laukhi and a farther 2km to the turn-off.

If you do plan a visit, and especially if you want to stay, ring ahead to get the latest information on access and the availability of facilities. Contact the park headquarters on ☎ 025-21488.

Places to Stay

The only formal accommodation is the *Koshi Tappu Wildlife Camp*, which is just outside the north-eastern corner of the reserve, 24km north of the barrage near the tiny village of Prakashpur and accessible from Inerwa on the Mahendra Hwy. The camp is located on a small waterway with excellent birdwatching possibilities from the bar! Because so few visitors come to this part of the world, it is an excellent place to escape the crowds for a few days.

The camp is very well set-up, and in a pleasant established garden. Accommodation is in very comfortable tented rooms, and there's shared bathroom facilities, a separate dining area serving excellent meals, and a bar. There's no electricity, and so the evenings are illuminated by atmospheric kero lamps.

Accommodation costs $175/250 per night, which includes guided bird walks, and an idyllic half-day rafting glide down the wide and slow-moving river. Most guests come on a package from Kathmandu, which involves flying to Biratnagar and transfers to the camp. Bookings can be made through Explore Nepal, PO Box 536, Kamaladi, Kathmandu (☎ 01-226130, fax 224237, email explore@mos.com.np).

For those who don't mind roughing it a bit, it is possible to stay with a few families who live at the *park headquarters*. This is village accommodation at its most basic. Don't expect any frills, and be sensitive to the fact that this is not tourist accommodation and the people may well be unfamiliar with what tourists usually expect in the way of food and facilities.

There is also basic *lodge* accommodation at Bhantabarl, the small village on the eastern side of the barrage.

Getting There & Away

Any buses travelling on the Mahendra Hwy can drop you at the park turn-off, from where it's a 3km walk to the park headquarters.

For the wildlife camp, if you don't have your own 4WD, take a bus to Inerwa on the Mahendra Hwy, and from there local buses

THE TERAI

go regularly to Prakashpur. The wildlife camp is a farther 1km, which you'll have to cover on foot; ask locally for directions.

RAJBIRAJ

Rajbiraj is a dusty uninteresting little town, but it lies on the edge of the Sapt Kosi flood plain, so the countryside and wickerwork villages to the east are fascinating. Rajbiraj is to the south of the main highway, but if you have private transport it's definitely worth the detour. You'd have to be pretty keen to build it into your itinerary if you are using local buses, but it could be done. Local buses from Janakpur and Biratnagar are frequent and cost around Rs 50.

There's only one place to stay, the *Sinha Lodge*, on the main road. It's very, very basic and singles/doubles are Rs 60/100.

JANAKPUR

☎ 041

Janakpur is a scruffy, dusty (or muddy) yet interesting town of temples, pools, sadhus,

rickshaws and rainbow-coloured saris. It's a tourist town, but the tourists are devout Indian pilgrims, not western backpackers.

Janakpur's religious significance is due to its role in the famous Hindu epic, the *Ramayana*. It is the legendary birthplace of Sita, an incarnation of Lakshmi, and the place of her marriage to Rama, who is one of Vishnu's most popular incarnations. At times, especially during festivals when strangely resonant vignettes from the *Ramayana* are played out in the streets, it can feel as if the ancient myth has come to life.

Janakpur is situated in what was once the kingdom of Mithila, a region now divided between Nepal and India. The Maithili language, which also has its own unique script, is spoken by approximately two million Nepalis; only Nepali is spoken by a greater number of people.

Janakpur is at least the third city to be built on this site, and most buildings are less than a century old. The city that was mythologised in the *Ramayana* existed around

---

Ramayana

The *Ramayana*, or romance of Rama, is among the best loved and most influential stories in Hindu literature. Handsome Rama embodies chivalry and virtue, and his wife, the beautiful Sita, exemplifies devotion and chastity. Together with Rama's ally, the faithful monkey god, Hanuman, they are heroes and exemplars of immense popularity and like all great mythical archetypes they have somehow found an enduring place in the human psyche.

It's likely the legend has at least a basis in fact, and was first retold around village hearths. The *Ramayana* was first permanently recorded in Sanskrit, possibly as long as 2400 years ago by a sage and poet, Valmiki. Since then it has become a part of people's lives and imaginations throughout the subcontinent and, in various forms, as far as Bali, where to this day it features in puppetry and dance.

Rama was a reincarnation of Vishnu, born at the request of the gods to do battle with the ghastly demon-king Ravana, the king of Lanka (possibly Sri Lanka). He was reincarnated at Ayodhya (350km west of Janakpur) as the eldest son of a wealthy king. Handsome, virtuous and strong, he grew up the idol of the people and especially of one of his half-brothers, Lakshmana.

In the kingdom of Mithila, good King Janak discovered baby Sita, the reincarnation of Lakshmi, lying in a furrow of a ploughed field. She too grew up to be wise and beautiful. So many men wanted to marry her that Janak set a test – a successful suitor had to bend the divine bow of Shiva. Rama, of course, drew the bow and he and Sita looked into each other's eyes and knew divine love.

700 BCE, but it apparently sank back into the forest, the population perhaps wiped out by disease. Simaraungarh grew up in its place, but it was destroyed by Muslims in the 14th century, and once again the region was reforested. Theologically, Janakpur is paired with Ayodhya, near Faizabad in Uttar Pradesh, where Rama is believed to have been born.

Modern Janakpur is a typical Terai town, although it is perhaps cleaner and less crowded than some others. The narrow lanes are interspersed with temples, pilgrim hostels (kutis) and both large and small sacred ponds (sagar and kunda). Legend says the ponds were created by King Janak for the use of the gods who came to the wedding of Rama and Sita. They take the place of a river for ritual bathing and are also used by the local dhobi caste who are clothes washers. Thanks to a successful development project, many are also stocked with the fish that provide an important supplement to the local diet.

The town authorities have managed to keep most traffic out of the centre of town, which makes it pleasant to wander around.

If you do have the time and the inclination to experience something of the Terai, Janakpur should be at the top of your list. It's possible to visit on the way to/from Kakarbhitta. However, although the only railway in Nepal connects Janakpur to the Indian town of Jaynagar, tourists are not allowed to cross the border (see the Around Janakpur section).

Orientation & Information

Janakpur is a hopeless tangle of narrow streets, so the best way to get your bearings is from the telecommunications tower and the large, elevated concrete water tank. The town itself lies to the east of the main road that runs through to Jaleshwar at the border.

The Janaki Mandir is just to the south of the water tank, and the bus station is to the south-west of the temple near the telecommunications tower. The train station is about

---

Ramayana

Rama and his three half-brothers were married in a single ceremony – the brothers to neighbouring princesses – and there was much feasting, flowers falling from heaven, gorgeous processions across the plains and so on. But this is where things took a turn for the worse.

After returning to Ayodhya, Rama and Sita were forced to leave the palace because of the intrigues of the detestable hunchback Manthara. While they wandered in exile, Rama and Lakshmana were distracted by a golden deer, and Sita was kidnapped and carried off to Lanka by the demon king. Imprisoned, Sita was forced to defend herself from the disgusting advances of Ravana.

Meanwhile, Rama and Lakshmana formed an alliance with a monkey kingdom. In particular they were served by the indomitable monkey god Hanuman. With Hanuman's loyal assistance Sita was finally rescued and the demon king, Ravana, destroyed.

Unfortunately, life didn't improve much for Sita who was forced to undergo an ordeal by fire to prove her chastity. Although Rama, now king of Ayodhya, believed her innocence, his people didn't and Sita was forced to go into exile again. Sita gave birth to Rama's twin sons and the family was later reunited, but Sita decided she had had enough of this mortal coil and was swallowed up by the earth.

There are many versions of the story recorded in many art forms and many different languages, including English. Trying to imagine the power and subtlety of the complete story by reading this condensation is a bit like trying to imagine a tree by looking at a match.

JANAKPUR

To Mahendra Highway (20km)

To Bijalpur

Purare Chowk

0   300   600 m

Ratan Saga Kunda

Bihar Kunda

Sita Kunda

Ramanand Chowk

Mills Area Chowk

To Jaynagar (29km)

Train Station

Kopal Mauchami Sagar

Ford Sagar

Bhanu Chowk

Station Road

Ganga Sagar

Dhanush Sagar

Zero Mile Chowk

Murali Chowk

To Jaleshwar (15km) & Indian Border (20km)

Campus Chowk

To Airport (200m)

Kuwa Village

PLACES TO STAY
5 Hotel Rama
10 Hotel Welcome
13 Sukh Sagar Hotel

PLACES TO EAT
16 Sanjog Restaurant

OTHER
1 Raj Yoga Ashram
2 Sajha Yatayat Bus Office
3 Big Monkey Temple
4 Cigarette Factory
6 RNAC Office
7 Nepal Bank
8 Tourist Office
9 Necon Air

11 Telegraph Office
12 Hospital
14 Ram Sita Bibaha Mandir
15 Janaki Mandir
17 Ram Mandir
18 Telecommunications Tower
19 Bus Station
20 Hospital
21 Gopal Dharamsala
22 Post Office
23 Nepal Rastra Bank
24 Police Station
25 Macha Palan Fisheries Project
26 Janakpur Women's Development Centre

THE TERAI

a 20 minute walk to the north-east of the large water tank.

There is a tourist office (☎ 20755) at Bhanu Chowk, not far from the railway station. Consider ringing to check the dates for major festivals. The office is open Monday to Friday 10 am to 5 pm, but closes an hour earlier from November to January.

Janaki Mandir

The temple to Sita (who is also known as Janaki) is believed to be built over the spot where her father, King Janak, found her lying in the furrow of a ploughed field. It's impressively large yet, surprisingly, you come across it from the winding Janakpur streets almost without warning.

Although it has no great architectural or historical merit – it was built in 1912 and might be described as baroque Mughal – it is nonetheless a fascinating place. There are instances of fine work, especially in some of the carved stone screens, and in the beautiful silver doors to the inner sanctum.

The inner sanctum is opened from 5 to 7 am and 6 to 8 pm, to reveal a flower bedecked statue of **Sita** that was apparently miraculously found in the Saryu River near Ayodhya. She is accompanied by Rama and his three half-brothers, Lakshmana, Bharat and Satrughna.

During the day, there are few people in the temple – some priests, sadhus and, if you're lucky, perhaps some musicians playing in the cloisters – but it comes alive in the evenings when Sita is displayed.

Ram Sita Bibaha Mandir

Virtually next door to the Janaki Mandir, but built with the traditional Nepali pagoda roof, this rather bizarre temple is built on the spot where Rama and Sita were married. Entry is Rs 1; leave cameras at the gate. The temple itself has glass walls so you can peer in at the kitsch life-sized models of Sita and Rama, his half-brothers and sisters-in-law.

Ram Mandir & Danush Sagar

Located in the city's oldest quarter, to the south-east of the Janaki Mandir, Ram Mandir is another Nepali-style temple that is the centrepoint for the Rama Navami celebrations. Immediately to its east is the Danush Sagar, which is considered to be one of the holiest ponds and is popular with pilgrims.

Other Temples & Ponds

There are numerous temples and ponds scattered around the outskirts of town. It is worth hiring a cycle-rickshaw to see them, although you could track them down on foot if you were energetic. They're reached by brick-paved roads that meander into the paddy fields. If you hire a rickshaw, allow a couple of hours and expect to pay around Rs 50.

Start at the temple that is widely known as the **Big Monkey Temple**. This place is easy to miss as it looks like an ordinary house. It's about 100m south of Ramanand Chowk. Hanuman, the monkey god, is worshipped in the form of a rhesus monkey kept in a depressing cage. Despite this, it could well be monkey heaven since the attendants and pilgrims press food on their mascot. The constant supply of delicacies no longer arouses much interest or excitement, but temptation (or boredom) triumphs and the monkey keeps munching on. The previous monkey grew to 60kg before finally succumbing to the affects of gross overfeeding and underexercising; its replacement is well on the way to following it.

Two of the most interesting and attractive ponds can be reached by following the brick-paved roads to the west. They are **Bihar Kunda** and **Ratan Saga Kunda**. The countryside is lush and tropical with coconut palms and huge trees framing the temples and ponds that are scattered across the fertile plains.

Janakpur Women's Development Centre

The Janakpur Women's Art Project (☎ 21080) was started to promote traditional Mithila painting skills and to empower the local women who live in a highly restrictive patriarchal society (see the Mithila Painting boxed text in this chapter).

The centre, on the southern outskirts of Janakpur, incorporates aspects of traditional architecture and the beautiful site is on the edge of an interesting village, a short rickshaw ride and walk from the centre of town. It is possible for visitors to see the women working at ceramics, painting, tapestry, silk-screen printing and sewing, and to purchase some of their striking creations at extremely reasonable prices; paintings start at Rs 200, ceramics at Rs 175. A visit is a must, and the centre is open daily except Saturday from 10 am to 5 pm. The centre also has a craft outlet near the Hotel Green-

wich Village in Kathmandu (see the Patan map).

Take a rickshaw from town to Macha Palan, a large fisheries project with a red and white sign in Nepali. The rickshaw should cost around Rs 10. Coming from town, a brick road on the left forms a T-junction just before the project. Follow it east to Kuwa village. Turn right at Kuwa village and continue until you reach a large, but unprepossessing temple. Turn left immediately before the temple and right immediately after it. Continue to the south; the road bends to the left, past a tank on the

Mithila Painting

Mithila culture is essentially a culture of the Gangetic plain, and the Hindu caste structure is strictly upheld. Most people are subsistence farmers, but land-holdings are usually very small, and many families live on the edge of starvation. Many are in the grip of moneylenders, or *zamindars*.

Zamindars, usually from the Brahmin (priest) or Kayastha (warrior, also Kshatriya) castes, occupy an almost feudal role as major landowners and through their traditional role as moneylenders. Their tenant farmers and debtors are effectively serfs trapped in a system of bonded labour.

Most Mithila people live in small villages, usually with no more than around a hundred households. House walls are made from bamboo or thatch plastered with a mixture of cow dung and mud. The roofs are thatched, sometimes tiled. Most houses have a fenced courtyard which is also sealed with mud and cow dung.

Mithila women are raised with the expectation that they will be workers in their husband's home, and are frequently married as children. After puberty they are veiled so that they cannot be seen by males outside their family. As a part of their cultural and religious tradition, the women paint striking murals on the external walls of their homes. Inside, pottery storage containers and internal pillars also carry designs.

Different castes and different regions have developed distinctive styles and symbols, which are passed down from mother to daughter. Traditionally, painting and decoration is not undertaken purely to create an aesthetic result, nor is it purely cathartic or expressive. Painting largely springs from cultural and religious motives. The act of painting, as a part of a ritual, can be more important than the finished result itself, and completed paintings can act as charms, prayers and meditation aids.

Paintings often derive from Hindu mythology and can use complex symbols (sometimes with a distinct mandala-like quality), simple apparently abstract figures (including hand stencils, peacocks, pregnant elephants and fish), or can take on a narrative quality (representing religious stories). High castes, including the Kayastha, have developed extremely elaborate, abstract forms. Lower-caste paintings are often simpler and more realistic, but they have an energetic expressionistic style, and retain a strong sense of formal design.

right. The centre is the only building in this vicinity, and it is enclosed behind a high, red-brick wall. The route sounds complicated, but ask directions if in doubt and you shouldn't have a problem. It's about a 10 minute walk from Macha Palan to the centre.

Special Events
On the fifth day of the waxing moon in late November/early December, thousands of pilgrims arrive to celebrate a re-enactment of Sita's marriage to Rama (Vivaha Panchami). This is also the occasion for an important fair and market that last a week. Rama's birthday (Rama Navami) in late March/early April is also accompanied by a huge procession.

Most Hindu festivals are major events in Janakpur. Deepawali is an interesting time to be in town, when the Mithila women repaint the murals on their houses. On the day before Holi, Parikrama involves a ritual walk around the town's ring road. Holi itself can get very boisterous and wild; women should take care.

Places to Stay & Eat
Janakpur is desperately in need of a couple of decent hotels.

Mithila Painting

Mithila paintings from Madubani in Bihar, India, have been discovered by the international art world. The most well known are the elaborate Kayastha wedding paintings that are presented to the groom as part of the build-up to an arranged marriage. Until fairly recently, little interest was taken in the art produced on Nepal's side of the border.

This changed with the foundation of the Janakpur Women's Art Project in 1989 which had the dual aim of promoting traditional Mithila painting skills and empowering the women painters. The project is housed in the Janakpur Women's Development Centre and it's possible to visit the centre to see the women working, and to buy what they produce. (See the entry under Janakpur.)

The project includes women of diverse castes and backgrounds and the art that is created reflects this variety: wedding paintings, pregnant elephants, gods, and abstract tattoo designs are just some of the subjects. Increasingly the paintings are changing to include scenes from the women's lives, including childbirth and marriage. In addition to paintings (acrylic on daphne paper) the women are also producing ceramics (plates and figures), papier-mâché, patchwork tapestry, silk-screen prints and woven wall hangings.

In Kathmandu, the project's goods are sold at Sana Hastakala, Mahaguthi, and a number of other reputable craft shops. See the Shopping sections in the Kathmandu, Patan & Bhaktapur chapter for more information. It's also possible to see examples of the women's work at the Kantipath branch of the Nepal Grindlays Bank in Kathmandu, and at the United Nations building in Pulchowk.

THE TERAI

Despite the fact that it is somewhat run-down, the **Hotel Welcome** (☎ 20646, fax 20922) on Station Rd is not a bad option. The rooms are tolerably grubby, although some of the deluxe ones have the most sickening decor. On the plus side, the staff are friendly and helpful and the restaurant is good. Singles/doubles with bath are Rs 220/275, for something a bit more comfortable (although this is relative) and with air-con, it's Rs 600/1100. Check-out is 24 hours after check-in.

Sukh Sagar Hotel (☎ 20488), very close to the Janaki Mandir, has large rooms which are passably clean, and reasonable value at Rs 150 with common bath, Rs 110/220 with attached bath. Next door there's a decent local restaurant, which does a passable dal bhat.

The best on offer is the pleasant **Hotel Rama** (☎ 20059), in the northern part of town by Mills Area Chowk. The rooms are a good size, and range in price from Rs 150 (very basic and gloomy) with common bath to Rs 350 for big, airy doubles with fan, attached bath and hot water, Rs 450 with air-cooler and Rs 800 with air-con. There's a reasonable although very dark restaurant here.

Sanjog Restaurant, down a side alley opposite the Danush Sagar, is basic, but for Janakpur it's about as good as it gets. The menu is very ambitious, although most dishes seem to be unavailable.

Getting There & Away
RNAC (☎ 20185) has six flights a week to Kathmandu for $77. Necon Air (☎ 20688) has five flights weekly.

Private buses for Kathmandu leave from the chaotic main bus station between 5 and 7 pm. There are half a dozen express buses to/from Kathmandu that cost Rs 206 and take about eight hours. Night buses to Pokhara also cost Rs 206. There are day buses to Birganj (Rs 88, from 4 am), Biratnagar (Rs 114, from 6 am to 12.30 pm) and Kakarbhitta (Rs 146, 7 am to 10 am).

The government-operated Sajha Yatayat buses leave from a stop to the west of town on the main highway at Ramanand Chowk; they have a day bus to Kathmandu leaving at 6.30 am, costing Rs 158 and taking around nine hours. There are departures at the same time from the Kathmandu bus terminal.

AROUND JANAKPUR
The fields and villages around Janakpur form a lush and magical mosaic. It's worth exploring on foot or bicycle, or by rickshaw or train. Unfortunately, there are no formal bicycle-hire places, but if you ask around something may turn up. Western visitors are rare, so tread gently, and always ask before taking photos.

It doesn't really matter in which direction you choose to go. Jaleshwar on the Nepali side of the border is a completely uninspiring town, but there are some interesting villages on the way. Other possibilities include the road that runs south to the airport, which turns to dirt and continues through a number of attractive villages, the road that runs north of the cigarette factory, and the road that runs west of Purare Chowk. **Dhanusa**, 15km to the north, marks the spot where Rama allegedly drew Shiva's magic bow.

Janakpur is the terminus for two train lines, one of which runs east to **Jaynagar** over the Indian border, and the other which runs north-west to Bijalpur, although only the former route carries passenger traffic. They're narrow-gauge trains and very slow, so they offer an interesting if somewhat crowded method of seeing the countryside.

To Jaynagar there are three daily services in each direction, so it is easy to put together a day trip. It's about 29km (four hours!) to Jaynagar, but tourists are not allowed to cross the border into India – get off in one of the villages along the way. Trains leave both Janakpur and Jaynagar at 6 and 11 am and 3 pm. Tickets are Rs 35 in 1st class and Rs 13 in 2nd class.

The first stop after Janakpur is **Parbaha** (Rs 4/10 in 2nd/1st class, 8km), and there are interesting villages on either side of the tracks – you could walk back to town. Another interesting stop is **Baidehi**, about an hour (Rs 5/14, 12km) from Janakpur, where you could alight and catch the Janakpur-bound train that comes through an hour later. Alternatively, you could continue all the way to **Khajuri** (Rs 9/25, 21km), about 8km from Jaynagar on the Nepali side of the border and catch the afternoon Janakpur train.

BIRGANJ
☎ 051

Birganj is one of the main border crossings between Nepal and India, and is one of Nepal's most important industrial cities. This is an unfortunate combination. It has been one of the most unattractive places on the planet for some time, but it is not resting on its laurels. It is growing rapidly and the pollution and squalor are getting worse. For much of the year the climate is oppressively hot, and during the monsoon the heat combines with the humidity to make the place almost unbearable.

Birganj seems to stretch northwards for miles, strung along the impossibly congested main road, although mercifully the heavy traffic bypasses the city centre on a recently constructed ring road. There are a large number of depressingly run-down factories, as the 'corridor' between Birganj and Hetauda is probably the most important centre for industrial development in Nepal. Among tanneries and other unattractive places there are a sugar factory and an agricultural implements factory.

There are immigrants from around Nepal and many from India; bear in mind that the only reason they come to Birganj is that the alternative of remaining in their place of birth is worse. The local language is Bhojpuri, which is spoken on both sides of the border.

Birganj is probably the most important entry point for Indian imports, but most travellers (especially those coming from Varanasi) enter through Sunauli to the west. Birganj remains the most convenient entry point, however, for those coming from Patna or Calcutta.

Fortunately, there are plenty of day and night buses to and from Kathmandu and Pokhara and points south (in India) so there should be no necessity to stay more than a night – hopefully not even that.

Orientation & Information

Birganj and Raxaul Bazaar (on the Indian side of the border) virtually run together, although it's a 30 minute rickshaw ride from one bus station to the other.

The Birganj bus station (the best or worse part of town, depending on whether you're going or coming) is on the ring road, about 500m east of the clocktower.

The various official offices on either side of the border are all open between 7 am and 7 pm, as is the bank on the Nepali side.

There's an official moneychanger on the main street, and it accepts major currencies (cash and travellers cheques).

Things to See

If you do find yourself with a couple of hours to kill in Birganj you could hire a rickshaw for an hour or two (at around Rs 30 an hour) and have a bit of a wander. The

BIRGANJ

To Hotel Samjhana (1km) & Kathmandu

To Bus Station (500m)

0   250   500 m

Tank

Main Road

1 Clocktower
2 Himanchal Cabin
3 Maystan Temple
4 Gita Temple
5 Bal Mandir
6 Nepal Rastra Bank
7 Government Offices
8 Hotel Prakash
9 Hotel Kailas
10 Hotel Diyalo
11 Prakash Lodge
12 Hotel Cottage Fulwari
13 Moneychanger
14 Lumbini Airways

To Customs & Immigration (3km) & Indian Border (4km)

town has a certain gruesome fascination and there are a couple of modern temples and muddy ponds. The most interesting is the **Bal Mandir**, a modern Buddhist temple about 1km west from the main road.

Places to Stay & Eat
The places to stay are in the centre of town, clustered around what was the old bus station. The really cheap places are a pretty dismal lot, and can't seriously be recommended. If you're broke and stuck, try the **Prakash Lodge**, a dirt-cheap place which is both dirty and cheap.

Hotel Kailas (☎ 23084, fax 22410) has a range of decent rooms and a good, air-con (mercifully), tandoori restaurant. A few smallish singles with shared bath start at Rs 100, otherwise rooms with bath start at Rs 250/430, rising to Rs 930/990 with air-con.

Almost next door is the **Hotel Diyalo** (☎ 22370, fax 25375), a well-run hotel with immaculate rooms that are reasonably priced for what you get. It also has a good restaurant. Singles/doubles with bath range from Rs 400/500 to Rs 600/700 with air-cooler and Rs 1200/1500 with air-con.

There's a decent, cheap **tandoori restaurant** between the Kailas and Diyalo hotels.

Farther along the same road is the **Hotel Cottage Fulwari**, with a range of OK rooms at Rs 400/450 with air-cooling and Rs 1100/1400 with air-con.

Hotel Samjhana (☎ 22122, fax 22535) is quite a distance from the bus station, but it has parking and decent food. This is the Birganj Ritz, and even has a swimming pool, although when we visited the water was a most uninviting shade of green. A room in the newer wing, with all mod cons including air-con costs Rs 1600/2000. The old section of the hotel is not particularly appealing, and rooms cost Rs 700/900. There is some room for bargaining if things are quiet.

Himanchal Cabin restaurant on the main street does South Indian food such as *dosas* (lentil and rice flour pancakes).

Getting There & Away
To/From India It's a 30 minute, Rs 15 rickshaw between the Birganj bus station and the border, and another 30 minutes and Indian Rs 20 between the border and the Raxaul Bazaar bus station. Expect to pay Rs 70 for the five hour journey to Patna from Raxaul Bazaar.

To/From Nepal Lumbini Airways (☎ 20453) has twice daily flights between Kathmandu and Simara, the airport for Birganj ($44). Cosmic Air and RNAC both have one flight per day.

There are plenty of day and night buses to and from Kathmandu. Anything between 20 and 40 buses leave Birganj each evening between 7 and 9 pm, arriving in Kathmandu around 5 am and costing Rs 145. A dozen or so day buses leave between 6 and 8 am and cost Rs 114.

There are also buses for Pokhara (Rs 120, 6.30 am to 2.30 pm; Rs 149, 7 and 8 pm; 10 hours), Janakpur (Rs 88, day buses), Sauraha (for Chitwan) for Rs 65.

Bureaucratic Blackmail in Birganj – Warning
In the past, the Nepali immigration officers at Birganj have been known to run a particularly infuriating scam. They insist they can only accept the $25 visa fee in cash US dollars. Although the bank or moneychangers at the border would happily change foreign currency and give an official foreign exchange encashment receipt, the immigration officials will under no circumstances accept rupees, or any other currency. This is definitely not official policy, but they have the magic stamp and so there's little you can do but be prepared. The best insurance is a visa already in your passport.

THE TERAI

Despite the fact that the Tribhuvan Hwy from Hetauda to Naubise looks like the best route to Kathmandu, all buses travel west to Narayanghat before they climb into the hills. It is possible to catch a bus from Hetauda (Rs 27 from Birganj) to Kathmandu that traverses the Tribhuvan Hwy – it's slow, but there are superb views. See the Hetauda section later in this chapter, and the Getting Around chapter.

Getting Around
Rickshaws cost around Rs 30 per hour, and this will be the charge if you get one to take you all the way through to Raxaul Bazaar (recommended).

HETAUDA
☎ 057
Hetauda is the starting point for a cableway that carries cement from the Terai to Kathmandu. It's quite an amazing construction, similar in concept to a ski lift. The current cableway dates from 1958 and can carry 25 tonnes per hour; it takes 15 hours for goods to travel the distance. Unless you want to catch a bus over the superb Tribhuvan Hwy, there's no need to stop. Normally, buses turn west to Narayanghat.

Places to Stay & Eat
Neelam Lodge (☎ 20900), on the Daman road near the main chowk in the centre of town and beside a big pipal tree, has clean singles/doubles for Rs 150/200 with attached bath (cold water) – good value.

Hotel Seema (☎ 20191), about 200m on the other side of the chowk, is a new place with decent rooms at Rs 120/180 with common bath, Rs 250/350 with bath and Rs 1200 for a deluxe air-con double room.

Motel Avocado (☎ 20429, fax 20611), on the way out of town on the Tribhuvan Hwy to Daman, has accommodation in a quiet, pleasant garden (with avocado trees). Rooms in an old Nissen hut are spacious, comfortable and rather idiosyncratic. They come with fans and attached bath, and cost Rs 350/500 (negotiable). There's also a three-storey wing of new deluxe rooms with

air-con, and these cost Rs 1200/1500. The restaurant here is quite good, and they also have interesting travellers' notebooks on cycling and motorcycling.

Getting There & Away
One Sajha Yatayat bus a day runs over the magnificent Tribhuvan Hwy via Daman. There are spectacular views and this route is well worth considering. The bus station in Hetauda is to the south-east of the main intersection and the Kathmandu via Daman bus leaves at 7 am. From the Kathmandu Bus Terminal the Sajha bus also leaves at 7 am (Rs 66, eight hours).

A number of private buses go to Kathmandu and Pokhara via Narayanghat and Tadi Bazaar. Buses to Tadi Bazaar take around three hours and cost Rs 60. There are numerous buses to Birganj for Rs 27.

DAMAN
Daman is 2322m above sea level, midway between Kathmandu and Hetauda. Its claim to fame is that it has, arguably, *the* most spectacular outlook on the Himalaya – there are unimpeded views of the entire range from Dhaulagiri to Mt Everest. If you have the opportunity it should not be missed.

There is a viewing tower with a telescope (small entry fee), which is part of a very uninspiring and cramped tented camp, a basic lodge/restaurant and not much else. On the Hetauda side of Daman there is a magnificent rhododendron forest – which would be particularly worth seeing in spring – then great views over the Terai to India.

Places to Stay & Eat
Daman Mountain Resort consists of a number of permanent tents clustered around the viewing tower. The cost to stay here is an expensive Rs 800 for a double! Much more sensible, but far more basic, is the nearby *Hotel Sherpa*, a friendly local hotel with double rooms at Rs 200. You can also get food here, as long as you don't want anything more complicated than dal bhat.

There's also another tent resort, the *Everest Panorama Resort* about 3km higher up

THE TERAI

the hill, but it is also quite expensive at Rs 1000 per person.

Getting There & Away

Daman is about three hours by car from Kathmandu and four hours from Hetauda. Unless you're on your way to/from Birganj, hiring a car and making a day trip from Kathmandu is the ideal way to get to Daman, but it won't be cheap. Think in terms of $60. If you have a group and it's clear weather, it would be worth it. Alternatively, this is one of the most spectacular (and most gruelling) mountain-bike routes in the world. See the Rajpath section in the Mountain Biking chapter for details.

From Daman there's one northbound (Kathmandu) and one southbound (Hetauda) Sajha Yatayat bus a day. Buses leave Kathmandu and Hetauda at 7 am (Rs 34).

TADI BAZAAR

In the Chitwan Valley between Hetauda and Narayanghat, the small town of Tadi Bazaar (sometimes spelt Tandi Bazaar) is nothing more than a junction town for Sauraha, the budget accommodation centre for Royal Chitwan National Park. For more details see the earlier section on the park.

Getting There & Away

See the Getting There & Away entry in the Royal Chitwan National Park section for details on transport to/from Tadi Bazaar and the nearby village of Sauraha.

NARAYANGHAT & BHARATPUR
☎ 056

Narayanghat is a fast-growing town on the banks of the large Narayani River, just downstream from the junction of the Kali Gandaki and Trisuli rivers. It has developed mainly because it lies at the intersection (Pul Chowk) of the Mahendra Hwy, which runs the length of the Terai, and the main road into the hills to Kathmandu and Pokhara. It is the administrative and trading centre for the whole district. Bharatpur is contiguous with Narayanghat, and has an airport.

Although on the map the most direct route from eastern Nepal to Kathmandu is the road from Hetauda to Naubise, most traffic takes the better road from Narayanghat to Mugling. The Tribhuvan Hwy (or Tribhuvan Rajpath) from Hetauda to Naubise is a great drive, but its endless narrow corners mean it's not appropriate for trucks and buses.

Narayanghat will, for most people, simply be a chai stop en route to Kathmandu, Chitwan or India, and apart from the river there's not much of interest in the town. However, it's not a bad spot to stop if you are exploring the Terai, and there's an interesting excursion to Devghat, a holy site north-west of town at the confluence of the Kali Gandaki and Trisuli rivers (see Around Narayanghat later).

Places to Stay & Eat

If due to bad luck or bad management you are forced to stay the night, there are a few choices. Right by the main intersection, very handy for buses, is the *Regal Rest House* (☎ 20755). Rooms with common bath are Rs 135/170, while with attached bath and hot water it's Rs 250/350. Don't stay here unless you can get a room at the back, as the road is very busy with buses coming and going at all hours of the day and night. There's a decent restaurant here.

A much more pleasant option, but also somewhat inconvenient, is the *Gainda Cottages* (☎ 20590) on the western bank of the Narayani (across the bridge and first right). It's not exactly luxurious, and mosquito repellent is a good idea, but the welcome is warm, the rooms are clean, and there's a courtyard garden area. Rooms are reasonable value at Rs 120/240 with common bath. Simple food is available.

There are some cheaper places around the northern bus station. The *Hotel River View* (☎ 21151) is a quiet, basic place which does indeed have a river view, although only from the upper floors. The rooms are a bit on the small side, but are good value at Rs 180 for a double with attached bath and mosquito nets.

Other than these places there are a couple of upmarket choices in Bharatpur, and these are handy for the airport. The *Hotel Narayani Safari* (☎ *20130, fax 21058*) is primarily used as a base for trips to Chitwan. It is well run and has air-con, a swimming pool, tennis court and an excellent restaurant. Singles/doubles cost $50/65, but discounts of 15% are offered.

Hotel Chitwan Keyman (☎ *20200*) is a modern place with a quiet rear garden, and very comfortable rooms with air-con and TV for $36/42, although a 30% discount should be possible.

A few kilometres out of town on the Kathmandu road is the *Lovely River Resort* (☎ *01-425042*), signposted 2km off the road along a dirt track. It's a very pleasant set up on the banks of the Trisuli River. Accommodation is in stone cottages, and costs Rs 800, which includes three meals.

Getting There & Away
RNAC (☎ 20326) has daily flights from Kathmandu to Bharatpur for $50.

As Narayanghat is such a major crossroad there are buses coming and going at all hours. Buses from Narayanghat to Pokhara leave from the bus park at the northern end of town on the road to Mugling. Buses to/from most Terai destinations and Kathmandu stop at the main T-junction just to the east of the bridge.

The Sajha Yatayat booking office is tucked away in the group of stalls next to the Gulf petrol station. Private night buses can be booked at the office with a green painted sign in the Gulf station; tickets for day buses can be bought from the desks set up outside the Regal Rest House.

From Kathmandu the fare is Rs 70 to Narayanghat, and you can catch just about any bus heading for the Terai.

From Narayanghat, there are Sajha day buses (most en route from Kathmandu) for Janakpur (Rs 100), Nepalganj (Rs 163), Bhairawa (Rs 55), Tansen (Palpa) (Rs 75) and Birganj (Rs 65).

Private buses from Narayanghat run to Kakarbhitta (Rs 263, 10 hours), Biratnagar (Rs 207, nine hours, leaving at 8 pm), Janakpur (Rs 119, six hours, 9 pm), Mahendranagar (Rs 306, 17 hours, 4.30 pm), Nepalganj (Rs 170/214 day/night, 10 hours, 7.30 am and 7 to 9 pm), Pokhara (Rs 73, five hours, several daytime departures) and Kathmandu (Rs 70/82, hourly from 7 am to 1 pm, many at night).

Crowded minibuses for Tadi Bazaar (Chitwan) leave from the side of the Mahendra Hwy just before the second intersection east of the main T-junction; they cost Rs 9 and take 30 minutes. Taxis to Chitrasali (for Chitwan) cost Rs 300.

NARAYANGHAT & BHARATPUR

To Butwal (110km)

Narayani River

To Lovely Resort (5km), Devghat (5km) & Mugling (36km)

Pulchowk

Narayanghat

Canal

0   0.5   1 km

Canal

Bharatpur

To Tadi Bazaar (15km) & Hetauda (70km)

Mahendra Highway

1 Hotel River View
2 Buses to Pokhara & Local Bus Station
3 Gainda Cottages
4 Temples
5 Necon Air Office
6 Nepal Bank
7 Sajha Yatayat Bus Office
8 Regal Rest House & Restaurant
9 Buses to Kathmandu
10 Minibuses for Tadi Bazaar
11 Hotel Chitwan Keyman
12 Hotel Narayani Safari
13 Nepal Airways Office

THE TERAI

AROUND NARAYANGHAT

Also known as Deoghat and Harihara Chhetra, **Devghat** is an ancient holy site that was first mentioned in the *Skanda Purana*. It's a suitably beautiful spot, with forest-clad hills, a large sandy beach, and a number of shady shrines and temples overlooking the swirling waters where the Kali Gandaki and Trisuli meet. The confluence of rivers, particularly when they are major tributaries of the Ganges, is always regarded as religiously significant by Hindus, as it is believed a third spiritual river also joins.

Many elderly high-caste Hindus come here to quietly live out their last days, and finally to be cremated on the river banks, thus gaining religious merit and hopefully avoiding a stay in hell while they wait for reincarnation. In fact, all sorts of religious rites, including marriages, are performed at Devghat and they often involve large family groups. The atmosphere is peaceful and tranquil, not at all gloomy.

Devghat is one of the main sites for the festival of Magh Sankranti, and pilgrims come from around Nepal and India to immerse themselves in the river (see the later Ridi Bazaar section). This festival takes place on the first day of the Nepali month of Magh, in mid-January, and celebrates the gradually lengthening days and the onset of warmer weather.

Western visitors (untouchables) are rare, and should bear in mind that caste-related ideas of ritual pollution may mean that some of the orthodox pilgrims and inhabitants could be offended by any contact. Do not enter homes or temples without invitation and do not touch anything that could be holy (which means almost everything!). There is nowhere to stay, and not even a chai stall, so bring drinks and food.

Getting There & Away

There are frequent minibuses to/from Narayanghat. By road, you head north from town on the Mugling road for 3km, turn left on a signposted dirt road just before a police checkpoint and continue for 2km, then take the right fork and continue for another 3km. It is possible to walk along the eastern bank of the river, although the track here is a bit overgrown and it's easiest to pick up and follow it from the Devghat end.

BUTWAL

☎ 071

Lying at the very foot of the Chure Hills, Butwal is at first appearances an unattractive, dirty town. The approach from Tansen, to the north, is dramatic: one moment you're in a narrow mountain gorge, the next you are surrounded by people, dust, rickshaws and Hindi film posters.

If you find yourself stranded for a night, or have a couple of hours to kill waiting for a bus, it's well worth a wander through the old part of town on the west bank of the Tinau River. Historically, Butwal once lay at the start of a trade route to Tibet and so has a good deal more history than most Terai towns. While there are no significant old buildings, the narrow, traffic-free streets of the old part of town are a million miles from new Butwal – kids play cricket in the street, women sit chatting in doorways and there is a general unhurried air. Walk across the main vehicle bridge, then head north through the old streets towards the hills, then cut back across the river on one of the two suspension foot/bicycle bridges.

Places to Stay & Eat

There are plenty of cheap hotels at Traffic Chowk on the main road in the centre of town, and this is also where long-distance buses stop. Pick of the cheapies is the *Hotel New Gandaki* (☎ 40928), which has scruffy rooms at Rs 120 for a double, Rs 200 with bath.

A quantum leap up the scale and well worth the difference is the modern *Hotel Kandara* (☎ 40380). This is a friendly place with a nice small garden with car parking at the rear. Clean rooms with bath are Rs 250/400, or with carpet and hot water it's Rs 400/720, and air-con Rs 1200 for a double. Avoid the front rooms as they cop the street noise. The attached *Fedee Restaurant* is not a bad place to eat.

Nearby is *Hotel Siddhartha* (☎ 40380), a clean and comfortable hotel with rooms at Rs 350/450 with bath.

Hotel Sindoor (☎ 40381) is an upmarket and expensive hotel catering to visiting big-wigs. Though overpriced and a bit gloomy, it's clean, quiet and unquestionably the best place in town. Singles/doubles here are $22/32; it wouldn't hurt to ask for a discount.

Getting There & Away
All the long-distance buses leave from Traffic Chowk on the main drag. The Sajha Yatayat booking office is just down from Traffic Chowk, opposite the modern temple built in traditional style. There are morning departures for Kathmandu at (Rs 132) and Nepalganj (Rs 132).

Private night buses are booked at the small shop with the red sign (Nepali writing) next to the Fedee Restaurant at Traffic Chowk. The booking office for day buses is between the Samrat and Siddhartha hotels, and also has a red sign in Nepali.

There are departures for Pokhara (eight hours) via Mugling (Rs 130, night) and via Tansen (Rs 102, morning). Buses also depart for Nepalganj (Rs 139, day and night), Janakpur (Rs 186), Narayanghat (Rs 53, throughout the day), Mahendranagar (Rs 228), Birganj (Rs 108), Gorkha (Rs 90) and Kathmandu (Rs 142).

There are also regular departures for Sunauli/Bhairawa (22km).

SUNAULI & BHAIRAWA
☎ 071
Sunauli (pronounced 'soo-*nor*-li') is a small, grubby collection of offices and hotels right on the Indian border. Bhairawa is a somewhat more substantial, dusty, bustling town nearly 4km inside Nepal; officially Bhairawa's name is Siddharthanagar, but this is rarely used.

There are three points in favour of visiting this part of the world. Firstly, Sunauli is by far the most popular and convenient border crossing between Nepal and northern and western India (including Varanasi, Agra and Delhi). Secondly, Bhairawa is the closest town to Lumbini, the birthplace of Buddha. And thirdly, although Sunauli and Bhairawa are hot and featureless, they are still relaxed and pleasant by comparison to Birganj, the next major crossing point to the east.

There is some small-scale industry, a couple of banks and government offices and plenty of shops. Most pre-arranged bookings to/from India involve a night's stop in Sunauli, and most individual travellers do the same.

Orientation & Information
Both the Nepali and Indian customs and immigration offices are open 24 hours, but between the hours of about 7 pm and 5 am you will have to wake them up, something they are quite accustomed to. You are free to walk across the border between the Indian and Nepali sides without going through any formalities, although attempting this with a backpack on would be asking for trouble.

Indian rupees are accepted readily in Sunauli and Bhairawa, and also in major centres such as Kathmandu and Pokhara. The exchange rate is set at Indian Rs 1 = Nepali Rs 1.60. Changing money is simple as there are a number of official private moneychangers on the Nepali side (open long hours). Outside these hours there are black-market operators who offer fairly poor rates. The bank on the Indian side of the border doesn't open until 10 am – after the buses have left – and is busy as hell. Nepali rupees are not easy to use in India, so spend or exchange them here if you are heading south.

There is a tourist office (☎ 20304) at the border. The Department of Tourism's *Visitors' Guide* (free) is worth picking up, but don't expect much more.

Bhairawa is a 20 minute rickshaw ride to the north. Most shops and businesses in Bhairawa are strung along Narayan Path or Bank Rd. The Siddhartha Hwy runs along the eastern edge of town to the border. Lumbini is 22km to the south-west, but there are frequent buses running along the route, and most people stay in Bhairawa if they plan to visit the site.

THE TERAI

Places to Stay & Eat

It doesn't really matter whether you stay in Bhairawa or Sunauli since it's easy and cheap to go between the two (see the Getting Around section).

Budget travellers in transit to or from India will find a couple of accommodation options in Sunauli, but there really is *nothing* to do, so consider staying in Bhairawa where there's a bit of life.

Sunauli There are about half a dozen options here, with not much between them. The *Nepal Guest House* has a reasonable restaurant, is reasonably priced and is passably clean. The place is something of a labyrinth and the rooms vary – ask to see several before you settle in. There are four-bed dorms with beds for Rs 30, doubles with fan and bath for Rs 150, and singles for Rs 100.

Hotel Paradise (☎ 22777) is OK and right next to the bus park, but make sure you get a room on the side away from the bus park as buses start leaving at around 4 am. Rooms are Rs 250/350 with bath.

Hotel Plaza is still relatively new and so has not yet slid into the shabby state that seems to befall most hotels in this part of the world before very long. It's good value at Rs 200/300.

Hotel Mamta (☎ 20312), about 300m from the border post, does not look very inspiring, but the rooms are reasonably clean. This is almost certainly where you'll find yourself if you've bought pre-arranged tickets through an agent. A single bed in a six-bed dorm costs Rs 40 and a single/double with common bath is Rs 80/150, and with attached bath Rs 120/200.

Apart from the restaurants attached to hotels, there are a few small restaurants.

Bhairawa *Hotel Shambala (☎ 20167)* on Bank Rd is not too bad, and charges Rs 250 for a double with common bath, Rs 350/450 for singles/doubles with attached bath, and Rs 1000/1200 with air-con.

Hotel Everest (☎ 20317) on the same road is a new place with clean and comfortable rooms. The charge is perhaps a bit high at Rs 500/700 with attached bath, but some bargaining may be possible.

Hotel Yeti (☎ 20551, fax 20893) is on the corner of Bank Rd and Siddhartha Hwy. This is where the tour groups that occasionally pass through stay. It's clean, there's a decent restaurant and, for what it delivers, the prices are reasonable – $20/25 for a single/double, or $30/35 with air-con, and a discount of 15% is offered. The only problem is the hotel overlooks a main intersection (where the buses stop) so it can be a bit noisy.

SUNAULI & BHAIRAWA

To Butwal (22km)

To Lumbini (22km)

To Airport (1.5km) & Lumbini (22km)

0   0.5   1 km

Bhairawa

Bank Road

Market Road

Paklihawa Road

Siddhartha Highway

Sunauli

INDIA   Nautanwa

1 Local Buses to Lumbini
2 Hotel Himalayan Inn
3 Necon Air
4 Hotel Yeti; Lumbini Airways; Buddha Air
5 Sajha Yatayat Office
6 RNAC Office
7 Hotel Everest
8 Hotel Shambala
9 Kasturi Restaurant
10 Hotel Nirvana
11 Hotel Mamta; Zorba The Buddha Restaurant
12 Hotel Plaza
13 Share Jeeps to Bhairawa
14 Nepal Guest House
15 Nepali Customs
16 Bus Park
17 Hotel Paradise
18 Nepali Immigration & Tourist Office
19 Indian Immigration Office

THE TERAI

Hotel Himalayan Inn (☎ 20347, fax 21540) is a bit out of town to the north on the Siddhartha Hwy. It's not too bad and has a restaurant and off-road parking. Singles/doubles with bath and air-con are $18/25, but a discount of 20% brings this back to something more reasonable.

Hotel Nirvana (☎ 20837, fax 21262, email nirva@ccsl.com.np) on Paklihawa Rd is a five-star place which seems very misplaced in scruffy Bhairawa. It's modern, clean, air-con and is well worth the money if you need this level of comfort. The restaurant serves OK meals, and there's a bar. Room rates are $95/105, but discounting can lower this by 30%.

Kasturi Restaurant, near the corner of Bank Rd and Narayan Path, is a pleasant high-ceilinged place with uniformed waiters and excellent vegetarian Indian food. Dishes like *pulau* and korma cost around Rs 30.

Getting There & Away

There are plenty of bus connections to destinations in both Nepal and India. Whether you have booked a 'through' ticket or not, everyone changes buses at the border and most people spend the night in Sunauli. There are no 'tourist' buses.

To/From India You catch buses to Indian cities from the Indian side of the border. There are direct buses to Varanasi for Indian Rs 90 to Rs 120, depending on the degree of luxury, and the journey takes about nine hours.

There are also buses to Gorakhpur where you can connect with the Indian broad-gauge railway (Indian Rs 30, three hours). From Gorakhpur, buses leave every half hour from 5 am to 7 pm; you'll need to catch a bus from Gorakhpur by 3 pm if you want to be sure of catching a night bus to Kathmandu the same day. See the Getting There & Away chapter for more information.

To/From Nepal RNAC (☎ 20175) operates four flights a week between Kathmandu and Bhairawa for $72. Buddha Air (☎ 21893) has daily flights. Necon Air (☎ 20498) also flies daily. The Bhairawa airport is just west of town.

Travelling north, most buses leave from Sunauli, stopping in Bhairawa, but buses can be booked and boarded at either place. In Sunauli there's a bus booking office at the bus stand, and buses can only be booked on the day of departure. This office opens at 3 am. In Bhairawa the bus companies' offices are around the intersection of Bank Rd and the Siddhartha Hwy. The Sajha Yatayat booking office is close to the Hotel Yeti, although these buses only operate to Kathmandu (Rs 120/148 by day/night, 6.45 and 8 am, 7 and 7.30 pm).

There are several private night and day buses to Pokhara and Kathmandu.

Buses for Pokhara (Rs 128/149 by day/night, nine hours) travel via Narayanghat and the trip is particularly beautiful (for great views of Machhapuchhare if you're heading north, get a seat on the left-hand side). A number of buses leave Sunauli between 4 and 10 am, and at 6.45 and 8 pm.

For Kathmandu there are also day and night buses from Sunauli, and there are at least seven buses each evening between 4.30 and 8 pm (Rs 128/159).

From Kathmandu, Sajha buses leave at 7.30 am and 7 pm. Private buses leave half-hourly from 6 to 9 am, and from 5 to 8 pm.

If you want to go to Royal Chitwan National Park from Sunauli, there are buses for Birganj (Rs 123, seven hours) that leave at 5.30 and 7.30 am. Get off at Tadi Bazaar if you're heading to Sauraha (Rs 80, four hours). There are plenty of local buses to Butwal for Rs 14.

There are also night buses to Janakpur (Rs 208), Biratnagar (Rs 297) and Kakarbhitta (Rs 337).

For transport to Lumbini see the Lumbini Getting There & Away section.

Getting Around

The only time you'll need transport will be to go between Sunauli and Bhairawa – four, hot, flat kilometres. A rickshaw costs around Rs 50 and takes 20 minutes, a share jeep Rs 3.

THE TERAI

LUMBINI

Lumbini is believed to be the birthplace of Siddhartha Gautama – the founder of Buddhism, known as Buddha, or the enlightened one. This is confirmed by the existence of an inscribed pillar erected 318 years after the event by the great Buddhist emperor Ashoka, and the presence of a number of ancient ruins.

Fittingly, Lumbini is an example of how ephemeral the results of human effort are. There's not much to see and it requires a serious effort of the imagination to conjure up the ghosts of the past. Lumbini is not a Bethlehem or Mecca – there is no city, no impressive architecture, no pilgrim-jammed car park, no heavily armed soldiers, no hustlers, not even a postcard stand.

In the end, it is the absence of all these things, and the peacefulness of Lumbini that make a visit worthwhile. In some ways, Tilaurakot (see that section later in this chapter), the site of Kapilavastu, the fortress-palace where Buddha was raised as a prince of the royal family, is more evocative.

It's curious that the Buddha should have been born and raised on a fertile tropical plain, a place of such contrast to the deserts of the Middle East where so many religions originated; strange that he should have been born a wealthy prince; and almost bizarre that this privileged life and rich countryside should have inspired a belief that suffering is synonymous with existence.

Allow yourself an hour or two to wander around and soak in the atmosphere. The important sights don't take long to cover – the Maya Devi Temple, the Ashokan Pillar, the Sacred Pond and the Tibetan and Theravada *viharas* (monasteries). Then find a shady spot where you can watch the parrots squabbling in the branches of the massive *bo* trees.

There are grandiose plans for the development of Lumbini, with the aim of creating a place of pilgrimage, and a tourist attraction. It will be interesting to see whether this can be achieved by government decree. A plan by Japanese architect Kenzo Tange was adopted in 1978, involving canals, gardens, a library and museum, monastic zones, a pilgrim lodge and a hotel. There has been some slow progress. The major earthworks are complete, there are a couple of buildings quite a distance from the site proper, which are forlornly empty, and a luxury hotel, which is actually operating.

History

The great Indian emperor Ashoka visited Lumbini in 245 BCE, and left a number of his famous inscribed pillars in the region. In 403 CE the region was visited by Fa Hsien a Chinese pilgrim who described a ruined Kapilavastu and a deserted countryside.

In 636 CE Hsuan Tang, another pilgrim, described 1000 derelict monasteries and Ashoka's pillar at Lumbini, shattered by lightning and lying on the ground. Derelict it may have been, but the site was still known in 1312 CE when Ripu Malla visited, possibly leaving the nativity statue which is still worshipped in the Maya Devi Temple.

Mughal invaders arrived in the region at the end of the 15th century, and in common with their zealous actions elsewhere on the subcontinent, it is likely that the remaining 'pagan' monuments at Kapilavastu and Lumbini were destroyed. The whole region returned to wilderness and the sites were lost to the jungle, until the governor of Palpa (Tansen), Khadga Shumsher Rana, who had a keen interest in archaeology, began the excavation of a pillar – which turned out to be Ashoka's Lumbini pillar – in late 1896.

Today, no trace of the Lumbini forest remains, but the pond where Maya Devi is believed to have bathed can still be seen, although in much restored form. The brick foundations of stupas and viharas dating from the 2nd century BCE can be seen around the pond. The Maya Devi Temple is built on ancient foundations, and these are now the site of an archaeological dig.

After the discovery of Lumbini, the ruins near Tilaurakot were identified as Kapilavastu. There has been some archaeological work, which has revealed the remains of moated city walls, impressive gates and the foundations for a palace complex.

Most of the surrounding countryside is now dominated by extremely poor Muslim peasant farmers. There are no Buddhists.

Ashokan Pillar

Emperor Ashoka is one of the greatest figures in Indian history. Throughout his massive empire he left pillars and rock-carved edicts, which to this day delineate the extent of his power. They can be seen in Delhi, Gujarat, Orissa, Uttar Pradesh, Madhya Pradesh – and Nepal.

The pillar at Lumbini commemorates Ashoka's pilgrimage to the birthplace of Buddha. It is 6m high, although half of it is underground, and it is inscribed with the following:

King Ashoka, the beloved of Gods, in the 20th year of the coronation, made a royal visit. A stone railing and a stone pillar were erected in honour of Buddha who was born here. Because Buddha was born here the village of Lumbini was freed from paying tax.

Maya Devi Temple

Until recently the Maya Devi Temple, parts of which were believed to be over 2000 years old, stood on the spot where the Buddha is though to have been born. A huge pipal tree, which was gradually tearing the temple apart, was believed by some to have been the tree that Maya Devi held while giving birth to Siddhartha.

In 1993 the tree was ripped out and the temple demolished to make archaeological excavations possible. At the time of writing these were still going on and the site has been sheltered by an ugly tin roof. In 1995 archaeologists claim to have found a commemorative stone atop a platform of seven layers of bricks 5m below the old temple floor and dating from the era of Ashoka. Buddhist literature says Ashoka placed a stone on top of bricks at the birthplace of Prince Siddhartha, who was later called Lord Buddha. Ancient writings say Buddha was born while his mother Maya Devi, the queen of nearby Kapilavastu kingdom, was travelling towards her parents' home, which is believed to be in Dewadaha. Passing through Lumbini, she went into labour, bathed in a sacred pond and walked 25 paces to deliver the child. The recently discovered stone is said to be the correct distance from the nearby pool.

When the temple was demolished the revered centrepiece of the temple, a stone carving showing the birth of Buddha, was moved to an ugly brick structure close by which looks like a public toilet block. Possibly dating from the Malla dynasty (about 14th century CE) the sculpture was the centre of a fertility rite, and it has almost been reduced to formlessness by the wear of constant puja. One can still make out Maya Devi, with her right hand raised to hold the pipal tree branch, as she gives birth. There is also a modern marble interpretation, along with a number of small sculptures left by devotees.

A major Hindu festival is held on the full moon of the Nepali month of Baisakh (April-May), when thousands of local Hindus come to worship Maya Devi as Rupa Devi, the mother goddess of Lumbini, and to celebrate Buddha as the ninth incarnation of Vishnu. The Buddhist celebration of Buddha's birthday, or Buddha Jayanti, is celebrated around the same time, but is lower key. During winter, when it's not too hot, Buddhist pilgrims from the Kathmandu Valley often come to worship on Purnima (the night of the full moon) and Astemi (the eighth night after the full moon).

Other Attractions

The square pool beside the temple is believed to be the spot where Maya Devi bathed before giving birth to Buddha; needless to say, it has been heavily restored. The foundations for a number of stupas and viharas dating from the 2nd century BCE to the 9th century CE lie in the vicinity.

There are also two modern temples although, unfortunately, neither are particularly interesting or well maintained – both are slated for demolition under the Lumbini Development Plan. One was built by the Nepali government in 1956, and the other was built in traditional Tibetan style in 1968.

THE TERAI

Siddhartha Gautama

Two and a half thousand years ago the region at the foot of the Himalaya was broken up into a number of small republics and principalities which were vassal states to larger empires based on the Gangetic plain. Siddhartha Gautama was the son of Suddhodana (of the Sakya clan) who ruled the republic of Kapilavastu, and Maya Devi (of the Koliya clan) the daughter of the ruler of the neighbouring state of Dewadaha. The ruins of Kapilavastu lie at Tilaurakot, 27km west of Lumbini, but Dewadaha has not been conclusively identified.

It is believed that Maya Devi was 10 months pregnant when she decided to visit her parents' house in Dewadaha. On the way from Kapilavastu, her entourage had to pass through the grove of Lumbini, which was a famous beauty spot with a pond surrounded by sal trees. On the day she reached Lumbini, in May 563 BCE the sal trees were in full bloom, so Maya Devi stopped to enjoy the scene and to bathe in the pond. Leaving the water, she suddenly felt labour pains. She raised her right hand and caught hold of the drooping branch of a pipal tree, and the baby was born.

Maya Devi returned to Kapilavastu where her son Siddhartha was given a sheltered, privileged upbringing. At the age of 29, while wandering in the town outside the palace walls, he came across an old man, a sick man, a corpse and a hermit. This confrontation with suffering and death impelled Siddhartha to renounce his luxurious life and to leave Kapilavastu.

He spent the next five years seeking to understand the nature of existence. Mostly he wandered as an itinerant ascetic – no doubt much like the Hindu sadhus of today – but he found that extreme self-denial did not provide him with any answers. Finally, after 49 days meditating under a bodhi tree at Bodhgaya he attained enlightenment. From Bodhgaya he travelled to Sarnath, near Varanasi, where he preached his first sermon.

The Buddha spent the next 46 years teaching his 'middle way'. Suffering, he taught, is a natural part of life, but suffering is caused by attachment, desire and delusion, and if these negative forces are controlled (by following the noble 'eightfold path'), it is possible to reach nirvana.

Although some people believe Buddha visited the Kathmandu Valley, there is no firm evidence for this. Most of his preaching was undertaken in northern India and across the Gangetic plain. He died at the age of 80 at Kushinagar, near Gorakhpur, about 100km southeast of Lumbini.

Despite his disavowal of divinity, the main sites associated with Buddha's life (Lumbini, Kapilavastu, Bodhgaya, Sarnath and Kushinagar) soon became centres for pilgrimage, and monasteries and temples sprang up. There are only sparse records of Lumbini's and Kapilavastu's histories, however.

The two large mounds on either side of the site are not impressive stupas, as you might suspect, but simply the spoils from modern archaeological digs.

Places to Stay & Eat

Most people simply make a day trip from Bhairawa, but there are a couple of places to stay and eat.

Lumbini Village Lodge is in Lumbini Mehalbar, the small market town about 1km east of the main site. The village is an undistinguished little place, with a lively market on Monday. The rest of the time it's a peaceful corner of the Terai. For what you get the prices are a bit steep; gloomy cell-like rooms are Rs 150/250. There is reasonable food at around Rs 30 for dal bhat.

There's very, *very* basic accommodation in the *dharamsala* (pilgrims' resthouse) between the two temples at the main site. Literally, all you get is a roof over your head and a bed (no mattress), and the toilets are vile. If you've got food and camping equipment and you do stay, pay a donation.

The best bet is the *Sri Lanka Pilgrims Rest House*, about 3km north of the site, beyond the sacred flame and just off the dirt road to Tilaurakot. This clean and modern place has spacious dorms with beds at $5, and you can often have a room to yourself. It would be handy to have a bicycle if you want to travel back and forth to the site.

At the top of the scale is the *Lumbini Hokke Hotel* (☎ & fax 20236), close to the Sri Lanka Pilgrims Rest House. It has been built with Japanese pilgrims in mind, and most of the rooms have been furnished in traditional Japanese style with tatami floors,

paper partitions and Japanese furniture. There are also a number of European-style rooms. All rooms are air-conditioned, and all have attached bathrooms. Considering the luxury, prices are not unreasonable, with singles/doubles at $79/120. Meals are expensive – lunch is $11 for nonguests; dinner $14. Mountain bikes are available for guests to use, but most people visit with their own transport, or as part of a tour.

Just by the main car park is the *Lumbini Garden Restaurant*, which, judging by its appearance, is not part of the Lumbini Development Plan – it's a modern red-brick eyesore. The prices are relatively high, but it's the only decent place to eat and the food is OK.

Getting There & Away
There are regular minibuses that make the 22km journey from Bhairawa to Lumbini

LUMBINI

To Lumbini Mehalbar (1km) & Bhairawa (22km)

Car Park

Mound

Mound

Sacred Pond

1 Eternal Flame
2 VIP Plantation
3 Ashokan Pillar
4 Maya Devi Temple
5 Maya Devi Shrine
6 Tibetan Gompa
7 Dharamsala
8 Lumbini Garden Restaurant
9 Theravada Temple
10 Bodhi Tree
11 Police Station
12 Mahendra Pillar
13 Old School
14 Lumbini Development Corporation

0   150   300 m

THE TERAI

for Rs 15, but they are agonisingly slow (1½ hours) and drop you off at Lumbini Mehalbar on the main road 1km from the main site. The roof is the place to be. The last bus back passes the turn-off at about 5 pm (check this time). They leave Bhairawa near the main intersection, across the road from the Hotel Yeti.

If you are in a group or have the funds it would be immensely preferable to hire a taxi-jeep (from Rs 300 to Rs 500). These prices include two hours waiting time, which should be sufficient for most people.

The best method of transport for budget travellers would be bicycle, but there are no formal rental places in Bhairawa. If you ask around (start at your hotel, then try bicycle repair shops), you might turn something up.

TAULIHAWA & TILAURAKOT

Tilaurakot is nothing more than a tiny hamlet 3km north of Taulihawa, which is a bustling Terai centre. Tilaurakot was once, however, the capital of the republic of Kapilavastu, where Buddha spent the first 29 years of his life.

Taulihawa is a vibrant town with the usual multicultural mix of peoples found in Terai cities. There is a temple complex known as **Tauleshwar**, now used by Shaivites, in the centre of town.

Although even less visited than Lumbini, Tilaurakot is in many ways the more atmospheric of the two spots. There is a small group of farming households outside the ruins of the city walls, which, along with their moat, can be clearly discerned. The whole complex is shaded by large trees and has the peaceful atmosphere of a park.

The scattered foundations that can be seen within the walls give only the most minimal indication that there was once a palace, but archaeologists have found 13 successive layers of human habitation, dating back to the 8th century BCE. Today the only sign of life is a small run-down shrine to a Hindu goddess, Somaya Mai.

The scene outside the walls could be unchanged from that which Siddhartha himself might have seen. Timeless patterns of sub-sistence farming unfold along the banks of the Banganga River, and on the north side of the river there is an expanse of untouched sal forest. It is not hard to imagine Siddhartha walking out through the imposing gateway of the palace and as he wandered, seeing an old man, a sick man, a corpse and a hermit ...

About 400m from the ruins, a small **museum** (closed on Tuesday and Saturday) displays some of the artefacts that were found at the site – including coins and pottery.

Places to Stay & Eat

There are plenty of food stalls in Taulihawa. *Lumbini Hotel*, on the road to Tilaurakot, is very basic but acceptably clean, and rooms cost Rs 50/80. There are no facilities at Tilaurakot.

Getting There & Away

A reasonable (though badly corrugated) dirt road links Taulihawa with Lumbini, 27km to the east. The road passes the Lumbini Hokke Hotel, and a number of Muslim villages. Slow and crowded local buses link Taulihawa with Bhairawa, but once again a bicycle is the best method of transport.

Tilaurakot is 3km north of Taulihawa. At the end of the bitumen the museum is on the left and the ruins are 400m away down a dirt track on the right. In winter it is possible to cross a ford over the Banganga River, and to continue 14km due north along a dirt road through the Sagar Forest, finally joining the Mahendra Hwy about 35km west of Butwal and 80km east of Lamahi (also spelt Lumihi).

TANSEN (PALPA)

☎ 075

Tansen is just off the Siddhartha Hwy, between Pokhara and Sunauli/Bhairawa. Historically, it has enjoyed a strategic position on the trade and pilgrim route between the hills and the plains.

Prior to the unification of Nepal under the Shahs, Tansen was the capital of the Palpa kingdom, which was ruled by the Sen dynasty. Prithvi Narayan Shah, the Gorkha king who founded modern Nepal, was the product of an arranged marriage between the Shah and Sen families.

For many years Palpa fought in alliance with Gorkha, and together the two states defeated the independent kingdoms of western Nepal. Finally in 1806, the last king of Palpa, Prithivipal Sen, was lured to Kathmandu and beheaded. Palpa was annexed, but Tansen remained the administrative centre for the region. A number of its subsequent governors were high-ranking members of the ruling Shah and, later, Rana families who were exiled from Kathmandu for plotting against the king of the day.

Tansen is still the administrative centre for a large region, but it sees few visitors, and as it is increasingly sidelined by the development on the Terai and at Pokhara, it is gently falling apart.

The town sprawls over a steep ridge and quite a few of the main streets are too steep for cars, which helps to keep some of the less pleasant aspects of the 20th century at bay. In the older sections of the town, attractive Newari buildings line cobbled streets that are reminiscent of parts of Kathmandu.

Most of the surrounding countryside is dominated by Magars, but there are also Bahuns and Chhetris. Newars form the majority in Tansen itself. They migrated from the Kathmandu Valley to take advantage of the new opportunities for trade between the hills and India that opened up in the 19th century – traditional crafts and agricultural surpluses were traded for the products of the British industrial revolution (especially cotton fabrics) that were flooding into India from Britain. Tansen is still famous for metalware, and for *dhaka*, the woven material that is made into *topis* (Nepali hats).

There are great views over the bowl-shaped **Madi Valley** from the town itself and a spectacular view of the Himalaya from the nearby hill, Srinagar Danda. There are some interesting walks in the surrounding countryside, including a two hour trek to the banks of the Kali Gandaki River and the vast, deserted Ranighat Palace. Tansen is a pleasant place to break the journey from Pokhara (110km, five hours!) to Bhairawa (55km, two hours).

Amar Narayan Temple

The Amar Narayan Temple is a classic three tiered pagoda-style temple, considered to be one of the most beautiful outside the Kathmandu Valley. There is some fine woodwork, with erotic figures on the roof struts, and beautifully carved doors.

The temple was built in 1806 CE by Amar Singh Thapa, the general who annexed Tansen to Nepal. Sadhus often stay in the resthouses around the temple on their way to Muktinath, north-west of Pokhara on the popular Annapurna Circuit. There's a large bat colony in the surrounding trees, and several tanks where local women do their washing.

Tansen Durbar

The palace of the provincial governor was built in the heavy-handed Rana style in 1927 and is now home to the local bureaucrats. The imposing, though dilapidated, entrance gate on the eastern side of the compound is called Baggi Dhoka, or Mul Dhoka. It is meant to be the biggest and tallest gate in Nepal, and its dimensions allowed the governor to make a suitably impressive entrance on an elephant.

A public square called **Sitalpati** lies just outside the gate; it's named after the building in the centre, which was, before renovation, an unusual octagonal shape.

Bhagwati Temple

The Bhagwati Temple, near the durbar, is a rather garish construction that was unsympathetically renovated after an earthquake in 1935, and again in 1974. It was built originally in 1815 to commemorate the Nepali victory over the British at Butwal. There are some smaller temples in the vicinity, dedicated to Shiva, Ganesh and Saraswati.

Places to Stay

There are some hotels around the bus station with singles/doubles for around Rs 80/100, but they're all pretty awful.

THE TERAI

Just a short walk up the hill there's a much better option. *Hotel The Bajra* (☎ 20443) is reasonably new and still quite clean – so far. Rooms with common bath are Rs 80/130 for singles/doubles, or with attached bath and hot water they're Rs 200/300.

Farther up the hill still are a couple more choices. *Hotel White Lake* (☎ 20503) has some excellent views away to the south, and the rooms are well appointed and good value at Rs 350/550.

Close by is the much cheaper *Hotel Gautam Siddhartha* (20280), which is basic, but clean and quiet. Rooms with twin beds are Rs 140.

The most luxurious option is about 2km away on the ridge above town. *Hotel Srinagar* (☎ 20045, fax 20467) is rather isolated, but it's comfortable and the views are sensational. It would be worth ringing in advance because the hotel deals mainly with groups and isn't all that used to people arriving unannounced. Singles/doubles with private bath are $26/35.

Getting There & Away

There is one bus a day from Pokhara for Rs 88, but there are others passing through from Butwal and the Terai. There are numerous buses to Butwal for Rs 22, and also to Sunauli/Bhairawa for Rs 40. Sajha Yatayat has one bus daily to Kathmandu at 6.15 am (Rs 131).

The north-south highway is magnificent, so if you can, find a place on the roof to appreciate the views. If you're inside and coming from Pokhara try to get a seat on the right side of the bus. The road to Butwal is subject to landslides during the monsoon, and traffic is often disrupted during this time.

TANSEN (PALPA)

1 Hotel Srinagar
2 Ganesh Temple
3 Hospital
4 Amar Narayan Temple
5 Sitalpati (Public Square)
6 Bhimsen Temple
7 Bhagwati Temple
8 Nepal Bank & Post Office
9 Tansen Durbar
10 Santosh Cinema
11 Gautam Siddhartha Hotel
12 Sajha Yatayat Bus Office
13 Hotel White Lake
14 Tribhuvan Campus
15 Hotel The Bajra
16 Bus Station
17 Hotel Gautam Siddhartha
18 Tundikhel (Parade Ground)

To Ridi Bazaar (28km)
To Ranighat Durbar
Srinagar Danda
To Pokhara (110km)
Birendra Park
Siddhartha Highway
Bártun
To Butwal (55km)

0   0.5   1 km

AROUND TANSEN
Srinagar Danda

Srinagar Danda is a 1600m hill directly north of town, and a steep half-hour walk from Sitalpati. From the pine-forested top there's a spectacular view over the gorge of the Kali Gandaki River to the Himalaya – the panorama stretches from Kanjiroba in the west, to Dhaulagiri, the Annapurnas, and Langtang in the east.

The Hotel Srinagar is a 20 minute walk west of the summit on the main ridge.

Ridi Bazaar

Ridi is a holy town, mainly populated by Newars, at the confluence of the Kali Gandaki and Ridi rivers. The confluence of tributaries to the Ganges is always regarded as holy, and Ridi has been further sanctified by the presence of *saligrams*, black ammonite fossils that have a spiral shape and are regarded as emblems of Vishnu. Saligrams are found in a number of places along the Kali Gandaki, most notably north of Jomsom around Muktinath.

Although Ridi's religious popularity has declined, cremations are still relatively frequent, and pilgrims come for ritual bathing, marriage ceremonies and other rites and rituals. Pilgrims believe that if they fast and worship for three days, and then take a ritual bath in the Kali Gandaki, all their sins will be forgiven.

The most important festival is Magh Sankranti, when many pilgrims come here to immerse themselves in the river (see the Devghat section earlier in this chapter). This festival takes place on the first day of the Nepali month of Magh, in mid-January, and celebrates the gradually lengthening days and the onset of warmer weather. Worshippers also gather every Ekadashi (the 11th day after the full moon). The festival of Ridi is held in November.

The commercial end of town is across the Ridi River; the **Rishikesh** (a manifestation of Vishnu) **Temple** is near the bus station. It is believed the temple was founded by Mukund Sen in the early 16th century, but the current temple dates from the 19th century. It is also believed that the statue of Rishikesh was discovered in the river, and that the figure of the god has gradually aged from boyhood to adulthood.

It is a 13km trek from Tansen to Ridi. You can leave the road just to the west of the Hotel Srinagar, and pick it up again about 7km from Ridi. Alternatively, it is 28km by road. Buses leave Tansen in the morning, take two hours and cost Rs 46.

Ranighat Durbar

Sometimes fancifully referred to as Nepal's Taj Mahal, Ranighat Durbar was built by Khadga Shamsher Rana in 1896. Khadga was exiled to Tansen and made governor for plotting to become prime minister. While he was in exile, he consoled himself by building a spectacular palace, supposedly in memory of his wife, Tej Kumari.

The palace is now a huge, white baroque ruin dramatically perched on a rocky crag above the Kali Gandaki River. It was used for 25 years as a luxurious dharamsala by aristocrats who ostensibly came to bathe in the Kali Gandaki, and no doubt to party and plot with Khadga. Khadga was an ambitious man and in 1921 he made another abortive attempt to seize power. As a result he was exiled farther away – this time in India. On his departure the building was stripped of its valuable furnishings, and has been gradually collapsing ever since.

The trail to Ranighat begins a short distance to the east of the Hotel Srinagar, at the edge of the pine forest. It's an attractive 7km hike down to the river and takes about two hours each way.

NEPALGANJ
☎ 081

The most important town in western Nepal, Nepalganj at times feels more Indian than Nepali. It's a border town that owes as much to trade (read smuggling) as it does to its position as a major administrative centre. It has more of an air of permanence than some other border towns and planners have had the good sense to run the highway to the west of the main town. Despite that, it's a distinctly unattractive place, with few redeeming features.

Nepalganj is a densely crowded city, and every possible ethnic group in Nepal is represented. There is an unusually large Muslim community, many of whom settled here to escape the violence of the 1857 Indian Uprising. The Muslim men are distinctive, with their long beards and skull caps, as are the women, some of whom dress in black and are completely veiled. The colourful throngs in the streets, however, include Shaivite sadhus, Tharu women (with tight bodices, bare midriffs and bright skirts), turbanned Sikhs, Bajis (Abadhi speakers from India), Bahuns, Chhetris, Newars, Magars, Gurungs, Thakuris and even Tibetans (who look a bit hot in their traditional gear).

A steady trickle of travellers come through Nepalganj on their way to or from western Nepal and Royal Bardia National Park (see later in this chapter), or to Jumla in western Nepal. It can also be a useful backdoor entry into Nepal from central Uttar Pradesh in India; Lucknow is about four hours away.

Orientation & Information

The airport is 6km north of Birendra Chowk (with the statue) and east of the main road. The long-distance bus station is also north of town. About 1km north of Birendra Chowk there's an accumulation of local buses (including buses for Mahendranagar) around a T-junction. Turn right and continue for another 500m and you come to the long-distance bus station (for Kathmandu and points east). Book your return ticket before you go into town to save yourself a trip.

The town is about 6km north of the border. The old, vaguely interesting part of town lies to the east of the main road around Tribhuvan Chowk, although virtually all the hotels are on the highway.

The various customs and immigration offices at the border all have different closing hours, but they are all open from 8 to 11 am and from 1 to 5 pm. There is a money-changer at the Mankamana Guest House and at least two banks in town.

Things to See & Do

The old part of town has the garish **Bageshwari Mandir**, honouring Kali. There's also a vibrant **bazaar** selling everything except kitchen sinks (although one of the metalworkers could probably knock one up if you needed it). It is well worth wandering around the centre of town. The crush of people, the smells, the food, the shops, the film posters and the rickshaws give a vivid taste of the subcontinent.

NEPALGANJ

PLACES TO STAY
5 New Hotel Punjabi
6 Hotel Nirala
8 Shanta Shakya Lodge
9 Mankamana Guest House
12 Star Lodge
20 New Bheri Hotel
22 Hotel Batika
23 Hotel Sneha

OTHER
1 Sajha Yatayat Bus Office
2 Long-Distance Bus Station
3 Mahendranagar Buses
4 Buddha Air
7 Tempos to Airport & Kohalpur
10 Nepal Rastra Bank
11 Necon Air
13 Bageshwari Mandir
14 Water Tower
15 RNAC Office
16 Mosque
17 Tongas (Horse Cart) to Indian Border
18 Nepal Bank
19 Hospital
21 Post Office

To Airport (5km) & Kohalpur (16km)

Birendra Chowk

Pond

Bazaar

Tribhuvan Chowk

To Indian Border (3km)

0.5   1 km

Places to Stay & Eat

The cheapies are centred around Birendra Chowk, the main intersection with the inevitable statue.

New Hotel Punjabi (☎ 20818) is probably the best bet. It has large comfortable rooms and is acceptably clean. Singles/doubles with private bath cost Rs 250/350; with shared bath they are Rs 100/150. The restaurant's Indian dishes are quite passable, and it's undoubtedly the best place to eat in town. The nearby *Mankamana Guest House* is also acceptable, with doubles with private bath (cold water) at Rs 150.

Somewhat quieter are the hotels on Garwhari Tole, which connect Birendra Chowk with the old part of town. The *Star Lodge* (☎ 22257) has rooms at Rs 95/130 with common bath, and attached bath at Rs 140/200.

Moving up the scale a bit is the *New Bheri Hotel* (☎ 20213), which offers the best value in town. The hotel is near the hospital in a quiet part of town, and has a pleasant garden. Room prices are $8/10 with bath and $16/20 with air-con, but with discounts you may have to pay only half that. It's a good place.

There are two reasonable top-end hotels, both south of town on the way to the Indian border on the highway. They're set back from the road so noise and parking aren't problems.

Hotel Sneha (☎/fax 20119) has a range of large, clean rooms, and helpful staff. A wing of high-standard rooms has been built around a courtyard behind the original hotel. Standard rooms are $18/24, and deluxe rooms with air-con are $30/36, plus 12% tax. Discounts of 15% are possible. You can also camp here for $5 per person if you have your own gear. There's a restaurant here, although the food is pretty uninspiring.

Virtually next door, the *Hotel Batika* (☎ 21360) has a number of comfortable rooms, but it's hard to see how they justify the price of $45/50. Forget it.

Getting There & Away

Air This is Royal Nepal Airlines Corporation's western headquarters and there's a modern airport, now somewhat run-down. Unfortunately, this doesn't mean that you are any more certain to arrive or depart on the promised hour or day than you are anywhere else in Nepal.

Flights from Nepalganj include:

Destination	RNAC (☎ 20239)	Lumbini (☎ 23360)
Kathmandu	$99, daily	$99, 2 weekly
Jumla	$57, daily	$57, weekly
Surkhet	$33, 7 weekly	$33, 2 weekly
Simikot	$88, 4 weekly	$88, weekly
Dhangadhi	$60, weekly	

Necon Air (☎ 20307) and Buddha Air (☎ 20745) fly to Kathmandu ($99) daily.

Bus Sajha Yatayat has two departures daily for Kathmandu; one leaves early morning, another early evening. They take about 14 hours and cost Rs 224/280 by day/night.

There are private night buses to Pokhara; they leave from 4.15 to 5.30 pm and cost Rs 277 via Mugling, Rs 250 via Tansen; the trip takes about 12 hours. You can get to Narayanghat for Rs 170/214 with day/night departures.

Buses for Mahendranagar leave at 7 am (Rs 195, seven to 10 hours). It's advisable to book at least one day in advance, although you can be lucky.

Getting Around

There are shared *tempos* from Birendra Chowk to the airport for Rs 6, or you can take one 'reserve' for Rs 50. A cycle-rickshaw costs around Rs 50 but takes up to half an hour. To the Indian border by cycle-rickshaw costs around Rs 30.

ROYAL BARDIA NATIONAL PARK

The Royal Bardia National Park is the largest untouched wilderness area in the Terai. It's bordered to the north by the crest of the Chure Hills and to the west by the large Geruwa River, a branch of the mighty Karnali, one of the major tributaries of the Ganges.

You stand a better chance of seeing a tiger here than anywhere else in Nepal (including Chitwan). It's a stunning place that seems a very long way from the 20th century – watching the sun rise over the forest from the back of an elephant is like having a box seat at the dawn of time.

About 70% of the 968 sq km park is covered with open sal forest, with the balance a mixture of grassland, savanna and riverine forest. The grassed areas *(phanta)* are excellent for game-viewing. Most people will visit in the hope of seeing a royal Bengal tiger, but there are also leopards, jungle cats, mongooses, sloth bears and blue cows (nilgai), plus langur and rhesus monkeys, as well as barking, spotted hog and sambar deer. The Asian one-horned rhinoceros was reintroduced from Chitwan in 1986, and though breeding successfully the numbers are still small. There are at least two wild

male elephants, and one is thought to be the largest in Asia.

The Geruwa River rushes through a gap in the hills at Chisopani, grey with silt and snow-melt. It's home to the famous mahseer game fish, gharial and mugger crocodiles, and the strange Gangetic dolphin.

More than 30 different mammals and 250 species of birds have been recorded in the park. Birds include numerous species of herons, storks, geese, ducks and parakeets as well as endangered birds like the Bengal florican and sarus crane.

In some ways Bardia is like Chitwan; the major difference is the degree of isolation and the limited number of visitors. The main disadvantage of Bardia is that it takes a day of travelling to get to or from Kathmandu, although it also takes a minimum of five hours to get to Chitwan. This means you need a minimum of four days: day one

ROYAL BARDIA NATIONAL PARK

– Kathmandu to Bardia; days two and three are for exploring the park, the river and the surrounding villages; day four – Bardia to Kathmandu.

Orientation & Information

The park headquarters are at Thakurdwara, about 20km south-west along a bumpy dirt road from Anbassa on the Mahendra Hwy. Anbassa is about 500m from the Motipur checkpoint, where the highway actually enters the park, and this in turn is 8km from Chisopani. Virtually all tourist activity is centred around the western spur of the park which takes in the forest and grasslands around the Geruwa River; the large eastern portion of the park is untouched.

The park office is open daily 8 to 10 am and 2 to 5 pm; the park itself is open from 6.30 am to 5.30 pm (7 pm in summer). Entry is the usual Rs 1000, and you can get a fishing permit for Rs 300 per rod. The national park also offers elephants at Rs 650 per person per hour from the park headquarters at Thakurdwara. The only trouble here is that you need at least 30 minutes by elephant to reach the 'core' area of the park for the best game viewing. It's also possible to enter the park on foot, although you need to take an experienced guide, something your lodge can arrange. Keep in mind that walking in the park is a potentially dangerous activity, which should only be undertaken if you are accompanied by an experienced guide.

Also at the park HQ is a small holding area for marsh muggers and gharial crocodiles that have been bred in captivity and are due to be released into the river.

Places to Stay

In recent years a few basic Chitwan-style 'jungle cottages' have sprung up around Thakurdwara. There's no electricity and accommodation is very basic, but this is the perfect spot to hole up for a few days and allow yourself to be lulled by the relaxing pace and atmosphere of Terai village life.

One of the best places is the solar-powered *Forest Hideaway Cottages* (☎ 084-29716, email forest-hideaway@geo.wlink.com.np),

a short walk along the northern park boundary from the park HQ and run by a helpful Scottish-Nepali couple. This place is also a licensed moneychanger (cash and cheques, no cards), and you can also make international and local phone calls. It's a comfortable little place set in a shady garden. There's a variety of mud-and-thatch cottages – basic cottages with two beds, mosquito nets and common bath are Rs 350 for a double, larger cottages are Rs 500, also with breakfast and common bath. Large cottages with a bathroom shared between two rooms are Rs 600 with breakfast. You can also camp here for Rs 150 for a double with breakfast, or Rs 75 in your own tent (no breakfast). Basic but perfectly adequate meals are available, and there's a bar. Jeep safaris can be arranged for Rs 1200 per person for four hours.

Right opposite the park entrance are the *Bardia Jungle Cottages* (☎ 29562), with a shady garden and good facilities. Cottages are Rs 200 with common bath, Rs 400 with bath. Meals are also available here.

There are a couple of even more basic places, including the *Hotel Racy Shade* and the adjacent *Hotel Bardia Natural Park*. Both have just a few mud and thatch cottages, and are about 500m from the park entrance.

There are a couple more places farther south along the river, but without your own transport they can be inconvenient. The *Bardia Wildlife Paradise* is a small place with a pleasant garden, and mud-and-thatch cottages at Rs 200 for a double, Rs 350 with attached bath. There's also a small dining room.

Dolphin Manor, close by, is aiming at the top end of the market but doesn't seem to know quite how to achieve that. The place looks only half completed, and has yet to take in a guest. If it finally gets up and running properly it could be quite pleasant.

Rhino Lodge (☎ 29720) is a little farther along again, and is about 4km from the park entrance. It consists of unattractive brick cottages set in a wide expanse of grassy garden with no shade. Accommodation prices are usually quoted in dollars, but you should be able to get a cottage for Rs 400 with bath.

At the top of the range is the **Tiger Tops Karnali Lodge**, run by Tiger Mountain (☎ 01-420322; fax 414075; PO Box 242, Durbar Marg, Kathmandu, email info@ tigermountain.com) the same company that runs the Tiger Tops Lodge in Chitwan. The lodge is built right on the park boundary and is built out of local materials in Tharu village style – simply outstanding. The staff is knowledgeable and helpful, without being intrusive. It's a place where you can abdicate all responsibility, relax and just enjoy.

It also has the only accommodation inside the park: the **Karnali Tented Camp**, which has a superb location overlooking the Geruwa River, not far from Chisopani in the north-west corner of the park. A camp it might be, rough it is not. The beds are comfortable, the food is good and the water is hot. Again activities revolve around the elephants, but another highlight is a float down the river – a birdwatcher's delight.

Although they aren't cheap, at $225/300 a night including all meals and activities (elephant rides, guided walks), they do offer an extraordinary experience. Those who have been to both Chitwan and Karnali almost unanimously vote Karnali superior. The tented camp closes from the middle of April to the end of September during the monsoon; the lodge is open all year.

Getting There & Away

The main highway is in excellent condition and the drive from Nepalganj takes less than 2½ hours, although local buses manage to take much longer. It's an interesting drive past thriving villages. For Thakurdwara, there are direct buses from Nepalganj at 11 am and 2.30 pm, taking three to four hours and costing Rs 70. Departures from Thakurdwara are at 8 and 9 am.

If you are staying at the Tiger Tops Karnali Lodge or Tented Camp, they can arrange jeep transfers from Nepalganj for $10.

Night buses bound for Mahendranagar from Kathmandu can drop you at Anbassa (Rs 350), although they get in between 3 and 6 am. Buses to Mahendranagar cost Rs 150, and to Pokhara (one daily, from Dhangadhi) Rs 350.

ROYAL SUKLA PHANTA WILDLIFE RESERVE

Sukla Phanta is smaller and more isolated than Bardia, yet similar in some respects. In the extreme south-west of the country, it covers 305 sq km of riverine flood plain, which includes open grass plains (phanta), forest (primarily sal), a lake and the Bahini River.

It is home to tigers, leopards, various species of deer (including an important colony of swamp deer, thought to number around 2000), gharial and mugger crocodiles, otters and a wide variety of birdlife.

The large swamp deer are found in large herds and it's not unusual to see three or more herds on even a short game drive in the southern part of the park in the *sukla phanta*, literally white grass plains, found in this area. Although the deer are found in large numbers, Indian poachers are a real problem. Army guards are stationed in this part of the park, however they have to patrol by bicycle, which limits their capacity to be effective.

This is probably one of the least visited reserves in Nepal, but if you are travelling between Nepal and India it is not too difficult to make a diversion, especially if you can afford to stay at the tented camp.

Information

The ranger's office is 3km past the airport (accessible by rickshaw from Mahendranagar). Entry is Rs 1000, and it is possible to organise elephant rides for Rs 650.

Places to Stay

Silent Safari (☎ 099-21230, fax 22220, PO Box 1, Mahendranagar) is currently the only company operating in the park. It is run by an ex-army colonel, the very personable Hikmat Bisht, a keen naturalist who has spent many years in and around the park and now divides his time between the camp (even when there are no guests) and his house in Mahendranagar. Visitors who come here are generally keen birders who don't mind roughing it a bit. Accommodation is in comfortable safari tents, and the price ($150 per person) includes meals, game drives and walks. Visits to local Tharu villages can also be arranged. The camp is open from October to June, and advance bookings are essential.

Getting There & Away
Silent Safari picks guests up from the airport at Mahendranagar or Dhangadhi ($10).

MAHENDRANAGAR
☎ 099

Mahendranagar is an uninspiring village that owes its existence to the nearby border crossing. There's absolutely nothing to see, and the locals are quite unused to dealing with tourists. A few words of Nepali are very useful. The surrounding countryside is inhabited by traditional Tharu communities, although here, as elsewhere, there is an increasing number of hill people.

Orientation & Information
The town is laid out to the south of the main highway with the bus park actually on the highway, about a 10 minute walk from the centre of the village. The main landmark is the King Mahendra Square with streets one to five leading off from one side.

Mahendranagar is about 5km from Mahakali River, which forms the Nepal-Indian border. The border is open 24 hours for pedestrians, but the barrage on the Indian side for vehicles is only open from 7 to 8 am, noon to 2 pm and again from 4 to 6 pm. It's a little-used border and the crossing is straightforward and quite fast.

Places to Stay & Eat
There are a few cheap hotels on the main street. *Hotel New Anand* (☎ 21693) is the best of them; it's friendly and has double rooms for Rs 280 with bath, and hot water by the bucket. Food is also available.

Around the corner from the New Anand is the cheaper *Green Lodge* (☎ 21950).

Rooms here are a bit rough, but would do in a pinch, and cost Rs 150 for a double with bath.

Mahendranagar's Hilton is the *Hotel Sweet Dream* (☎ 22313), on the highway about a five minute walk east of the bus station. The rooms in this recently built hotel are large and have carpets. The cost is Rs 400 for a double with bath, and this is pretty good value. There's also a restaurant here.

Getting There & Away
The road from the border to Nepalganj is a mess. The first 40km, to Ataria, where there is a turn-off to Dhangadhi, is diabolical, with an old single lane of bitumen now so pot-holed that it's worse than no bitumen at all. From Ataria to Chisopani the road is good bitumen, although there are still quite a number of creeks which have to be forded. Until the bridges are completed (don't hold your breath, although the Indians may be starting work on these soon), the road is a slow, dry-weather-only proposition. The last few kilometres to Chisopani along the banks of the Karnali River are the worst on the entire highway.

There are daily direct buses from Kathmandu to Mahendranagar at 12.30 pm. The trip takes a gruelling 18 hours and costs Rs 383. From Mahendranagar departures are around 2 pm. There are also buses from Mahendranagar to Dhangadhi and Nepalganj.

To/From India Buses leave Mahendranagar roughly every half hour for the border. It's a 1km walk (or rickshaw ride) between the Nepali and Indian posts, and then a farther kilometre to the Indian town of Banbassa.

Banbassa is on the Indian rail system, and there are also buses to Almora and Delhi. There are at least three direct buses a day to Delhi (Indian Rs 80, 11 hours).

DHANGADHI
☎ 091

Dhangadhi is rarely visited by westerners, but it is possible to cross the border here and to hook up with the Indian railway for places like Lucknow. The local people are friendly, but there's really nothing to see. The border crossing here is quite busy, as it is a major entry point for goods coming by truck.

Places to Stay

There are a few basic places to stay; but the town is not well set up for travellers. The

Hotel Taruan has been recommended, but don't expect too much.

Getting There & Away

RNAC (☎ 21205) has flights to Nepalganj (four weekly). There are daily bus connections with Nepalganj and Kathmandu.

RICHARD I'ANSON

STAN ARMINGTON

RICHARD I'ANSON

Mountaineering
The majesty of Nepal's peaks has lead countless mountaineers to risk their lives.

Clockwise from top left: Chilly weather, despite the sun; this method of carrying is typical of mountain people; Mustang – beautiful, isolated and on the banks of the upper Kali Gandaki; Tibetan prayer flags flutter, releasing prayers to the heavens.

The Himalaya & Mountaineering

The word Himalaya is Sanskrit for 'abode of snows' and Nepal's stretch of the Himalaya includes eight peaks over 8000m, including the highest of them all, mighty Mt Everest (8848m). Known to the Tibetans as Qomolangma and to the Nepalis as Sagarmatha, the world's highest place was the overpowering attraction which drew in Nepal's first modern tourists – the mountaineers.

During the 1950s and 60s most of the important Nepali peaks were conquered, but just because it is no longer possible to be the first to set foot on top has certainly not diminished the attraction of Himalayan mountaineering. Climbing these giants today is often an adventurous sporting activity, whereas 40 years ago it required huge and well sponsored expeditions.

There are 14 peaks over 8000m in the world, and of the 10 highest no less than eight are in Nepal, although some of the peaks actually straddle borders – Everest is in Nepal and China for example, Kanchenjunga (8598m) is in Nepal and India. The heights of the 14 highest peaks in the world, followed by the highest peaks in South America, North America, Africa, Russia, Antarctica, Europe, Australia and the United Kingdom can be seen in the Mountain Heights diagram.

Nepal's magnificent mountains can be enjoyed in three distinctly different fashions. The easiest way is to simply look at them. This can be done by flying past them – either on regular flights or the daily tourist-season mountain flights. Or you can admire them from the various popular mountain viewpoints such as Nagarkot or Dhulikhel near Kathmandu or Sarangkot above Pokhara. Getting to these viewpoints is covered in the appropriate chapters.

If simply looking at the mountains isn't enough you can get right in among them by trekking. Trekking is not mountain climbing: apart from high passes on certain treks and the approach to the Everest base camp you are unlikely to go above 3500m. Trekking, however, does provide breathtaking views. Full details on trekking are given in the Trekking chapter.

Finally, there is mountain climbing and while getting to the top of an 8000m peak is strictly for the professionals, there are plenty of 'trekking peaks' which small-scale amateur expeditions can readily attempt. This is not to say that mountaineering in Nepal can be easy – climbing mountains this high always involves an element of risk – but getting to the top of a worthwhile Himalayan peak doesn't necessarily require millionaire status or big commercial backers.

MOUNTAINEERING

Mountaineering became a fashionable pursuit in Europe during the second half of the 19th century and, having knocked off the great Alpine peaks, the much greater heights of the Himalaya were an obvious new challenge. An Englishman named WW Graham made a mountaineering visit to Nepal in 1883 and reached the top of a 6000m peak. He was followed by another Englishman, Tom Longstaff, who climbed 7215m Trisuli in 1907. For the next 20 years this remained the highest summit reached in the world. An Italian attempt on K2 in Pakistan two years later was the first of the huge Himalayan expeditions with hundreds of porters.

Mountain Flights

Every morning during the clear dry-season months, Royal Nepal Airlines' and Everest Air's mountain flights offer panoramic dawn views of the Himalaya. Passengers on the Everest Air flight are all guaranteed a window seat, and the hour-long flight from Kathmandu costs $99. If the weather is clear, the views are stunning.

First Attempts on Everest

During the 1920s and 30s, reaching the top of Mt Everest came to be seen as the major goal, but apart from the difficulties inherent in reaching such heights there were also political constraints. Nepal continued to be totally secluded and attempts on Everest were all made from the Tibetan side.

British assaults were made in 1921, 1922 and 1924. The 1922 expedition used oxygen to reach 8326m, while the 1924 expedition fell just 300m short of the top, reaching 8572m without the use of oxygen. Apart from numerous climbers and support staff, the 1924 expedition utilised no less than 350 porters. Such massive numbers of porters and support staff set a pattern which was to continue until recent years.

The discovery of the body of British climber Mallory frozen near the summit is a new chapter in one of the enduring mysteries of mountaineering history. In 1925 Mallory and Irvine disappeared within sight of the top. Did they reach the it? No one can be sure. However, Mallory did leave behind his famous explanation of mountaineering –

he said he was climbing Everest 'because it's there'. Further expeditions followed through the 1920s and 30s but no real progress was made, although the 8000m level was breached a number of times. Maurice Wilson added his name to the Everest legends, and the Everest death roll, when he died during a bizarre solo attempt on the mountain in 1934.

Post WWII Attempts

The west's new-found affluence after its recovery from WWII, together with more modern equipment, vastly improved oxygen apparatus, new mountaineering skills and the reopening of Nepal, led to a golden age of Himalayan mountaineering.

There hadn't been any Himalayan mountaineering in the 1940s, and through the 30s only two significant summits had been reached – Kamet at 7761m in 1931 and Nanda Devi at 7822m in 1936. Interestingly, the Kamet summit group included HW Tilman and the Nanda Devi group included Eric Shipton, whose descriptions of their trekking and mountaineering experi-

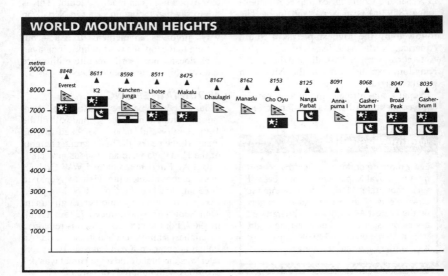

WORLD MOUNTAIN HEIGHTS

ences helped to spark the current interest in trekking. Shipton was said to have planned his lightweight expeditions on the back of an envelope.

The pre-war failures were abruptly reversed in the 1950s, beginning with Maurice Herzog's valiant French expedition on Annapurna in 1950. His team's horrific storm-plagued struggle turned an already extremely difficult climb into an epic of human endurance – but for the first time mountaineers had reached the top of an 8000m peak. After descending the mountain they then had a month-long struggle through the monsoon with the expedition doctor having to perform amputations of frostbitten fingers and toes as they went.

Herzog's book *Annapurna* (Jonathan Cape, London, 1952) remains a classic of mountaineering literature. It's indicative of how things have changed in Nepal that Herzog had trouble even finding his way to the mountain! Today thousands of trekkers pass by the Annapurnas every year and, where Herzog once had to search desperately for supplies for his hungry climbers, there are

now comfortable lodges offering bed and breakfast to trekking parties.

Conquest of Everest

Everest was also getting its share of attention, and in 1951 a climber who would soon become very famous took part in an exploratory expedition to the mountain – he was New Zealander Edmund Hillary. Another name, soon to be equally famous, appeared on the list of climbers on the Swiss Everest expedition of 1952 when Sherpa climber Norgay Tenzing reached 7500m. The conquest of Everest finally took place in 1953 when the British team led by John Hunt put those two climbers, Tenzing and Hillary, on top of the world's highest peak.

Repeat performances came much easier than the first time and the second success came in 1956 when a Swiss party reached the summit. In 1960 it was the People's Republic of China which managed the feat, this time from the Tibetan side. A huge US expedition with the climbers backed up by nearly 1000 porters got to the top in 1963, and in 1965 it was the turn of an Indian

WORLD MOUNTAIN HEIGHTS

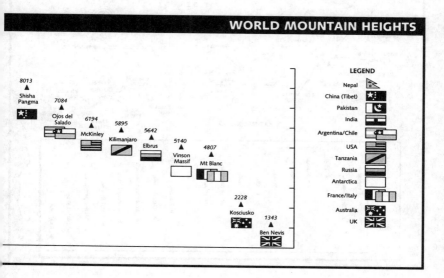

LEGEND

Nepal
China (Tibet)
Pakistan
India
Argentina/Chile
USA
Tanzania
Russia
Antarctica
France/Italy
Australia
UK

8013
Shisha Pangma

7084
Ojos del Salado

6194
McKinley

5895
Kilimanjaro

5642
Elbrus

5140
Vinson Massif

4807
Mt Blanc

2228
Kosciusko

1343
Ben Nevis

expedition. Another huge party, this time from Japan, was on top in 1970 and one utterly fearless climber ensured his place in the Everest history books by making an extremely rapid descent on skis! Further attempts included the massive Italian expedition which reached the summit in 1973 and the victorious Japanese women's party which celebrated International Women's Year by putting a woman climber on top.

The success of the 1953 British expedition to Everest had begun a trend for larger and larger expeditions. Proponents of this form of 'siege' mountaineering believed that this was the only way to conquer the great Himalayan peaks. A series of camps would be established higher and higher up the mountain with constant 'carries' of supplies eventually resulting in climbers reaching the top. This theory of Himalayan climbing reached its ultimate expression with the 1973 Italian Everest expedition when 64 climbers were backed up by 100 sherpas and nearly 2000 porters! Helicopters ferried supplies and, hardly surprisingly, this massive effort put nine people on the summit in two parties.

The few climbers who did reach the summit from these expeditions required a huge pyramid of supporters below them. The effect on the country could be devastating as forests fell to provide firewood for the expeditions and vast amounts of mountaineering equipment and garbage were left behind. The Everest base camp has been aptly titled the 'world's highest garbage dump'. Lightweight expeditions had been successful, but Helmut Bhul's solo climb to the summit of Nanga Parbat in Pakistan and his lightweight expedition to the top of Broad Peak were looked upon more as being aberrations requiring superhuman effort rather than as

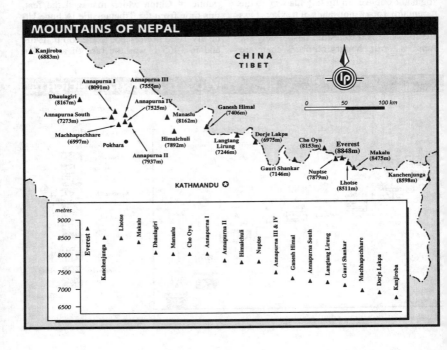

MOUNTAINS OF NEPAL

pointers towards a different way of doing things.

New-Style Mountaineering

Inevitably, a reaction set in and, while the checklist of important summits was methodically knocked over by huge and expensive expeditions, young climbers were perfecting a wholly different style of climbing on the peaks of Europe and North America. Getting to the top was no longer the sole aim, you had to reach the top with style.

The 'easy' ridge routes to the top were ignored while climbers scaled the most difficult faces, combining athletic skills and high-tech equipment. British mountaineer Chris Bonnington was the chief protagonist for this style of climbing and his brilliant conquest of the southern face of Annapurna in 1970, followed by an expertly organised race up the hitherto unthinkable south-western face of Everest in 1975, were supreme examples of this trend.

Lightweight Expeditions

Attempting the difficult faces and routes was one trend, but lightweight expeditions were another. In 1978 the Austrian expedition to Everest put Reinhold Messner and Peter Habler on top without the use of oxygen. Once this 'impossible' feat had been achieved other climbers also found they could reach the top without oxygen and, freed from the necessity of carting heavy oxygen cylinders up the mountains, much smaller parties could now attempt the big mountains.

Only two years later Reinhold Messner made a solo ascent of Everest, climbing the north face on the Tibetan side in the fastest ascent ever made.

In early 1990 Tim McCartney-Snape, an Australian, went several steps further. He walked and climbed from sea level, at the Bay of Bengal, to the top of Mt Everest, alone and without oxygen.

Mountaineering Today

Himalayan mountaineering today not only provides a great deal of free publicity for tourism to Nepal, it's also a very useful source of income for the government. If you want to attempt a Himalayan peak there's a fee to be paid to the government even before you get your climbing permit, and the higher and more famous the mountain the higher the fee that must be paid. Everest is currently $50,000 and is usually 'booked out' for years ahead. Annually, 600 to 900 climbers come to Nepal to try their luck, but there are still many sizeable peaks which have not been successfully climbed, and some which haven't even been attempted.

Today mountaineering is a sport pure and simple – there's no noise made about its scientific value. In fact the successes and failures of the various expeditions are regularly reported on the sports pages of the *Rising Nepal*. Of course it's also a decidedly dangerous sport: over 200 climbers have reached the top of Everest (some of them three, four and even five times), but about 100 climbers have died in the attempt. Some other mountains in Nepal have an even worse record: almost as many climbers have lost their lives climbing Annapurna as have managed to reach the top.

Permits To climb any mountain peaks that are open to expeditions, a mountaineering team should obtain permission from the Ministry of Tourism's Mountaineering Section (☎ 211286), Tripureshwar, Kathmandu. Every team must be represented by a licensed trekking agency in Nepal.

TREKKING PEAKS

There are many smaller mountains in Nepal called 'trekking peaks' (ranging from 5587m to 6654m) which keen trekkers can climb. Most Everest base camp trekkers make the ascent of Kala Pattar for the view of Everest and at 5545m this would be a substantial peak anywhere else in the world. In his book *Many People Come, Looking, Looking* (The Mountaineers, Seattle, 1980) Galen Rowell tells of a little jaunt up a 6500m peak as a pre-lunch side trip while crossing the Thorung La on the Annapurna Circuit Trek.

The trekking peaks are:

Peak	Height
Chulu East	6584m
Chulu West	6419m
Hiunchuli	6441m
Imja Tse	6183m
Kangja Chuli	5844m
Khongma Tse (or Mehra)	5849m
Kusum Kanguru	6367m
Kwangde	6011m
Lubuje	6119m
Mardi Himal	5587m
Mera Peak	6654m
Paldor Peak	5896m
Parchemuche	6187m
Pisang	6091m
Pokalde	5806m
Ramdung	5925m
Singu Chuli (or Fluted Peak)	6501m
Tharpu Chuli (or Tent Peak)	5663m

By Himalayan standards these are minor peaks, but some of them provide challenging snow and ice climbing. To climb trekking peaks, a permit is required from the Nepal Mountaineering Association, Kamaladi, PO Box 1435, Kathmandu.

Fees (or royalties, as they are often referred to) depend on the altitude of the peak, starting at $1000 for peaks below 6501m and rising $500 for every 500m increment to $3000 for peaks from 7501m to 8000m.

Climbing gear can be bought or rented in Kathmandu, and while tents, stoves, sleeping bags and down gear should pose no problems, socks, shoes, clothing and freeze-dried food are likely to be harder to find.

Bill O'Connor's book *The Trekking Peaks of Nepal* gives a detailed description of climbing each of the peaks plus the trek to the mountain. Equipment, applications, procedures, weather, health and other matters are also comprehensively covered.

Trekking

For the people in the hills of Nepal, walking has always been the main method of getting from A to B. There were no roads into the hill country from the Terai and India until the Tribhuvan Hwy to Kathmandu was constructed in the 1950s. Pokhara was not connected to the outside world by road until the 1970s. Even today the vast majority of villages can only be reached on foot, although every year the roads penetrate farther into Nepal's endless ranges of hills.

The Nepali people, making their way from village to village on the well-worn trails, were only joined by western visitors when Himalayan mountaineering came into vogue. It was the accounts of those pioneering mountaineers, who had to make their way to the base of the great peaks on foot, which inspired the first trekkers. The word 'trekking' was first applied to Nepali hiking trips in the 1960s and the enormous popularity of trekking today has developed since that time.

Trekking in Nepal means a walking trip following trails, many of which have been used for communication and trade for centuries. Trekking is not mountaineering. Some of the popular trekking trails are used by mountaineering expeditions on their approach marches, but most are used by Nepalis for everyday travel and trade. A trekking trip can be any length you choose – there are popular short treks around the Kathmandu and Pokhara valleys which only take a day to complete, there are short treks of two or three days, or there are longer treks lasting from a week to a month. You could even string a series of popular treks together and walk for months on end.

Three major attractions account for trekking's enormous popularity – the scenery, the people, and the flora and fauna.

Scenery

There is no question that Nepal offers some of the most spectacular and beautiful scen-

ery in the world. Of course it's the mountains that are best known, and the exploits of mountain photographers have made Everest, Machhapuchhare, Ama Dablam, and other mountains instantly recognisable to keen walkers all over the world. Nepal has a near monopoly on the world's highest peaks – eight of the 10 highest are found in Nepal and a number of the popular trekking routes offer you wonderful views or even visits to the base camps used by mountaineering expeditions. Mountain flights may give you superb views, but there is absolutely nothing like waking up on a crystal-clear Himalayan day and seeing an 8000m peak towering over you, seemingly just an arm's length away.

The mountains may be the most obvious scenic attraction, but trekkers soon find there are plenty of other treats for the eye. The hill country is often breathtakingly beautiful with pretty little villages, attractive houses, neat fields and interesting temples. As you climb higher the subtropical lowlands give way to meadows, stretches of forest, swift-flowing rivers and deep canyons before you reach the cold and often barren regions at the foot of the great peaks. The views change with the seasons, whether it is the cycle of planting and harvesting or the brilliant displays of wildflowers in spring and autumn.

People

Trekking in Nepal is not like hiking through the often uninhabited countryside of a North American, Australian or European national park. People are constantly passing by on the trails, and along many routes there are regularly spaced villages to pause in. In the villages you can meet people from a wide diversity of ethnic groups. The outgoing nature, general friendliness and good humour of Nepalis is often noted by trekkers. Colourful festivals can make trekking at certain times of year even more enjoyable.

Of course, your trekking companions can be another important part of the trekking experience. A long trek can be a great opportunity to enjoy yourself with good friends. Despite stories you may have heard about the Himalaya being overrun with hordes of trekkers the reality is generally very different. Certainly there may be many trekkers during the peak seasons on the most popular routes, particularly the Jomsom Trek, but compared to the crowds visiting national parks in the west the numbers are often minuscule.

About Trekking

Although Nepal offers plenty of opportunity for short treks lasting a day or less, most treks last considerably longer. From Pokhara or around the Kathmandu Valley you can make a variety of two, three or four-day

Trekking & Cultural Awareness

Trekkers should respect Nepali culture and traditions. Dress modestly – women should not wear short or revealing clothes (loose pants or a calf-length dress are ideal) and men should not go shirtless. Don't put down what you may see as shortcomings in the Nepali lifestyle; remember that life in western countries has many problems and drawbacks as well. Every visitor's maxim should be: Nepal is here to change you, not for you to change it.

Before bargaining, try to establish a fair price by talking to guides and other travellers. Paying too much feeds inflation, while paying too little denies the locals a reasonable return for their efforts and investments. Not everything is subject to bargaining: respect standard food, bed and entry charges and follow the going rate for services.

Bargaining should never be treated as a matter of life and death importance – it's usually regarded as an integral part of a transaction and is, ideally, an enjoyable social exchange. Nepalis do not ever appreciate aggressive behaviour. A good deal is when both parties are happy. Try to remember that Rs 5 might make quite a difference to the seller, but in hard currency it amounts to less than 10 US cents.

Regrettably, some nationalities have established such a reputation for unpleasant, mean-minded bargaining that they are no longer welcome in many lodges or restaurants. Israelis will find that previous hard-core shoestring travellers have created a negative impression that may well take a long time to erase.

Don't encourage begging children; tell them Na raamro, 'not good', and remember that hand-outs can create dependence and other negative side effects. (See the Begging boxed text under Society & Conduct in the Facts about Nepal chapter.)

walks, but Nepal's most popular treks take at least a week. For the very popular Everest base camp and Annapurna Circuit treks you have to allow three weeks. Don't take on one of these classic long treks too lightly: the end of the first week is not the ideal time to discover you're not keen on walking.

INFORMATION

Two organisations offer free, up-to-date information on trekking conditions, health risks and how to minimise your impact on the environment; both are conveniently located in Thamel in Kathmandu. The Kathmandu Environment Education Project (KEEP; for details see the Environmental Information boxed text) is open 10 am to 5 pm except Saturday and holidays. It has a library and sells iodine bottles, biodegradable soap and other environmentally friendly equipment; they also have an excellent notice board. The Himalayan Rescue Association (HRA) Information Centre is close by, open daily except Saturday 9 am to 5 pm. They have information about altitude sickness and useful notebooks with up-to-date information from other trekkers. Both offices are excellent places to advertise for trekking companions.

For those who want trekking information, particularly related to independent trekking, probably the best source of impartial information in Kathmandu are the slide shows held regularly in the Kathmandu Guest House by Chris Beall, a British freelance photographer, writer, trek leader and long-time resident of Nepal. The slide shows give an introduction into Nepal and its various trekking regions, and there's a question-and-answer session afterwards where you can get up-to-date information on trail conditions, and forthright advice as to what trails and style of trekking would most suit your budget, fitness and interests, something it can be difficult to get out of a trekking agency who simply want to hook a customer. The shows cost Rs 300 (including tea/coffee and biscuits), and if they are on you'll see posters up at various locations in Thamel, most notably the Kathmandu Guest House.

WHEN TO GO

Put very simply, the best time to trek is from October to May (the dry season) and the worst time is from June to September (the monsoon). This generalisation does not allow for the peculiarities of individual treks, however. Some people even claim that the undeniable difficulties of trekking

---

Environmental Information

On the positive side, trekking plays a vital role in the economy of mountain areas. Without the influx of cash, many more people would be forced to abandon the villages for the cities, which are already suffering from rapid population increase. A number of impressive organisations are attempting to deal with the problems, including the Annapurna Conservation Area Project (ACAP), which has done a great deal to encourage sustainable development in the Annapurna region.

For more information on minimising your impact, visit the trekkers' information centres run by the Kathmandu Environmental Education Project (KEEP) and Himalayan Rescue Association (HRA). Most Thamel bookshops also stock *Trekking Gently in the Himalaya* by Wendy Brewer Lama (Rs 30), a small booklet that has essential tips for trekkers.

Information centre addresses are:

Annapurna Conservation Area Project
   (ACAP), King Mahendra Trust for Nature
   Conservation,
   (☎ 526571, fax 526570)
   PO Box 3712, Jawlakhel, Patan
Himalayan Rescue Association (HRA)
   (☎ 262746, email hra@aidpost.mos
   .com.np)
   PO Box 4944, Thamel, Kathmandu
Kathmandu Environmental Education
   Project (KEEP)
   (☎ 259275, email tours@keep.wlink
   .com.np)
   PO Box 9178, Thamel, Kathmandu

TREKKING

during the monsoon are outweighed by the virtual absence of western trekkers.

The first two months of the dry season, October and November, are probably the ideal period for trekking in Nepal. The air, freshly washed by the monsoon rains, is crystal clear, the mountain scenery is superb and the weather is still comfortably warm. At low altitudes in October it can actually be quite balmy, and trekkers may find they complete a whole trek in T-shirt weather.

December, January and February are still good months for trekking, but the cold can be bitter at high altitudes. Getting up to the Everest base camp can be a real endurance test and the Thorung La pass on the Annapurna Circuit is usually blocked by snow.

March and April offer better weather but at the price of hazy visibility on long-distance views. By this time of year the weather has been dry for a long time and dust is starting to hang in the air. The poorer quality of the Himalayan views is compensated for by the superb wild flowers, particularly Nepal's wonderful rhododendrons.

By May it starts to get very hot, dusty and humid, and the monsoon is definitely just around the corner. From June to September the trails can be dangerously slippery due to the monsoon rains, and raging rivers often wash away bridges and stretches of trail. Nepal's famous *jukha* (leeches) are an unpleasant feature of the wet season, but with care, trekking can still be possible and there are certainly fewer trekkers on the trail.

TRAIL CONDITIONS

Most trekkers want to get away from roads as quickly as possible, and although roads reach farther into the hill country every year, it is still possible to leave them quickly behind. Nepali trails are often steep and taxing. The old adage that 'the shortest path between two points is a straight line' appears to have been firmly drummed into Nepalis, irrespective of any mountains which may get in the way! In compensation, the trails are often very well maintained. Busy trails up steep slopes are often flagged with stones every step of the way.

Walking the trails of Nepal often entails a great deal of altitude gain and loss, and it is as well to remember that even the base of the great mountains of the Himalaya can be very high. Most treks which go through populated areas stick to between 1000m and 3000m, although the Everest Base Camp Trek and the Annapurna Circuit Trek both reach over 5000m. On high treks like these it is wise to ensure adequate acclimatisation, and the old maxim of 'walking high, sleeping low' is good advice: your night halt should be at a lower level than the highest point reached in the day.

A typical day's walk lasts from five to seven hours and involves a number of ascents and descents. It's rare to spend much time at the same level. On an organised camping trek the day is run to a remarkably tight schedule. A typical pattern would be: up at 6 am, start walking at 7 am, stop for lunch at 10 am, start after lunch at noon, stop walking at 3 pm. Nepalis rise early, eat very little for breakfast, eat a large lunch in the late morning and a second meal before dark, then retire early – you are best off following a similar schedule. Although a little rudimentary knowledge of the Nepali language will help to make your trek easier and more interesting, finding your way is rarely difficult on the major trekking routes and English is fairly widely spoken. See the language chapter for tips.

ACCOMMODATION & FOOD

Organised treks camp each night and all you have to do is eat and crawl into your tent. Even erecting the tent is handled by the trekking crew who put it up for you at the site selected by your *sirdar* or group leader.

Independent trekkers usually stay in the small lodges, guesthouses or village inns which have appeared along almost all the main trails. At first this sort of accommodation was simply a matter of local teahouses letting you unroll your sleeping bag on the floor. Today along some of the most popular trails the lodges are quite luxurious and offer private rooms, extensive menus and even showers. It's possible to make quite long treks relying entirely on local food and accommodation. Nevertheless, it's still a good idea to carry a sleeping bag as lodges sometimes run out of bedding at peak season, and their bedding can contain unwanted sleeping companions.

On a typical organised trek your only concern with food is sitting down to eat it. The porters carry all the food along with them, and there will be a cook with well-drilled assistants who can turn out meals of often stunning complexity. Baking a cake on a kerosene stove is just one of the tricks trekking party cooks like to perform to display their virtuosity.

Independent trekkers will find numerous places to eat along the most popular trails, although it's often wise to carry some emergency food supplies like cheese, dried fruit or chocolate bars. Food may vary from rice and dal *(dal bhat)* at simple teahouses to surprisingly good meals on the more popular trails. KEEP and other environmentally concerned organisations point out that dal bhat is nutritious, easily prepared, available everywhere, and requires a minimum of fuel for preparation. In most places they will give you a second helping of dal bhat for free. You lessen your impact and usually eat better if you try to adapt to the local diet. On the Everest and Annapurna treks it's unlikely that you will walk more than an hour or two without coming across some sort of establishment that can offer tea, soft drinks, beer, and often a full meal.

The standard of cuisine on the Jomsom Trek is so westernised that it has been dubbed 'the apple pie trail' because that dish features on so many village-inn menus. It's surprising how many places even have cold beer available as well; before you complain about the price contemplate the fact that somebody had to carry that bottle of beer all the way there and will probably have to carry the empty bottle back again!

If you're going right off the beaten track and exploring remote areas like Makalu and Kanchenjunga in the east or Jumla and Dolpo in the west, you must be very self-sufficient. In these relatively untouched areas there is probably very little surplus food for sale and the practice of catering to western trekkers has not yet developed. Teahouses are rare and when they occur are very rudimentary and sanitation conditions leave a lot to be desired.

HEALTH

See the Health section in the Facts for the Visitor chapter for more information on trekking health. Acute mountain sickness (AMS) or altitude sickness is the major concern on high-altitude treks, but for the majority of trekkers health problems are likely to be minor, such as stomach upsets and blisters. While paranoia is not required, common-sense precautions are.

Basic rules for healthy trekking include taking care that water is always safe to drink. The best method is to treat water with iodine, as this is safe (although not exactly delicious!) and does not require the use of firewood or kerosene. Diarrhoea is one of the comparatively minor problems which can ruin a trek so take care in what you eat and make sure your medical kit has a medication such as Lomotil or Imodium and also an antibiotic such as norfloxacin.

The food on an organised trekking expedition is unlikely to cause any problems, but village-inn trekkers are at risk.

At high altitudes the burning power of the sun is much stronger, so make sure you have a pair of good sunglasses, and a maximum-protection sunscreen for your skin. If there is any likelihood that you'll be walking over snow, sunglasses are insufficient – you need mountaineering glasses with side pieces, or at the very least, rig up pieces of cardboard on the frames of your glasses to cut the glare. Ensure that your porters also have adequate eye-wear. Blisters can take the fun out of trekking so make sure your shoes and socks are comfortable and come prepared with Band-aids and moleskins just in case they aren't. Many people suffer from knee and ankle strains, particularly if they are carrying their own pack. If you have a predisposition for these injuries, carry elastic supports or bandages.

TREKKING

Make sure you are in good health before departing as there is very little medical attention along the trails and rescue helicopters are not only very expensive but *must* be cleared for payment in advance! Your embassy can do this if you have registered with them (see the Safety section below). See the individual treks for more information on possible medical assistance. In general, Himalayan hospitals can offer only very limited facilities and expertise.

The Himalayan Rescue Association (HRA) in Thamel, Kathmandu can offer valuable advice on trekking issues and has an excellent pamphlet on AMS.

SAFETY
In the mid-1970s it was possible to claim that Nepal was totally immune from theft, assaults and other assorted vices of western 'civilisation'. Unfortunately that claim can no longer be made and in a number of places it would be unwise to trek alone, or

in small groups, and a sharp eye should be kept on your possessions.

If you're intending to trek independently and don't have a partner it's usually relatively easy to find one. Notice boards around Kathmandu or Pokhara often have signs up from people looking for partners. In Kathmandu, the KEEP Information Centre and the Kathmandu Guest House have particularly good boards. You could also hire a guide, not necessarily just to show the way, but also as a trekking companion.

Usually, the farther you get from population centres the fewer problems there will be, although assaults in remote places are not unheard of. Several basic rules should be followed: Don't trek alone, don't make ostentatious displays of valuable possessions and don't leave lodge doors unlocked or valuables unattended. If you hire porters make sure they are reputable by hiring them through a lodge or trekking agency or by getting good first-hand recommendations

---

Garbage & Waste

While trekkers certainly contribute to the problems of firewood use and the appearance of rubbish along the trails, they are not the only culprits. As modern nonbiodegradable packaging becomes increasingly common in Nepal, garbage is starting to appear even along village trails untravelled by western trekkers.

You can do several things that will reduce the amount of rubbish and pollution in the hills. One important contribution you can make is to reduce the volume of waste plastic in village rubbish heaps by not drinking bottled mineral water; carry a water bottle and treat the water with iodine. The empty plastic bottles are becoming a major problem – the Annapurna Conservation Area Project (ACAP) estimated that in 1995 alone 200,000 of these were dumped in the Annapurna region!

Independent trekkers should always carry their garbage out or dispose of it properly. You can burn it, but you should remember that the fireplace in a Nepali home is a sacred institution and throwing rubbish into it would be a great insult.

Toilet paper is a particularly unpleasant sight along trails: if you must use it, carry it out in a plastic bag until you can burn it. Better yet, carry a small plastic trowel to bury the shit (well away from any streams) and a small plastic water container so that – like the vast majority of people in the world – you can clean yourself with water instead.

Those travelling with organised groups should ensure that toilet tents are properly organised, and that rubbish is carried out.

Check on the company's policies before you sign up.

about a person. A porter or guide found at a street corner can easily disappear along the trail with all your gear – even if they are carrying a slew of letters from past clients certifying to their honesty.

Women should choose all trekking companions carefully and treat with caution any offer of a massage in a remote hotel.

Walking at high altitudes on rough trails can be dangerous. Watch your footing on slippery trails, and never underestimate the capacity of the weather to change extremely rapidly for the worse – at any time of the year. If you are crossing high passes where snow is a possibility, never walk with less than three people, carry a supply of emergency rations, have a map and compass (and know how to use them), and have sufficient equipment to deal with cold, wet, blizzard conditions.

All embassies and consulates strongly recommend that their citizens register with them before they head off into the wilderness. They have standard forms that record your name, rough itinerary, insurance details and next of kin, and can obviously speed up a search, or a medical evacuation. These are usually kept at the embassies' reception desks and take two minutes to complete. You can avoid a trip to the embassy by filling in a registration forms at either the KEEP or the HRA Trekkers' Information Centre. They regularly forward the forms to the appropriate embassies.

Preparations in Nepal

PERMITS

Up until very recently, trekking anywhere more than a day's walk from the main roads required a trekking permit. Changes in the visa regulations (see Facts for the Visitor) in 1999 mean that for trekking in the Everest, Annapurna and Langtang regions a permit is no longer required. These three regions cover the vast majority of trekking routes taken by visitors to Nepal.

Treks in more remote areas (see table following) still require a permit. If you are trekking with an organised group this will be arranged for you. If you're doing it yourself it is possible to obtain the permit the same day, although you must make your application as early as possible in the morning. Be prepared for a distinctly tiring battle with bureaucracy.

Trekking permits are issued in Kathmandu and Pokhara, and can only be extended in those cities. Permits can be

---

Trekking, Firewood & Forest Depletion

The depletion of forest is a severe problem throughout the Himalaya, and is a particular problem in Nepal. Trekkers can definitely do their part to aid Himalayan conservation. You can minimise the use of firewood by staying in lodges that use kerosene or fuel-efficient wood stoves and solar-heated hot water. Avoid using large open fires for warmth – wear additional clothing instead. Keep showers to a minimum, and spurn showers altogether if wood is burnt to produce the hot water.

Consolidate cooking time (and wood consumption) by ordering the same items at the same time as other trekkers. Dal bhat is usually readily available for large numbers of people, does not require special lengthy cooking time and is nutritious and inexpensive. Remember that local meals are prepared between 10 and 11 am, so eating then will usually not require an additional fire. Treat your drinking water with iodine, rather than boiling it.

Those travelling with organised groups should ensure that kerosene is always used for cooking.

obtained from Kathmandu's immigration office, open 10 am to 1 pm Monday to Thursday and 10 am to noon on Friday for applications. You have to go back later to retrieve your passport. It's wise to start the process early as it can be time-consuming.

If you plan to trek in two different remote areas, two trekking permits are needed. Trekking permits and application forms are colour coded depending on the region in which you plan to trek; be sure to get the right form when you start the process. Two passport photos are required with each application; fees, though quoted in US dollars, are payable only in rupees.

Area	Fee
Everest, Annapurna & Langtang	No permit required
Jumla (& others)	$5 per week for first four weeks, $10 per week after that
Kanchenjunga* & Lower Dolpo*	$10 per week for first four weeks, $20 per week after that
Upper Mustang* † & Upper Dolpo* †	$700 for up to 10 days, groups only
Manaslu* †	$75 per week low season, $90 high season
Humla*	$90 for seven days then $15 per day

* Treks to these regions must be fully equipped treks arranged by a trekking agency.

† A government liaison officer must accompany treks to this region.

Finally, if you plan to trek through a national park, wildlife reserve or conservation area – this will be necessary in the case of almost all treks – you will need to pay a park entrance fee. You can buy an entrance ticket in advance at the National Parks office located in the basement of the Sanchaya Kosh shopping centre in Thamel in Kathmandu, or the Immigration Office in Pokhara, or you can just pay the fee when you arrive at the park entrance station. Currently, there is a Rs 1000 entry fee for national parks and conservation areas, including the Annapurna Conservation Area.

MONEY
Except in Khumbu and on the Annapurna Trek, changing foreign money is likely to be very difficult if not impossible. Bring enough money for the whole trek and don't count on being able to change Rs 1000 notes easily.

EQUIPMENT
It's always best to have your own equipment since you will be familiar with it and know for certain that it works. If there is some equipment which you do not have, however, you can buy or rent it from one of Nepal's many trekking shops. Much of the equipment available is of excellent quality and the rental charges are generally not excessive, but large deposits are often required (usually equal to a generous valuation of the equipment itself). Never leave your passport as a deposit.

Rental rates vary depending on quality, but per day prices are roughly as follows:

Item	Rate
mattress	Rs 6 – 10
sleeping bag	Rs 20 – 40
down jacket	Rs 15 – 40
pack	Rs 15 – 30
tent	Rs 50 – 150

Kathmandu is still the centre for trekking equipment and there are many outlets around Thamel. Pokhara and Namche Bazaar also have trekking equipment places. The equipment available in Nepal used to be mainly expedition leftovers, but now there is also a great deal of new equipment. Some trekking gear, including sleeping bags, down jackets, duffel bags, rucksacks, camera cases, ponchos and wind jackets are manufactured in

Kathmandu and sold in Thamel trekking shops at very reasonable prices. Much of this locally produced gear is decorated with well-known brand names such as North Face, Karimor, Lowe Pro and Gore-Tex, but don't be deceived into thinking you're getting top quality merchandise at a bargain price. Even so, most items are well made and stand up to the rigours of trekking.

Approximate retail prices for new Nepal-made gear with fake brand names are as follows:

Item	Cost
sleeping bag	Rs 5500
down jacket	Rs 5000
rain/wind jacket	Rs 1300
pile jacket	Rs 1200 – 1500
day pack	Rs 1000 – 2500
expedition pack	Rs 3500
duffel bag	Rs 350 – 450

Clothing

The clothing you require depends on where and when you trek. If you're going to the Everest base camp in the middle of winter you must be prepared for very cold weather with down gear, mittens and the like. On the other hand, if you're doing a short, low-altitude trek early or late in the season the weather is likely to be fine for T-shirts and perhaps a sweater, or better yet a pile jacket, to pull on in the evenings. If you don't have your own sleeping bag or down jacket, these can be rented in Kathmandu; however, they may not be particularly clean.

Apart from ensuring you have adequate clothing to keep warm, the important considerations are that your feet are comfortable and that you can keep dry if it rains or snows. Uncomfortable shoes or blistered feet are the worst possible trekking discomfort. Make sure your shoes fit well and are comfortable for long periods. Running shoes are adequate for low-altitude (below 3000m), warm-weather treks where you won't encounter snow, though they lack ankle support. Otherwise the minimum standard of footwear is

lightweight trekking boots, and these can be bought new (imported) in Kathmandu at Rs 2000 to Rs 3000.

Books & Maps

Books and maps are readily available in Kathmandu and Pokhara bookshops.

See Lonely Planet's *Trekking in the Nepal Himalaya* by Stan Armington for the complete story on trekking. It has comprehensive advice on equipment selection, an excellent medical section oriented towards trekking and the mountains, and comprehensive route descriptions not only of the popular treks covered more briefly in this book, but also of a number of interesting but less heavily used routes.

The *Schneider* maps, named after their cartographer, are the best available trekking maps. They cover the entire Everest trek, Langtang and Annapurna, but they are expensive at Rs 1000 each. The locally produced Mandala series has colour maps for a number of regions including *Helambu & Langtang*, *Round Annapurna* and *Khumbu* priced at Rs 80 to Rs 150. For less popular routes, you'll have to rely on the older dye-line maps at Rs 80 each.

All the trekking maps, including the Schneider maps, suffer from a number of problems. For a start the trails change faster than the maps: you may well find a new trail in use or a route change necessitated by an avalanche or flood. Equally disorienting is the fact that Nepali villages are often hard to pinpoint (they sprawl over hills and down valleys) and often have very different names depending on which map you look at or whom you ask. Treat any map with scepticism.

Other Gear

In winter or at high altitudes a high-quality sleeping bag will be necessary. However, if you are going on an organised trek check exactly what equipment is supplied: it's a waste of time bringing your own sleeping bag if the company supplies one. If you need to hire one, it may be grubby; check for fleas or worse.

Rain is rare during most of the trekking season, though disturbances in the Bay of Bengal can cause massive rainstorms during the autumn, and there are sure to be a few rainy days in spring. You should be prepared for it by carrying waterproof gear, or at least an umbrella. The rainy season just before and after the monsoon also brings leeches and it's nice to have some salt or matches to deal with them.

Take a torch (flashlight) for those inevitable calls of nature on moonless nights.

Cigarettes and matches are popular small gifts to have with you on treks if you are travelling with porters, but beware of encouraging children begging for 'one rupee' or a 'school pen'.

INDEPENDENT TREKKING

At one extreme, independent trekking can mean simply trekking from lodge to lodge along the main trekking trails with one or more friends. All you need is your trekking permit and your walking gear and off you go. The popular trekking trails all have accommodation along their entire length. People have even walked the complete Annapurna Circuit without a sleeping bag, although this is asking for trouble and is definitely not recommended.

For most moderately fit people, guides and porters are not necessary on the Annapurna or Mt Everest treks. A good guide/porter will enhance your experience, but a bad one will just make life more complicated.

Independent Trekking with Children

In 1994 Linda and I decided to have a family holiday in Nepal. We had both travelled and trekked extensively in Nepal – without kids – and thought it would be a good place to return to with our two children – Ella aged six and Vera 2½. It turned out to be an excellent choice, although there were moments when we doubted our sanity in carting two kids halfway across the world, exposing them to all manner of bugs, not to mention the pollution of Kathmandu, just so we could see some mountains with snow on them. At times Ella was inclined to agree: 'What's so special about them, Dad?', was her response at one stage, after having the snow-capped mountains pointed out to her by excited parents for the fifth time in as many minutes on the spectacular plane ride between Kathmandu and Pokhara.

One of the main goals of our trip was to do a week-long trek in the mountains. Many people we spoke to thought it was perhaps a bit of an ambitious thing to undertake with two small children, but this just made us more determined to give it a go – we could always turn back if it didn't work out. Our base point was to be Pokhara, seven bumpy and dusty but cheap hours by bus, or one easy, spectacular and not-too-expensive hour by plane (we opted for the latter) from Kathmandu.

As we were travelling on a fairly tight budget, we couldn't afford an organised trek where everything is taken care of for you. Instead we organised it all ourselves.

We approached many of the trekking agencies in Pokhara, and finally settled on one which we felt had its act together sufficiently to arrange for porters and transport to the trail head. Our plan was that we would have three porters – two to carry rucksacks, and a third to carry Vera most of the time, and Ella when she got tired of walking.

As it turned out, Ella walked virtually the whole way, which was a great effort, and Vera was carried in a *doko* (a large, conical, cane basket) on a porter's back. She felt safe being up off the ground, and was emboldened enough to pull faces at trekkers and locals we passed along the trail. Her mode of travel certainly made her a curiosity to locals and foreigners alike. To wedge her in safely we sat her first in her child-pack, placed this in the basket, and then

There are many factors that influence how much you spend on an independent trek. In most places, dormitory accommodation costs around Rs 20 to Rs 50, a simple meal of rice and dal around Rs 30 to Rs 50 – note that as you get farther from the road on the Annapurna Circuit and in the Everest region, prices can be more than twice as high. After a long day hiking, however, most people will weaken when confronted by a cold beer, an apple pie or a hot shower and these will dramatically add to your costs. Around $10 per day in the Annapurnas and Everest region is about right, and this includes the occasional luxury items you might treat yourself to.

According to some studies, competition on the Annapurna Circuit is so intense, and the need for money so desperate, that lodges have been known to provide food and accommodation at below cost. In almost all lodges prices are fixed and are more than reasonable. Remember this – and the real value of the rupee – if you start to get carried away with bargaining.

Guides & Porters

If you can't (or don't want to) carry a decent-sized pack, if you have children or elderly people in your party, or if you plan to walk in regions where you have to carry in food and tents, help should be considered. It's fairly easy to find guides and porters, but it is hard to be certain of their honesty and ability.

Independent Trekking with Children

filled the gaps with sleeping bags and items of warm clothing we shed as the day wore on.

The porters were great with the kids, and although we felt a bit like a travelling show at times, it was worth hiring enough porters to free us of any major load. At $5 per porter per day, it was money well spent.

Overall the trek went very well, but we realised early on that we had overestimated how far we would be able to walk in one day. Once we slowed down and basically let Ella set the pace, things were fine. The walking itself was not too strenuous, largely because of our slow pace, but we did get up to 3500m, and even at this altitude the children's breathing was being affected. In six days we were able to comfortably walk from Birethanti to Ghorapani/Deorali on the Jomsom Trek, cut across to Ghandruk on the Annapurna Circuit and return to Birethanti.

Staying in the teahouses along the way was a highlight for the kids. On arrival they would disappear into the candle-lit, smoky interiors of the kitchen, and usually emerge beaming some time later, brandishing a boiled potato or some other morsel kindly given by the hard-working women of the house.

The major problem we faced on the trek was a bout of giardia which Vera contracted, and this led to our second biggest problem: what to do with all the soiled disposable nappies. They're a bugger of a thing to get rid of at the best of times; in small villages in the mountains they are a disaster. The only really sound solution is to use cloth nappies. On a practical level this is very difficult (although not impossible), so with the disposables you need to roll the used ones up very tightly, store them in a strong plastic bag and carry them out to a place where you can dispose of them properly. This is not as offensive as it sounds!

Empty, plastic mineral-water bottles are another problem in the mountains, and it's recommended that you buy iodine tablets to purify your water. Some powdered flavouring helps to disguise the awful taste, but our two children steadfastly refused anything other than plain bottled water.

Hugh Finlay

TREKKING

Unless you have first-hand recommendations, you're best to hire someone through a guesthouse or agency. Arranging expeditions where guides, porters, tents and food are required can be very time-consuming and can quickly become extremely complicated. In such cases you're definitely best off putting this in the hands of a professional.

There is a distinct difference between a guide and a porter. A guide should speak English, know the terrain and the trails, and supervise porters, but will probably not be interested in carrying a load or doing menial tasks like cooking and putting up tents. Porters are generally hired for load-carrying, although an increasing number speak some English and know the trails well enough to act as guides.

If halfway through a trek you decide you do need some help (illness, problems with high altitude or ordinary old blisters might

contribute) it will generally be possible to find someone. Most lodges can arrange a porter, particularly in large villages or near a hill-country airstrip where there are often porters who have just been paid off from a trekking party and are looking for another load to carry. Large organised trekking parties carry most of their own food and as the food is used up, fewer porters are needed and the extra porters are paid off along the route – so you can find experienced porters in the most unlikely places.

Whether you're making the arrangements yourself or dealing with an agency, make sure you clearly establish where you will go, how long you will take, how much you are going to pay and what you will be obliged to supply along the way. Traditionally you pay for a guide's food and porters pay for their own food out of their wages. With a guide, you are better off agreeing on

Organised Trekking with Children

Taking children trekking in Nepal can be surprisingly enjoyable. Both of our children's treks were of the organised variety.

Tackling a long, high-altitude trek like the Annapurna Circuit with small children might be asking too much. With our children we planned on shorter treks (we didn't want them getting fed up) which avoided very high altitudes. We also opted for organised treks to make it easier for both sides – we didn't have to worry about finding food and shelter and the kids were likely to eat better.

Our first trek with children was the short Annapurna Skyline Trek (see the Pokhara chapter) when our daughter Tashi was eight and our son Kieran was six. Back home, like most kids, they seemed to think getting from the car to the video recorder a long walk, but in fact they walked the whole way and still had energy for frantic games with the porters and local village kids after we set up camp each night.

Our enthusiasm must have been catching because three years later we found ourselves back in Nepal, this time with seven friends and neighbours and six children (two aged six, two aged eight, one 10-year-old and one 11-year-old). This time we opted for the Helambu Trek as it is reasonably short, doesn't go too high and is not too heavily trekked. Malla Treks in Kathmandu, who organised the trek for us, made it even more interesting by sending along a bunch of Nepali children, who also happened to be on school vacation. Our resulting 'international trek' was a great learning experience, and once again our kids turned out to be hardier than we'd expected. On one day only, when a misunderstanding with the porters resulted in us having to climb a 3500m pass late in the day, did the two six-year-olds require a little carrying. Apart from that, the whole noisy mob walked the entire eight days.

Tony Wheeler

a daily rate for food rather than paying as you go. Arrangements where you pay for the guide or porter's accommodation and food can end up being surprisingly expensive. The amount of food a hungry Nepali porter can go through, when you're footing the bill, can be simply stunning.

You may also be responsible for outfitting guides and porters to cope with cold and snow. If you are going above the snow line you must make absolutely certain that porters have goggles, shoes, shelter and appropriate clothing. There are still regular horror stories about ill-equipped porters tackling the Thorung La (the pass between Manang and Muktinath on the Annapurna Circuit). Frostbite, snow blindness and death have resulted.

If you make arrangements with one of the small trekking agencies in Kathmandu expect to pay Rs 150 to Rs 200 per day for a guide, Rs 150 to Rs 350 per day for a porter. If you find a porter yourself or through a guesthouse, the costs will be lower. Local agencies are listed in the following section.

ORGANISED TREKKING

Organised treks can also vary greatly in standards and costs. At one extreme there are the big international adventure travel companies that market trips in the west. You book your trek through them and everything is organised and arranged before you leave home. Your cost will probably include flights to and from Nepal, accommodation in Kathmandu before and after the trek, tours and other activities as well as the trek itself. A fully organised trek will provide virtually everything: tents, sleeping bags, food, porters and an experienced English-speaking sirdar (trail boss), sherpa guides and usually a western trek leader. All you need to worry about is your day-pack and camera.

Companies organising trekking trips in Nepal include some well-known names such as Mountain Travel, Wilderness Travel or Above the Clouds in the USA, World Expeditions or Peregrine Adventures in Australia, and Explore Worldwide in the UK.

Although the trek leaders may be experienced western walkers from the international company the actual organisation in Nepal will probably be by a locally based trekking company.

Local Trekking Agencies

It's quite possible to arrange a fully organised trip when you get to Nepal (and save a lot of money), but if you have a large group it's best to make the arrangements well in advance. Many trekking companies in Nepal can put together a fully equipped trek if you give them a few days notice. With the best of these companies a trek may cost upwards of $60 or $70 a day and you'll trek in real comfort with tables, chairs, dining tents, toilet tents and other luxuries.

Some of the large trekking agencies based in Nepal that have been recommended include:

Ama Dablam Trekking
  (☎ 415372, fax 416029)
  PO Box 3035, Lazimpat
International Trekkers
  (☎ 371397, fax 371561)
  PO Box 1273, Chabahil
Malla Treks
  (☎ 410089, fax 423143, email trekinfo@
  mallatrk.mos.com.np)
  PO Box 5227, Lainchaur
Mountain Travel Nepal
  (☎ 411225, fax 414075, email info@
  tigermountain.com)
  PO Box 170, Kathmandu
Thamserku Trekking
  (☎ 420044, fax 412323)
  PO Box 3124, Kamal Pokhari

There are more than 300 trekking agencies in Nepal, ranging from those tied up with international adventure travel companies, down to small agencies who specialise in handling independent trekkers. These small agencies will often be able to fix you up with individual porters or guides. A group trek organised through one of these smaller trekking agencies might cost $30 to $50 a day. Group treks staying at village inns along the route can be cheaper still (around $25 a day including a guide and food).

TREKKING

TREKKING

Trekking agencies that have been recommended in this category include:

Asian Trekking
(☎ 415506, fax 411878, email asiant@
asian-trekking.com)
Thamel, PO Box 3022, Kathmandu
Himalayan Hill Treks & River Tours
(☎ 520609, fax 521057, email brian@
hilltrek.mos.com.np)
PO Box 1066, Kathmandu
Lama Excursions
(☎ 425812, fax 425813)
Chanddol, Maharajganj, PO Box 2485,
Kathmandu
Lucky Trek & Expedition Nepal
(☎ 259415, fax 258950)
Thahity Chowk, PO Box 6632, Kathmandu
Nepal Himal Treks
(☎ 413305) Baluwatar, PO Box 4528,
Kathmandu
Sherpa Co-operative Trekking
(☎ 224068, fax 227983)
Durbar Marg, PO Box 1338, Kathmandu

TREKS

There are countless long treks in Nepal, many of which still see only a handful of western walkers each year. Many of the previously off-limits areas have been opened up, but only for trekkers in organised groups: upper Mustang, upper Dolpo, Manaslu, Humla and the Kanchenjunga base camp in the north-east of the country.

The six very popular longer treks, described in detail in this chapter, are the Everest Base Camp Trek, Helambu, Langtang and Jomsom treks, the Annapurna Circuit and the Annapurna Sanctuary Trek.

Everest Base Camp Trek

The Everest Base Camp Trek takes about three weeks and reaches a maximum height of 5545m at Kala Pattar, a small peak offering fine views of Mt Everest. Although the final part of the trek is through essen-

The Yeti

Like Big Foot in North America, the Loch Ness monster in Scotland or even the elusive bunyip in Australia, the yeti or abominable snowman is much hunted but little seen. The yeti is a shy humanoid creature which lives high in the most remote regions of the Himalaya. There are countless yeti legends told by the Sherpas and other hill peoples. They tell of its legendary strength, its ability to carry off yaks and even abduct people.

Nobody has ever managed to get a clear photograph of the yeti: footprints in the snow are generally the only indication that a yeti has been by, although hastily gnawed yak bones also add to the yeti legend.

Of course, there are plenty of scientific explanations for yetis. The footprints may have been a human print or some other natural footprint which has appeared to grow larger as the snow melts. Rigorous studies have been made of the yeti scalps found in various monasteries, in particular the one at the Khumjung Monastery, and they have all turned out to be fakes. Keep your camera loaded though, a good photo of a yeti (even a small yeti) will probably be worth a fortune.

tially uninhabited areas, small lodges operate during the trekking season so it's quite suitable for independent trekkers. The flights in or out of Lukla at the start and/or finish of the trek can be a real problem.

Helambu Trek
The Helambu Trek, a one-week trek that can start from and finish in the Kathmandu Valley, does not offer superb mountain scenery but is culturally interesting. The maximum height reached is 3490m and there is plenty of accommodation along the route, although it's still a good idea to carry a sleeping bag.

Langtang Trek
The Langtang Trek lasts 10 to 12 days if you walk in and out, but it can be varied by crossing a high pass down to the Helambu region. There are fine views, interesting villages, and although there are some relatively uninhabited stretches, accommodation is available. The maximum height reached is 4300m.

Jomsom Trek
The Jomsom Trek, from Pokhara up the Kali Gandaki valley, is among the most popular in Nepal with superb scenery, interesting people and the best trailside accommodation in the country. It takes a week to reach Muktinath, the end point of the trek. Walking back takes another week or you can fly from Jomsom. Muktinath, the high point of the trek, is at 3800m.

Annapurna Circuit
It takes nearly three weeks to walk the entire Annapurna Circuit, but for scenery and cultural diversity this is the best trek in Nepal. It crosses to the north of the main Himalayan Range, on to the Tibetan plateau, and crosses a 5416m pass. The last week of the trek is the Jomsom Trek in reverse.

Annapurna Sanctuary Trek
The Annapurna Sanctuary Trek into the centre of the Annapurna Range also starts from Pokhara, and offers unparalleled mountain scenery. The trek takes 10 to 14 days and reaches a maximum height of 4095m at the Annapurna base camp. Finding shelter in the uninhabited sanctuary area was a real problem at one time, but recently numerous lodges have sprung up along the route.

Everest Base Camp Trek

Everybody knows of Mt Everest and that's the simple reason why the Everest Base Camp Trek is so popular. The trek has a number of stunning attractions, but it also has some distinct drawbacks which might well deter potential trekkers were it not for the undeniable plus point of being able to say you've been to the base of the highest mountain in the world.

The attractions include spectacular scenery and the outgoing Sherpa people of the Solu Khumbu, the region where Mt Everest and its attendant lesser peaks are located. The drawbacks include the long, hard slog to get there and the acclimatisation problems caused by the region's considerable altitude.

It's not until you get right into the Solu Khumbu region that the Everest trek really gets interesting. The first part of the trek is not only a hard slog, but is also pretty sparse in the breathtaking views department. The hard slog comes about because the trek doesn't follow valleys – like the Annapurna treks – instead the Everest trek cuts across the valleys. So for day after day it's a tiring process of dropping down one side of a steep valley and climbing up again on the other. By the time you reach the base camp your ascents will total almost 9000m, the full height of Everest from sea level!

The Everest trek starts in the Nepali-speaking Hindu lowlands and ends in the Tibetan-Buddhist highlands where the Sherpas are renowned for their enterprise, hard work, civic responsibility and devotion to the practice of Buddhism. In their often

TREKKING

TREKKING

EVEREST TREKS

inhospitable land, the potato, a relatively recent introduction, is the main crop, but these days trekking and mountaineering is the backbone of the Sherpa economy. More than half the population in the region is now involved with tourism and Namche Bazaar looks more like an alpine resort than a Sherpa village.

Most Everest trekkers opt to fly one way to avoid having to repeat all those ups and downs. This introduces its own problems as flights to Lukla are notorious for cancellations, waiting lists and short-tempered trekkers. If you have the time, walk in from Jiri and fly out from Lukla. If you want to make a shorter trip you can fly in to Lukla, trek to Everest and then fly out, taking 15 days to trek to Kala Pattar or you can just visit Thami, Namche Bazaar and Tengpoche in a week or so.

The Everest trek may not be quite as good as the Pokhara area for village-inn treks, but plenty of accommodation is available during the trekking season even in the normally uninhabited areas around the high peaks.

Medical Services There are small hospitals in Jiri, Phaplu and Khunde while the Himalayan Rescue Association has a medical facility in Pheriche.

THE TREK
Access: Kathmandu via Lamosangu to Jiri
The Everest trek has been getting steadily shorter over the years. The members of the 1953 British expedition which put Hillary and Tenzing on the top started their walk to Everest at Bhaktapur in the Kathmandu Valley. Today you can take the Kodari road to Lamosangu, 78km from Kathmandu, and turn off there to Jiri, a farther 110km. Buses to Jiri leave from the Kathmandu City bus terminal in the mornings (Rs 120, around 10 to 12 hours). Keep a close eye on your luggage.

Jiri at 1860m is a relatively new town which has expanded since the road was completed. It has a weekly market on Saturday and there are many hotels in the town centre near the bus stop and also on the ridge near the market site. The bus stops at the far end of town so you walk back to find somewhere to stay. The *Sagarmatha Hotel*, the *Sherpa Guide Lodge* and the *Cherdung Lodge* are all on the main road and all have basic rooms for less than Rs 200.

Day 1: Jiri to Bhandar
The walk starts with a climb to the ridge top at 2370m then drops down to Shivalaya at 1750m. Before the Jiri road was opened the trek used to go through Those, which at that time was the busiest market town between Lamosangu and Namche Bazaar. It's still possible to walk from Jiri to Those and Shivalaya.

From Shivalaya you climb again to Sangbadanda at 2150m, Kosaribas at 2500m, then to Deorali, a pass at 2705m. There are hotels here, or you can descend again to Bhandar at 2150m. This Sherpa settlement has a gompa and a number of hotels. It's possible to take a short detour between Sangbadanda and Bhandar to visit Thodung at 3090m where there's a cheese factory, established with Swiss aid in the 1950s.

Day 2: Bhandar to Sete
The trail drops down to the Likhu Khola and crosses the river at 1490m, and tracks along it to Kenja (1570m). The trail now starts the long climb to Lamjura La. The first part of the climb is quite steep, then it traverses to Sete, an abandoned gompa at 2575m. From here on the villages are almost all inhabited by Sherpas and have both Nepali and Sherpa names (the Sherpa village names are given in brackets).

Day 3: Sete to Junbesi
It's a long but gradual climb to the Lamjura pass at 3530m. You're rewarded with frost and often snow along the trail in winter or with flowering rhododendrons in the spring. Goyem at 3300m on your way to the pass is a good lunch stop. The pass is the highest point between Jiri and Namche Bazaar and from the top you descend to Tragdobuk at 2860m, then to the pretty Sherpa village of Junbesi (Jun) at 2675m. It has a monastery,

some good hotels and is a good place for a rest day with some interesting walks in the vicinity.

Day 4: Junbesi to Nuntala

The trail climbs to a ridge at 2980m where for the first time you can see Everest, then on to Salung at 2650m. A lower trail from Junbesi leads to the hospital and airstrip at Phaplu and the district headquarters and bazaar at Salleri. From Salung the trail descends to the Ringmo Khola at 2570m. Then it's up to Ringmo where apples and other fruit are grown; the *Apple House* offers apple juice, pie and *rakshi* (rice spirit). The trail from here to Namche Bazaar was built in the 1980s and avoids many of the steep descents and ascents of the old route.

A short climb from Ringmo takes you to the 3071m Trakshindo La, then the trail drops down past the gompa of the same name, and on to Nuntala (Manidingma) at 2250m where there are numerous hotels offering a variety of standards.

Day 5: Nuntala to Bupsa

The trail descends to the Dudh Kosi at 1480m and crosses it to follow the other bank. The trail climbs to Jubing (Dorakbuk) at 1680m and continues over a ridge to Khari Khola (Khati Thenga) at 2070m. You should arrive in Khari Khola early enough to push on up the steep hill to Bupsa (Bumshing) at 2300m. There are several hotels on the top of the ridge and a few less sumptuous hotels at Kharte, 20 minutes walk beyond Bupsa, and in the rhododendron forests beyond.

Day 6: Bupsa to Ghat

From Bupsa the trail climbs gradually, offering views of the Dudh Kosi 1000m below at the bottom of the steep-sided valley, until it reaches a ridge at 2840m overlooking Puiyan (Chitok). The trail is very narrow in places as it makes its way down to Puiyan at 2730m in a side canyon of the Dudh Kosi valley. Climb to a ridge at 2750m then drop down to Surkhe (Buwa) at 2290m. Shortly beyond Surkhe is the turn-off to Lukla with its airstrip.

The trail continues to climb through Mushe (Nangbug) and Chaunrikarka (Dungde) at 2630m to Chablung (Lomdza), then contours along the side of the Dudh Kosi valley before descending to Ghat (Lhawa) at 2530m. This is a longish day; you may want to take advantage of the many hotels in Chaunrikarka and Chablung if you don't feel like pushing on.

Day 7: Ghat to Namche Bazaar

Climb past Ghat's gompa and large collection of mani stones, then trek along the river to Phakding at 2800m, a huge collection of lodges that provide the first night stop for people who have flown in to Lukla.

The trail crosses the river on a long swaying bridge, then leads you along the river to Benkar at 2700m. It recrosses the river and climbs to Chomoa, with the curious *Hatago Lodge*, created by an eccentric Japanese gentleman. It's a short climb up to Monjo, where there are a number of good places to stay. Show your trek permit and entrance ticket at the Sagarmatha National Park entrance station, then drop down to cross the Dudh Kosi. On the other side it's a short distance to Jorsale (Thumbug) at 2810m, then the trail crosses back to the east side of the river before climbing to the high suspension bridge over the Dudh Kosi.

It's a steady climb from here to Namche Bazaar at 3440m. As this is the first climb to an altitude where AMS may be a problem, take it easy and avoid rushing.

Namche Bazaar is the main centre in the Solu Khumbu region and has shops, restaurants, a bakery, hotels with hot showers, pool hall, a national park visitor centre (well worth a visit), a police checkpoint (where your trekking permit will be inspected), a moneychanger and even a bank. Namche Bazaar and the surrounding villages have an ample supply of hydro-electricity, which is used for lighting and cooking as well as video parlours. The *Cafe Danfe*, *Khumbu Lodge*, *Tawa Lodge* and *Trekkers Inn* offer food as good as any restaurant in Kathmandu. There is a colourful market each Saturday.

Day 8: Namche Bazaar
There is plenty to do around Namche Bazaar and a day should be spent here acclimatising. Remember that the victims of altitude sickness are often the fittest and healthiest people who foolishly overextend themselves. It's important to do a strenuous day walk to a higher altitude as part of your acclimatisation, coming back down to Namche to sleep. For this purpose the day walk to Thami (to the west) is worthwhile.

In Namche pay a visit to the Sagarmatha Pollution Control Committee office to find out about the conservation efforts that are being made in the region, and also visit the national park visitor centre on the ridge above town.

Day 9: Namche Bazaar to Tengpoche
The slightly longer route from Namche Bazaar to Tengpoche via Khumjung and Khunde is more interesting than the direct one. It starts by climbing up to the Shyangboche airstrip. Above it is the *Everest View Hotel*, a Japanese scheme to build a deluxe hotel with great views of the highest mountains on earth. The hotel has had a chequered history, but is once again open, with rooms at $135, plus an extra charge for oxygen if needed!

From the hotel or the airstrip you continue to Khumjung (3790m) and then rejoin the direct trail to Tengpoche. The trail descends to the Dudh Kosi at 3250m where there are three small lodges and a series of picturesque water-driven prayer wheels. A steep ascent brings you to Tengpoche at 3870m. The famous gompa, a photographer's favourite with its background of Ama Dablam, Everest and other peaks, was burnt down in 1989. It has been rebuilt as a large, impressive structure. There's a camping area, a number of places to stay, and during the November-December full moon the colourful Mani Rimdu festival is held here with much singing and dancing.

Day 10: Tengpoche to Pheriche
Beyond Tengpoche the altitude really starts to tell. The trail drops down to Devuche,

crosses the Imja Khola and climbs past superb mani stones to Pangboche at 3860m. The gompa here is worth visiting and the village is a good place for a lunch stop.

The trail then climbs to Pheriche at 4240m where there is a trekkers' aid post and possible medical assistance. Pheriche has a number of hotels and restaurants which usually feature exotic dishes left over from international mountaineering expeditions.

Day 11: Pheriche
Another acclimatisation day should be spent at Pheriche. As at Namche, a solid day walk to a higher altitude is better than just resting; Dingboche and Chhukung (4730m) are possible destinations. You could also make a day trip to Nangkartshang Gompa or up past Dingboche. Either walk offers good views.

Day 12: Pheriche to Lobuje
The trail climbs to Phalang Karpo at 4340m then Duglha at 4620m before reaching the summer village of Lobuje at 4930m. The lodge accommodation here is all dormitory-style and the altitude, the cold and the crowding combine to ensure less than restful nights.

Day 13: Lobuje to Gorak Shep
The trail continues to climb to Gorak Shep at 5160m. The return trip from Lobuje to Gorak Shep takes a couple of hours, enough time to continue to Kala Pattar (Black Rock) – or you can overnight in Gorak Shep and reach Kala Pattar the next morning. At 5545m this small peak offers the best view you'll get of Everest without climbing it.

Although there is usually accommodation at Gorak Shep it's nothing to write home about, so it's a better plan to return to Lobuje for the night. The altitude hits nearly everybody; getting back down to Lobuje or even better to Pheriche makes a real difference.

Day 14: Gorak Shep to Lobuje
If you want to actually get to the base camp then it's about six hours round trip from

Gorak Shep, and there's no view, so if you only have the energy for one side trip, then make it Kala Pattar.

The descent to Lobuje is easy, but seems endless because of the many uphill climbs from Gorak Shep. The night, however, will be much more comfortable than the previous one.

Day 15: Lobuje to Dingboche
Staying the night at Dingboche instead of Pheriche makes an interesting alternative. It's a 'summer village' at 4410m with four large lodges.

Days 16, 17 & 18: Dingboche to Lukla
The next three days retrace your steps down to Lukla via Tengpoche and Namche Bazaar. There is extreme pressure for a seat on flights out of Lukla, so be sure to have an advance booking, and be there the night before your flight to reconfirm (the airline offices are generally open from 5 to 6 pm, but sometimes it's 6 to 7 pm). Then be prepared for a torrid time at the airstrip as frustrated trekkers vie for the limited seats. This is especially so when flights have been cancelled for a few consecutive days due to poor visibility, and there is a huge backlog of passengers all wanting to get back to Kathmandu. Lukla has a number of places to stay including the relatively expensive *Trekkers Cabin* and the *Sagarmatha Resort*, and life revolves around watching flights come and go.

Day 19: Lukla to Kathmandu
If the gods are with you, your flight comes in and your reservation hasn't been cancelled. Then, after it took you so many days to get here by road and foot, your aircraft only takes 35 minutes to fly you back.

VARIATIONS & SIDE-TRIPS
See the Other Treks section later in this chapter for information on the long trek south from the Solu Khumbu region to Hile, an interesting alternative to going straight back to Kathmandu. Alternatives to hanging around in Lukla waiting for flights or

walking all the way back to Jiri are also possible but not very satisfactory. Going down to Phaplu, two or three days south of Lukla, is unlikely to get you out any faster. It's a four or five-day walk down to Lamidanda from where there are several flights a week to Biratnagar and Kathmandu.

Experienced trekkers could take the little-frequented Barabise to Mali route in, avoiding the Jiri road completely. Another interesting side-trip is the nine-day round trip from Namche Bazaar to Gokyo and back. This trek ends at another Kala Pattar with fine, but different, views of Everest. You can even combine both Kala Pattars by crossing the 5420m Cho La, but you had better bring your ice axe and crampons and know how to use them.

A shorter side trip from Namche Bazaar is to Thami, the gateway to Tesi Lapcha and the Rolwaling Himal. You can do a round trip to Thami in one very long day, although it's better to stay overnight in order to catch the morning views.

Helambu & Langtang Treks

Although they are not as well known and popular as the Everest Base Camp Trek or the Annapurna Circuit these two treks offer a number of distinct advantages. The treks are north of the Kathmandu Valley, so both are easily accessible from Kathmandu. Indeed you can leave your hotel in Kathmandu and set foot on the Helambu trail within an hour. The Helambu Trek only takes a week so it is ideal for people who do not have the time for one of the longer treks. Since it stays at relatively low altitudes it does not require fancy cold-weather equipment and clothing.

The Langtang Trek, on the other hand, gives you the opportunity to get right in among the Himalayan peaks and to walk through remote and relatively unpopulated areas. If you want real adventure then these two treks can be linked by high-altitude passes, either via the Gosainkund lakes or across the 5106m Ganja La.

Medical Services The only medical facility on the Helambu and Langtang treks is the Dhunche dispensary.

HELAMBU TREK

The Helambu Trek only takes seven days, starts from Sundarijal at the eastern end of the Kathmandu Valley and does not climb above 3500m. It makes a loop through the Sherpa-populated Helambu region to the north-east of Kathmandu and only the first day's walk is repeated on the return trip. The trek's main drawback is that it does not offer fine Himalayan views, like some other treks, but it can be trekked on a village-inn basis as there are guesthouses and lodges in many of the villages along the trail. The Sherpa people of the Helambu region are friendly and hospitable, just like their better known kinfolk of the Solu Khumbu region.

As in Solu Khumbu, the potato is a vitally important crop and not only forms a large part of the local diet but is also exported to the Nepali lowland in exchange for rice and other produce.

Day 1: Sundarijal to Pati Bhanjyang

There's no direct bus to Sundarijal, 15km from Kathmandu, but you can get to the start of the trail by taxi, or get a bus to Jorpati, just beyond Bodhnath, and catch a Sundarijal bus at the road junction. At Sundarijal you enter the Shivapuri Watershed & Wildlife Reserve, the organisation that administers the area.

From Sundarijal the trail starts off up concrete steps beside the pipeline which brings drinking water down to the valley. Eventually the trail leaves the pipeline from near the dam and reaches Mulkharka, sprawling up the ridge around 1895m, 600m above Sundarijal. There are superb views back over the valley and some convenient tea shops for rest and refreshment.

The trail continues to climb, but less steeply, through Chisopani (2300m) then drops down to Pati Bhanjyang at 1770m.

Chisopani is rather like a grubby little truck stop without the trucks but the mountain views in the morning can be very fine. Take care of your possessions here, it's still rather close to the Kathmandu Valley. There are lodges at Chisopani and at Pati Bhanjyang which also has a police checkpoint where your trekking permit may be inspected.

Day 2: Pati Bhanjyang to Khutumsang

The trail rises and falls through Chipling at 2170m then over a 2470m pass and down past a large chörten to the village of Gul Bhanjyang (2140m). From here the trail climbs again to reach a 2620m pass before descending along a rocky route to Khutumsang at 2470m. The Rs 1000 entry fee to the Langtang National Park is collected at the office here, although it's better to buy a permit in Kathmandu before starting out. There are lodges at Gul Bhanjyang and Khutumsang or there's the *Dragon Lodge* beside a pleasant meadow about 45 minutes before Khutumsang.

Day 3: Khutumsang to Tharepati

The trail follows a ridge line with views of the Langtang and Gosainkund peaks through sparsely populated forests to Magen Goth with an army checkpoint before finally reaching the Tharepati La at 3490m. The trail to Gosainkund branches off north-west from here. Tharepati has several lodges including the very nicely situated *Himaliya Lodge* on the Khutumsang side.

Day 4: Tharepati to Tarke Gyang

From the pass the trail turns east and descends rapidly down a ravine to the pretty Sherpa village of Malemchigaon at 2530m. There are a number of lodges in the village and a very brightly painted gompa.

From Malemchigaon the trail continues to drop, crossing the Malemchi Khola by a bridge at 1890m and then making the long climb up the other side of the valley to Tarke Gyang at 2600m. This is the largest village in Helambu and the prosperous Sherpas who live here specialise, among other things, in turning out 'instant antiques' for gullible

HELAMBU & LANGTANG TREKS

trekkers. There are a number of lodges including the pleasant *Mount View Hotel* on the Malemchigaon side of the village. Tarke Gyang makes a good place for a rest day or you can take a side-trip up to the peak (3771m) overlooking the village. This is the end of the route down from the Ganja La.

Day 5: Tarke Gyang to Kiul

From Tarke Gyang there is a very pleasant alternative return route, described after the final day of this trek description. On the loop trek the wide and well-used trail descends through rhododendron forests and past Buddhist chörtens and mani walls to Kakani at 2070m and Thimbu at 1580m. By the time you reach Kiul at 1280m you have left the Sherpa highlands and entered the warmer lowland areas where rice is grown. Kiul is at a lower altitude than Kathmandu.

Day 6: Kiul to Pati Bhanjyang

There is a large road under construction in this portion of the valley in preparation for the development of a tunnel that will take water from here to the Kathmandu Valley. The trekking route is likely to be confused and dusty while construction is under way.

The trail descends along a river, crossing it on the second suspension bridge at just 1190m then joining a wide trail at Mahenkal and following it to Talamarang at 940m. Here the trail follows the Talamarang Khola for some distance, the trail (hard to find at times) climbs steeply to Batache and then Thakani, on the ridge top, at 1890m. From here the trail follows the ridge to Pati Bhanjyang (1770m) where the Helambu circuit is completed.

Day 7: Pati Bhanjyang via Sundarijal to Kathmandu

The final day retraces the first day's walk.

Alternative Routes from Tarke Gyang

An alternative route can be followed from Tarke Gyang through Sermathang and then along a long ridge through Kakani and Dubhachaur to join the road at Malemchi Pul Bazaar, south of Talamarang. This route is very pleasant as far as Malemchi and attracts relatively few trekkers. There are numerous lodges at Sermathang and Malemchi but the choice is limited elsewhere.

From Malemchi the final stretch is along a dusty roadway which brings you out on the Kathmandu to Kodari road at Panchkhal, from where you will have to take a bus 55km back to Kathmandu via Dhulikhel. You can usually get a ride on a bus or truck down the road from Malemchi and this route does avoid having to duplicate the final stretch from Pati Bhanjyang through Sundarijal.

Another Helambu alternative is to start and finish from Malemchi Pul Bazaar (via Panchkhal on the main road), completing the shorter loop through Malemchi, Talamarang, Kiul, Tarke Gyang, Sermathang and Malemchi.

The alternative routes are as follows:

Day 5: Tarke Gyang to Sermathang

The easy trail descends gently through a beautiful forest to Sermathang (2620m), the centre of an important apple-growing area. Sermathang is more spread out than the closely spaced houses of Tarke Gyang and there are fine views of the valley of the Malemchi Khola to the south. Trekking permits are checked at Sermathang and if you do the trek in the reverse direction this is where you must pay the Rs 1000 entry fee to the Langtang National Park. There are a number of lodges at Sermathang.

Day 6: Sermathang to Malemchi Pul Bazaar

From Sermathang the trail continues to descend to Dubhachaur (1500m) then steeply down to Malemchi (830m) where it meets the road. The village has a collection of lodges and teahouses. You should be able to get transport (including buses) from here to Panchkhal on the Kodari road, where you change to a bus to Kathmandu.

LANGTANG TREK

Langtang Lirung (7246m) is visible to the north of Kathmandu on clear days. The Langtang trek takes up to two weeks and leads to the foot of glaciers high in the Langtang Valley. The trail passes through Tibetan and Tamang villages and offers fine views of the Ganesh Himal. Though the trek passes through comparatively lightly populated and undeveloped areas, it is still possible to stay at village inns along the route. Ascending from just 541m at Trisuli Bazaar to 3800m at Kyanjin Gompa the trail passes through an ever-changing climate and offers trekkers an exceptional diversity of scenery and culture.

Access: Kathmandu via Trisuli to Dhunche

It's 72km from Kathmandu to Trisuli Bazaar – about four hours by car or six by bus. The road is paved but very winding and offers some fine mountain views. Ranipauwa is the only large village along the route. From Trisuli the 50km road to Dhunche is steep, winding and rather hairy, passing through Betrawati and Thare. There are two buses per day from Kathmandu to Dhunche (12 hours).

Dhunche is a pretty village at 1950m and here you will have your trekking permit checked and must pay the entrance fee to the Langtang National Park, although it's preferable to buy the permit in Kathmandu before starting your trek. The road continues from here, winding its way over a mountain pass to the village of Somdang, at the foot of Ganesh Himal.

Day 1: Dhunche to Syabru

Soon after Dhunche the trail leaves the road and follows the Trisuli Khola south-east, crossing it and climbing steeply then leaving the Gosainkund trail and following a ridge to Bharku at 1860m. Most of the Trisuli River's water comes from the Bhote Kosi, from Tibet. (Bhote Kosi means 'river from Tibet'.) From Bharku you climb to 2300m and enter the Langtang Valley with views of Himalayan peaks to the west, north and east. The trail descends rapidly to Syabru at 2100m where there are numerous lodges.

There is an alternative route to Langtang by continuing the drive past Dhunche to Syabrubesi and then trekking up the Langtang Valley through Syapargaon, joining the primary route near Changtang.

Day 2: Syabru to Changtang

The trail descends through forest to the Langtang Khola at 1890m then follows the river upstream, crossing from the southern to northern bank to reach Changtang, popularly known as Lama Hotel, at 2380m. There are is at least five lodges here, including the *Lama Hotel*, and a few camping spots.

Day 3: Changtang to Langtang

The trail continues to follow the Langtang Khola, climbing steeply, at times very steeply, to Ghora Tabela at 3000m where there are fine views of Langtang Lirung. Although there is no permanent settlement here, there is the good *Lovely Lodge*, and your trekking permit and national park entry permit will be checked again here.

From Ghora Tabela the trail climbs more gradually to Langtang at 3500m. The national park headquarters is here and Langtang and the villages around are in Tibetan style with stone walls around the fields and herds of yaks. The best lodge here is the *Village View Lodge*.

Day 4: Langtang to Kyanjin Gompa

Passing through small villages it only takes the morning to climb to Kyanjin Gompa at 3800m where there is a monastery, lodges (best is the *Hotel Yala Peak*) and a cheese factory. There are a number of interesting walks from the gompa and if you are intending to continue over the Ganja La to Helambu you should spend some time here acclimatising. From the gompa you can climb to 4300m on the glacial moraine to the north for superb views of Langtang Lirung. Day walks can also be made to Yala or farther up the valley for more spectacular views.

Alternative Routes from Kyanjin Gompa

There are a number of alternative routes back to Kathmandu. There are occasional helicopter flights from the nearby STOL airstrip but these are usually chartered sight-seeing trips and it's unlikely that you could get a seat on one. You can simply retrace your route back down the valley to Dhunche or, if the season and weather permits, attempt the high route via the Gosainkund Lakes to Helambu. If you have a tent, stove and food, you could tackle the Ganja La.

Across the Ganja La Walking from the Kyanjin Gompa at the end of the Langtang route south to Tarke Gyang in Helambu involves crossing the 5106m Ganja La. The pass is usually blocked by snow from December to March and at any time a bad weather change can make crossing the pass decidedly dangerous. The walk takes four days and between Kyanjin and Tarke Gyang there is no permanent settlement. The final climb to the pass on both sides is steep and exposed. During most of the year there is no water for two days south of the pass, so you must be prepared for all these complications.

Warning This is one of the more difficult passes in Nepal and should not be attempted without a knowledgeable guide, adequate acclimatisation, good equipment and some mountaineering experience.

Gosainkund The trek via Gosainkund is another way of crossing between Langtang and Helambu. Again, adequate preparation is necessary, but there are teahouses along the route, so finding food and accommodation is not a problem in the trekking season. There is often snow on the Gosainkund trail, so the route becomes impassable during much of the winter.

It takes four days to walk from Dhunche, at the start of the Langtang Trek, to Tharepati in Helambu. The trek can also be made from Helambu or by turning off the Langtang route from Syabru, and it's an excellent choice as a return route from the Langtang trek.

Gosainkund is the site for a great pilgrimage in August each year – this is the height of the monsoon, not a pleasant time for trekking. The large rock in the centre of the lake is said to be the remains of a Shiva shrine and it is also claimed that a channel carries water from the lake directly to the tank at the Kumbeshwar Temple in Patan, 60km to the south.

Day 1 takes you from Dhunche at 1950m to Chandan Bari (Sing Gompa) at 3350m. The route from Syabru to the gompa can be confusing. The second day's walk climbs steeply with fine mountain views then drops down to Saraswati Kund at 4100m, the first of the Gosainkund lakes. The second lake is Bhairav Kund, the third is Gosainkund itself at 4380m. There are seasonal teahouses at Gosainkund, and also stone shelters used by pilgrims during the festival at the August full moon. During the season, teahouses operate along the route from the Sing Gompa to the lakes.

On Day 3 the trail climbs from the Gosainkund still higher to the four lakes near the Laurebina La at 4610m, then drops down to Gopte at 3430m where there are seasonal teahouses. It was in the Gopte area that an Australian trekker got lost in 1991 and was not found for 43 days (it should be pointed out that he ended up in this predicament by straying from the major – and even minor – trails, and basically disregarded all the safety rules). Nearby is the place where a Thai International Airbus became lost in 1992 and crashed into a mountain.

The final day's walk descends to a stream and then climbs to Tharepati at 3490m. From Tharepati you can either take the direct route south to Pati Bhanjyang and Kathmandu or head west to Tarke Gyang and Helambu.

Jomsom, Annapurna Circuit & Other Pokhara Treks

Pokhara is the starting or finishing point for some of the best trekking in Nepal and the long Annapurna Circuit trek is the most popular trek in the country.

Spot the yeti (Gokyo Ri, Everest).

RICHARD I'ANSON

Tamang child, Langtang.

GARETH MCCORMACK

Picturesque Tengpoche Monastery.

RICHARD I'ANSON

Trekking & Rafting
The unforgettable sights of Nepal's diverse wilderness – magnificent peaks, spectacular gorges and raging rapids.

The reasons for the area's popularity are numerous but topping the list is convenience. You can start your trek from Pokhara – there's no long, uncomfortable bus rides or problematic flights to the starting point. Also, because the Annapurna Range is so very close to Pokhara you are in the mountains almost immediately.

The treks in this part of the country offer a great deal of cultural and geographic diversity; indeed the Jomsom and Annapurna Circuit treks both go to the north of the Himalayan watershed, into the dry desert area which is properly part of the Tibetan plateau. Finally, these treks are the best in Nepal for independent trekkers and a network of lodges and guesthouses can be found all along the main trails. The entire region is administered by the Annapurna Conservation Area Project (ACAP) which is working to conserve the natural and cultural resources of the area.

The Pokhara area also offers a number of one-day treks or short three or four-day treks. These are covered in the Around Pokhara section of the Pokhara chapter. There are three popular longer treks from Pokhara, all of which follow the same route at some point.

The **Annapurna Sanctuary Trek** takes you right in among the mountains of the Annapurna Range to the Machhapuchhare base camp. This trek takes about 10 days. The **Jomsom Trek** takes about seven days in each direction, but it is possible to fly back to Pokhara from Jomsom. Most trekkers continue a day farther to the holy temple of Muktinath. Finally, the **Annapurna Circuit** takes a full three weeks and completely encircles the Annapurna Range. The last seven days of the circuit walk from Muktinath to Pokhara are the same as the Jomsom trek, but in reverse.

The Annapurna Range is the centre for all these Pokhara treks. For most of Nepal's length, the Himalaya form the border between Nepal and China. The Annapurna mountains are different in that the border is well to the north so the Jomsom and Annapurna Circuit treks both go north of the

Himalayan watershed, into the high-altitude desert which is characteristic of the Tibetan plateau.

JOMSOM TREK

The Jomsom Trek is essentially the final third of the Annapurna Circuit. It follows the Kali Gandaki valley between the soaring peaks of Annapurna and Dhaulagiri and finally emerges to the north of the main Himalayan range, on the dry, desert-like Tibetan plateau. The final destination is the holy temple of Muktinath, a farther day's walk beyond Jomsom. The return to Pokhara can either be made by retracing your steps down the Kali Gandaki valley or by flying from Jomsom to Pokhara.

Access: Pokhara to Naya Pul

Like many other treks in Nepal this one is getting shorter as roads gradually extend farther into the mountains. Eventually it will probably be possible to drive all the way to Jomsom. A road has been pushed through the hills from Pokhara to Baglung. Buses leave for Baglung from the bus station in Bag Bazaar at the northern end of Pokhara. Take the bus up the ridge to Naudanda and then down into the Modi Khola valley and get off at Naya Pul ('new bridge').

Day 1: Naya Pul to Tikedungha

From Naya Pul it's a short walk up the Modi Khola to the large village of Birethanti at 1065m, where you can really see how civilised this trek is. Birethanti has a bakery, bank and even sidewalk cafes! A trail to Ghandruk turns off here. Birethanti has excellent hotels but you may want to continue farther to shorten the next day's long climb. Sticking to the northern side of the Bhurungdi Khola, the trail climbs to Hille and nearby Tikedungha at 1525m. Both Tikedungha and Hille have places to stay.

It's still possible to walk all the way to Birethanti of course. You can reach Naudanda by walking through Sarangkot (see the Pokhara chapter for details) and along the ridge to Kaski, which has the ruins of a small palace, and on to Naudanda. There are fine views of the whole Annapurna Range and back over Pokhara and Phewa Tal from this large village. Naudanda has a choice of hotels and a trekking permit checkpoint, so for day-trekkers without a permit this is the end of the line. From Naudanda, follow the road for a bit, then turn off past Lumle to Chandrakot and drop to Birethanti.

You can also avoid the long climb over the Ghorapani hill by taking the bus on to Baglung. From here it's a two-day walk up the Kali Gandaki valley to Tatopani. You can also continue on a rough, unpaved road by bus or taxi to Beni and save another half day of walking.

Day 2: Tikedungha to Ghorapani

From Tikedungha the trail climbs very steeply to Ulleri, a large Magar village at 2070m. It continues to ascend, but more gently, through fine forests of oak and rhododendron to Banthanti at 2250m and then Nangathanti at 2460m. Another hour brings you to Ghorapani at 2775m.

Only a short walk beyond Ghorapani is the Deorali pass (*deorali* also means 'pass') with spectacular views. An hour's climb from here will take you to Poon (or Pun) Hill, one of the best Himalayan viewpoints in Nepal. There are hotels at Ghorapani and at Deorali. *Ghora* means 'horse' and *pani*

means 'water' and indeed, long caravans of pack horses are regularly seen all along the Jomsom Trek. A trail also runs from Ghorapani/Deorali to Ghandruk. This part of the trek is plagued by leeches during the monsoon and there may be snow on the trail in the winter.

Day 3: Ghorapani to Tatopani

The trail descends steeply to Chitre at 2390m where there are more lodges offering accommodation. From here the hills are extensively terraced as the trail drops down through Sikha, a large village with shops and hotels at 1980m, and then descends gently to Ghara at 1705m. A farther steep descent of 500m takes you to the Ghar Khola where the trail crosses the river on a suspension bridge and then climbs up above the Kali Gandaki before crossing that too.

Turning north the trail soon reaches Tatopani at 1180m. It's a busy population centre, although it was flooded by a lake which built up behind a landslide in 1998 and so a lot of the town is being rebuilt. Tatopani offers some of the best food along the whole trail, and you can even get a cold beer to go with it. *Tato* means 'hot' and *pani* is 'water', a name earned courtesy of the hot springs by the river. Tatopani is a popular destination for a shorter trek out of Pokhara.

Saligrams

The black fossils of marine animals known as saligrams are found at several points along the Kali Gandaki, most notably in the area north of Jomsom around Muktinath, but also at Ridi Bazaar and Devghat. These ammonite fossils date back to the Jurassic period over 100 million years ago and provide dramatic evidence that the mighty Himalaya was indeed once under water.

Saligrams are considered holy emblems. They are sometimes believed to represent Vishnu, and are often held during worship and when making a vow. In Pokhara, the image of the goddess Durga (Parvati) in her Binde Basini Bhagwati form is a saligram.

You will see many on sale in Pokhara or along the Jomsom trail. Think twice before buying them: firstly, it is actually illegal to collect them, because the government is concerned about potential damage to Nepal's fossil record, secondly, they're overpriced, and thirdly, adding rocks to your backpack is never a good idea!

Day 4: Tatopani to Kalopani

The trail follows the Kali Gandaki valley all the rest of the way to Jomsom. The river cuts a channel between the peaks of Annapurna I and Dhaulagiri, thus qualifying the Kali Gandaki valley for the title of the world's deepest gorge. The two 8000m mountaintops are only 38km apart and the river flows between them at a height of less than 2200m.

The Kali Gandaki valley is also the home for the Thakalis, a group noted for their trading and business expertise, particularly in running hotels and lodges not only here in their homeland but also in Pokhara and elsewhere in Nepal.

From Tatopani the trail climbs gradually to Dana at 1400m. This is where the difficult track branches off to Maurice Herzog's base camp, used for his historic ascent of Annapurna in 1950.

The trail continues to climb to Rupse Chhahara (1550m) and at one stage takes a precarious route through a very steep and narrow section of the gorge. Another suspension bridge crosses the river at 1935m and the trail then goes through Ghasa at 2080m, the first Thakali village.

A steep climb through forest takes you to the Lete Khola, then to the village of Lete at 2470m, with a superb view of the eastern flank of Dhaulagiri, and finally to Kalopani at 2560m. Kalopani has great mountain views and some comfortable lodges to view them from.

Day 5: Kalopani to Marpha

From Kalopani the trail crosses to the east side of the Kali Gandaki, before crossing back again at Larjung. This village at 2560m has interesting alleyways and tunnels between the houses, an attempt to avoid the fierce winds that often whistle down the Kali Gandaki valley. Khobang is the next village, with a gompa above it, and the mountain views on this stretch are the best to be seen.

Tukuche at 2590m is one of the most important Thakali villages, once a meeting place for traders from Tibet. Despite the growth of tourism in this area Tukuche is still a quieter, smaller place than it was during the era of trade with Tibet.

From here the landscape changes as you enter the drier and more desert-like country north of the Himalayan watershed. It also gets windier: gentle breezes from the north in the early morning shift to a gale from the south as the morning wears on. Marpha, at 2665m, virtually huddles behind a ridge to keep out of the wind! The village also has some of the most luxurious accommodation to be found along the trail and is a good alternative to staying in Jomsom. A government-established project between Tukuche and Marpha grows fruit and vegetables for the whole region.

Day 6: Marpha to Kagbeni

Marpha to Jomsom The trail continues along the valley side, rising gradually before crossing over a low ridge to Jomsom.

Jomsom At 2713m, Jomsom is the major centre in the region and has a hospital and the inevitable trekking-permit checkpoint. If you're heading in the opposite direction on the Annapurna Circuit you must get your permit stamped here as it will be checked farther south. This is the last Thakali village – those farther north are inhabited by people of Tibetan descent.

Jomsom has regular flights to Pokhara ($50).

Jomsom to Kagbeni If you have time, it's worth following the trail along the river to the medieval-looking village of Kagbeni at 2810m. This very Tibetan-influenced settlement has a number of good lodges, and is as close as you can get to Lo Monthang, the capital of the legendary kingdom of Mustang farther to the north without paying a $700 permit fee.

Day 7: Kagbeni to Muktinath

From Kagbeni the trail climbs steeply to rejoin the direct trail before Khingar is reached at 3200m. The trail climbs through a desert landscape then past meadows and streams to

TREKKING

ANNAPURNA TREKS

ANNAPURNA TREKS

CHINA
TIBET

0   5   10 km

TREKKING

Phugaon

Himlung Himal
(7126m) ▲

Cheo Himal ▲
(6820m)

Rest House

Nar

Kang Guru
(6981m) ▲

Larkya La
(5100m)

Pisang Peak
(6091m) ▲

Ngawal

Bimtang

Larkya Peak
(6249m) ▲

Ghyaru

Hongde ✈

Upper
Pisang

Gho

Manaslu North ▲
(7154m)

Naike Peak
(5515m)

Pisang

Bhratang

Kotho

Telekhu

Thanchok

Tilje

Phungi ▲
(6398m)

Manaslu
(8156m) ▲

Annapurna IV
(7525m) ▲

Chame

Bagarchhap

Manaslu
Glacier

Annapurna II
(7937m) ▲

Lattemarang

Dhanakyu

Thonje

Dharapani

Temang

Karte

Ngadi Chuli ▲
(7879m)

Pungyen
Glacier

Lamjung
Himal
(6986m) ▲

Tal

Lidanda
Glacier

Namun
Bhanjyang
(5784m) ᕼ

Sattale

Chamje

Mimi
Pokhari

Siklis

Jagat

Syange

Lili Bir

Bahundanda

Thak

Lampata

Ngadi

Bara Pokhari

Ghanpokhara

Bhulbule

Usta

Khudi

Pasgaon

Baragaon

Kalikastan

Rabidanda

Taksar

Besi
Sahar

Taksar

Thulokot

Gorje

Baglung Pani

Chaur

Chiti

Begnas
Tal

Mathi
Thana

Sheklung

Nalma

Gaonsahar

Phalensangu

Sisuwa

Rupa Tal

Chisopani

Chisankhu

Deorali

Bhote Odar

To Kathmandu

Kunchha

Paundi

To Dumre

the interesting village of Jharkot at 3500m. A farther climb brings you to Ranipauwa, the accommodation area of Muktinath, at 3710m.

Muktinath is a pilgrimage centre for Buddhists and Hindus. You'll see Tibetan traders as well as sadhus from the far south of India. The shrines, in a grove of trees, include a Buddhist gompa and the Vishnu temple of Jiwala Mayi. An old temple nearby shelters a spring and natural gas jets which provide Muktinath's famous eternal flame. It's the earth-water-fire combination that accounts for Muktinath's great religious significance.

From Muktinath you can retrace your steps to Pokhara, or simply to Jomsom and hope to catch a flight from there. It is possible to continue beyond Muktinath and cross the Thorung La to walk the rest of the Annapurna Circuit but this long walk is better made in the opposite direction – it's a long, hard climb of 1600m from Muktinath to the pass.

AROUND ANNAPURNA TREK

Since it opened to foreign trekkers in 1977, the three-week trek around Annapurna has become the most popular trek in Nepal. It passes through country inhabited by a wide diversity of peoples, it offers spectacular mountain scenery and it goes to the north of the main Himalayan range on to the high and dry Tibetan plateau. To many independent trekkers it also offers the considerable advantage of having accommodation available each night. The only drawback perhaps are the tedious checkpoints on this trek – between ACAP and the police there is a checkpoint to pass almost every day!

The circuit is usually walked in a counter-clockwise direction because of difficulties crossing the Thorung La. Travelling clockwise the longer ascent and shorter descent from west to east is too much for many people to manage in one day. The Thorung La at 5416m is often closed by snow from mid-December to mid-March and bad weather can move in at any time. Trekkers should be prepared to turn back due to the weather or if they suffer from altitude sickness. If you

take porters over this pass you must make sure they are adequately equipped for severe cold and snow.

Most people start the circuit from Dumre, on the Kathmandu to Pokhara road. There are jeeps and buses that ply the miserably rough road north from Dumre as far as Besi Sahar.

After you cross the Thorung La from Manang to Muktinath the final seven days of the circuit trek are the same as the Jomsom Trek from Pokhara, but in reverse.

Access

Kathmandu to Dumre It's a long and somewhat tedious drive from Kathmandu to the turn-off at Dumre. Starting from Pokhara is much easier since Dumre is 137km from Kathmandu but only 70km from Pokhara.

Dumre to Besi Sahar From Dumre, at 440m, buses and 4WDs run regularly to Besi Sahar at 820m.

Day 1: Besi Sahar to Bahundanda

The trail drops, then climbs to Khudi at 790m. This is the first Gurung village that you reach (many of Nepal's Gurkha soldiers are Gurungs). From Khudi the trail offers fine views of Himalchuli and Ngadi Chuli (aka Manaslu II and before that Peak 29) as it climbs to Bhulbhule at 830m. You enter the Annapurna Conservation Area here and must register at the ACAP checkpoint.

The trail goes to Ngadi before reaching Lampata at 1135m and nearby Bahundanda at 1310m. Bahundanda has a few shops, several hotels, and a telephone office.

Day 2: Bahundanda to Chamje

From Bahundanda the trail drops steeply to Syange at 1190m. The trail crosses the Marsyangdi Khola on a suspension bridge and then follows the river to the stone village of Jagat before climbing through forest to Chamje at 1430m.

Day 3: Chamje to Bagarchhap

The rocky trail follows the Marsyangdi steadily uphill to Tal at 1675m, the first village in the Manang district. The trail crosses a wide, flat valley then climbs a stone stairway to 1860m before dropping down to another crossing of the Marsyangdi. The trail continues up and down to Dharapani at 1890m, which is marked by a stone entrance chörten typical of the Tibetan-influenced villages from here northwards.

Bagarchhap at 2160m has flat-roofed stone houses of typical Tibetan design although the village is still in the transition zone before the dry highlands. A landslide roared through the centre of this village in late 1995 and wiped out much of the village, including two lodges.

Day 4: Bagarchhap to Chame
The trail, often rough and rocky, climbs to Lattemarang at 2360m and then continues through forest, but near the river, to Kotho at 2590m. Chame at 2630m is the headquarters of the Manang district and its buildings include many hotels and a bank. There are fine views of Annapurna II as you approach Chame and two small hot springs by the town.

Day 5: Chame to Pisang
The trail runs through deep forest in a steep and narrow valley, crosses a river on a long bridge at 2840m and then another bridge at 3040m. Views include the first sight of the soaring Paungda Danda rock face. The trail continues to climb to Pisang which sprawls between 3190 and 3300m and has many lodges.

Day 6: Pisang to Manang
The walk is now through the drier upper part of the Manang district, cut off from the full effect of the monsoon by the Annapurna Range. The people of this area herd yaks and raise crops for part of the year, but they also continue to enjoy special trading rights gained way back in 1784. Today they exploit these rights with shopping trips to Bangkok and Hong Kong where they buy electronic goods and other modern equipment to resell in Nepal. Not surprisingly they are shrewd traders and hard bargainers.

From Pisang there are two trails, north and south of the Marsyangdi River, which meet up again at Mungji. The southern route by Hongde, with its airstrip, at 3325m involves less climbing than the northern route via Ghyaru, though there are better views on the trail that follows the northern bank of the river. The trail continues from Mungji past the picturesque but partially hidden village of Bryaga at 3475m to nearby Manang at 3500m where there are a number of lodges and a Himalayan Rescue Association post.

Day 7: Acclimatisation Day in Manang
It's important to spend a day acclimatising in Manang before pushing on to the Thorung La. There are some fine day walks and magnificent views around the village, and it's best to gain altitude during the day, returning back down to Manang to sleep. The Manangbhot people's legendary trading skills are seen at their keenest here – buy with caution!

Day 8: Manang to Letdar
From Manang it's an ascent of nearly 2000m to the Thorung La. The trail climbs steadily through Tengi, leaving the Marsyangdi Valley and continuing along the Jarsang Khola valley. The vegetation becomes steadily more sparse as you reach Letdar at 4250m.

Day 9: Letdar to Thorung Phedi
Finally, you descend to cross the river at 4310m and then climb up to Thorung Phedi at 4420m. There are two hotels here and at the height of the season as many as 200 trekkers a day may cross over the Thorung La and beds can be in short supply. Some trekkers find themselves suffering from altitude sickness symptoms at Phedi.

If you find yourself in a similar condition you must retreat downhill; even the descent to Letdar can make a difference.

Day 10: Phedi to Muktinath
Phedi means 'foot of the hill' and that's where it is, at the foot of the 5416m Thorung La. The trail climbs steeply but is

regularly used and easy to follow. The altitude and snow can be problems: when the pass is snow-covered it is often impossible to cross. It takes about four to six hours to climb up to the pass, marked by chörtens and prayer flags. The effort is worthwhile as the view from the top is magnificent. From the pass you have a tough 1600m descent to Muktinath.

Many start out for the pass far too early at 3 am. This is not necessary and is potentially dangerous due to the risk of frostbite if you are hanging around waiting in the cold snow for too long. A better starting time is around 5 am.

Days 11-16: Muktinath to Pokhara

The remaining seven days of the trek simply follow the Pokhara-Jomsom-Muktinath route but in the opposite direction. Completing the Annapurna Circuit in 16 days allows for only one rest and acclimatisation day at Manang. It's very easy to slot a few additional days into the schedule.

ANNAPURNA SANCTUARY TREK

The walk up to the Annapurna base camp is a classic walk right into the heart of the mountains. The walk ends at a point where you are virtually surrounded by soaring Himalayan peaks. At one time this trek was a real expedition into an uninhabited wilderness area, but now there is a string of lodges that operate during the trekking season. The return trip can take as little as 10 or 11 days but usually takes a full 14 days, and the walk to the base camp can be tacked on as a side-trip from the Jomsom or Annapurna Circuit treks.

There are several possible routes to the sanctuary, all meeting at Chhomrong. The diversion from the Jomsom and Annapurna Circuit treks is made from Ghorapani to Ghandruk.

The route to the Annapurna Sanctuary is occasionally blocked by avalanches. Check with the ACAP offices in Ghandruk or Khuldighar for a report on current trail conditions, and do not proceed into the sanctuary if there is heavy rain or snow.

Access

Pokhara to Phedi The walk from Pokhara leaves the Jomsom and Annapurna Circuit routes at Phedi – you can take a bus or taxi.

Day 1: Phedi to Tolka

From Phedi the trail climbs to Dhampus (1750m) which stretches for several kilometres from 1580 to 1700m and has a number of widely spaced hotels. Theft is a real problem in Dhampus, so take care.

The trail then climbs to Pothana (1990m), descends steeply through a forest to Bichok. It finally emerges in the Modi Khola valley and continues to drop to Tolka.

Day 2: Tolka to Chhomrong

From Tolka the trail descends a long stone staircase, and then climbs a ridge to the Gurung village of Landruk at 1620m. The trail descends again for about 10 minutes, and then splits – north to Chhomrong and the sanctuary, or downhill to Ghandruk.

The sanctuary trail turns up the Modi Khola valley, through Naya Pul (1340m), climbs up to Jhinu Danda (1750m) and up again to Taglung (2180m), where it joins the Ghandruk to Chhomrong trail.

Chhomrong (1950m), the last permanent settlement in the valley, has a choice of hotels, and an ACAP office.

Day 3: Chhomrong to Bamboo Lodge

The trail drops down to the Chhomrong Khola, then climbs to Kuldi at 2520m where there is an ACAP checkpoint and information centre. Continue on to Bamboo Lodge (2340m), a collection of four hotels. This stretch of trail has many leeches early and late in the trekking season.

Day 4: Bamboo Lodge to Himalayan Hotel

The trail climbs through bamboo, then rhododendron forests to Doban (2630m) and on to Himalayan Hotel at 2900m.

Day 5: Himalayan Hotel to Machhapuchhare Base Camp

From Himalayan Hotel it's on to Hinko at 3160m. There is accommodation in Deorali

(3230m), on the ridge above Hinko. This is the stretch of trail that is most subject to avalanches.

At Machhapuchhare base camp (which isn't really a base camp since climbing the mountain is not permitted) at 3720m there is seasonal accommodation.

Day 6: Machhapuchhare Base Camp to Annapurna Base Camp

The climb to the Annapurna base camp (4095m) takes about two hours, and is best done early in the day before clouds roll in and make visibility a problem. There are four lodges here, which get ridiculously crowded at the height of the season.

Back to Pokhara

On the return trip you can retrace your steps, or divert from Chhomrong to Ghandruk and on to Ghorapani to visit Poon Hill and follow the Annapurna Circuit or Jomsom route back to Pokhara.

The Ghorapani to Ghandruk walk is a popular way of linking the Annapurna Sanctuary Trek with treks up the Kali Gandaki valley. It's also used for shorter loop walks out of Pokhara (see the Around Pokhara section of the Pokhara chapter).

Other Treks

The Everest Base Camp Trek in the east, the Langtang and Helambu treks to the north of Kathmandu and the three Pokhara area treks in central Nepal between them are used by the vast majority of all trekkers. Yet there are other alternatives taking you to areas still relatively unvisited.

KANCHENJUNGA BASE CAMPS

The trekking route up to the Kanchenjunga North and South base camps in the extreme north-eastern corner of the country is open to trekkers, but you have to go with a recognised agency. The starting point can be Basantapur or Taplejung by road, or Tumlingtar or Taplejung by air.

MAKALU BASE CAMP

It's a long but fine trek from Hile or Tumlingtar up the Arun River to the Makalu base camp in eastern Nepal. The area is protected by the recently established Makalu-Barun National Park and its conservation area.

SOLU KHUMBU TO HILE

As an alternative to flying back to Kathmandu from Lukla, or walking back to Jiri, the Everest Base Camp Trek can be extended by walking for 11 days east and then south to Hile. From Hile you can travel by road through Dhankuta and Dharan to Biratnagar from where there are buses and flights to Kathmandu.

DOLPO

Trekking to the Dolpo region has only been permitted since mid-1989. The region lies to the west of the Kali Gandaki valley. A special permit is needed, and you must be well equipped and self sufficient. From Pokhara it's a tough 14-day trek to Phoksundo Lake, and beyond it is 'inner Dolpo' the site of Shey Gompa. A special permit ($700) is required to trek into this area.

RARA LAKE

The eight-day round trip trek from Jumla to the Rara Lake and back still gets very few trekkers, largely because trekking here requires real planning since flights are difficult to get on, porters are hard to find and little food is available.

MUSTANG

Mustang has lured trekkers for many years, and has only recently been opened. It was closed, both because of guerrilla war along the border with Tibet, and because of the ecological sensitivity of the region. The area is part of the Tibetan plateau, and is high, dry and beautiful. It lies to the north-west of the Kali Gandaki, beyond Kagbeni, which is the farthest point west on the Jomsom Trek. It is only possible to enter with an organised group, and permits are a steep $700 for 10 days, with extra days at $70.

TREKKING

Mountain Biking

This chapter was originally written by John Prosser, and was updated this edition by Peter Stewart, a keen mountain biker and adventurer who has explored much of Nepal's biking routes and ridden many parts of wider Asia. In 1995 he came to Nepal and soon after was managing Himalayan Mountain Bikes, which he now owns, organising cycling tours around Nepal and many parts of Asia.

Ah, mountain biking! Strong wheels, knobbly tyres, a wide selection of gears and overall strength – the mountain bike is an ideal, go anywhere, versatile machine for exploring Nepal. These attributes make it possible to escape paved roads, and to ride tracks and ancient walking trails to remote, rarely visited areas of the country. Importantly, they allow independent travel – you can stop whenever you like – and they liberate you from crowded buses and claustrophobic taxis.

Nepal's tremendously diverse terrain and its many tracks and trails are ideal for mountain biking. It's only in recent years that Nepal has gained recognition for the biking adventures it offers – challenging mountain roads that climb thousands of metres to reach spectacular viewpoints, followed by unforgettable, exhilarating descents. The Terai has flat, smooth roads, and mountain biking is an excellent way of getting to the Royal Chitwan National Park. For the adventurous there are large areas of the country still to be explored by mountain bike.

The Kathmandu Valley still offers the best and most consistent biking of any region, with its vast network of tracks, trails and back roads. Mountain biking offers the perfect way to visit the people of the Kathmandu Valley and their wealth of temples, stupas and medieval towns. A mountain bike really comes into its own when you get off the beaten track and discover idyllic Newari villages that have preserved their

HIGHLIGHTS

- Biking to heights that initially seem unachievable, with the world's greatest 8,000m peaks hovering in the distance, seemingly within arm's reach

- Winding your way through and around cities such as Kathmandu and Bhaktapur which seem to have been designed with mountain bikes in mind

- Covering in a day what takes days by foot, at a pace that allows an intimacy with your surroundings, the people and their culture

- Exploring enchanting villages reached via thrilling mountain trails over high passes with superb vistas

traditional and rural lifestyle. Even today, it's possible to cycle into villages in the Kathmandu Valley that have not seen a visitor on a foreign bike.

Many trails are narrow, century-old walkways that are not shown on maps, so you need a good sense of direction when venturing out without a guide. To go unguided offers some risks and you should learn a few important words of Nepali to assist in seeking directions. It's also important to know the name of the next village you wish to reach. However, it's no simple task in gaining the right directions and any mispronunciations can result in tragic misdirections. The most detailed Kathmandu Valley map is commonly referred to as the 'German map' (also Schneider and Nelles Verlag), and is widely available in Kathmandu. Most other maps are poor reproductions of these with inaccurate contours, roads and village names.

TRAIL CONDITIONS
Traffic travels (generally) on the left-hand side, even though it's not uncommon to find

a vehicle approaching head-on, and smaller vehicles giving way to larger ones. Bikes are at the bottom of the list, and definitely come off second best if they mess with Tata trucks! Nepali roads carry a vast array of vehicles: auto-rickshaws, tempos, buses, motorbikes, cars, trucks, tractors ... Once you've thrown in a few holy cows, wheelbarrows, dogs, wandering children, chickens and rickshaws all moving at different speeds and in different directions, under a barrage of blowing horns, you have a typical chaotic Nepali street scene!

The centre of Kathmandu, unfortunately, is becoming a very unpleasant place to ride due to pollution and heavy traffic – if you are sensitive to traffic fumes, consider bringing some sort of mask.

Extreme care should be taken near villages as young children play on the trails – and roads! A philosophy of 'others can watch out for me' seems to exist for locals who set foot on roads, thus pedestrians (and drivers) do not look and appear to have little awareness of surrounding traffic. On the trails, animals should be approached with caution. Don't even try to predict what a buffalo, dog or chicken will do. A good bike helmet is a sensible accessory.

A few intrepid mountain bikers have taken bikes into trekking areas hoping to find great riding. What they have discovered is that these areas are generally not suitable for mountain biking and they carry their bikes for 80% of the time! Trails are unreliable, and are subject to avalanche and frequent obstacles. To say 'I did it' may be enough, however there are other equally great locations that can be ridden. In addition, there are always trekkers, porters and local people clogging up the trails. Bikers just add one more problem to these heavy-traffic areas in peak season.

Riders who have taken bikes to such places as the Everest base camp or around the Annapurna Circuit will know of the long carries. If you decide to indulge in such a bike trek have a good shoulder pad and be thoughtful of others sharing the trail.

Local buses are useful if you wish to avoid some of the routes that carry heavy traffic. You can place your bike on the roof for an additional charge (between Rs 40 to Rs 80 depending on the length of the journey and the bus company). If you're lucky, rope may be available and the luggage boy will assist you. Make sure the bike is held securely to cope with the rough roads and that it's lying as flat as possible to prevent it catching low wires or tree branches. Unless you travel with foam padding it is hard to avoid the scratches to the frame but a day pack may come in handy. Supervise it's loading and protect the rear derailleur from being damaged. Remembers more baggage is likely to be loaded on top once you're inside.

With domestic flights, if you pack your bike correctly (removing both wheels and pedals) it is possible to load them in the cargo hold of most airlines. Check with the airline first.

EQUIPMENT

If you plan to do more than use roads it may be a good idea to bring your own bike. To a large degree the only bikes you can hire in Nepal are low quality Indian so-called mountain bikes not suitable for the rigours of trail riding. In addition, rental shops do not supply helmets, pannier bags, luggage racks, spare parts, pumps or tools for on-road repairs. Quality, imported bikes are slowly becoming available for rent through tour operators. See Getting Around in the Kathmandu, Patan & Bhaktapur and Pokhara chapters for information on bike hire.

Your bike can be carried as part of your baggage allowance on international flights. You are required to deflate the tyres and turn the handle bars parallel with the frame and remove the pedals. Passage through Nepali customs is quite simple once you reassure airport officers that it is 'your' bike and it will be returning with you.

If you bring your bike it is essential to bring tools and spare parts, as these are largely unavailable in Nepal. Unfortunately, carrying a complete tool kit and spares for every situation may be impractical. An established mountain bike tour operator (such as Himalayan Mountain Bikes in Kathmandu) with a mechanic, workshop and a full range of bike tools can help. Fortunately, what the standard local bike repair shops lack in spare parts and knowledge of the latest fads, they make up in their ability to improvise. For basic adjustments their standard of skill is usually high, but you still need to maintain a watchful eye on your equipment.

Once on the trails you're on your own, so plan for all situations and be ready to improvise.

WHAT TO BRING

Although not a complete list, a few items worth considering include:

Lightweight clothing (eg Coolmax and Gortex), windproof windbreaker, stiff-soled shoes that suit riding and walking, cycling tops and shorts, warm hat and gloves, sun protection, sunglasses, camelback or water bottles, torch (flashlight), fleecy top for evenings, cycle gloves, helmet, basic range of bike tools, spare parts (inner tubes), mini pump, energy bars and electrolyte water additives, bike bell, medium sized money bag.

Sleeping bags, mats, tents and panniers can be hired in Kathmandu cheaply. More thin layers of clothes offer better protection and convenience than thick, bulky items.

TRAIL ETIQUETTE

Arriving in a new country for a short time where social and cultural values are vastly different from those of our home country does not allow much time to gain an appreciation of these matters. So consider a few pointers to help you on your way and develop mutual respect and understanding.

Clothing

Tight fitting Lycra bike clothing, although functional, is a shock to the locals who maintain a very modest approach to dressing. Such clothing is embarrassing and offensive to Nepalis.

A simple way to overcome this is by wearing a pair of comfortable shorts and a T-shirt over your bike gear. This is especially applicable to women bikers as women in Nepal generally dress conservatively. Arms and legs should be covered when entering a temple or monastery.

On the Trails

Trails can often be filled with locals going about their daily work of farming, carting food, portering, playing, passing the time of day and shepherding their stock. A small hammer bell attached to your handlebars and used as a warning of your approach, reducing your speed and a friendly call of 'cycle ioh!' (cycle coming!) goes a long way in keeping all on the trails happy and safe. Children love the novelty of the bikes, fancy helmets, the colours and novel clothing and will come running from all directions to greet you. They also love to grab hold of the back of your bike and run with you. You need to maintain a watchful eye so no-one gets hurt.

Environment

Although the awareness of environmental matters is generally not high for many local people, seeing visitors respecting the land and environment can be a great example. So don't destroy the trails and vegetation, or litter. Leave things as you found them – or better than you found them.

ORGANISED BIKE TOURS

There are a small number of companies offering guided trips on mountain bikes. They provide high-quality bikes, local and western guides, pannier bags, helmets and all the necessary equipment. There is usually a minimum of four clients per trip although for shorter tours two is often sufficient. For the shorter tours (two to three days) vehicle support is not required while for longer tours vehicles are provided at an extra cost.

Himalayan Mountain Bikes (HMB)
(☎ 437437, fax 419237, email bike@hmb .wlink.com.np) Operating since 1988, HMB has offices in Kathmandu and Pokhara, but also operates throughout Asia. The Thamel office is at the entrance to Northfield Cafe and adjoin-

ing Pilgrims Book House. The Pokhara office (☎ 22219) is in Lakeside near the Hungry Eye Hotel. HMB offers a full range of tours from one day (around $30) to three or four day tours (around $45 per day) and up to 21-day fully catered trips (around $80 per day), and also does customised group tours.

Dawn Till Dusk
(☎ 418733, fax 419870, email info@ frontier.wlink.com)
Kathmandu Guest House compound. Similar tours to HMB. The only outfit with good quality imported mountain bikes for hire.

Touring Routes

THE SCAR ROAD

The Scar Road can be considered as one of the Kathmandu Valley's classic mountain bike adventures. It's got the lot and offers a challenging ride for all levels of experience. It's a 70km round trip which for the average biker will take around six hours.

Leaving Kathmandu, head towards Balaju, on the Ring Rd only 2km north of Thamel, and onto the Trisuli road. At this point you start to climb out of the valley on a sealed road towards Kakani, 23km away at an altitude of 2073m. The road twists and turns at an even gradient past the Nagarjun Forest Reserve (or Rani Ban), which provides the road with a leaf canopy.

Once you're through the initial pass and out of the valley, the road continues in a north-westerly direction and offers a view of endless terraced fields to your left. On reaching the summit of the ridge turn right (at a clearly marked T-intersection), instead of continuing down to Trisuli Bazaar. If you go too far you reach a checkpoint just 100m beyond. At this point magnificent views of Ganesh Himal give the required inspiration to complete the remaining 4km of steep and deteriorating blacktop to the crown of the hill just past the *Tara Gaon Kakani Hotel* in Kakani, for a well deserved rest.

It is possible to spend the night at this overpriced hotel or two other basic teahouse style lodges, so as to take advantage of sunrise and sunset from this great spot. See the Kakani section of the Around the Kathmandu Valley chapter for details.

After admiring the view from the hotel's garden terrace, descend for just 30m beyond the gate and take the first left onto a jeep track. This track takes you through the popular picnic grounds frequented on Saturday by Kathmandu locals. Continue through in an easterly direction towards Shivapuri. The track narrows after a few kilometres near a metal gate on your left. Through the gate, you are faced with some rough stone steps and a 10 minute push/carry up and over the hilltop to an army checkpoint. Here it's necessary to pay a Rs 300 reserve entry fee. Exit the army camp turning right where the Scar Road is clearly visible in front of you. You are now at the day's highest point – approximately 2200m.

Taking the right-hand track you start to descend dramatically along an extremely steep, rutted single trail with several water crossings. The trail is literally cut into the side of the hill, with sharp drops on the right which challenge a rider's skill and nerve. As you hurtle along, take time to admire the view of the sprawling Kathmandu Valley below, it's one of the best. Maybe stop to look!

The trail widens, after one long gnarly climb before the saddle, then it's relatively flat through the protected Shivapuri watershed area. This beautiful mountain biking section lasts for nearly 25km before the trail descends into the valley down a 7km spiral on a gravel road. This joins a paved road, to the relief of jarred wrists, at Budhanilkantha, where you can buy refreshments. From here it's back to civilisation as the sealed road descends gently for the remaining 15km back into the bustle of Kathmandu via Lazimpat.

DHULIKHEL

This two or three day circular tour takes you through a classic selection of valley sights. The first day from Kathmandu to Dhulikhel, an interesting hilltop town at 1500m, is 32km; the second day is 58km.

From Thamel, head out of town in the direction of Pashupatinath and once onto the

Ring Rd proceed towards Tribhuvan air-port. Follow the western boundary of the airport past the very end of the airport run-way to the south. Here the road descends just after branching left followed by a straight run through to the edge of Bhakta-pur and the beginning of the Arniko Hwy.

The Arniko Hwy was built by the Chinese and carries an enormous amount of traffic, including dilapidated Chinese-donated elec-tric trolley buses. It is a far nicer ride along the old road via the village of Sano Thimi (Small Thimi), which is famous for its pot-tery and handicrafts, and runs parallel to the main road just to the north. This you can do by taking the first left off the main highway and onto a narrower sealed road that heads back towards the airport on it's east side. At the next main intersection (1.8km on) make the right turn before continuing on to com-plete the 16km to the medieval town of Bhaktapur.

Mountain bikes are a great way to explore Bhaktapur's narrow streets (Rs 300 city entry fee). After time in this magical past kingdom, continue east. Facing Bhaktapur's 30m high Nyatapola Temple, in Taumadhi Tole, take the exit from the square on your right-hand side. This narrow street twists and turns on its way out of the city. After leaving the brick-paved streets, join a tar-mac road and continue straight on, bearing south-east.

The tarmac ends and the road continues in the form of a compacted track towards the rural village of Nala. This route is an ex-cellent alternative to the Arniko Hwy and takes you through a beautiful corner of the valley. The track climbs gradually, and be-comes progressively steeper near the top. A gentle 3km downhill gradient brings you to rural Nala with its pretty temples.

From Nala head right, via the Bhagvati Temple, and continue for a couple of kilo-metres to Banepa. Turn left and continue along the paved main road for a further 5km to Dhulikhel, which is visible on your right-hand side as you approach, after passing through a truck/bus checkpoint. This com-pletes the first day. See the Around the Kathmandu Valley chapter for more infor-mation on Dhulikhel.

Namobuddha

Namobuddha is a popular day trek starting and finishing in Dhulikhel and offers superb trail riding with spectacular views of the Himalaya. To start your ride from Dhu-likhel's main square, which has a small tank, head south-east along a paved road in the di-rection of the Kali Temple set on a hillside above the town. The paved road ends and starts to climb the hill in the form of a rough jeep track. The track twists its way up a test-ing 3km to reach the temple, which is a spectacular viewpoint. From the temple you can see the track snake its way across the terraced landscape.

Continue along the track, which provides fun downhill runs before it starts a 5km climb towards Namobuddha. After complet-ing the climb, descend for a short while until you reach a T-junction at Kavre village. Turn right and Namobuddha will appear shortly after on the left, so completing a 12km jour-ney from Dhulikhel. Refreshments are available in the small shops near the stupa, which provides an interesting place to rest before continuing to Panauti. It's worth mak-ing the 15 minute walk to the monastery above the stupa. The stupa is frequented by many Buddhists and Hindu's alike as a major pilgrimage point of the Kathmandu Valley

Leaving Namobuddha you continue down the track, which takes you through a series of turns – a great mountain bike de-scent. The track finally drops to the bottom of the valley and undulates for 14km from the village of Shanku to the historic town of Panauti. This ancient Newari town has some of the oldest temples in Nepal – cross the footbridge if you want to explore fur-ther. See the Around the Kathmandu Valley chapter for information about Panauti.

Leaving Panauti you join a paved road that's a flat run along the valley to the main road at Banepa. From this point you can re-turn to Kathmandu, 26km via the Arniko Hwy, or ride the 3.5km back to Dhulikhel, completing a 33km circuit.

KODARI & TIBETAN BORDER

It is possible to continue 82km along the Arniko Hwy from Dhulikhel to the Friendship Bridge at Kodari (1500m) that marks the Tibetan border. This is a three or (more likely) a four day return trip from Dhulikhel.

From Dhulikhel you immediately begin an adrenaline filled descent (almost 900m) into the Panchkhal Valley, on a slick sealed road, with majestic views of the Himalaya adding to a thrilling ride. A couple of short climbs interrupt the descent as you cycle to Dolalghat, a popular starting point for Sun Kosi rafting trips.

After 20km you cross the bridge over the Indrawati River and climb out of the Panchkhal Valley to join the Bhote Kosi, on your left, which you follow for the rest of the journey. Owing to landslide damage there is a mixture of surfaced and unsurfaced roads. Traffic can be quite heavy along this section as it is also the road to Jiri, a popular starting point for the Everest Base Camp Trek. The road climbs at a gentle gradient as it follows the river.

A couple of kilometres past the turn-off to Jiri is Lamosangu, 23km from Dolalghat. Lamosangu provides a far more pleasant place to spend the night than Barabise thanks to the fact that fewer buses stop. See the Lamosangu section in the Around the Kathmandu Valley chapter for information on accommodation.

The next day's ride continues past Barabise where the road changes into a compacted track with a top layer of dust. Recent roadwork along here has improved things, but still the dust cover is transformed into choking clouds when buses pass; in wet weather it turns to mud. Care should be taken during heavy rain as this section of the road is particularly susceptible to landslides. The valley's sides begin to steepen and it gradually changes into a beautiful gorge with spectacular waterfalls. The track climbs practically the entire 34km to Tatopani to complete the second day, after which you can visit the hot springs just a few minutes outside the town to the north. Again, see the Around Kath-

mandu Valley chapter for information on accommodation.

Tatopani is 5km from the border post of Kodari. As it climbs towards the Friendship Bridge, this section of the ride is probably the most beautiful. It is possible (but dependant on border guards) to cycle beyond the bridge and climb a rough and steep track to the Chinese customs checkpoint (11km) just outside Khasa, which is visible from the bridge. It should be possible to return as far as Lamosangu the same day, taking advantage of a mainly downhill ride.

The ride back to Dhulikhel is then 43km and includes the long climb out of Dolalghat which you should allow time for. An option here is jump on a local bus with your bike. Depending on how you feel after the climb, you can stay in Dhulikhel or complete the trip by returning the 37km to Kathmandu.

THE RAJPATH

The Tribhuvan Hwy (or Rajpath as it is popularly known) was the first highway to connect Kathmandu with the rest of the world. The road switchbacks 150 spectacular kilometres from Kathmandu to Hetauda. Most traffic from the Terai and India uses the highway between Narayanghat and Mugling which, although longer, is actually quicker. The Rajpath has a great mixture of light traffic and magnificent scenery, culminating at Daman with an incomparable Himalayan view. It's a classic ride over a 2488m pass on a rough sealed road.

The ride begins on the Kathmandu-Pokhara (Prithvi) Hwy, which gives the only access to the valley. After leaving the valley, the highway descends to Naubise, at the bottom of the Mahesh Khola valley, 27km from Kathmandu, where the Rajpath intersects with the Kathmandu-Pokhara (Prithvi) Hwy. Take the Rajpath, which forks to the left and is well signposted for Hetauda. Start a 35km climb to Tistung at a height of 2030m. You climb through terraced fields, carved into steep hillsides. On reaching the pass at Tistung you descend for 7km into the beautiful Palung Valley before the final steep 9km climb to Daman, at a height of 2322m.

This day's ride (almost all climbing) takes between six and nine hours in the saddle. Thus, with an early start it is possible to stay in Daman, which will give you the thrill of waking up to the broadest Himalayan panorama Nepal has to offer. On a clear morning you can see from Dhaulagiri to Everest, a view worth the pedal. The following day the road climbs a further 3km to the top of the pass, at 2488m. At this point, you can savour the prospect of an exhilarating 2300m descent in 60km!

As you descend towards the Indian plains, laid out before you to the south, you will notice a contrast with the side you climbed – the south side is lush and semitropical. With innumerable switchbacks and a bit of speed you should watch out for the occasional bus and truck looming around a blind corner. The road eventually flattens out when you make a right turn to cross a newly constructed bridge and the first main river crossing. The rest of the journey is a gently undulating route alongside a river – a further 10km brings you to Hetauda. See the Hetauda section in the Terai chapter for details on accommodation. After a night's rest you can continue along the Rajpath towards India or turn right at the statue of the king in the centre of town and head towards Royal Chitwan National Park.

HETAUDA TO NARAYANGHAT & MUGLING

Hetauda is just to the east of Royal Chitwan National Park, which has a wide selection of accommodation, both in the park and in the town of Sauraha, as well as a great range of activities. See Royal Chitwan National Park section in the Terai chapter for more details. You are prohibited from riding inside the park, but are allowed to ride directly to your resort.

This is vastly different riding to that of Kathmandu, or the other sections described herein, and in the summer months (say May to September) it can be a very hot ride. From Hetauda as you cycle along the flat, smooth road towards Narayanghat enjoying the lush subtropical scenery, watch for resort signposts on your left-hand side. Machan Wildlife Resort's turn-off is 40km from Hetauda, and the resort is reached after a further 4km of beautiful trail riding with three river crossings. Alternatively, a further 23km from the Machan turn-off brings you to the Chitwan Jungle Lodge turn-off. A further 14km brings you to Tadi Bazaar and the turn-off for Sauraha, reached by an interesting 6km jeep track.

Narayanghat, 20km from Sauraha on the banks of the Narayani River, gives a choice of further routes. From here you can return to Kathmandu or Pokhara via Mugling. Although some would say this section from Narayanghat to Mugling is probably best avoided on a bike due to heavy bus and truck traffic, it is nonetheless a very beautiful section of road to ride and traffic during many times of the day can be light. The alternative is to catch a bus. If you're heading to Pokhara (96km) it may be a good idea to miss the busy highway between Mugling and Pokhara by catching a bus in Mugling. Here, the road is much improved and vehicles travel a lot faster in what is still quite dusty conditions.

POKHARA

Pokhara is famous for its beauty, relaxed atmosphere and the spectacular views of the Annapurnas and Manaslu Himal and the splendour of the unclimbed Machhapuchhare. The surrounding area provides excellent opportunities for trail riding around lakes and rivers and towards the mountains. The riding, however, is less consistent or contiguous than that around Kathmandu, resulting in shorter trips. The area is also less populated than the Kathmandu Valley, so although there are fewer trails, villages and temples to explore, the rides are more tranquil and the traffic is hardly noticeable.

Sarangkot

The ride to Sarangkot, visible directly north from Pokhara Lakeside, provides an excellent, challenging day trip. This is in fact the bike leg of the Annapurna Triathlon.

Leave early and ride along Lakeside (towards the mountains) to the last main intersection and sealed road. Make a right which returns to central Pokhara. After 2km you turn left and continue straight on (north). After a further 2km there is a smaller sealed road to the left, signposted as the road to Sarangkot. This winds it's way along a ridge into Sarangkot, providing outstanding views of the Himalaya that seem close enough to reach out and touch. After 6km a few tea shops mark a welcome refreshment stop just were the stone steps commence the walking trail to the summit. From here it's a jeep track which closely hugs the edge of the mountain overlooking Phewa Tal. Continue until you join a 'Y' intersection which doubles back sharply to the right and makes the final climb to Sarangkot Point. From this point you can also continue straight ahead, riding the narrower motorbike trails leading to Naudanda.

What was in past years only a single track is now motorable. However, it still makes for a great day out on the bike mixing challenging climbs and fast rocky downhills always with a stunning panorama. After the Sarangkot turn-off the trail soon begins to climb to Kaski, towards the hill immediately in front of you. This section to Kaski takes around 30 to 60 minutes, and you may need to push your bike on the steeper section near the crown of the hill. Over the top you follow the trail through to Naudanda. You are now at around 1590m having gained around 840m altitude from Pokhara. The trail is rocky in parts and will test your equipment to the extreme, so don't consider riding this trail on a cheap hire bike.

The view from the ridge at Naudanda is spectacularly beautiful. Dhaulagiri, Manaslu, the Annapurnas and Machhapuchhare create a classic Himalayan panorama, especially on a cool, clear morning. To the south you can look down over Pokhara and Phewa Tal.

From Naudanda

Having reached Naudanda from Sarangkot Point you have the choice of continuing left or right. Heading left (if you are facing north) the sealed Pokhara-Baglung Hwy continues along the spine of the ridge and connects Pokhara with Lumle (a popular starting point for trekking in the Annapurnas). If you choose to head towards Lumle and onto Beni you have a mostly downhill run on sealed roads except for the last 10km into Beni. Riding onto Birethanti may be a good mid-point if Beni is too far. This is an initial 5km followed by a 20km switchback downhill. There are nice lodges in Birethanti (walk in from Birat) for an overnight stop before returning to Pokhara.

On your return from Naudanda it is 32km to Pokhara. You can either return via the Sarangkot trail (described earlier) or follow the highway back. The latter starts with a twisting 6km descent into the Madi Khola valley. The highway has an excellent asphalt surface and descends gently as it follows the river, allowing an enjoyable coast almost all the way back to Pokhara.

MOUNTAIN BIKING

Rafting & Kayaking

The bulk of this chapter was written and researched by David Allardice, the operations manager for Wet Dreams (formerly Ultimate Descents), a company which organises rafting and kayaking journeys in Nepal. The Information section was written by Ravi Fry.

Nepal has earned the reputation of being one of the best places in the world for rafting and kayaking. Its mountain scenery has drawn trekkers and climbers for many years; these same mountains shape an incredible variety of white-water challenges for paddlers.

A series of the world's most outstanding river journeys are found here, ranging from steep, adrenaline-charged mountain streams to classic big volume wilderness expeditions. The combination of spectacular rivers, mountain scenery and a rich cultural heritage makes Nepal an obvious river runner's destination.

No other country has such a choice of trips on wild rivers with warm water, a subtropical climate (with no bugs!), and huge white-sand beaches that are ideal for camping.

Rivers are graded for difficulty on an international scale from class 1 to 6, with class 1 defined as easy-moving water with few obstacles, and class 6 being considered nearly impossible to negotiate and a hazard to life – something best attempted after your lover leaves you.

As long as you are in reasonable physical shape and aren't afraid of water you can safely go rafting on rivers with gradings from class 1 to 3. For more difficult and exciting class 4 rivers, you should be active, confident in water, and preferably have some rafting experience. Class 5 is a very large step up from class 4: long continuous sections of powerful white water, strenuous paddling, steep constricted channels, powerful waves and the possibility of overturning a raft. Swimming in a class 5 rapid poses a significant risk.

Rafting in Nepal has an image of extremely difficult white water, which is well justified at times of high water flow (during the monsoon), but at most flows there are many class 3 to 4 rivers. There are also many easier class 1 and class 2 rivers where you can float along admiring the scenery and running a few small rapids.

WHEN TO GO

The best times for rafting are September to early December, and March to early June. From early September to early October, and May to June, the rivers can be extremely high with monsoon run-off. Any expeditions attempted at this time require a very experienced rafting company with an intimate knowledge of the river and strong teams, as high flows are potentially the most dangerous times to be on a river.

From mid-October onwards the weather is settled and this is one of the most popular times to raft. In December many of the rivers become too cold to enjoy unless you have wetsuits, and the days are short with the start of winter – a time to consider shorter trips. The summer season from March to early June has lower water flows to begin with, which generally means the rapids aren't as powerful. The rivers rise again in May with pre-monsoon storms and some snow-melt, then it's high water time again.

From June to August the monsoon rains arrive and the rivers carry 10 times their low-water flows, and can flood with 60 to 80 times as much. High flows can obviously make rivers much more difficult. Few rivers should be attempted at flood levels.

There is a definite relationship between volume, gradient and difficulty. River levels can fluctuate dramatically at any time, although as a general rule weather patterns in Nepal are quite stable.

TYPES OF RAFTING TRIPS

For many people a rafting trip in Nepal will be their first white-water experience. There are many different kinds of rafting trips, and it is important to select a river that suits your interests and ability. The style of trip, difficulty of the river and length of time you have are all factors to consider.

Any raft can be paddled, or rigged with an oar frame and rowed. With an oar frame the guide normally sits in the middle and rows, while the other passengers enjoy the scenery – and hold on through the rapids.

Shaping the Future of River Running in Nepal

With no regulating body, it's up to you to help shape the sport and future of Nepal's rivers. Your comments, feedback and attitude can have a very positive effect on what happens in the future.

A few guidelines:

Rural Nepal is still very conservative so make sure you adhere to a minimum dress code and respect local customs, they in turn will have more respect for you. This is especially important if you visit a temple or village. See the Society & Conduct section in Facts about Nepal.

Show respect for the environment and make sure that your group and company does the same. Camp sites should be kept scrupulously clean. Burn all burnable waste. Bury organic waste below the high water mark, or dispose it in the river – it feeds the fish. Well constructed toilet pits should be away from camp and below the high water level; everyone should use them. Toilet paper should be burnt. Leave only footprints.

Use only as much driftwood as you need, and do not use wood that would otherwise be used by villagers. Your trip should not place an additional burden on an already taxed environment, so if there is no driftwood available, use an alternative fuel like gas or kerosene. See also the Environmental Information; Trekking, Firewood & Forest Depletion; and Garbage & Waste boxed texts in the Trekking chapter.

It's worthwhile making sure that you know where your valuables are at all times. Don't leave gear lying around the camp site – put it inside your tent. Don't take any valuables you don't need on the river, instead store them in Kathmandu or Pokhara. Many of the operators will store them for you. As a general rule, local people don't leave their belongings lying around and there is a reason for it.

If you feel that any part of your trip varied considerably from what you where sold, or was unsafe and not run with respect to the environment and cultures then do something about it. Support companies that run safe and responsible trips, and all companies will have to follow these examples to stay in business.

If you have any suggestions or complaints, write to the Nepal Association of Rafting Agents (NARA; ☎ 01-221197) PO Box 2585, Kathmandu, or to the Nepal River Conservation Trust (☎ 01-271894) PO Box 6720, Kathmandu.

With a paddle raft the guide normally sits at the back calling instructions and steering, while the crew provides the power. Most active people prefer the teamwork and group participation of paddle rafting. With a strong team a paddle raft can probably run harder rapids than an oar raft, and the sense of achievement cannot be compared.

Rafting trips vary from quite luxurious trips where you are rowed down the river and staff do everything for you (pitch camp, cook and so on), to trips where you participate in the running of the expedition – pitching tents, loading the rafts and helping with the cooking. The quality of the rafting equipment is another variable, and can make a huge difference to the comfort and safety of participants.

EXPEDITION INFORMATION

Anyone who is seriously interested in rafting and kayaking, and especially anyone contemplating a private expedition, should get hold of *White Water Nepal*, an excellent guidebook by Peter Knowles & David Allardice. It should be possible to get copies of the book in Kathmandu. It has very detailed information on river trips, with 60 maps, river profiles and hydrographs, plus advice on equipment and health – in short all the information a prospective river runner could want.

Independent Rafting & Kayaking

Anyone who plans to raft or kayak privately should also contact local rafting companies to get up-to-date information. Himalayan rivers are dynamic, and rivers and their rapids change every monsoon.

Getting Your Gear to Nepal

Most airlines will carry short kayaks on the same basis as surfboards or bicycles – there's no excess baggage charge, so long as you are within the weight limits. If you are a group, negotiate a deal at the time of booking. If there is just one or two of you, just turn up, put all your bulky light gear in the kayak, with heavy items in your carry-on luggage, and smile sweetly! (If you phone them in advance they have to quote the rule book and start talking air cargo).

Permits Rafters and kayakers are required to have rafting permits, which are obtained from the Ministry of Tourism, Tripureshwar Marg, Kathmandu (near the National Stadium) and cost $5. There's a list of rivers where rafting is permitted (including all the rivers in the following section), but this is constantly being expanded, so it's best to check the situation when you arrive.

Organised Rafting & Kayaking

If you go on an organised rafting trip the necessary permits will be arranged for you. All specialised equipment is normally supplied. Usually you will only need light cotton clothing, with a slightly warmer change for nights. A swim-suit, sun hat, sunscreen, and light tennis shoes or sandals that will stay on your feet are all necessary, but can also be bought in Kathmandu. For overnight trips a sleeping bag is necessary, but this can easily be hired. Temperatures on some rivers vary, so check with the company you are booking with – they will recommend what to bring.

There are about 90 companies in Kathmandu claiming to be rafting operators. A few are well-established older companies with good reputations, and the rest are newer companies, often formed by guides breaking away and starting their own operations, and sometimes people with very little experience of rivers. Although these new companies can be enthusiastic and good, they can also be shoestring operations that may not have adequate resources in terms of equipment and staff.

Most of the small travel agencies simply sell trips on commission; often they have no real idea about the details of what they are selling and are only interested in getting bums on seats. To further confuse the situation, there are also sometimes complicated subcontracting arrangements between companies. It is immensely preferable to deal with the rafting company directly.

If time is limited you may choose to book

a trip before you leave home, however all the operators accept bookings in Kathmandu. Booking in Kathmandu gives you the opportunity to meet your fellow rafters and guides before you make a commitment. Trips depart on a regular basis (at least one long trip a week during the season), and the best companies will refer you to a friendly competitor if they don't have any suitable dates.

Trips range in price from $15 to $70 a day, and generally you get what you pay for. At $15 you don't get much at all. It is better to pay a bit more and have a good, safe trip, than to save $100 and have a lousy, dangerous trip. Bear in mind that trips in Nepal are generally less than half the cost of similar trips in the USA, so in relative terms all the prices are extremely reasonable. If you plan to do a more difficult trip it's particularly important to choose a company that has the experience, skills and equipment to run a safe and exciting expedition.

With the constant change in rafting companies it's difficult to make individual recommendations; the fact that a company is not recommended here does not necessarily mean it will not deliver an excellent trip. Nonetheless, the following companies have been recommended for their professionalism. Their prices range from $40 to $70 a day.

Equator Rafting
(☎ 01-414803, fax 411933) Thamel, Kathmandu. This is a smaller company with experienced staff, and specialises in long participatory rafting and kayaking trips.
Himalayan Encounters
(☎ 01-417426, fax 417133) Kathmandu Guest House compound, Thamel, Kathmandu. This company is associated with Encounter Overland, and has earned a solid reputation through many Trisuli and Sun Kosi trips.
Himalayan River Exploration
(☎ 01-418491, fax 414075) Hattisar, Kathmandu. This company is part of the Tiger Mountain organisation (one of Nepal's original companies) and is an upmarket operation, running a lot of catered trips with rowing rigs.
Himalayan Wonders
Namche Bazaar Building, Thamel, Kathmandu. This new company is at the budget end of rafting.

Raging River Runner
(☎ 01-214712, fax 229983) Jyatha, Thamel. Another recommended budget company.
Wet Dreams
(☎/fax 01-414765, PO Box 14431 Kathmandu, email rivers@ultimate.wlink.com.np) opposite Helena's Restaurant, Thamel. Formerly known as Ultimate Descents, this group has been in operation for more than a decade. They specialise in participatory rafting and kayaking trips and have pioneered many of the most challenging commercial trips available in Nepal.

SAFETY
Safety is the most important part of any river trip. Unfortunately, there are no minimum safety conditions enforced by any official body in Nepal. This makes it very important to choose a professional rafting company. Not all rafting companies are created equal.

If a group has recently returned from a trip, speak to its members. This will give you reliable information about the quality of equipment, the guides, the food, and the transportation. Question the company about things like how they get to and from the river, the number of hours spent paddling or rowing, where the camps are set up (near to villages?), food provided (rafting promotes a very healthy appetite), who does the cooking and work around the camp, the cooking fuel used (wood?), what happens to rubbish, hygiene precautions taken, and nighttime activities. Many companies have a photo file or video in their office which can give an impression of the equipment, safety and how they operate trips. Ask a lot of questions.

The following check list is based on the experience of many international guides.

Raft Numbers
There should be a minimum of two rafts per trip. If anyone does fall out of a raft (known as a 'swimmer' in the trade) the second raft can help with the rescue. In higher water, three rafts are safer than two. Many experts also agree that one or two safety kayakers can replace the second raft, though the kayakers need to be white-water professionals with the training, skill and experience not

only to run the most difficult rapids on the river, but also to be able to perform rescues in these rapids. Good safety kayakers are invaluable on steeper rivers where they can often get to a swimmer in places no other craft could manage a rescue.

Check how many people have booked and paid for a trip, and the maximum number that will be taken.

Safety Kayakers

Having good kayakers along will not only add to the safety of the trip, but they may also teach people to kayak on the easier river sections. For more adventurous people, some of the inflatable kayaks and catamarans that are turning up in Nepal are an excellent way to get the feel of controlling your own craft. These are a lot of fun, but it's important if you have these craft on a trip that the guides have the experience to know which rapids are safe to run. If you are interested in kayaking, a few companies have kayaks and kayaking gear for hire and also run instruction programs.

Raft Guides

The person leading the trip must be a qualified, trained guide with a minimum of 50 days rafting experience. They should also have done at least five previous trips on the river on which they are guiding. All raft guides should have done the river before.

If possible, speak with the guide who will lead the trip. This will give you a chance to form an impression of the people you will be spending time with and the type of trip they run. Ask them about their previous experience. Overseas experience or training allows the guides to keep up with the latest advances and safety training. Kayaking experience adds additional depth to a guide's skills.

All guides should have a current first aid certificate and be trained in CPR.

Equipment

Quality equipment is important, both for safety and comfort. Modern self-bailing rafts are essential for more difficult trips.

Good life jackets and helmets are mandatory on any white-water trip. Modern plastic and alloy paddles are preferable to locally made wooden ones. Roll-top dry bags will keep your gear dry even if the raft flips, and waterproof camera containers will allow you to take photos all the way down the river. The companies should also supply tents. Ask how old the equipment is.

Ask what first-aid gear, supplies, spare parts and repair equipment is carried. On a river it's important that the guides are capable of dealing with any situation that occurs – more so if it is a long wilderness expedition. Many a trip has gone astray due to lack of preparation, not having the right equipment, or insufficient training to deal with the variety of situations that can arise.

On the River

At the river your guide should give you a comprehensive safety talk and paddle training before you launch off downstream. The more you know the safer it is. If you don't get a good safety talk it is probably cause for concern.

- Always wear your life jacket in rapids. Wear your helmet whenever your guide tells you, and make sure that both the helmet and jacket are properly adjusted and fitted.
- Keep your feet and arms inside the raft. If the raft hits a rock or wall and you are in the way, the best you'll escape with is a laceration.
- If you do swim in a rapid, get into the 'white-water swimming position' – on your back, with your feet downstream and up where you can see them. Hold onto your paddle as this will make you more visible. Relax and breathe when you aren't going through waves. Turn over and swim at the end of the rapid when the water becomes calmer. Self rescue is the best rescue.

Selecting a River

Before you decide what river you'll do, you need to decide what it is you want out of the river trip to begin with. There are trips available from two to 12 days on different rivers, all offering dramatically different experiences.

First off, don't believe that just because its a river it's going to be wet 'n wild. Some rivers, such as the Sun Kosi, which are incredible full-on white-water trips in September and October are basically flat and uneventful in the low water of early spring. On the flip side of that, early spring can be a superb time to raft rivers such as the Marsyangdi or Bhote Kosi, which would be suicidal during high flows. The Karnali is probably the only river which offers continually challenging white water at all flows, though in the high water months of September and May, it's a significantly more challenging endeavour.

There is much more to rivers than just white water, but the climate in Nepal being what it is, many companies will promote whichever river they're running at the time as the pinnacle of white-water excitement. Not all companies run all rivers, especially the more technical and demanding ones, and some companies shouldn't be running any rivers at all, but such is life. Buyer beware.

Longer trips such as the Sun Kosi (in the autumn) and the Karnali have the advantages of offering some real heart thumping white water with the incredible journeying aspect of a long river trip. With more time on the river things are more relaxed, relationships progress at a more natural pace, and memories become firmly entrenched for a lifetime. Long after the white water has blurred into one long white-knuckled thrill ride, the memories of a moonrise over the river and the friends you inevitably make will remain. After spending the better part of their adult lives on different rivers, most hard-core river people can still distinctly remember the long expeditions they've been on; it's a much more involving and enveloping experience than a short two or three-day trip. River trips are much more than gravity powered roller-coaster rides: they're journeys traversed on very special highways. For many people they become a way of life.

If a long trip is simply impossible due to financial or time constraints, don't undervalue the shorter ones. Anyone who has ever taken a paddle-raft or kayak down the Bhote Kosi (at any flow) would be hard

RIVERS OF NEPAL

CHINA
TIBET

INDIA

KATHMANDU

Pokhara

Nepalganj

Biratnagar

0   100   200 km

RAFTING & KAYAKING

pressed to find anything better to do with two days in Nepal. There are also medium length options which are perfect for people who want to experience river journeying but have limited time.

The following section describes the main commercially rafted rivers in Nepal. It is by no means a complete list, and private boaters who have the experience and equipment to run their own expeditions would be best advised to consult the aforementioned river guide book, *White Water Nepal*.

KARNALI

The Karnali is a gem, combining a lowland trek with some of the prettiest canyons and jungle scenery available in Nepal. Most experienced river people who have boated the Karnali find it one of the best all-round river trips they've ever done. In high water, the Karnali is a serious commitment, combining *huge*, though fairly straightforward, rapids with a seriously remote location. At low water the Karnali is still a fantastic trip. The rapids become smaller, but the steeper gradient and constricted channel of the Karnali keep it interesting.

Being the longest and largest river in all of Nepal, the Karnali drains a huge and well-developed catchment. Spring snow-melts can drive the river up dramatically in a matter of hours – as the river rises the difficulty increases exponentially. The river flows through some steep and constricted canyons where the rapids are close together, giving little opportunity to correct for potential mistakes. Pick your company carefully.

The trip starts with a long but interesting bus ride over to the remote far west of Nepal. If you're allergic to bus rides, it's possible to fly to Nepalganj and cut the bus transport down to about five hours on the way over, and two hours on the way back. From the frontier town of Surkhet there is a lovely two day trek through lowland Sal forests to the village of Sauli. From Sauli it's 180km to the next road access at Chisopani, on the northern border of the Royal Bardia National Park.

The river section takes about seven days, giving plenty of time to explore some of the side canyons and waterfalls which come into the river valley. Better-run trips also include a lay over day, where the expedition stays at the same camp site for two nights.

The combination of long bus rides and trekking puts some people off, but anyone who has ever done the trip invariably raves about it. Finish with a visit to the Royal Bardia National Park at the end for an unbeatable combination.

SUN KOSI

This is the longest river trip offered in Nepal, traversing 270km through the beautiful Mahabharat Range on it's meandering way from the put in at Dolalghat to the take out at Chatara, far down on the Gangetic Plain. It's quite an experience to begin a river trip just three hours out of Kathmandu, barely 60km from the Tibetan border, and end the trip looking down the hot, dusty gun barrel of the north Indian plain just nine or 10 days later. Because it's one of the easiest trips to organise logistically, it's also one of the least expensive for the days you spend on a river.

The Sun Kosi starts off fairly relaxed, with class 2 and small class 3 rapids to warm up on during the first couple of days. Savvy guides will take this opportunity to get the teams working together with precision, as on the third day the rapids become more powerful and frequent, and those on high water trips find themselves astonished at just how big a wave in a river can get. While the lower sections of large volume rivers are usually rather flat, the Sun Kosi reserves some of its biggest and best rapids for the last days. At the right flow it's an incredible combination of white water, scenery, villages, and truly quiet and introspective evenings along what many people consider to be one of the world's 10 classic river journeys.

TRISULI

Just out of Kathmandu, the Trisuli is where the bulk of the commercial trips operate due to the easy access. Without a doubt this is the cheapest trip available in Nepal – if you sign onto a $20 a day raft trip, this is where you'll end up, and it's no wonder.

What makes the Trisuli so cheap is also what makes it one of the least desirable rafting trips in the country. The easy access is provided by the Prithvi Hwy, which is the only highway connecting Kathmandu and India, and it runs right alongside the river. During most flows the rapids are straightforward and spread well apart. The large number of companies operating on the river drives the prices down, but it also detracts considerably from the experience of the trip. Beaches are often heavily used and abused, with garbage, toilet paper and fire pits well assimilated into the sand. This, combined with the noise and pollution of the highway, makes the Trisuli a less than ideal rafting experience.

It's not all bad news though. During the monsoon months the Trisuli changes character completely as huge run-offs make the river swell and shear like an immense ribbon of churning ocean. There are fewer companies running at this time of the year, and the garbage and excrement of the past season is well on it's way to Bangladesh as topsoil.

The best white water is found on the section between Baireni and Mugling, and trips on the Trisuli can be combined with trips to Pokhara or Chitwan.

KALI GANDAKI

The Kali Gandaki is an excellent alternative to the Trisuli, as there is no road alongside, and the scenery, villages, and temples all combine to make it a great trip.

The rapids on the Kali Gandaki are much more technical and continuous than on the Trisuli (class 3 to 4 depending on the flows), and in high water it's no place to be unless you are an accomplished kayaker experienced in avoiding big holes. At medium and lower flows, it's a fun and challenging river with rapids keeping you busy for three full days.

Being one of the holiest rivers in Nepal, every river junction on the Kali Gandaki is dotted with cremation sites and aboveground burial mounds. If you've been wondering what's under that pile of rocks, we recommend against exploring. Due to the recent construction of a dam at the confluence with the Andhi Khola, what was once a four to five day trip has now become a three day trip, starting at Baglung and taking out at the dam site. At very high flows it will probably be possible to run the full five day trip to Ramdhighat by just portaging the dam site. This option would add some great white water and you could visit the wonderful derelict palace at Ranighat, which is slowly being taken over by the surrounding jungle. It's a fantastic place to stop and have a look around.

If you are able to raft to Ramdhighat on the Siddhartha Hwy between Pokhara and Sunauli, you could continue on to the confluence with the Trisuli at Devghat. This adds another 130km and three or four more days. The lower section below Ramdhighat doesn't have much white water, but it is seldom rafted and offers a very isolated area with lots of wildlife.

SETI

The Seti is an excellent two-day trip in an isolated area, with beautiful jungle and plenty of easy rapids. Beware of companies who market this as a hot white-water trip. While it's a beautiful river valley well worth rafting, it's not a white-water bonanza.

The logical starting point is Damauli on the Kathmandu-Pokhara (Prithvi) Hwy between Mugling and Pokhara. This would give you 32km of rafting to the confluence with the Trisuli River. This is an excellent trip for learner/intermediate kayakers.

It is possible to raft a higher section, starting at Dule Gouda, which would add another 30km, but considering the quality of the rapids it probably isn't worth it. Beware if you decide to try the upper section of the river as it disappears underground above Dule Gouda! Perhaps this is what they refer to as class 6.

BHOTE KOSI

Just three hours from Kathmandu, the Bhote Kosi is one of the best two-day raft trips to be found anywhere in the world. The Bhote is one of the most recently opened rivers in Nepal, and represents the forefront of river rafting.

The Bhote Kosi is the steepest river rafted in Nepal – technical and totally committing. With a gradient of 80 feet per mile (24m per 1.6km), it's a full eight times as steep as the Sun Kosi, which it feeds farther downstream. The rapids are steep and continuous class 4, with a lot of continuous class 3 in between.

The normal run is from approximately Hwy Km 95 (above Barabise) to the dam at Lamosangu. The river has been kayaked above this point, but a raft trip here would not be recreational. At high flows several of the rapids become solid class 5, and consequences for mistakes on the entire river will become serious.

This river is one of the most fun things you can do right out of Kathmandu and a great way to get an adrenaline fix during the low water months, but it should only be attempted with a company who has a lot of experience on the Bhote Kosi, and is running the absolute best safety equipment and guides.

UPPER SUN KOSI

Not to be confused with the Bhote Kosi which finishes at Lamosangu, the upper Sun Kosi is a fun 20km stretch of easy class 2 water and beautiful scenery. From Khadichour to Dolighat the river is crystal blue, with brilliant beaches on which to picnic. A great place for a short family trip.

MARSYANGDI

The Marsyangdi is one of the best whitewater runs in the world. The trip starts with a class 5 bus ride from Dumre to Besisahar, which is a good opportunity to steel your nerves and awaken your fight-or-flight responses. If you make it to Besisahar intact, you're in for a beautiful trek up to the village of Ngadi, with great views of the Manaslu and the Annapurnas ahead of you the whole time. The scenery is fantastic.

From Ngadi downstream to the end of the trip at Bimalnagar, it's pretty much solid white water. Rapids are steep, technical, and consecutive, making the Marsyangdi a serious undertaking. Like the Bhote Kosi, successful navigation of the Marsyangdi is dependent on companies having previous experience on the river, and using the absolute best guides and equipment. Rafts must be self bailing, and should be running with a minimum of weight and gear on board. Professional safety kayakers should be considered a standard safety measure on this river.

For people looking for a six to seven day trip with lots of demanding white water and great mountain scenery, the Marsyangdi is hard to beat.

OTHER RIVERS

The **Bheri**, which is in the west, is a great float trip with incredible jungle scenery and lots of wildlife. This is one of the best fishing rivers and can be combined with a visit to the Royal Bardia National Park. The **Arun** from Tumlingtar makes an excellent three-day wilderness trip, although the logistics of getting to the starting point are pretty complicated.

There is a plethora of rivers which could be rafted and kayaked in Nepal, but government permission is another matter. Things change quickly and capriciously in this part of the world, and the best advice is to check local information sources (several of them) to see what's running. One that we hope will open soon is the **Tamur** which drains all the mountains in the far east of Nepal. Well worth waiting for.

Language

It's quite easy to get by with English in Nepal; most of the people the average visitor will have to deal with in the Kathmandu Valley and in Pokhara will speak some English. Along the main trekking trails, particularly the Annapurna Circuit, English is widely understood.

However, it's interesting to learn at least a little Nepali and it's quite an easy language to pick up. Nepali is closely related to Hindi and, like Hindi, is a member of the Indo-European group of languages. If you want to know a bit more Nepali than the phrases and vocabulary included in this chapter, the Lonely Planet *Nepali phrasebook* is a handy introduction to the language.

Although Nepali is the national language of Nepal and is the linking language between all the country's ethnic groups, there are many other languages spoken. The Newars of the Kathmandu Valley, for example, speak Newari; other languages are spoken by the Tamangs, Sherpas, Rais, Limbus, Magars, Gurungs and other groups. In the Terai, bordering India, Hindi and Maithili, another Indian language of this region, are often spoken (see the table on this page for a breakdown of the languages spoken by Nepalis as their first language).

Even if you learn no other Nepali, there is one word every visitor soon picks up – *namaste* (pronounced 'na-ma-stay'). Strictly translated it means 'I salute the god in you', but it's used as an everyday greeting encompassing everything from 'Hello' to 'How are you?' and even 'See you again soon'. Properly used, it should be accompanied with the hands held in a prayer-like position, the Nepali gesture which is the equivalent of westerners shaking hands.

Studying Nepali

Nepali pronunciation is relatively straightforward. Peace Corps and other aid workers pick up a working knowledge of the language very quickly and there are language courses available which will enable you to

Languages of Nepal	
Language	**% of Total Population**
Nepali	50.3
Maithili	11.9
Bhojpuri	7.5
Tharu	5.4
Tamang	4.9
Newari	3.4
Rai	2.4
Magar	2.3
Abadhi	2.0
Limbu	1.4
Gurung	1.2
Sherpa	0.7
Other	8.6

get by with just four to eight weeks of intensive study. See the Courses section in the Facts for the Visitor chapter for details.

Pronunciation
Vowels

a	as the 'u' in 'hut'
ā	as the 'ar' in 'garden'
e	as the 'e' in 'best' but longer
i	as the 'i' in 'sister' but longer
o	as the 'o' in 'sold'
u	as the 'u' in 'put'
ai	as the 'i' in 'mine'
au	as the 'ow' in 'cow'

Consonants

Most Nepali consonants are quite similar to their English counterparts. The exceptions are the so-called retroflex consonants and the aspirated consonants. Retroflex sounds are made by curling the tongue back to touch the roof of the mouth with the tip as you make the sound; they are indicated in this guide by an underdot, eg ṭ, *Kaṭhmaṇḍu*.

Aspirated consonants are sounded more forcefully than they would be in English and are made with a short puff of air; they are indicated in this guide by an 'h' after the consonant, eg **kh**, *khānuhos* (please).

Both retroflex and aspirated consonants are best learned by having a Nepali demonstrate them for you. You could start with the word *kaṭhmaṇḍu*, which contains both retroflex and aspirated consonants.

Greetings & Civilities

Hello/Goodbye.	*namaste*
How are you?	*tapāilai kasto chha?*
Excuse me.	*hajur*
Please (give me).	*dinuhos*
Please (you have).	*khānuhos*
Thank you.	*dhanyabad*

Unlike in the west, verbal expressions of thanks are not the cultural norm in Nepal. Although neglecting to say 'Thank you' may make you feel a little uncomfortable, it is rarely necessary in a simple commercial transaction; foreigners going round saying *dhanyabad* all the time sounds distinctly odd to Nepalis.

Basics

I	*ma*
Yes. (I have)	*chā*
No. (I don't have)	*chhaina*
OK.	*theekcha*
Where?	*kahā?*
here	*yahā*
there	*tyahā*
good/pretty	*ramro*
Do you speak English?	*tapāi angreji bolna saknu hunchha?*
I only speak a little Nepali.	*ma ali nepāli bolchhu*
I understand.	*ma bujhchu*
I don't understand.	*maile bujhina*
Please say it again.	*pheri bhanuhos*
Please speak more slowly.	*tapāi bistārai bolnuhos*
I don't need it.	*malai chahina*
I don't have it.	*ma sanga chhaina*
Wait a minute.	*ek chhin parkhanos*

Getting Around

bus	*bus*
taxi	*taxi*
boat	*nāu*
ticket	*tikaṭ*

How can I get to ...?	*... kolāgi kati paisā lāgchha?*
Is it far from here?	*yahābata ke tādhā chha?*
Can I walk there?	*hiḍera jāna sakinchhu?*
I want to go to ...	*ma ... jānchhu*
Where does this bus go?	*yo bus kahā jānchha?*
How much is it to go to ...?	*... jāna kati parchha?*
I want a one-way/ return ticket.	*jāne/jāne-āune tikaṭ dinuhos.*
Does your taxi have a meter?	*tapāi ko taxi mā meter chha?*

Accommodation

Where is a ...?	*... kahā chha?*
guesthouse	*pāhuna ghar*
hotel	*hoṭel*
camp site	*shivir*
lodge	*laj*
What is the address?	*thegānā ke ho?*
Please write down the address.	*thegānā lekhunuhos*
Can I get a place to stay here?	*yahā bās paunchha?*
May I look at the room?	*kothā herna sakchhu?*
How much is it per night?	*ek rātko, kati paisā ho?*
Does it include breakfast?	*bihānako khāna samet ho?*
room	*kothā*
clean	*safā*
dirty	*mailo*
fan	*pankhā*
hot water	*tāto pāni*

Around Town

bank	*baink*
... embassy	*... rājdutāvas*
museum	*samgrāhālaya*
police	*prahari*
post office	*post afis*
stamp	*tikaṭ*
envelope	*kham*
tourist office	*turist afis*

What time does it open/close?	*kati baje kholchha/ banda garchha?*
I want to change some money.	*paisā sātnu manlāgchha*

Trekking

Which way is ...?	*... jāne bato kata parchha?*
Is there a village nearby?	*najikai gaun parchha?*
How many hours/ days to ...?	*... kati ghanṭā/din?*
Where is the porter?	*bhariya kata gayo?*
I want to sleep.	*malai sutna man lagyo*
I'm cold.	*malai jado lagyo*
Please give me (water).	*malai (pani) dinuhos*

way/trail	*sāno bāṭo*
bridge	*pul*
downhill	*orālo*
uphill	*ukālo*
left	*bāyā*
right	*dāyā*
cold	*jāḍo*
teahouse	*bati*

Food & Drink

I'm a vegetarian.	*ma sākāhari hun*
What is this/that?	*yo/tyo ke ho?*

food/meal	*khāna*
bread (loaf)	*(pau) roṭi*
rice/cooked rice	*chāmal/bhāt*
meat	*māsu*
green, leafy vegetable	*sāg*
vegetable (cooked)	*tarkāri*
lentils	*dāl*
egg	*phul/anḍā*
fruit	*phala*
sugar	*chini*
salt	*nun*
pepper	*marich*
curd	*dhai*
milk	*dudh*
tea	*chiyā*
drinking water	*khāna pāni*

Emergencies

Help!	*guhār!*
It's an emergency!	*āpaṭ paryo!*
There's been an accident!	*durghaṭanā bhayo!*
Please call a doctor.	*dākṭarlai bolāunuhos*
Where is the (public) toilet?	*shauchālaya kahā chha?*
I'm lost.	*ma harāye*

Shopping

Where is the market?	*bazar kata parchha?*
What is it made of?	*kele baneko?*
How much?	*kati?*
That's enough.	*pugyo*
I like this.	*malai yo ramro lagyo*
I don't like this.	*malai yo ramro lagena*

money	*paisa*
cheap	*sasto*
expensive	*mahango*
less	*kam*
more	*badhi*
little bit	*alikati*

Health

Where can I find a good doctor?	*rāmro dākṭar kaha pāincha?*
Where is the nearest hospital?	*yahā aspatāl kahā chha?*
I don't feel well.	*malai sancho chhaina*
I have diarrhoea.	*dishā lāgyo*
I have altitude sickness.	*lekh lāgyo*
I have a fever.	*joro āyo*
I'm having trouble breathing.	*sās pherna sakdina*

medicine	*ausadhi*
pharmacy	*ausadhi pasal*

I have ...	*malāi ... lāgyo*
asthma	*damko byathā*
diabetes	*madhu meha*
epilepsy	*chāre rog*

Times & Dates

What time is it?	*kati bajyo?*
It's one o'clock.	*ek bajyo*
minute	*minet*
hour	*ghantā*
day	*din*
today	*āja*
yesterday	*hijo*
tomorrow	*bholi*
now	*ahile*
week	*haptā*
month	*mahinā*
What day is it today?	*āja ke bār?*
Today is ...	*āja ... ho*
Monday	*som bār*
Tuesday	*mangal bār*
Wednesday	*budh bār*
Thursday	*bihi bār*
Friday	*sukra bār*
Saturday	*sani bār*
Sunday	*āita bār*

Numbers

1	*ek*
2	*dui*
3	*teen*
4	*chār*
5	*panch*
6	*chha*
7	*sāt*
8	*āth*
9	*nau*
10	*das*
20	*bees*
30	*tees*
40	*chālis*
50	*pachās*
60	*sātthi*
70	*satari*
80	*assi*
90	*nabbe*
100	*saya*
200	*dui saya*
500	*panch saya*
1000	*hazār*
100,000	*lākh*
one million	*das lākh*
ten million	*crore*

Glossary

Beware of the different methods of transliterating Nepali and the other languages spoken in Nepal. There are many and varied ways of spelling Nepali words. In particular the letters 'b' and 'v' are often interchanged. The god Bhairab becomes Bhairav or the thunderbolt symbol changes from *vajra* to *bajra*.

ACAP – Annapurna Conservation Area Project.

Adi Buddha – the original self-generated Buddha of Tantric Buddhism who created the Dhyani Buddhas.

Aditya – ancient Vedic sun god.

Agni – ancient Vedic god of the hearth and fire. He rides a chariot drawn by parrots and his four arms hold flames, a ball of fire, a trident and a rosary.

Agnipura – Buddhist symbol for fire.

Aksobhya – the Dhyani Buddha of the east; his vehicle is an elephant and he is often seen with one hand touching the ground in the gesture known as subduing Mara.

Amitabha – the Dhyani Buddha of the west; his animal is the peacock.

Amoghasiddhi – the Dhyani Buddha of the north, his consort is Green Tara and in Nepali stupas he sits under a seven-hooded snake canopy.

AMS – Acute mountain sickness, or altitude sickness. See Environmental Hazards in the Facts for the Visitor chapter.

Ananda – the Buddha's chief disciple.

Ananta – the cosmic serpent upon which Vishnu reclines.

Annapurna – the goddess of abundance and an incarnation of Mahadevi.

arak – a fermented drink made from potatoes or grain.

Ashoka – Indian Buddhist emperor who spread the religion throughout the subcontinent.

Ashta Matrikas – the eight mother goddesses.

asla – river trout.

Asuras – demons ruled by Rawana, king of Lanka in the *Ramayana*. The name can be a suffix as in Mahisasura.

Avalokiteshvara – as Gautama Buddha is the Buddha of our era, so is Avalokiteshvara the Bodhisattva of our era. In Nepal he has become a Hindu/Buddhist god of mercy whose incarnation is Machhendranath or Manjushri.

avataar – an incarnation of a deity living on earth.

bahal – a Buddhist monastery, usually two storeys high and built around a courtyard. There are a great number of bahals in the towns of the Kathmandu Valley but few of them continue to function as monasteries. Many are used as schools.

bahil – a simpler version of a bahal.

bakba – Tibetan clay mask.

bajra – see *vajra*.

Balarama – Krishna's brother.

Balkumari – one of Bhairab's consorts.

Banrhas – Buddhist hereditary priesthood.

bazaar – market area; a market town is called a bazaar or bazar.

BCE – before common era.

bell – see *ghanta*.

bel tree – it is a Newari custom to 'marry' young girls to a bel tree so that they can never be widowed.

betel – mildly intoxicating concoction of areca nut and lime which is wrapped in betel leaf and chewed. The red splashes you see on the ground throughout south Asia are spat out by betel chewers. Regular betel chewing leads to dark-red stained teeth.

Bhairab – the 'terrific' or fearsome Tantric form of Shiva in Nepal. Bhairab has 64 manifestations.

Bhadrakali – a Tantric goddess who is also a consort of Bhairab.

Bhagavad Gita – Krishna's lessons to Arjuna, part of the *Mahabharata*.

bhati – term for a teahouse in Nepal.

Bhimsen – a deity noted for his strength and bravery.

Bhote – high-altitude desert valleys north of the Himalaya bordering Tibet. In Nepal Tibetans are known as Bhotes.

Bhot – Nepali for Tibet.

bodhi tree – or bo tree, a pipal tree under which the Buddha was sitting when he attained enlightenment.

Bodhisattva – a near-Buddha who renounces the opportunity to attain nirvana in order to aid humankind.

Bön – the animist religion of Tibet prior to Buddhism.

Brahmin – the highest Hindu caste, said to originate from Brahma's head. Priests are drawn from this caste although Brahmins may have many other occupations.

CE – common era.

chaitya – small stupa which usually contains a mantra rather than a Buddhist relic.

chakra – Vishnu's disc-like weapon, one of the four symbols he holds.

chang – Tibetan rice beer.

chapati – unleavened Indian bread.

Chaturmukha – Shiva lingam with four images of the god's face.

chautara – stone platforms around trees which serve as shady places for porters to rest.

Chenrezig – Tibetan name for Avalokiteshvara.

Chhetri – the second caste of Nepali Hindus and the prince and warrior caste to which the Ranas and the Shah kings belonged. Chhetris are said to originate from Brahma's arms.

chirag – ceremonial oil lamp.

Chitrakar – special caste of Newari painters.

Chomolongma – see *Qomolangma*.

chörten – Tibetan Buddhist stupa.

chowk – a courtyard or marketplace such as Indra Chowk, the old market area of Kathmandu.

chuba – long woollen Sherpa coat.

chura – beaten rice.

curd – yoghurt.

Dalai Lama – incarnation of a Bodhisattva who is the spiritual leader of Tibetan Buddhists.

Damais – a caste of tailors who perform music at weddings.

danda – hill.

Dattatraya – deity who is thought of as an incarnation of Vishnu, Shiva's teacher, or the Buddha's cousin.

deval – Nepali word for temple.

Devanagari – Sanskrit Nepali script.

Devi – the short form of Mahadevi, the shakti to Shiva.

dhaki – handwoven cotton cloth.

dal – lentil soup; the main source of protein in the Nepali diet.

dhami – priest claiming occult powers, a sorcerer.

dharma – Buddhist teachings.

dharamsala – resthouse for pilgrims.

dhoka – door or gate.

dhwaja – metal ribbon streaming out from the roof of a temple and acting as a pathway for the gods.

dhyana – meditation.

Dhyani Buddhas – the original Adi Buddha created five Dhyani Buddhas who in turn create the universe of each human era. Amitabha is the Dhyani Buddha of our era. See the Dhyani Buddhas boxed text in the Around the Kathmandu Valley chapter for more information.

dighur – Thakali cooperative economic system where members of a group pool their money to support one person's plans.

doko – basket carried by porters.

doonga – boat.

dorje – Tibetan word for *vajra* or *bajra*.

durbar – palace.

Durga – fearsome manifestation of Parvati, Shiva's consort.

Dwarapala – door guardian figure.

dyochen – a form of temple enshrining Tantric deities.

dzopkyo – male cross between a yak and a cow; also zopkiok.

dzum – female offspring of a yak and a cow; also zhum.

dzu-tch – large yeti that eats cattle.

ek – Nepali number one, a symbol of the unity of all life.

Ekamukha – Shiva lingam with one image of the god's face.

freaks – 1960s term from the overland era for the young western travellers who could be found congregating in Bali, Kabul, Goa and Kathmandu.

gaines – beggar musicians.

gajur – bell-shaped top to a bahal.

ganas – Shiva's 'companions'.

Ganesh – Shiva and Parvati's son, instantly recognisable by his elephant head.

Ganga – goddess of the Ganges.

ganja – hashish.

Garuda – the man-bird vehicle of Vishnu.

Gautama Buddha – the Buddha of our era.

Gelugpa – Yellow Hat order of Tibetan Buddhism. This is the reformed order headed by the Dalai Lama.

gada – club-like weapon of Vishnu.

ghanta – Tantric bell which is the female equivalent of the dorje.

ghat – steps beside a river. A 'burning ghat' is used for cremations.

ghee – clarified butter.

gompa – Tibetan Buddhist monastery.

gopis – cowherd girls. (Krishna had a lot of fun with his gopis.)

Gorakhnath – 11th-century yogi now said to be an incarnation of Shiva.

gurkha – Nepali mercenaries who have long formed a part of the British army. The name comes from the region of Gorkha.

Gurkhali – British army name for the Nepali language.

gurr – traditional Sherpa potato dish.

Gurungs – western hill people, predominantly from around Gorkha and Pokhara.

Guthi – Newari community group offering mutual support to its members.

Hanuman – monkey god.

Harisiddhi – a fearsome Tantric goddess.

harmika – eyes on a stupa which face the four cardinal directions, or the 13 steps of a stupa steeple, symbolising the 13 stages to enlightenment.

hashish – dried marijuana plant resin.

himal – range or massif with permanent snow.

hiti – water conduit or tank with waterspouts.
hookah – water pipe for smoking.

impeyan pheasant – Nepal's national bird.
incarnation – a particular life form; in the case of mortals, determined by karma. Vishnu has 10 different incarnations.
Indra – king of the Vedic gods, god of rain.

Jagannath – Krishna as 'Lord of the World'.
Jambhala – god of wealth; look for his money bag and his attendant mongoose.
Jamuna – goddess of the River Jamuna.
Janai – sacred thread which high-caste Hindu men wear looped over their left shoulder and replace once each year; also Munja.
jatra – festival, as in Indra Jatra.
Jaya Varahi – Vishnu's consort when the god takes on his boar incarnation.
jhankri – sorcerer.
Jogini – mystical goddesses, counterparts to the 64 manifestations of Bhairab.
jukha – Nepali word for leech.

Kala – see *Mara*.
kalakuta – the poison which Shiva swallowed when he was in the form of Nilakantha.
kalasa – a pot, or a pot-shaped top to a temple.
Kali – most terrifying manifestation of Parvati.
Kalki – Vishnu's 10th, and as yet unseen, incarnation when he will come riding a white horse and wielding a sword to destroy the world.
Kalpa – a day in the age of Brahma.
Kam Dev – Shiva's 'companion'.
Karkotak – chief naga of the Kathmandu Valley.
karma – Buddhist and Hindu law of cause and effect which continues from one life to another.
Kartikkaya – god of war and son of Shiva, his animal is the cock or peacock and he carries a variety of weapons. Also known as Skanda or Kumar.
kata – the Tibetan prayer shawl which should be presented to an important Buddhist personage when introduced.
Kaukala – a form of Shiva in his fearsome aspect; he carries a trident with the skeleton of Vishnu's gatekeeper impaled upon it: a result of banning Shiva from Vishnu's palace!
KEEP – Kathmandu Environmental Education Project.
Khas – Hindu hill people.
khola – stream or tributary.
khukuri – traditional curved knife of the Gurkhas.
kinkinimali – temple wind bells.
kosi – river.
kot – fort.
Krishna – the fun-loving eighth incarnation of Vishnu.

Kshatriyas – Indian equivalent of the Chhetri caste.
Kshepu – snake-eating figure often seen on toranas.
Kubera – see *Jambhala*.
kundalini – female energy principle.
Kumar – see *Kartikkaya*.
Kumari – the living goddess, a peaceful incarnation of Kali.
kunda – water tank fed by springs.

la – mountain pass.
Lakshmi – goddess of prosperity and Vishnu's consort.
laliguras – Nepali word for rhododendron, the national flower.
lama – Tibetan Buddhist monk or priest.
lingam – phallic symbol of Shiva's creative powers.
Locana – consort of the Dhyani Buddha, Aksobhya.
Lokeshvara – Lord of the World, an aspect of Avalokiteshvara but often mingled with the Hindu gods in Nepal. He appears as Nilakantha, an aspect of Shiva, and as Nateshvara, much like Natraj, the dancing Shiva whose cosmic dance created the world.

machan – a lookout tower used to view wildlife.
Machhendranath – patron god of the Kathmandu Valley and an incarnation of Avalokiteshvara or Lokeshvara.
Mahabharata – one of the major Hindu epics.
Mahadeva (Mahadeo) – another name for Shiva; *maha* translates as 'great', *deva* as 'god'.
Mahadevi – Great Goddess, sometimes known simply as Devi, the shakti to Shiva.
Mahakala – protector of the mandala and a Tantric equivalent of Shiva; literally, 'great black one'.
maharishi – great teacher.
Mahayana – form of Buddhism (the 'greater vehicle') prevalent through East Asia, Tibet and Nepal.
Mahayuga – each day of Brahma (see *Kalpa*) is divided into 1000 Mahayugas or Great Ages.
Mahisasura – buffalo demon killed by Durga.
mahseer – game fish of the Terai rivers.
Maitreya – a Buddha who will come in a future era.
Makara – mythical water monster, often appears as a waterspout on buildings.
Mali – Newari gardener caste.
Malla – royal dynasty of the Kathmandu Valley responsible for most of the important temples and palaces of the valley towns.
mandala – geometrical and astrological representation of the world.
mandap – roofless Tantric shrine.
mandir – Nepali word for temple.
Manjushri – god who cut open the Chobar Gorge

so that the Kathmandu Lake could become the Kathmandu Valley.

mani – stone carved with the Tibetan Buddhist chant om mani padme hum.

mantra – prayer formula or chant.

Mara – Buddhist god of death, has three eyes and holds the Wheel of Life.

math – Hindu priest's house.

mela – a country fair.

mithuna – Sanskrit term usually referring to a depiction of gods engaged in intercourse in erotic art; yab-yum in Tibetan.

moksha – spiritual release, Hindu equivalent of nirvana.

momos – meat/vegetable filled pasta.

mudra – symbolic hand gesture of the gods.

Munja – see Janai.

naga – serpent deity. The nine nagas have control over water, and are often seen over house entrances to keep evil spirits away.

nagini – female naga.

Nagpura – Buddhist symbol for water.

nak – female yak.

namaste – traditional Hindu greeting (hello or goodbye), often accompanied by a small bow with the hands brought together at chest or head level, as a sign of respect.

Nandi – the bull, vehicle of Shiva.

Narayan – Vishnu as the sleeping figure on the cosmic ocean. From his navel Brahma appears and goes on to create the universe. Narayan is Vishnu's most important appearance in Nepal but it is simply another name for Vishnu, not another incarnation.

Narsingha (Narsimha) – man-lion incarnation of Vishnu.

Newars – people of the Kathmandu Valley.

Nilakantha – blue-throated form of Shiva, a result of swallowing poison that would have destroyed the world.

nirvana – final escape from the cycles of existence.

Nriteshwar – god of dance.

Nyingmapa – one of the three Red Hat orders of Tibetan Buddhism.

om mani padme hum – sacred Buddhist mantra which means 'hail to the jewel in the lotus'.

oriflammes – prayer flags; the wind carries off the prayers written on them.

padma – lotus flower.

Padmapani – literally 'lotus in hand'; a manifestation of Avalokiteshvara as he appears in many Nepali viharas, holding a tall lotus stalk.

Padmasambhava – Bodhisattva who founded the Nyingmapa Tibetan Buddhist order.

pagoda – multistoreyed Nepali temple, which was later exported to China and Japan.

panchayat – the nonparty parliament of Nepal until 1990.

Panduravasini – consort of the Dhyani Buddha Amitabha.

Parvati – Shiva's consort.

pashmina – goat's wool blanket or shawl.

Pashupati – Shiva as Lord of the Animals.

patakas – see dhwaja.

path (pati) – small raised platform to shelter pilgrims.

patuka – waistcoat to carry things.

pith – open shrine for a Tantric goddess.

prajna – female counterparts of male Buddhist deities.

pokhari – large water tank.

Prajnaparamita – consort of the Dhyani Buddhas Vairocana and Aksobhya.

prasad – food offering.

prayer flags – each carries a sacred mantra which is 'said' when the flag flutters.

prayer wheels – cylindrical wheel inscribed with a Buddhist prayer or mantra which is 'said' when the wheel spins. There are even water-driven prayer wheels.

Prithvi – Vedic earth goddess.

puja (pooja) – religious offering or prayer.

Puranas – Hindu holy books of around 400 BCE which heralded the shift from the Vedic gods to the Hindu trinity of Brahma, Vishnu and Shiva.

puri – town.

Qomolangma – the Tibetan name for Mt Everest; literally, 'Mother Goddess of the World'. Also spelt Chomolongma.

rajpath – road or highway, literally 'king's road'.

rakshi – rice spirit.

Rama – Vishnu's seventh incarnation, and hero of the Ramayana.

Ramayana – Hindu epic which recounts the adventures of Rama, Sita, Hanuman and the demon king Rawana.

Rana – hereditary prime ministers who ruled Nepal from 1841 to 1951.

rath – the temple chariot in which the idol is conveyed in processions.

Ratnasambhava – Dhyani Buddha of the south.

Rawana (Ravana) – the demon king of Lanka in the Ramayana.

rikhi doro – golden thread worn around the waist by Shiva devotees.

rimpoche – abbot of a gompa.

Rudra – Vedic god of lightning, an early version of Shiva.

sadhus – wandering Hindu holy men, generally Shaivites who have given up everything to follow the trail to religious salvation. Many sadhus come from India to visit Pashupatinath, the great Shiva temple of Nepal.

Sagarmatha – Nepali name for Mt Everest.

Sakyamuni – another name for Gautama Buddha.

sal – tree of the lower Himalayan foothills.

saligrams – black ammonite fossils of Jurassic period sea creatures, proof that the Himalaya was once under water.

sankha – conch shell symbol of Vishnu.

sanyasin – religious ascetic who has cut all ties with normal society.

saranghi – small violin played by the Gaines.

Saraswati – goddess of learning and the creative arts, and consort of Brahma. She can often be identified by the flute-like instrument, called a *vina*.

satal – pilgrim's house.

sha bhakley – a Tibetan meat pie.

Shaivites – followers of Shiva who cover their faces in ashes, paint three horizontal lines on their forehead and carry a begging bowl and Shiva's symbolic trident.

Shakti – dynamic female element in male-female relationships; a goddess.

Shantipura – Buddhist symbol for the sky.

Sherpas – literally 'people from the east', the Sherpas are Buddhist hill people famed for their stalwart work with mountaineering expeditions. With a small 's' sherpa means trek leader.

Sherpanis – female Sherpas.

Sheshnag – some believe that this snake, not Ananta, is the one which Vishnu reclines on.

shikhara – Indian-style temple with tall corncob-like spire.

Shitala Mai – ogress who became a protector of children.

Shiva – most powerful Hindu god, the creator and destroyer.

Shivaratri – birthday of Shiva.

Simhanada – a form of Avalokiteshvara who rides a lion.

sindur – red dust and mustard oil mixture used for offerings.

sirdar – leader/organiser of a trekking party.

Sita – Rama's wife in the *Ramayana*.

Skanda – see *Kartikkaya*.

Solu Khumbu – Everest region of eastern Nepal where the majority of the Sherpas live.

sonam – the karma acquired through successive incarnations.

STOL – short-take-off-and-landing aircraft used on mountain airstrips.

stupa – hemispherical Buddhist religious structure; always walk around stupas clockwise.

Sudras – the lowest Nepali caste, said to originate from Brahma's feet.

sundhara – fountain with golden spout.

Surya – see *Aditya*.

suttee (sati) – practice of widows throwing themselves on their husband's funeral pyre.

tabla – hand drum.

tahr – wild mountain goat.

tal – lake.

Taleju Bhawani – Nepali goddess, an aspect of Mahadevi and the family deity of the Malla kings of the Kathmandu Valley. There are Taleju temples in the old royal palaces of Kathmandu, Patan and Bhaktapur.

Tantric Buddhism – form of Buddhism which evolved in Tibet during the 10th to 15th centuries.

Tara – White Tara is the consort of the Dhyani Buddha Vairocana; Green Tara is associated with Amoghasiddhi. Either way she is a very popular figure in the Buddhist pantheon and may also be adopted by Hindus as Shiva's wife in her peaceful mood.

tempos – small Indian three-wheeled transports commonly used in Kathmandu (similar to the Thai *samlor*).

Terai – flat land south of the Himalaya in Nepal.

Thakalis – people of the Kali Gandaki Valley who specialise in running hotels.

thangka –Tibetan religious painting on cotton, usually of mandalas or Tantric deities.

third eye – symbolic eye on Buddha figures, used to indicate the Buddha's clairvoyant powers.

tika – red sandalwood paste spot marked on the forehead, particularly for religious occasions.

thugpa – thick Tibetan soup.

tole – street or quarter of a town, sometimes used to refer to a square such as Kel Tole in Kathmandu or Tachupal Tole in Bhaktapur.

topi – traditional Nepali cap.

torana – portico above temple doors which can indicate the god to whom the temple is dedicated.

Tribhuvan – king who ended the Rana period and Nepal's long seclusion in 1951.

trisul – trident weapon symbol of Shiva.

tsampa – barley-flour porridge of the Sherpas.

Tulku – Tibetan Buddhist reincarnation of a great lama.

tulsi – sacred basil plant.

tunal – carved temple strut.

Uma – one of the peaceful incarnations of Shiva's consort Parvati.

Uma Maheshwar – Shiva and Parvati in a pose where Shiva sits cross-legged and Parvati sits on his thigh and leans against him.

Upanishads – ancient Vedic scripts, the last part of the Vedas.

urna – the bump on the forehead of a Buddha or Bodhisattva.

vahana – a god's animal mount or vehicle.

Vairocana – the central Dhyani Buddha and the 'embodiment of perfection'.

Vaisya – caste of merchants and farmers, said to originate from Brahma's thighs.

Vaishnavites – followers of Vishnu.

vajra – the 'thunderbolt' symbol of Buddhist power in Nepal; *(dorje* in Tibetan).

Vajra Jogini – a Tantric goddess, shakti to a Bhairab.

Vajrapani – literally 'thunderbolt in hand', a manifestation of Avalokiteshvara holding a thunderbolt.

Vajrayana – literally 'vehicle of the thunderbolts'; this is a variety of Buddhism which involves magical spells.

Vamana – see *Vikrantha*.

Varahi – Vishnu's boar incarnation.

Varuna – ancient Vedic god of wisdom and morality.

Vasudhara – wife of Jambhala the god of wealth; she rides a chariot drawn by a pig.

Vasupura – Buddhist symbol for the earth.

Vayupura – Buddhist symbol for the air.

Vedas – ancient spiritual texts, the orthodox Hindu scriptures.

Vedic gods – ancient Hindu gods described in the Vedas.

vehicle – the animal with which a Hindu god is associated. Shiva's vehicle is a bull, Ganesh's is a mouse while Vishnu's is the man-bird Garuda.

vihara – Buddhist religious buildings and pilgrim accommodation.

Vikrantha – Vishnu's fifth incarnation when he appeared as a dwarf, then grew so large that he could cross the universe in three strides.

Vishnu – the preserver, one of the three main Hindu gods.

Vishnu Chaturmurti – four-faced Vishnu with faces of a lion, boar, human and demon.

Wheel of Life – held by Mara, the god of death. The wheel's concentric circles show a stage of existence, those who are chained to the cycles of existence, the forces which keep the wheel turning or the desires which keep humankind chained to the cycle.

yab-yum – Tantric erotica.

yak – main beast of burden and form of cattle above 3000 metres.

yakshas – attendant deities.

Yama – Vedic god of death, son of Aditya or Surya; his messenger is the crow.

yeti – the abominable snowman.

yi-dam – protective deities of the Buddhas; they have a fierce form in contrast to the peacefulness of the Buddhas.

yoni – female sexual symbol, equivalent of a lingam.

Yuga – each Mahayuga is divided into four Yugas.

zamindar – absentee landlord and/or moneylender.

zhum – see *dzum*.

zopkiok – see *dzopkyo*.

Acknowlegments

THANKS

Many thanks to the travellers who used the last edition and wrote to us with helpful hints, useful advice and interesting anecdotes:

Katleen & Luc, Chris Albert, Jon Aldridge, Alexej Alvariza, Rafa Artavia, Frans van Assendelft, Jorg Ausfelt, Sue Bailey, Mark Baker, Les Ballard, Eve Ballenegger, Helen Banks, Andrew Bell, Nicole Bellefleur, Silke Belzer, Marten Berglund, W H Bergner, Vicki Bielski, Gary Blanchard, Pamela Bode, Nick Bourne, Dan Brake, Ian & Sarah Brenchley, Karel Brevet, Meg Brown, Belinda Brown, Andrew Burke, Francesca Camisoli, A Chapman, Melanie Cheng, T Cook, Natalie Cook, Kevin Cosgriff, Anne Cox, Michael Cridland, Sean Cross, Michel J van Dam, Adam Danek, Victoria & Christopher Darue, John Darwin, Laura Davidson, Harry Dawson, Anthony Doerga, Neelke Doorn, Jack Dyson, Michael Eckert, Maarten van Egmond, Dirk & Isabelle Engels, Don & Achara Entz, Susan Esmonde, Camilla Fredberg, Gary Garthwait, Amanda Gilliam, Robert Gillman, Bea Goemans, Sabijin Gorter-Wijnheijmer, Joanna Grabiak, Nienke Groen, Deah Gulley, Rachael Gulliver, Prema Gurung, Jason van Haard, Luke Haas, Mari Hagberg, Stuart Hamilton, Helle Hansen, Roger La Haye, Trea & Kevin Heapes, Pete Helfrich, Victoria Henkin, Marion Hercock, Anna Hicks, Kaye Hill, Ignace Hindrick, Paula Hirschoff, Vanessa Smith Holburn, Zoe Holloway, R Holtes, Birgitta Holzel, Mark Horsley, Rod How, Nadine & Mike Hudson, Kelly Hunt, Dirk Huyge, Prema Gurung Imazawa, Barbara Int-Hout, Aurianne Jacobs, Kjaer Johansen, Helen Johnston, Brett Jones, Rachael Jones, Sture Jonsson, Dan Kalafatas, Renko Karruppannan, Gideon Katz, Jitso Keizer, Daniel Kern, Cathy Kim, Ruth King, Errol Korn, Albert Kromkamp, Jakob Kroon, Mike Kryne, Igal Kutin, Yeong Kwok, Paul Lachapelle, Brian Lacy, Raymond Lae, Nicole McGaffney- Lee, Jeffrey Lee, Elspeth Logan, Manoeal Lopez, Rachel MacHenry, Kathy Madson, Jennifer Magarity, Stefano Maggini, Jane Mara, Paloma Marugan, Lee Soo May, Trevor Mazzucchelli, Liz McMillan, Karin Mendoza, Jane & Ramsey Mikhail, Karsten Mikkelsen, Rosemarie Milsom, Toby Milwright, Ardalan Mirahmadi, Kerstin Mockrish, S P Moore, Vincenzo Morelli, Matthew John Nash, Doris Neilson, Dieter Neujahr, Lily Neve, Serene Ng, Bonnie Ng, Paul O'Kelly, Helle Olesed, Conny Olde Olthof, Jolanda Onderwater, Stefan Orani, Joe Osentoski, J C O'Sullivan, Mark Outerbridge, Richard & Israr Parker, Sangita Patel, G Paul, Emma Pavey, Michael & Denni Pearson, Claire Pellit, Andreas Pfletschinger, Bernard Phelps, Liezel Pilling, JonniLu Pool, Marcelo Houacio Pozzo, Jaliya Rasaputra, Simon Reed, Jose Remmers, Jan Rensen, Elizabeth Rhoades, Karen Van Riemsdyk, Joe Rizzo, Natasha Robinson, Ellie Roelofs, Herwig Rombauts, Rick Ronald, Leif Ronby Pedersen, Michael Rose, Ruth Rosselson, Michael Rubio, Jay Ruchamkin, Gabriela Rutz, Menno Sasker, Elizabeth Savir, John Saynor, Peter Schroeder, Thorsten Schuller, Bill Searl, Grishma Shah-Elzinga, Surendra Shahi, Noa Shefet, P T Sherpa, Ailsa Siemens, Barbara Siliquini, Serge Sintzoff, Laura Skilton, Nathalie van der Slikke, Chris Slocombe, Sue Smith, Yael Soffer, Thomasina Stanford, Ben Stewart-Koster, Leonie Stockwell, Jan Strubbe, Koen Stynen, Lisa Tapert, Alice Teasdale, Hari Thapaliya, Fern Thomas, Neil Thompson, Hari Timilsina, Fredrik Tukk, Ian Tupper, Mark Turin, Phil Vaughan, Mike Venables, Aron Wahl, Ali Wale, Colin A Walker, Paul Weaver, Brad Wetmore, John Whelpton, Jon Willis, Julian Woodridge, Andrew Woolnough, Karl Yeomans, Tv Zuilen, T Van Zuren.

LONELY PLANET

Phrasebooks

Lonely Planet phrasebooks are packed with essential words and phrases to help travellers communicate with the locals. With colour tabs for quick reference, an extensive vocabulary and use of script, these handy pocket-sized language guides cover day-to-day travel situations.

- handy pocket-sized books
- easy to understand Pronunciation chapter
- clear & comprehensive Grammar chapter
- romanisation alongside script to allow ease of pronunciation
- script throughout so users can point to phrases for every situation
- full of cultural information and tips for the traveller

'... vital for a real DIY spirit and attitude in language learning'
– *Backpacker*

'the phrasebooks have good cultural backgrounders and offer solid advice for challenging situations in remote locations'
– *San Francisco Examiner*

Arabic (Egyptian) • Arabic (Moroccan) • Australian *(Australian English, Aboriginal and Torres Strait languages)* • Baltic States *(Estonian, Latvian, Lithuanian)* • Bengali • Brazilian • British • Burmese • Cantonese • Central Asia (Uyghur, Uzbek, Kyrghiz, Kazak, Pashto, Tadjik • Central Europe *(Czech, French, German, Hungarian, Italian, Slovak)* • Eastern Europe *(Bulgarian, Czech, Hungarian, Polish, Romanian, Slovak)* • Ethiopian (Amharic) • Fijian • French • German • Greek • Hebrew • Hill Tribes • Hindi & Urdu • Indonesian • Italian • Japanese • Korean • Lao • Latin American Spanish • Malay • Mandarin • Mediterranean Europe *(Albanian, Croatian, Greek, Italian, Macedonian, Maltese, Serbian, Slovene)* • Mongolian • Nepali • Pidgin • Pilipino (Tagalog) • Portugese • Quechua • Russian • Scandinavian Europe *(Danish, Finnish, Icelandic, Norwegian, Swedish)* • South-East Asia *(Burmese, Indonesian, Khmer, Lao, Malay, Tagalog Pilipino, Thai, Vietnamese)* • South Pacific Languages • Spanish (Castilian) *(also includes Catalan, Galician and Basque)* • Sri Lanka • Swahili • Thai • Tibetan • Turkish • Ukrainian • USA *(US English, Vernacular, Native American languages, Hawaiian)* • Vietnamese • Western Europe *(Basque, Catalan, Dutch, French, German, Greek, Irish, Italian, Portuguese, Scottish Gaelic, Spanish (Castilian), Welsh)*

LONELY PLANET

Guides by Region

Lonely Planet is known worldwide for publishing practical, reliable and no-nonsense travel information in our guides and on our Web site. The Lonely Planet list covers just about every accessible part of the world. Currently there are 16 series: Travel guides, Shoestring guides, Condensed guides, Phrasebooks, Read This First, Healthy Travel, Walking guides, Cycling guides, Watching Wildlife guides, Pisces Diving & Snorkeling guides, City Maps, Road Atlases, Out to Eat, World Food, Journeys travel literature and Pictorials.

AFRICA Africa on a shoestring • Cairo • Cape Town • Cape Town City Map • East Africa • Egypt • Egyptian Arabic phrasebook • Ethiopia, Eritrea & Djibouti • Ethiopian (Amharic) phrasebook • The Gambia & Senegal • Healthy Travel Africa • Kenya • Malawi • Morocco • Moroccan Arabic phrasebook • Mozambique • Read This First: Africa • South Africa, Lesotho & Swaziland • Southern Africa • Southern Africa Road Atlas • Swahili phrasebook • Tanzania, Zanzibar & Pemba • Trekking in East Africa • Tunisia • Watching Wildlife East Africa • Watching Wildlife Southern Africa • West Africa • World Food Morocco • Zimbabwe, Botswana & Namibia
Travel Literature: Mali Blues: Traveling to an African Beat • The Rainbird: A Central African Journey • Songs to an African Sunset: A Zimbabwean Story

AUSTRALIA & THE PACIFIC Auckland • Australia • Australian phrasebook • Australia Road Atlas • Bushwalking in Australia •Cycling New Zealand • Fiji • Fijian phrasebook • Healthy Travel Australia, NZ and the Pacific • Islands of Australia's Great Barrier Reef • Melbourne • Melbourne City Map • Micronesia • New Caledonia • New South Wales & the ACT • New Zealand • Northern Territory • Outback Australia • Out to Eat – Melbourne • Out to Eat – Sydney • Papua New Guinea • Pidgin phrasebook • Queensland • Rarotonga & the Cook Islands • Samoa • Solomon Islands • South Australia • South Pacific • South Pacific phrasebook • Sydney • Sydney City Map • Sydney Condensed • Tahiti & French Polynesia • Tasmania • Tonga • Tramping in New Zealand • Vanuatu • Victoria • Watching Wildlife Australia • Western Australia
Travel Literature: Islands in the Clouds: Travels in the Highlands of New Guinea • Kiwi Tracks: A New Zealand Journey • Sean & David's Long Drive

CENTRAL AMERICA & THE CARIBBEAN Bahamas, Turks & Caicos • Baja California • Bermuda • Central America on a shoestring • Costa Rica • Costa Rica Spanish phrasebook • Cuba • Dominican Republic & Haiti • Eastern Caribbean • Guatemala • Guatemala, Belize & Yucatán: La Ruta Maya • Healthy Travel Central & South America • Jamaica • Mexico • Mexico City • Panama • Puerto Rico • Read This First: Central & South America • World Food Mexico • Yucatán
Travel Literature: Green Dreams: Travels in Central America

EUROPE Amsterdam • Amsterdam City Map • Amsterdam Condensed • Andalucía • Austria • Baltic States phrasebook • Barcelona • Barcelona City Map • Berlin • Berlin City Map • Britain • British phrasebook • Brussels, Bruges & Antwerp • Budapest • Budapest City Map • Canary Islands • Central Europe • Central Europe phrasebook • Corfu & the Ionians • Corsica • Crete • Crete Condensed • Croatia • Cycling Britain • Cycling France • Cyprus • Czech & Slovak Republics • Denmark • Dublin • Dublin City Map • Eastern Europe • Eastern Europe phrasebook • Edinburgh • Estonia, Latvia & Lithuania • Europe on a shoestring • Finland • Florence • France • Frankfurt Condensed • French phrasebook • Georgia, Armenia & Azerbaijan • Germany • German phrasebook • Greece • Greek Islands • Greek phrasebook • Hungary • Iceland, Greenland & the Faroe Islands • Ireland • Istanbul • Italian phrasebook • Italy • Krakow • Lisbon • The Loire • London • London City Map • London Condensed • Madrid • Malta • Mediterranean Europe • Mediterranean Europe phrasebook • Moscow • Mozambique • Munich • Norway • Out to Eat – London • Paris • Paris City Map • Paris Condensed • Poland • Portugal • Portuguese phrasebook • Prague • Prague City Map • Provence & the Côte d'Azur • Read This First: Europe • Romania & Moldova • Rome • Russia, Ukraine & Belarus • Russian phrasebook • Scandinavian & Baltic Europe • Scandinavian Europe phrasebook • Scotland • Sicily • Slovenia • South-West France • Spain • Spanish phrasebook • St Petersburg • St Petersburg City Map • Sweden • Switzerland • Trekking in Spain • Tuscany • Ukrainian phrasebook • Venice • Vienna • Walking in Britain • Walking in France • Walking in Ireland • Walking in Italy • Walking in Spain • Walking in Switzerland • Western Europe • Western Europe phrasebook • World Food France • World Food Ireland • World Food Italy • World Food Spain
Travel Literature: Love and War in the Apennines • The Olive Grove: Travels in Greece • On the Shores of the Mediterranean • Round Ireland in Low Gear • A Small Place in Italy

INDIAN SUBCONTINENT Bangladesh • Bengali phrasebook • Bhutan • Delhi • Goa • Healthy Travel Asia & India • Hindi & Urdu phrasebook • India • Indian Himalaya • Karakoram Highway • Kerala • Mumbai

LONELY PLANET

Mail Order

Lonely Planet products are distributed worldwide. They are also available by mail order from Lonely Planet, so if you have difficulty finding a title please write to us. North and South American residents should write to 150 Linden St, Oakland, CA 94607, USA; European and African residents should write to 10a Spring Place, London NW5 3BH, UK; and residents of other countries to Locked Bag 1, Footscray, Victoria 3011, Australia.

(Bombay) • Nepal • Nepali phrasebook • Pakistan • Rajasthan • Read This First: Asia & India • South India • Sri Lanka • Sri Lanka phrasebook • Tibet • Tibetan phrasebook • Trekking in the Indian Himalaya • Trekking in the Karakoram & Hindukush • Trekking in the Nepal Himalaya
Travel Literature: The Age of Kali: Indian Travels and Encounters • Hello Goodnight: A Life of Goa • In Rajasthan • A Season in Heaven: True Tales from the Road to Kathmandu • Shopping for Buddhas • A Short Walk in the Hindu Kush • Slowly Down the Ganges

ISLANDS OF THE INDIAN OCEAN Madagascar & Comoros • Maldives • Mauritius, Réunion & Seychelles

MIDDLE EAST & CENTRAL ASIA Bahrain, Kuwait & Qatar • Central Asia • Central Asia phrasebook • Dubai • Hebrew phrasebook • Iran • Israel & the Palestinian Territories • Istanbul • Istanbul City Map • Istanbul to Cairo on a shoestring • Jerusalem • Jerusalem City Map • Jordan • Lebanon • Middle East • Oman & the United Arab Emirates • Syria • Turkey • Turkish phrasebook • World Food Turkey • Yemen
Travel Literature: Black on Black: Iran Revisited • The Gates of Damascus • Kingdom of the Film Stars: Journey into Jordan

NORTH AMERICA Alaska • Boston • Boston City Map • California & Nevada • California Condensed • Canada • Chicago • Chicago City Map • Deep South • Florida • Hawaii • Hiking in Alaska • Hiking in the USA • Honolulu • Las Vegas • Los Angeles • Miami • Miami City Map • New England • New Orleans • New York City • New York City City Map • New York City Condensed • New York, New Jersey & Pennsylvania • Oahu • Out to Eat – San Francisco • Pacific Northwest • Puerto Rico • Rocky Mountains • San Francisco • San Francisco City Map • Seattle • Southwest • Texas • USA • USA phrasebook • Vancouver • Virginia & the Capital Region • Washington, DC City Map • World Food Deep South, USA
Travel Literature: Caught Inside: A Surfer's Year on the California Coast • Drive Thru America

NORTH-EAST ASIA Beijing • Cantonese phrasebook • China • Hiking in Japan • Hong Kong • Hong Kong City Map • Hong Kong Condensed • Hong Kong, Macau & Guangzhou • Japan • Japanese phrasebook • Korea • Korean phrasebook • Kyoto • Mandarin phrasebook • Mongolia • Mongolian phrasebook • Seoul • South-West China • Taiwan • Tokyo
Travel Literature: In Xanadu: A Quest • Lost Japan

SOUTH AMERICA Argentina, Uruguay & Paraguay • Bolivia • Brazil • Brazilian phrasebook • Buenos Aires • Chile & Easter Island • Colombia • Ecuador & the Galapagos Islands • Healthy Travel Central & South America • Latin American Spanish phrasebook • Peru • Quechua phrasebook • Read This First: Central & South America • Rio de Janeiro • Rio de Janeiro City Map • Santiago • South America on a shoestring • Santiago • Trekking in the Patagonian Andes • Venezuela
Travel Literature: Full Circle: A South American Journey

SOUTH-EAST ASIA Bali & Lombok • Bangkok • Bangkok City Map • Burmese phrasebook • Cambodia • Hanoi • Healthy Travel Asia & India • Hill Tribes phrasebook • Ho Chi Minh City • Indonesia • Indonesian phrasebook • Indonesia's Eastern Islands • Jakarta • Java • Lao phrasebook • Laos • Malay phrasebook • Malaysia, Singapore & Brunei • Myanmar (Burma) • Philippines • Pilipino (Tagalog) phrasebook • Read This First: Asia & India • Singapore • Singapore City Map • South-East Asia on a shoestring • South-East Asia phrasebook • Thailand • Thailand's Islands & Beaches • Thailand, Vietnam, Laos & Cambodia Road Atlas • Thai phrasebook • Vietnam • Vietnamese phrasebook • World Food Thailand • World Food Vietnam

ALSO AVAILABLE: Antarctica • The Arctic • The Blue Man: Tales of Travel, Love and Coffee • Brief Encounters: Stories of Love, Sex & Travel • Chasing Rickshaws • The Last Grain Race • Lonely Planet Unpacked • Not the Only Planet: Science Fiction Travel Stories • Lonely Planet On the Edge • Sacred India • Travel with Children • Travel Photography: A Guide to Taking Better Pictures

Index

Abbreviations

NP – National Park

WR – Wildlife Reserve

Text

Bold indicates maps.
Tibetan place names in brackets.

Boxed Text

MAP LEGEND

BOUNDARIES

————··—————··— International
————··——————··— Provincial
————·—·—————·— Regional

HYDROGRAPHY

Coastline
River, Creek
Lake
Intermittent Lake
Salt Lake
Canal
Spring, Rapids
Waterfalls
Swamp

ROUTES & TRANSPORT

Freeway
Highway
Major Road
Minor Road
City Freeway
City Highway
City Road
City Street, Lane

⇒==== Tunnel
+—+—○—+—+ Train Route & Station
—○—Ⓜ—○— Metro & Station
+—+—+—+—+ Cable Car or Chairlift
———————— Walking Track
·············· Walking Tour
———————— Described Trek
———————— Ferry Route

AREA FEATURES

Building
✿ Park, Gardens
+ + × × Cemetery

Market
Beach, Desert
Urban Area

MAP SYMBOLS

○ **CAPITAL** ....National Capital	✈ ....Airport	☂ ....National Park
◎ **CAPITAL** ......Provincial Capital	⌒ ...Ancient or City Wall	← ....One Way Street
● **City** ....City	∴ ....Archaeological Site	‡ ....Pagoda
● **Town** ....Town	⌒ ....Cave	)(..........................Pass
● **Village** ....Village	⌒ ...Cliff or Escarpment	★ ....Police Station
○ ....Point of Interest	◎ ....Embassy	✉ ....Post Office
	⊞ ....Hindu Temple	🏛 ....Stately Home
■ ....Place to Stay	✚ ....Hospital	⏦ ....Stupa
⚑ ....Camping Ground	🅗 ....Lookout	☎ ....Telephone
⚏ ....Caravan Park	🏯 ....Monastery	◪ ....Temple
⌂ ....Hut or Chalet	▲ ....Monument	▣ ....Tomb
	Ⓒ ....Mosque	❶ ......Tourist Information
▼ ....Place to Eat	▲ ....Mountain or Hill	◗ ....Transport
⬤ ....Pub or Bar	🏛 ....Museum	🐾 ....Zoo

Note: not all symbols displayed above appear in this book

LONELY PLANET OFFICES

Australia
PO Box 617, Hawthorn, Victoria 3122
☎ 03 9819 1877 fax 03 9819 6459
email: talk2us@lonelyplanet.com.au

UK
10a Spring Place, London NW5 3BH
☎ 020 7428 4800 fax 020 7428 4828
email: go@lonelyplanet.co.uk

USA
150 Linden St, Oakland, CA 94607
☎ 510 893 8555 TOLL FREE: 800 275 8555
fax 510 893 8572
email: info@lonelyplanet.com

France
1 rue du Dahomey, 75011 Paris
☎ 01 55 25 33 00 fax 01 55 25 33 01
email: bip@lonelyplanet.fr
www.lonelyplanet.fr

World Wide Web: www.lonelyplanet.com *or* AOL keyword: lp
Lonely Planet Images: lpi@lonelyplanet.com.au